AN INTRODUCTION TO THE INTERNATIONAL CRIMINAL COURT

FOURTH EDITION

WILLIAM A. SCHABAS OC MRIA

CAMBRIDGE
UNIVERSITY PRESS

CAMBRIDGE UNIVERSITY PRESS
Cambridge, New York, Melbourne, Madrid, Cape Town,
Singapore, São Paulo, Mexico City

Cambridge University Press
The Edinburgh Building, Cambridge CB2 8RU, UK

Published in the United States of America by Cambridge University Press, New York

www.cambridge.org
Information on this title: www.cambridge.org/9780521767507

First published 2001
Second edition 2004
Third edition 2007
Fourth edition 2011
3rd printing 2012

Printed and Bound in the United Kingdom by the MPG Books Group

A catalogue record for this publication is available from the British Library

ISBN 978-0-521-76750-7 Hardback
ISBN 978-0-521-15195-5 Paperback

AN INTRODUCTION TO THE
INTERNATIONAL CRIMINAL COURT

The Inte ... on
of huma ... n-
ity and ... ng
or unab ... r-
nationa ... he
Interna ... d-
ing the ...

This ... rt
and the ... es
the situ ... ly,
Democ ... an
Republ ... ot
to proc ... so
addres ... ct-
iveness ... of
and su ...

WILLI ... w
at the ... sh
Centre ... de
in Inte ... th
Penalt ... ns
Interno ... ra
Leone (... on
the Ro ... m,
and ch ... ... of the Board of Trustees of the United Nations ... ry
Fund for Technical Cooperation in the Field of Human Rights.

CONTENTS

PREFACE

On 17 July 1998, at the headquarters of the Food and Agriculture Organization of the United Nations in Rome, 120 States voted to adopt the Rome Statute of the International Criminal Court. Less than four years later – far sooner than even the most optimistic observers had imagined – the Statute had obtained the requisite sixty ratifications for its entry into force, which took place on 1 July 2002. By mid-2010, the number of States Parties stood at 111.[1] By then, the Court was a thriving, dynamic international institution, with an annual budget of about €100 million and a staff of more than 500. Its first trial was nearing completion, and two others were in their initial stages.

The Rome Statute provides for the creation of an international criminal court with power to try and punish for the most serious violations of human rights in cases when national justice systems fail at the task. It constitutes a benchmark in the progressive development of international human rights, whose beginning dates back more than sixty years, to the adoption on 10 December 1948 of the Universal Declaration of Human Rights by the third session of the United Nations General Assembly.[2] The previous day, on 9 December 1948, the Assembly had adopted a resolution mandating the International Law Commission to begin work on the draft statute of an international criminal court,[3] in accordance with Article VI of the Genocide Convention.[4]

Establishing this international criminal court took considerably longer than many at the time might have hoped. In the early years of the Cold War, in 1954, the General Assembly essentially suspended work on the project.[5] Tensions between the two blocs made progress impossible, both

---

[1] A list of States Parties to the Statute appears in Appendix 2 to this volume.
[2] GA Res. 217 A (III), UN Doc. A/810.
[3] Study by the International Law Commission of the Question of an International Criminal Jurisdiction, GA Res. 216 B (III).
[4] Convention on the Prevention and Punishment of the Crime of Genocide, (1951) 78 UNTS 277.
[5] GA Res. 897 (X) (1954).

sides being afraid they might create a tool that could advantage the other. The United Nations General Assembly did not resume its consideration of the proposed international criminal court until 1989.[6] The end of the Cold War gave the concept the breathing space it needed. The turmoil created in the former Yugoslavia by the end of the Cold War provided the laboratory for international justice that propelled the agenda forward.[7]

The final version of the Rome Statute is not without serious flaws, and yet it 'could well be the most important institutional innovation since the founding of the United Nations'.[8] The astounding progress of the project itself during the 1990s and into the first decade of the twenty-first century indicates a profound and in some ways mysterious enthusiasm from a great number of States. Perhaps they are frustrated at the weaknesses of the United Nations and regional organizations in the promotion of international peace and security. To a great extent, the success of the Court parallels the growth of the international human rights movement, much of whose fundamental philosophy and outlook it shares. Of course, the Court also attracted the venom of the world's superpower, the United States of America. But Washington's opposition to the institution has abated, and increasingly appears as a temporary aberration of the Bush years. Alongside the growing enthusiasm of the United States for the Court, however, are troubling signs of discontent in African States, which had been among the keenest supporters in the early years.

The new International Criminal Court sits in The Hague, along-side its long-established cousin, the International Court of Justice. The International Court of Justice is the court where States litigate matters relating to their disputes as States. The role of individuals before the International Court of Justice is marginal, at best. As will be seen, not only does the International Criminal Court provide for prosecution and punishment of individuals, it also recognizes a legitimate participation for the individual as victim. In a more general sense, the International Criminal Court is concerned, essentially, with matters that might generally be described as serious human rights violations. The International Court of Justice, on the other hand, spends much of its judicial time on delimiting international boundaries and fishing zones, and similar

---

[6] GA Res. 44/89.

[7] Statute of the International Criminal Tribunal for the former Yugoslavia, UN Doc. S/RES/827, Annex.

[8] Robert C. Johansen, 'A Turning Point in International Relations? Establishing a Permanent International Criminal Court', (1997) 13 Report No. 1, 1 (Joan B. Kroc Institute for International Peace Studies, 1997).

matters. Yet, because it is exposed to the same trends and developments that sparked the creation of the International Criminal Court, the International Court of Justice finds itself increasingly involved in human rights matters.[9]

Whether or not one is supportive of the International Criminal Court, any knowledgeable specialist has to admit that in the history of public international law it is a truly extraordinary phenomenon. From an exceedingly modest proposal in the General Assembly in 1989,[10] derived from an atrophied provision of the 1948 Genocide Convention,[11] the idea has grown at a pace faster than even its most steadfast supporters have ever predicted. At every stage, the vast majority of participants in the process of creating the Court have underestimated developments. For example, during the 1998 Rome Conference, human rights NGOs argued that the proposed threshold for entry into force of sixty ratifications was an American plot to ensure that the Court would never be created. Convincing one-third of States to join the Court seemed impossible. Prominent delegations insisted that the Court could only operate if it had universal jurisdiction, predicting that a compromise by which it could only prosecute crimes committed on the territory of a State Party or by a national of a State Party would condemn it to obscurity and irrelevance. Countries in conflict or in a post-conflict peace process, where the Court might actually be of some practical use, would never ratify the Rome Statute, they argued.[12] Their perspective viewed the future court as an institution that would be established and operated by a relatively small number of countries in the North. Its field of operation, of course, was going to be the South.

---

[9] Recent cases have involved violations of human rights law and international humanitarian law in the Democratic Republic of Congo and the Occupied Palestinian Territories, genocide in the Former Yugoslavia, the use of nuclear weapons, self-determination in East Timor, the immunity of international human rights investigators, prosecution of government ministers for genocide and crimes against humanity, and imposition of the death penalty in the United States. In 2005, for the first time in its history, the International Criminal Court ruled that important human rights conventions, such as the International Covenant on Civil and Political Rights, the African Charter of Human and Peoples' Rights and the Convention on the Rights of the Child, had been breached by a State: *Case Concerning Armed Activities on the Territory of the Congo (Democratic Republic of the Congo v. Uganda)*, 19 December 2005, para. 219.

[10] GA Res. 44/89.

[11] Convention for the Prevention and Punishment of the Crime of Genocide, (1951) 78 UNTS 277, Art. VI.

[12] See, e.g., UN Doc. A/CONF.183/C.1/SR.7, paras. 48–51; UN Doc. A/CONF.183/C.1/SR.8, para. 7.

And yet, slightly more than a decade after the adoption of the Rome Statute, there are more than 110 States Parties, ninety more than the safe threshold that human rights NGOs and many national delegations thought was necessary to ensure entry into force within a foreseeable future. As for the fabled universal jurisdiction, despite exercising jurisdiction only over the territory and over nationals of States Parties, the real Court now has plenty of meat on the bone: Sierra Leone, Colombia, Uganda, the Democratic Republic of the Congo, Central African Republic, Guinea, Côte d'Ivoire, Afghanistan, Cambodia, Macedonia and Burundi are all States Parties, to name a few of the possible candidates for Court activity. In other words, the lack of universal jurisdiction has proven to be no obstacle whatsoever to the operation of the institution.

The phenomenal support for the Court following entry into force of the Rome Statute, evidenced by the rapid pace of ratification and entry into force, has been followed by a period of rather lacklustre and somewhat disappointing performance. Initially, the Prosecutor projected that the Court would complete its first trial by late 2005.[13] But, five years later, it was still struggling to finish a case. The *ad hoc* tribunals, for the former Yugoslavia, Rwanda and Sierra Leone, were far more productive at comparable periods in their evolution. The reasons for this are probably complex and multifaceted. The Rome Statute adds some additional procedural hurdles to prosecution, but this does not adequately explain the situation. There has been a reluctance of supporters of the Court to discuss this subject. For example, the agenda of the Review Conference, held eight years after the Statute's entry into force, included a 'stocktaking' that was focused on the role of States rather than on the performance of the institution.

The literature on the International Criminal Court is already abundant. It includes three commentaries,[14] some monographs[15] and several

---

[13] 'Draft Programme Budget for 2005', ASP/3/2, para. 159, p. 49.

[14] Antonio Cassese, Paola Gaeta and John R. W. D. Jones, eds., *The Rome Statute of the International Criminal Court: A Commentary*, Oxford: Oxford University Press, 2002; Otto Triffterer, ed., *Commentary on the Rome Statute of the International Criminal Court, Observers' Notes, Article by Article*, 2nd edn, Munich: C. H. Beck; Baden-Baden: Nomos; Oxford: Hart, 2008; William Schabas, *The International Criminal Court: A Commentary on the Rome Statute*, Oxford: Oxford University Press, 2010.

[15] Leila Nadya Sadat, *The International Criminal Court and the Transformation of International Law: Justice for the New Millennium*, Ardsley, NY: Transnational Publishers, 2002; and Bruce Broomhall, *International Justice and the International Criminal Court: Between Sovereignty and the Rule of Law*, Oxford: Oxford University Press, 2003; Benjamin N. Schiff, *Building the International Criminal Court*, New York: Cambridge University Press, 2008.

collections of essays, all addressed essentially to specialists.[16] The goal of this work is both more modest and more ambitious: to provide a succinct and coherent introduction to the legal issues involved in the creation and operation of the International Criminal Court, and one that is accessible to non-specialists. References within the text signpost the way to rather more detailed sources when readers want additional analysis. As with all international treaties and similar documents, students of the subject are also encouraged to consult the original records of the 1998 Diplomatic Conference and the meetings that preceded it. But the volume of these materials is awesome, and it is a challenging task to distil meaningful analysis and conclusions from them.

In the earlier editions, I have thanked many friends and colleagues, and beg their indulgence for not doing so again here. I want to give special thanks to my students at the Irish Centre for Human Rights of the National University of Ireland, Galway, many of whom have contributed to my ongoing study of the Court with original ideas and analyses. Several of them have published journal articles and monographs on specific issues concerning the Court and, more generally, international criminal law, and without exception these works have been cited somewhere in this text. The enthusiasm and encouragement of Sinead Moloney and Finola O'Sullivan of Cambridge University Press is greatly appreciated. Finally, of course, thanks are mainly due to Penelope, for her mythical patience.

WILLIAM A. SCHABAS OC MRIA

Oughterard, County Galway

20 June 2010

[16] Roy Lee, ed., *The International Criminal Court, The Making of the Rome Statute, Issues, Negotiations, Results*, The Hague: Kluwer Law International, 1999; Herman von Hebel, Johan G. Lammers and Jolien Schukking, eds., *Reflections on the International Criminal Court: Essays in Honour of Adriaan Bos*, The Hague: T. M. C. Asser, 1999; Flavia Lattanzi and William A. Schabas, eds., *Essays on the Rome Statute of the International Criminal Court*, Rome: Editrice il Sirente, 2000; Dinah Shelton, ed., *International Crimes, Peace, and Human Rights: The Role of the International Criminal Court*, Ardsley, NY: Transnational Publishers, 2000; Roy Lee, ed., *The International Criminal Court: Elements of Crimes and Rules of Procedure and Evidence*, Ardsley, NY: Transnational Publishers, 2001; Mauro Politi and Giuseppe Nesi, eds., *The Rome Statute of the International Criminal Court: A Challenge to Impunity*, Aldershot: Ashgate, 2001; and Lattanzi and Schabas, *Essays on the Rome Statute*; Carsten Stahn and Goran Sluiter, *The Emerging Practice of the International Criminal Court*, Leiden: Brill, 2009; and José Doria, Hans-Peter Gasser and M. Cherif Bassiouni, eds., *The Legal Regime of the International Criminal Court: Essays in Honour of Professor Igor Blishchenko*, Leiden and Boston: Martinus Nijhoff, 2009.

ABBREVIATIONS

ASP	Assembly of States Parties
CHR	Commission on Human Rights
GA	General Assembly
ICC	International Criminal Court
ICJ	International Court of Justice
ICTR	International Criminal Tribunal for Rwanda
ICTY	International Criminal Tribunal for the former Yugoslavia
ILC	International Law Commission
LRTWC	*Law Reports of the Trials of the War Criminals*
SC	Security Council
SCSL	Special Court for Sierra Leone
TWC	*Trials of the War Criminals*

1

Creation of the Court

War criminals have been prosecuted at least since the time of the ancient Greeks, and probably well before that. The idea that there is some common denominator of behaviour, even in the most extreme circumstances of brutal armed conflict, confirms beliefs drawn from philosophy and religion about some of the fundamental values of the human spirit. The early laws and customs of war can be found in the writings of classical authors and historians. Those who breached them were subject to trial and punishment. Modern codifications of this law, such as the detailed text prepared by Columbia University professor Francis Lieber that was applied by Abraham Lincoln to the Union army during the American Civil War, proscribed inhumane conduct, and set out sanctions, including the death penalty, for pillage, raping civilians, abuse of prisoners and similar atrocities.[1] Prosecution for war crimes, however, was only conducted by national courts, and these were and remain ineffective when those responsible for the crimes are still in power and their victims remain subjugated. Historically, the prosecution of war crimes was generally restricted to the vanquished or to isolated cases of rogue combatants in the victor's army. National justice systems have often proven themselves to be incapable of being balanced and impartial in such cases.

The first genuinely international trial for the perpetration of atrocities was probably that of Peter von Hagenbach, who was tried in 1474 for atrocities committed during the occupation of Breisach. When the town was retaken, von Hagenbach was charged with war crimes, convicted and beheaded.[2] But what was surely no more than a curious experiment

---

[1] Instructions for the Government of Armies of the United States in the Field, General Orders No. 100, 24 April 1863.

[2] Georg Schwarzenberger, *International Law as Applied by International Courts and Tribunals: The Law of Armed Conflict*, vol. II, London: Stevens & Sons Limited, 1968, p. 463; M. Cherif Bassiouni, 'From Versailles to Rwanda in 75 Years: The Need to Establish a Permanent International Court', (1997) 10 *Harvard Human Rights Journal* 11.

in medieval international justice was soon overtaken by the sanctity of State sovereignty resulting from the Peace of Westphalia of 1648. With the development of the law of armed conflict in the mid-nineteenth century, concepts of international prosecution for humanitarian abuses slowly began to emerge. One of the founders of the Red Cross movement, which grew up in Geneva in the 1860s, urged a draft statute for an international criminal court. Its task would be to prosecute breaches of the Geneva Convention of 1864 and other humanitarian norms. But Gustav Monnier's innovative proposal was much too radical for its time.[3]

The Hague Conventions of 1899 and 1907 represent the first significant codification of the laws of war in an international treaty. They include an important series of provisions dealing with the protection of civilian populations. Article 46 of the Regulations that are annexed to the Hague Convention IV of 1907 enshrines the respect of '[f]amily honour and rights, the lives of persons, and private property, as well as religious convictions and practice'.[4] Other provisions of the Regulations protect cultural objects and the private property of civilians. The preamble to the Conventions recognizes that they are incomplete, but promises that, until a more complete code of the laws of war is issued, 'the inhabitants and the belligerents remain under the protection and the rule of the principles of the law of nations, as they result from the usages established among civilized peoples, from the laws of humanity, and the dictates of the public conscience'. This provision is known as the Martens clause, after the Russian diplomat who drafted it.[5]

The Hague Conventions, as international treaties, were meant to impose obligations and duties upon States, and were not intended to create criminal liability for individuals. They declared certain acts to be illegal, but not criminal, as can be seen from the absence of any suggestion that there is a sanction for their violation. Yet, within only a few years, the Hague Conventions were being presented as a source of the law of war crimes. In 1913, a commission of inquiry sent by the Carnegie Foundation to investigate atrocities committed during the

---

[3] Christopher Keith Hall, 'The First Proposal for a Permanent International Criminal Court', (1998) 322 *International Review of the Red Cross* 57.

[4] Convention Concerning the Laws and Customs of War on Land (Hague IV), 3 *Martens Nouveau Recueil* (3d) 461. For the 1899 treaty, see Convention (II) with Respect to the Laws and Customs of War on Land, 32 Stat. 1803, 1 Bevans 247, 91 British Foreign and State Treaties 988.

[5] Theodor Meron, 'The Martens Clause, Principles of Humanity, and Dictates of Public Conscience', (2000) 94 *American Journal of International Law* 78.

Balkan Wars used the provisions of the Hague Convention IV as a basis for its description of war crimes.[6] Immediately following World War I, the Commission on Responsibilities of the Authors of War and on Enforcement of Penalties, established to examine allegations of war crimes committed by the Central Powers, did the same.[7] But actual prosecution for violations of the Hague Conventions would have to wait until Nuremberg. Offences against the laws and customs of war, known as 'Hague Law' because of their roots in the 1899 and 1907 Conventions, are codified in the 1993 Statute of the International Criminal Tribunal for the former Yugoslavia[8] and in Article 8(2)(b), (e) and (f) of the Statute of the International Criminal Court.

As World War I wound to a close, public opinion, particularly in England, was increasingly keen on criminal prosecution of those generally considered to be responsible for the war. There was much pressure to go beyond violations of the laws and customs of war and to prosecute, in addition, the waging of war itself in violation of international treaties. At the Paris Peace Conference, the Allies debated the wisdom of such trials as well as their legal basis. The United States was generally hostile to the idea, arguing that this would be *ex post facto* justice. Responsibility for breach of international conventions, and above all for crimes against the 'laws of humanity' – a reference to civilian atrocities within a State's own borders – was a question of morality, not law, said the United States delegation. But this was a minority position. The resulting compromise dropped the concept of 'laws of humanity' but promised the prosecution of Kaiser Wilhelm II 'for a supreme offence against international morality and the sanctity of treaties'. The Versailles Treaty formally arraigned the defeated German emperor and pledged the creation of a 'special tribunal' for his trial.[9] Wilhelm of Hohenzollern had fled to neutral Holland which refused his extradition, the Dutch Government considering that the charges consisted of retroactive criminal law. He lived out his life there and died, ironically, in 1941, when his country of refuge was falling under German occupation in the early years of World War II.

---

[6] Report of the International Commission to Inquire into the Causes and Conduct of the Balkan Wars, Washington DC: Carnegie Endowment for International Peace, 1914.

[7] *Violations of the Laws and Customs of War, Reports of Majority and Dissenting Reports of American and Japanese Members of the Commission of Responsibilities, Conference of Paris, 1919*, Oxford: Clarendon Press, 1919.

[8] Statute of the International Criminal Tribunal for the former Yugoslavia, UN Doc. S/RES/827 (1993), Annex, Art. 3.

[9] Treaty of Peace between the Allied and Associated Powers and Germany ('Treaty of Versailles'), (1919) TS 4, Art. 227.

The Versailles Treaty also recognized the right of the Allies to set up military tribunals to try German soldiers accused of war crimes.[10] Germany never accepted the provisions, and subsequently a compromise was reached whereby the Allies were to prepare lists of German suspects, but the trials would be held before the German courts. An initial roster of nearly 900 was quickly whittled down to about forty-five, and in the end only a dozen were actually tried. Several were acquitted; those found guilty were sentenced to modest terms of imprisonment, often nothing more than time already served in custody prior to conviction. The trials looked rather more like disciplinary proceedings of the German army than any international reckoning. Known as the 'Leipzig Trials', the perceived failure of this early attempt at international justice haunted efforts in the inter-war years to develop a permanent international tribunal and were grist to the mill of those who opposed war crimes trials for the Nazi leaders. But two of the judgments of the Leipzig court involving the sinking of the hospital ships *Dover Castle* and *Llandovery Castle*, and the murder of the survivors, mainly Canadian wounded and medical personnel, are cited to this day as precedents on the scope of the defence of superior orders.[11]

The Treaty of Sèvres of 1920, which governed the peace with Turkey, also provided for war crimes trials.[12] The proposed prosecutions against the Turks were even more radical, going beyond the trial of suspects whose victims were either Allied soldiers or civilians in occupied territories to include subjects of the Ottoman Empire, notably victims of the genocide of the Armenian people. This was the embryo of what would later be called crimes against humanity. However, the Treaty of Sèvres was never ratified by Turkey, and no international trials were undertaken. The Treaty of Sèvres was replaced by the Treaty of Lausanne of 1923 which contained a 'Declaration of Amnesty' for all offences committed between 1 August 1914 and 20 November 1922.[13]

---

[10] *Ibid.*, Arts. 228–230.

[11] *German War Trials, Report of Proceedings Before the Supreme Court in Leipzig*, London: His Majesty's Stationery Office, 1921. See also James F. Willis, *Prologue to Nuremberg: The Politics and Diplomacy of Punishing War Criminals of the First World War*, Westport, CT: Greenwood Press, 1982; Gerd Hankel, *Die Leipziger Prozesse*, Hamburg: Hamburger Edition, 2003.

[12] (1920) UKTS 11; (1929) 99 (3rd Series), DeMartens, *Recueil général des traités*, No. 12, p. 720 (French version).

[13] Treaty of Lausanne Between Principal Allied and Associated Powers and Turkey, (1923) 28 LNTS 11.

Although these initial efforts to create an international criminal court were unsuccessful, they stimulated many international lawyers to devote their attention to the matter during the years that followed. Baron Descamps of Belgium, a member of the Advisory Committee of Jurists appointed by the Council of the League of Nations, urged the establishment of a 'high court of international justice'. Using language borrowed from the Martens clause in the preamble to the Hague Conventions, Descamps recommended that the jurisdiction of the court include offences 'recognized by the civilized nations but also by the demands of public conscience [and] the dictates of the legal conscience of civilized nations'. The Third Committee of the Assembly of the League of Nations declared that Descamps' ideas were 'premature'. Efforts by expert bodies, such as the International Law Association and the International Association of Penal Law, culminated, in 1937, in the adoption of a treaty by the League of Nations that contemplated the establishment of an international criminal court.[14] But, failing a sufficient number of ratifying States, that treaty never came into force.

The Nuremberg and Tokyo trials

In the Moscow Declaration of 1 November 1943, the Allies affirmed their determination to prosecute the Nazis for war crimes. The United Nations Commission for the Investigation of War Crimes, composed of representatives of most of the Allies, and chaired by Sir Cecil Hurst of the United Kingdom, was established to set the stage for post-war prosecution. The Commission prepared a 'Draft Convention for the Establishment of a United Nations War Crimes Court', basing its text largely on the 1937 treaty of the League of Nations, and inspired by work carried out during the early years of the war by an unofficial body, the London International Assembly.[15] But it was the work of the London Conference, convened at the close of the war and limited to the four major powers, the United Kingdom, France, the United States and the Soviet Union, that laid the groundwork for the prosecutions at Nuremberg. The Agreement for the Prosecution and Punishment of Major War Criminals of the European Axis, and Establishing the Charter of the International Military Tribunal

---

[14] Convention for the Creation of an International Criminal Court, League of Nations OJ Spec. Supp. No. 156 (1936), LN Doc. C.547(I).M.384(I).1937. V (1938).

[15] Draft Convention for the Establishment of a United Nations War Crimes Court, UN War Crimes Commission, Doc. C.50(1), 30 September 1944.

(IMT) was formally adopted on 8 August 1945. It was promptly signed by representatives of the four powers. The Charter of the International Military Tribunal was annexed to the Agreement.[16] This treaty was eventually adhered to by nineteen other States who, although they played no active role in the Tribunal's activities or the negotiation of its statute, sought to express their support for the concept and indicate the wide international acceptance of the norms the Charter set out.[17]

In October 1945, indictments were served on twenty-four Nazi leaders. Their trial – known as the Trial of the Major War Criminals – began the following month. It concluded nearly a year later, with the conviction of nineteen defendants and the imposition of sentence of death in twelve cases. The Tribunal's jurisdiction was confined to three categories of offence: crimes against peace, war crimes and crimes against humanity. The Charter of the International Military Tribunal had been adopted after the crimes had been committed, and for this reason it was attacked as constituting *ex post facto* criminalization. Rejecting such arguments, the Tribunal referred to the Hague Conventions, for the war crimes, and to the 1928 Kellogg–Briand Pact, for crimes against peace.[18] The judges also answered that the prohibition of retroactive crimes was a principle of justice, and that it would fly in the face of justice to leave the Nazi crimes unpunished. This argument was particularly important with respect to the category of crimes against humanity, for which there was little real precedent, apart from the famous declaration by the three Allied powers in 1915 condemning the Turkish persecution of the Armenians. In the case of some war crimes charges, the Tribunal refused to convict after hearing evidence of similar behaviour by British and American soldiers.[19]

---

[16] Agreement for the Prosecution and Punishment of Major War Criminals of the European Axis, and Establishing the Charter of the International Military Tribunal (IMT), Annex, (1951) 82 UNTS 279. See Arieh J. Kochavi, *Prelude to Nuremberg: Allied War Crimes Policy and the Question of Punishment*, Chapel Hill, NC, and London: University of North Carolina Press, 1998; *Report of Robert H. Jackson, United States Representative to the International Conference on Military Trials*, Washington DC: US Government Printing Office, 1949.

[17] Australia, Belgium, Czechoslovakia, Denmark, Ethiopia, Greece, Haiti, Honduras, India, Luxembourg, the Netherlands, New Zealand, Norway, Panama, Paraguay, Poland, Uruguay, Venezuela and Yugoslavia.

[18] The Kellogg–Briand Pact was an international treaty that renounced the use of war as a means to settle international disputes. Previously, war as such was not prohibited by international law. States had erected a network of bilateral and multilateral treaties of non-aggression and alliance in order to protect themselves from attack and invasion.

[19] *France et al. v. Goering et al.*, (1946) 22 IMT 203; (1946) 13 ILR 203; (1946) 41 *American Journal of International Law* 172. The judgment itself, as well as the transcript of the

In December 1945, the four Allied powers enacted a somewhat modified version of the Charter of the International Military Tribunal, known as Control Council Law No. 10.[20] It provided the legal basis for a series of trials before military tribunals that were run by the occupying regime, as well as for subsequent prosecutions by German courts that continued for several decades. Control Council Law No. 10, which was really a form of domestic legislation because it applied to the prosecution of Germans by the courts of the civil authorities, largely borrowed the definition of crimes against humanity found in the Charter of the Nuremberg Tribunal, but omitted the latter's insistence on a link between crimes against humanity and the existence of a state of war, thereby facilitating prosecution for pre-1939 atrocities committed against German civilians, including persecution of the Jews and euthanasia of the disabled. Several important thematic trials were held pursuant to Control Council Law No. 10 in the period 1946–8 by American military tribunals. These focused on groups of defendants, such as judges, doctors, bureaucrats and military leaders.[21]

In the Pacific theatre, the victorious Allies established the International Military Tribunal for the Far East. Japanese war criminals were tried under similar provisions to those used at Nuremberg. The bench was more cosmopolitan, consisting of judges from eleven countries, including India, China and the Philippines, whereas the Nuremberg judges were appointed by the four major powers, the United States, the United Kingdom, France and the Soviet Union. Judge Pal of India wrote a lengthy dissenting opinion that reflected his profound anti-colonialist sentiments.

hearings and the documentary evidence, are reproduced in a forty-volume series published in English and French and available in most major reference libraries, as well as on the website of the Library of Congress (www.loc.gov/rr/frd/Military_Law/NT_major-war-criminals.html). The literature on the Nuremberg trial of the major war criminals is extensive. Probably the best modern account is Telford Taylor, *The Anatomy of the Nuremberg Trials*, New York: Alfred A. Knopf, 1992.

[20] Control Council Law No. 10, Punishment of Persons Guilty of War Crimes, Crimes Against Peace and Against Humanity, 20 December 1945, *Official Gazette of the Control Council for Germany*, No. 3, 31 January 1946, pp. 50–5.

[21] Frank M. Buscher, *The US War Crimes Trial Program in Germany, 1946–1955*, Westport, CT: Greenwood Press, 1989. The judgments in the cases, as well as much secondary material and documentary evidence, have been published in two series, one by the United States Government entitled *Trials of the War Criminals*, the other by the United Kingdom Government entitled *Law Reports of the Trials of the War Criminals*. Both series are readily available in reference libraries.

At Nuremberg, Nazi war criminals were charged with what the prosecutor called 'genocide', but the term did not appear in the substantive provisions of the Statute, and the Tribunal convicted them of 'crimes against humanity' for the atrocities committed against the Jewish people of Europe. Within weeks of the judgment, efforts began in the General Assembly of the United Nations to push the law further in this area. In December 1946, a resolution was adopted declaring genocide a crime against international law and calling for the preparation of a convention on the subject.[22] Two years later, the General Assembly adopted the Convention for the Prevention and Punishment of the Crime of Genocide.[23] The definition of genocide set out in Article II of the 1948 Convention is incorporated unchanged in the Rome Statute of the International Criminal Court, as Article 6. But, besides defining the crime and setting out a variety of obligations relating to its prosecution, Article VI of the Convention said that trial for genocide was to take place before 'a competent tribunal of the State in the territory of which the act was committed, or by such international penal tribunal as may have jurisdiction with respect to those Contracting Parties which shall have accepted its jurisdiction'. An early draft of the Genocide Convention prepared by the United Nations Secretariat had actually included a model statute for a court, based on the 1937 treaty developed within the League of Nations, but the proposal was too ambitious for the time and the conservative drafters stopped short of establishing such an institution.[24] Instead, a General Assembly resolution adopted the same day as the Genocide Convention, on 9 December 1948, called upon the International Law Commission to prepare the statute of the court promised by Article VI.[25]

The International Law Commission

The International Law Commission is a body of experts, named by the United Nations General Assembly, charged with the codification and progressive development of international law. Besides the mandate

---

[22] GA Res. 96 (I).

[23] Convention on the Prevention and Punishment of the Crime of Genocide, (1951) 78 UNTS 277.

[24] William A. Schabas, *Genocide in International Law: The Crime of Crimes*, 2nd edn, Cambridge: Cambridge University Press, 2009, pp. 62–3.

[25] Study by the International Law Commission of the Question of an International Criminal Jurisdiction, GA Res. 216 B (III).

to draft the statute of an international criminal court derived from Article VI of the Genocide Convention, in the post-war euphoria about war crimes prosecution the General Assembly had also asked the Commission to prepare what are known as the 'Nuremberg Principles', a task it completed in 1950,[26] and the 'Code of Crimes Against the Peace and Security of Mankind', a job that took considerably longer. The final version of the Code of Crimes was only adopted by the International Law Commission in 1996. Much of the work on the draft statute of an international criminal court and the draft code of crimes went on within the Commission in parallel, almost as if the two tasks were hardly related. The two instruments can be understood by analogy with domestic law. They correspond in a general sense to the definitions of crimes and general principles found in criminal or penal codes (the 'code of crimes'), and the institutional and procedural framework found in codes of criminal procedure (the 'statute').

Meanwhile, alongside the work of the International Law Commission, the General Assembly also established a committee charged with drafting the statute of an international criminal court. Composed of seventeen States, it submitted its report and draft statute in 1952.[27] A new committee, created by the General Assembly to review the draft statute in the light of comments by Member States, reported to the General Assembly in 1954.[28] The International Law Commission made considerable progress on its draft code and actually submitted a proposal in 1954.[29] Then, the General Assembly suspended the mandates, ostensibly pending the sensitive task of defining the crime of aggression.[30] By then,

---

[26] The Principles begin with an important declaration: 'Any person who commits an act which constitutes a crime under international law is responsible therefor and liable to punishment.' They proceed with statements excluding the defences of official capacity, superior orders and retroactive criminal law, they define the categories of crimes against peace, war crimes, and crimes against humanity, and provide that complicity in such crimes is also punishable.

[27] Report of the Committee on International Criminal Court Jurisdiction, UN Doc. A/2135 (1952).

[28] Report of the Committee on International Criminal Court Jurisdiction, UN Doc. A/2645 (1954).

[29] Yearbook ... 1954, vol. I, 267th meeting, para. 39, p. 131 (ten in favour, with one abstention). On the 1954 draft code in general, see D. H. N. Johnson, 'Draft Code of Offences Against the Peace and Security of Mankind', (1955) 4 International and Comparative Law Quarterly 445.

[30] GA Res. 897 (IX) (1954).

political tensions associated with the Cold War had made progress on the war crimes agenda virtually impossible.

The General Assembly eventually adopted a definition of aggression, in 1974,[31] but work did not immediately resume on the proposed international criminal court. In 1981, the General Assembly asked the International Law Commission to revive activity on its draft code of crimes.[32] Doudou Thiam was designated the Special Rapporteur of the Commission, and he produced annual reports on various aspects of the draft code for more than a decade. Thiam's work, and the associated debates in the Commission, addressed a range of questions, including definitions of crimes, criminal participation, defences and penalties.[33] A substantially revised version of the 1954 draft code was provisionally adopted by the Commission in 1991, and then sent to Member States for their reaction.

But the code did not necessarily involve an international jurisdiction. That aspect of the work was only initiated in 1989, the year of the fall of the Berlin Wall. Trinidad and Tobago, one of several Caribbean States plagued by narcotics problems and related transnational crime issues, initiated a resolution in the General Assembly directing the International Law Commission to consider the subject of an international criminal court within the context of its work on the draft code of crimes.[34] Special Rapporteur Doudou Thiam made an initial presentation on the subject in 1992. By 1993, the Commission had prepared a draft statute, this time under the direction of Special Rapporteur James Crawford. The draft statute was examined that year by the General Assembly, which encouraged the Commission to complete its work. The following year, in 1994, the Commission submitted the final version of its draft statute for an international criminal court to the General Assembly.[35]

The International Law Commission's draft statute of 1994 focused on procedural and organizational matters, leaving the question of

---

[31] GA Res. 3314 (XXIX) (1974).   [32] GA Res. 36/106 (1981).

[33] These materials appear in the annual reports of the International Law Commission.

[34] GA Res. 44/89.

[35] James Crawford, 'The ILC's Draft Statute for an International Criminal Tribunal', (1994) 88 *American Journal of International Law* 140; James Crawford, 'The ILC Adopts a Statute for an International Criminal Court', (1995) 89 *American Journal of International Law* 404. For the International Law Commission's discussion of the history of the draft statute, see Report of the International Law Commission on the Work of Its Forty-Sixth Session, 2 May–22 July 1994, UN Doc. A/49/10, chapter II, paras. 23–41.

defining the crimes and the associated legal principles to the code of crimes, which it had yet to complete. Two years later, at its 1996 session, the Commission adopted the final draft of its 'Code of Crimes Against the Peace and Security of Mankind'.[36] The draft statute of 1994 and the draft code of 1996 played a seminal role in the preparation of the Rome Statute of the International Criminal Court. The International Criminal Tribunal for the former Yugoslavia has remarked that 'the Draft Code is an authoritative international instrument which, depending upon the specific question at issue, may (i) constitute evidence of customary law, or (ii) shed light on customary rules which are of uncertain content or are in the process of formation, or, at the very least, (iii) be indicative of the legal views of eminently qualified publicists representing the major legal systems of the world'.[37]

The *ad hoc* tribunals

While the draft statute of an international criminal court was being considered in the International Law Commission, events compelled the creation of a court on an *ad hoc* basis in order to address the atrocities being committed in the former Yugoslavia. Already, in mid-1991, there had been talk in Europe of establishing a tribunal to try Saddam Hussein and other Iraqi leaders following the Gulf War. In late 1992, as war raged in Bosnia, a Commission of Experts established by the Security Council identified a range of war crimes and crimes against humanity that had been committed and that were continuing. It urged the establishment of an international criminal tribunal, an idea that had originally been recommended by Lord Owen and Cyrus Vance, who themselves were acting on a proposal from French constitutional judge Robert Badinter. The proposal was endorsed by the General Assembly in a December 1992 resolution. The rapporteurs appointed under the Moscow Human Dimension Mechanism of the Conference on Security and Cooperation in Europe, Hans Corell, Gro Hillestad Thune and Helmut Türk, took the initiative to prepare a draft statute. Several governments also

---

[36] Timothy L. H. McCormack and G. J. Simpson, 'The International Law Commission's Draft Code of Crimes Against the Peace and Security of Mankind: An Appraisal of the Substantive Provisions', (1994) 5 *Criminal Law Forum* 1; John Allain and John R. W. D. Jones, 'A Patchwork of Norms: A Commentary on the 1996 Draft Code of Crimes Against the Peace and Security of Mankind', (1997) 8 *European Journal of International Law* 100.

[37] *Furundžija* (IT-95-17/1-T), Judgment, 10 December 1998, para. 227.

submitted draft proposals or otherwise commented upon the creation of a tribunal.[38]

On 22 February 1993, the Security Council decided upon the establishment of a tribunal mandated to prosecute 'persons responsible for serious violations of international humanitarian law committed in the territory of the former Yugoslavia since 1991'.[39] The draft proposed by the Secretary-General was adopted without modification by the Security Council in its Resolution 827 of 8 May 1993. According to the Secretary-General's report, the tribunal was to apply rules of international humanitarian law that are 'beyond any doubt part of the customary law'.[40] The Statute clearly borrowed from the work then underway within the International Law Commission on the statute and the code of crimes, in effect combining the two into an instrument that both defined the crimes and established the procedure before the court. The Tribunal's territorial jurisdiction was confined within the frontiers of the former Yugoslavia. Temporally, it was entitled to prosecute offences beginning in 1991, leaving its end-point to be established by the Security Council.

In November 1994, acting on a request from Rwanda, the Security Council voted to create a second *ad hoc* tribunal, charged with the prosecution of genocide and other serious violations of international humanitarian law committed in Rwanda and in neighbouring countries during the year 1994.[41] Its Statute closely resembles that of the International Criminal Tribunal for the former Yugoslavia, although the war crimes provisions reflect the fact that the Rwandan genocide took place within the context of a purely internal armed conflict. The resolution creating the Tribunal expressed the Council's 'grave concern at the reports indicating that genocide and other systematic, widespread and flagrant violations of international humanitarian law have been committed in Rwanda', and referred to the reports of the Special Rapporteur for Rwanda of the United Nations Commission on Human Rights, as well as the preliminary report of the Commission of Experts, which the Council had established earlier in the year.

---

[38] For a general overview of the Tribunal, see the companion to this volume: William A. Schabas, *The UN International Criminal Tribunals, Former Yugoslavia, Rwanda and Sierra Leone*, Cambridge: Cambridge University Press, 2006.

[39] UN Doc. S/RES/808 (1993).

[40] Report of the Secretary-General Pursuant to Paragraph 2 of Security Council Resolution 808 (1993), UN Doc. S/25704.

[41] UN Doc. S/RES/955 (1994).

The Yugoslav and Rwandan Tribunals are in effect joined at the hip, sharing not only virtually identical statutes but also some of their institutions. The Security Council built in overlapping provisions, so that initially the Prosecutor was the same for both tribunals, as was the composition of the Appeals Chamber.[42] The consequence, at least in theory, was economy of scale as well as uniformity of both prosecutorial policy and appellate jurisprudence. The first major judgment by the Appeals Chamber of the Yugoslav Tribunal, the *Tadić* jurisdictional decision of 2 October 1995, clarified important legal issues relating to the creation of the body.[43] It also pointed the Tribunal towards an innovative and progressive view of war crimes law, going well beyond the Nuremberg precedents by declaring that crimes against humanity could be committed in peacetime and by establishing the punishability of war crimes during internal armed conflicts.

Subsequent rulings of the *ad hoc* tribunals on a variety of matters fed the debates on the creation of an international criminal court. The findings in *Tadić* with respect to the scope of war crimes were essentially incorporated into Article 8 of the Rome Statute of the International Criminal Court. The *obiter dictum* of the Appeals Chamber of the Yugoslav Tribunal declaring that crimes against humanity could be committed in time of peace and not just in wartime, as had been the case at Nuremberg, was also endorsed, in the text of Article 7. But other judgments, such as a controversial holding that excluded recourse to a defence of duress,[44] prompted drafters of the Rome Statute to enact a provision ensuring precisely the opposite.[45] The issue of 'national security' information, ignored by the International Law Commission, was thrust to the forefront of the debates after the Tribunal ordered Croatia to produce

---

[42] In 2000, the Statute of the International Criminal Tribunal for Rwanda was amended to allow for the appointment of two appellate judges. They sit in The Hague, and, together with five colleagues from the International Criminal Tribunal for the former Yugoslavia, they make up the Appeals Chamber of the two bodies. See UN Doc. S/RES/1329 (2000), Annex. In 2003, the Security Council further amended the Statute so that the Rwanda Tribunal would have its own Prosecutor: UN Doc. S/RES/1503 (2003). A few days later, the Security Council appointed Hassan Bubacar Jallow as ICTR Prosecutor: UN Doc. S/RES/1505 (2003).

[43] *Tadić* (IT-94-1-AR72), Decision on the Defence Motion for Interlocutory Appeal on Jurisdiction, 2 October 1995. There is no equivalent judgment from the Rwanda Tribunal. A motion raising similar issues to those in *Tadić* was dismissed by the Trial Chamber, but appeal of the ruling was discontinued. See *Kanyabashi* (ICTR-96-15-T), Decision on the Defence Motion on Jurisdiction, 18 June 1997.

[44] *Erdemović* (IT-96-22-A), Sentencing Appeal, 7 October 1997.

[45] Rome Statute of the International Criminal Court, (2002) 2187 UNTS 90, Art. 31(1)(d).

government documents,[46] and resulted in one of the lengthiest and most enigmatic provisions in the final Statute.[47] The Rome Conference also departed from some of the approaches taken by the Security Council itself, choosing, for example, to recognize a limited defence of superior orders whereas the Council's drafters had preferred simply to exclude this with an unambiguous provision. But the Tribunals did more than simply set legal precedent to guide the drafters. They also provided a reassuring model of what an international criminal court might look like. This was particularly important in debates concerning the role of the Prosecutor. The integrity, neutrality and good judgment of Richard Goldstone and his successor, Louise Arbour, answered those who warned of the dangers of a reckless and irresponsible 'Dr Strangelove prosecutor'.

Although by the mid-1990s attention had shifted from the *ad hoc* tribunals to the establishment of the permanent court, the creation of temporary institutions was not ruled out after the Rome Statute was adopted. In 2000, the Security Council instructed the Secretary-General to establish such an institution to deal with atrocities committed in Sierra Leone during the 1990s. It was a leaner and more focused version of the *ad hoc* tribunals, reflecting growing concerns within the Security Council about the cost of international justice. The International Criminal Court was already in the process of being established, but its temporal jurisdiction clause ruled out prosecutions for crimes committed prior to entry into force. Thus, the International Criminal Court was not in a position to assume responsibility for prosecutions concerning the Sierra Leone civil war. As a result, the Special Court for Sierra Leone was born in January 2002.[48]

In 2005, the United States argued for the establishment of yet another *ad hoc* tribunal.[49] The purpose was to address atrocities committed in the Darfur region of western Sudan. But, because there was no issue about the temporal jurisdiction of the International Criminal Court, given that all of the relevant events had occurred since the Rome Statute's entry into

---

[46] *Blaškić* (IT-95-14-AR108*bis*), Objection to the Issue of Subpoenae Duces Tecum, 29 October 1997.

[47] Rome Statute, Art. 72.

[48] Agreement between the United Nations and the Government of Sierra Leone on the Establishment of a Special Court for Sierra Leone, (2002) 2178 UNTS 138. The establishment of the Special Court for Sierra Leone is discussed in some detail in one of the Court's early rulings: *Kallon et al.* (SCSL-2004-15, 16 and 17-AR72-E), Decision on Constitutionality and Lack of Jurisdiction, 13 March 2004.

[49] UN Doc. S/PV.5158, p. 3.

force on 1 July 2002, there was very strong momentum from other States to refer the case to the new Court rather than to create another institution. In the result, the United States backed down, and the Darfur situation was referred by the Security Council to the International Criminal Court.[50]

In 2007, the fourth *ad hoc* tribunal, named the Special Tribunal for Lebanon, was established.[51] It is meant to address a wave of terrorist assassinations in Lebanon that began in February 2005 with the murder of Rafiq Hariri, the former Prime Minister of Lebanon, and twenty-two others. The matter is plainly within the temporal jurisdiction of the International Criminal Court, but there are difficulties with the subject-matter jurisdiction. When the Tribunal was being conceived, there may also have been some concern with a Darfur-like referral of a 'situation' in Lebanon that might raise the issue of Israeli war crimes committed in southern Lebanon during the July 2006 war, when in fact the intention was to limit the tribunal's activities to terrorist bombings of which Syria was an important suspect. Some might argue that terrorist acts, including assassinations, may fall within the scope of crimes against humanity, although this is not necessarily obvious. The report of the Secretary-General to the Security Council acknowledged the existence of a debate on this point.[52] But, although international, by virtue of its creation, the Tribunal can only prosecute crimes under Lebanese law. It uses a French-inspired procedural model that includes pre-trial judges and the possibility of *in absentia* trials.

Finally, the international community continues to explore a concept known as 'hybrid courts'.[53] These are institutions set up within the framework of national law, but with a strong international participation.

---

[50] UN Doc. S/RES/1593 (2005).   [51] Pursuant to UN Doc. S/RES/1757 (2007).

[52] Report of the Secretary-General on the Establishment of a Special Tribunal for Lebanon, UN Doc. S/2006/893, paras. 22–3; Report of the Secretary-General on the Establishment of a Special Tribunal for Lebanon, Addendum, Statement by Mr Nicolas Michel, Under-Secretary-General for Legal Affairs, the Legal Counsel, at the Informal Consultations Held by the Security Council on 20 November 2006, UN Doc. S/2006/893/Add.1.

[53] Laura A. Dickinson, 'The Promise of Hybrid Courts', (2003) 97 *American Journal of International Law* 295: 'Such courts are "hybrid" because both the institutional apparatus and the applicable law consist of a blend of the international and the domestic. Foreign judges sit alongside their domestic counterparts to try cases prosecuted and defended by teams of local lawyers working with those from other countries. The judges apply domestic law that has been reformed to accord with international standards.' The distinction between 'international' and 'hybrid' tribunals is made in the Secretary-General's August 2004 Report: The Rule of Law and Transitional Justice in Conflict and Post-Conflict Societies, UN Doc. S/2004/616, paras. 40, 45 and 46.

In particular, they often involve the presence of foreign judges and prosecutors, and apply provisions drawn from international law. In terms of content, they bear many resemblances to the international tribunals. But they are profoundly different in form, because they are not created by international law and they do not stand above the national legal order.

Drafting of the Rome Statute

In 1994, the United Nations General Assembly decided to pursue work towards the establishment of an international criminal court, taking the International Law Commission's draft statute as a basis.[54] It convened an Ad Hoc Committee, which met twice in 1995.[55] Debates within the Ad Hoc Committee revealed rather profound differences among States about the complexion of the future court, and some delegations continued to contest the overall feasibility of the project, although their voices became more and more subdued as the negotiations progressed. The International Law Commission draft envisaged a court with 'primacy', much like the *ad hoc* tribunals for the former Yugoslavia and Rwanda. If the court's prosecutor chose to proceed with a case, domestic courts could not pre-empt this by offering to do the job themselves. In meetings of the Ad Hoc Committee, a new concept reared its head, that of 'complementarity', by which the court could only exercise jurisdiction if domestic courts were unwilling or unable to prosecute. Another departure of the Ad Hoc Committee from the International Law Commission draft was its insistence that the crimes within the court's jurisdiction be

---

[54] All of the basic documents of the drafting history of the Statute, including the draft statute prepared by the International Law Commission, have been reproduced in M. Cherif Bassiouni, ed., *The Statute of the International Criminal Court: A Documentary History*, Ardsley, NY: Transnational Publishers, 1998. Professor Bassiouni has also produced a much more comprehensive three-volume collection of the documents: M. Cherif Bassiouni, ed., *The Legislative History of the International Criminal Court: Introduction, Analysis and Integrated Text*, Ardsley, NY: Transnational Publishers, 2005. The proceedings of the Rome Conference have been officially published by the United Nations in a three-volume edition: UN Doc. A/CONF.183/13. Most of the preparatory documents, including the 'non-papers' that are not officially recorded, can be found in the 'Legal Tools' section of the Court's website (www.legal-tools.org).

[55] Generally, on the drafting of the Statute, see M. Cherif Bassiouni, 'Negotiating the Treaty of Rome on the Establishment of an International Criminal Court', (1999) 32 *Cornell International Law Journal* 443; Adriaan Bos, 'From the International Law Commission to the Rome Conference (1994–1998)', in Antonio Cassese, Paola Gaeta and John R. W. D. Jones, eds., *The Rome Statute of the International Criminal Court: A Commentary*, vol. I, Oxford: Oxford University Press, 2002, pp. 35–64.

defined in some detail and not simply enumerated. The International Law Commission had contented itself with listing the crimes subject to the court's jurisdiction – war crimes, aggression, crimes against humanity and genocide – presumably because the draft code of crimes, on which it was also working, would provide the more comprehensive definitional aspects. Beginning with the Ad Hoc Committee, the nearly fifty-year-old distinction between the 'statute' and the 'code' disappeared. Henceforth, the statute would include detailed definitions of crimes as well as elaborate provisions dealing with general principles of law and other substantive matters. The Ad Hoc Committee concluded that the new court was to conform to principles and rules that would ensure the highest standards of justice, and that these should be incorporated in the statute itself rather than being left to the uncertainty of judicial discretion.[56]

It had been hoped that the Ad Hoc Committee's work would set the stage for a diplomatic conference where the statute could be adopted. But it became evident that this was premature. At its 1995 session, the General Assembly decided to convene a 'Preparatory Committee', inviting participation by Member States, non-governmental organizations and international organizations of various sorts. The 'PrepCom', as it became known, held two three-week sessions in 1996, presenting the General Assembly with a voluminous report comprising a hefty list of proposed amendments to the International Law Commission draft.[57] It met again in 1997, this time holding three sessions. These were punctuated by informal intersessional meetings, of which the most important was surely that held in Zutphen, in the Netherlands, in January 1998. The 'Zutphen draft' consolidated the various proposals into a more or less coherent text.[58] The 'Zutphen draft' was reworked somewhat at the final session of the PrepCom, and then submitted for consideration by the Diplomatic Conference.[59] Few provisions of the original International

---

[56] Report of the Ad Hoc Committee on the Establishment of an International Criminal Court, UN Doc. A/50/22. See Roy Lee, 'The Rome Conference and Its Contributions to International Law', in Roy Lee, ed., *The International Criminal Court: The Making of the Rome Statute, Issues, Negotiations, Results*, The Hague: Kluwer Law International, 1999, pp. 1–39 at p. 7; Tuiloma Neroni Slade and Roger S. Clark, 'Preamble and Final Clauses', in Lee, *ibid.*, pp. 421–50 at pp. 436–7.

[57] Report of the Preparatory Committee on the Establishment of an International Criminal Court, UN Doc. A/51/22.

[58] Report of the Inter-Sessional Meeting from 19 to 30 January 1998 in Zutphen, The Netherlands, UN Doc. A/AC.249/1998/L.13.

[59] Report of the Preparatory Committee on the Establishment of an International Criminal Court, Addendum, UN Doc. A/CONF.183/2/Add.1.

Law Commission proposal had survived intact. Most of the Articles in the final draft were accompanied with an assortment of options and alternatives, surrounded by square brackets to indicate a lack of consensus, foreboding difficult negotiations at the Diplomatic Conference.[60] Some important issues such as 'complementarity' – recognition that cases would only be admissible before the new court when national justice systems were unwilling or unable to try them – were largely resolved during the PrepCom process. The challenge to the negotiators at the Diplomatic Conference was to ensure that these issues were not reopened. Other matters, such as the issue of capital punishment, had been studiously avoided during the sessions of the PrepCom, and were to emerge suddenly as impasses in the final negotiations.

Pursuant to General Assembly resolutions adopted in 1996 and 1997,[61] the Diplomatic Conference of Plenipotentiaries on the Establishment of an International Criminal Court convened on 15 June 1998 in Rome, at the headquarters of the Food and Agriculture Organization. More than 160 States sent delegates to the Conference, in addition to a range of international organizations and literally hundreds of non-governmental organizations. The enthusiasm was quite astonishing, with essentially all of the delegations expressing their support for the concept. Driving the dynamism of the Conference were two new constituencies: a geographically heterogeneous caucus of States known as the 'like-minded'; and a well-organized coalition of non-governmental organizations.[62] The 'like-minded caucus', initially chaired by Canada, had been active since the early stages of the PrepCom, gradually consolidating its positions while at the same time expanding its membership. By the time the Rome Conference began, the 'like-minded caucus' included more than sixty of the 160 participating States.[63] The 'like-minded' were committed

---

[60] See M. Cherif Bassiouni, 'Observations Concerning the 1997–98 Preparatory Committee's Work', (1997) 25 *Denver Journal of International Law and Policy* 397.

[61] UN Doc. A/RES/51/207; UN Doc. A/RES/52/160.

[62] On the phenomenal and unprecedented contribution of non-governmental organizations, see William R. Pace and Mark Thieroff, 'Participation of Non-Governmental Organizations', in Lee, *The International Criminal Court*, pp. 391–8; William Bourdon, 'Rôle de la société civile et des ONG', in *La Cour pénale internationale*, Paris: La Documentation française, 1999, pp. 89–96; Marlies Glasius, *The International Criminal Court, A Global Civil Society Achievement*, London and New York: Routledge, 2006.

[63] Andorra, Argentina, Australia, Austria, Belgium, Benin, Bosnia-Herzegovina, Brunei, Bulgaria, Burkina Faso, Burundi, Canada, Chile, Congo (Brazzaville), Costa Rica, Croatia, Czech Republic, Denmark, Egypt, Estonia, Finland, Gabon, Georgia, Germany, Ghana, Greece, Hungary, Ireland, Italy, Jordan, Korea (Republic of), Latvia, Lesotho,

to a handful of key propositions that were substantially at odds with the premises of the 1994 International Law Commission draft and, by and large, in conflict with the conception of the court held by the permanent members of the Security Council. The principles of the 'like-minded' were: an inherent jurisdiction of the court over the 'core crimes' of genocide, crimes against humanity and war crimes (and, perhaps, aggression); the elimination of a Security Council veto on prosecutions; an independent prosecutor with the power to initiate proceedings *proprio motu*; and the prohibition of reservations to the statute. While operating relatively informally, the like-minded quickly dominated the structure of the Conference. Key functions, including the chairs of most of the working groups, as well as membership in the Bureau, which was the executive body that directed the day-to-day affairs of the Conference, were taken up by its members. Canada relinquished the chair of the 'like-minded' when the legal advisor to its foreign ministry, Philippe Kirsch, was elected president of the Conference's Committee of the Whole.

But there were other caucuses and groupings at work, many of them reflections of existing formations within other international bodies, like the United Nations. The caucus of the Non-Aligned Movement (NAM) was particularly active in its insistence that the crime of aggression be included within the subject-matter jurisdiction of the court. A relatively new force, the Southern African Development Community (SADC), under the dynamic influence of post-apartheid South Africa, took important positions on human rights, providing a valuable counterweight to the Europeans in this field. The caucus of the Arab and Islamic States was active in a number of areas, including a call for the prohibition of nuclear weapons, and support for inclusion of the death penalty within the statute. The beauty of the like-minded caucus, indeed the key to its great success, was its ability to cut across the traditional regionalist lines. Following the election of the Labour government in the United Kingdom in 1997, the like-minded caucus even managed to recruit a permanent member of the Security Council to its ranks.

The Rome Conference began with a few days of formal speeches from political figures, United Nations officials and personalities from the growing ranks of those actually involved in international criminal

Liechtenstein, Lithuania, Luxembourg, Malawi, Malta, Namibia, the Netherlands, New Zealand, Norway, the Philippines, Poland, Portugal, Romania, Samoa, Senegal, Sierra Leone, Singapore, Slovakia, Slovenia, Solomon Islands, South Africa, Spain, Swaziland, Sweden, Switzerland, Trinidad and Tobago, United Kingdom, Venezuela and Zambia.

prosecution, including the presidents of the two *ad hoc* tribunals and their Prosecutor.[64] Then the Conference divided into a series of working groups with responsibility for matters such as general principles, procedure and penalties. Much of this involved details, unlikely to create insurmountable difficulties to the extent that the delegates were committed to the success of the endeavour. But a handful of core issues – jurisdiction, the 'trigger mechanism' for prosecutions, the role of the Security Council – remained under the wing of the Bureau. These difficult questions were not publicly debated for most of the Conference, although much negotiating took place informally.

One by one, the provisions of the statute were adopted 'by general agreement' in the working groups, that is, without a vote. The process was tedious, in that it allowed a handful of States or even one of them to hold up progress by refusing to join the consensus. The chairs of the working groups would patiently negotiate compromises, drawing on comments by States that often expressed their views on a provision but then indicated their willingness to be flexible. Within a week of the beginning of the Conference, the working groups were forwarding progress reports to the Committee of the Whole, indicating the provisions that had already met with agreement. These were subsequently examined by the Drafting Committee, chaired by Professor M. Cherif Bassiouni, for terminological and linguistic coherence in the various official language versions of the statute.

But, as the weeks rolled by, the key issues remained to be settled, of which the most important were the role of the Security Council, the list of 'core crimes' over which the court would have inherent jurisdiction, and the scope of its jurisdiction over persons who were not nationals of States Parties. These had not been assigned to any of the working groups, and instead were handled personally by the chair of the Committee of the Whole, Philippe Kirsch. With two weeks remaining, Kirsch issued a draft that set out the options on these difficult questions. The problem, though, was that many States belonged to the majority on one question but dissented on others. Finding a common denominator, that is, a workable statute that could reliably obtain the support of two-thirds

---

[64] For a detailed discussion of the proceedings at the Rome Conference, see Philippe Kirsch and John T. Holmes, 'The Rome Conference on an International Criminal Court: The Negotiating Process', (1999) 93 *American Journal of International Law* 2; Roy Lee, 'The Rome Conference and Its Contributions to International Law', in Lee, *The International Criminal Court*, pp. 1–39, particularly pp. 21–3; and Philippe Kirsch, 'The Development of the Rome Statute', in Lee, *The International Criminal Court*, pp. 451–61.

of the delegates in the event that the draft statute was ever to come to a vote, remained daunting. Suspense mounted in the final week, with Kirsch promising a final proposal that in fact he only issued on the morning of 17 July, the day the Conference was scheduled to conclude. By then it was too late for any changes. Like a skilled blackjack player, Kirsch had carefully counted his cards, yet he had no guarantee that his proposal might not meet unexpected opposition and lead, inexorably, to the collapse of the negotiations. Throughout the final day of the Conference, delegates expressed their support for the 'package', and resisted any attempts to alter or adjust it out of fear that the entire compromise might unravel. The United States tried unsuccessfully to rally opposition, convening a meeting of what it had assessed as 'waverers'. Indeed, hopes that the draft statute might be adopted by consensus at the final session were dashed when the United States exercised its right to demand that a vote be taken. The result was 120 in favour, with twenty-one abstentions and seven votes against. The vote was not taken by roll call, and only the declarations made by States themselves indicate who voted for what. The United States, Israel and China stated that they had opposed adoption of the statute.[65] Among the abstainers were several Arab and Islamic States, as well as a number of delegations from the Commonwealth Caribbean.

In addition to the Rome Statute of the International Criminal Court,[66] on 17 July 1998 the Diplomatic Conference also adopted a Final Act,[67] providing for the establishment of a Preparatory Commission by the United Nations General Assembly. The Commission was assigned a variety of tasks, of which the most important were the drafting of the Rules of Procedure and Evidence,[68] which provide details on a variety of procedural and evidentiary questions, and the Elements of Crimes,[69] which elaborate upon the definitions of offences in Articles 6, 7, 8 and 8*bis* of the Statute. The Commission met the deadline of 30 June 2000, set for it by the Final Act, for the completion of the Rules

---

[65] UN Doc. A/CONF.183/SR.9, paras. 28, 33 and 40; Lee, *The International Criminal Court*, pp. 25–6; and Giovanni Conso, 'Looking to the Future', in Lee, *The International Criminal Court*, pp. 471–7. For the positions of the United States and China, see also UN Doc. A/C.6/53/SR.9.

[66] The text of the Statute adopted at the close of the Rome Conference contained a number of minor errors, essentially of a technical nature. There have been two attempts at correction of the English-language version of the Statute: UN Doc. C.N.577.1998.TREATIES-8 (10 November 1998) and UN Doc. C.N.604.1999.TREATIES-18 (12 July 1999).

[67] UN Doc. A/CONF.183/10.   [68] Provided for in Art. 51 of the Rome Statute.

[69] Provided for in Art. 9 of the Rome Statute.

and the Elements.[70] Other tasks included drafting an agreement with the United Nations on the relationship between the two organizations, preparation of a host State agreement with the Netherlands, and documents to direct or resolve a range of essentially administrative issues, such as the preliminary budget. An Agreement on the Privileges and Immunities of the International Criminal Court was also adopted. It provides the personnel of the Court with a range of special measures analogous to those of United Nations personnel and diplomats. It is up to individual States to sign and ratify this treaty.[71] The Preparatory Commission held ten sessions, concluding its work in July 2002 just as the Statute was entering into force, although it did not formally dissolve until September 2002.

---

[70] Elements of Crimes, ASP/1/3, pp. 108–55; Rules of Procedure and Evidence, ASP/1/3, pp. 10–107.

[71] Agreement on the Privileges and Immunities of the International Criminal Court, ASP/1/3, pp. 215–32. See Phakiso Mochochoko, 'The Agreement on Privileges and Immunities in the International Criminal Court', (2002) 25 *Fordham International Law Journal* 638.

2

The Court becomes operational

The Statute required sixty ratifications or accessions for entry into force. The date of entry into force – 1 July 2002 – is an important one, if only because the Court cannot prosecute crimes committed prior to entry into force. Entry into force also began the real formalities of establishing the Court, such as the election of judges and Prosecutor. States were also invited to sign the Statute, which is a preliminary step indicating their intention to ratify. They were given until the end of 2000 to do so, and some 139 availed themselves of the opportunity.[1] Even States that had voted against the Statute at the Rome Conference, such as the United States and Israel, ultimately decided to sign. Many of those which had abstained in the vote on 17 July 1998 also signed. States wishing to join the Court who did not deposit their signatures by the 31 December 2000 deadline are said to accede to, rather than ratify, the Statute.[2]

Senegal was the first to ratify the Statute, on 2 February 1999, followed by Trinidad and Tobago two months later. The pace of ratification was speedier and more dramatic than anyone had realistically expected. By the second anniversary of the adoption of the Statute, fourteen ratifications had been deposited. By 31 December 2000, when the signature process ended, there were twenty-seven parties. On the third anniversary of adoption, the total stood at thirty-seven. Significant delays between signature and ratification were to be expected, because most States needed to undertake significant legislative changes in order to comply with the obligations imposed by the Statute, and it was normal for them to want to resolve these issues before formal ratification. Specifically, they were required to provide for cooperation with the Court in terms of investigation, arrest and transfer of suspects. A significant number of States

---

[1] A list of signatories and of States Parties appears in Appendix 2 to this volume.
[2] There have been nine accessions: Afghanistan, Cook Islands, Dominica, Japan, Montenegro, St Kitts and Nevis, Serbia, Suriname and Timor Leste.

prohibit the extradition of their own nationals, a situation incompatible with the requirements of the Statute, and legislative changes were necessary to resolve the conflict. In addition, because the Statute is predicated on 'complementarity', by which States themselves are presumed to be responsible for prosecuting suspects found on their own territory, some felt obliged to bring their substantive criminal law into line, enacting the offences of genocide, crimes against humanity and war crimes as defined in the Statute and ensuring that their courts can exercise universal jurisdiction over these crimes.[3]

The magic number of sixty ratifications was reached on 11 April 2002. In fact, because several were planning to ratify at the time, the United Nations organized a special ceremony at which ten States deposited their instruments simultaneously. The Statute provides for entry into force on the first day of the month after the sixtieth day following the date of deposit of the sixtieth instrument of ratification.[4] Accordingly, the Statute entered into force on 1 July 2002.

The Assembly of States Parties was promptly convened for its first session, which was held on 3–10 September 2002. The Assembly formally adopted the Elements of Crimes and the Rules of Procedure and Evidence in versions unchanged from those that had been approved by the Preparatory Commission two years earlier. A number of other important instruments were also adopted, and plans made for the election of the eighteen judges and the Prosecutor. Nominations for these positions closed at the end of November 2002, with more than forty candidates for judge but none for the crucially important position of Prosecutor. Elections of the judges were completed by the Assembly during the first week of February 2003, at its resumed first session. In a totally unprecedented development for international courts and tribunals, more than one-third of the judges elected in February 2003 were women.[5] The first Prosecutor, Luis Moreno-Ocampo of Argentina, was elected in April 2003.

---

[3] William A. Schabas, 'The Follow Up to Rome: Preparing for Entry into Force of the International Criminal Court Statute', (1999) 20 *Human Rights Law Journal* 157; S. Rama Rao, 'Financing of the Court, Assembly of States Parties and the Preparatory Commission', in Lee, *The International Criminal Court*, pp. 399–420 at pp. 414–20; Bruce Broomhall, 'The International Criminal Court: A Checklist for National Implementation', (1999) 13*quater Nouvelles études pénales* 113.

[4] Rome Statute of the International Criminal Court, (2002) 2187 UNTS 90, Art. 126(1).

[5] See Assembly of States Parties to the Rome Statute of the International Criminal Court, First Session, New York, 3–10 September 2002, Official Records, ASP/1/3.

The rise and fall of United States opposition

Even prior to entry into force, it became increasingly clear that a show-down was looming between the United States and the Court. During the negotiations to establish the Court, the United States had made many constructive and helpful contributions. Nevertheless, it was unhappy with the final result. Many assessments of the position of the United States often reduce it to the simple proposition that Washington wants to protect its own citizens from the jurisdiction of the Court.[6] A distinct but related argument contests the legality of the Court's alleged jurisdiction over third States. In an official statement, one American diplomat said 'the United States respects the decision of those nations who have chosen to join the ICC; but they in turn must respect our decision not to join the ICC or place our citizens under the jurisdiction of the court'.[7] This is, of course, a perfectly logical response by Washington to a Court that it does not like. But, it does not respond to the rather obvious observation that the United States sought to establish a Court that it would be able to support and that would, consequently, exercise jurisdiction over United States nationals. As Monroe Leigh pointed out, '[o]nly very late in the negotiations did the United States introduce this objection as a fundamental obstacle to its acceptance of the treaty'.[8] The implication is that the issue was not genuinely central to American concerns. In fact, exclusion of United States nationals from the jurisdiction of the Court was never a policy objective of the United States when the Statute was being drafted.

The muddle of arguments against the International Criminal Court from the United States no doubt reflects some of the differences within Washington's policy-making community. Conservative Republicans, like John Bolton, present a litany of justifications for United States opposition that are in large part nothing more than a general hostility to multilateral diplomacy and international organizations. The complex discourse advanced by the United States is at times confusing. It is necessary to separate serious objections from more trivial ones, and

---

[6] For example, Marina Halberstam, in 'Association of American Law Schools Panel on the International Criminal Court', (1999) 36 *American Criminal Law Review* 223 at 257.

[7] 'US under Secretary of State for Political Affairs Marc Grossman, American Foreign Policy and the International Criminal Court, Remarks to the Center for Strategic and International Studies', 6 May 2002, available at www.state.gov/p/9949pf.htm.

[8] Monroe Leigh, 'The United States and the Statute of Rome', (2001) 95 *American Journal of International Law* 124 at 127.

to distinguish what are really no more than technical criticisms. John Bolton was right when he said that 'never before has the United States been asked to place [the power of law enforcement] outside the complete control of our government without our consent'.[9]

In order to comprehend the logic behind the opposition of the United States towards the International Criminal Court, it is helpful to consider what the United States actually wanted. In 1994, when the International Law Commission presented its report on an international criminal court to the General Assembly,[10] the United States was well disposed to the proposal.[11] In a general sense, the International Law Commission draft provided for an international criminal court that fitted neatly within the Charter of the United Nations and that was, accordingly, subordinate to the Security Council. It might be described as a permanent version of the *ad hoc* tribunal for the former Yugoslavia established a year earlier by the Security Council. As Ambassador David Scheffer, who led the United States delegation at Rome, has noted:

> [t]he ILC's final draft statute for the ICC addressed many of the US object-ives and constituted, in our opinion, a good starting point for far more detailed and comprehensive discussions. Though not identical to US posi-tions, the ILC draft recognized that the Security Council should deter-mine whether cases that pertain to its functions under Chapter VII of the UN Charter should be considered by the ICC, that the Security Council must act before any alleged crime of aggression could be prosecuted against an individual, and that the prosecutor should act only in cases referred either by a state party to the treaty or by the Council.[12]

The experts at the International Law Commission conceived of a per-manent court seamlessly positioned within the framework of the Charter of the United Nations. Specifically, the International Law Commission addressed potential points of friction between the future court and the Security Council. For the United States, this was a court that made sense.

---

[9] 'The United States and the International Criminal Court, John R. Bolton, Under Secretary for Arms Control and International Security, Remarks at the Aspen Institute, Berlin, Germany, 16 September 2002', available at www.state.gov/t/us/rm/13538.htm.

[10] Report of the International Law Commission on the Work of Its Forty-Sixth Session, 2 May–22 July 1994, UN Doc. A/49/10, Chapter II. See James Crawford, 'The ILC Adopts a Statute for an International Criminal Court', (1995) 89 *American Journal of International Law* 404.

[11] UN Doc. A/CN.4/458/Add.7.

[12] David J. Scheffer, 'The United States and the International Criminal Court', (1999) 93 *American Journal of International Law* 12 at 13.

To the extent the final product promised to be along the lines projected by the International Law Commission, the United States was willing to contribute to the effort. The focus on the role of the Security Council appears in other major policy declarations of United States officials during the course of the negotiations.[13] Thoughtful academic commentators who support the government's position also seem to grasp the centrality of the Security Council issue. In a recent article, Jack Goldsmith has condemned 'the ICC's unprecedented attempt to check the power of the Security Council'.[14]

But the dynamics of the post-Cold War world revealed an underlying malaise with the Security Council's monopoly on such matters. The result at Rome was a new international institution, distinct from the United Nations and yet exercising authority in a field that had previously been occupied, albeit on a piecemeal basis, by the Security Council. In a sense, the Rome Statute was an attempt by many States to effect indirectly what could not be done directly, namely, reform of the United Nations and amendment of the Charter. This unprecedented challenge to the Security Council accounts for the difficulties with the United States. But it also contributes to understanding and explaining the astonishing success of the organization. It is precisely because of this bold and exciting challenge to the existing mechanisms of the United Nations that so many States have enthusiastically joined the new venture. Had the Rome Statute been more accommodating to the Security Council, and had it more closely resembled the 1994 draft of the International Criminal Court, the United States might be a State Party. But this would have dampened the enthusiasm of other States. Overall, there might well have been considerably fewer States Parties than there are today.[15]

---

[13] William J. Clinton, 'Remarks at the University of Connecticut in Storrs', 15 October 1995, 2 Pub. Papers 1595, 159; 'Statement by Jamison S. Borek, Deputy Legal Advisor to the Sixth Committee of the General Assembly', 1 November 1995; Bill Richardson, 'Statement in the Plenary Session of the UN Diplomatic Conference of Plenipotentiaries on the Establishment of an International Criminal Court', 19 June 1998; Lincoln P. Bloomfield Jr, Assistant Secretary for Political-Military Affairs, in a speech to the Consultative Assembly of Parliamentarians for Global Action, New York, 12 September 2003.

[14] Jack Goldsmith, 'The Self-Defeating International Criminal Court', (2003) 70 *University of Chicago Law Review* 89 at 101.

[15] For further discussion of this, see William A. Schabas, 'United States Hostility to the International Criminal Court: It's All About the Security Council', (2004) 15 *European Journal of International Law* 701.

One of the final acts of the Clinton administration was to sign the Statute, literally at the eleventh hour, on the evening of 31 December 2000.[16] The administration had been somewhat divided on the issue, as elements within the Department of State – some of them fundamentally sympathetic to the Court – tried to 'fix' the Statute and thereby facilitate United States support or, at the very least, a modicum of benign tolerance. The Bush administration, which took office a few weeks later, was overtly hostile to the Court. It approached the United Nations Secretariat to see if the signature could be revoked. But, while international law does not permit a treaty to be 'unsigned', the Vienna Convention on the Law of Treaties clearly envisages a situation where a State, subsequent to signature, has changed its mind. According to Article 18 of the Vienna Convention, a signatory State may not 'defeat the object and purpose of a treaty prior to its entry into force' until it has made clear its intent not to become a party to the treaty.[17] This is what the Bush administration did on 6 May 2002, in a communication filed with the United Nations Secretary-General.[18]

---

[16] The chief negotiator for the United States, David Scheffer, offered several reasons for signature, including maintaining the country's influence within the ongoing negotiations, influencing national judges and prosecutors to take a positive view of the Court, and enhancing the country's 'leadership on international justice issues'. See David J. Scheffer, 'Staying the Course with the International Criminal Court', (2002) 35 *Cornell International Law Journal* 47. Ambassador Scheffer left the Department of State when the administration changed in 2001, and subsequently took a public position favouring ratification by the United States. On the United States position, see also William K. Lietzau, 'The United States and the International Criminal Court: International Criminal Law After Rome: Concerns from a US Military Perspective', (2001) 64 *Law and Contemporary Problems* 119; Ruth Wedgwood, 'The International Criminal Court: An American View', (1999) 10 *European Journal of International Law* 93; Gerhard Hafner, Kristen Boon, Anne Rübesame and Jonathan Huston, 'A Response to the American View as Presented by Ruth Wedgwood', (1999) 10 *European Journal of International Law* 108; and David Forsythe, 'The United States and International Criminal Justice', (2002) 24 *Human Rights Quarterly* 974.

[17] Vienna Convention on the Law of Treaties, (1979) 1155 UNTS 331.

[18] The statement reads: 'This is to inform you, in connection with the Rome Statute of the International Criminal Court adopted on July 17, 1998, that the United States does not intend to become a party to the treaty. Accordingly, the United States has no legal obligations arising from its signature on December 31, 2000. The United States requests that its intention not to become a party, as expressed in this letter, be reflected in the depositary's status lists relating to this treaty.' Israel did much the same thing on 28 August 2002. On 'unsigning' treaties, see Harold Hongju Koh, 'On American Exceptionalism', (2003) 55 *Stanford Law Review* 1479; Edward T. Swaine, 'Unsigning', (2003) 55 *Stanford Law Review* 2061; and David C. Scott, 'Presidential Power to "Un-Sign" Treaties', (2002) 69 *University of Chicago. Law Review* 1447.

The 'unsigning' was only a precursor for more aggressive challenges to the Court. Most of this took the form of measures aimed at protecting what were euphemistically referred to as 'US peacekeepers'.[19] The United States pressured a number of States to reach bilateral agreements whose purpose was to shelter American nationals from the Court. These were made pursuant to Article 98(2) of the Statute, which prevents the Court from proceeding with a request to surrender an accused if this would require the requested State to breach an international agreement that it has made with another State. The provision was actually intended to recognize what are known as 'host State agreements' and 'status of forces agreements'.[20] Such instruments give a kind of immunity to foreign military forces based in another State, or to various international and non-governmental organizations. The new agreements that the United States was pushing went much further, because they applied to all of its citizens within the State in question. Perhaps these were consistent with a technical reading of Article 98(2), although they were not at all what was meant when the provision was adopted. American diplomats succeeded in bullying more than 100 States – almost half of them not even parties to the Statute, for whom such obligations were irrelevant – into signing these agreements. However, those States with the most significant numbers of American residents, such as Canada, Mexico and those of Western Europe, for whom there might be some real significance to the possibility of enforcement of surrender orders issued by the Court, have refused to entertain what they have understood as a more or less indirect attack on the Court. On 25 September 2002, the European Parliament opposed the bilateral immunity agreements being proposed by the United States, saying that they were inconsistent with the Rome Statute. But in 2005, as part of the *quid pro quo* for United States abstention on the referral of the Darfur situation to the Court, a preambular paragraph in Security Council Resolution 1593 took note of the existence of the Article 98(2) agreements, giving them a degree of legitimacy. During the debate, the representative of the United States said:

> As is well known, in connection with our concerns about the jurisdiction of the Court and the potential for politicized prosecutions, we have concluded agreements with 99 countries – over half the States Members

[19] See Sean D. Murphy, 'Efforts to Obtain Immunity from ICC for US Peacekeepers', (2002) 96 *American Journal of International Law* 725.

[20] David Scheffer, 'Article 98(2) of the Rome Statute: America's Original Intent', (2005) 3 *Journal of International Criminal Justice* 333.

of this Organization – since the entry into force of the Rome Statute to protect against the possibility of transfer or surrender of United States persons to the Court. We appreciate that the resolution takes note of the existence of those agreements and will continue to pursue additional such agreements with other countries as we move forward.[21]

Most of the States Parties to the Rome Statute who were present during the debate acquiesced, making no comment on the reference to the Article 98(2) agreements.[22]

Worse was yet to come, however. Within a few days of the Statute's entry into force, the United States announced that it would veto all future Security Council resolutions concerning peacekeeping and collective security operations until the Council adopted a resolution that would, in effect, exclude members of such operations from the jurisdiction of the Court.[23] As early as May 2002, it had threatened to withdraw peacekeeping troops from East Timor if there was no immunity.[24] The debate erupted as the Council was about to renew the mandate of its mission in Bosnia and Herzegovina. Even with the proposed resolution, United Nations peacekeepers, as well as the much larger contingent of United States armed forces and those of other States that belong to the NATO-led Stabilization Force (SFOR), remained subject to the jurisdiction of the International Criminal Tribunal for the former Yugoslavia. The United States was really concerned about other parts of the world. The blackmail succeeded, but to outraged protests from many States, including such traditional friends as Germany and Canada.[25]

Finally, on 2 August 2002, President Bush signed into law the American Service Members' Protection Act. Referring to the Rome Statute, the preamble to the Act declares: 'Not only is this contrary to the most fundamental principles of treaty law, it could inhibit the ability of the US to use its military to meet alliance obligations and participate in multinational operations including humanitarian interventions to save civilian lives.' The Act prohibits agencies of the United States

---

[21] UN Doc. S/PV.5158, p. 4.　　[22] Brazil was the one exception: *ibid.*, p. 11.

[23] UN Doc. S/RES/1422 (2002). See Mohamed El Zeidy, 'The United States Dropped the Atomic Bomb of Article 16 of the ICC Statute: Security Council Power of Deferrals and Resolution 1422', (2002) 35 *Vanderbilt Journal of Transnational Law* 1503; Aly Mokhtar, 'The Fine Art of Arm-Twisting: The US, Resolution 1422 and Security Council Deferral Power under the Rome Statute', (2004) 4 *International Criminal Law Review* 295.

[24] Colum Lynch, 'US Seeks Court Immunity for E. Timor Peacekeepers', *Washington Post*, 16 May 2002, p. A22; Colum Lynch, 'US Peacekeepers May Leave E. Timor', *Washington Post*, 18 May 2002, p. A20.

[25] UN Doc. S/PV.4568.

Government from cooperating with the Court, imposes restrictions on participation in United Nations peacekeeping activities, prohibits United States military assistance to States Parties to the Statute, and authorizes the use of force to free any United States citizen who is detained or imprisoned by or on behalf of the Court.[26] It was soon christened the 'Hague Invasion Act' by its many critics who imagined a scenario of the Marines landing on the beaches of Scheveningen in an attempt to rescue some latter-day Henry Kissinger.

These developments proved to be little more than squalls, and the Court has weathered them without major mishap. At times, it seemed as if opposition from the United States only enhanced the enthusiasm of other countries for the Court. They may have reasoned that there must be something positive about an institution that can annoy the United States so much. Its opposition amounts to a failure for United States diplomacy, not unlike the position it took in the 1950s with respect to human rights treaties within the United Nations. For two decades, the United States refused to participate in the development of the human rights instruments, before eventually accepting them.[27] After withdrawing completely from negotiations with respect to the International Covenant on Civil and Political Rights in 1953, and thereby denying itself a role in influencing the content of the instrument as it was being drafted, the United States eventually signed the Covenant, in the late 1970s, and then ratified it, in 1992. A similar tale can be told of the 1948 Genocide Convention, which the United States took forty years to ratify.[28]

The first sign that United States opposition to the International Criminal Court was flagging came in June 2004, when it decided not to argue for renewal of the Security Council resolution that it had pushed through two years earlier. Security Council Resolution 1422 had been adopted in accordance with Article 16 of the Rome Statute. Many argued that this was a misuse of the provision,[29] but the fact remains that the Resolution passed unanimously. Article 16 specifies that any 'deferral' of prosecution by the Security Council must be renewed every twelve

---

[26] Sean D. Murphy, 'American Servicemembers' Protection Act', (2002) 96 American Journal of International Law 975.

[27] Louis Henkin, 'US Ratification of Human Rights Conventions: The Ghost of Senator Bricker', (1995) 89 American Journal of International Law 341.

[28] Lawrence J. Leblanc, The United States and the Genocide Convention, Durham, NC: Duke University Press, 1991.

[29] Kai Ambos, 'International Criminal Law Has Lost Its Innocence', (2002) 3 German Law Journal 382; Carsten Stahn, 'The Ambiguities of Security Council Resolution 1422', (2003) 14 European Journal of International Law 85.

months. This is indeed what occurred the following year, in June 2003.[30] But three States – France, Germany and Syria – abstained on Resolution 1487. It was essentially symbolic opposition; France could have blocked the resolution with its veto, just as any seven members could have denied the requisite majority. Nevertheless, the 2003 vote suggested that annual renewal of the Article 16 deferral resolution could not be assumed. The following year, revelations about torture being conducted in Abu Ghraib prison by United States military personnel shocked the world. Shamed and humbled by the tales of abuse, and nervous about growing opposition within the Security Council, the United States decided to drop the resolution. What once seemed a serious challenge to the authority of the Court now looks like little more than a hiccup.

The following year, in March 2005, the United States abstained when the Security Council voted to refer the situation in Darfur, in western Sudan, to the International Criminal Court, in accordance with Article 13(b) of the Statute.[31] The United States can, of course, veto any resolution in the Security Council, a power of which it makes frequent use. Its abstention is therefore a form of acquiescence. Explaining her country's position to the Security Council at the time Resolution 1593 was adopted, the United States representative said 'we do not agree to a Security Council referral of the situation in Darfur to the ICC', but added that '[w]e decided not to oppose the resolution because of the need for the international community to work together in order to end the climate of impunity in the Sudan and because the resolution provides protection from investigation or prosecution for United States nationals and members of the armed forces of non-State parties'. She said that, although 'the United States believes that the better mechanism would have been a hybrid tribunal in Africa, it is important that the international community speak with one voice in order to help promote effective accountability'.[32]

During 2005 and 2006, it became increasingly clear that yet another component of the United States strategy to fight the Court was not working. Certain elements of the United States military began publicly challenging the campaign to promote bilateral immunity agreements, in accordance with Article 98(2) of the Rome Statute. In order to induce States to sign such treaties, American diplomats had been threatening

---

[30] UN Doc. S/RES/1487 (2003). Similar provisions were also incorporated into a resolution setting up a Multilateral Force in Liberia: UN Doc. S/RES/1497 (2003).
[31] UN Doc. S/RES/1593 (2005).   [32] UN Doc. S/PV.5158, p. 3.

to withdraw forms of military assistance. When some countries called their bluff, China was poised to replace whatever the United States was denying. American generals soon realized that they had shot themselves in the foot.[33] In late November 2006, President Bush waived the penalties imposed upon countries that refused to reach bilateral immunity agreements.

Although there was much angst about the immunity agreements among States Parties and the supporters of the Court in the NGO and academic communities, the issue proved to be of little real significance. In practice, these agreements never operated as an obstacle to the Court. In 2010, at the Review Conference, they were barely mentioned during the so-called 'stocktaking' exercise on cooperation.[34] The whole business was little more than a storm in a teacup.

On 14 June 2006, the *Wall Street Journal* reported on an interview with John Bellinger, the Legal Adviser to the Secretary of State:

> US officials concede they can't delegitimize a court that now counts 100 member countries, including such allies as Australia, Britain and Canada. While insisting the Bush administration will never allow Americans to be tried by the court, 'we do acknowledge that it has a role to play in the overall system of international justice,' John Bellinger, the State Department's chief lawyer, said in an interview … In a May speech, Mr Bellinger said 'divisiveness over the ICC distracts from our ability to pursue these common goals' of fighting genocide and crimes against humanity.[35]

In July 2008, when members of the Security Council, including several States Parties to the Rome Statute, contemplated invoking Article 16 in order to block proceedings against Sudanese President Omar Al-Bashir, the United States abstained in the vote 'because the language added to the resolution would send the wrong signal to Sudanese President Al-Bashir and undermine efforts to bring him and others to justice'.[36] Things had come full circle. From abusive resort to Article 16 in 2002 and 2003, the

---

[33] See, e.g., Statements by General Bantz J. Craddock, Head of United States Southern Command, before the House Armed Services Committee, 16 March 2006, and before the Senate Armed Services Committee, 19 September 2006; Vice Admiral James G. Stavridis, nominee for Commander, United States Southern Command, before the Senate Armed Services Committee, 19 September 2006.

[34] Declaration on Cooperation, RC/Decl.2; Stocktaking of International Criminal Justice, Cooperation, Summary of the Roundtable Discussion, RC/ST/CP/1.

[35] Jess Bravin, 'US Warms to Hague Tribunal: New Stance Reflects Desire to Use Court to Prosecute Darfur Crimes', *Wall Street Journal*, 14 June 2006.

[36] UN Doc. S/PV.5947, p. 8.

United States had become the most uncompromising defender of the integrity of the Statute.

The election of Barack Obama in 2008 no doubt contributed to this trend, and soon long-time supporters of the Court were occupying important positions within the United States administration. In November 2009, the United States returned to the observer seat in the Court's Assembly of States Parties that it had left empty since 2002. It participated actively in the Review Conference in June 2010. The recent friendship of the United States with the Court cannot solely be explained by political changes within that country, because the shift actually began early in the second Bush administration. Rather, the United States has warmed to the Court because its sphere of activity, essentially in central Africa, is within the comfort zone of United States interests and foreign policy.

The United States is unlikely to ratify the Rome Statute in the foreseeable future. Even with the political will of the administration, the constitution sets a very high threshold of two-thirds of the Senate. Although not a State Party, the United States can still continue to contribute to the Court in many ways. The relatively brief period of antagonism that characterized a period during the Bush administration stands out as a great diplomatic defeat for the United States.

Developing a prosecution strategy

Within days of taking office in early 2003, Prosecutor Luis Moreno-Ocampo issued a 'Draft Policy Paper' and invited comments.[37] He convened two days of public hearings in The Hague, on 17–18 June 2003, for discussion of his proposed priorities and strategies. In September 2003, the finished version of the 'Paper on Some Policy Issues before the Office of the Prosecutor' appeared. Moreno-Ocampo noted that, in determining where to initiate prosecutions, he would have to take into account the practical realities, including questions of security on the ground' and 'the necessary means of investigation and possibilities for protection of witnesses'.[38]

Under the principle of 'complementarity', defined in Article 17 of the Rome Statute, the Court may only proceed with a case when the

---

[37] Draft Paper on Some Policy Issues before the Office of the Prosecutor, for Discussion at the Public Hearing in The Hague on 17 and 18 June 2003.

[38] *Ibid.*, p. 2.

State responsible for prosecution can be shown to be 'unwilling or unable' to proceed. Referring to the concept of complementarity with national justice systems, Moreno-Ocampo said he would encourage States to initiate their own proceedings before national judicial institutions. 'As a general rule, the policy of the Office of the Prosecutor will be to undertake investigations only where there is a clear case of failure to act by the State or States concerned', he wrote.[39] Moreno-Ocampo said:

> The principle of complementarity represents the express will of States Parties to create an institution that is global in scope while recognising the primary responsibility of States themselves to exercise criminal jurisdiction. The principle is also based on considerations of efficiency and effectiveness since States will generally have the best access to evidence and witnesses.[40]

Moreover, 'the system of complementarity is principally based on the recognition that the exercise of national criminal jurisdiction is not only a right but also a duty of States'.[41]

But the Prosecutor also suggested a somewhat different philosophy, by which the Court's operations might result from cooperation rather than antagonism:

> [T]here may be cases where inaction by States is the appropriate course of action. For example, the Court and a territorial State incapacitated by mass crimes may agree that a consensual division of labour is the most logical and effective approach. Groups bitterly divided by conflict may oppose prosecutions at each others' hands and yet agree to a prosecution by a Court perceived as neutral and impartial.[42]

Nevertheless, he said, '[a]s a general rule, however, the policy of the Office in the initial phase of its operations will be to take action only where there is a clear case of failure to take national action'.[43]

The policy paper indicated that the targets of prosecution would be 'the leaders who bear most responsibility for the crimes'. Wherever possible, the Prosecutor would encourage national prosecutions for lower-ranking perpetrators. According to the Prosecutor, the global character of the Court, its statutory provisions and its logistical constraints all direct its investigative and prosecutorial efforts and resources onto 'those who bear the greatest responsibility, such as the leaders of the State or

[39] *Ibid.*   [40] *Ibid.*, p. 5.   [41] *Ibid.*   [42] *Ibid.*   [43] *Ibid.*

organization allegedly responsible for those crimes'.[44] He warned of an 'impunity gap', where perpetrators who did not qualify as 'those who bear the greatest responsibility' might escape accountability.[45] This general approach continues to be enriched by other public documents issued by the Office of the Prosecutor, including two periodic reports on prosecutorial strategy.[46]

The term 'those who bear the greatest responsibility' seems to have originated in the Security Council resolution proposing the establishment of the Special Court for Sierra Leone.[47] At the time, the United Nations Secretary-General said this was an indication of a limitation on the number of accused by reference to their command authority and the gravity and scale of the crime. Kofi Annan proposed, as an alternative, 'that the more general term "persons most responsible" should be used'.[48] But the Security Council did not agree, replying that its 'those who bear the greatest responsibility' terminology should be retained, in order to limit the focus of the Special Court 'to those who played a leadership role'.[49] The Special Court for Sierra Leone has since interpreted the terms in light of the drafting history, holding that the leadership role of an accused rather than the severity of the crime or its massive scale should determine jurisdiction.[50] According to the Prosecutor of the International Criminal Court, 'the Office will select for prosecution those situated at the highest echelons of responsibility, including those who ordered, financed, or otherwise organized the alleged crimes'.[51] The Appeals Chamber appears to take a somewhat different view of this. It said it was difficult to understand how the deterrent effect of the Court could be enhanced if perpetrators other than leaders could not be brought before the Court. 'It seems more logical to assume that the deterrent effect of the Court is highest if no category of perpetrators is *per se* excluded from potentially being brought before the Court.'[52] The Appeals Chamber continued:

---

[44] *Ibid.*, p. 7.   [45] *Ibid.*, p. 5.

[46] Office of the Prosecutor, Report on Prosecutorial Strategy, 14 September 2006; Prosecutorial Strategy 2009–2012, 1 February 2010, The Hague.

[47] UN Doc. S/RES/1315 (2000).

[48] Report of the Secretary-General on the Establishment of a Special Court for Sierra Leone, UN Doc. S/2000/915, para. 29.

[49] Letter Dated 22 December 2000 from the President of the Security Council Addressed to the Secretary-General, UN Doc. S/2000/1234, p. 1.

[50] *Fofana* (SCSL-2004-14-PT), Decision on the Preliminary Defence Motion on the Lack of Personal Jurisdiction Filed on Behalf of the Accused Fofana, 3 March 2004, para. 40.

[51] Prosecutorial Strategy 2009–2012, 1 February 2010, The Hague, para. 19.

[52] *Situation in the Democratic Republic of the Congo* (ICC-01/04), Judgment on the Prosecutor's Appeal Against the Decision of Pre-Trial Chamber I Entitled 'Decision on the Prosecutor's Application for Warrants of Arrest, Article 58', 13 July 2006, para. 73.

The imposition of rigid standards primarily based on top seniority may result in neither retribution nor prevention being achieved. Also the capacity of individuals to prevent crimes in the field should not be implicitly or inadvertently assimilated to the preventive role of the Court more generally. Whether prevention is interpreted as a long-term objective, i.e., the overall result of the Court's activities generally, or as a factor in a specific situation, the preventive role of the Court may depend on many factors, much broader than the capacity of an individual to prevent crimes. The predictable exclusion of many perpetrators on the grounds proposed by the Pre-Trial Chamber could severely harm the preventive, or deterrent, role of the Court which is a cornerstone of the creation of the International Criminal Court, by announcing that any perpetrators other than those at the very top are automatically excluded from the exercise of the jurisdiction of the Court.[53]

The Prosecutor justified his strategic approach to targets by reference to various provisions of the Rome Statute. He noted the references to 'the most serious crimes of concern to the international community as a whole' in the preamble and in Article 5. He also pointed to Article 17, which circumscribes the concept of complementarity, and which authorizes the Court to declare inadmissible a case that 'is not of sufficient gravity to justify further action by the Court'. The Prosecutor said that '[t]he concept of gravity should not be exclusively attached to the act that constituted the crime but also to the degree of participation in its commission'.[54] Finally, he noted that Article 53 empowers the Prosecutor to decline to investigate or prosecute when this would not serve 'the interests of justice'.

Early in his mandate, on 16 July 2004, the Prosecutor issued a statement on the 'communications' he had received in accordance with Article 15, informing him of allegations that might lead to the exercise of his *proprio motu* authority. According to Article 15 of the Rome Statute:

1. The Prosecutor may initiate investigations proprio motu on the basis of information on crimes within the jurisdiction of the Court.
2. The Prosecutor shall analyze the seriousness of the information received. For this purpose, he or she may seek additional information from States, organs of the United Nations, intergovernmental or non-governmental organizations, or other reliable sources that he or she deems appropriate, and may receive written or oral testimony at the seat of the Court ...

[53] *Ibid.*, paras. 74–5.
[54] Paper on Some Policy Issues Before the Office of the Prosecutor, p. 7.

Prosecutor Moreno-Ocampo said that, since July 2002, the Office of the Prosecutor had received 499 communications from sixty-six different countries. Many of these were patently inadmissible because they concerned matters outside the jurisdiction of the Court. For example, some fifty communications related to acts perpetrated prior to 1 July 2002. Others dealt with crimes that were not within the Court's subject-matter jurisdiction, such as environmental damage, drug trafficking, money laundering, tax evasion and judicial corruption. He said that thirty-eight complaints concerned aggression in Iraq, noting that the Court was prohibited from exercising jurisdiction over that crime by the Statute itself.

Prosecutor Moreno-Ocampo indicated that his office had selected the situation in Ituri, Democratic Republic of the Congo, as the most urgent situation to be investigated. The Statement said that the Office of the Prosecutor had received six communications regarding the situation in Ituri, including two detailed reports from non-governmental organizations.[55] Aside from the Ituri situation, the Prosecutor's statement did not mention explicitly any other State Party to the Statute as a candidate for prosecution. In September 2003, in his report to the Assembly of States Parties, the Prosecutor confirmed that Ituri was the focus of his activity.[56]

Prosecutor Moreno-Ocampo's July 2003 report on Article 15 communications clearly suggested that his *proprio motu* powers would be the source of the first cases before the Court. This was no surprise to Court watchers. It had been expected since the Rome Conference. Indeed, many had argued that, without the *proprio motu* powers, the Court would never get a case. But, instead, the Prosecutor soon took up situations that had been referred to him by States, in accordance with Article 14 of the Rome Statute. Obviously, the States in question, Uganda and the Democratic Republic of the Congo, had their own strategic objectives. Put simply, these appear to have been to use the Court in order to prosecute rebel bands within their own territory. It was not something that had been seriously contemplated when the Rome Statute was drafted.[57] Tamely

---

[55] Communications Received by the Office of the Prosecutor of the ICC, Press Release No. pids.009.2003-EN, 16 July 2003.

[56] Second Assembly of States Parties to the Rome Statute of the International Criminal Court, Report of the Prosecutor of the ICC, Mr Luis Moreno-Ocampo, 8 September 2003.

[57] There had been talk about 'waiver', when a State would decide not to challenge claims it was unwilling or unable to proceed. But this is not at all the same thing as a State invoking the triggering provisions of the Statute to, in effect, make a complaint against itself.

complying with these State Party referrals, he appeared to lose sight of his own prosecutorial priorities, as set out in the initial policy paper. Moreover, rather than encourage the two States to attempt prosecutions within their national justice systems, as the policy paper suggested, he eagerly took up the prosecutions himself, as if it hardly mattered whether domestic courts could handle the cases.

Uganda and the Lord's Resistance Army

Before the year 2003 was over, the Prosecutor announced that a situation had been referred to the Court by a State Party, in accordance with Articles 13(a) and 14. Moreover, this was a referral by a State of a situation within its own borders. On 16 December 2003, the Government of Uganda referred the situation in northern Uganda.[58] Seven months later, on 28 June 2004, Prosecutor Moreno-Ocampo announced his conclusion that there was a 'reasonable basis' to proceed with an investigation. He said that there was credible evidence that widespread and systematic attacks had been committed against the civilian population since July 2002, including the abduction of thousands of girls and boys. Information indicated that rape and other crimes of sexual violence, torture, child conscription, and forced displacement continue to take place. The Prosecutor said he had concluded a cooperation agreement in order to facilitate the investigation and to execute arrest. The Prosecutor assembled a team of twelve investigators and lawyers. It conducted more than fifty missions to Uganda with a view to gathering evidence. Some twenty missions were also undertaken to meet with local leaders, and a meeting was held in The Hague with national authorities and local community leaders.

On 6 May 2005, the Prosecutor submitted applications for five arrest warrants, in accordance with Article 58 of the Rome Statute. These were subsequently amended, and considered by the three judges of Pre-Trial Chamber II on 18 May 2005,[59] and in hearings during the month

---

[58] For the background to the conflict, see Mohamed El Zeidy, 'The Ugandan Government Triggers the First Test of the Complementarity Principle: An Assessment of the First State's Party Referral to the ICC', (2005) 5 *International Criminal Law Review* 83.

[59] A single judge is authorized to issue arrest warrants (Rome Statute, Art. 57(2)). However, the Pre-Trial Chamber considered it appropriate, under the circumstances, that the Prosecutor's application be examined by the full bench: *Situation in Uganda* (ICC-02/04-6), Decision on the Exercise of Functions by the Full Chamber in Relation to an Application by the Prosecutor under Article 58, 18 May 2005.

of June. The application contained general allegations about the Lord's Resistance Army, indicating it had been directing attacks against the Ugandan army (Uganda People's Defence Force or UPDF) and local militias (known as Local Defence Units or LDUs) as well as against civilian populations. The Pre-Trial Chamber noted that the existence and acts of the Lord's Resistance Army, as well as their impact on Uganda's armed forces and civilian communities, had been reported by the Government of Uganda and its agencies and by several independent sources, including the United Nations, foreign governmental agencies, non-governmental organizations and world media.[60] Sealed arrest warrants were issued on 8 July 2005 against five leaders of the Lord's Resistance Army: Joseph Kony, Vincent Otti, Raska Lukwiya, Okot Odhiambo and Dominic Ongwen.[61]

Several specific crimes against humanity were alleged, including 'unlawful killings',[62] enslavement, rape, sexual enslavement and 'inhuman acts' (inflicting serious bodily injury and suffering). Many war crimes were also charged: unlawful killings and cruel treatment (contrary to common Article 3 of the Geneva Conventions), intentional directing of an attack against a civilian population, and against individual civilians not taking direct part in hostilities, pillage, enlisting children under the age of fifteen years into armed forces or groups or using them to participate actively in hostilities. In most cases, the accused were charged with having 'ordered' the commission of these crimes, pursuant to Article 25(3)(b) of the Rome Statute. The Prosecutor did not invoke the concept of 'joint criminal enterprise' set out in Article 25(3)(d), which has proven to be so potent in prosecutions at the International Criminal Tribunal for the former Yugoslavia. Nor did he claim any application of the principle of superior responsibility, described in Article 28 of the Rome Statute, despite what would seem to be its obvious application to the case of five rebel leaders.

---

[60] *Ibid.*, para. 6.
[61] *Situation in Uganda* (ICC-02/04–87), Decision on the Prosecutor's Application for Warrants of Arrest under Article 59, 8 July 2005. The Prosecutor was unhappy with a procedural aspect of the 8 July 2005 decision authorizing the arrest warrants, and applied for leave to appeal. Relying upon the jurisprudence of the *ad hoc* tribunals for the former Yugoslavia, Rwanda and Sierra Leone, the Pre-Trial Chamber adopted a restrictive interpretation of the scope of interlocutory appeal and dismissed the motion: *Situation in Uganda* (ICC-02/04-01/05), Decision on Prosecutor's Application for Leave to Appeal in Part Pre-Trial Chamber II's Decision on the Prosecutor's Applications for Warrants of Arrest under Article 59, 19 August 2005.
[62] The Rome Statute's definition of crimes against humanity refers to 'murder', not 'unlawful killing'.

On 9 September 2005, the Prosecutor applied to have the warrants unsealed.[63] The Pre-Trial Chamber so decided on 13 October 2005, and the warrants became known to the general public the following day.[64] Issuance of the warrants helped drive the rebel leaders to sue for peace. Hostilities came to an end in August 2006. Peace negotiations were carried out in Juba, in southern Sudan, from 2006 to 2008. On a visit to the Court, the Ugandan Minister for Security, Amama Mbabazi, noted that the issuance of warrants had contributed to bringing the Lord's Resistance Army leaders to the negotiating table. In September 2006, Jan Egelund, the United Nations Under-Secretary-General for Humanitarian Affairs and Emergency Relief, made similar observations in a briefing to the Security Council.[65] Speaking to the Assembly of States Parties in November 2006, Prosecutor Moreno-Ocampo said:

> The Court's intervention has galvanized the activities of the states concerned … Thanks to the unity of purpose of these states, the LRA has been forced to flee its safe haven in southern Sudan and has moved its headquarters to the DRC border. As a consequence, crimes allegedly committed by the LRA in Northern Uganda have drastically decreased. People are leaving the camps for displaced persons and the night commuter shelters which protected tens of thousands of children are now in the process of closing. The loss of their safe haven led the LRA commanders to engage in negotiations, resulting in a cessation of hostilities agreement in August 2006.[66]

In other words, issuance of the arrest warrants had contributed to conflict resolution in northern Uganda. The situation was reminiscent of the situation faced by Richard Goldstone, Prosecutor of the International Criminal Tribunal for the former Yugoslavia, in July 1995. While the war in Bosnia and Herzegovina was still raging, he obtained indictments against Serb leaders Radovan Karadžić and Ratko Mladić. Goldstone was later chastised by United Nations Secretary-General Boutros Boutros-Ghali for failing to consult at a political level. He replied that as a prosecutor it was not his job to take political factors into account.[67]

---

[63] *Situation in Uganda* (ICC-02/04–01/05–20), Prosecutor's Application for Unsealing of the Warrants of Arrest, 9 September 2005.

[64] *Situation in Uganda* (ICC-02/04–01/05–52), Decision on the Prosecutor's Application for Unsealing of the Warrants of Arrest, 13 October 2005.

[65] UN Doc. S/PV.5525, p. 4.

[66] Opening Remarks, Luis Moreno-Ocampo, Fifth Session of the Assembly of States Parties, 23 November 2006.

[67] Richard J. Goldstone, *For Humanity: Reflections of a War Crimes Investigator*, New Haven and London: Yale University Press, 2000, pp. 102–3.

Nevertheless, the indictments helped to isolate Karadžić and Mladić, and may well have contributed to the successful outcome of peace negotiations at Dayton later that same year.

But if the charges against the Lord's Resistance Army might have helped to provoke peace negotiations, they also soon proved to be a potential obstacle to their successful completion.[68] Jan Egelund reported to the Security Council that, in meetings with internally displaced persons, civil society and the parties themselves, the 'International Criminal Court indictments were the number one subject of discussion ... All expressed a strong concern that if the indictments were not lifted, they could threaten the progress in these most promising talks ever for northern Uganda.'[69] The rebel leaders quite predictably insisted that the arrest warrants be withdrawn as a condition for the peace settlement. President Yoveri Museveni of Uganda, who had triggered the prosecutions two years earlier when he referred the situation in northern Uganda to the Court, asked the Prosecutor to withdraw the warrants. He promised those who had been charged that they would have immunity from arrest in Uganda.[70] Richard Goldstone remarked:

> It would be fatally damaging to the credibility of the international court if Museveni was allowed to get away with granting amnesty. I just don't accept that Museveni has the right to use the International Criminal Court like this.[71]

Opinions were sharply divided on how to react to the demands from the Lord's Resistance Army, and from President Museveni. Some took the extreme view that under no conditions could there be any compromise with prosecution, whatever the consequences in terms of prolonging the conflict. Others saw it more strategically, noting the positive contribution to the peace process of the arrest warrants. They argued that the warrants should be maintained, at least as long as they continue

---

[68] This is discussed by Kasaija Phillip Apuuli, 'The International Criminal Court (ICC) and the Lord's Resistance Army (LRA) Insurgency in Northern Uganda', (2005) 15 *Criminal Law Forum* 408; Kasaija Phillip Apuuli, 'The ICC Arrest Warrants for the Lord's Resistance Army Leaders and Peace Prospects for Northern Uganda', (2006) 4 *Journal of International Criminal Justice* 179; Manisuli Ssenyonjo, 'Accountability of Non-State Actors in Uganda for War Crimes and Human Rights Violations: Between Amnesty and the International Criminal Court', (2005) 10 *Journal of Conflict and Security Law* 405.

[69] UN Doc. S/PV.5525, p. 4.

[70] Chris McGreal, 'African Search for Peace Throws Court into Crisis', *Guardian*, 9 January 2007.

[71] *Ibid.*

to have this effect, although without making it a question of absolute principle. The problem had been foreseen when the Rome Statute was being drafted, but no solution had been found. South Africa, in particular, insisted that the Court should not prohibit a domestic peace process that involves some form of amnesty or immunity from prosecution. This had worked successfully, under the stewardship of Nelson Mandela, Desmond Tutu and others. But there was concern that any compromise in this respect would leave the door open to the ugly amnesties that characterized transitional processes in Latin America during the 1980s. There is some authority for the view that so-called 'blanket amnesties' are prohibited by customary international law,[72] although the argument is seriously flawed,[73] and seems to be inconsistent with State practice.

In February 2008, agreement was reached whereby war crimes were to be prosecuted by a new division of the High Court of Uganda, apparently excluding the International Criminal Court from the scene. The Pre-Trial Chamber reacted immediately by asking the Government of Uganda to provide information on the status of the arrest warrants in light of the 'Agreement on Accountability and Reconciliation' reached at Juba.[74] The Government of Uganda replied that '[t]he establishment of the special division of the High Court and the enactment of the relevant legislation shall take place after the signing of the final peace agreement'. Furthermore, '[t]he special division of the High Court is not meant to supplant the work of the International Criminal Court and accordingly those individuals who were indicted by the International Criminal Court will have to be brought before the special division of the High Court for trial'.[75] In any event, the rebel leader, Joseph Kony, never signed the agreement. It seems the refusal of the International Criminal Court to suspend or withdraw the arrest warrants was a factor in the breakdown in the peace process.

---

[72] *Kallon* (SCSL-04-15-AR72(E)) and *Kamara* (SCSL-04-16-AR72(E)), Decision on Challenge to Jurisdiction: Lomé Accord Amnesty, 13 March 2004. See also *Kondewa* (SCSL-04-14-AR72(E)), Separate Opinion of Justice Robertson, 25 May 2004.

[73] Mark Freeman, *Necessary Evils: Amnesties and the Search for Justice*, New York: Cambridge University Press, 2009; Louise Mallinder, *Amnesty, Human Rights and Political Transitions, Bridging the Peace and Justice Divide*, Oxford: Hart, 2008.

[74] *Situation in Uganda* (ICC-02/04–01/05), Request for Information from the Republic of Uganda on the Status of Execution of the Warrants of Arrest, 29 February 2008.

[75] *Situation in Uganda* (ICC-02/04–01/05), Report by the Registrar on the Execution of the 'Request for Information from the Republic of Uganda on the Status of Execution of the Warrants of Arrest', 28 March 2008, Annex 2, p. 3.

The Pre-Trial Chamber then appointed defence counsel for the four remaining accused, and encouraged proceedings on the admissibility of the cases. The Prosecutor insisted that there were no national proceedings relating to the four cases. The Pre-Trial Chamber concluded there was 'total inaction' by the Ugandan courts,[76] a ruling subsequently upheld by the Appeals Chamber.[77] At the Review Conference, in June 2010, the president of the War Crimes Division said Uganda's courts were perfectly capable of prosecuting the Lord's Resistance Army leaders, but that a *modus vivendi* had been reached with the International Criminal Court.

The warrants remain unexecuted. Three of the defendants have been reported dead, and proceedings have been formally terminated in the case of one of them.[78] The other three defendants, including Joseph Kony, are reported to be no longer in Uganda. After two decades of conflict, peace has returned to northern Uganda

Civil war in the Democratic Republic of the Congo

The Uganda 'self-referral' inspired the Prosecutor to attempt the same strategy in the Democratic Republic of the Congo. This was the situation he had indicated as his first priority, in July 2003. Then, he was planning to proceed on the basis of his *proprio motu* powers, in accordance with Article 15 of the Rome Statute. This changed on 3 March 2004, when the Democratic Republic of the Congo followed Uganda's example and referred the situation in the Ituri region to the Court. In its letter of referral, the Democratic Republic of the Congo said that 'les autorités compétentes ne sont malheureusement pas en mesure de mener des enquêtes sur les crimes mentionnés ci-dessus ni d'engager les poursuites nécessaires sans la participation de la Cour Pénale Internationale'.[79] In other words, Congo was not only referring the case but indicating that it conceded the admissibility of the case. It did not, however, indicate whether this was because it was unwilling or because it was unable to proceed.

---

[76] *Situation in Uganda* (ICC-02/04–01/05), Decision on the Admissibility of the Case under Article 19(1) of the Statute, para. 52.

[77] *Situation in Uganda* (ICC-02/04–01/05 OA 3), Judgment on the appeal of the Defence against the 'Decision on the Admissibility of the Case under Article 19(1) of the Statute' of 10 March 2009, 16 September 2009.

[78] *Lukwiya* (ICC-02/04–01/05), Decision to Terminate the Proceedings Against Raska Lukwiya, 11 July 2007.

[79] Letter of Joseph Kabila to the Prosecutor, 3 March 2004.

On 17 June 2004, the Prosecutor informed the Presidency of the referral. On 21 June 2004, after citing an estimated 5,000 to 8,000 unlawful killings committed in the region since 1 July 2002, he announced the opening of a formal investigation.

The procedure at the International Criminal Court is significantly different than that of the *ad hoc* tribunals. It is more of a hybrid of inquisitorial and adversarial systems than its predecessors.[80] The Rome Statute establishes a robust Pre-Trial Chamber that in some ways is analogous to the role of the *juge d'instruction* in systems derived from continental European models. The interests of both the defence and the victims are present and represented at a much earlier stage in proceedings than under the procedure applicable before the *ad hoc* tribunals. The initial experiment with these innovative mechanisms took place under the direction of a French magistrate, Claude Jorda. As President of Pre-Trial Chamber I,[81] he made no secret of his intention to depart from the model of the *ad hoc* tribunals, mainly by enhanced judicial supervision of the Prosecutor in the pre-investigation and investigation stages.

On 17 February 2005, without any particular initiative from the Prosecutor, Pre-Trial Chamber I announced that it would convene a status conference. The Pre-Trial Chamber referred to earlier communications with the Prosecutor, and cited the latter's own Policy Document in support of the call for the meeting. It said this was necessary in order to ensure the protection of victims and witnesses, and the preservation of evidence.[82] The Prosecutor strenuously objected to the authority of the Pre-Trial Chamber to take this initiative at such an early stage in the proceedings.[83]

---

[80] On the conflict of systems at the *ad hoc* tribunals, see Megan Fairlie, 'The Marriage of Common and Continental Law at the International Criminal Tribunal for the former Yugoslavia and its Progeny, Due Process Deficit', (2004) 4 *International Criminal Law Review* 243.

[81] *Situation in the Democratic Republic of Congo* (ICC-01/04), Election of the Presiding Judge of Pre-Trial Chamber I, 16 September 2004.

[82] *Situation in the Democratic Republic of Congo* (ICC-01/04), Décision de convoquer une conférence de mise en état, 17 February 2005. See Michela Miraglia, 'The First Decision of the ICC Pre-Trial Chamber, International Criminal Procedure under Construction', (2006) 4 *Journal of International Criminal Justice* 188.

[83] *Situation in the Democratic Republic of Congo* (ICC-01/04), Prosecutor's Position on Pre-Trial Chamber I's 17 February 2005 Decision to Convene a Status Conference, 8 March 2005; *Situation in the Democratic Republic of Congo* (ICC-01/04), Decision on the Prosecutor's Application for Leave to Appeal, 14 March 2005; *Situation in the Democratic Republic of Congo* (ICC-01/04), Décision concernant la demande d'autorisation d'interjeter appel déposée par le Procureur, 17 March 2005.

With both defence counsel and victims quarrelling before the Pre-Trial Chamber, all that was missing was a defendant. On 10 February 2006, the Prosecutor's application for an arrest warrant directed at Thomas Lubanga Dyilo, filed a month earlier on 13 January 2006, was granted by the Pre-Trial Chamber.[84] This followed an *ex parte* hearing on 2 February 2006. Lubanga had apparently been in custody in the Democratic Republic of the Congo for nearly a year prior to issuance of the arrest warrant. He had been in detention in the *Centre pénitentiaire et de réeducation de Kinshasa* since 19 March 2005, although the Prosecutor was concerned that he might soon be released. A second arrest warrant, directed against another rebel leader, Bosco Ntaganda, was initially dismissed by the Pre-Trial Chamber on the ground that he was not sufficiently important in the hierarchy,[85] but the ruling was reversed on appeal.[86]

The *Lubanga* arrest warrant concerned the recruitment of child soldiers. It noted that between July 2002 and December 2003 members of the *Forces patriotiques pour la libération du Congo*, of which Lubanga was the leader, had repeatedly enlisted children under fifteen years of age, who were brought to various training camps. The arrest warrant said there were also reasonable grounds to believe that, during the same period, children under fifteen participated actively in hostilities. In his remarks to the Assembly of States Parties, in November 2006, Prosecutor Moreno-Ocampo described the charges:

> The case against Thomas Lubanga Dyilo is a case about children. It is a case about young children. The Prosecution evidence will show that children as young as seven, eight and nine years old were also victims of these types of crimes. Many of the children were abducted. Abducted on the road. Abducted from schools. Abducted from their parents' houses. In the presence of their families. The families did not resist. They did not resist because they were threatened with death. They feared being killed. Other children joined the FPLC troops voluntarily. They did so for a variety of reasons, such as the desire for revenge of orphans whose families were killed by the militias opposing the FPLC. Such as the wish to gain

---

[84] *Lubanga* (ICC-01/04–01/06), Decision on the Prosecutor's Application for a Warrant of Arrest, 10 February 2006.

[85] *Situation in the Democratic Republic of the Congo* (ICC-01/04), Decision on the Prosecutor's Application for Warrants of Arrest, Article 58, 10 February 2006.

[86] *Situation in the Democratic Republic of the Congo* (ICC-01/04), Judgment on the Prosecutor's Appeal Against the Decision of Pre-Trial Chamber I Entitled 'Decision on the Prosecutor's Application for Warrants of Arrest, Article 58', 13 July 2006.

social status. Such as the need for protection and shelter, and basic survival. Such as having access to food. The children were instructed to kill the enemies regardless of whether they were combatants or civilians. The commanders forced children, boys and girls, to fight at the frontlines. Forced by threats of execution. Many child soldiers were killed. Others were seriously wounded. The Prosecution will present to the Court details of the individual cases of six children who were victims of these crimes. As the Prosecution will show, their experiences reflect those of hundreds of other children.[87]

Commenting on the warrant in a press statement, Prosecutor Moreno-Ocampo said that '[f]orcing children to be killers jeopardises the future of mankind'.[88]

While the Prosecutor worked with the authorities of Democratic Republic of the Congo in order to ensure the accused person's transfer to The Hague, the *Lubanga* arrest warrant remained under seal.[89] Lubanga was brought to The Hague by French military aircraft, with the assistance of the United Nations mission (MONUC). On 20 March 2006, Lubanga came before the Pre-Trial Chamber, the first defendant ever to appear before the International Criminal Court, for the purpose of establishing that he had been informed of the crimes he was alleged to have committed, and that he knew of his rights under the Statute, including the right to apply for interim release. The Statute requires that a hearing to confirm the charges be held within a reasonable time.[90] The Pre-Trial Chamber set 17 June 2006 for the hearing. 'Three months are necessary for you to become familiar with the mass of documents', said presiding Judge Jorda, 'in order to proceed on a fair basis.'

The three months proved to be much too short, and the convening of the confirmation hearing was postponed twice, because of witness-protection issues as well as the need for adequate disclosure of evidence to the defence. It finally began on 9 November 2006, and concluded at the end of the month.

---

[87] Opening Remarks, Luis Moreno-Ocampo, Fifth Session of the Assembly of States Parties, 23 November 2006.

[88] Statement by Luis Moreno-Ocampo, Press Conference in relation to the surrender to the Court of Mr Thomas Lubanga Dyilo, 18 March 2006.

[89] It was made public once Lubanga was in the Court's custody: *Lubanga* (ICC-01/04–01/06–37), Decision to Unseal the Warrant of Arrest Against Mr Thomas Lubanga Dyilo and Related Documents, 17 March 2006.

[90] Rome Statute, Art. 61(1).

For the first time in the history of international criminal justice, the victims were also represented, in accordance with a decision authorizing their participation issued by the Pre-Trial Chamber earlier in the year. During the confirmation hearing, counsel for the victims presented observations in opening and closing, and attended the hearings in their entirety. Predictably, the victims' representatives argued in favour of confirming the charges against Lubanga.

On 29 January 2007, Pre-Trial Chamber I confirmed the charges against Lubanga concerning the enlistment, conscription and active use of child soldiers.[91] He became the first person to be committed for trial before the International Criminal Court. Lubanga's trial date was repeatedly postponed, and it did not in fact begin until early 2009, two years after the confirmation hearing decision. A simmering issue about disclosure of exculpatory evidence eventually exploded, in June 2008, when the Trial Chamber ordered a stay of proceedings.[92] The Prosecutor had refused to disclose evidence obtained early in the investigation from confidential sources. According to Article 53(4)(e), the Prosecutor may '[a]gree not to disclose, at any stage of the proceedings, documents or information that the Prosecutor obtains on the condition of confidentiality and solely for the purpose of generating new evidence, unless the provider of the information consents'. The United Nations mission in the Congo, as well as some NGOs, had furnished information under assurances of confidentiality, and the Prosecutor had conceded that there might possibly be exculpatory information contained in this material. Defence counsel responded by invoking Article 67(2), which imposes a duty on the Prosecutor to disclose any exculpatory evidence. Forced to resolve this apparent conflict between two provisions of the Statute, the Trial Chamber came down on the side of the defence. After months of negotiations, the United Nations and the other information providers modified their positions, and a solution was found permitting the trial to proceed. Presentation of the case for the prosecution continued from January 2009 until early the following year. The trial will probably be completed during 2010.

---

[91] *Lubanga* (ICC-01/04–01/06), Decision on the Confirmation of the Charges, 29 January 2007.

[92] *Lubanga* (ICC-01/04–01/06), Decision on the Consequences of Non-Disclosure of Exculpatory Materials Covered by Article 54(3)(e) Agreements and the Application to Stay the Prosecution of the Accused, Together with Certain Other Issues Raised at the Status Conference on 10 June 2008, 13 June 2008.

Three other defendants have also been charged in the *Situation in the Democratic Republic of the Congo*. The second person to be accused, Bosco Ntaganda, remains at large. Arrest warrants against two others, Germain Katanga and Mathieu Ngudjolo Chui, were issued in July 2007.[93] Katanga was commander of the Force de Résistance Patriotique en Ituri, while Ngudjolo led the Front des Nationalistes et Intégrationnistes. They are charged with a number of counts of crimes against humanity and war crimes allegedly committed in an assault on the village of Bogoro in 2003. The two cases were joined.[94] After the charges were confirmed by the Pre-Trial Chamber,[95] the trial began in January 2010.

Darfur referred by the Security Council

The third 'situation' to come before the Court, that of Darfur in western Sudan, is the result of a Security Council referral in accordance with Article 13(b) of the Rome Statute. Sudan signed the Statute on 8 September 2000, but has not yet deposited its ratification. In early September 2004, United States Secretary of State Colin Powell called upon the Security Council to take action with regard to what he described as genocide underway in Darfur.[96] Powell explicitly invoked Article VIII of the 1948 Genocide Convention, which authorizes States Parties to 'call upon the competent organs of the United Nations to take such action under the Charter of the United Nations as they consider appropriate for the prevention and suppression of acts of genocide or any of the other acts enumerated in article III'.[97]

Responding to Powell's appeal, Security Council Resolution 1564 of 18 September 2004 mandated the establishment of 'an international

---

[93] *Katanga* (ICC-01/04–01/07), Warrant of Arrest for Germain Katanga, 2 July 2007; *Ngudjolo* (ICC-01/04–02/07), Warrant of Arrest for Mathieu Ngudjolo Chui, 6 July 2007.

[94] *Katanga et al.* (ICC-01/04–02/07), Decision on the Joinder of the Cases Against Germain Katanga and Mathieu Ngudjolo Chui, 10 March 2008; *Katanga et al.* (ICC-01/04–01/07 OA 6), Judgment on the Appeal Against the Decision on Joinder Rendered on 10 March 2008 by the Pre-Trial Chamber in The Prosecutor v. Germain Katanga and Mathieu Ngudjolo Chui Cases, 9 June 2008.

[95] *Katanga et al.* (ICC-01/04–01/07), Decision on the Confirmation of Charges, 30 September 2008.

[96] Secretary Colin L. Powell, Testimony before the Senate Foreign Relations Committee, Washington DC, 9 September 2004.

[97] Convention on the Prevention and Punishment of the Crime of Genocide, (1951) 78 UNTS 277.

commission of inquiry in order immediately to investigate reports of violations of international humanitarian law and human rights law in Darfur by all parties, to determine also whether or not acts of genocide have occurred, and to identify the perpetrators of such violations with a view to ensuring that those responsible are held accountable'.[98] The Commission of Inquiry called for in the Security Council resolution was promptly created by the United Nations Secretary-General. Chaired by the distinguished international legal scholar Antonio Cassese, who had also been the first president of the International Criminal Tribunal for the former Yugoslavia, among other distinctions, the Commission reported back to the Secretary-General on 25 January 2005. The Commission disagreed with Powell, concluding that the atrocities that had been committed in the Darfur region of Sudan were not acts of genocide but rather crimes against humanity. Noting that proceedings before the *ad hoc* tribunals were too slow and therefore not an acceptable option, the Commission called for prosecution by the International Criminal Court.[99] Several weeks after the Darfur Commission issued its report, and following protracted negotiations during which the United States put forward several alternative options for internationalized prosecution, the United Nations Security Council responded to the report by referring 'the situation in Darfur since 1 July 2002' to the International Criminal Court.[100] The resolution states that the Government of Sudan and the other parties to the conflict are under an international obligation to 'cooperate fully with and provide any necessary assistance to the Court and the Prosecutor'.[101] Other States are 'urged' to assist the Court with respect to enforcement of the resolution. The United States, Algeria, Brazil and China all abstained in the vote on Resolution 1593.[102]

In his December 2005 report,[103] Prosecutor Moreno-Ocampo said his office had issued requests for assistance to eleven States and seventeen

---

[98] UN Doc. S/RES/1564 (2004), para. 12.

[99] *Ibid.*, para. 569. See Luigi Condorelli and Annalisa Ciampi, 'Comments on the Security Council Referral of the Situation in Darfur to the ICC', (2005) 3 *Journal of International Criminal Justice* 590; William A. Schabas, 'Darfur and the "Odious Scourge": The Commission of Inquiry's Findings on Genocide', (2005) 18 *Leiden Journal of International Law* 871.

[100] UN Doc. S/RES/1593 (2005), para. 1.

[101] *Ibid.*, para. 2.

[102] Robert Cryer, 'Sudan, Resolution 1593 and International Criminal Justice', (2006) 19 *Leiden Journal of International Law* 195.

[103] The Security Council resolution referring the Darfur situation requires the Prosecutor to make regular reports on progress in the case.

non-governmental and intergovernmental organizations. He noted that witnesses to the crimes under investigation had been identified in seventeen countries, that 'well over a hundred potential witnesses have been screened and a number of formal statements have been taken'. At a diplomatic briefing held on 23 March 2006, the Prosecutor said:

> Darfur presents new challenges for the Court. The security situation in Darfur means that any national or international investigations in Darfur at this time would cause risks for victims. No one can conduct a judicial investigation in Darfur. A comparative advantage for the ICC is that we can more easily investigate from the outside. We have interviewed witnesses in more than 10 countries. We are planning to present a clear picture of the crimes in our next report to the Security Council, in June. We have recently conducted two missions to the Sudan, in November last year and in February. We have discussed cooperation and admissibility. We have interviewed persons. The Sudan will be sending us further information that we have requested.[104]

But, more than a year after the referral, there were still no arrest warrants. Frustrated by the slow pace of the Prosecutor, in July 2006 the Pre-Trial Chamber assigned to the Darfur situation decided to seek a second opinion.[105] The unprecedented initiative was ostensibly based upon Article 57(3)(c), which authorizes the Chamber 'where necessary [to] provide for the protection and privacy of victims and witnesses [and] the preservation of evidence'. But, in reality, the judges were questioning the Prosecutor's claim that he could not conduct investigations within Darfur because of the security situation. Two *amici curiae* were asked for their views: Professor Antonio Cassese, chair of the United Nations Commission of Inquiry whose report provoked the Darfur referral, and Louise Arbour, United Nations High Commissioner for Human Rights. Their reports were submitted in August and September 2006. Each took the position that the Prosecutor had exaggerated the security problems involved in investigating within Darfur. In a journal article published at about the same time, Professor Cassese referred critically to the '[e]exceedingly prudent attitude of the ICC Prosecutor'.[106]

---

[104] Sixth Diplomatic Briefing of the International Criminal Court, Compilation of Statements, 23 March 2006.

[105] *Situation in Darfur, Sudan* (ICC-02/05), Decision Inviting Observations in Application of Rule 103 of the Rules of Procedure and Evidence, 24 July 2006.

[106] Antonio Cassese, 'Is the ICC Still Having Teething Problems?', (2006) 4 *Journal of International Criminal Justice* 434 at 438.

Professor Cassese's report discussed the investigation in general, making a number of observations about the focus of the inquiry, the types of witnesses who should be interviewed, and even the legal basis for prosecution. He signalled the importance of establishing the chain of command so as to hold accountable those responsible for addressing the violations within the Sudanese military, under the principle of command or superior responsibility. With respect to the specific issue of conducting an investigation within Darfur, Professor Cassese recommended 'targeted and brief interviews of victims and witnesses'. He also proposed that Sudanese officials be summoned to The Hague to testify before the Pre-Trial Chamber.[107] High Commissioner Arbour told the Pre-Trial Chamber that 'it is possible to conduct investigations of human rights violations during an armed conflict in general, and in Darfur in particular, without putting victims at unreasonable risk'.[108] The Prosecutor seemed stung by the remarks. He replied with observations to the Pre-Trial Chamber arguing that parts of the reports 'encroach upon the discretion of the Prosecutor'.[109] But, in his report to the Assembly of States Parties in November 2006,[110] and to the Security Council in December 2006,[111] the Prosecutor did not even mention the skirmish with the Pre-Trial Chamber and the admonitions of Antonio Cassese and Louise Arbour.

In April 2007, more than two years after the Security Council referral, the Pre-Trial Chamber issued two arrest warrants, one directed to a senior government official and the other to a militia leader, on charges of crimes against humanity and war crimes.[112] Nothing happened. Despite

---

[107] *Situation in Darfur, Sudan* (ICC-02/05), Observations on Issues Concerning the Protection of Victims and the Preservation of Evidence in the Proceedings on Darfur Pending before the ICC, 25 August 2006.

[108] *Situation in Darfur, Sudan* (ICC-02/05), Observations of the United Nations High Commissioner for Human Rights Invited in Application of Rule 103 of the Rules of Procedure and Evidence, 10 October 2006, para. 64.

[109] *Situation in Darfur, Sudan* (ICC-02/05), Prosecutor's Response to Cassese's Observations on Issues Concerning the Protection of Witnesses and the Preservation of Evidence in the Proceedings on Darfur Pending before the ICC, 11 September 2006, para. 9. Also *Situation in Darfur, Sudan* (ICC-02/05), Prosecutor's Response to Arbour's Observations on Issues Concerning the Protection of Witnesses and the Preservation of Evidence in the Proceedings on Darfur Pending before the ICC, 19 October 2006.

[110] Opening Remarks, Luis Moreno-Ocampo, Fifth Session of the Assembly of States Parties, 23 November 2006.

[111] UN Doc. S/PV.5589.

[112] *Harun* (ICC-02/05–01/07), Warrant of Arrest for Ahmad Harun, 17 April 2007; *Kushayb* (ICC-02/05–01/07), Warrant of Arrest for Ali Kushayb, 27 April 2007.

the order to cooperate from the Security Council, the Government of Sudan refused to hand over the two accused persons. Frustrated by the situation, in July 2008 the Prosecutor decided to move up the chain of command. He applied for an arrest warrant against the country's president, Omar Al-Bashir. The following March, the Pre-Trial Chamber authorized a warrant on charges of crimes against humanity, but refused to add the counts of genocide that were sought.[113] The Prosecutor was successful in an appeal based on the test applied by the Pre-Trial Chamber, and the genocide issue was remitted to the Pre-Trial Chamber for reconsideration.[114]

The charges against Al-Bashir provoked a firestorm. The African Union called upon the Security Council to apply Article 16 of the Rome Statute and 'defer the process initiated by the ICC'.[115] A Security Council resolution adopted several days later noted the African Union's position in the preamble, '*having in mind* concerns raised by members of the Council regarding potential developments subsequent to the application by the Prosecutor of the International Criminal Court of 14 July 2008, and *taking note* of their intention to consider these matters further ...'.[116] In the Security Council debate, Libya and Indonesia supported deferral, and even the United Kingdom said: 'We will not stand in the way of a Security Council discussion of whether there is a case for invoking Article 16 of the Rome Statute in relation to President Al-Bashir, but that discussion will raise profound questions about the relationship between peace and justice. It is not something that the Security Council should rush into.'[117] Noting that the African Union's views were shared by the Non-Aligned Movement, the Organization of the Islamic Conference and the League of Arab States, Russia observed that these organizations

---

[113] *Bashir* (ICC-02/05–01/09), Decision on the Prosecution's Application for a Warrant of Arrest Against Omar Hassan Ahmad Al Bashir, 4 March 2009.

[114] *Bashir* (ICC-02/05–01/09 OA), Judgment on the Appeal of the Prosecutor Against the 'Decision on the Prosecution's Application for a Warrant of Arrest Against Omar Hassan Ahmad Al Bashir', 3 February 2010.

[115] African Union Peace and Security Council Decision (PSC/MIN/Comm (CXLII)), 21 July 2008, paras. 3, 5, 9, 11(i). Also African Union Assembly Decision on the Application by the International Criminal Court Prosecutor for the Indictment of the President of the Republic of the Sudan (Dec.221 (XII)), 3 February 2009, paras. 2, 3; and Peace and Security Council Decision (PSC/PR/Comm (CLXXV)), 5 March 2009, paras. 4–6. See A. Ciampi, 'The Proceedings Against President Al Bashir and the Prospects of Their Suspension under Article 16 ICC Statute', (2008) 6 *Journal of International Criminal Justice* 885.

[116] UN Doc. S/RES/1828 (2008).   [117] *Ibid.*, p. 3.

'represent quite simply the views of two-thirds of the international community'.[118]

The African Union reacted in July 2009 with a resolution stating that it 'DEEPLY REGRETS that the request by the African Union to the Security Council to defer the proceedings initiated against President Bashir of the Sudan in accordance with Article 16 of the Rome Statute of the ICC has neither been heard nor acted upon, and in this regard, REITERATES ITS REQUEST to the UN Security Council'.[119] The Decision stated that 'in view of the fact that the request by the African Union has never been acted upon, the AU Member States shall not cooperate' in the arrest and surrender of President Bashir.[120] The political tension with many African States, including many States Parties to the Statute, resulting from the Al-Bashir arrest warrant continues to simmer. In May 2010, Al-Bashir was re-elected President of Sudan.

In addition to the three accused associated with the government, the Prosecutor has also pursued charges against rebel leaders. When anti-government forces attacked peacekeeping personnel associated with the African Union Mission in Sudan, the Prosecutor applied for three arrest warrants.[121] One of the accused essentially surrendered to the Court, and a summons to appear was issued instead of an arrest warrant.[122] Abu Garda was discharged following the confirmation hearing, which concluded there were not 'substantial grounds' that would justify a trial. The Pre-Trial Chamber concluded there was insufficient evidence of an armed group under Abu Garda's command and control in Haskanita at the time of the attack, and that the evidence tended to point to other rebel commanders in the area.[123] The Prosecutor's application for leave to appeal the ruling was denied.[124] The other two rebel leaders appeared voluntarily in June 2010.[125]

[118] *Ibid.*

[119] Decision on the Meeting of the African States Parties to the Rome Statute of the International Criminal Court (ICC), Doc. Assembly/AU/13 (XIII), para. 9.

[120] *Ibid.*, para. 10.

[121] *Situation in Darfur, Sudan* (ICC-02/05), Summary of the Prosecutor's Application under Article 58, 20 November 2008.

[122] *Abu Garda* (ICC-02/05–02/09), Summons to Appear, 7 May 2009.

[123] *Abu Garda* (ICC-02/05–02/09), Decision on the Confirmation of the Charges, 8 February 2010, paras. 147–8.

[124] *Abu Garda* (ICC-02/05–02/09), Decision on the 'Prosecution's Application for Leave to Appeal the "Decision on the Confirmation of Charges"', 23 April 2010.

[125] As Darfur rebel commanders surrender to the Court, ICC Prosecutor 'welcomes compliance with the Court's decisions and with Resolution 1593 (2005) of the Security Council', ICC-OTP-20100616-PR548, 13 June 2010.

Central African Republic

The Central African Republic was the third State Party to make a self-referral to the Court. The Central African Republic ratified the Rome Statute on 3 October 2001, and therefore the Court may exercise jurisdiction over its territory and its nationals from 1 July 2002. The Prosecutor received a referral from a representative of President Bozizé on 21 or 22 December 2004, which he communicated to the President of the Court the following day. The referral was announced publicly on 7 January 2005. In late 2005, a mission from the Office of the Prosecutor visited the country, but it was decided to await developments within the domestic justice system before reaching a conclusion on whether to proceed with an investigation. In mid-December 2006, in response to a request for a progress report from the Pre-Trial Chamber,[126] the Prosecutor said that the matter was being dealt with 'as expeditiously as possible'.[127]

In May 2008, the Office of the Prosecutor learned that a Congolese politician suspected of atrocities in the Central African Republic was visiting Belgium. Jean-Pierre Bemba Gombo was the leader of the Mouvement de Libération du Congo. In 2002, the organization assisted President Ange-Felix Patasse of the Central African Republic in repressing a coup attempt. The charges involved attacks on civilians in several localities that took place in late 2002 and early 2003, and included rapes. At the Court's request, Jean-Pierre Bemba Gombo was arrested by Belgian authorities and then transferred to The Hague. Bemba was charged with crimes against humanity and war crimes.[128] Charges against Bemba were confirmed in June 2009.[129] They involve an application of the doctrine of command responsibility, pursuant to Article 28 of the Statute, the first time this has occurred at the Court. A trial date set for April 2010 was postponed until July of that year.

---

[126] *Situation in the Central African Republic* (ICC-01/05–1), Decision Requesting Information on the Status of the Preliminary Examination of the Situation in the Central African Republic, 30 November 2006.

[127] *Situation in the Central African Republic* (ICC-01/05–1), Prosecution's Report Pursuant to Pre-Trial Chamber III's 30 November 2006 Decision Requesting Information on the Status of the Preliminary Examination of the Situation in the Central African Republic, 15 December 2006.

[128] *Bemba* (ICC-01/05–01/08), Decision on the Prosecutor's Application for a Warrant of Arrest Against Jean-Pierre Bemba Gombo, 10 June 2008.

[129] *Bemba* (ICC-01/05–01/08), Decision Pursuant to Article 61(7)(a) and (b) of the Rome Statute on the Charges of the Prosecutor Against Jean-Pierre Bemba Gombo, 15 June 2009.

Kenya's post-electoral violence

Following the post-electoral violence that took place in Kenya in early 2008, the Prosecutor applied to the Pre-Trial Chamber for authorization to initiate an investigation, in accordance with Article 15 of the Statute. His application, filed in November 2009, was the first exercise of the *proprio motu* power of the Prosecutor since the beginning of the Court. On 31 March 2010, the Pre-Trial Chamber authorized the Prosecutor to investigate the situation. One of the judges, Hans-Peter Kaul, would have rejected the application on the ground that the element of 'state or organizational plan or policy' that is required for charges of crimes against humanity had not been established.[130]

Other situations

Activities also continue with respect to Côte d'Ivoire, which has not ratified the Statute but which has made a declaration in accordance with Article 12(3), allowing a non-party State to lodge a declaration with the Registrar accepting the jurisdiction of the Court for specific crimes. Other situations that the Prosecutor has said are being considered are Georgia, Afghanistan, Guinea and Palestine.[131]

In February 2006, the Office of the Prosecutor issued a statement declaring that it had dismissed communications concerning Venezuela and Iraq. Although the Prosecutor concluded that war crimes, including killing, had been committed by British forces associated with military operations since the 2003 invasion, he said they did not reach the required gravity threshold, given that the number of victims was relatively small compared with other situations under consideration, such as northern Uganda.[132]

Early in his mandate, the Prosecutor pointed towards economic actors as being those who might 'bear the greatest responsibility', and therefore merit his attention:

> One important area of investigation will involve financial links with crimes. The investigation of financial transactions, for example for the

---

[130] *Situation in Kenya* (ICC-01/09), Decision Pursuant to Article 15 of the Rome Statute on the Authorization of an Investigation into the Situation in the Republic of Kenya, 31 March 2010.

[131] Report of the International Criminal Court, UN Doc. A/64/356, paras. 44–51.

[132] Update on Communications Received by the Prosecutor, 10 February 2006.

purchase of arms used in murder, may well provide evidence proving the commission of atrocities. Here again the interaction between State authorities and the Office of the Prosecutor will be crucial: national investigative authorities may pass to the Office evidence of financial transactions which will be essential to the Court's investigations of crimes within the Court's jurisdiction; for its part, the Office may have evidence of the commission of financial crimes which can be passed to national authorities for domestic prosecutions. Such prosecutions will be a key deterrent to the commission of future crimes, if they can curb the source of funding. And all assistance of this kind provided by national authorities to the Office of the Prosecutor will help to keep the Court cost-effective.[133]

This might shift his focus from the warlords of central Africa to the entrepreneurs and financiers of Europe and elsewhere who fuel the conflicts. But this initial hint at a new direction for prosecutions has received no subsequent confirmation in the public activities of the Office of the Prosecutor, or in the Prosecutor's statements.

The International Criminal Court has positioned itself at the centre of what it calls the 'emerging system of international criminal justice'.[134] There are several manifestations of this. In 2006, the Court provided interpreters and specialized advice to the International Criminal Tribunal for Rwanda, when it held a hearing in the Netherlands. The Court has furnished detention and courtroom facilities for the trial of Charles Taylor by the Special Court for Sierra Leone. Exceptionally, in accordance with a Security Council resolution, the Taylor trial is being held outside Sierra Leone, in The Hague.[135] The Court also loaned its Deputy Prosecutor for Investigations, Serge Brammertz, to the United Nations, where he served as Commissioner of the International Independent Investigation Commission into terrorist crimes in Lebanon committed in 2005 and 2006. Brammertz had been granted a leave of absence by the Prosecutor, in accordance with Article 42(2) of the Rome Statute.

The Court has adopted a mission statement as part of its 'Strategic Plan'. It states: 'As an independent judicial institution in the emerging international justice system, the International Criminal Court will: Fairly, effectively and impartially investigate, prosecute and conduct

---

[133] Paper on Some Policy Issues Before the Office of the Prosecutor, pp. 2–3.
[134] Report of the International Criminal Court, UN Doc. A/60/177, para. 3; Report of the International Criminal Court, UN Doc. A/61/217, para. 57.
[135] UN Doc. S/RES/1688 (2006).

trials of the most serious crimes; Act transparently and efficiently; and Contribute to long lasting respect for and the enforcement of international criminal justice, to the prevention of crime and to the fight against impunity.'[136] The Strategic Plan explains that, while the Court's mandate is derived from the Rome Statute, '[t]he mission statement expresses how the Court will realize the aims of the Statute and reflects the context in which the Court operates, its core functions, and the impact it is intended to have'.[137] The Mission Statement relates this to what it calls the 'One Court principle'. Accordingly, although the Court is composed of separate and functionally independent organs, 'the Court's staff and elected officials form part of the same institution and share a common mission. They work together as one Court on matters of common concern.'[138]

The influence of the Rome Statute will extend deep into domestic criminal law, enriching the jurisprudence of national courts and challenging prosecutors and judges to display greater zeal in the repression of serious violations of human rights. National courts have shown, in recent years, a growing enthusiasm for the use of international law materials in the application of their own laws. A phenomenon of judicial globalization is afoot. The Statute itself, and eventually the case law of the International Criminal Court, will no doubt contribute in this area. The International Criminal Tribunal for the former Yugoslavia, in *Prosecutor* v. *Furundžija*, described the Statute's legal significance as follows:

> [A]t present it is still a non-binding international treaty (it has not yet entered into force). It was adopted by an overwhelming majority of the States attending the Rome Diplomatic Conference and was substantially endorsed by the General Assembly's Sixth Committee on 26 November 1998. In many areas the Statute may be regarded as indicative of the legal views, i.e. *opinio juris* of a great number of States. Notwithstanding article 10 of the Statute, the purpose of which is to ensure that existing or developing law is not 'limited' or 'prejudiced' by the Statute's provisions, resort may be had *com grano salis* to these provisions to help elucidate customary international law. Depending on the matter at issue, the Rome Statute may be taken to restate, reflect or clarify customary rules or crystallize them, whereas in some areas it creates new law or modifies existing law. At any event, the Rome Statute by and large may be taken

---

[136] *Ibid.*, para. 18.   [137] *Ibid.*, para. 19.   [138] *Ibid.*, para. 12.

as constituting an authoritative expression of the legal views of a great number of States.[139]

In the same vein, another Trial Chamber described the draft Elements of Crimes to be 'helpful in assessing the state of customary international law'. It added that those States attending the Rome Conference, regardless of whether they had signed the Statute, were eligible to participate in the sessions of the Preparatory Commission that adopted the Elements of Crimes in July 2000. 'From this perspective', said the Trial Chamber, 'the document is a useful key to the *opinio juris* of the States.'[140]

The International Criminal Court is now embarked on what promises to be an exciting period of judicial interpretation and even law-making.[141] In addition to clarifying many of the complex procedural issues, the Court will interpret provisions that are central to its operations and that were intentionally left ambiguous by negotiators at the Rome Diplomatic Conference. Underlying much of the debate is a philosophical divide between adversarial and inquisitorial approaches, between interventionist judges who believe they must guide the prosecution and those who consider that their role is more passive.

As the Court approaches the ten-year mark of the entry into force of the Rome Statute, that it has only finished one or two trials with perhaps another one or two in the works may be disappointing to many of its supporters. The Court has missed the targets that it had set itself. A year after taking office, in 2004, the Prosecutor proposed a budget that was based upon the proposition that '[i]n 2005, the Office plans to conduct one full trial, begin a second and carry out two new investigations'.[142] A flow chart derived from the Prosecutor's forecasts indicated that the first trial before the Court would be completed by August 2005.[143] He became somewhat less ambitious in 2006, when a three-year strategic plan proclaimed the expectation that the Court would *complete* two 'expeditious

---

[139] *Furundžija* (IT-95-17/IT), Judgment, 10 December 1998, para. 227. For an example of the draft statute of the Court being cited as a guide to evolving customary international law, see the reasons of Justice Michel Bastarache of the Supreme Court of Canada in *Pushpanathan v. Canada (Minister of Citizenship and Immigration)* [1998] 1 SCR 982, paras. 66–8.

[140] *Krstić* (IT-98-33-T), Judgment, 2 August 2001, para. 541.

[141] *Case Concerning Armed Activities on the Territory of the Congo (New Application: 2002)* (*Democratic Republic of the Congo v. Rwanda*), Jurisdiction of the Court and Admissibility of the Application, Separate Opinion of Judge Ad Hoc Dugard, 3 February 2006, para. 9.

[142] Draft Programme Budget for 2005, ASP/3/2, para. 159.   [143] *Ibid.*, p. 49.

trials by 2009, and ... conduct four to six new investigations'.[144] In fact, by 2009 not even one trial was even close to completion. The second strategic plan, covering the period 2009–12, said the goal was to complete three trials and to start a fourth.[145]

This does not compare very favourably with the precedents. We all recall how the Nuremberg indictments were served on defendants in October 1945, a little more than two months after the London Conference agreed on the definition of the crimes and the architecture of the International Military Tribunal.[146] In more recent times, the first indictments of the International Criminal Tribunal for the former Yugoslavia were issued in November 1994,[147] approximately five months after Prosecutor Richard Goldstone took office, and one year after the Tribunal's judges were elected. Several major trials had been fully completed, including the appeals, by the time the Tribunal reached its eighth birthday. The initial indictments of the International Criminal Tribunal for Rwanda date to November 1995,[148] twelve months after the Security Council resolution establishing the Tribunal. It, too, was well advanced with several completed trials in the same period. The first arrests by the Special Court for Sierra Leone were made in March 2003,[149] about eight months after the election of the judges and the arrival of the Prosecutor in Freetown. Indeed, the Special Court began its work at almost the same time as the entry into force of the Rome Statute, and it has practically completed its work.

Deterrence is supposed to be one of the purposes of international criminal justice in general, and the International Criminal Court in particular. The theme has often figured in the public statements of the Prosecutor. In the *Lubanga* arrest warrant decision, the Pre-Trial Chamber spoke of 'maximizing' the 'deterrent effects of the activities

---

[144] Report on Prosecutorial Strategy, 14 September 2006, p. 3.

[145] Prosecutorial Strategy, 2009–2012, 1 February 2010, The Hague, para. 25.

[146] *France et al.* v. *Goering et al.*, (1946) 22 IMT 203.

[147] *Dragan Nikolić* (IT-94-2-I), Indictment, 4 November 1994.

[148] *Kayishema et al.* (ICTR-95-1-I), Indictment, 22 November 1995. Also Report of the International Criminal Tribunal for the Prosecution of Persons Responsible for Genocide and Other Serious Violations of International Humanitarian Law Committed in the Territory of Rwanda and Rwandan Citizens Responsible for Genocide and Other Such Violations Committed in the Territory of Neighbouring States Between 1 January and 31 December 1994, UN Doc. A/51/399-S/1996/778, para. 44; Navanethem Pillay, 'The Rwanda Tribunal and Its Relationship to National Trials in Rwanda', (1998) 13 *American University International Law Review* 1469.

[149] E.g., *Taylor* (SCSL-2003-01-I), Indictment, 7 March 2003.

of the Court'.[150] It cited the 'deterrent function' to justify the 'key role' of the gravity threshold in determining whether a case was admissible.[151] Deterrence remains somewhat of an enigma for experts in criminal justice. It will never be easy to establish whether the Court really deters effectively, because, while we can readily point to those who are not deterred, it is nearly impossible to identify those who are. Of course, we would like to assume that the Prosecutor and the Pre-Trial Chamber are right, and that the activities of the Court do in fact deter the atrocities that plague central Africa and other parts of the world. But, if this is really the case, why are they moving so slowly? If they really believed their actions were a deterrent, surely they would be in more of a hurry.

The International Criminal Court is perhaps the most innovative and exciting development in international law since the creation of the United Nations. The Statute is one of the most complex international instruments ever negotiated, a sophisticated web of highly technical provisions drawn from comparative criminal law combined with a series of more political propositions that touch the very heart of State concerns with their own sovereignty. Without any doubt, its creation is the result of the human rights agenda that has steadily taken centre stage within the United Nations since Article 1 of its Charter proclaimed the promotion of human rights to be one of its purposes. From a hesitant commitment in 1945, to an ambitious Universal Declaration of Human Rights in 1948, we have now reached a point where individual criminal liability is established for those responsible for serious violations of human rights, and where an institution is created to see that this is more than just some pious wish.

---

[150] *Lubanga* (ICC-01/04–01/06–8), Decision on the Prosecutor's Application for a Warrant of Arrest, 10 February 2006, para. 54.
[151] *Ibid.*, para. 60.

3

Jurisdiction

The term 'jurisdiction' is used in several places in the Rome Statute to identify the scope of the Court's authority. Article 5 is entitled 'Crimes within the jurisdiction of the Court', and provides a list of punishable offences. Article 11 indulges the lawyer's fetish for Latin expressions. It is labelled 'Jurisdiction ratione temporis', although the plain English 'temporal jurisdiction' would have done just as well. Article 12 is entitled 'Preconditions to the exercise of jurisdiction', but it actually sets out what are described as 'territorial jurisdiction' and 'personal jurisdiction'. Article 19 requires the Court to 'satisfy itself that it has jurisdiction in any case brought before it'. Pre-Trial Chamber I did this quite explicitly when it authorized the issuance of the arrest warrant against Thomas Lubanga.[1] The concept of jurisdiction also arises with regard to national justice systems. Article 17 requires the Court to defer to national prosecutions, unless the 'State which has jurisdiction' over the offence in question is unwilling or unable genuinely to investigate and prosecute. In the same context, Article 18 speaks of the State that 'would normally exercise jurisdiction over the crimes concerned'.

States exercise jurisdiction in the field of criminal law on five bases: territory, protection, nationality of offender (active personality), nationality of victim (passive personality), and universality.[2] Territory is the most common, if for no other reason than that it is the only form of jurisdiction where the State can be reasonably sure of actually executing the process of its courts. In the *Lotus* case, Judge Moore of the Permanent Court of International Justice indicated a presumption favouring the

---

[1] *Ibid.*, para. 19. See also *Situation in Uganda* (ICC 02/04–01/05), Decision on the Prosecutor's Application That the Pre-Trial Chamber Disregard as Irrelevant the Submission Filed by the Registry on 5 December 2005, 9 March 2006, paras. 22–3.

[2] *United States v. Yunis*, 681 F Supp 896 at 900–1 (DDC 1988). See Yoram Dinstein, 'The Universality Principle and War Crimes', in Michael N. Schmitt and Leslie C. Green, eds., *The Law of Armed Conflict: Into the Next Millennium*, Newport, RI: Naval War College, 1998, pp. 17–37.

forum delicti commissi, the place where the crime was committed.[3] One of the earliest criminal law treaties, the Treaty of International Penal Law, signed at Montevideo on 23 January 1889, stated that: 'Crimes are tried by the Courts and punished by the laws of the nation on whose territory they are perpetrated, whatever may be the nationality of the actor, or of the injured.'[4] Sometimes territory may be given a rather broad scope, so as to encompass acts which take place outside the State's territory but which have a direct effect upon it.[5] Jurisdiction based on the nationality of the victim or the offender, as well as on the right of a State to protect its interests, is somewhat rarer. The Permanent Court of International Justice, in the *Lotus* case, left unresolved the issue of the right of States to exercise jurisdiction based on the nationality of the victim (passive personality jurisdiction) rather than that of the offender (active personality jurisdiction),[6] which is well established.

The Nuremberg Tribunal exercised jurisdiction 'to try and punish persons who, acting in the interests of the European Axis countries, whether as individuals or as members of organizations', had committed one of the crimes within the Tribunal's subject-matter jurisdiction.[7] Thus, its jurisdiction was personal in nature; defendants had to have acted in the interests of the European Axis countries. The jurisdiction of the International Criminal Tribunal for the former Yugoslavia is confined to crimes committed on the territory of the former Yugoslavia, subsequent to 1991.[8] The jurisdiction is therefore territorial in nature. The International Criminal Tribunal for Rwanda has jurisdiction over crimes committed in Rwanda during 1994, and over crimes committed by Rwandan nationals in neighbouring countries in the same period.[9] Accordingly, its jurisdiction is both territorial and personal.

The basic difference with these precedents is that the International Criminal Court was created with the consent of those who are themselves subject to its jurisdiction. They have agreed that crimes

---

[3] *SS Lotus* (*France* v. *Turkey*), PCIJ, 1927, Series A, No. 10, p. 70.

[4] (1935) 29 *American Journal of International Law* 638.

[5] *United States* v. *Noriega*, 746 F Supp 1506 (SD Fla 1990). See Lynden Hall, '"Territorial" Jurisdiction and the Criminal Law', (1972) *Criminal Law Review* 276.

[6] *SS Lotus* (*France* v. *Turkey*), PCIJ, 1927, Series A, No. 10, p. 70.

[7] Agreement for the Prosecution and Punishment of Major War Criminals of the European Axis, and Establishing the Charter of the International Military Tribunal (IMT), Annex, (1951) 82 UNTS 279, Art. 6.

[8] Statute of the International Criminal Tribunal for the former Yugoslavia, UN Doc. S/RES/827, Annex.

[9] Statute of the International Criminal Tribunal for Rwanda, UN Doc. S/RES/955, Annex.

committed on their territory, or by their nationals, may be prosecuted. These are the fundamentals of the Court's jurisdiction. The jurisdiction that the international community has accepted for its new Court is narrower than the jurisdiction that individual States are entitled to exercise with respect to the same crimes. Moreover, the drafters of the Rome Statute sought to limit the ability of the Court to try cases over which it has, at least in theory, jurisdiction. Consequently, they have required that the State's own courts get the first bite at the apple. Only when the domestic justice system is 'unwilling' or 'unable' to prosecute can the International Criminal Court take over.[10] This is what the Statute refers to as admissibility.

Universal jurisdiction – *quasi delicta juris gentium* – applies to a limited number of crimes for which any State, even absent a personal or territorial link with the offence, is entitled to try the offender. In customary international law, these crimes include piracy,[11] the slave trade, and traffic in children and women. Recognition of universal jurisdiction for these crimes was largely predicated on the ground that they were often committed in *terra nullius*, where no State could exercise territorial jurisdiction. More recently, some multilateral treaties have also recognized universal jurisdiction for particular offences such as hijacking and other threats to air travel,[12] piracy,[13] attacks upon diplomats,[14] nuclear safety,[15] terrorism,[16] apartheid,[17] torture[18] and enforced disappearance.[19] The application of universal jurisdiction is also widely accepted for genocide, crimes against humanity and war crimes, that

[10] Mohamed El Zeidy, 'The Principle of Complementarity: A New Machinery to Implement International Criminal Law', (2002) 23 *Michigan Journal of International Law* 869.

[11] *United States* v. *Smith*, 18 US (5 Wheat.) 153 at 161–2 (1820).

[12] Hague Convention for the Suppression of Unlawful Seizure of Aircraft, (1971) 860 UNTS 105; Montreal Convention for the Suppression of Unlawful Acts Against the Safety of Civil Aviation, (1976) 974 UNTS 177.

[13] Convention on the Law of the Sea, (1994) 1833 UNTS 3, Art. 105.

[14] Convention on the Prevention and Punishment of Crimes Against Internationally Protected Persons Including Diplomatic Agents, (1977) 1035 UNTS 167.

[15] Convention on the Physical Protection of Nuclear Material of 1980, (1984) 1456 UNTS 101.

[16] European Convention on the Suppression of Terrorism, (1978) 1137 UNTS 99; International Convention Against the Taking of Hostages, (1983) 1316 UNTS 205.

[17] International Convention on the Suppression and Punishment of the Crime of Apartheid, (1976) 1015 UNTS 243, Art. IV(b).

[18] Convention Against Torture and Other Cruel, Inhuman or Degrading Treatment or Punishment, (1987) 1465 UNTS 85, Art. 10.

[19] International Convention for the Protection of All Persons from Enforced Disappearance, UN Doc. A/61/488, annex, Art. 9(2).

is, for the core crimes of the Rome Statute, although a recent decision of the International Court of Justice provoked a variety of individual opinions on the subject, leaving the matter not only unresolved but also still in some doubt.[20] The *ad hoc* tribunals have adopted Rules enabling them to transfer cases to any national jurisdiction prepared to prosecute the case. Rule 11*bis* of the Rules of Procedure and Evidence of the International Criminal Tribunal for Rwanda authorizes referral to 'any State that is willing to prosecute the accused in its own courts'. The corresponding provision in the Rules of Procedure and Evidence of the International Criminal Tribunal for the former Yugoslavia uses the phrase 'willing and adequately prepared to accept such a case'. Earlier versions of Rule 11*bis* only allowed referral to the State where the crime was committed, or where the accused had been arrested. The judges of the *ad hoc* tribunals, who are the authors of the Rules, have confirmed the validity of universal jurisdiction for genocide, crimes against humanity and war crimes.[21] There has been no objection to this by members of the Security Council.

During the drafting of the Rome Statute, some argued that what States could do individually in their own national justice systems they could also do collectively in an international body.[22] Consequently, if they have the right to exercise universal jurisdiction over the core crimes of genocide, crimes against humanity and war crimes, they ought also to be able to create an international court that can do the same. If the Statute were to provide for universal jurisdiction in such a way, it was asserted, then the new international court would have the authority to try anybody found on the territory of a State Party, even if the crime had been committed elsewhere and if the accused was not a national

---

[20] *Arrest Warrant of 11 April 2000 (Democratic Republic of the Congo v. Belgium)*, Judgment, 15 February 2002. See Nicolaos Strapatsas, 'Universal Jurisdiction and the International Criminal Court', (2002) 29 *Manitoba Law Journal* 1; Claus Kreß, 'Universal Jurisdiction over International Crimes and the Institut de Droit International', (2006) 4 *Journal of International Criminal Justice* 1; Mohamed El Zeidy, 'Universal Jurisdiction in Absentia: Is It a Legal Valid Option for Repressing Heinous Crimes?', (2003) 37 *International Lawyer* 835; Antonio Cassese, 'When May Senior State Officials Be Tried for International Crimes?: Some Comments on the Congo v. Belgium Case', (2002) 13 *European Journal of International Law* 853.

[21] *Bucyibaruta* (ICTR-2005-85-I), Décision relative à la requête du Procureur aux fins de renvoi de l'acte d'accusation contre Laurent Bucyibaruta aux autorités françaises, 20 November 2007, para. 5.

[22] Daniel D. Ntanda Nsereko, 'The International Criminal Court: Jurisdictional and Related Issues', (1999) 10 *Criminal Law Forum* 87 at 101.

of the State Party.[23] But such an approach met with two objections.[24] First, some States felt the solution too ambitious and likely to discourage ratifications. It is true that, in practice, universal jurisdiction is rarely exercised by States, and many would probably prefer not to be pushed into matters that in the past, for diplomatic or other reasons, they have sought to avoid. Secondly, a few States quarrelled with the legality of an international court that could exercise universal jurisdiction.[25] The United States in particular argued that there was no rationale in law for such a court, and insisted that the only legal basis would be active personal jurisdiction, that is, the court would only be entitled to try nationals of a State Party. Thereby, a State could shield its nationals from the jurisdiction of the Court, even for crimes committed abroad, by simply withholding ratification. The United States threatened that, if universal jurisdiction were to be incorporated in the Statute, it would have to oppose the Court actively.

Indeed, the United States remains unhappy with the solution reached at Rome whereby the Court may exercise jurisdiction over crimes committed within the territory of a State Party or by a national of a State Party.[26] As recently as March 2005, it declared in the Security Council: '[T]he United States continues to fundamentally object to the view that the ICC should be able to exercise jurisdiction over the nationals, including government officials, of States not party to the Rome Statute.'[27] The view that this lies at the core of United States objections is, however, an exaggeration. If the United States had agreed with the end product adopted on 17 July 1998, Washington would have had little real problem with the prospect of its own nationals being subject to its jurisdiction. The other international tribunals, for the former Yugoslavia, Rwanda and Sierra Leone, all of which are supported by the United States, can exercise jurisdiction over nationals of the United States.

---

[23] E.g., UN Doc. A/CONF.183/SR.3, para. 21 (Czech Republic), para. 42 (Latvia), para. 76 (Costa Rica); UN Doc. A/CONF.183/SR.4, para. 12 (Albania), paras. 20–1 (Germany); UN Doc. A/CONF.183/SR.6, para. 4 (Belgium), para. 69 (Luxembourg); UN Doc. A/ CONF.183/SR.8, para. 18 (Bosnia and Herzegovina), para. 62 (Ecuador).

[24] Morten Bergsmo, 'The Jurisdictional Regime of the International Criminal Court (Part II, Articles 11–19)', (1998) 6 *European Journal of Crime, Criminal Law and Criminal Justice* 29; Ruth B. Philips, 'The International Criminal Court Statute: Jurisdiction and Admissibility', (1999) 10 *Criminal Law Forum* 61.

[25] UN Doc. A/CONF.183/SR.9, para. 28 (United States), para. 37 (China).

[26] David Scheffer, 'The United States and the International Criminal Court', (1999) 93 *American Journal of International Law* 12.

[27] UN Doc. S/PV.5158, p. 3.

The compromise in Article 12, by which the Court has jurisdiction over nationals of States Parties and over crimes committed on their territory, was ruthlessly criticized by many at the time who said it would doom the Court to impotence.[28] Only angelic States – the Scandinavians, Canada, Ireland, the Netherlands, and so on – would join the Court on such a basis, it was argued. As for States facing war and internal strife, they would cautiously remain outside the Court and thereby protect themselves from its reach, at least with regard to crimes committed on their territories. Others took the more moderate view that Article 12 represented an unfortunate but inevitable compromise. For Professor Sharon Williams, the provision '[i]s far from perfect but was all that was possible at the time'.[29]

As the pace of ratification accelerated in 2000 and 2001, there was an astonishing and unforeseen development. The very States expected to steer clear of the Court because of their obvious vulnerability to prosecution started to produce instruments of ratification at United Nations headquarters. The first was Fiji, which had known severe civil conflict in the late 1990s. It was followed by Sierra Leone, where civil war had raged from 1991 until the Lomé Peace Agreement of 1999, only to heat up once again in 2000. By the time the magic number of sixty ratifications was reached, several other countries that had known violent conflict and atrocity in recent years had joined the Court: Cambodia, Macedonia, the Democratic Republic of the Congo, Bosnia and Herzegovina, Yugoslavia and Croatia. Colombia, Afghanistan and Burundi soon followed.

These ratifications were totally unexpected, particularly by those who insisted that the Court should be premised on universal jurisdiction because conflict-afflicted States, primarily in the South, would never join. Obviously, they disprove the arguments that were advanced at Rome by those who were critical of the compromise on jurisdiction in Article 12. They suggest that States are ratifying the Statute precisely

[28] For a discussion by one of the most vocal advocates of universal jurisdiction, Hans-Peter Kaul, who is now a judge of the Court, see Hans-Peter Kaul, 'Preconditions to the Exercise of Jurisdiction', in Antonio Cassese, Paola Gaeta and John R. W. D. Jones, eds., *The Rome Statute of the International Criminal Court: A Commentary*, vol. I, Oxford: Oxford University Press, 2002, pp. 583–616. Also Marlies Glasius, *The International Criminal Court, A Global Civil Society Achievement*, London and New York: Routledge, 2006, pp. 61–76.

[29] Sharon A. Williams, 'Article 12 (Preconditions to the Exercise of Jurisdiction)', in Otto Triffterer, ed., *Commentary on the Rome Statute of the International Criminal Court, Observers' Notes, Article by Article*, Baden-Baden: Nomos, 1999, pp. 329–41.

because they view the Court as a promising and realistic mechanism capable of addressing civil conflict, human rights abuses and war. This is entirely consistent, of course, with the logic of those who have argued over the years that international justice contributes to peace and security.

Indeed, we might ask in hindsight whether sixty ratifications would have been achieved so quickly had the broad universal jurisdiction proposal actually been adopted. The problem with the universal jurisdiction approach is that it leaves little incentive for States to join the Court. One way or another, whether or not States ratify the Statute, if the Court is based on universal jurisdiction, crimes committed on their territory are subject to its jurisdiction in any case. On the other hand, under the current regime as set out in Article 12, States must ratify the Statute if they wish to send a message of deterrence that war crimes, crimes against humanity and genocide will not go unpunished on their territories. This they seem to be doing, in ever-increasing numbers. In other words, far from dooming the Court to inactivity, the limited jurisdictional scheme of Article 12 would appear to have contributed to the rate of ratification.

This debate about jurisdiction of the Court was labelled the 'State consent' issue during the drafting process. The International Law Commission had adopted an approach to jurisdiction whereby States would have to 'opt in' to jurisdiction on specific crimes. Jurisdiction was not to be conferred automatically simply because a State ratified the future Statute.[30] This was not unlike the Statute of the International Court of Justice, whereby States belong to the Court and are parties to the Statute but must make additional declarations in order to accept jurisdiction.[31] The International Law Commission draft allowed for one exception, in the case of genocide, at least for parties to the 1948 Genocide Convention. It was predicated on the fact that the 1948 Genocide Convention specifically contemplated an international criminal court with jurisdiction over the crime.[32]

As debate unfolded in the Ad Hoc Committee, in 1995, and later in the Preparatory Committee, there was a trend towards enlarging the scope of the 'inherent jurisdiction' of the Court from genocide to crimes against

[30] Report of the International Law Commission on the Work of Its Forty-Sixth Session, 2 May–22 July 1994, UN Doc. A/49/10, Art. 22(1).
[31] Statute of the International Court of Justice, Art. 36(2)–(5).
[32] Convention on the Prevention and Punishment of the Crime of Genocide, (1951) 78 UNTS 277, Art. VI.

humanity and war crimes. Accompanying this development, and contributing to it, was a tendency to move away from including 'treaty crimes', such as terrorism and drug trafficking, in the subject-matter jurisdiction of the court. Thus, as the scope of the crimes narrowed to those upon which there was genuine consensus as to their severity and significance, the argument that the court should have automatic jurisdiction over all crimes within its subject-matter jurisdiction became more compelling.[33] Article 12, entitled 'Preconditions to the exercise of jurisdiction', was the result of this difficult debate.[34]

1. A State which becomes a Party to this Statute thereby accepts the jurisdiction of the Court with respect to the crimes referred to in article 5.
2. In the case of article 13, paragraph (a) or (c), the Court may exercise its jurisdiction if one or more of the following States are Parties to this Statute or have accepted the jurisdiction of the Court in accordance with paragraph 3:
   (a) The State on the territory of which the conduct in question occurred or, if the crime was committed on board a vessel or aircraft, the State of registration of that vessel or aircraft;
   (b) The State of which the person accused of the crime is a national.
3. If the acceptance of a State which is not a Party to this Statute is required under paragraph 2, that State may, by declaration lodged with the Registrar, accept the exercise of jurisdiction by the Court with respect to the crime in question. The accepting State shall cooperate with the Court without any delay or exception in accordance with Part 9.

Issues of jurisdiction take several forms, each of which must be considered separately. They are temporal (*ratione temporis*) jurisdiction, personal (*ratione personae*) jurisdiction, territorial (or *ratione loci*) jurisdiction, and subject-matter (*ratione materiae*) jurisdiction.

Temporal (*ratione temporis*) jurisdiction

The Court is a prospective institution in that it cannot exercise jurisdiction over crimes committed prior to the entry into force of the Statute.

---

[33] Elizabeth Wilmshurst, 'Jurisdiction of the Court', in Lee, *The International Criminal Court*, pp. 127–41.

[34] Hans-Peter Kaul, 'Special Note: The Struggle for the International Criminal Court's Jurisdiction', (1998) 6 *European Journal of Crime, Criminal Law and Criminal Justice* 48. See also Vera Gowlland-Debbas, 'The Relationship Between the Security Council and the Projected International Criminal Court', (1998) 3 *Journal of Armed Conflict Law* 97; Pietro Gargiulo, 'The Controversial Relationship Between the International Criminal

In this respect, it differs from all of its predecessors. Previous international criminal tribunals were established primarily to deal with atrocities committed before their creation, although they have also been given a prospective jurisdiction.[35] Article 11(1) of the Rome Statute declares that '[t]he Court has jurisdiction only with respect to crimes committed after the entry into force of this Statute', that is, beginning 1 July 2002. The Statute seems to return to the issue in Article 24, which declares that no person shall be criminally responsible for conduct prior to the entry into force of the Statute. Articles 24 and 11 are in fact quite closely related. At the Rome Conference, 'temporal jurisdiction and non-retroactivity' were discussed under a single agenda item, and at one point during the drafting process the chair of the Working Group on General Principles proposed that the concepts be merged in a single provision.[36]

Ruling on whether it had jurisdiction in the *Lubanga* case, Pre-Trial Chamber I addressed the question of the temporal application of the Statute:

> Considering that '[t]he Statute entered into force for the [Democratic Republic of the Congo] on 1 July 2002, in conformity with article 126(1) of the Statute, the [Democratic Republic of the Congo] having ratified the Statute on 11 April 2002', the second condition would be met pursuant to article 11 of the Statute if the crimes underlying the case against Mr Thomas Lubanga Dyilo were committed after 1 July 2002. As the case against Mr Thomas Lubanga Dyilo referred to crimes committed between July 2002 and December 2003, the Chamber considers that the second condition has also been met.[37]

Court and the Security Council', in Flavia Lattanzi and William A. Schabas, eds., *Essays on the Rome Statute of the International Criminal Court*, Rome: Editrice il Sirente, 2000, pp. 67–104.

[35] Both the Nuremberg and Tokyo tribunals were purely retroactive. The International Criminal Tribunal for the former Yugoslavia is retroactive, to a date more than two years prior to its creation, but it is also prospective. The International Criminal Tribunal for Rwanda is essentially retroactive, although its temporal jurisdiction continues for a few weeks after establishment by the Security Council. The Special Court for Sierra Leone is also retroactive, to a date several years prior to its creation, but it too is also prospective.

[36] UN Doc. A/CONF.183/C.1/SR.8, para. 74; UN Doc. A/CONF.183/C.1/SR.35, para. 28; UN Doc. A/CONF.183/C.1/SR.39, para. 4; Per Saland, 'International Criminal Law Principles', in Lee, *The International Criminal Court*, pp. 189–216 at p. 197.

[37] *Lubanga* (ICC-01/04–01/06–8), Decision on the Prosecutor's Application for a Warrant of Arrest, 10 February 2006, para. 26.

The Security Council resolution referring the Darfur situation refers explicitly to 'the situation in Darfur since 1 July 2002'.[38] Presumably, the Security Council was simply confirming that it could not refer a situation prior to that date. But perhaps, by the precise reference to 1 July 2002, some will argue that the Security Council was reserving its authority to refer a situation prior to the entry into force of the Statute, on the premise that its power under the Charter of the United Nations trumps any provision in the Rome Statute,

Reporting on the 1,732 communications received as of early 2006, the Prosecutor said that 5 per cent of them concerned events prior to 1 July 2002, and were therefore outside the temporal jurisdiction of the Court.[39] Explaining why he was declining to proceed with communications concerning international crimes committed in Venezuela, the Prosecutor stated:

> A considerable number of the allegations referred to incidents that are alleged to have taken place prior to 1 July 2002, in particular in connection with incidents occurring in the context of the short-lived coup in April 2002. These events occurred prior to the temporal jurisdiction of the Court and cannot be considered as the basis for any investigation under the Statute.[40]

In the case of States that become parties to the Statute subsequent to its entry into force, the Court has jurisdiction over crimes committed after the entry into force of the Statute with respect to that State.[41] For example, Colombia ratified the Statute in August 2002, several weeks after its entry into force on 1 July 2002. The Statute only entered into force for Colombia on 1 November 2002, in accordance with Article 126, and the Court cannot therefore prosecute any cases that are based on the Colombian ratification for the period between 1 July and 1 November 2002. This does not exclude it acting with respect to crimes committed in Colombia during that period, but the Court must then establish its jurisdiction on some other basis, for example where the perpetrator is a

---

[38] UN Doc. S/RES/1593 (2005), para. 1.

[39] Update on Communications Received by the Office of the Prosecutor of the ICC, undated (but issued in February 2006), p. 2. See also Communications Received by the Office of the Prosecutor of the ICC, 16 July 2003, p. 1.

[40] Letter of Prosecutor dated 9 February 2006 (Venezuela), p. 3.

[41] Rome Statute of the International Criminal Court, (2002) 2187 UNTS 90, Art. 11(2).

national of another State Party, or where the situation is referred by the Security Council.

There is an exception to the general rule concerning the temporal application of the Statute, because it is possible for a State to make an *ad hoc* declaration recognizing the Court's jurisdiction over specific crimes, even if the State is not a party to the Statute.[42] Such declarations, formulated in accordance with Article 12(3) of the Statute, would appear to be retroactive by their very nature. On 27 February 2004, Uganda made such a statement, which it labelled 'Declaration on Temporal Jurisdiction'. Uganda accepted the exercise of the Court's jurisdiction for crimes committed following the entry into force of the Statute on 1 July 2002. The legality of the declaration appears to have been assumed by Pre-Trial Chamber III, which took note of it when it confirmed the arrest warrant against Joseph Kony.[43]

The Statute has been criticized for its inability to reach into the past and prosecute atrocities committed prior to its coming into force. The answer to this objection is entirely pragmatic. Few States – even those who were the Court's most fervent advocates – would have been prepared to recognize a court with such an ambit. The idea was unmarketable and was never seriously entertained during the drafting. But the failure to prosecute retroactively does not wipe the slate clean and grant a form of impunity to previous offenders. Those responsible for atrocities committed prior to entry into force of the Rome Statute may and should be punished by national courts. Where the State of nationality or the territorial State refuse to act, an increasing number of States now provide for universal jurisdiction over such offences.[44] Other options include the establishment by treaty of an international court, like the Special Court for Sierra Leone, whose legal basis is an agreement between the Government

---

[42] *Ibid.*, Art. 12(3).

[43] *Situation in Uganda* (ICC-02/04–53), Warrant of Arrest for Joseph Kony Issued on 8 July 2005 as Amended on 27 September 2005, para. 32. Also *Situation in Uganda* (ICC-02/04–54), Warrant of Arrest for Vincent Otti, 8 July 2005, para. 32; *Situation in Uganda* (ICC-02/04–55), Warrant of Arrest for Raska Lukwiya, 8 July 2005, para. 20; *Situation in Uganda* (ICC-02/04–56), Warrant of Arrest for Okot Odhiambo, 8 July 2005, para. 22; *Situation in Uganda* (ICC-02/04–57), Warrant of Arrest for Dominic Ongwen, 8 July 2005, para. 20.

[44] On this subject generally, see Naomi Roht-Arriaza, ed., *Impunity and Human Rights in International Law and Practice*, New York and London: Oxford University Press, 1995; Steven R. Ratner and Jason S. Abrams, *Accountability for Human Rights Atrocities in International Law: Beyond the Nuremberg Legacy*, Oxford: Clarendon Press, 1997.

of Sierra Leone and the United Nations,[45] the latter acting pursuant to a Security Council resolution.[46]

The issue of jurisdiction *ratione temporis* should not be confused with the question of retroactive crimes. International human rights law considers the prohibition of retroactive crimes and punishments to be one of its most fundamental principles. Known by the Latin expression *nullum crimen nulla poena sine lege*, this norm forbids prosecution of crimes that were not recognized as such at the time they were committed. There are, of course, varying interpretations as to the scope of the principle.[47] The Nuremberg Tribunal could point to existing legal texts, such as the Hague Convention IV of 1907, in the case of war crimes, and the Kellogg–Briand Pact, in the case of crimes against peace. But, while these described certain acts as being contrary to international law, they did not define them as generating individual criminal liability. Inspired by the writings of Hans Kelsen, the Nuremberg Tribunal answered the charge only indirectly, noting that *nullum crimen sine lege* was a principle of justice, and that it would be unjust to let the Nazi leaders go unpunished.[48] Since then, similar pronouncements can be found in the *Eichmann* case of 1961 and even recently in the *Erdemović* judgment of the International Criminal Tribunal for the former Yugoslavia.[49]

In any event, *nullum crimen* is set out in Articles 22 and 23. Specifically, Article 22(1) declares: 'A person shall not be criminally responsible under this Statute unless the conduct in question constitutes, at the time it takes place, a crime within the jurisdiction of the Court.' Why Article 22(1) is necessary may initially seem puzzling, given the general jurisdictional prohibition on crimes committed prior to the entry into force of the Statute. After all, this is not a court like those at Nuremberg or Tokyo, or the *ad hoc* tribunals established for Yugoslavia and Rwanda,

---

[45] Agreement between the United Nations and the Government of Sierra Leone on the Establishment of a Special Court for Sierra Leone, (2002) 2178 UNTS 138. See Micaela Frulli, 'The Special Court for Sierra Leone: Some Preliminary Comments', (2000) 11 *European Journal of International Law* 857; Robert Cryer, 'A "Special Court" for Sierra Leone?', (2001) 50 *International and Comparative Law Quarterly* 435; Avril McDonald, 'Sierra Leone's Shoestring Special Court', (2002) 84 *International Review of the Red Cross* 121; and S. Beresford and A. S. Muller, 'The Special Court for Sierra Leone: An Initial Comment', (2001) 14 *Leiden Journal of International Law* 635.

[46] UN Doc. S/RES/2000/1315.

[47] See Aly Mokhtar, 'Nullum Crimen, Nulla Poena Sine Lege: Aspects and Prospects', (2005) 26 *Statute Law Review* 41.

[48] Hans Kelsen, 'Will the Judgment in the Nuremberg Trial Constitute a Precedent in International Law?', (1947) 1 *International Law Quarterly* 153 at 165.

[49] *Erdemović* (IT-96-22-T), Sentencing Judgment, 29 November 1996, para. 35.

all of them set up with a view to judging crimes already committed.[50] But, where a State has made an *ad hoc* declaration recognizing the jurisdiction of the Court, with respect to a crime committed in the past, a defendant might argue that one or another of the provisions of Articles 6, 7, 8 and 8*bis* is not recognized as a norm of customary international law and is therefore not punishable by the Court. Likewise, this question might arise where the Security Council gives jurisdiction to the Court,[51] the same argument raised by defendants before the *ad hoc* tribunals in The Hague and Arusha.[52] But the argument, though not totally frivolous, has never really succeeded before international courts in the past and is unlikely to cut much ice with the Court in the future. The standard adopted by the European Court of Human Rights with respect to retroactive crimes is that they must be both accessible and reasonably foreseeable by an offender.[53] Inevitably, the Prosecutor will adopt this reasoning, and argue that, from the moment the Statute was adopted, or at the very least from the moment it entered into force, individuals have received sufficient warning that they risk being prosecuted for such offences, and that the Statute itself (in Article 12(3)) contemplates such prosecution even with respect to States that are not yet parties to the Statute.

In principle, where criminal conduct has commenced before the starting point of temporal jurisdiction, 'a conviction may be based only on that part of such conduct having occurred' since the date in question.[54] This does not preclude the admission of evidence of events that occurred previously in order to clarify the context, establish by inference the elements of criminal conduct occurring subsequently, or demonstrate

---

[50] That the Court only operates prospectively would seem to resolve problems concerning retroactive prosecution, but this has not stopped defence lawyers from raising an imaginative, if patently flawed, argument. During the *Lubanga* confirmation hearing, defence counsel claimed 'that the mere fact that the offence is listed in the Rome Statute does not in itself satisfy the principle of legality if the requirements of specificity, certainty, and accessibility and foreseeability have not been complied with'. *Lubanga* (ICC-01/04–01/06), Transcript, 26 November 2006. The objection was dismissed by Pre-Trial Chamber I: *Lubanga* (ICC-01/04–01/06), Decision on the Confirmation of the Charges, 29 January 2007, paras. 301–3.

[51] Rome Statute, Art. 13(b).

[52] *Tadić* (IT-94-1-AR72), Decision on the Defence Motion for Interlocutory Appeal on Jurisdiction, 2 October 1995.

[53] *SW* v. *United Kingdom*, Series A, No. 335-B, 22 November 1995, paras. 35–6. See also *CR* v. *United Kingdom*, Series A, No. 335-B, 22 November 1995, paras. 33–4; *Kononov* v. *Latvia*, No. 36376/04 [GC], Judgment, 17 May 2010.

[54] *Nahimana et al.* (ICTR-99-52-A), Judgment, 28 November 2007, para. 41.

a deliberate pattern of conduct.[55] The question of 'continuing crimes' arose during the Rome Conference. There were unsuccessful proposals to add the words 'unless the crimes continue after this date' so as to ensure the punishability of continuing crimes.[56] Such a circumstance might present itself, for example, in the case of an 'enforced disappearance', which is a crime against humanity punishable under Article 7. Someone might have disappeared prior to entry into force of the Statute but the crime would continue after entry into force to the extent that the disappearance persisted. It might also be argued that this is the case where a population had been forcibly transferred or deported, and was being prohibited from returning home. Transfers and deportations fall within the scope of all three categories of crimes punishable under the Statute. Verbs such as 'committed', 'occurred', 'commenced' or 'completed', in Article 24, were ways in which the problem might have been addressed, but this proved difficult to cope with in all six working languages in an appropriate manner. Eventually, the 'unresolvable matter' was resolved by the chair of the Working Group on General Principles, who proposed simply avoiding the troublesome verb in the English version. Thus, the issue of 'continuing crimes' remains undecided and it will be for the Court to determine how it should be handled.[57] The Drafting Committee appended an intriguing footnote to paragraph 1 of Article 24, reading: 'The question has been raised as regards a conduct which started before the entry into force and continues after the entry into force.'[58] It was an extremely unusual step for the Drafting Committee to insert a footnote. This may well have been a late-night compromise aimed at appeasing a handful of delegates who were obsessed with the question of continuous offences. Later, the Preparatory Committee addressed the matter with respect to enforced disappearance through a footnote in the Elements of Crimes: 'This crime falls under the jurisdiction of the Court only if the attack referred to in elements 7 and 8 occurs after the entry into force of the Statute.'[59] But the question remains alive

---

[55] *Bikindi* (ICTR-01-72-T), Judgment, 2 December 2008, para. 27; *Nahimana* (ICTR-99-52-A), Judgment, 28 November 2007, para. 315.

[56] UN Doc. A/CONF.183/C1/SR.9, para. 73.

[57] Per Saland, 'International Criminal Law Principles', in Lee, *The International Criminal Court*, pp. 189–216 at pp. 196–7; Raul Pangalangan, 'Article 24', in Triffterer, ed., *Commentary*, pp. 735–41 at pp. 739–40.

[58] UN Doc. A/CONF.183/C.1/L.65/Rev.1, p. 2; Report of the Drafting Committee, UN Doc. A/CONF.183/13(Vol. III), p. 150, n. 6. There was no footnote in the final version adopted by the Conference: UN Doc. A/CONF.183/C.1/L.76/Add.3, pp. 1–2.

[59] Elements of Crimes, Crimes Against Humanity, Article 7(1)(i), Crime Against Humanity of Enforced Disappearance of Persons, n. 24.

with regard to the war crime of transferring populations into occupied territories, for example.

The Statute does not clarify the temporal jurisdiction in the case of amendments. It might be argued that an amendment to the Statute is punishable as of 1 July 2002, based upon a literal reading of Article 11(1). In the case of the crime of aggression, the Review Conference made the non-retroactivity of prosecutions explicit.[60] It did not do the same with respect to the new war crimes concerning the use of prohibited weapons. This may bolster an argument that these are punishable as of the entry into force of the Statute with respect to a given State rather than from the entry into force of the amendment itself. References in the preamble to the resolution to customary international law provide an answer to charges that the law might not have been accessible or foreseeable.[61]

Personal (*ratione personae*) jurisdiction

The International Criminal Court exercises jurisdiction over nationals of a State Party who are accused of a crime, in accordance with Article 12(2)(b), regardless of where the acts are perpetrated. The Court can also prosecute nationals of non-party States that accept its jurisdiction on an *ad hoc* basis by virtue of a declaration of the State of nationality,[62] or pursuant to a decision of the Security Council. Creating jurisdiction based on the nationality of the offender is the least controversial form of jurisdiction and was the absolute minimum proposed by some States at the Rome Conference. Cases may arise where the concept of nationality has to be considered by the Court. In accordance with general principles of public international law, the Court should look at whether a person's links with a given State are genuine and substantial, rather than it being governed by some formal and perhaps even fraudulent grant of citizenship.[63]

At the 2010 Review Conference, two exceptions to the general rule in Article 12 on personal jurisdiction were created. The Conference

---

[60] Understandings Regarding the Amendments to the Rome Statute of the International Criminal Court on the Crime of Aggression, RC/10/Add.1, paras. 1–3.

[61] Resolution Amending Article 8 of the Rome Statute, RC/DC/1/Add.1, PP8, PP9.

[62] Rome Statute, Art. 12(3); and Rules of Procedure and Evidence, ASP/1/3, pp. 10–107, Rule 44.

[63] *Nottebohm Case (Second Phase)*, Judgment of 6 April 1955, [1955] ICJ Reports 24; *Proposed Amendments to the Naturalization Provisions of the Constitution of Costa Rica*, Advisory Opinion OC-4/84, 19 January 1984, Series A, No. 4, para. 35.

adopted an amendment to Article 8 with respect to the use of certain prohibited weapons and an entirely new provision on the crime of aggression, Article 8*bis*. The Court may only exercise jurisdiction with respect to nationals of States that ratify or accept these amendments. It is prohibited from exercising jurisdiction over nationals of States Parties that do not ratify or accept the amendment, as well as over nationals of non-party States, even if the acts are perpetrated on their own territory. This amounts to the very restrictive approach to jurisdiction that was pushed by the United States at the Rome Conference in 1998.

This more limited jurisdiction is a consequence of debates concerning the mechanism for changes or additions to the Rome Statute. Article 121(5) governs amendments to the subject-matter jurisdiction of the Court. It specifies that the Court is not to exercise its jurisdiction regarding a crime covered by the amendment when committed by the nationals or the territory of a State Party that has not ratified or accepted the amendment. The Review Conference confirmed its 'understanding that in respect to this amendment the same principle that applies in respect of a State Party which has not accepted the amendment applies also in respect of States that are not parties to the Statute'.[64] Article 15*bis* confirms the same rule with respect to the crime of aggression.

The prosecutions to date appear to be based solely on territory, and not nationality. In the prosecutions concerning Uganda and the Democratic Republic of the Congo, there are no allegations that the accused persons are nationals of a State Party. Nor did the Security Council give the Court jurisdiction over the acts of Sudanese nationals committed outside of Sudan, even where these might be germane to the conflict in Darfur. It adopted such an approach when the International Criminal Tribunal for Rwanda was established, authorizing the international tribunal to prosecute crimes on Rwandan territory and crimes committed by Rwandan nationals in neighbouring States.[65] However, when it issued the arrest warrant in *Bemba*, the Pre-Trial Chamber noted that, although it was satisfied that the alleged crimes were committed on the territory of a State Party, 'Mr Bemba is believed to be a national of the Democratic Republic of the Congo ("DRC"), a State which is also a party to the Statute.'[66]

---

[64] Resolution Amending Article 8 of the Rome Statute, RC/DC/1/Add.1, PP2.
[65] UN Doc. S/RES/955 (1994).
[66] *Bemba* (ICC-01/05–01/08), Decision on the Prosecutor's Application for a Warrant of Arrest Against Jean-Pierre Bemba Gombo, 10 June 2008, para. 15.

The Prosecutor has examined the possibility of cases based on nationality rather than territory, but has rejected them. In his first report on communications submitted in accordance with Article 15, the Prosecutor noted that there had been several allegations of acts perpetrated by nationals of coalition forces during the invasion of Iraq, in 2003.[67] He pursued this in more depth in his second report, in February 2006, and especially in the statement concerning Iraq-related prosecutions. There he indicated that inquiries had been made concerning nationals of the United Kingdom with respect to acts perpetrated on the territory of Iraq, a non-party State.[68]

An exception to the general principle of jurisdiction over nationals is explicitly set out in the Rome Statute with respect to persons under the age of eighteen at the time of the offence.[69] Much energy was expended on the issue in tedious debates during the sessions of the Preparatory Committee and the Diplomatic Conference.[70] The Working Group on General Principles agreed to impose a 'jurisdictional solution' and to provide, in Article 26, that the Court would simply be unable to prosecute persons who were under eighteen at the time of the commission of the crime.[71] The International Criminal Tribunal for the former Yugoslavia has noted that Article 26 is purely jurisdictional in nature, rejecting as 'completely unfounded in law' the proposition that there was no criminal responsibility for crimes committed by persons under the age of eighteen under either conventional or customary international law.[72]

Less explicit, but certainly just as imperative, is the exclusion of jurisdiction over persons benefiting from forms of immunity. The issue is much misunderstood, due in part to the fact that there are two relevant provisions in different parts of the Statute, Articles 27 and 98, and the fact that the bilateral agreements negotiated by the United States are often said to grant a form of immunity. These agreements do not in fact create immunity for nationals of the United States; they simply purport to relieve a State Party from an obligation to arrest and transfer individuals with American citizenship subject to a request from the Court.

---

[67] Communications Received by the Office of the Prosecutor of the ICC, 16 July 2003, p. 2.

[68] Letter of Prosecutor dated 9 February 2006 (Iraq).

[69] Rome Statute, Art. 26.

[70] Per Saland, 'International Criminal Law Principles', in Lee, *The International Criminal Court*, pp. 189–216 at pp. 200–2.

[71] UN Doc. A/CONF.183/C.1/WGGP/L.1, p. 2. For the debate in the Committee of the Whole of the Rome Conference, see A/CONF.183/C.1/SR.2, paras. 3–44.

[72] *Orić* (IT-03-68-T), Judgment, 30 June 2006, para. 400.

If Albania, for example, receives a request from the Court to arrest and transfer an American national, it may invoke its Article 98(2) agreement with the United States and decline to comply without necessarily violating its duties under the Rome Statute.

Article 98(1) applies to 'obligations under international law with respect to the State or diplomatic immunity of a person or property of a third State'. It does not create immunity, but it acknowledges that obligations relating to diplomatic immunity, resulting either from treaty law or customary law, may create a potential conflict in the event of a request from the Court, and provides a solution that amounts to deference for the existing immunity. The Court is prohibited, pursuant to Article 98(1), from proceeding with a request for surrender or assistance if this would require a requested State to act inconsistently with its obligations under international law as concerns a third State, unless the latter consents. Diplomatic immunity falls into such a category. This means that, while a State Party to the Statute cannot shelter its own head of State or foreign minister from prosecution by the International Criminal Court, the Court cannot request the State to cooperate in surrender or otherwise with respect to a third State, that is, a non-party State. Nothing prevents the State Party from doing this if it so wishes, and, once a head of State has been taken into the actual custody of the Court, he or she would be treated like any other defendant.

The Court itself has extended the scope of Article 98(1) so as to address the issue of personnel of the United Nations. This is in the spirit of its relationship with the United Nations, but it is also a tacit recognition of the supremacy of the Charter of the United Nations, which itself calls for the recognition of privileges and immunities to those working for the organization, over the Rome Statute. The Relationship Agreement with the United Nations, which was negotiated between the Court and the United Nations pursuant to Article 2 of the Rome Statute, contains the following provision:

Article 19. Rules concerning United Nations privileges and immunities

If the Court seeks to exercise its jurisdiction over a person who is alleged to be criminally responsible for a crime within the jurisdiction of the Court and if, in the circumstances, such person enjoys, according to the Convention on the Privileges and Immunities of the United Nations and the relevant rules of international law, any privileges and immunities as are necessary for the independent exercise of his or her work for the United Nations, the United Nations undertakes to cooperate fully with the Court

and to take all necessary measures to allow the Court to exercise its jurisdiction, in particular by waiving any such privileges and immunities in
accordance with the Convention on the Privileges and Immunities of the
United Nations and the relevant rules of international law.

Similarly, the Court is also prohibited from proceeding in a request
for surrender that would require a State Party to act inconsistently with
certain international agreements reached with a third State. The provision – Article 98(2) – was intended to ensure that a rather common class
of treaties known as 'status of forces agreements' (or SOFAs) would not
be undermined or neutralized by the Statute. SOFAs are used to ensure
that peacekeeping forces or troops based in a foreign country are not
subject to the jurisdiction of that country's courts. Some ingenious lawyers in the United States Department of State have attempted to pervert
Article 98(2), drafting treaties that shelter all American nationals from
the Court. Several States Parties have succumbed to Washington's pressure and agreed to such arrangements.

Article 27(2) of the Rome Statute also refers to immunity, but the
context is of a substantive rather than procedural nature. According to
Article 27(2), '[i]mmunities or special procedural rules which may attach
to the official capacity of a person, whether under national or international law, shall not bar the Court from exercising its jurisdiction over
such a person'. Despite initial appearances,[73] there is no conflict between
Article 27(2) and Article 98(1). The effect of Article 27(2) is to foreclose
States Parties from invoking immunities before the Court, and to make a
defence of immunity unavailable to an accused national of a State Party.
It is probably going too far to suggest that Article 27(2) applies to nationals of non-party states. Any immunities that they may have as a result of
customary or treaty law cannot be removed simply because a group of
States have decided, by treaty, that such immunities cannot be invoked
before an institution of their own creation. Nevertheless, when it issued
the arrest warrant decision against President Al-Bashir of Sudan, the
Pre-Trial Chamber rather summarily dismissed the possibility that as
head of state of a non-party State he might benefit from immunity under
customary international law.[74]

---

[73] According to Professor Bassiouni, who chaired the Drafting Committee at the Rome
Conference, Arts. 27(2) and 98 should have been merged into a single provision in
order to avoid confusion: M. Cherif Bassiouni, 'Negotiating the Treaty of Rome on the
Establishment of an International Criminal Court', (1999) 32 *Cornell International Law
Journal* 443 at 454.

[74] *Bashir* (ICC-02/05–01/09), Decision on the Prosecution's Application for a Warrant of
Arrest Against Omar Hassan Ahmad Al Bashir, 4 March 2009, para. 41. For academic

Finally, the Court cannot exercise jurisdiction over individuals where the Security Council has decided to exclude them from the Court's jurisdiction. It has, in fact, done this on two occasions. Resolution 1497, adopted in August 2003, declares 'that current or former officials or personnel from a contributing State, which is not a party to the Rome Statute of the International Criminal Court, shall be subject to the exclusive jurisdiction of that contributing State for all alleged acts or omissions arising out of or related to the Multinational Force or United Nations stabilization force in Liberia, unless such exclusive jurisdiction has been expressly waived by that contributing State'.[75] There were three abstentions when the resolution was adopted, by Mexico, Germany and France. The German and French representatives said that the paragraph in question was incompatible with international law.[76]

Along much the same lines, Resolution 1593, adopted in March 2005, which refers the situation in Darfur to the Court, states that 'nationals, current or former officials or personnel from a contributing State outside Sudan which is not a party to the Rome Statute of the International Criminal Court shall be subject to the exclusive jurisdiction of that contributing State for all alleged acts or omissions arising out of or related to operations in Sudan established or authorized by the Council or the African Union, unless such exclusive jurisdiction has been expressly waived by that contributing State'.

Territorial (*ratione loci*) jurisdiction

The Court has jurisdiction over crimes committed on the territory of States Parties, regardless of the nationality of the offender. This general principle is set out in Article 12(2)(a) of the Statute. It also has jurisdiction over crimes committed on the territory of States that accept its jurisdiction on an *ad hoc* basis, in accordance with Article 12(3), as well as where jurisdiction is conferred by the Security Council, pursuant to Article 13(b) but also acting in accordance with Chapter VII of the Charter of the United Nations. The 1948 Genocide Convention provides some precedent for the idea that an international criminal

---

critique of this aspect of the decision, see Paola Gaeta, 'Does President Al Bashir Enjoy Immunity from Arrest?', (2009) 7 *Journal of International Criminal Justice* 315 at 323–5.

[75] UN Doc. S/RES/1497 (2003), para. 7. See Salvatore Zappalà, 'Are Some Peacekeepers Better Than Others? UN Security Council Resolution 1497 (2003) and the ICC', (2003) 1 *Journal of International Criminal Justice* 671.

[76] UN Doc. S/PV.4803, pp. 4 and 7.

court will have jurisdiction over crimes committed on the territory of a State Party. Article VI of the Convention envisages just such an eventuality. There is an exception to this general rule in the case of crimes resulting from amendments to the Statute, adopted in accordance with Article 121(5).[77]

Territory, for the purposes of criminal law jurisdiction, is a term that needs to be defined. Obviously, it will extend to the land territory of the State. The Statute also considers the concept of territory to include crimes committed on board vessels or aircraft registered in the State Party.[78] This is a rather common and widely accepted extension of the concept of territorial jurisdiction. Logically, territorial jurisdiction should extend to the airspace above the State, and to its territorial waters and, possibly, its exclusive economic zone. But the actual scope of these grey areas remains to be determined. There are really no useful precedents from the case law of previous international criminal tribunals. Solutions to these issues will be sought in the practice of national justice systems, although this varies considerably and it is difficult to establish any common rules that are generally accepted. Whatever the result, some territories are necessarily beyond the reach of the Court: the high seas, Antarctica and outer space. If atrocities are committed in these places, jurisdiction will have to be established on the basis of the nationality of the offender.

Many national jurisdictions extend the concept of territorial jurisdiction to include crimes that create effects upon the territory of a State. For example, it could be argued that, in the case of a conspiracy to commit genocide,[79] the Court might have jurisdiction even if the conspirators actually hatched their plan outside the territory where the crime was to take place. Similarly, an order to take no prisoners (denial of quarter), which is a crime in and of itself even if nobody acts upon the order,[80] could be committed outside the territory of a State but might be deemed to fall within the jurisdiction of the Court if its effects were felt on the territory. The case becomes somewhat clearer with respect to accusations of incitement and abetting. Nevertheless, given the silence of the Statute about effects jurisdiction, there are compelling arguments in favour of a strict construction of Article 12 and the exclusion of such a concept.

---

[77] This is discussed above under the heading 'Personal (ratione personae) jurisdiction'.
[78] Rome Statute, Art. 12(2)(a).   [79] *Ibid.*, Arts. 6 and 25(d).
[80] *Ibid.*, Art. 8(2)(b)(xii) and (e)(x).

It is not improbable that the judges of the International Criminal Court find themselves determining where international borders are placed, and making pronouncements about title to specific territory. It is said that somewhat more than 50 per cent of international boundaries are disputed. Obviously, the places where these disputes are most acute are also likely to be the trouble spots on which the Court's attention will focus. Two examples from the Middle East should suffice. Suppose that the leaders of the Palestinian Authority declare independence and, at the same time, accede to the Rome Statute. The Court would have jurisdiction over the 'territory' of an independent Palestine, of which most if not all of the actual boundaries might well be contested. Because Israel is not a State Party to the Rome Statute, it has obviously not conferred jurisdiction on the Court over its territory generally. Although the matter is under study by Israeli officials and politicians, it seems unlikely that Israel will ratify the Rome Statute in the foreseeable future. At present, the only neighbouring State that has ratified the Rome Statute is Jordan. Thus, the Court might find itself adjudicating where the borders of an independent Palestine actually lie.

Even before Palestinian independence, the question could arise in another way. The International Criminal Court can exercise jurisdiction over the territory of Jordan, but not that of Israel. Israel has occupied the West Bank since 1967. Prior to that date, Jordan exercised sovereignty over the West Bank. Two decades after the occupation by Israel, in 1988, Jordan declared that it had abandoned its claims to sovereignty over the West Bank. It would be worth scrutinizing the actions of Jordan at the time it renounced its claims, so as to verify if these were done properly and if they are legally effective. If its acts of renunciation were not adequate, then there is an arguable case that the West Bank is still technically part of Jordanian territory with the result that the International Criminal Court may exercise jurisdiction over acts and omissions perpetrated on that territory subsequent to entry into force of the Rome Statute. Of course, even if this argument could be sustained, it would still be necessary to convince a State Party or the Prosecutor of the Court to trigger a case.

At the time of ratification a few States made declarations concerning the territorial scope of the Rome Statute. In contrast with many other multilateral international instruments, there is no specific provision for this in the Statute. The Netherlands made a harmless but reassuring statement to the effect that the Statute applies not only to its European territory but also to the Netherlands Antilles and Aruba. More troublesome was Denmark's declaration that it does not intend the Statute to apply to the Faroe Islands and Greenland.[81] While this was no doubt motivated by admirable sentiments of respect for local autonomy, it had the effect of excluding the reach of the Court from a territory which, on its own, has no right to correct the situation, because neither the Faroe Islands nor Greenland are sovereign States and as a result they cannot accede to the Statute. Were a case to arise, the Court might well take the lead from analogous cases before the European Court of Human Rights[82] and rule the Danish declaration to be an illegal reservation without any effect, in accordance with Article 120 of the Statute, thereby recognizing jurisdiction over the disputed territories. The special rapporteur of the International Law Commission on the question of reservations has written that 'a statement by which a State purported to exclude the application of a treaty to a territory meant that it sought "to exclude or to modify" the legal effect which the treaty would normally have, and such a statement therefore constituted, according to the Special Rapporteur, a "true" reservation, rationae loci'.[83] The problem has become largely hypothetical, because Denmark withdrew the declaration in 2006.

Acceptance of jurisdiction by a non-party State

In addition to the territorial and personal jurisdiction that results from ratification of the Statute with respect to a State Party, Article 12(3) also contemplates the possibility of a non-party State accepting the jurisdiction of the Court on an *ad hoc* basis. The provision requires such a State to lodge a declaration with the Registrar by which it accepts the exercise of jurisdiction by the Court 'with respect to the crime in question'. The Statute describes such a State as an 'accepting State'. The final sentence in Article 12(3) says that '[t]he accepting State shall cooperate with the Court without any delay or exception in accordance with Part 9'. However, there does not seem to be any consequence should an accepting State fail to cooperate as required.[84]

---

[81] See also the declaration by New Zealand concerning Tokelau.

[82] *Loizidou* v. *Turkey* (Preliminary Objections), Series A, No. 310.

[83] Report of the International Law Commission on the Work of Its Fiftieth Session, 20 April–12 June 1998, 27 July–14 August 1998, UN Doc. A/53/10 and Corr.1, para. 498.

[84] On Art. 12(3), see Carsten Stahn, Mohamed El Zeidy and Héctor Olásolo, 'The International Criminal Court's Ad Hoc Jurisdiction Revisited', (2005) 99 *American Journal of International Law* 421; Steven Freeland, 'How Open Should the Door Be? – Declarations by Non-States Parties under Article 12(3) of the Rome Statute of the

David Scheffer has argued that the proper interpretation of the Rome Statute is to limit the jurisdiction of the Court with respect to crimes committed on the territory of a State Party to nationals of a State Party. The argument relies heavily on a construction of the intent behind Article 12(3), as well as other provisions. He has suggested that, if such an interpretation were to be confirmed, it would lessen much of the opposition to the Court from countries like the United States.[85] The text of Article 12(3) is ambiguous in its reference to a declaration by a non-party State with respect to a 'crime in question'. Does this refer to one of the crimes listed in Article 5? In other words, are non-party States to make declarations accepting the jurisdiction of the Court with respect to one or more of genocide, crimes against humanity and war crimes? Such an interpretation seems consistent with the use of the term 'crimes' in paragraph 1 of Article 12. Or is the provision to mean the acceptance of jurisdiction with respect to a specific incident or situation? According to one writer, the understanding of the drafters was that it referred to a 'situation'.[86] A consequence of this interpretation is to eliminate the perverse situation in which a non-party State might attempt to make a one-sided declaration, aimed at an adversary but at the same time designed to shelter its own behaviour.

It was precisely in order to prevent abusive and one-sided use of Article 12(3) that the Assembly of States Parties has modified its application somewhat. Rule 44 of the Rules of Procedure and Evidence states:

Declaration provided for in article 12, paragraph 3
1. The Registrar, at the request of the Prosecutor, may inquire of a State that is not a Party to the Statute or that has become a Party to the Statute after its entry into force, on a confidential basis, whether it intends to make the declaration provided for in article 12, paragraph 3.

International Criminal Court', (2006) 75 *Nordic Journal of International Law* 211; Carsten Stahn, 'Why Some Doors May Be Closed Already: Second Thoughts on a "Case-by-Case" Treatment of Article 12(3) Declarations', (2006) 75 *Nordic Journal of International Law* 243.

[85] David Scheffer, 'How to Turn the Tide Using the Rome Statute's Temporal Jurisdiction', (2004) 2 *Journal of International Criminal Justice* 26.

[86] Hans-Peter Kaul, 'Preconditions to the Exercise of Jurisdiction', in Antonio Cassese, Paola Gaeta and John R. W. D. Jones, eds., *The Rome Statute of the International Criminal Court: A Commentary*, vol. I, Oxford: Oxford University Press, 2002, pp. 583–616. Also M. Cherif Bassiouni, 'Negotiating the Treaty of Rome on the Establishment of an International Criminal Court', (1999) 32 *Cornell International Law Journal* 443 at 453–4.

> 2. When a State lodges, or declares to the Registrar its intent to lodge, a declaration with the Registrar pursuant to article 12, paragraph 3, or when the Registrar acts pursuant to sub-rule 1, the Registrar shall inform the State concerned that the declaration under article 12, paragraph 3, has as a consequence the acceptance of jurisdiction with respect to the crimes referred to in article 5 of relevance to the situation and the provisions of Part 9, and any rules thereunder concerning States Parties, shall apply.

The provision in the Rules was promoted by the Americans in an attempt to 'fix' what they considered to be the perverse consequences of Article 12(3).[87] The United States argued that Article 12(3) would allow a Saddam Hussein to invoke the jurisdiction of the Court for crimes committed by the United States in Iraq, and yet prevent it from doing the same with atrocities committed by the regime against the people of the country.[88] The Rule means such a one-sided manipulation of the jurisdiction is impossible. Some supporters of the American position have taken the view that reciprocity flows automatically from the logic of a 'sensible reading' of Article 12(3) in any event, and that there is no need for a rule to clarify things.[89] Others claim that, even with Rule 44, the problem persists. According to Jack Goldsmith:

> This vague provision does not, as many have stated, guarantee that Article 12(3) parties will consent to jurisdiction for all crimes related to the consent. But even if it did, the Iraqs of the world could consent under Article 12(3) and simply not show up. Rule 44(3) improves the anomaly of Article 12(3), but does not fix it.[90]

There have been three declarations pursuant to Article 12(3), by Côte d'Ivoire, Uganda and the Palestinian Authority. Côte d'Ivoire signed the Rome Statute on 30 November 1998, but it has never ratified the instrument and is not a State Party. In 2006, the Prosecutor said that he would send a mission to Côte d'Ivoire 'when security permits'.[91] He has

---

[87] David J. Scheffer, 'The United States and the International Criminal Court', (1999) 93 *American Journal of International Law* 12 at 18–20.

[88] David J. Scheffer, 'A Negotiator's Perspective on the International Criminal Court', (2001) 167 *Military Law Review* 1 at 8.

[89] Ruth Wedgwood, 'The United States and the International Criminal Court: Achieving a Wider Consensus Through the "Ithaca Package"', (1999) 32 *Cornell International Law Journal* 535 at 541.

[90] Jack Goldsmith, 'The Self-Defeating International Criminal Court', (2003) 70 *University of Chicago Law Review* 89, n. 11.

[91] Sixth Diplomatic Briefing of the International Criminal Court, Compilation of Statements, 23 March 2006.

suggested that the declaration and the threat of prosecution have already had a deterrent effect in Côte d'Ivoire.[92] As for Uganda, in support of his application for arrest warrants of leaders of the Lord's Resistance Army, the Prosecutor included a 'Declaration on Temporal Jurisdiction', dated 27 February 2004, whereby the Republic of Uganda accepted the exercise of the Court's jurisdiction for crimes committed following the entry into force of the Statute on 1 July 2002. Because Uganda ratified the Rome Statute on 14 June 2002, it only entered into force with respect to Uganda on 1 September 2002, two months after the entry into force of the Statute itself. Although no explicit provision allows for a State Party to backdate the effect of its ratification, Article 12(3) of the Rome Statute authorizes a non-party State to accept jurisdiction over specific crimes. Presumably, Article 12(3) is the authority for Uganda's 'Declaration of Temporal Jurisdiction'.

Following the Israeli campaign directed against Hamas militants in Gaza in late 2008 and early 2009, the Minister of Justice of the Palestinian Authority filed a declaration with the Court:

> Declaration recognizing the jurisdiction of the International Criminal Court
>
> In conformity with Article 12, paragraph 3 of the Statute of the International Criminal Court, the Government of Palestine hereby recognizes the jurisdiction of the Court for the purpose of identifying, prosecuting and judging the authors and accomplices of acts committed on the territory of Palestine since 1 July 2002.
>
> As a consequence, the Government of Palestine will cooperate with the Court without delay or exception, in conformity with Chapter IX of the Statute.
>
> This declaration, made for an indeterminate duration, will enter into force upon its signature.
>
> Material supplementary to and supporting this declaration will be provided shortly in a separate communication.[93]

The Palestinian declaration raises a number of difficult legal issues. Palestine is not a Member State of the United Nations, and its claim to be a State within the meaning of Article 12(3) is debatable.[94] Even if it

---

[92] 'Building a Future on Peace and Justice, Address by Mr Luis Moreno-Ocampo, Prosecutor of the International Criminal Court, Nuremberg', 24–25 June 2007.

[93] Palestinian National Authority, Ministry of Justice, Office of the Minister, Declaration Recognizing the Jurisdiction of the International Criminal Court, 21 January 2009.

[94] See e.g. Report of the United Nations Fact-Finding Mission on the Gaza Conflict, UN Doc. A/HRC/12/48, para. 1632.

is recognized as a State at some point in time, there is a question as to whether it can retroactively give jurisdiction to the Court over its territory for periods of time when it was not a State. Finally, the actual limits of the territory of Palestine are also a matter of dispute.

Article 12(3) is the residue of a provision in the 1994 draft statute of the International Law Commission by which State consent was contemplated on a case-by-case basis. Article 12(3) allows the Court to exercise jurisdiction if a non-party State makes a declaration 'with respect to the crime in question' committed on its territory or by one of its nationals. The reference to 'crime' rather than 'situation' implies that this is not analogous to a referral by a State Party or by the Security Council. The language used in Articles 12 and 13 suggests that what is envisaged is an investigation that has already been initiated by the Prosecutor, that is then followed by a request that the State concerned consent to jurisdiction. The fact that the Prosecutor has not initiated proceedings confirms his understanding that Côte d'Ivoire's declaration does not mean the case has been referred to the Court, and that its jurisdiction has been triggered.

The Prosecutor might well make greater use of Article 12(3). It is a way of addressing impunity in territories that may not yet be subject to the jurisdiction of the Court. For example, could not the Prosecutor, given his pro-active approach to inciting referrals, invite Cuba to make a declaration under Article 12(3) concerning a portion of its sovereign territory that has been under foreign occupation for more than a century, and where there are credible allegations of large-scale violations of human rights? Another situation crying out for an Article 12(3) declaration is the Golan, which is Syrian territory occupied by Israel for more than forty years. Syria has signed but not ratified the Statute; nevertheless, it could give jurisdiction to the Court over Golan by making such a declaration.

Even in such cases, the Court is obviously without jurisdiction to prosecute a crime committed prior to the entry into force of the Statute. Similar issues could arise in the opposite direction if Israel were to make a declaration under Article 12(3), thereby accepting the jurisdiction of the Court with respect to a specific crime committed on its territory.

Subject-matter (*ratione materiae*) jurisdiction

The International Criminal Court has jurisdiction over four categories of international crimes: genocide, crimes against humanity, war crimes and the crime of aggression. In both the preamble to the Statute and Article 5, these are variously described as 'the most serious crimes of concern to the international community as a whole'. Elsewhere, the Statute describes them as 'unimaginable atrocities that deeply shock the conscience of humanity' (preamble), 'international crimes' (preamble) and 'the most serious crimes of international concern' (Art. 1).[95]

The concept of 'international crimes' has been around for centuries. They were generally considered to be offences whose repression compelled some international dimension. Piracy, for example, was committed on the high seas. This feature of the crime necessitated special jurisdictional rules as well as cooperation between States. Similar requirements obtained with respect to the slave trade, trafficking in women and children, trafficking in narcotic drugs, hijacking, terrorism and money-laundering. Today we are more likely to use the term 'transnational crime' for such offences. It was indeed this sort of crime that inspired Trinidad and Tobago, in 1989, to reactivate the issue of an international criminal court within the General Assembly of the United Nations.[96] Many transnational crimes are already addressed in a rather sophisticated scheme of international treaties, and for this reason the drafters of the Rome Statute referred to them as 'treaty crimes'.

The four crimes subject to the jurisdiction of the International Criminal Court are somewhat more recent in origin than many of the so-called 'treaty crimes' or transnational crimes, in that their recognition and subsequent development is closely associated with the human rights movement that arose subsequent to World War II. To a large extent they are 'international' crimes for much the same reason as the earlier generation of treaty crimes. They too escape prosecution under the ordinary criminal justice system, although in the case of genocide, crimes against humanity, war crimes and aggression it is not so much because they are territorially inaccessible or are committed over several territories as that they are left unpunished by the very State where the crime was committed. The explanation for this is political, not technical: the State of territorial jurisdiction is usually unwilling to prosecute because it is itself complicit in the criminal behaviour.

---

[95] For an extensive review of the crimes punishable by the Court, see Machteld Boot, *Genocide, Crimes Against Humanity, War Crimes: Nullum Crimen Sine Lege and the Subject Matter Jurisdiction of the International Criminal Court*, Antwerp: Intersentia, 2002.

[96] GA Res. 44/89.

The Rome Statute suggests that there is another explanation for the international dimension of the crimes within the Court's jurisdiction. Their heinous nature elevates them to a level where they are of 'concern' to the international community. They dictate prosecution because humanity as a whole is the victim. Moreover, humanity as a whole is entitled, indeed required, to prosecute them for essentially the same reasons as we now say that humanity as a whole is concerned by violations of human rights that were once considered to lie within the exclusive prerogatives of State sovereignty.

But aren't all serious crimes of violence against the person of concern to the international community? Certainly, many heinous crimes committed within States go unnoticed by the international community. This is surely not because of the objective gravity of the crime, but rather because the national justice system acts effectively to address the issue. Terrorist crimes are a good example. They may often involve hundreds of deaths, in appalling circumstances, and they feature in the headlines of the world's newspapers. But they are of little concern to international justice because the crime is adequately prosecuted by the domestic courts.

Thus, the rationale for the classification of international prosecution cannot be oversimplified. The need to ensure that there is no impunity for State-sponsored crimes and the objective heinousness of the offence act as somewhat competing justifications for the exercise. Among the legal consequences of classifying an offence as an international crime are the possible exercise of universal jurisdiction, a duty to prosecute or extradite, a prohibition on statutory limitation and a justification for prosecution before international courts.

All four crimes within the jurisdiction of the Court were prosecuted, at least in an earlier and somewhat embryonic form, by the Nuremberg Tribunal and the other post-war courts. At Nuremberg and Tokyo, they were called crimes against peace, war crimes and crimes against humanity.[97] The term 'crimes against peace' is now replaced by 'aggression'; while probably not identical, the two terms largely overlap. Although the term 'genocide' already existed at the time of the Nuremberg trial, and it was used by the prosecutors of the International Military Tribunal, the indictments against Nazi criminals for the

---

[97] Agreement for the Prosecution and Punishment of Major War Criminals of the European Axis, and Establishing the Charter of the International Military Tribunal (IMT), Annex, (1951) 82 UNTS 279.

genocide of European Jews were based on the cognate charge of 'crimes against humanity'. But, in contemporary usage, the crime of 'genocide' is now essentially subsumed within the broader concept of 'crimes against humanity'.

The definitions of crimes within the Nuremberg Charter are relatively laconic. The scope of the four categories of crimes as they are now conceived has evolved considerably since that time. Post-Nuremberg, the concepts of crimes against humanity and war crimes have also undergone significant development and enlargement. For example, crimes against humanity can now take place in peacetime as well as during armed conflict, and war crimes are punishable whether they are committed in non-international or in international armed conflict. The evolution in the conceptions is reflected in the length of the definitions in the Rome Statute. But other factors are also at work. It was easier to define the crimes at Nuremberg because it was the prosecutors who were doing the defining. When States realize they are setting a standard by which they themselves, or their leaders and military personnel, may be judged, they seem to take greater care and insist upon many safeguards. The evolution in international criminal law towards longer and longer definitional provisions does not necessarily mean that the norms are being broadened. The relatively short war crimes definition in the Statute of the International Criminal Tribunal for the former Yugoslavia, as interpreted by the Appeals Chamber, is much larger in scope than its equivalent in the Rome Statute, with its detailed enumeration.[98] Arguments in favour of more extensive texts also relied upon principles of procedural fairness in criminal law, recognized by contemporary human rights law. At Rome, States argued that the 'principle of legality' dictated detailed and precise provisions setting out the punishable crimes.

The definition of the crimes in the Rome Statute is in some cases the result of recent human rights treaties, such as the 1984 Convention Against Torture[99] or the earlier Apartheid Convention.[100] But most of the development in the definition of these crimes is attributed to the

---

[98] For example, Art. 3 of the Statute of the International Criminal Tribunal for the former Yugoslavia, with its general criminalization of serious violations of international humanitarian law, is clearly much more comprehensive than the detailed codification of Art. 8 of the Rome Statute.

[99] Convention Against Torture and Other Cruel, Inhuman or Degrading Treatment or Punishment, (1987) 1465 UNTS 85.

[100] International Convention on the Suppression and Punishment of the Crime of Apartheid, (1976) 1015 UNTS 243.

evolution of customary law, whose content is not always as easy to identify with clarity. The definitions of crimes set out in Articles 6–8*bis*, as
completed by the Elements of Crimes, correspond in a general sense to
the state of customary international law.[101] The four categories of crimes
are drawn from existing definitions and use familiar terminology. The
drafters might have chosen to dispense with these old terms – crimes
against humanity, war crimes, crimes against peace – in favour of a genuinely original codification, defining the Court's subject-matter jurisdiction as being over 'serious violations of human rights'[102] or 'atrocity
crimes'.[103] But they did not take such a route. Nevertheless, while the cor-
respondence with customary international law is close, it is far from perfect. To answer concerns that the Statute's definitions of crimes be taken
as a codification of custom, Article 10 of the Statute declares: 'Nothing in
this Part shall be interpreted as limiting or prejudicing in any way existing or developing rules of international law for purposes other than this
Statute.'[104] Those who argue that customary law goes beyond the Statute,
for example by prohibiting the use of certain weapons that are not listed
in Article 8, can rely on this provision.[105] It will become more and more
important in the future, because customary law should evolve and the
Statute may not be able to keep pace with it. For example, it is foreseeable
that international law may raise the age of prohibited military recruitment from fifteen, or consider certain weapons to be prohibited, or
regard the death penalty and even life imprisonment as a form of torture
or cruel, inhuman or degrading treatment or punishment. As a result of
Article 10, the Statute cannot provide comfort to those who argue against
this evolution of customary law. But, of course, the logic of Article 10
cuts both ways. To those who claim that the Statute sets a new minimum

---

[101] The Canadian legislation implementing the Rome Statute declares that 'crimes described
in Articles 6 and 7 and paragraph 2 of Article 8 of the Rome Statute are, as of July 17,
1998, crimes according to customary international law': Crimes Against Humanity and
War Crimes Act, SC 2000, c. 24, ss. 4(4) and 6(4).

[102] See, on this, L. C. Green, '"Grave Breaches" or Crimes Against Humanity', (1997/8) 8
United States Air Force Academy Journal of Legal Studies 19; William J. Fenrick, 'Should
Crimes Against Humanity Replace War Crimes?', (1999) 37 *Columbia Journal of
Transnational Law* 767.

[103] David Scheffer, 'The Future of Atrocity Law', (2002) 35 *Suffolk Transnational Law
Review* 389; David Scheffer, 'Genocide and Atrocity Crimes', (2007) 2 *Genocide Studies
and Prevention* 31.

[104] See also Understandings Regarding the Amendments to the Rome Statute of the
International Criminal Court on the Crime of Aggression, RC/10/Add.1, para. 4.

[105] Note also the definitions of crimes, which begin with the phrase 'For the purpose of this
Statute …'.

standard, for example in the field of gender crimes, conservative jurists will plead Article 10 and stress the differences between the texts in the Statute and their less prolix ancestors in the Geneva Conventions and related instruments. In the *Bashir* arrest warrant decision, the Pre-Trial Chamber noted the requirement of a contextual element for the crime of genocide in the Elements of Crimes adopted pursuant to the Rome Statute, but signalled the absence of such a contextual element in the case law of the *ad hoc* tribunals. According to the Pre-Trial Chamber: 'It is in this scenario that, in the view of the Majority, article 10 of the Statute becomes meaningful insofar as it provides that the definition of the crimes in the Statute and the Elements of Crimes shall not be interpreted "as limiting or prejudicing in any way existing or developing rules of international law for purposes other than this Statute".'[106] The Pre-Trial Chamber used Article 10 in order to reject arguments that it should interpret Article 6 of the Statute in light of what might be said to constitute customary international law, where there appeared to be a discrepancy with the applicable law imposed by the Statute and the Elements of Crimes. Judge Wolfgang Schomburg of the Appeals Chamber of the International Criminal Tribunal for the former Yugoslavia wrote that 'even though I am fully aware of Article 10' of the Rome Statute, 'it must be pointed out that the Rome Statute does not have a provision referring to terrorization against a civilian population. If indeed this crime was beyond doubt part of customary international law, in 1998 (!) states would undoubtedly have included it in the relevant provisions of the Statute or in their domestic legislation implementing the Statute.'[107]

There would be little disagreement with the proposition that the Court is not designed to try all perpetrators of the four core crimes. It will be concerned not only with 'the most serious crimes' but also with the most serious criminals, generally leaders, organizers and instigators. Lower-level offenders are unlikely to attract the attention of a prosecutor whose energies must be concentrated, if only because of budgetary constraints. Article 17(1)(d) of the Statute says that the Court must declare a case inadmissible if it is not 'of sufficient gravity'. The Prosecutor, in the exercise of his or her discretion as to whether to proceed with a case, is instructed to forego prosecution when '[a] prosecution is not in the interests of justice, taking into account all the circumstances, including

---

[106] *Bashir* (ICC-02/05–01/09), Decision on the Prosecution's Application for a Warrant of Arrest Against Omar Hassan Ahmad Al Bashir, 4 March 2009, para. 127.

[107] *Galić* (IT-98-29-A), Separate and Partially Dissenting Opinion of Judge Schomburg, 30 November 2006, para. 20 (references omitted).

the gravity of the crime, the interests of victims and the age or infirmity of the alleged perpetrator, and his or her role in the alleged crime'.[108]

All of the definitions of crimes within the jurisdiction of the Court have some form of built-in threshold that will help to focus these decisions and limit the discretion of the Prosecutor. In the case of genocide, the result is achieved by the intentional element that is part of the definition of the crime. The offender must intend to destroy the targeted group in whole or in part. Many of those who participate in a genocide may well fall outside this definition. Although they are actively involved, they may lack knowledge of the context of the crime or the plan for its perpetration and for that reason lack the requisite intent. In the case of crimes against humanity, this issue is addressed somewhat differently, with a criterion by which the offence must be part of a 'widespread or systematic attack'. Both genocide, by its very nature, and crimes against humanity, by the 'widespread or systematic' qualification, have a quantitative dimension. They are not isolated crimes, and will in practice only be prosecuted when planned or committed on a large scale. In contrast, war crimes do not, in a definitional sense, require the same quantitative scale. A single murder of a prisoner of war or a civilian may constitute a war crime, but it is hard to envisage a single murder constituting genocide or a crime against humanity, at least in the absence of some broader context. For this reason, the Rome Statute attempts to narrow the scope of war crimes with a short introductory paragraph or *chapeau* at the beginning of Article 8: 'The Court shall have jurisdiction in respect of war crimes in particular when committed as a part of a plan or policy or as part of a large-scale commission of such crimes.' Many States were opposed to any such limitation on the scope of war crimes,[109] and only agreed to the provision if the words 'in particular' were included. It should not be taken as any new restriction on the customary definition of war crimes but rather as a technique to limit the jurisdiction of the Court.[110]

The Statute does not propose any formal hierarchy among the four categories of crime. There are suggestions, within customary international

---

[108] Rome Statute, Art. 53(2)(c).

[109] UN Doc. A/CONF.183/SR.2, para. 61 (Sweden); UN Doc. A/CONF.183/C.1/SR.4, para. 59 (Germany); UN Doc. A/CONF.183/C.1/SR.4, para. 110 (New Zealand), para. 111 (Czech Republic) and para. 112 (Ireland).

[110] According to the Prosecutor, '[t]his threshold is not an element of the crime, and the words "in particular" suggest that this is not a strict requirement. It does, however, provide Statute guidance that the Court is intended to focus on situations meeting these requirements.' Letter of Prosecutor dated 9 February 2006 (Iraq), p. 8.

law, the case law of international tribunals and the Statute itself, that, even among these 'most serious crimes', some are more serious than others. At Nuremberg, the judges of the International Military Tribunal said that crimes against peace was 'the supreme international crime differing only from other war crimes in that it contains within itself the accumulated evil of the whole'.[111] It might be argued that war crimes are less important than both genocide and crimes against humanity because Article 124 of the Statute allows States temporarily to 'opt out' of jurisdiction for war crimes at the time of ratification. Also, two of the defences that are codified by the Statute, superior orders and defence of property,[112] are admissible only in the case of war crimes, implying that justification may exist for war crimes where it can never exist for genocide and crimes against humanity. The crime of 'direct and public incitement' exists only in the case of genocide;[113] the drafters at Rome rejected suggestions that this inchoate form of criminality, drawn from Article III of the 1948 Genocide Convention, be broadened to encompass crimes against humanity and war crimes.

Before the *ad hoc* tribunals for the former Yugoslavia and Rwanda, the judges appear to be divided on whether or not there is a hierarchy between the different categories of offences, although a majority seems unfavourable to the concept.[114] Nevertheless, the tribunals consistently impose the most serious penalties when an individual is convicted of genocide, and the lightest when the conviction lies for war crimes. Moreover, in the negotiation of plea agreements, both Prosecutor and defendant seem to agree that it is beneficial for an accused to have a genocide charge withdrawn and to plead guilty 'only' to crimes against humanity, suggesting that there is a hierarchy, at least at this subjective level.[115]

The subject-matter jurisdiction of the International Criminal Court may be amended, in accordance with Article 121. This may be done either in the regular meetings of the Assembly of States Parties or at a Review

---

[111] *France et al.* v. *Goering et al.*, Judgment, 30 September–1 October 1946, (1947) 41 *American Journal of International Law* 172 at 186.

[112] Rome Statute, Arts. 33(1) and 31(1)(c), respectively.

[113] *Ibid.*, Art. 25(3)(e).

[114] *Erdemović* (IT-96-22-A), Sentencing Appeal, 7 October 1997, (1998) 111 ILR 298; *Kupreškić et al.* (IT-95-16-T), Judgment, 14 January 2000; *Tadić* (IT-94-1-A and IT-94-1-A*bis*), Judgment in Sentencing Appeals, 26 January 2000; *Furundžija* (IT-96-17/1-A), Judgment, 17 July 2000.

[115] See, e.g., *Plavšić* (IT-00-39 and 40/1), Sentencing Judgment, 27 February 2003; *Rutaganira* (Case No. ICTR-95-1C-T), Jugement portant condamnation, 14 March 2005.

Conference. The possibility of amending the list of crimes at a Review Conference is explicitly foreseen.[116] Some offences, while theoretically within the jurisdiction of the Court, are subject to further decisions and agreements. For example, the war crimes provision dealing with use of weapons and methods of warfare of a nature to cause superfluous injury or unnecessary suffering, or which are inherently indiscriminate, can only become operational when a list of such weapons and methods is included in an annex to the Statute.[117] A proposal from Belgium to adopt such an annex at the first Review Conference was not pursued. In fact, Belgium chose to drop the idea of an annex in favour of a full-blown amendment to the text of the Statute in order to avoid difficulties created by the amendment process.[118] Incorporation of the crime of aggression is also contemplated by Article 5(2) of the Statute. With the adoption of amendments at the first Review Conference, Article 5(2) was deleted.[119]

Although the original impetus to revive the international criminal court project, in 1989, came from States concerned with matters such as international drug-trafficking and terrorism, there was ultimately no consensus on including the 'treaty crimes' within the jurisdiction of the Court and they were excluded at the Rome Conference. These are called 'treaty crimes' because they have been proscribed in a variety of multilateral conventions dealing with terrorist crimes, drug crimes and crimes against United Nations personnel.[120] Proposals at the Rome Conference to include drug-trafficking[121] and terrorism[122] did not meet with sufficient consensus. Some considered that these crimes should be excluded because they are not 'as serious' as genocide, crimes against humanity and war crimes.[123] There was also concern that there would be interference with existing international or transnational efforts at the

---

[116] Rome Statute, Art. 123(1).   [117] *Ibid.*, Art. 8(2)(b)(xx).

[118] Belgium: Proposal of Amendments, UN Doc. C.N.733.2009.TREATIES-8.

[119] Amendments to the Rome Statute of the International Criminal Court on the Crime of Aggression, RC/10, para. 1.

[120] See especially Report of the Preparatory Committee on the Establishment of an International Criminal Court, Addendum, UN Doc. A/CONF.183/2/Add.1 (1998), Art. 5.

[121] Proposal Submitted by Barbados, Dominica, Jamaica, and Trinidad and Tobago on Article 5, UN Doc. A/CONF.183/C.1/L.48.

[122] Proposal Submitted by Algeria, India, Sri Lanka and Turkey on Article 5, UN Doc. A/CONF.183/C.1/L.27/Corr.1.

[123] Daniel D. Ntanda Nsereko, 'The International Criminal Court: Jurisdictional and Related Issues', (1999) 10 *Criminal Law Forum* 87 at 91–2. See also Neil Boister, 'The Exclusion of Treaty Crimes from the Jurisdiction of the Proposed International Criminal Court: Law, Pragmatism, Politics', (1998) 3 *Journal of Armed Conflict Law* 27.

repression of such crimes.[124] In the final version of the Statute, certain crimes against United Nations personnel were incorporated within the definition of war crimes, but that is about all.[125] The Final Act of the Rome Conference, adopted at the same time as the Statute, includes a resolution on treaty crimes recommending that the Review Conference consider means to enable the inclusion of crimes of terrorism and drug crimes.[126] However, attempts to incorporate these categories of crimes in the Rome Statute during the first Review Conference were abandoned by their promoters.[127]

The attacks of 11 September 2001 revived interest in the incorporation of terrorist crimes within the Statute. Certainly, many so-called terrorist acts will fall within the ambit of crimes against humanity, or war crimes, and perhaps even genocide, as these crimes are defined in the Statute. Many authorities in the field of international criminal law characterized the destruction of the World Trade Centre and the accompanying loss of life as a crime against humanity.[128] Antonio Cassese was somewhat circumspect, observing cautiously that 'it may happen that states gradually come to share this characterisation'.[129] The problem with a distinct crime of terrorism lies in definition, it being often said that 'one person's terrorist is another's freedom fighter'. Terrorism seems to have more to do with motive than with either the mental or physical elements of a crime, and this is something that is not generally part of the definitions of offences.

As the judicial activities of the International Criminal Court develop, it becomes increasingly evident that it will only be able to deal with a very limited number of cases. If it can handle only a handful of the most serious cases of the most serious crimes committed by leaders and organizers, it seems entirely unrealistic to think that new criminal law paradigms, such as drug-trafficking or terrorism, could be added to the jurisdiction.

---

[124] E.g., UN Doc. A/CONF.183/SR.9, para. 31 (United States).

[125] Rome Statute, Art. 8(2)(e)(iii), (b)(vii) and (3)(iii).

[126] Final Act of the United Nations Diplomatic Conference of Plenipotentiaries on the Establishment of an International Criminal Court, UN Doc. A/CONF.183/13 (Vol. I), pp. 67–79, Annex II(E), OP1.

[127] Report of the Bureau on the Review Conference, ASP/8/43, paras. 15–22.

[128] For example, Geoffrey Robertson, *The Times*, 18 September 2001, p. 18; Alain Pellet, *Le Monde*, 21 September 2001, p. 12.

[129] Antonio Cassese, 'Terrorism Is Also Disputing Some Crucial Legal Categories of International Law', (2001) 12 *European Journal of International Law* 993 at 995.

The strongest argument for excluding such crimes is that they do not suffer from a problem of impunity in a manner similar to that of the other categories. Genocide, crimes against humanity, war crimes and the crime of aggression all became international crimes not so much because of their scale or horror as because they were perpetrated by the governments themselves, or with their complicity. For that reason, they went unpunished. The courts of the jurisdiction that would ordinarily prosecute would not assume such duties because they were part of a State that was itself involved in the criminal acts. The same problem does not generally exist with respect to terrorism and drug-trafficking, where the international dimension is essentially one of inter-State cooperation rather than the reluctance of a State to prosecute. To the extent that there is impunity for drug crimes and terrorism, it is a failure of law enforcement and mutual legal assistance, rather than the lack of an appropriate national jurisdiction that is willing and able to investigate or prosecute.

For the purposes of interpreting and applying the definitions of crimes found in Articles 6, 7, 8 and 8*bis* of the Rome Statute, reference must also be made to the Elements of Crimes, a fifty-page document adopted in June 2000 by the Preparatory Commission, subsequently endorsed in September 2002 by the Assembly of States Parties at its first session,[130] and amended at the first Review Conference in 2010.[131] The Elements of Crimes are a source of applicable law for the Court,[132] but as a form of subordinate legislation they must also be consistent with the Statute itself. The whole concept originated with the United States delegation, and while at Rome many greeted it with some suspicion, the idea seemed rather less harmful than many other Washington-based initiatives and it was incorporated in the Statute without great opposition. Fundamentally, the Elements reflect the continuing anxiety among States of any degree of judicial discretion. Thus, in addition to prolix definitions of crimes, the Elements further fetter the possibilities of judicial interpretation. On a more positive note, they are somewhat easier to amend than the Statute itself. Adopted by the Assembly of States Parties, they allow for the possibility of 'tweaking' the definitions of crimes when this seems desirable without the requirement of a full-blown amendment.

---

[130] Pursuant to Art. 9 of the Rome Statute. The Elements of Crimes are published in the report of the first session of the Assembly of States Parties: ASP/1/3, pp. 108–55.

[131] Amendments to the Elements of Crimes, RC/10, Annex II.

[132] Rome Statute, Art. 21(1)(a).

When it issued the arrest warrant against Al-Bashir, the majority of the Pre-Trial Chamber said it considered that the Elements of Crimes 'must be applied unless the competent Chamber finds an irreconcilable contradiction' with the Statute, in which case 'the provisions contained in the Statute must prevail'.[133] The majority said 'this interpretation is not inconsistent with a literal interpretation of Article 9(1) of the Statute, which states that "elements of the crimes shall assist the Court in the interpretation and application of articles 6, 7 and 8"'.[134] Judge Ušacka, dissenting, said she disagreed with the majority's contention that the Elements of Crimes must be applied, absent a contradiction with the Statute. She said that, although Article 21(1) states that the Court 'shall' apply the Elements of Crimes, the introduction to the Elements states that it is to 'assist the Court'. She added that 'several commentators have stated that the Elements of Crimes are not binding upon the Court'.[135]

Genocide

The word 'genocide' was coined in 1944 by Raphael Lemkin in his book on Nazi crimes in occupied Europe.[136] Lemkin felt that the treaty regime aimed at the protection of national minorities established between the two world wars had important shortcomings, amongst them the failure to provide for prosecution of crimes against groups. The term 'genocide' was adopted the following year by the prosecutors at Nuremberg (although not by the judges), and in 1946 genocide was declared an international crime by the General Assembly of the United Nations.[137] The General Assembly also decided to proceed with the drafting of a treaty on genocide.

At the time, it was considered important to define genocide as a separate crime in order to distinguish it from crimes against humanity. The latter term referred to a rather wider range of atrocities, but it also

---

[133] *Bashir* (ICC-02/05–01/09), Decision on the Prosecution Application for a Warrant of Arrest againt Omar Hassan Ahmad Al Bashir, 4 March 2009, para. 128.

[134] *Ibid.*, para. 129.

[135] *Bashir* (ICC-02/05–01/09), Separate and Partly Dissenting Opinion of Judge Anita Ušacka, 4 March 2009, para. 17.

[136] Raphael Lemkin, *Axis Rule in Occupied Europe: Laws of Occupation, Analysis of Government, Proposals for Redress*, Washington DC: Carnegie Endowment for World Peace, 1944.

[137] GA Res. 96 (I).

had a narrow aspect, in that the prevailing view was that crimes against humanity could only be committed in association with an international armed conflict. The General Assembly wanted to go a step further, recognizing that one atrocity, namely, genocide, would constitute an international crime even if it were committed in time of peace. The price to pay, however, was an exceedingly narrow definition of the mental and material elements of the crime, and of the punishable acts. It was also hoped, by those who took the initiative in the General Assembly, that genocide would be recognized as a crime of universal jurisdiction, subject to prosecution by courts other than those where the crime took place. In this pursuit they were unsuccessful. The negotiated agreement was set out in the Convention on the Prevention and Punishment of the Crime of Genocide, adopted by the General Assembly on 9 December 1948.[138] The Convention entered into force slightly more than two years later after obtaining twenty ratifications. The Convention itself has been described as the quintessential human rights treaty.[139]

The distinction between genocide and crimes against humanity is less significant today, because the recognized definition of crimes against humanity has evolved and now unquestionably refers to atrocities committed in peacetime as well as in wartime. At the present time, genocide constitutes the most aggravated form of crime against humanity.[140] The International Criminal Tribunal for Rwanda has labelled it 'the crime of crimes'.[141] Not surprisingly, then, it is the first crime set out in the Rome Statute and the only one to be adopted by the drafters with virtually no controversy.[142] Although literature on the subject is replete with

---

[138] Convention on the Prevention and Punishment of the Crime of Genocide, (1951) 78 UNTS 277.

[139] Report of the International Law Commission on the Work of Its Forty-Ninth Session, 12 May–18 July 1997, UN Doc. A/52/10, para. 76. See also *Kayishema and Ruzindana* (ICTR-95-1-T), Judgment, 21 May 1999, para. 88.

[140] On the crime of genocide, see Nehemiah Robinson, *The Genocide Convention: A Commentary*, New York: Institute of Jewish Affairs, 1960; Pieter Nicolaas Drost, *Genocide: United Nations Legislation on International Criminal Law*, Leiden: A. W. Sijthoff, 1959; William A. Schabas, *Genocide in International Law: The Crime of Crimes*, 2nd edn, Cambridge: Cambridge University Press, 2009; and Paola Gaeta, ed., *The Genocide Convention*, Oxford: Oxford University Press, 2009.

[141] *Kambanda* (ICTR-97-23-S), Judgment and Sentence, 4 September 1998, para. 16; *Serashago* (ICTR-98-39-S), Sentence, 2 February 1999, para. 15; *Jelisić* (IT-95-10-A), Partial Dissenting Opinion of Judge Wald, 5 July 2001, para. 1; *Stakić* (IT-97-29-T), Decision on Rule 98*bis* Motion for Judgment of Acquittal, 31 October 2002, para. 22.

[142] UN Doc. A/CONF.183/C.1/SR.3, paras. 2, 18 and 20 (Germany), para. 22 (Syria), para. 24 (United Arab Emirates), para. 26 (Bahrain), para. 28 (Jordan), para. 29 (Lebanon),

proposals to amend the definition of genocide, at the Rome Conference, only Cuba argued that it might be altered by the inclusion of political and social groups.[143]

Genocide is defined in Article 6 of the Rome Statute.[144] The provision is essentially a copy of Article II of the Genocide Convention. The definition set out in Article II, although often criticized for being overly restrictive and difficult to apply to many cases of mass killing and atrocity, has stood the test of time. The decision of the Rome Conference to maintain a fifty-year-old text is convincing evidence that Article 6 of the Statute constitutes a codification of a customary international norm.

Article 6 of the Rome Statute, and Article II of the Genocide Convention, define genocide as consisting of five specific acts committed with the intent to destroy a national, ethnical, racial or religious group as such. The five acts are: killing members of the group; causing serious bodily or mental harm to members of the group; imposing conditions on the group calculated to destroy it; preventing births within the group; and forcibly transferring children from the group to another group. The definition has been incorporated in the penal codes of many

para. 30 (Belgium), para. 31 (Saudi Arabia), para. 33 (Tunisia), para. 35 (Czech Republic), para. 38 (Morocco), para. 40 (Malta), para. 41 (Algeria), para. 44 (India), para. 49 (Brazil), para. 54 (Denmark), para. 57 (Lesotho), para. 59 (Greece), para. 64 (Malawi), para. 67 (Sudan), para. 72 (China), para. 76 (Republic of Korea), para. 80 (Poland), para. 84 (Trinidad and Tobago), para. 85 (Iraq), para. 107 (Thailand), para. 111 (Norway), para. 113 (Côte d'Ivoire), para. 116 (South Africa), para. 119 (Egypt), para. 122 (Pakistan), para. 123 (Mexico), para. 127 (Libya), para. 132 (Colombia), para. 135 (Iran), para. 137 (United States), para. 141 (Djibouti), para. 143 (Indonesia), para. 145 (Spain), para. 150 (Romania), para. 151 (Senegal), para. 153 (Sri Lanka), para. 157 (Venezuela), para. 161 (Italy), para. 166 (Ireland) and para. 172 (Turkey).

[143] *Ibid.*, para. 100.

[144] Lyal S. Sunga, 'The Crimes within the Jurisdiction of the International Criminal Court (Part II, Articles 5–10)', (1998) 6 *European Journal of Crime, Criminal Law and Criminal Justice* 61 at 66–8; Hermann von Hebel and Daryl Robinson, 'Crimes within the Jurisdiction of the Court', in Roy S. Lee, ed., *The International Criminal Court: The Making of the Rome Statute: Issues, Negotiations, and Results*, The Hague: Kluwer Law International, 1999, pp. 79–126 at pp. 89–90; William A. Schabas, 'Article 6', in Triffterer, ed., *Commentary*, pp. 143–57; Emanuela Fronza, 'Genocide in the Rome Statute', in Lattanzi and Schabas, *Essays on the Rome Statute*, pp. 105–38; Christine Byron, 'Genocide', in Dominic McGoldrick, Peter Rowe and Eric Donnelly, eds., *The Permanent International Criminal Court: Legal and Policy Issues*, Oxford and Portland, OR: Hart Publishing, 2004, pp. 143–77; Machteld Boot, *Nullum Crimen Sine Lege and the Subject Matter Jurisdiction of the International Criminal Court, Genocide, Crimes Against Humanity, War Crimes*, Antwerp: Intersentia, 2002, pp. 401–54.

countries, although actual prosecutions have been rare. The 1961 trial of Adolf Eichmann in Israel was conducted under a legal provision modelled on Article II of the Genocide Convention. Only in late 1998, after the adoption of the Rome Statute, were the first significant judgments of the *ad hoc* tribunals issued dealing with interpretation of the norm.

It is often said that what distinguishes genocide from all other crimes is its mental element, described as the *dolus specialis* or 'special intent'. In effect, all three crimes that are defined by the Rome Statute provide for prosecution for killing or murder. What sets genocide apart from crimes against humanity and war crimes is that the act, whether killing or one of the other four acts defined in Article 6, must be committed with the intent to destroy in whole or in part a national, ethnical, racial or religious group as such.

The perpetrator's intent must be 'to destroy' the group. During the debates surrounding the adoption of the Genocide Convention, the forms of destruction were grouped into three categories: physical, biological and cultural. Cultural genocide was the most troublesome of the three, because it could well be interpreted in such a way as to include the suppression of national languages and similar measures. The drafters of the Convention considered that such matters were better left to human rights declarations on the rights of minorities and they actually voted to exclude cultural genocide from the scope of the definition. However, it can be argued that a contemporary interpreter of the definition of genocide should not be bound by the intent of the drafters back in 1948. The words 'to destroy' can readily bear the concept of cultural as well as physical and biological genocide, and bold judges might be tempted to adopt such progressive construction. Recent decisions of the International Criminal Tribunal for the former Yugoslavia[145] and of the German Constitutional Court[146] suggest that the law may be evolving in this direction. Other judgments, including the February 2007 ruling of the International Court of Justice,[147] adopt a more restrictive interpretation.[148] In any event, evidence of 'cultural genocide' has already

---

[145] *Krstić* (IT-98-33-T), Judgment, 2 August 2001, para. 580; *Krstić* (IT-98-33-A), Judgment, 19 April 2004. See particularly the Partially Dissenting Opinion of Judge Shahabuddeen, which was followed in *Blagojević et al.* (IT-02-60-T), Judgment, 17 January 2005.

[146] *Nikolai Jorgic, Bundesverfassungsgericht* (Federal Constitutional Court), Fourth Chamber, Second Senate, 12 December 2000, 2 BvR 1290/99, para. (III)(4)(a)(aa).

[147] *Case Concerning the Application of the Convention on the Prevention and Punishment of the Crime of Genocide (Bosnia and Herzegovina v. Serbia and Montenegro)*, Judgment, 26 February 2007, para. 187.

[148] *Brdjanin* (IT-99-36-T), Judgment, 1 September 2004.

proven to be an important indicator of the intent to perpetrate physical genocide.[149]

The definition of genocide contains no formal requirement that the punishable acts be committed as part of a widespread or systematic attack, or as part of a general or organized plan to destroy the group. This would seem, however, to be an implicit characteristic of the crime of genocide, although in the *Jelisić* case a Trial Chamber of the International Criminal Tribunal for the former Yugoslavia entertained the hypothesis of the lone genocidal maniac.[150] In the same case, the Appeals Chamber confirmed that 'the existence of a plan or policy is not a legal ingredient of the crime. However, in the context of proving specific intent, the existence of a plan or policy may become an important factor in most cases.'[151] The Darfur Commission, established by the United Nations in 2004, concluded that genocide was not being committed in Sudan essentially because it failed to find evidence of a State plan or policy.[152]

Probably in reaction to the position taken at the Yugoslav Tribunal, the Elements of Crimes adopted by the Assembly of States Parties require that an act of genocide 'took place in the context of a manifest pattern of similar conduct directed against that group or was conduct that could itself effect such destruction'.[153] As a result, the law applied by the International Criminal Court with respect to aggression may not mirror that of the *ad hoc* Tribunals. For example, an emphasis on specific intent is entirely appropriate where the general approach to the crime contemplates an individual who may be acting alone, and who may target isolated victims, in the absence of a plan or policy. However, the relevance of 'specific intent' declines dramatically when the starting point in the inquiry is a plan or policy. Then, the more significant question is whether the offender had knowledge of the plan or policy. Reliance upon the contextual element set out in the Elements of Crimes focuses the debate about the mental element of the perpetrator on knowledge

---

[149] *Karadžić and Mladić* (IT-95-5-R61, IT-95-18-R61), Consideration of the Indictment within the Framework of Rule 61 of the Rules of Procedure and Evidence, 11 July 1996, para. 94.

[150] *Jelisić* (IT-95-10-T), Judgment, 14 December 1999, para. 100.

[151] *Jelisić* (IT-95-10-A), Judgment, 5 July 2001, para. 48. The Appeals Chamber's *obiter dictum* was followed in *Sikirica et al.* (IT-95-8-I), Judgment on Defence Motions to Acquit, 3 September 2001, para. 62.

[152] Report of the International Commission of Inquiry on Violations of International Humanitarian Law and Human Rights Law in Darfur, UN Doc. S/2005/60, para. 518.

[153] Elements of Crimes, ASP/1/3, pp. 113–15.

more than intent. Such an approach, described in the literature as the 'knowledge-based approach',[154] received a significant nod of approval from Pre-Trial Chamber I in the *Bashir* arrest warrant decision.[155]

With the words 'in whole or in part', the definition indicates a quantitative dimension. The quantity contemplated must be significant, and an intent to kill only a few members of a group cannot be genocide. The prevailing view is that, where only part of a group is destroyed, it must be a 'substantial' part.[156] There is much confusion about this, because it is often thought that there is some precise numerical threshold of real victims before genocide can take place. But the reference to quantity is in the description of the mental element of the crime, and what is important is not the actual number of victims, rather that the perpetrator intended to destroy a large number of members of the group. Where the number of victims becomes genuinely significant is in the proof of such a genocidal intent. The greater the number of real victims, the more logical the conclusion that the intent was to destroy the group 'in whole or in part'.

Another interpretation has emerged by which genocide is also committed if a 'significant part' of the group is destroyed. This significant part may consist of persons of 'special significance' to the group, such as the leadership of the group,[157] although in one case a Trial Chamber of the Yugoslav Tribunal extended the approach to cover men of military age.[158] Some judgments have also established that 'in part' means the crime may be committed in a very small geographic area against a group defined by its borders, such as the Muslim population of the town of Srebrenica, which was attacked by Bosnian Serb forces in July 1995.[159]

---

[154] Alexander Greenawalt, 'Rethinking Genocidal Intent: The Case for a Knowledge-Based Interpretation', (1999) 99 *Columbia Law Review* 2288; Claus Kreß, 'The Darfur Report and Genocidal Intent', (2005) 3 *Journal of International Criminal Justice* 578 at 565–73; Claus Kreß, 'The Crime of Genocide Under International Law', (2006) 6 *International Criminal Law Review* 461 at 492–7; Claus Kreß, 'The International Court of Justice and the Elements of the Crimes of Genocide', (2007) 18 *European Journal of International Law* 619 at 625–7. See also Hans Vest, 'A Structure-Based Concept of Genocidal Intent', (2007) 5 *Journal of International Criminal Justice* 781.

[155] *Bashir* (ICC-02/05–01/09), Decision on the Prosecution's Application for a Warrant of Arrest Against Omar Hassan Ahmad Al Bashir, 4 March 2009, para. 139, n. 154.

[156] *Jelesić* (IT-95-10-T), Judgment, 14 December 1999, para. 82.

[157] *Sikirica et al.* (IT-95-8-I), Judgment on Defence Motions to Acquit, 3 September 2001, para. 80.

[158] *Krstić* (IT-98-33-T), Judgment, 2 August 2001, para. 595.

[159] *Ibid.*, para. 590.

The destruction must be directed at one of the four groups listed in the definition: national, ethnical, racial or religious. The enumeration has often been criticized because of its limited scope. In effect, proposals to include political and social groups within the definition were rejected in 1948 and, again, during the drafting of the Rome Statute. But dissatisfaction with the narrowness of the four terms was reflected in the first conviction for genocide by the International Criminal Tribunal for Rwanda. It stated that the drafters of the Genocide Convention meant for the definition to apply to all 'permanent and stable' groups, a questionable interpretation because it so clearly goes beyond the text.[160] The 'stable and permanent' gloss on the definition of genocide was not followed by other Trial Chambers of the International Criminal Tribunal for Rwanda, and finds no echo in the case law of the International Criminal Tribunal for the former Yugoslavia.[161]

The four terms themselves are not easy to define. Moreover, the common meaning of such concepts as 'racial groups' has changed considerably since 1948. Taken as a whole, the four terms correspond closely to what human rights law refers to as ethnic or national minorities,[162] expressions that themselves have eluded precise definition. The real difficulty with attempting to find precise definition of the terms is its reliance on an objective conception of the protected groups. Almost without exception, the international tribunals have opted for a subjective approach, by which the groups are defined according to the attitudes of those who persecute them rather than pursuant to some scientifically verifiable list of parameters. For example, the Darfur Commission concluded that the persecuted tribes of western Sudan were subsumed within the scope of the crime of genocide to the extent that victim and persecutor 'perceive each other and themselves as constituting distinct groups'.[163] This essentially subjective view towards the identification of groups contemplated by the definition of genocide has gained increasing acceptance in the case law of the international tribunals.[164] The point

---

[160] *Akayesu* (ICTR-96-4-T), Judgment, 2 September 1998 (1998) 37 ILM 1399, para. 515. But, in other cases before the Rwanda Tribunal, this approach has not been adopted: *Kayishema and Ruzindana* (ICTR-95-1-T), Judgment, 21 May 1999, para. 94. See also *Rutaganda* (ICTR-96-3-T), Judgment, 6 December 1999.

[161] See, however, the Darfur Commission, which endorses the approach: Report of the International Commission of Inquiry on Violations of International Humanitarian Law and Human Rights Law in Darfur, UN Doc. S/2005/60, para. 498.

[162] *Krstić* (IT-98-33-T), Judgment, 2 August 2001, para. 556.

[163] *Ibid.*, para. 509.

[164] *Semanza* (ICTR-97-20-T), Judgment and Sentence, 15 May 2003, para. 317; *Kajelijeli* (ICTR-98-44A-T), Judgment and Sentence, 1 December 2003, para. 811.

here is that the victims were being persecuted not because the *Janjaweed* militias saw them as a 'permanent and stable group', but rather because they considered them to be a 'national, ethnical, racial or religious group'. Once the subjective approach, which relies essentially on the perpetrator's perception of the victim group, is adopted, there is no longer a need to enlarge, by interpretation, the accepted definition of the crime of genocide. The responsibility for genocide lies with racists, and they attack groups not because they are 'stable and permanent' but because they perceive them to be national, racial, ethnic or religious.

The description of the crime of genocide concludes with the puzzling words 'as such'. These were added in 1948 as a compromise between States that felt genocide required not only an intentional element but also a motive. The two concepts are not equivalent. Individuals may commit crimes intentionally, but for a variety of motives: greed, jealousy, hatred and so on. Proof of motive creates an additional obstacle to effective prosecution, and it is for this reason that several delegations opposed requiring it as an element of the crime. According to the Appeals Chamber of the International Criminal Tribunal for Rwanda, the words 'as such' are 'an important element of genocide', and were included in the 1948 Convention in order to reconcile divergent views as to whether or not motive should be an element of the crime:

> The term 'as such' has the *effet utile* of drawing a clear distinction between mass murder and crimes in which the perpetrator targets a specific group because of its nationality, race, ethnicity or religion. In other words, the term 'as such' clarifies the specific intent requirement. It does not prohibit a conviction for genocide in a case in which the perpetrator was also driven by other motivations that are legally irrelevant in this context.[165]

The definition of the mental element or *mens rea* of the crime of genocide, found in the *chapeau* of the provision, is followed by five paragraphs listing the punishable acts of genocide. The list is an exhaustive one, and cannot properly be extended to other acts of persecution directed against ethnic minorities. Such atrocities – for example, 'ethnic cleansing', as it is now known – will for this reason probably be prosecuted as crimes against humanity rather than as genocide.[166]

[165] *Niyitegeka* (ICTR-96-14-A), Judgment, para. 53 (references omitted).
[166] Note, for example, that the Prosecutor of the International Criminal Tribunal for the former Yugoslavia indicted Slobodan Milošević for crimes against humanity

Killing is at the core of the definition and is without doubt the most important of the five acts of genocide. The *ad hoc* tribunals have held that the term killing is synonymous with murder or intentional homicide[167] (although the Elements of Crimes say that the term 'killing' is 'interchangeable' with 'causing death', which seems to leave room for unintentional homicide). The second act of genocide, causing serious bodily or mental harm, refers to acts of major violence falling short of homicide. In the *Akayesu* decision, the Rwanda Tribunal gave rape as an example of such acts. The Elements are even more detailed, stating that such conduct may include 'acts of torture, rape, sexual violence or inhuman or degrading treatment'.[168] The third act of genocide, imposing conditions of life calculated to destroy the group, applies to cases like the forced marches of the Armenian minority in Turkey in 1915. But none of the acts defined in Article 6 consists of genocide if not accompanied by the specific genocidal intent. In cases where the intent falls short of the definition, prosecution may still lie for crimes against humanity or war crimes.

Crimes against humanity

Although occasional references to the expression 'crimes against humanity' can be found dating back several centuries, the term was first used in its contemporary context in 1915. The massacres of Turkey's Armenian population were denounced as 'new crimes against humanity and civilisation' in a declaration of three Allied powers pledging that those responsible would be held personally accountable.[169] But, in the post-war peace negotiations, there were objections that this was a form of retroactive criminal legislation and no prosecutions were ever undertaken on an international level for the genocide of the Armenians. The term 'crimes against humanity' reappeared in 1945 as one of three categories of offence within the jurisdiction of the Nuremberg Tribunal. Once again, the arguments about retroactivity resurfaced, but they were successfully rebuffed.

---

and not genocide with respect to allegations of 'ethnic cleansing' in Kosovo during 1999: *Milošević et al.* (IT-99-37-I), Indictment, 22 May 1999.
[167] *Akayesu* (ICTR-96-4-T), Judgment, 2 September 1998, paras. 228–9.
[168] Elements of Crimes, Art. 6(b), para. 1, n. 3.
[169] United Nations War Crimes Commission, *History of the United Nations War Crimes Commission and the Development of the Laws of War*, London: His Majesty's Stationery Office, 1948, p. 35.

In 1945, there was little legal difficulty with international prosecution of Nazi war criminals for acts committed against civilians in occupied territories. International law already proscribed persecution of civilians within occupied territories, and it was a short step to define these as international crimes. The 1907 Hague Convention set out general principles concerning the treatment of civilians under occupation, but most of these were already well-accepted components of customary international law. Yet, when Allied lawyers met in 1943 and 1944 to prepare the post-war prosecutions, many of them considered it legally unsound to hold the Nazis responsible for crimes committed against Germans within the borders of Germany. Not without considerable pressure from Jewish non-governmental organizations, there was an important change in thinking and it was agreed to extend the criminal responsibility of the Nazis to internal atrocities under the rubric 'crimes against humanity'. But the Allies were uncomfortable with the ramifications that this might have with respect to the treatment of minorities within their own countries, not to mention their colonies. For this reason, they insisted that crimes against humanity could only be committed if they were associated with one of the other crimes within the Nuremberg Tribunal's jurisdiction, that is, war crimes and crimes against peace.[170] In effect, they had imposed a requirement or nexus, as it is known, between crimes against humanity and international armed conflict. Lyle Sunga describes the Nuremberg Charter's approach to crimes against humanity as the Siamese twin of war crimes, unnaturally joined.[171] Indeed, we refer to the Nuremberg prosecutions as 'war crimes trials', and the restrictive terminology requiring a nexus with armed conflict continues to haunt the international prosecution of human rights atrocities, many of which are actually committed during peacetime.

Dissatisfaction with such a limitation emerged within weeks of the Nuremberg judgment. The United Nations General Assembly decided to define the most egregious form of crime against humanity, namely, genocide, as a distinct offence that could be committed in time of peace

---

[170] Report of Robert H. Jackson, United States Representative to the International Conference on Military Trials, Washington DC: US Government Printing Office, 1949; Egon Schwelb, 'Crimes Against Humanity', (1946) 23 British Yearbook of International Law 178; Roger S. Clark, 'Crimes Against Humanity at Nuremberg', in G. Ginsburgs and V. N. Kudriavstsev, eds., The Nuremberg Trial and International Law, Dordrecht and Boston: Martinus Nijhoff, 1990, pp. 177–212.

[171] Lyal S. Sunga, 'The Crimes within the Jurisdiction of the International Criminal Court (Part II, Articles 5–10)', (1998) 6 European Journal of Crime, Criminal Law and Criminal Justice 61 at 68.

as well as in wartime. Over the years since 1945, there were several variants on the definition of crimes against humanity, some of them eliminating the nexus with armed conflict.[172] This prompted many to suggest that, from the standpoint of customary law, the definition had evolved to cover atrocities committed in peacetime. But the Security Council itself muddied the waters in 1993 when it established the International Criminal Tribunal for the former Yugoslavia. Article 5 of that court's Statute says that crimes against humanity must be committed 'in armed conflict, whether international or internal in character'. A year later, however, the Security Council did not insist upon the nexus when it established the International Criminal Tribunal for Rwanda.[173] In 1995, in its celebrated *Tadić* jurisdictional decision, the Appeals Chamber of the International Criminal Tribunal for the former Yugoslavia described the nexus as 'obsolescent', and said that 'there is no logical or legal basis for this requirement and it has been abandoned in subsequent State practice with respect to crimes against humanity'.[174] Since then, the Appeals Chamber has described the nexus with armed conflict set out in Article 5 of the Statute of the Yugoslav Tribunal as being 'purely jurisdictional'.[175]

Article 7 of the Rome Statute codifies this evolution in the definition of crimes against humanity, although an argument that customary international law still requires the nexus is not inconceivable, based upon the fact that at Rome 'a significant number of delegations argued vigorously that crimes against humanity could only be committed during an armed conflict'.[176] Indeed, several Arab States initially said they could only agree with crimes against humanity in international armed conflict, and not non-international armed conflict, although their position

---

[172] Agreement for the Prosecution and Punishment of Major War Criminals of the European Axis, and Establishing the Charter of the International Military Tribunal (IMT), Annex, (1951) 82 UNTS 279, Art. 6(c); International Military Tribunal for the Far East, TIAS No. 1589, Annex, Charter of the International Military Tribunal for the Far East, Art. 5(c); Control Council Law No. 10, Punishment of Persons Guilty of War Crimes, Crimes Against Peace and Against Humanity, 20 December 1945, *Official Gazette of the Control Council for Germany*, No. 3, 31 January 1946, pp. 50–5, Art. II(1) (c); Statute of the International Criminal Tribunal for the former Yugoslavia, UN Doc. S/RES/827 (1993), Annex, Art. 5; Statute of the International Criminal Tribunal for Rwanda, UN Doc. S/RES/955 (1994), Annex, Art. 4.

[173] Statute of the International Criminal Tribunal for Rwanda, UN Doc. S/RES/955, Annex, Art. 3.

[174] *Tadić* (IT-94-1-AR72), Decision on the Defence Motion for Interlocutory Appeal on Jurisdiction, 2 October 1995, para. 140.

[175] *Kunarac et al.* (IT-96-23 and IT-96-23/1-A), Judgment, 12 June 2002, para. 83.

[176] Hermann von Hebel and Daryl Robinson, 'Crimes within the Jurisdiction of the Court', in Roy S. Lee, ed., *The International Criminal Court: The Making of the Rome*

appeared to evolve as the debates wore on. In an explanation of its vote at the conclusion of the Rome Conference, China said that it was still opposed to the inclusion of crimes against humanity without a link to international armed conflict.[177] As with the definition of genocide, there is nothing specific in the text of the Rome Statute to indicate that the crime can be committed in the absence of international armed conflict, but this is undoubtedly implicit.

Article 7 begins with an introductory paragraph or *chapeau* stating: 'For the purpose of this Statute, "crime against humanity" means any of the following acts when committed as part of a widespread or systematic attack directed against any civilian population, with knowledge of the attack.' Like genocide, then, there is an important threshold that elevates the 'acts' set out later in the provision to the level of crimes against humanity. First among them, and the subject of great controversy at the Rome Conference, is the requirement that these acts be part of a 'widespread or systematic attack'. Some of the earlier proposals had required that the attack be widespread *and* systematic. The push to present these two conditions as alternatives was supported by the first major judgment of the International Criminal Tribunal for the former Yugoslavia only a year earlier, in the *Tadić* case.[178] But the apparent broadening of the threshold may be a deception, because further on in Article 7 the term 'attack' is defined as 'a course of conduct involving the multiple commission of acts referred

Statute: Issues, Negotiations, and Results, The Hague: Kluwer Law International, 1999, pp. 79–126 at p. 92; UN Doc. A/CONF.183/C.1/SR.3, para. 176. See also, on Art. 7 of the Rome Statute, Darryl Robinson, 'Crimes Against Humanity: Reflections on State Sovereignty, Legal Precision and the Dictates of the Public Conscience', in Lattanzi and Schabas, *Essays on the Rome Statute*, pp. 139–70; Machteld Boot, Rodney Dixon and Christopher K. Hall, 'Article 7', in Triffterer, ed., *Commentary*, pp. 159–273; M. Cherif Bassiouni, *Crimes Against Humanity in International Law*, 2nd edn, The Hague: Kluwer Law International, 1999; Darryl Robinson, 'Defining "Crimes Against Humanity" at the Rome Conference', (1999) 93 *American Journal of International Law* 43; Timothy L. H. McCormack, 'Crimes Against Humanity', in Dominic McGoldrick, Peter Rowe and Eric Donnelly, eds., *The Permanent International Criminal Court: Legal and Policy Issues*, Oxford and Portland, OR: Hart Publishing, 2004, pp. 179–202; Philippe Currat, *Les crimes contre l'humanité dans le Statut de la Cour pénale internationale*, Geneva: Schulthess Medias Juridiques, 2006; Machteld Boot, *Nullum Crimen Sine Lege and the Subject Matter Jurisdiction of the International Criminal Court, Genocide, Crimes Against Humanity, War Crimes*, Antwerp: Intersentia, 2002, pp. 455–536.

[177] UN Doc. A/CONF.183/SR.9, para. 38.

[178] *Tadić* (IT-94-1-T), Opinion and Judgment, 7 May 1997, para. 656. Also Report of the Secretary-General Pursuant to Paragraph 2 of Security Council Resolution 808 (1993), UN Doc. S/25704 (1993), para. 48.

to in paragraph 1 against any civilian population, pursuant to or in furtherance of a State or organizational policy to commit such attack'. It seems, therefore, that the term 'attack' has both widespread and systematic aspects. In addition, the attack must be directed against a civilian population, distinguishing it from many war crimes, which may be targeted at combatants or at civilians. The attack need not be a military attack.[179]

The attack must also be carried out 'pursuant to or in furtherance of a State or organizational policy to commit such attack'. This phrase appears to suggest that crimes against humanity may in some circumstances be committed by non-State actors. Historically, it was generally considered that crimes against humanity required implementation of a State policy. This requirement was gradually attenuated, a legal development that paralleled the expansion of war crimes into the area of non-international armed conflict. In *Tadić*, the Yugoslav Tribunal said that, at customary law, crimes against humanity could also be committed 'on behalf of entities exercising de facto control over a particular territory but without international recognition or formal status of a "de jure" state, or by a terrorist group or organization'.[180] The reflection of these views in Article 7 of the Rome Statute is an example of the influence of the case law of the *ad hoc* tribunals upon the drafters.

However, Professor Cherif Bassiouni, who chaired the drafting committee at the Rome Conference, disagrees that Article 7 enlarges the concept of crimes against humanity so as to cover non-state actors. In his recent three-volume work, *The Legislative History of the International Criminal Court*, he argues:

> Contrary to what some advocates advance, Article 7 does not bring a new development to crimes against humanity, namely, its applicability to non-state actors. If that were the case, the mafia, for example, could be charged with such crimes before the ICC, and that is clearly neither the letter nor the spirit of Article 7. The question arose after 9/11 as to whether a group such as al-Qaeda, which operates on a worldwide basis and is capable of inflicting significant harm in more than one state, falls within this category. In this author's opinion, such a group does not qualify for inclusion within the meaning of crimes against humanity as defined in Article 7,

---

[179] Elements of Crimes, Art. 7, Introduction, para. 3.
[180] *Tadić* (IT-94-1-T), Opinion and Judgment, 7 May 1997, para. 654.

and for that matter, under any definition of that crime up to Article 6(c) of
the IMT, notwithstanding the international dangers that it poses ... The
text [of Article 7(2)] clearly refers to state policy, and the words 'organisa-
tional policy' do not refer to the policy of an organisation, but the policy of
a state. It does not refer to non-state actors.[181]

The most authoritative statement against Professor Bassiouni's position is that of the Appeals Chamber of the International Criminal
Tribunal for the former Yugoslavia, buried in a footnote in its judgment in *Kunarac*. The Appeals Chamber was addressing the issue
from the standpoint of customary international law, because of its
well-known approach to interpreting the Rome Statute by which its
provisions are deemed to be consistent with custom.[182] After noting that '[t]here has been some debate in the jurisprudence of this
Tribunal as to whether a policy or plan constitutes an element of the
definition of crimes against humanity', the Appeals Chamber said
that practice 'overwhelmingly supports the contention that no such
requirement exists under customary international law'.[183] The Appeals
Chamber cited a number of authorities in support: Article 6(c) of the
Nuremberg Charter, the Nuremberg Judgment, national cases from
Australia, Israel and Canada, the Secretary-General's report on the
draft Statute of the Tribunal and various materials of the International
Law Commission. Unfortunately, there is no detailed explanation, and
it is often not very clear how and why these references buttress the
Appeals Chamber's position. Moreover, the Appeal Chamber did not
even mention the text of Article 7(2) of the Rome Statute, and what
influence it might have upon the determination of customary international law. Echoing earlier pronouncements of the International
Law Commission, the Appeals Chamber set the low-end threshold of
crimes against humanity as being more than merely 'isolated or ran-
dom acts'.[184] The case law of the International Criminal Tribunal for
the former Yugoslavia makes it impossible to exclude serial killers and
the acts of organized crime syndicates from the ambit of crimes against
humanity. The International Criminal Court has already been called

[181] M. Cherif Bassiouni, *The Legislative History of the International Criminal Court:
Introduction, Analysis and Integrated Text*, vol. I, Ardsley, NY: Transnational Publishers,
2005, pp. 151–2. See also M. Cherif Bassiouni, *Crimes Against Humanity*, 2nd edn, The
Hague: Kluwer Law International, 1999, pp. 243–81.
[182] *Tadić* (IT-94-1-A), Judgment, 15 July 1999, para. 287 (see also para. 296).
[183] *Kunarac et al.* (IT-96-23/1-A), Judgment, 12 June 2002, para. 98, n. 114.
[184] *Ibid.*, para. 96.

upon to interpret this 'State or organizational plan or policy' requirement, positioning it with respect to the case law of the International Criminal Tribunal for the former Yugoslavia, which has rejected the relevance of such a criterion.[185] According to Pre-Trial Chamber I, the requirement of an organizational policy is aimed at ensuring that an attack, 'even if carried out over a large geographical area or directed against a large number of victims, must still be thoroughly organized and follow a regular pattern'.[186] For Pre-Trial Chamber II, '[s]uch a policy may be made by groups of persons who govern a specific territory or by any organization with the capability to commit a widespread or systematic attack against a civilian population. The policy need not be formalized.'[187] For the Pre-Trial Chamber, 'an attack which is planned, directed or organized – as opposed to spontaneous or isolated acts of violence – will satisfy this criterion'.[188]

According to Pre-Trial Chamber I, the attack must be conducted 'in furtherance of a common policy involving public or private resources. Such a policy may be made either by groups of persons who govern a specific territory or by any organization with the capability to commit a widespread or systematic attack against a civilian population'.[189] It referred in particular to the ill-fated 1991 report of the International Law Commission on the Code of Crimes in this respect, reprising the words '[p]rivate individuals with de facto power or organized in criminal gangs or groups'.[190] Pre-Trial Chamber II divided on the scope of the concept of 'organizational policy'. Judge Kaul, dissenting, said that 'even though the constitutive elements of statehood need not be established those "organizations" should partake of some characteristics of a State. Those characteristics eventually turn the private "organization" into an entity which may act like a State or has quasi-State abilities.'[191] He said that groups such as organized crime, mobs, groups of armed

---

[185] See the remarks by Antonio Cassese, 'Areas Where Article 7 Is Narrower Than Customary International Law', in Cassese, *The Rome Statute*, pp. 375–6.

[186] *Ibid.*, para. 398.

[187] *Bemba* (ICC-01/05–01/08), Decision Pursuant to Article 61(7)(a) and (b) of the Rome Statute on the Charges of the Prosecutor Against Jean-Pierre Bemba Gombo, 15 June 2009, para. 81.

[188] *Ibid.*

[189] *Katanga et al.* (ICC-01/04–01/07), Decision on the Confirmation of the Charges, 30 September 2008, para. 398.

[190] *Ibid.*, para. 398, n. 507.

[191] *Situation in Kenya* (ICC-01/09), Dissenting Opinion of Judge Hans-Peter Kaul, 31 March 2010, para. 51.

civilians and criminal gangs would generally fall outside the scope of Article 7(2)(a).[192]

The perpetrator of crimes against humanity must have 'knowledge of the attack'. This mental element, which is in addition to the general knowledge and intent to commit the underlying crime, seems to be less demanding than the 'specific intent' required for genocide. Most writers refer to it as the 'contextual element', something that connects the specific act with the broader context of the particular crimes. According to Maria Kelt and Herman von Hebel,

> there was considerable debate [during the negotiations of the Elements of Crimes] as to whether [the contextual elements] really were 'material elements' – and if so whether they were (fully) covered by the mental element of article 30 – or whether they formed a separate type of element. Some participants thought, for example, that there might be a category of elements that are neither material nor mental, but which should be considered 'jurisdictional' or 'merely jurisdictional'. Ultimately, however, an explicit decision as to whether these elements were 'material elements' became unnecessary, as for each contextual element some corresponding mental element [however, lower than that provided for under Article 30] was specified in most cases, which, as a result ... rendered the other question moot.[193]

An individual who participates in crimes against humanity but who is unaware that they are part of a widespread or systematic attack on a civilian population may be guilty of murder and perhaps even of war crimes but cannot be convicted by the International Criminal Court for crimes against humanity. However, according to the Elements of Crimes, this does not require 'that the perpetrator had knowledge of all characteristics of the attack or the precise details of the plan or policy of the State or organization'.[194]

The definition of crimes against humanity makes no mention of the motive for such crimes, unlike earlier models for the definition that imply such a requirement. Some States had argued for the contrary view, insisting that they were supported by customary international law, but they gave way to the majority on this point.[195] This issue, too, remained

---

[192] *Ibid.*, para. 52.
[193] Maria Kelt and Herman von Hebel, 'What Are the Elements of Crimes?', in Roy Lee, ed., *The International Criminal Court: Elements of Crimes and Rules of Procedure and Evidence*, Ardsley, NY: Transnational Publishers, pp. 13–18 at p. 15.
[194] Elements of Crimes, para. 2.
[195] Hermann von Hebel and Daryl Robinson, 'Crimes within the Jurisdiction of the Court', in Roy S. Lee, ed., *The International Criminal Court: The Making of the Rome*

controversial until a 1999 judgment of the Appeals Chamber of the Yugoslav Tribunal declared that there was no particular motive requirement for crimes against humanity in general (the act of 'persecution' has a motive requirement built into its definition).[196] This does not mean, of course, that motive is never relevant to the prosecution of crimes against humanity. Where it can be shown that an accused had a motive to commit the crime, this may be a compelling indicator of guilt, just as the absence of any motive may raise a doubt about guilt. Motive is also germane to the establishment of an appropriate sentence for the crime.[197]

The *chapeau* or introductory portion of paragraph 1 of Article 7 is followed by an enumeration of eleven acts of crimes against humanity. At Nuremberg, the list was considerably shorter. It has been enriched principally by developments in international human rights law. Accordingly, there are subparagraphs dealing with specific types of crimes against humanity that have already been the subject of prohibitions in international law, namely, apartheid, torture and enforced disappearance. Some terms that were recognized at the time of Nuremberg have also been developed and expanded. For example, to 'deportation' are now added the words 'forcible transfer of population', recognizing our condemnation of what in recent years has been known as 'ethnic cleansing', particularly when this takes place within a country's own borders. However, proposals to include other new acts of crimes against humanity, including economic embargo, terrorism and mass starvation, did not rally sufficient support at the Rome Conference.

The most dramatic example of enlarging the scope of crimes against humanity is found in the very substantial list of 'gender crimes'. The Nuremberg Charter did not even recognize rape as a form of crime against humanity, at least explicitly, although this was corrected by judicial interpretation as well as in the texts of subsequent definitions. The Rome Statute goes much further, referring to '[r]ape, sexual slavery, enforced prostitution, forced pregnancy, enforced sterilization, or any other form of sexual violence of comparable gravity'.[198] 'Sexual slavery' seems to overlap with the stand-alone crime against humanity of 'enslavement'.

Statute: Issues, Negotiations, and Results, The Hague: Kluwer Law International, 1999, pp. 79–126 at pp. 93–4.

[196] *Tadić* (IT-94-1-A), Judgment, 15 July 1999.

[197] For example, Rules of Procedure and Evidence, ASP/1/3, pp. 10–107, Rule 145(2)(v).

[198] For detailed analysis of the gender crime provisions in crimes against humanity, see Kelly Dawn Askin, 'Crimes Within the Jurisdiction of the International Criminal Court', (1999) 10 *Criminal Law Forum* 33; Cate Steains, 'Gender Issues', in Lee, *The*

According to a Trial Chamber of the International Criminal Tribunal for the former Yugoslavia, '[t]he setting out of the violations in separate subparagraphs of the ICC Statute is not to be interpreted as meaning, for example, that sexual slavery is not a form of enslavement. This separation is to be explained by the fact that the sexual violence violations were considered best to be grouped together.'[199] The Elements of Crimes attempt to define 'sexual slavery': 'The perpetrator exercised any or all of the powers attaching to the right of ownership over one or more persons, such as by purchasing, selling, lending or bartering such a person or persons, or by imposing on them a similar deprivation of liberty.' A footnote states: 'It is understood that such deprivation of liberty may, in some circumstances, include exacting forced labour or otherwise reducing a person to a servile status as defined in the Supplementary Convention on the Abolition of Slavery, the Slave Trade, and Institutions and Practices Similar to Slavery of 1956. It is also understood that the conduct described in this element includes trafficking in persons, in particular women and children.'[200]

The term 'forced pregnancy' was the most problematic when the Statute was being drafted, because some believed it might be construed as creating an obligation upon States to provide women who had been forcibly impregnated with access to abortion.[201] A definition of the term was agreed to: '"Forced pregnancy" means the unlawful confinement, of a woman forcibly made pregnant, with the intent of affecting the ethnic composition of any population or carrying out other grave violations of international law. This definition shall not in any way be interpreted

International Criminal Court, pp. 357–90; and Barbara C. Bedont, 'Gender-Specific Provisions in the Statute of the ICC', in Lattanzi and Schabas, Essays on the Rome Statute, pp. 183–210. See also Nicole Eva Erb, 'Gender-Based Crimes under the Draft Statute for the Permanent International Criminal Court', (1998) 29 Columbia Human Rights Law Review 401; Patricia Viseur Sellers and Kaoru Okuizuma, 'International Prosecution of Sexual Assaults', (1997) 7 Transnational Law and Contemporary Problems 45.

[199] Kvočka et al. (IT-98-30/1-T), Judgment, 2 November 2001, para. 541, n. 1333.

[200] Elements of Crimes, ASP/1/3, p. 108, e.g., Arts. 7(1)(g)-(2), 8(2)(b)(xxii)-2 and 8(2)(e)(vi)-2. This is discussed in Knut Dörmann, Elements of War Crimes under the Rome Statute of the International Criminal Court, Sources and Commentary, Cambridge: Cambridge University Press, 2002, pp. 328–9.

[201] UN Doc. A/CONF.183/C.1/SR.3, para. 32 and UN Doc. A/CONF.183/C.1/SR.5, para. 21 (Saudi Arabia); UN Doc. A/CONF.183/C.1/SR.5, para. 71 (Iran). The Holy See attempted to introduce a reference to 'human beings' in the preamble that was widely viewed as an attempt to raise the abortion issue, and was rejected for this reason: Tuiloma Neroni Slade and Roger S. Clark, 'Preamble and Final Clauses', in Lee, The International Criminal Court, pp. 421–50 at p. 426.

as affecting national laws relating to pregnancy.'[202] The second sentence was added to reassure some States that the Rome Statute would not conflict with anti-abortion laws.[203] It is also possible to prosecute sexual violence as an act of torture. In *Kunarac*, the Appeals Chamber of the International Criminal Tribunal for the former Yugoslavia said that sexual violence necessarily gives rise to severe pain or suffering, whether physical or mental, adding that it was not necessary to provide visual evidence of suffering by the victim, as this could be assumed.[204]

Rape is not defined in the Rome Statute, and at the time the drafters may have felt it was obvious enough to be left to the judges to figure out. Within a few months of the adoption of the Rome Statute, judgments of the *ad hoc* tribunals had developed two somewhat different definitions of the crime of rape. The first was proposed by the Rwanda Tribunal in *Akayesu*, which warned that 'the central elements of the crime of rape cannot be captured in a mechanical description of objects and body parts'.[205] It defined the crime as 'a physical invasion of a sexual nature, committed on a person under circumstances which are coercive'.[206] The definition was broad enough to encompass forced penetration by the tongue of the victim's mouth, which most legal systems would not stigmatize as a rape, although it might well be prosecuted as a form of sexual assault. Subsequently, a Trial Chamber of the Yugoslav Tribunal reverted to a more mechanical and technical definition, holding rape to be 'the sexual penetration, however slight: (a) of the vagina or anus of the victim by the penis of the perpetrator or any other object used by the perpetrator; or (b) of the mouth of the victim by the penis of the perpetrator'.[207] The Elements of Crimes lean towards the second of these approaches, but with some slight divergences: 'The perpetrator invaded the body of a person by conduct resulting in penetration, however slight, of any part of the body of the victim or of the perpetrator with a sexual organ, or of the anal or genital opening of the victim with any object or any other part of the body.' Many legal systems consider that only a woman may be a victim of rape. The Elements of Crimes

---

[202] Rome Statute, Art. 7(2)(f).

[203] Steains, 'Gender Issues', p. 368. But, for a somewhat different view, that seems to allow a contrary interpretation of the text, see Bedont, 'Gender-Specific Provisions', pp. 198–9.

[204] *Kunarac et al.* (IT-96-23 and IT-96-23/1-A), Judgment, 12 June 2002, para. 150.

[205] *Akayesu* (ICTR-96-4-T), Judgment, 2 September 1998, para. 325.

[206] *Ibid.*, para. 326. See also *Delalić et al.* (IT-96-21-T), Judgment, 16 November 1998, paras. 477–8.

[207] *Furundžija* (IT-95-17/1-T), Judgment, 10 December 1998, para. 185.

provide a signal that men may also be victims of the crime in a foot-note indicating that '[t]he concept of "invasion" is intended to be broad enough to be gender-neutral'.[208]

Although Article 7 expands the scope of crimes against humanity, in some respects it may also limit it. For example, the Statute defines persecution as a punishable act: 'Persecution against any identifiable group or collectivity on political, racial, national, ethnic, cultural, religious, gender as defined in paragraph 3, or other grounds that are universally recognized as impermissible under international law, in connection with any act referred to in this paragraph or any crime within the jurisdiction of the Court.' The list of groups or collectivities is considerably larger than any previous definitions. However, the words 'in connection with any act referred to in this paragraph or any crime within the jurisdiction of the Court' narrows its scope considerably. This is a departure from previous definitions, although it probably reflects recent judicial interpretations which require acts of persecutions to be 'of the same gravity or severity as the other enumerated crimes' in the provision on crimes against humanity.[209] A Trial Chamber of the Yugoslav Tribunal said that, 'although the Statute of the ICC may be indicative of the *opinio juris* of many States, Article 7(1)(h) is not consonant with customary international law', and rejected in particular the requirement that persecution be connected with a crime within the jurisdiction of the Court or another act of crime against humanity as too narrow.[210] Yet, by comparison with earlier interpretations of crimes against humanity, the Appeals Chamber of the Yugoslav Tribunal has described the provision as 'expansive'.[211]

Defining 'persecution' perplexed the Rome drafters, with many judging it to be ambiguous and vague. The result is a compromise. The Elements of Crimes explain that, in the act of persecution, the perpetrator 'severely deprived, contrary to international law, one or more persons

---

[208] Elements of Crimes, Art. 7(1)(e), para. 1 and n. 15.

[209] *Kvočka et al.* (IT-98-30/1-T), Judgment, 2 November 2001, para. 185; *Kupreškić et al.* (IT-95-16-T), Judgment, 14 January 2000, paras. 618–19; *Kordić et al.* (IT-95-14/2-T), Judgment, 26 February 2001, paras. 193–5; *Kordić et al.* (IT-95-14/2-A), Judgment, 17 December 2004, para. 102.

[210] *Kupreškić et al.* (IT-95-16-T), Judgment, 14 January 2000, paras. 579–81. On this issue, see Mohamed Elewa Badar, 'From the Nuremberg Charter to the Rome Statute: Defining the Elements of Crimes Against Humanity', (2004) 5 *San Diego International Law Journal* 73 at 125–7.

[211] *Blaškić* (IT-95-14-A), Judgment, 29 July 2004, para. 148, n. 310.

of fundamental rights'.[212] A judgment of the International Criminal Tribunal for the former Yugoslavia holds that the crime against humanity of persecution 'derives its unique character from the requirement of a specific discriminatory intent'.[213] The case law has defined persecution as an act or omission that discriminates in fact and that denies or infringes on a fundamental right laid down in international customary or treaty law.[214]

Where the Rome Statute leaves the door open for some evolution is in the final paragraph of the list of crimes against humanity, dealing with 'other inhumane acts'. In the case law of the *ad hoc* tribunals, concern has been expressed that 'this category lacks precision and is too general to provide a safe yardstick for the work of the Tribunal and hence, that it is contrary to the principle of the "specificity" of criminal law'.[215] According to Professor Kai Ambos, the provision is 'a classic example of punishment by analogy in contradiction to the lex stricta requirement under Article 22(2) of the ICC Statute'.[216]

The International Criminal Tribunal for the former Yugoslavia has suggested that the legal parameters of 'other inhumane acts' be found in a set of basic rights appertaining to human beings drawn from the norms of international human rights law. It views 'other inhumane acts' as a residual category, providing crimes against humanity with the flexibility to cover serious violations of human rights that are not specifically enumerated in the other paragraphs of the definition, on the condition that they be of comparable gravity. The examples given by the Tribunal of inhumane acts not specifically listed in the definition of crimes against humanity in the Statute of the Yugoslav Tribunal are the forcible transfer of groups of civilians, enforced prostitution and the enforced disappearance of persons.[217]

In the *Akayesu* decision, the Rwanda Tribunal used 'other inhumane acts' to encompass such behaviour as forced nakedness of Tutsi women.[218] The Yugoslav Tribunal concluded that the compulsory bussing of

---

[212] Elements of Crimes, Art. 7(1)(h), para. 1.

[213] *Krnojelac* (IT-97-25-T), Judgment, 15 March 2002, para. 436.   [214] *Ibid.*

[215] *Kupreškić et al.* (IT-95-16-T), Judgment, 14 January 2000, para. 563. See also *Stakić* (IT-97-24-T), Decision on Rule 98*bis* Motion for Judgment of Acquittal, 31 October 2002, para. 131.

[216] Kai Ambos, 'Remarks on the General Part of International Criminal Law', (2006) 4 *Journal of International Criminal Justice* 660 at 670.

[217] *Kupreškić et al.* (IT-95-16-T), Judgment, 14 January 2000, para. 566.

[218] *Akayesu* (ICTR-96-4-T), Judgment, 2 September 1998.

thousands of women, children and elderly persons from Potocari, in the Srebrenica enclave, consisted of an 'inhumane act'. Those being bussed were not told where they were going, some were struck and abused by Serb soldiers as they boarded the buses, the buses themselves were over-crowded and unbearably hot, and stones were thrown at them as they travelled. After disembarking, the victims had to march several kilo-metres through a 'no man's land'.[219]

But, under the Rome Statute, the concept of 'other inhumane acts' may actually be narrowed by the addition of the words 'of a similar char-acter intentionally causing great suffering, or serious injury to body or to mental or physical health'. It is open to question whether the acts of sex-ual indignity condemned by the Rwanda Tribunal would now fit within the restrictive language of the Rome Statute. The provision was criti-cized by a Trial Chamber of the Yugoslav Tribunal for failing 'to provide an indication, even indirectly, of the legal standards which would allow us to identify the prohibited inhumane acts'.[220]

Article 7 concludes with two further paragraphs that endeavour to define some of the more difficult terms of paragraph 1. Accordingly, the term 'attack' is defined, as explained above, as well as 'extermination', 'enslavement', 'deportation or forcible transfer of population', 'torture', 'forced pregnancy', 'persecution', 'the crime of apartheid' and 'enforced disappearance of persons'. Some of these definitions reflect customary law, but some clearly go further. They are also influenced by, and have themselves influenced, the case law of the *ad hoc* tribunals.

For example, Article 7(2)(b) describes the crime against humanity of 'extermination' as 'the intentional infliction of conditions of life, inter alia the deprivation of access to food and medicine, calculated to bring about the destruction of part of a population'. Noting that previous judgments had not defined the term, a Trial Chamber of the Yugoslav Tribunal adopted the definition proposed in the Rome Statute. It said that insertion of this provision means 'that the crime of extermination may be applied to acts committed with the intention of bringing about the death of a large number of victims either directly, such as by killing the victim with a firearm, or less directly, by creat-ing conditions provoking the victim's death'. The Trial Chamber also referred to the Elements of Crimes, which state that 'the perpetrator

---

[219] *Krstić* (IT-98-33-T), Judgment, 2 August 2001, paras. 50–2 and 519.
[220] *Kupreškić et al.* (IT-95-16-T), Judgment, 14 January 2000, para. 565.

[should have] killed one or more persons' and that the conduct should have been committed 'as part of a mass killing of members of a civilian population'.[221]

Torture is defined by Article 7(2)(e) as 'the intentional infliction of severe pain or suffering, whether physical or mental, upon a person in the custody or under the control of the accused; except that torture shall not include pain or suffering arising only from, inherent in or incidental to, lawful sanctions'. There is nothing here to suggest the perpetrator must be in some official capacity, or that the torture must be conducted for a prohibited purpose. Yet, Article 1 of the Convention Against Torture and Other Cruel, Inhuman or Degrading Treatment or Punishment includes, in its definition of torture, the requirement that it be inflicted 'for such purposes as obtaining from him or a third person information or a confession, punishing him for an act he or a third person has committed or is suspected of having committed, or intimidating or coercing him or a third person, or for any reason based on discrimination of any kind, when such pain or suffering is inflicted by or at the instigation of or with the consent or acquiescence of a public official or other person acting in an official capacity'. The *ad hoc* tribunals have regularly described the definition in the Convention Against Torture as a reflection of customary international law.[222] However, recent decisions take the view, consistent with the text of the Rome Statute, that customary international law does not require that torture be committed by a person acting in an official capacity.[223] In one ruling, a Trial Chamber of the Yugoslav Tribunal specifically referred to the Rome Statute as evidence that customary law does not impose an official capacity criterion as part of the crime of torture.[224]

A special provision defines 'gender', not only for the purposes of crimes against humanity but also for whenever else it may be used in the Statute. In a formulation borrowed from the 1995 Beijing Conference, Article 7 states that 'it is understood that the term "gender" refers to the two sexes, male and female, within the context of society'.[225]

---

[221] *Krstić* (IT-98-33-T), Judgment, 2 August 2001, para. 498.

[222] *Furundžija*, Judgment, 17 July 2000, para. 111.

[223] *Kunarac et al.* (IT-96-23 and IT-96-23/1-A), Judgment, 12 June 2002, para. 148.

[224] *Kvočka et al.* (IT-98-30/1-T), Judgment, 2 November 2001, n. 296.

[225] On the debate surrounding the term 'gender', see Steains, 'Gender Issues', pp. 371–5. But, for a somewhat different view, that seems to allow a contrary interpretation of the text, see Bedont, 'Gender-Specific Provisions', pp. 198–9.

War crimes

The lengthiest provision defining offences within the jurisdiction of the International Criminal Court is Article 8, entitled 'War crimes'.[226] This is certainly the oldest of the four categories. War crimes have been punished as domestic offences probably since the beginning of criminal law.[227] Moreover, they were the first to be prosecuted pursuant to international law. The trials conducted at Leipzig in the early 1920s, as a consequence of Articles 228–230 of the Treaty of Versailles, convicted a handful of German soldiers of 'acts in violation of the laws and customs of war'. The basis in international law for these offences was the Regulations annexed to the 1907 Hague Convention IV.[228] And, while that instrument had not originally been conceived of as a source of individual criminal responsibility, its terms had been the basis of the definitions of war crimes by the 1919 Commission on Responsibilities. Certainly, from that point on, there is little argument about the existence of war crimes under international law.

War crimes were subsequently codified in the Nuremberg Charter, where they are defined in a succinct provision:

> [Violations of the laws or customs of war] shall include, but not be limited to, murder, ill-treatment or deportation to slave labour or for any other purpose of civilian population of or in occupied territory, murder or ill-treatment of prisoners of war or persons on the seas, killing of hostages, plunder of public or private property, wanton destruction of cities, towns or villages, or devastation not justified by military necessity.[229]

---

[226] Hermann von Hebel and Daryl Robinson, 'Crimes within the Jurisdiction of the Court', in Roy S. Lee, ed., *The International Criminal Court: The Making of the Rome Statute: Issues, Negotiations, and Results*, The Hague: Kluwer Law International, 1999, pp. 79–126 at pp. 103–22; Gabriella Venturini, 'War Crimes', in Lattanzi and Schabas, *Essays on the Rome Statute*, pp. 171–82; Roberta Arnold, Elisabeth Bennion, Michael Cottier, Knut Dörmann, Patricia Viseur Sellers and Andreas Zimmermann, 'Article 8', in Triffterer, ed., *Commentary*, pp. 275–503.

[227] Leslie C. Green, 'International Regulation of Armed Conflict', in M. Cherif Bassiouni, ed., *International Criminal Law*, 2nd edn, Ardsley, NY: Transnational Publishers, 2003, vol. I, pp. 355–91.

[228] Convention Concerning the Laws and Customs of War on Land (Hague IV), 18 October 1907, 3 *Martens Nouveau Recueil* (3d) 461.

[229] Agreement for the Prosecution and Punishment of Major War Criminals of the European Axis, and Establishing the Charter of the International Military Tribunal (IMT), Annex, (1951) 82 UNTS 279, Art. 6(c).

Four years later, in the 'grave breaches' provisions of the four Geneva Conventions of 1949, a second codification was advanced:

> wilful killing, torture or inhuman treatment, including biological experiments, wilfully causing great suffering or serious injury to body or health, unlawful deportation or transfer or unlawful confinement of a protected person, compelling a protected person to serve in the forces of a hostile Power, or wilfully depriving a protected person of the rights of fair and regular trial prescribed in the present Convention, taking of hostages and extensive destruction and appropriation of property, not justified by military necessity and carried out unlawfully and wantonly.[230]

Both of these provisions do not by any extent cover the entire range of serious violations of the laws of war. They extend only to the most severe atrocities, and their victims must be, by and large, civilians or non-combatants. Moreover, these provisions only contemplate armed conflicts of an international nature.

Until the mid-1990s, there was considerable confusion about the scope of international criminal responsibility for war crimes. Some considered that the law of war crimes had been codified and that consequently, since 1949, the concept was limited to grave breaches of the Geneva Conventions. But the Conventions only covered what is known as 'Geneva law', addressing the protection of the victims of armed conflict. War crimes as conceived at Nuremberg were derived from 'Hague law', which focused on the methods and materials of warfare. In any case, beyond these two categories there seemed to be little doubt that international criminal responsibility did not extend to internal armed conflicts. Indeed, when the 1949 Geneva Conventions were updated with two Additional Protocols in 1977, the drafters quite explicitly excluded any suggestion that there could be 'grave breaches' during a non-international armed conflict.

This conception of the law of international criminal responsibility was reflected in the Statute of the International Criminal Tribunal for the

[230] Convention (I) for the Amelioration of the Condition of the Wounded and Sick in Armed Forces in the Field, (1949) 75 UNTS 31, Art. 49; Convention (II) for the Amelioration of the Condition of Wounded, Sick and Shipwrecked Members of Armed Forces at Sea, (1950) 75 UNTS 85, Art. 50; Convention (III) Relative to the Treatment of Prisoners of War, (1950) 75 UNTS 135, Art. 129; Convention (IV) Relative to the Protection of Civilian Persons in Time of War, (1950) 75 UNTS 287, Art. 156. The provision varies slightly in the four Conventions.

former Yugoslavia, adopted in May 1993.[231] At the time, the Secretary-General made it clear that the Statute would not innovate and that it would confine itself to crimes generally recognized by customary international law. Accordingly, there were two separate provisions, Article 2, covering 'grave breaches' of the Geneva Conventions, and Article 3, addressing the 'Hague law' violations of the 'laws and customs of war'. The text presented to the General Assembly by the International Law Commission, in 1994, had nothing on war crimes committed in such situations.[232] But movement was afoot, and, when it adopted the Statute of the International Criminal Tribunal for Rwanda in November 1994, the Security Council recognized the punishability of war crimes in internal armed conflict.[233] The Secretary-General noted that the Security Council was taking a 'more expansive approach to the choice of the applicable law than the one underlying the statute of the Yugoslav Tribunal', in that it was including crimes regardless of whether they were considered part of customary international law and whether customary international law entailed individual criminal responsibility with respect to war crimes in non-international armed conflict.[234]

A year later, in its first major judgment, the Appeals Chamber of the International Criminal Tribunal for the former Yugoslavia stunned international lawyers by issuing a broad and innovative reading of the two categories of war crimes in the Statute of the Tribunal, affirming that international criminal responsibility included acts committed during internal armed conflict.[235] In *Tadić*, the judges in effect read this in as a component of the rather archaic term 'laws or customs of war'. These developments were on the ground that this was dictated by the evolution of customary law. This exercise in judicial law-making was open to criticism not only for departing from the text of the Statute but also as a form of retroactive legislation. The debate about whether to include war crimes in non-international armed conflict continued throughout the

---

[231] Statute of the International Criminal Tribunal for the former Yugoslavia, UN Doc. S/RES/827, Annex.

[232] Report of the International Law Commission on the Work of Its Forty-Sixth Session, Draft Statute for an International Criminal Court, UN Doc. A/49/10.

[233] Statute of the International Criminal Tribunal for Rwanda, UN Doc. S/RES/955, Annex, Art. 4.

[234] Report of the Secretary-General Pursuant to Paragraph 5 of Security Council Resolution 955 (1994), UN Doc. S/1995/134, para. 12.

[235] *Tadić* (IT-94-1-AR72), Decision on Defence Motion for Interlocutory Appeal on Jurisdiction, 2 October 1995.

drafting of the Statute.[236] Eventually, doubts about the broadening of the scope of war crimes were laid to rest at the Rome Conference in 1998, when States confirmed that they were prepared to recognize responsibility for war crimes in non-international armed conflict. The dichotomy is not entirely resolved, however, because not all war crimes punishable in international armed conflict are also punishable in non-international armed conflict. As Pre-Trial Chamber I has noted, the drafters of Article 8 intended that it provide broader coverage with respect to international armed conflict.[237]

Article 8 of the Rome Statute is one of the most substantial provisions in the Statute, and is all the more striking when compared with the relatively laconic texts of the Nuremberg Charter and the Geneva Conventions. To some extent it represents a progressive development over these antecedents, because it expressly covers non-international armed conflicts. Furthermore, several war crimes are defined in considerable detail, focusing attention on their forms and variations. Yet such detailed definition may also serve to narrow the scope of war crimes in some cases. In the future, judges will have greater difficulty undertaking the kind of judicial law-making that the Yugoslav Tribunal performed in the *Tadić* case, and this will make it harder for justice to keep up with the imagination and inventiveness of war criminals. Indeed, the *Tadić* Appeals Chamber, with its bold initiatives at judge-made law, may well have frightened States who then resolved that they would leave far less room for such developments in any statute of an international criminal court. Of course, the definitions in the Rome Statute can always be amended, but the process is cumbersome.

The drafters of the Rome Statute drew upon the existing sources of war crimes law, and these are reflected in the structure of Article 8, although the law would have been considerably more accessible and coherent had they attempted to rewrite this complex body of norms in a more simple form. As it now stands, Article 8 consists of four categories of war crimes, two of them addressing international armed conflict and two of them non-international armed conflict. Not only are the specific acts set out in excruciating detail, but the actual categories impose a

---

[236] E.g., Report of the Ad Hoc Committee on the Establishment of an International Criminal Court; UN Doc. A/50/22, paras. 74–6; Report of the Preparatory Committee on the Establishment of an International Criminal Court, vol. I, UN Doc. A/51/22, para. 78.

[237] *Lubanga* (ICC-01/04–01/06), Decision on the Confirmation of the Charges, 29 January 2007, para. 284.

difficult exercise of assessment of the type of armed conflict involved. Courts will be required to distinguish between international and non-international conflicts, and this is further complicated by the fact that within the subset of non-international conflicts there are what initially appear to be two distinct categories. The judgments of the Yugoslav Tribunal have already shown just how difficult this task of qualification can be.

This is notably the case with so-called 'gender crimes'. Rape has always been considered a war crime, although it was not mentioned as such in either the Nuremberg Charter or the Geneva Conventions,[238] which probably reflects the fact that it was not always prosecuted with great diligence. The Rome Statute provides a detailed enumeration of rape and similar crimes, the result of vigorous lobbying by women's groups prior to and during the Rome Conference. The real question is whether this rather prolix provision actually offers women better protection than the somewhat archaic yet potentially larger terms of Geneva Convention IV: 'Women shall be especially protected against any attack on their honour, in particular against rape, enforced prostitution, or any form of indecent assault.'[239]

As all criminal lawyers know, there is a dark side to detailed codification. The greater the detail in the provisions, the more loopholes exist for able defence arguments. It may well be wrong to interpret the lengthy text of Article 8 as an enlargement of the concept of war crimes. In *Kupreškić*, the Yugoslav Tribunal warned that '[a]n exhaustive categorization would merely create opportunities for evasion of the letter of the prohibition'.[240] The extremely precise and complex provisions of Article 8 are mainly due to the nervousness of States about the scope of war crimes prosecutions, and arguably have the effect of narrowing the potential scope of prosecutions. Much of this was cloaked in arguments about the need for precision in legal texts and the sanctity of the principle of legality. The detailed terms of Article 8 may indirectly contribute to impunity in their inability to permit dynamic or evolutive

---

[238] See, e.g., the 'Leiber Code', Instructions for the Government of Armies of the United States in the Field, General Orders No. 100, 24 April 1863, Arts. 44 and 47. See also Theodor Meron, 'Rape as a Crime under International Humanitarian Law', (1993) 87 *American Journal of International Law* 424.

[239] Convention (IV) Relative to the Protection of Civilian Persons in Time of War, (1950) 75 UNTS 287, Art. 27.

[240] *Kupreškić et al.* (IT-95-16-T), Judgment, 14 January 2000, para. 563.

interpretations. As the Appeals Chamber of the Yugoslav Tribunal recently recalled, citing Nuremberg, the laws of armed conflict 'are not static, but by continual adaptation follow the needs of a changing world'.[241]

In customary law, a major distinction between war crimes and the other categories, crimes against humanity, genocide and aggression, is that the latter three have jurisdictional thresholds while the former does not. Crimes against humanity must be 'widespread' or 'systematic', and genocide and aggression requires a very high level of specific intent. War crimes, on the other hand, can in principle cover even isolated acts committed by individual soldiers acting without direction or guidance from higher up. While genocide and crimes against humanity would seem to be *prima facie* serious enough to warrant intervention by the Court, this will not always be the case for war crimes. As a result, Article 8 begins with what has been called a 'non-threshold threshold'.[242] The Court has jurisdiction over war crimes 'in particular when committed as a part of a plan or policy or as part of a large-scale commission of such crimes'. The language brings war crimes closer to crimes against humanity. The Rome Conference found middle ground with the words 'in particular', thereby compromising between those favouring a rigid threshold and those opposed to any such limitation on jurisdiction.[243]

According to the Appeals Chamber of the International Criminal Court, 'the requirement of large-scale commission under the Statute is *alternative* to the requirement of commission as part of a policy'.[244] Moreover, it has observed 'the statutory requirement of either large-scale commission or part of a policy is not absolute but qualified by the expression "in particular"'.[245] For Pre-Trial Chamber II, 'the term "in particular" makes it clear that the existence of a plan, policy or

---

[241] *Kunarac et al.* (IT-96-23 and IT-96-23/I-A), Judgment, 12 June 2002, para. 67.

[242] Hermann von Hebel and Daryl Robinson, 'Crimes within the Jurisdiction of the Court', in Roy S. Lee, ed., *The International Criminal Court: The Making of the Rome Statute: Issues, Negotiations, and Results*, The Hague: Kluwer Law International, 1999, pp. 79–126 at p. 124.

[243] *Ibid.*, pp. 107–8.

[244] *Situation in the Democratic Republic of the Congo* (ICC-01/04), Judgment on the Prosecutor's Appeal Against the Decision of Pre-Trial Chamber I Entitled 'Decision on the Prosecutor's Application for Warrants of Arrest, Article 58', 13 July 2006, para. 70. See also *Lubanga* (ICC-01/04–01/06), Decision on the Prosecutor's Application for a Warrant of Arrest, Article 58', 24 February 2006, para. 46.

[245] *Ibid.*

large-scale commission is not a prerequisite for the Court to exercise jurisdiction over war crimes but rather serves as a practical guideline for the Court'.[246] In practice, the Pre-Trial Chambers have virtually ignored Article 8(1) in their decisions on issuance of arrest warrants and confirmation of charges.

The threshold established by Article 8(1) has proven to be more important to the Office of the Prosecutor. For example, in his statement on communications concerning alleged war crimes committed in Iraq, the Prosecutor accepted that there was a reasonable basis that there were an estimated four to twelve victims of wilful killing and a limited number of victims of inhuman treatment, totalling in all less than twenty persons, attributable to nationals of States Parties. He explained:

> For war crimes, a specific gravity threshold is set down in Article 8(1), which states that 'the Court shall have jurisdiction in respect of war crimes in particular when committed as part of a plan or policy or as part of a large-scale commission of such crimes'. This threshold is not an element of the crime, and the words 'in particular' suggest that this is not a strict requirement. It does, however, provide Statute guidance that the Court is intended to focus on situations meeting these requirements. According to the available information, it did not appear that any of the criteria of Article 8(1) were satisfied.[247]

In the result, the Prosecutor decided that there was no basis to proceed with an investigation, and he dismissed the communication. The Prosecutor returned to the issue in his application for arrest warrants concerning the September 2007 attack on the African Union Mission in Sudan, which involved the killing of twelve peacekeepers and the wounding of eight others. He referred to the threshold of Article 8(1), noting the finding of the Appeals Chamber that it 'should not be construed narrowly' and explaining that in applying the provision 'the issues of the nature, manner and impact of the attack are critical'. In this matter, however, he chose to proceed, noting that '[i]ntentional [sic] directing attacks against peacekeeping operations constitute exceptional serious offences'.[248] Whether the attack was part of a 'large-scale

---

[246] *Bemba* (ICC-01/05–01/08), Decision Pursuant to Article 61(7)(a) and (b) of the Rome Statute on the Charges of the Prosecutor Against Jean-Pierre Bemba Gombo, 15 June 2009, para. 211.

[247] Office of the Prosecutor, Letter Concerning Communication on the Situation in Iraq, The Hague, 9 February 2006, p. 8.

[248] *Situation in Darfur, Sudan* (ICC-02/05), Summary of the Prosecutor's Application under Article 58, 20 November 2008, para. 7.

commission' or pursuant to a 'plan or policy' was not really addressed. The matter was not at all considered by the Pre-Trial Chamber when it issued a summons to appear based upon this application, surprisingly given the reference to Article 8(1) in the Prosecutor's application.[249] Perhaps it is further confirmation of the practical insignificance of the provision. A comparison of the Prosecutor's application of the provision in the two situations, Iraq and Sudan, also suggests that Article 8(1) is an expedient to be invoked opportunistically rather than a meaningful legal norm.

The preliminary issue to be determined in charges under Article 8 is the existence of an armed conflict, be it international or non-international. In terms of time, some war crimes can be committed after the conclusion of overt hostilities, particularly those relating to the repatriation of prisoners of war. Therefore, war crimes can actually be perpetrated when there is no armed conflict or, in other words, after the conclusion of the conflict. From the standpoint of territory, war crimes law applies in some cases to the entire territory of a State, and not just the region where hostilities have been committed. The International Criminal Tribunal for the former Yugoslavia has held that 'an armed conflict exists whenever there is a resort to armed force between States or protracted armed violence between governmental authorities and organized armed groups or between such groups within a State'.[250]

The Elements of Crimes clarify that, while the Prosecutor must establish the threshold elements of war crimes, he or she need not prove that the perpetrator had knowledge of whether or not there was an armed conflict, or whether it was international or non-international. According to the Elements, '[t]here is only a requirement for the awareness of the factual circumstances that established the existence of an armed conflict that is implicit in the terms "took place in the context of and was associated with"'.[251]

Not every act listed under Article 8 and committed while a country is at war will constitute a punishable crime before the Court. There must also be a nexus between the act perpetrated and the conflict. This implied

---

[249] *Abu Garda* (ICC-02/05–02/09), Decision on the Prosecutor's Application under Article 58, 7 May 2009.

[250] *Tadić* (IT-94-1-AR72), Decision on the Defence Motion for Interlocutory Appeal on Jurisdiction, 2 October 1995, para. 70. See also *Tadić* (IT-94-1-T), Opinion and Judgment, 7 May 1997, para. 561; and *Aleksovski* (IT-95-14/1-T), Judgment, 25 June 1999, para. 43.

[251] Elements of Crimes, Art. 8, Introduction.

requirement has been developed in the case law of the *ad hoc* tribunals. In *Kunarac*, a Trial Chamber of the Yugoslav Tribunal explained that:

> the criterion of a nexus with the armed conflict … does not require that the offences be directly committed whilst fighting is actually taking place, or at the scene of combat. Humanitarian law continues to apply in the whole of the territory under the control of one of the parties, whether or not actual combat continues at the place where the events in question took place. It is therefore sufficient that the crimes were closely related to the hostilities occurring in other parts of the territories controlled by the parties to the conflict. The requirement that the act be closely related to the armed conflict is satisfied if, as in the present case, the crimes are committed in the aftermath of the fighting, and until the cessation of combat activities in a certain region, and are committed in furtherance or take advantage of the situation created by the fighting.[252]

According to early case law from the Court, the armed conflict 'must play a substantial role in the perpetrator's decision, in his ability to commit the crime or in the manner in which the conduct was ultimately committed'.[253] But, '[i]t is not necessary, however, for the armed conflict to have been regarded as the ultimate reason for the criminal conduct, nor must the conduct have taken place in the midst of the battle'.[254] In *Akayesu*, the Appeals Chamber of the International Criminal Tribunal for Rwanda held that there were no particular restrictions on persons who could be charged with war crimes. It overruled the Trial Chamber, which had refused to convict local officials of war crimes, despite accepting the existence of an internal armed conflict within Rwanda in 1994. For the Trial Chamber, even proof that an accused wore military clothing, carried a rifle, and assisted the military is insufficient to establish that he 'acted for either the Government or the [Rwandese Patriotic Front] in the execution of their respective conflict objectives'.[255] According to the Appeals Chamber, 'international humanitarian law would be lessened and called into question' if certain persons were exonerated from

---

[252] *Kunarac et al.* (IT-96-23 and IT-96-23/1-A), Judgment, 22 February 2001, para. 568. See also *Kvočka et al.* (IT-98-30-T), Judgment, 2 November 2001, para. 123.

[253] *Lubanga* (ICC-01/04–01/06), Decision on the Confirmation of the Charges, 29 January 2007, para. 287; *Katanga et al.* (ICC-01/04–01/07), Decision on the Confirmation of the Charges, 30 September 2008, para. 380.

[254] *Katanga et al.* (ICC-01/04–01/07), Decision on the Confirmation of the Charges, 30 September 2008, para. 380; *Lubanga* (ICC-01/04–01/06), Decision on the Confirmation of the Charges, 29 January 2007, para. 287.

[255] *Akayesu* (ICTR-96-4-A), Judgment, 2 September 1998, paras. 640–3.

individual criminal responsibility for war crimes under the pretext that they did not belong to a specific category.[256]

The first category of war crimes enumerated in Article 8 is that of 'grave breaches' of the Geneva Conventions. The four Geneva Conventions were adopted on 12 August 1949, replacing the earlier and rather more summary protection contained in the two Geneva Conventions of 1929. The four Conventions are distinguished by the group of persons being protected: Convention I protects wounded and sick in land warfare; Convention II protects wounded, sick and shipwrecked in sea warfare; Convention III protects prisoners of war; and Convention IV protects civilians. Probably the most significant difference between the two generations of treaties is that the 1949 Conventions finally provided a detailed protection of civilian non-combatants. But another very important development in the 1949 treaties was the recognition of individual criminal responsibility for certain particularly severe violations of the treaties, known as 'grave breaches'. This was an incredible innovation at the time, the recognition by States that they were obliged to investigate and prosecute or extradite persons suspected of committing 'grave breaches', irrespective of their nationality or the place where the crime was committed. By comparison, only months earlier the United Nations General Assembly had refused, in the case of genocide, to recognize such broad obligations, as well as a right to prosecute on the basis of universal jurisdiction. The obligation set out in the 'grave breach' provisions of the Geneva Conventions is often characterized by the Latin phrase *aut dedere aut judicare*, meaning 'extradite or prosecute'.

The 'grave breaches' of the 1949 Conventions are limited in scope. According to the fourth or 'civilian' Convention, grave breaches consist of:

> wilful killing, torture or inhuman treatment, including biological experiments, wilfully causing great suffering or serious injury to body or health, unlawful deportation or transfer or unlawful confinement of a protected person, compelling a protected person to serve in the forces of a hostile Power, or wilfully depriving a protected person of the rights of fair and regular trial prescribed in the present Convention, taking of hostages and extensive destruction and appropriation of property, not justified by military necessity and carried out unlawfully and wantonly.[257]

---

[256] *Akayesu* (ICTR-96-4-A), Judgment, 1 June 2001, para. 443.
[257] Convention (IV) Relative to the Protection of Civilian Persons in Time of War, (1950) 75 UNTS 287, Art. 147.

The other three Conventions contain somewhat shorter enumerations, but the fundamentals remain the same. In terms of application, however, what was in 1949 a very radical step of defining international crimes and responsibilities was accompanied by a narrowness in application: 'grave breaches' could only be committed in the course of international armed conflict.

The 'grave breaches' of the Geneva Conventions are set out in Article 8(2)(a) of the Rome Statute. Nothing in paragraph (a) insists that these apply only to international armed conflict, although the context suggests that this must necessarily be the case.[258] The *chapeau* describes grave breaches as acts committed 'against persons or property protected under the provisions of the relevant Geneva Convention'. There are no significant changes in the wording between the provisions of the four Conventions and the Rome Statute. In the *Tadić* decision, the Yugoslav Tribunal held that the grave breaches regime applied only to international armed conflict, even though this was not stated in the Tribunal's Statute.[259] An armed conflict may take place within the borders of a single State and yet it may still be international in nature if, for example, the troops of another State intervene in the conflict and even where some participants in the internal armed conflict act on behalf of this other State.[260]

Victims of 'grave breaches' must be 'protected persons'. In the case of the first three Conventions, this means members of the armed forces of a party to the international armed conflict who are no longer engaged in hostilities due to injury or capture. With respect to the fourth Convention, protected persons must be 'in the hands of a Party to the conflict or Occupying Power of which they are not nationals'. The Yugoslav Tribunal has declared that even 'nationals', in the traditional international law sense, are protected if they cannot rely upon the protection of the State

---

[258] The international armed conflict is made explicit in the Elements of Crimes. The Elements also specify that 'the term "international armed conflict" includes military occupation' (at p. 19, n. 34).

[259] *Tadić* (IT-94-1-AR72), Decision on the Defence Motion for Interlocutory Appeal on Jurisdiction, 2 October 1995, para. 80. See also *Blaškić* (IT-95-14-T), Judgment, 3 March 2000, para. 74. But see the dissenting opinion of Judge Abi-Saab in *Tadić, ibid.*; *Delalić et al.* (IT-96-21-A), Judgment, 20 February 2001, para. 202; dissenting opinion of Judge Rodrigues in *Aleksovski* (IT-95-14/1-T), Judgment, 25 June 1999, paras. 29–49; *Kordić et al.* (IT-95-14/2-PT), Decision on the Joint Defence Motion to Dismiss the Amended Indictment for Lack of Jurisdiction Based on the Limited Jurisdictional Reach of Articles 2 and 3, 2 March 1999.

[260] *Blaškić* (IT-95-14-T), Judgment, 3 March 2000, para. 76.

of which they are citizens because, for example, they belong to a national minority that is being victimized.[261] According to the Elements of Crimes, the perpetrator need not know the nationality of the victim, it being sufficient that he or she knew that the victim belonged to an adverse party to the conflict.[262] Pre-Trial Chamber I has said 'it is not necessary for the perpetrator to have evaluated and concluded that the victim was in fact a protected person under any of the Geneva Conventions'.[263]

Because there is so little case law in the application of the Geneva Conventions, many of the terms used in the Statute (and the Conventions) still await judicial interpretation. For example, what is the difference between ordinary 'killing', a familiar expression in national criminal law systems, and 'wilful killing', the term used in the Conventions? And what of 'appropriation of property', which must be carried out not only 'unlawfully' but also 'wantonly'?[264] Subsequent to the adoption of the Statute, participants in the Preparatory Commission devoted a great deal of attention to specifying the scope of these provisions. In their work, they were guided mainly by the Commentaries to the Geneva Conventions, prepared by the International Committee of the Red Cross during the 1950s. The Commentaries are based largely on the *travaux préparatoires* of the Conventions and constitute the principal interpretative source thereof.

Although refusing to proceed with an investigation, on the ground that the acts are not of sufficient gravity, the Prosecutor concluded that there was a 'reasonable basis' (the term used in Articles 15, 18 and 53) that two grave breaches had been committed by British troops in Iraq following the 2003 invasion, namely, wilful killing (Art. 8(2)(a)(i)) and torture or inhumane treatment (Art. 8(2)(a)(ii)). He said that information available to his Office indicated four to twelve victims of wilful killing, and a 'limited number of victims of inhuman treatment totalling in all less than twenty persons'.[265]

The second category of war crimes that is listed in Article 8 of the Rome Statute is '[o]ther serious violations of the laws and customs

---

[261] *Tadić* (IT-94-1-A), Judgment, 15 July 1999, paras. 164–6.

[262] Elements of Crimes, Art. 8(2)(a)(i), para. 3, n. 33.

[263] *Katanga et al.* (ICC-01/04–01/07), Decision on the Confirmation of the Charges, 30 September 2008, para. 297.

[264] For the origins of this term, see Mohamed Elewa Bader, 'Drawing the Boundaries of Mens Rea in the Jurisprudence of the International Criminal Tribunal for the Former Yugoslavia', (2006) 6 *International Criminal Law Review* 313 at 334–5.

[265] Letter of Prosecutor dated 9 February 2006 (Iraq), p. 8.

applicable in international armed conflict, within the established framework of international law'. The wording makes it quite explicit that this category, found in paragraph (b), is, like the crimes in paragraph (a), confined to international armed conflict. The list consists of crimes generally defined as 'Hague law', because these are principally drawn from the Regulations annexed to the 1907 Hague Convention IV.[266] The other important source of law is Additional Protocol I to the Geneva Conventions, which was adopted in 1977, and whose application is confined to international armed conflicts.[267] Additional Protocol I expanded somewhat upon the definition of grave breaches in the 1949 Conventions, although it also slightly watered down the obligations upon States that flow from them. Interestingly, the Rome Statute includes some of these new 'grave breaches' within paragraph (b) rather than in paragraph (a) of Article 8(2), but it does not include all of them.[268] Nor does Article 8(2)(b) include all serious violations of Additional Protocol I. In *Galić*, Judge Schomburg of the Yugoslav Tribunal's Appeals Chamber argued that 'spreading terror among the civilian population', which is prohibited by Article 51(2) of Additional Protocol I, was not a war crime at customary international law, on the grounds that no such crime had been included in Article 8(2)(b) of the Rome Statute.[269]

Unlike the four Geneva Conventions, which have benefited from near-universal ratification, Additional Protocol I still enjoys far less unanimity, and its reflection in Article 8 of the Rome Statute testifies to the ongoing uncertainty with respect to its definitions of 'grave breaches' and other serious violations. Additional Protocol I applies to a somewhat broader range of conflicts than the four Geneva Conventions, and the Prosecutor might well argue before the International Criminal Court that the specific provisions in Article 8 derived from Additional Protocol I can be committed in 'armed conflicts which peoples are fighting against colonial domination and alien occupation and against racist regimes in the exercise of their right of self-determination'.[270]

---

266 Convention Concerning the Laws and Customs of War on Land (Hague IV), 3 *Martens Nouveau Recueil* (3d) 461.

267 Protocol Additional to the 1949 Geneva Conventions and Relating to the Protection of Victims of International Armed Conflicts, (1979) 1125 UNTS 3.

268 For example, unjustifiable delay in repatriation of prisoners of war or civilians (Additional Protocol I, Art. 85(4)(b)) or apartheid (Additional Protocol I, Art. 85(4)(c)).

269 *Galić* (IT-98-29-A), Separate and Partially Dissenting Opinion of Judge Schomburg, 30 November 2006, para. 20.

270 Additional Protocol I, Art. 1(4).

There is no requirement under Article 7(2)(b), unlike the situation for 'grave breaches' under Article 7(2)(a), that the victims be 'protected persons'. Indeed, the overall focus of Hague law is on combatants themselves as victims. Hague law is concerned not so much with the innocent victims of war as with its very authors, the combatants. More than Geneva law, then, it is the continuation of ancient rules of chivalry and similar systems reflecting a code of conduct among warriors. In fact, some of the language sounds positively anachronistic. In the past, this was also the source used by the Commission on Responsibilities that explored the notion of war crimes following World War I, as well as of the post-World War II tribunals at Nuremberg, Tokyo and elsewhere. Unlike the Geneva Conventions, which have a rigorous codification of 'grave breaches', the notion of 'serious violations of the laws and customs of war' is rather malleable and has evolved over the years.

The term 'within the established framework of international law' is a bit mysterious. One of the main commentaries on the Statute confines itself to the observation that it is 'unclear',[271] while the other is entirely silent on the matter.[272] At the time of ratification of the Rome Statute, the United Kingdom formulated a declaration:

> The United Kingdom understands the term 'the established framework of international law', used in article 8(2)(b) and (e), to include customary international law as established by State practice and opinio iuris. In that context the United Kingdom confirms and draws to the attention of the Court its views as expressed, inter alia, in its statements made on ratification of relevant instruments of international law, including the Protocol Additional to the Geneva Conventions of 12th August 1949, and relating to the Protection of Victims of International Armed Conflicts (Protocol I) of 8th June 1977.

The United Kingdom was particularly concerned about reaffirming certain positions taken at the time of ratification of Additional Protocol I, namely, its view that nuclear weapons are not prohibited, and its right to take reprisals against States that violate norms of international humanitarian law. The declaration is also a reaction to the consequences of a finding by the International Criminal Tribunal for the former Yugoslavia on the subject of reprisals.[273]

---

[271] William J. Fenrick, 'Article 8', in Triffterer, ed., *Commentary*, pp. 575–7.

[272] Michael Bothe, 'War Crimes', in Cassese, *The Rome Statute*, pp. 379–426 at pp. 395–7.

[273] *Kupreškić et al.* (IT-95-16-T), Judgment, 14 January 2000, para. 527. In reaction to the decision, the United Kingdom military manual reads: '[T]he court's reasoning [in *Kupreškić*]

In addition to those provisions reflecting the terms of the Hague Regulations and Additional Protocol I, there are also some 'new' crimes in paragraph (b). These were in a sense codified by the drafters at Rome, and it is not improbable that those accused in the future will argue that they were not part of customary law applicable at the time the Statute was adopted. Among the new provisions included in Article 8(2)(b) are those concerning the protection of humanitarian or peacekeeping missions[274] and prohibiting environmental damage.[275] Probably the most controversial provision was subparagraph (viii), defining as a war crime 'the transfer, directly or indirectly, by the Occupying Power of parts of its own civilian population into the territory it occupies, or the deportation or transfer of all or parts of the population of the occupied territory within or outside this territory'. The provision governs not only population transfer within the occupied territory, but also the transfer by an occupying power of parts of its own civilian population into the occupied territory.[276] Israel felt itself particularly targeted by the provision, and, in a speech delivered on the evening of 17 July at the close of the Rome Conference, it announced it had voted against the Statute because of its irritation that a crime not previously considered to be part of customary international law had been included in the instrument because of political exigencies.[277] But including transfer of a civilian population to an occupied territory within the definition of war crimes is perfectly consistent with the approach of the Appeals Chamber of the International Criminal Tribunal for the former Yugoslavia in *Tadić*, whereby serious

---

is unconvincing and the assertion that there is a prohibition in customary law flies in the face of most of the state practice that exists. The UK does not accept the position as stated in this judgment.' United Kingdom Ministry of Defence, *The Manual of Law of Armed Conflict*, Oxford and New York: Oxford University Press, 2004, p. 421, n. 62.

[274] Rome Statute, Art. 8(b)(iii).   [275] *Ibid.*, Art. 8(b)(iv).

[276] Hermann von Hebel and Daryl Robinson, 'Crimes within the Jurisdiction of the Court', in Roy S. Lee, ed., *The International Criminal Court: The Making of the Rome Statute: Issues, Negotiations, and Results*, The Hague: Kluwer Law International, 1999, pp. 79–126 at p. 112.

[277] 'Israel has reluctantly cast a negative vote. It fails to comprehend why it has been considered necessary to insert into the list of the most heinous and grievous war crimes the action of transferring [a] population into occupied territory. The exigencies of lack of time and intense political and public pressure have obliged the Conference to by-pass very basic sovereign prerogatives to which we are entitled.' UN Diplomatic Conference Concludes in Rome with Decision to Establish Permanent International Criminal Court, UN Press Release L/ROM/22, 17 July 1998, at Explanations of Vote. Also UN Doc. A/CONF.183/SR.9, para. 34. When Israel signed the Statute, on 31 December 2000, it made a declaration protesting 'the insertion into the Statute of formulations tailored to meet the political agenda of certain states'.

violations of the Geneva Conventions that are not deemed to be 'grave breaches' may nevertheless constitute violations of the laws or customs of war.

It is a violation of the Statute to launch an intentional attack directed against civilians, or against civilian objects, or against personnel, installations, material, units or vehicles involved in a humanitarian assistance or peacekeeping mission in accordance with the Charter of the United Nations.[278] Responding to communications alleging war crimes committed by British subjects in Iraq, the Prosecutor focused much of his analysis on subparagraph (iv) of Article 8(2)(b) which criminalizes '[i]ntentionally launching an attack in the knowledge that such attack will cause incidental loss of life or injury to civilians or damage to civilian objects or widespread, long-term and severe damage to the natural environment which would be clearly excessive in relation to the concrete and direct overall military advantage anticipated'. This addresses what is known colloquially as 'collateral damage'. The provision is derived from Article 51(5)(b) of Additional Protocol I. The Prosecutor said that the material concerning allegations of such illegal attacks was characterized by a lack of information indicating clear excessiveness in relation to military advantage and a lack of information indicating the involvement of nationals of States Parties. The report notes that '[t]he available information suggests that most of the military activities were carried out by non-States Parties'.[279]

The use of human shields also finds its first formal criminalization in international law. Article 8(2)(b)(xxiii) refers to 'utilising the presence of a civilian or other protected person to render certain points, areas or military forces immune from military operations'. The provision was cited by the Appeals Chamber of the International Criminal Tribunal for the former Yugoslavia as evidence of the prohibition of this practice under customary international law.[280]

Several of the provisions of paragraph (b) deal with prohibited weapons. These include poison or poisoned weapons, asphyxiating, poisonous or other gases, and bullets that expand or flatten easily in the human body.[281] The casual reader of the Statute might get the impression that it

---

[278] Rome Statute, Art. 8(2)(b)(i), (ii) and (iii).

[279] Letter of Prosecutor dated 9 February 2006 (Iraq), p. 6.

[280] *Blaškić* (IT-95-14-A), Judgment, 29 July 2004, para. 653, n. 1366.

[281] Roger S. Clark, 'Methods of Warfare That Cause Unnecessary Suffering or Are Inherently Indiscriminate: A Memorial Tribute to Howard Berman', (1998) 28 *California Western International Law Journal* 379.

was drafted in the nineteenth century, as these horrific weapons seem rather obsolete alongside modern-day weapons, including those of mass destruction, like land mines, chemical and biological weapons, and nuclear weapons. Such, however, are the consequences of diplomatic negotiations, especially in the context of an international system where a handful of States monopolize the production and control of the most nefarious weapons. The nuclear powers resisted any language that might impact upon their own prerogatives, such as a reference to weapons that might in the future be deemed contrary to customary international law. They had already had a close scrape in the International Court of Justice in 1996, which came near to an outright prohibition of nuclear weapons.[282] Several delegations argued that the Rome Statute should be consistent with the advisory opinion of the International Court of Justice. More generally, there was much support for either direct or indirect language that would prohibit nuclear weapons. As a result, the nuclear powers insisted upon specifying that 'material and methods of warfare which are of a nature to cause superfluous injury or unnecessary suffering or which are inherently indiscriminate' also be the subject of a comprehensive prohibition included in an annex to the Statute, yet to be prepared.[283] With the exclusion of nuclear weapons, some of the non-nuclear States in the developing world objected to language that would explicitly prohibit the 'poor man's atomic bomb', that is, chemical and biological weapons. The result, then, is a shameful situation where poisoned arrows and hollow bullets are forbidden yet nuclear, biological and chemical weapons, as well as anti-personnel land mines, are not.[284]

---

[282] *Legality of the Threat or Use of Nuclear Weapons (Request by the United Nations General Assembly for an Advisory Opinion)*, [1996] ICJ Reports 226.

[283] Rome Statute, Art. 8(2)(b)(xx).

[284] Hermann von Hebel and Daryl Robinson, 'Crimes within the Jurisdiction of the Court', in Roy S. Lee, ed., *The International Criminal Court: The Making of the Rome Statute: Issues, Negotiations, and Results*, The Hague: Kluwer Law International, 1999, pp. 79–126 at pp. 113–16. Egypt, upon signing the Statute, made the following declaration: 'The provisions of the Statute with regard to the war crimes referred to in Article 8 in general and Article 8, paragraph 2(b) in particular shall apply irrespective of the means by which they were perpetrated or the type of weapon used, including nuclear weapons, which are indiscriminate in nature and cause unnecessary damage, in contravention of international humanitarian law.' New Zealand said something similar, expressly citing the advisory opinion of the International Court of Justice in the *Nuclear Weapons* case to the effect that 'the conclusion that humanitarian law did not apply to such weapons "would be incompatible with the intrinsically humanitarian character of the legal principles in question which permeates the entire law of armed conflict and applies to all forms of warfare and to all kinds of weapons, those of the past, those of

Replying to communications concerning the use of cluster munitions in Iraq, the Prosecutor recalled that 'their use *per se* does not constitute a war crime under the Rome Statute'.[285] He stressed that a war crime could nevertheless be established in the case of the use of cluster bombs to the extent they are employed in a manner satisfying the elements of other war crimes. He proposed to consider the use of cluster munitions within the framework of other provisions of Article 8(2)(b), which deal with indiscriminate attacks and disproportionate harm to civilians. He noted that the United Kingdom Ministry of Defence claimed that nearly 85 per cent of weapons released by its aircraft were precision-guided, 'a figure which would tend to corroborate effort to minimize casualties'.[286] It is an odd comment. Article 8(2)(b)(iv) talks about an intentional attack committed with knowledge of clearly excessive collateral damage. Use of targeted weapons can hardly be a defence to such a charge.

As with crimes against humanity, the 'laws and customs of war' provision significantly develops the area of sexual offences. The text is essentially new law.[287] It prohibits rape, sexual slavery, enforced prostitution, forced pregnancy, enforced sterilization or any other form of sexual violence also constituting a grave breach of the Geneva Conventions. Another provision consisting of new law makes it a crime to conscript or enlist children under the age of fifteen into the national armed forces or to use them to participate actively in hostilities. This wording is drawn from the 1989 Convention on the Rights of the Child[288] as well as from Additional Protocol I.[289] The term 'recruiting' appeared in an earlier draft, but was replaced with 'conscripting or enlisting' to suggest

the present and those of the future'". See also the statement by Sweden. France, on the other hand, issued a declaration on the same subject at the time of ratification: 'The provisions of Article 8 of the Statute, in particular paragraph 2(b) thereof, relate solely to conventional weapons and can neither regulate nor prohibit the possible use of nuclear weapons nor impair the other rules of international law applicable to other weapons necessary to the exercise by France of its inherent right of self-defence, unless nuclear weapons or the other weapons referred to herein become subject in the future to a comprehensive ban and are specified in an annex to the Statute by means of an amendment adopted in accordance with the provisions of articles 121 and 123.' The United Kingdom was only slightly more circumspect, referring to statements that it had made at the time of ratification of humanitarian treaties that, in effect, reserve the possibility of using nuclear weapons.

[285] Letter of Prosecutor dated 9 February 2006 (Iraq), p. 5.

[286] *Ibid.*, p. 7.   [287] Rome Statute, Art. 8(2)(b)(xxii).

[288] Convention on the Rights of the Child, GA Res. 44/25, Annex, Art. 38.

[289] Protocol Additional to the 1949 Geneva Conventions of 12 August 1949, and Relating to the Protection of Victims of International Armed Conflicts, (1979) 1125 UNTS 3, Art. 77(2).

something more passive, such as putting the name of a person on a list. Secondly, the word 'national' was added before 'armed forces' to allay concerns of several Arab States who feared that the term might cover young Palestinians joining the *intifadah* revolt.[290] Interestingly, the provision in the Convention on the Rights of the Child has been deemed too moderate by many States. In May 2000, the United Nations General Assembly adopted a protocol to the Convention increasing the age to eighteen.

Thomas Lubanga Dyilo, the first accused person to appear before the Court, was charged pursuant to these provisions, as well as equivalent crimes listed in the portions of Article 8 concerning non-international armed conflict. In the arrest warrant, the charges were phrased in the alternative, making a determination of whether the conflict in the Democratic Republic of the Congo was international or non-international of little importance in the prosecution.[291] However, months after the arrest when it issued the document containing the charges, the Office of the Prosecutor took the position that the conflict was purely non-international in nature, and withdrew the charge based upon Article 8(2)(b).[292] The Pre-Trial Chamber disagreed, and reinstated the charges concerning enlistment, conscription and active use of child soldiers in an international armed conflict.[293]

This was not, however, the first international prosecution based on the relevant provisions in the Rome Statute. The Special Court for Sierra Leone, parts of whose Statute are derived from Article 8 of the Rome Statute, including the child soldier offences, has conducted trials for such crimes. When the Statute of the Special Court for Sierra Leone was being drafted, in 2000 and 2001, the Secretary-General of the United Nations opposed reproducing the child soldier enlistment provisions of the Rome Statute. He said these had a 'doubtful customary nature',[294] and that it was preferable to criminalize the acts of '[a]bduction and

---

[290] Hermann von Hebel and Daryl Robinson, 'Crimes within the Jurisdiction of the Court', in Roy S. Lee, ed., *The International Criminal Court: The Making of the Rome Statute: Issues, Negotiations, and Results*, The Hague: Kluwer Law International, 1999, pp. 79–126 at p. 118.

[291] *Lubanga* (ICC-01/04–01/06), Mandat d'arrêt, 10 February 2006.

[292] *Lubanga* (ICC-01/04–01/06), Document Containing the Charges, Article 61(3)(a), 28 August 2006, para. 7.

[293] *Lubanga* (ICC-01/04–01/06), Decision on the Confirmation of the Charges, 29 January 2007, p. 132.

[294] Report of the Secretary-General on the Establishment of a Special Court for Sierra Leone, UN Doc. S/2000/915, para. 18.

forced recruitment of children under the age of 15 years'.[295] According
to the Secretary-General: 'While the definition of the crime as "conscripting" or "enlisting" connotes an administrative act of putting one's
name on a list and formal entry into the armed forces, the elements of
the crime under the proposed Statute of the Special Court are: (a) abduction, which in the case of the children of Sierra Leone was the original
crime and is in itself a crime under common Article 3 of the Geneva
Conventions; (b) forced recruitment in the most general sense – administrative formalities, obviously, notwithstanding; and (c) transformation
of the child into, and its use as, among other degrading uses, a "child-
combatant".'[296] The Security Council disagreed, and insisted that Article
4(c) of the Statute of the Special Court for Sierra Leone be modified 'so
as to conform it to the statement of the law existing in 1996 and as currently accepted by the international community',[297] in other words, to
the text found in the Rome Statute.

The Appeals Chamber of the Special Court for Sierra Leone dismissed
a defence challenge arguing that the child soldier provisions should not
apply to acts perpetrated prior to 17 July 1998, the date the Rome Statute
was adopted, on the grounds that they could not be considered to be
part of customary law and that therefore a prosecution would breach the
prohibition of retroactive criminal punishment (*nullum crimen nulla
poena sine lege*).[298] Judge Geoffrey Robertson preferred the reasoning of
the Secretary-General at the time the Statute was drafted, and issued a
dissenting opinion:

> It might strike some as odd that the state of international law in 1996
> in respect to criminalization of child soldiers was doubtful to the UN
> Secretary-General but very clear to the President of the Security Council
> only two months later. If it was not clear to the Secretary-General and
> his legal advisors that international law had by 1996 criminalized the
> enlistment of child soldiers, could it really have been any clearer to Chief
> Hinga Norman or any other defendant at that time, embattled in Sierra
> Leone?[299]

---

[295] *Ibid.*, p. 22.   [296] *Ibid.*, para. 18.
[297] Letter dated 22 December 2000 from the President of the Security Council addressed to
the Secretary-General, UN Doc. S/2000/1234, p. 2.
[298] *Norman* (SCSL-04-14-AR72(E)), Decision on Preliminary Motion Based on Lack of
Jurisdiction (Child Recruitment), 31 May 2004.
[299] *Norman* (SCSL-04-14-AR72(E)), Dissenting Opinion of Justice Robertson, 31 May
2004, para. 6. Among the authorities Judge Robertson invoked was the opinion stated
in the previous paragraph of the first edition of this work, describing the child soldier
provisions as 'new law' (at para. 32).

The terms 'enlistment' and 'conscription' are employed in the Rome Statute, rather than 'recruitment', which appears in international human rights law.[300] According to Pre-Trial Chamber I, 'conscription' and 'enlistment' are two forms of recruitment, the former involving compulsion and the latter being essentially voluntary.[301] As for 'active participation', Pre-Trial Chamber I said this required a link to the hostilities. Delivery of food to an air force base, or use of children as domestics in married officers' quarters, would not be a punishable crime under this provision.[302]

The two succeeding categories of war crimes in Article 8, defined in subparagraphs (2)(c) and 2(e), apply to non-international armed conflict, a far more controversial area of international law, at least in an historical sense. As early as 1949, and even before, States were prepared to recognize international legal obligations, including international criminal responsibility, arising between them. However, they were far more hesitant when it came to internal conflict or civil war, which many considered to be nobody's business but their own. In the *Tadić* jurisdictional decision, the Appeals Chamber of the International Criminal Tribunal for the former Yugoslavia pointed to evidence that atrocities committed in internal armed conflict had been proscribed by international law as early as the terror bombing of civilians during the Spanish Civil War.[303] The 1949 Geneva Conventions refer to non-international armed conflict in only one provision, known as 'common Article 3' because it is identical in all four Conventions. Attempts to expand the scope of common Article 3 in 1977, by the adoption of Additional Protocol II, were only moderately successful.[304] The Protocol elaborates somewhat on the laconic terms of common Article 3, but does not extend the concept of

---

[300] Convention on the Rights of the Child, UN Doc. A/RES/44/25, Annex, Art. 38(3); Optional Protocol to the Convention on the Rights of the Child on the Involvement of Children in Armed Conflicts, UN Doc. A/RES/54/263, Annex.

[301] *Lubanga* (ICC-01/04–01/06), Decision on the Confirmation of the Charges, 29 January 2007, para. 246. The Pre-Trial Chamber endorsed the detailed discussion of the provision in *Norman* (SCSL-04-14-AR72(E)), Dissenting Opinion of Justice Robertson, 31 May 2004.

[302] *Lubanga* (ICC-01/04–01/06), Decision on the Confirmation of the Charges, 29 January 2007, para. 262.

[303] *Tadić* (IT-94-1-AR72), Decision on the Defence Motion for Interlocutory Appeal on Jurisdiction, 2 October 1995, paras. 100–1. See also *Strugar et al.* (IT-01-42-PT), Decision on Defence Preliminary Motion Challenging Jurisdiction, 7 June 2002, para. 13.

[304] Protocol Additional II to the 1949 Geneva Conventions and Relating to the Protection of Victims of Non-International Armed Conflicts, (1979) 1125 UNTS 3.

'grave breaches' to non-international armed conflict, nor does it recognize prisoner of war status in such wars.

Therefore, subject to a few minor exceptions, paragraphs (c) and (d) of Article 8(2) apply to non-international armed conflicts contemplated by common Article 3 of the four Geneva Conventions, while paragraphs (e) and (f) apply to non-international armed conflicts within the scope of Additional Protocol II. The threshold of application of common Article 3 is somewhat lower. The scope of both provisions is limited in a negative sense, it being stated that they apply to armed conflicts not of an international character, but not 'to situations of internal disturbances and tensions, such as riots, isolated and sporadic acts of violence or other acts of a similar nature'. But the Additional Protocol II crimes listed in paragraph (e) apply to 'armed conflicts that take place in the territory of a State when there is protracted armed conflict between governmental authorities and organized armed groups or between such groups'. The slight difference between these two thresholds has been a matter of considerable debate, and the better view would seem to be that there are no material distinctions between them.[305] According to Theodor Meron:

> The reference to protracted armed conflict was designed to give some satisfaction to those delegations that insisted on the incorporation of the higher threshold of applicability of Article 1(1) of Additional Protocol II. It may be noted that this language tracks language contained in paragraph 70 of the *Tadić* decision on interlocutory appeal on jurisdiction of the ICTY (2 October 1995). Attempts to interpret protracted armed conflict as recognizing an additional high threshold of application should be resisted.[306]

---

[305] In fact, Art. 8(2)(e) of the Rome Statute appears to be slightly broader than Additional Protocol II, in requiring that the conflict be 'protracted', whereas the Protocol requires rebels to control territory. However, the two thresholds in the Statute concerning non-international armed conflict, described in subparagraphs (2)(d) and (f), do not have any material differences. I am grateful to Anthony Cullen, one of my PhD students, for explaining this to me. Pre-Trial Chamber I appeared to take this approach in *Lubanga* (ICC-01/04–01/06), Decision on the Confirmation of the Charges, 29 January 2007, paras. 229–37. See Anthony Cullen, 'The Definition of Non-International Armed Conflict in the Rome Statute of the International Criminal Court: An Analysis of the Threshold of Application Contained in Article 8(2)(f)', (2008) 12 *Journal of Conflict and Security Law* 419; and Anthony Cullen, *The Concept of Non-International Armed Conflict in International Humanitarian Law*, Cambridge: Cambridge University Press, 2010.

[306] Theodor Meron, 'Crimes under the Jurisdiction of the International Criminal Court', in Herman von Hebel, Johan G. Lammers and Jolien Schukking, eds., *Reflections on the International Criminal Court: Essays in Honour of Adriaan Bos*, The Hague: T. M. C.

There is a further limitation on the common Article 3 crimes: 'Nothing in paragraphs 2(c) and (d) shall affect the responsibility of a Government to maintain or re-establish law and order in the State or to defend the unity and territorial integrity of the State, by all legitimate means.' These thresholds, drawn from the Geneva Conventions and Additional Protocol II, have been constantly criticized for their narrow scope. In effect, in cases of internal disturbances and tensions, atrocities may be punishable as crimes against humanity but they will not be punishable, at least by the International Criminal Court, as war crimes.

The common Article 3 crimes listed in paragraph (c), like the 'grave breaches' in paragraph (a), must be committed against 'protected persons'. The latter are defined, for the purposes of common Article 3, as 'persons taking no active part in the hostilities, including members of armed forces who have laid down their arms and those placed *hors de combat* by sickness, wounds, detention or any other cause'. The punishable acts consist of murder, mutilation, cruel treatment and torture, outrages upon personal dignity, taking of hostages and summary executions. They represent, in reality, a common denominator of core human rights. The International Committee of the Red Cross has often described common Article 3 as a 'mini-convention' of the laws applicable to non-international armed conflict. According to the Appeals Chamber of the International Criminal Tribunal for the former Yugoslavia, the rules contained in common Article 3 are the 'quintessence' of the humanitarian norms contained in the Geneva Conventions as a whole. They 'also constitute a minimum yardstick, in addition to the more elaborate rules which are also to apply to international conflicts; and they are rules which, in the Court's opinion, reflect what the [International Court of Justice] in 1949 called "elementary considerations of humanity"'.[307]

The crimes listed in paragraph (e) are largely drawn from Additional Protocol II, and address attacks that are intentionally directed against civilians, culturally significant buildings, hospitals and Red Cross and Red Crescent units and other humanitarian workers such as peacekeeping missions. Nevertheless, not all serious violations of Additional Protocol II are included in Article 8 of the Statute.[308] A detailed

---

Asser, 1999, pp. 47–56 at p. 54. Also Michael Bothe, 'War Crimes', in Cassese, *The Rome Statute*, pp. 379–426 at p. 423.

[307] *Delalić et al.* (IT-96-21-A), Judgment, 20 February 2001, para. 140.

[308] For a discussion on these omissions in the sessions of the Preparatory Committee, see Christopher Keith Hall, 'The Fifth Session of the UN Preparatory Committee on the Establishment of an International Criminal Court', (1998) 92 *American Journal*

codification of sexual or gender crimes, similar to the one in paragraph (b), is also included. There is a prohibition on child soldiers under the age of fifteen. It has an equivalent provision in Article 8(2)(b), making the norm seamless as far as any distinction between international and non-international armed conflict might be argued by a future accused. The crime has been charged in the first case to proceed before the Court, where the accused is charged in the alternative under the two provisions.[309] A number of offences concern the conduct of belligerents amongst themselves that echo the provisions applicable to international armed conflict.

In addition to the *Lubanga* prosecution for enlistment, conscription and active use of child soldiers, the arrest warrants issued so far by the Court contain several counts of war crimes alleged to have been committed in non-international armed conflict. These relate to the civil war in northern Uganda. Joseph Kony was charged with murder (Art. 8(2)(c)(i)), cruel treatment of civilians (Art. 8(2)(c)(i)), intentionally directing an attack against a civilian population (Art. 8(2)(e)(i)), pillaging (Art. 8(2)(e)(v)), inducing rape (Art. 8(2)(e)(vi)), and the forced enlisting of children (Art. 8(2)(e)(vii)). Vincent Otti was charged with murder (Art. 8(2)(c)(i)), cruel treatment of civilians (Art. 8(2)(c)(i)), intentionally directing an attack against a civilian population (Art. 8(2)(e)(i)), pillaging (Art. 8(2)(e)(v)) and the forced enlisting of children (Art. 8(2)(e)(vii)). Okot Odhiambo was charged with murder (Art. 8(2)(c)(i)), intentionally directing an attack against a civilian population (Art. 8(2)(e)(i)), pillaging (Art. 8(2)(e)(v)) and the forced enlisting of children (Art. 8(2)(e)(vii)). Dominic Ongwen and Raska Lukwiya are charged with cruel treatment of civilians (Art. 8(2)(c)(i)), intentionally directing an attack against a civilian population (Art. 8(2)(e)(i)) and pillaging (Art. 8(2)(e)(v)).

Even a casual glance at the war crime provisions reveals that those applicable to non-international armed conflict are significantly shorter than the list that pertains to international armed conflict. In particular, there are no provisions dealing with the use of prohibited weapons in non-international armed conflict. At the 2010 Review Conference, three paragraphs were added to Article 8(2)(e) that correspond to Articles

---

of International Law 331 at 336; and Christopher Keith Hall, 'The Third and Fourth Sessions of the UN Preparatory Committee on the Establishment of an International Criminal Court', (1998) 92 *American Journal of International Law* 124.

[309] The *Lubanga* prosecution for enlistment of child soldiers is discussed earlier in this section, under international armed conflict.

8(2)(b)(xvii), (xviii) and (xix), creating a symmetry between the texts governing non-international and international armed conflict with respect to three categories of prohibited weapons. These are the categories upon which States have been able to agreement, and are based on relatively ancient norms, such as the prohibition of the use of poison weapons and dum-dum bullets. Unfortunately, it seems impossible to go further, and extend this category of crimes to cover the more devastating forms of modern-day weapons such as anti-personnel mines and cluster munitions. At the 2010 Review Conference, some States insisted on a distinction between international armed conflict and non-international armed conflict, to the extent that law enforcement authorities may use hollow-tipped bullets in order to avoid collateral damage. Thus, weapons deemed to cause unnecessary suffering and superfluous harm on the battlefield of an international armed conflict may actually serve a humanitarian purpose in a hostage-taking or similar circumstance. As a result, understandings were included at the time the 2010 amendments were adopted.[310]

The crime of aggression

The crime of aggression is defined in Article 8*bis* of the Rome Statute, a provision that was adopted at the 2010 Review Conference. It must be read together with Articles 15*bis* and 15*ter*, which govern the exercise of jurisdiction over the crime of aggression. Until the final minutes of the Review Conference, the fate of the proposed amendments remained uncertain. Ultimately, the two permanent members of the Security Council who had been most steadfastly opposed to the new provisions to the extent that they encroached upon the prerogatives of the Council, the United Kingdom and France, joined the consensus of the other delegations. The amendments represent a singular achievement that confirms the continuing dynamism of the Court. They return to the logic of the Nuremberg trial, where the judges wrote:

> War is essentially an evil thing. Its consequences are not confined to the belligerent states alone, but affect the whole world. To initiate a war of aggression, therefore, is not only an international crime; it is the supreme international crime differing only from other war crimes in that it contains within itself the accumulated evil of the whole.[311]

---

[310] Resolution Amending Article 8 of the Rome Statute, RC/DC/1/Add.1, PP10.

[311] *France et al.* v. *Goering et al.*, (1946) 22 IMT 203 at 427.

During the drafting of the Rome Statute, it was principally the non-aligned countries who insisted that aggression remain within the jurisdiction of the Court. These States pursued a 'compromise on the addition of aggression as a generic crime pending the definition of its elements by a preparatory committee or a review conference at a later stage'.[312] The Bureau of the Rome Conference suggested, on 10 July 1998, that, if generally acceptable provisions and definitions were not developed forthwith, aggression would have to be dropped from the Statute.[313] This provoked much discontent among the delegates, and forced the Bureau to reconsider the matter.[314] Literally on the final day of the conference, agreement was reached that authorized the Court to exercise jurisdiction over aggression once the crime is defined and its scope designated in a manner consistent with the purposes of the Statute and the ideals of the United Nations. Article 5(1)(d) of the Statute lists 'the crime of aggression' as one of four crimes within the jurisdiction of the Court. But it must be read with paragraph 2 of that provision:

> The Court shall exercise jurisdiction over the crime of aggression once a provision is adopted in accordance with articles 121 and 123 defining the crime and setting out the conditions under which the Court shall exercise jurisdiction with respect to this crime. Such a provision shall be consistent with the relevant provisions of the Charter of the United Nations.

The 2010 amendments were added to the Statute in pursuit of the objective set in Article 5(2). Article 5(2) is deleted from the Statute by the 2010 amendments.

Prosecutions for 'crimes against peace', a more ancient term used to describe the concept of aggression, were undertaken at Nuremberg and Tokyo.[315] During the Rome Conference, both German and Japanese

---

[312] *Terraviva*, 13 July 1998, No. 21, p. 2; UN Press Release L/ROM/16, 13 July 1998.

[313] UN Doc. A/CONF.183/C.1/L.59.

[314] See, e.g., UN Doc. A/CONF.183/C.1/SR.33, para. 17 (Movement of Non-Aligned Countries), para. 29 (Syria), para. 63 (Ghana), para. 73 (Germany); UN Doc. A/CONF.183/C.1/SR.34, para. 9 (Trinidad and Tobago), para. 43 (Azerbaijan), para. 54 (Southern African Development Community), para. 61 (Iran), para. 68 (Cuba), para. 72 (Jordan), para. 94 (Sudan), para. 98 (Poland); UN Doc. A/CONF.183/C.1/SR.35, para. 1 (Egypt), para. 10 (Greece), para. 12 (Nigeria), para. 18 (Tunisia), para. 29 (Afghanistan), para. 30 (Algeria), para. 33 (Indonesia), para. 47 (Tanzania), para. 57 (Qatar), para. 58 (Philippines), para. 64 (Iraq), para. 70 (Mozambique), para. 83 (Madagascar); UN Doc. A/CONF.183/C.1/SR.36, para. 9 (Angola), para. 11 (Congo), para. 19 (Oman), para. 27 (Malta), para. 32 (Zimbabwe), para. 38 (Bolivia), para. 45 (Cameroon).

[315] See Historical Review of Developments Relating to Aggression, PCNICC/2002/SGCA/L.1 and Add.1.

delegations insisted that aggression be included, expressing bewilder-
ment over the fact that it had been an international crime in 1945 –
indeed, the supreme international crime, according to the Nuremberg
Tribunal – yet seemed to be one of only secondary importance half a
century later.[316] In the early years of the international criminal court
project, difficulties in subsequent definition of aggression led to a suspension of the work of the International Law Commission on the Code
of Crimes in 1954. A definition was eventually adopted by the General
Assembly in the early 1970s.[317] Nevertheless, the General Assembly
resolution was not designed as an instrument of criminal prosecution,
although it provides a useful starting point in the question for definition
of 'the crime of aggression'.[318] Because it had been prosecuted successfully at Nuremberg and Tokyo, there can be no doubt that the crime of
aggression forms part of customary international law. In 2003, in his
opinion to British Prime Minister Tony Blair on the legal issues involved
in invading Iraq, Attorney General Goldsmith warned of possible prosecution for the crime of aggression, which he recalled was recognized
customary international law and which therefore automatically formed
part of the country's domestic law.[319] The British House of Lords, in R. v.
Jones, later confirmed that the crime of aggression formed part of customary international law.[320]

Early in the sessions of the Preparatory Commission, a Working
Group on aggression was set up, and it met throughout the life of the
Commission in an effort to make progress on the matter. Its work was then
continued by the Special Working Group on the Crime of Aggression,
which was set up under the authority of the Assembly of States Parties.
The final report of the Special Working Group was delivered in 2009.[321]

---

[316] Report of the Ad Hoc Committee on the Establishment of an International Criminal
    Court, UN Doc. A/50/22, paras. 63–71; Report of the Preparatory Committee on
    the Establishment of an International Criminal Court, UN Doc. A/51/22, vol. I,
    paras. 65–73.
[317] GA Res. 3314 (XXIX) (1974).
[318] Lyal S. Sunga, 'The Crimes within the Jurisdiction of the International Criminal Court
    (Part II, Articles 5–10)', (1998) 6 European Journal of Crime, Criminal Law and Criminal
    Justice 61 at 65.
[319] Lord Goldsmith, Attorney General, Iraq: Resolution 1441, 7 March 2003, para. 34.
[320] R. v. Jones et al. [2006] UKHL 16.
[321] Report of the Special Working Group on the Crime of Aggression, ASP/7/SWGCA/2.
    The work of the Special Working Group generated a great deal of academic com-
    mentary, including Roger S. Clark, 'The Crime of Aggression', in Carsten Stahn and
    Goran Sluiter, The Emerging Practice of the International Criminal Court, Leiden: Brill,
    2009, pp. 709–23; Roger S. Clark, 'The Crime of Aggression and the International

Its tireless work over nearly a decade had resulted in the clarification of a number of issues as well as the identification of questions that remained unresolved, requiring a political solution at the Review Conference. In particular, the definition of the crime of aggression that it had developed was deemed acceptable by the Review Conference, and was adopted without change. The issues relating to the exercise of jurisdiction and to the entry into force of the amendments were more challenging. New approaches emerged at the Review Conference that were eventually part of the final compromise.

The definition of aggression in Article 8*bis* of the Rome Statute results from a combination of two approaches, deemed 'generic' and 'specific'. In this sense, it resembles the structure of the definitions of genocide and crimes against humanity. Paragraph 1 provides a generic definition of the crime, while paragraph 2 sets out a list of specific acts. The list is reproduced from General Assembly Resolution 3314(XXIX). Article 8*bis*(1) limits the perpetration of the crime of aggression to 'a person in a position effectively to exercise control over or to direct the political or military action of a State'. The same principle reappears in Article 25(3)*bis*, which was also adopted as part of the 2010 amendments: 'In respect of the crime of aggression, the provisions of this article shall apply only to persons in a position effectively to exercise control over or to direct the political or military action of a State.' None of the other crimes in the Rome Statute limits the notion of perpetrators in this way. Indeed, the defence of superior orders is specifically excluded for the

Criminal Court', in José Doria, Hans-Peter Gasser and M. Cherif Bassiouni, eds., *The Legal Regime of the International Criminal Court: Essays in Honour of Professor Igor Blishchenko*, Leiden and Boston: Martinus Nijhoff, 2009, pp. 661–99; Astrid Reisinger Coracini, 'Evaluating Domestic Legislation on the Customary Crime of Aggression under the Rome Statute's Complementarity Regime', in Carsten Stahn and Goran Sluiter, *The Emerging Practice of the International Criminal Court*, Leiden: Brill, 2009, pp. 725–54; Mauro Politi and Giuseppe Nesi, *The International Criminal Court and the Crime of Aggression*, Aldershot: Ashgate, 2004; Sergey Sayapin, 'The Definition of the Crime of Aggression for the Purpose of the International Criminal Court: Problems and Perspectives', (2008) 13 *Journal of Conflict and Security Law* 333; Robert Schaeffer, 'The Audacity of Compromise: The UN Security Council and the Pre-conditions to the Exercise of Jurisdiction by the ICC with Regard to the Crime of Aggression', (2009) 9 *International Criminal Law Review* 411; Anja Seibert-Fohr, 'Das Verbrechen der Aggression im Rom-Statut: Fragen der Vertragsänderung und Jurisdiktion', (2008) 8 *Zeitschrift für Internationale Strafrechtsdogmatik* 361; Nicolaos Strapatsas, 'Rethinking General Assembly Resolution 3314 (1974) as a Basis for the Definition of Aggression Under the Rome Statute of the ICC', in Olaoluwa Olusanya, ed., *Rethinking International Criminal Law: The Substantive Part*, Groningen: Europa Law, 2007, pp. 155–79; Noah Weisbord, 'Prosecuting Aggression', (2008) 49 *Harvard International Law Journal* 161.

other crimes by Article 33. Presumably, Article 33 is irrelevant to the prosecution of aggression because of its limitation to the political and military leadership.

The leadership requirement probably has the consequence of excluding accomplices, such as powerful allies of a small State that would encourage it to attack another country in what could be little more than a proxy war. For example, the occupation of East Timor by Indonesia in 1974 might readily meet the proposed definition of aggression. It is widely believed to have been conducted at the instigation of United States President Gerald Ford and Secretary of State Henry Kissinger, who visited Jakarta only hours before the attack and apparently authorized it to proceed.[322] It is a shame if the Rome Statute appears to exclude similar cases of incitement or abetting of aggression, which are ordinarily punishable with respect to the other crimes within the Court's jurisdiction.

The other important limitation in Article 8*bis*(1) is the requirement that an act of aggression 'by its character, gravity and scale, constitutes a manifest violation of the Charter of the United Nations'. This is completed by two paragraphs in the Elements of Crimes: '3. The term "manifest" is an objective qualification. 4. There is no requirement to prove that the perpetrator has made a legal evaluation as to the "manifest" nature of the violation of the Charter of the United Nations.' Finally, at the Review Conference, two understandings were reached that are relevant to this issue:

1. It is understood that aggression is the most serious and dangerous form of the illegal use of force; and that a determination whether an act of aggression has been committed requires consideration of all the circumstances of each particular case, including the gravity of the acts concerned and their consequences, in accordance with the Charter of the United Nations.

2. It is understood that in establishing whether an act of aggression constitutes a manifest violation of the Charter of the United Nations, the three components of character, gravity and scale must be sufficient to justify a 'manifest' determination. No one component can be significant enough to satisfy the manifest standard by itself.

The United States had submitted a much longer list of understandings, its intention being to further narrow the scope of the definition and in particular to carve out a justification for aggression when allegedly

---

[322] See Christopher Hitchens, *The Trial of Henry Kissinger*, New York: Verso Books, 2002.

conducted for humanitarian purposes, but these were not acceptable to most States. The language in Understanding 6 is derived from General Assembly Resolution 3314(XXX). The version proposed by the Americans also contained a phrase referring to the purpose of the aggression, but was quickly withdrawn by the United States when delegates pointed out that Resolution 3314 contained no such language. A proposal from Iran to include a reference to the Charter was graciously accepted by the United States.

The reference, in Article 5(2) of the Rome Statute, to the fact that the definition 'shall be consistent with the relevant provisions of the Charter of the United Nations' was a 'carefully constructed phrase' that was 'understood as a reference to the role the Council may or should play'.[323] The underlying issue is the fact that Article 39 of the Charter of the United Nations declares that determining situations of aggression falls to the Security Council: 'The Security Council shall determine the existence of any threat to the peace, breach of the peace, or act of aggression'. In the final session of the Rome Conference, the British representative said that 'the United Kingdom interpreted the reference to aggression in Article 5 and, in particular, the last sentence of paragraph 2 of that article, which mentioned the Charter of the United Nations, as a reference to the requirement of prior determination by the Security Council that an act of aggression had occurred'.[324] During the Review Conference, the permanent members of the Security Council returned again and again to Article 39, insisting that the only way that jurisdiction over aggression could be exercised was with the prior authorization of the Council.

It has often been noted that, although the Security Council's role in this issue is uncontested, this does not preclude other bodies from making such determinations. It would seem, for example, that the International Court of Justice may make a determination that an act of aggression has been committed. In his Separate Opinion in the case of *Congo* v. *Uganda*, Judge Bruno Simma wrote:

> It is true that the United Nations Security Council, despite adopting
> a whole series of resolutions on the situation in the Great Lakes region

---

[323] Hermann von Hebel and Daryl Robinson, 'Crimes within the Jurisdiction of the Court', in Roy S. Lee, ed., *The International Criminal Court: The Making of the Rome Statute: Issues, Negotiations, and Results*, The Hague: Kluwer Law International, 1999, pp. 79–126 at p. 85.

[324] UN Doc. A/CONF.183/SR.9, para. 51.

(cf. paragraph 150 of the Judgment) has never gone as far as expressly qualifying the Ugandan invasion as an act of aggression, even though it must appear as a textbook example of the first one of the definitions of 'this most serious and dangerous form of the illegal use of force' laid down in General Assembly resolution 3314 (XXIX). The Council will have had its own – political – reasons for refraining from such a determination. But the Court, as the principal *judicial* organ of the United Nations, does not have to follow that course. Its very raison d'être is to arrive at decisions based on law and nothing but the law, keeping the political context of the cases before it in mind, of course, but not desisting from stating what is manifest out of regard for such non-legal considerations. This is the division of labour between the Court and the political organs of the United Nations envisaged by the Charter![325]

Leaving the Security Council as the arbiter of situations of aggression implies that the Court can only prosecute aggression once the Council has pronounced on the subject. Such a view seems an incredible encroachment upon the independence of the Court, and would almost certainly mean, for starters, that no permanent member of the Security Council would ever be subject to prosecution for aggression.[326] Moreover, no Court can leave determination of such a central factual issue to what is essentially a political body. As Judge Schwebel of the International Court of Justice noted, a Security Council determination of aggression is not a legal assessment but is based on political considerations. The Security Council is not acting as a court.[327]

The Review Conference rejected the view that there is a Security Council monopoly on determination of acts of aggression. It divided the process into two distinct provisions. Article 15*ter* governs referral to the Court by the Security Council, while Article 15*bis* applies to referral to the Court by a State Party or the exercise of jurisdiction at the initiative of the Prosecutor acting *proprio motu*. There is a form of priority given to the Security Council, in that, before proceeding on his own, the Prosecutor must first verify whether the Security Council has yet determined that an act of aggression has taken place. If it has not, the

---

[325] *Case Concerning Armed Activities on the Territory of the Congo (Democratic Republic of the Congo v. Uganda)*, 19 December 2005, Separate Opinion of Judge Simma, para. 3. See also Separate Opinion of Judge Elaraby.

[326] Lionel Yee, 'The International Criminal Court and the Security Council: Articles 13(b) and 16', in Lee, *The International Criminal Court*, pp. 143–52 at pp. 144–5.

[327] *Military and Paramilitary Activities in and Against Nicaragua (Nicaragua v. United States)*, Merits, [1986] ICJ Reports 14 at 290.

Prosecutor must then wait six months before taking further action.[328] The Security Council may also block prosecution by invoking Article 16 of the Statute. Accepting this priority for the Security Council represented a major concession by many States; on the other hand, when the United Kingdom and France joined consensus at the Review Conference in the adoption of Article 8*bis*, they too were effecting a dramatic shift in their position on the prerogatives of the Security Council.

If prosecution for the crime of aggression is triggered by a State Party or results from the Prosecutor exercising *proprio motu* authority, there is a so-called 'jurisdictional filter'. The Pre-Trial Division must authorize the commencement of the investigation. This is similar to the mechanism that applies to *proprio motu* prosecution for the other three crimes pursuant to Article 15 of the Statute, the only difference being that in the case of aggression the task belongs not to the Pre-Trial Chamber, which is composed of three judges, but to the Division, which has a minimum of six judges.[329] Indeed, Article 15*bis* explicitly references Article 15.

Although the problem may have been underestimated during the work of the Special Working Group, the question of entry into force of the amendments took on a central role in the negotiations at the Review Conference. The amending process is governed by Article 121. It states a general rule, by which amendments to the Statute enter into force when they have been ratified or accepted by seven-eighths of the States Parties.[330] A special norm applies to amendments to the subject-matter jurisdiction: amendments to the crimes themselves enter into force for a State that ratifies or accepts the amendment, making that State's nationals subject to prosecution; otherwise, nationals of States Parties that do not accept the amendments are immunized from prosecution for the crimes contained therein, even when committed on the territory of a State Party that has ratified or accepted the amendment. Moreover, on a literal reading of Article 121(5), the nationals of a non-party State seem to be exposed to prosecution for the new crime when committed on the territory of the State Party that has ratified or accepted the amendment. This has the consequence of sheltering the nationals of a State Party that does not ratify or accept an amendment, but not those of a non-party State. Some have said this was intended as an incentive to States to join the Court. Others consider it to be an incoherent result of the last chaotic days of the Rome Conference, when the text of Article 121(5) emerged.

---

[328] Rome Statute, Art. 15*bis*(6), (7), (8).   [329] *Ibid.*, Art. 39(1).
[330] *Ibid.*, Art. 121(4).

The 2010 amendments adopt what can only be described as a *sui generis* approach to entry into force. On the one hand, the resolution to which the amendments are annexed states that they are to enter into force 'in accordance with article 121, paragraph 5'. Confirming the so-called 'negative understanding' of Article 121(5), the amendments specify that they are without application to the nationals or the territory of a non-party State.[331] Thus, while the nationals of a non-party State are immunized from prosecution, even for aggression committed against a State Party, they are not protected if attacked by a State Party to which the amendment applies. This should be an incentive for non-party States to join the Court. If an act of aggression is committed by a State Party (against another State Party), the Court may exercise jurisdiction unless the aggressor State has previously made a declaration that it does not accept the jurisdiction of the Court over the crime of aggression.[332] This reflects the 'positive understanding' of Article 121(5). Although the amendment itself does not make this clear, the resolution adopted at the Review Conference specifies that 'any State Party may lodge a declaration referred to in article 15*bis* prior to ratification or acceptance'.[333]

There are some further layers of complexity to the entry into force process. The Court may only exercise jurisdiction once the amendment has been ratified or accepted by thirty States Parties.[334] Moreover, the Court may not exercise jurisdiction until 1 January 2017, and only then if two-thirds of the States Parties take a decision to this effect.[335] This delayed entry into force provision was the final compromise at the 2010 Review Conference. An Understanding adopted at the Review Conference specifies that, where prosecution is based upon referral by a State Party or the *proprio motu* authority of the Prosecutor, this applies 'only with respect to crimes of aggression committed after a decision in accordance with article 15*bis*, paragraph 3 is taken, and one year after the ratification or acceptance of the amendments by thirty States Parties, whichever is later'.[336]

This *sui generis* regime for entry into force is fully applicable in the case of referral by a State Party or exercise of *proprio motu* authority by the Prosecutor. However, in the case of Security Council referral, an

---

[331] *Ibid.*, Art. 15*bis*(5).   [332] *Ibid.*, Art. 15*bis*(4).
[333] The Crime of Aggression, RC/Res.4.   [334] Rome Statute, Arts. 15*bis*(2) and 15*ter*(2).
[335] *Ibid.*, Arts. 15*bis*(3) and 15*ter*(3).
[336] Understandings Regarding the Amendments to the Rome Statute of the International Criminal Court on the Crime of Aggression, RC/10/Add.1, para. 3.

Understanding adopted as part of the amending process declares: 'It is understood that the Court shall exercise jurisdiction over the crime of aggression on the basis of a Security Council referral in accordance with article 13, paragraph (b), of the Statute irrespective of whether the State concerned has accepted the Court's jurisdiction in this regard.' This makes the issue of ratification or acceptance of the amendments, and the opt-out declaration contemplated by Article 15*bis*(4), by the aggressor State irrelevant to Security Council referral. Indeed, Security Council referral may also cover aggression by a non-party State. It would seem, therefore, that the only requirement for the entry into force of the Security Council referral provisions in Article 15*ter* is ratification or acceptance by thirty States[337] and the decision to be taken by two-thirds of States Parties after 1 January 2017.[338] This is inconsistent with both paragraphs 4 and 5 of Article 121 of the Rome Statute. Nothing prevented the Review Conference from amending Article 121, and this seems to be what it has done indirectly. The authority would seem to be Article 5(2), in that it mandates the Review Conference to amend the provisions of the Statute so as to incorporate the crime of aggression.

Other offences

The Court is also given jurisdiction over what are called 'offences against the administration of justice', when these relate to proceedings before the Court.[339] The Statute specifies that such offences must be committed intentionally. These are: perjury or the presentation of evidence known to be false or forged; influencing or interfering with witnesses; corrupting or bribing officials of the Court or retaliating against them; and, in the case of officials of the Court, soliciting or accepting bribes. The Court can impose a term of imprisonment of up to five years or a fine upon conviction. States Parties are obliged to provide for criminal offences of the same nature with respect to offences against the administration of justice that are committed on their territory or by their nationals.

The Court can also 'sanction' misconduct before the Court, such as disruption of its proceedings or deliberate refusal to comply with its directions. But, unlike the case of 'offences against the administration of justice', the measures available are limited to the temporary or

---

[337] Rome Statute, Art. 15*ter*(3).   [338] *Ibid.*, Art. 15*ter*(4).
[339] Rome Statute, Art. 70; Rules of Procedure and Evidence, Rules 162–169 and 172.

permanent removal from the courtroom and a fine of up to €2,000.[340]
Regulation 29 of the Regulations of the Court provides:

1. In the event of non-compliance by a participant with the provisions of
   any regulation, or with an order of a Chamber made thereunder, the
   Chamber may issue any order that is deemed necessary in the interests
   of justice.
2. This provision is without prejudice to the inherent powers of the
   Chamber.

It is not clear what these inherent powers may be. The subject of inherent powers of the international criminal tribunals is one of considerable
controversy in the case law and the literature.[341] When it informed the
Security Council of a lack of cooperation by the Government of Sudan,
the Pre-Trial Chamber said that this was in exercise of its 'inherent
powers'.[342]

---

[340] Rome Statute, Art. 71; Rules of Procedure and Evidence, Rules 170–172.
[341] E.g., *Kanyabashi* (ICTR-96-15-A), Dissenting Opinion of Judge Shahabuddeen, 3 June
    1999, p. 17; *Nsengiyumva* (ICTR-96-12-A), Dissenting Opinion of Judge Shahabuddeen,
    3 June 1999; Michael Bohlander, 'International Criminal Tribunals and Their Power to
    Punish Contempt and False Testimony', (2001) 12 *Criminal Law Forum* 91.
[342] *Harun et al.* (ICC-02/05–01/07), Decision Informing the United Nations Security
    Council About the Lack of Cooperation by the Republic of the Sudan, 25 May 2010,
    p. 6.

4

Triggering the jurisdiction

In earlier experiments with international criminal justice, a tribunal was established and its prosecutor assigned to identify deserving cases. There was no need to 'trigger' the jurisdiction, because the target of prosecution was already defined by the enabling legislation. Thus, the International Military Tribunal at Nuremberg was assigned to prosecute 'the major war criminals of the European Axis'. It was left to the prosecutor to determine whom those individuals might be. Similarly, the prosecutors of the United Nations international criminal tribunals for the former Yugoslavia, Rwanda, Sierra Leone and Lebanon were given essentially free reign to identify their targets. But this was not terribly difficult, given that the exercise of prosecutorial discretion was so carefully circumscribed by the jurisdiction of the Court itself. The members of the Security Council who created the International Criminal Tribunal for the former Yugoslavia did not feel particularly threatened by the exercise of prosecutorial discretion because they had created an institution whose jurisdiction was limited to crimes committed on the territory of the former Yugoslavia. In effect, the resolution itself that established the Tribunal was also its 'trigger'.

The situation is quite different with respect to the International Criminal Court.[1] The Court's focus of prosecution is not pre-determined, as has been the case with the earlier *ad hoc* institutions. Determination of the International Criminal Court's 'trigger' of jurisdiction proved to be highly contentious during the negotiations. The initial proposal submitted by the International Law Commission to the General Assembly in 1994 contemplated two basic means of unleashing prosecution: 'referral of a matter' by the Security Council or a 'complaint' by a State Party that genocide or another crime within the jurisdiction of the court has been

---

[1] There is now a monograph on this subject: Héctor Olásolo, *The Triggering Procedure of the International Criminal Court*, Leiden and Boston: Martinus Nijhoff, 2005.

committed.[2] In the case of Security Council referral, the mechanism was essentially analogous to the one already established for the International Criminal Tribunal for the former Yugoslavia. Indeed, the International Law Commission seemed to view the proposed court as little more than a standing or permanent version of the *ad hoc* institution that already existed for the former Yugoslavia (and that would soon be created for Rwanda). The International Law Commission draft also enabled a State Party to refer a situation. This was seen as an inter-State complaint mechanism, similar to what exists at the International Court of Justice and various international human rights bodies, like the European Court of Human Rights and the Human Rights Committee. Here, the consent of both the referring State and the referred State was required. A sole exception concerned a complaint of genocide, if the two States concerned were parties to the 1948 Convention for the Prevention and Punishment of the Crime of Genocide, because it was assumed that ratification of that instrument was in some sense equivalent to consent to the jurisdiction.

Like other important parts of the Rome Statute, there are significant differences between the 1994 International Law Commission draft and the final version. The Rome Statute proposes three ways of 'triggering' the jurisdiction. First, a State Party may also refer a 'situation' to the Court, provided this concerns the nationals or the territory of a State Party or, in the case of a non-party State, there is acceptance of the jurisdiction of the Court pursuant to Article 12(3). Secondly, referral of a 'situation' by the Security Council remains without change from the International Law Commission draft statute of 1994. Finally – and this is the great innovation – the Prosecutor may initiate charges acting *proprio motu*, that is, on his or her own initiative. Here, he or she may select any situation as long as it is within the jurisdiction of the Court. In other words, he or she may choose from crimes committed on the territory of any of the more than 110 States Parties to the Statute as well as crimes committed by nationals of any of those States Parties anywhere else in the world. Accordingly, Article 13, which is entitled 'Exercise of jurisdiction', states:

> The Court may exercise its jurisdiction with respect to a crime referred to in article 5 in accordance with the provisions of this Statute if:
> (a) A situation in which one or more of such crimes appears to have been committed is referred to the Prosecutor by a State Party in accordance with article 14;

---

[2] Report of the International Law Commission on the Work of Its Forty-Sixth Session, 2 May–22 July 1994, Chapter II, UN Doc. A/49/10, Arts. 23(1) and 25(1) and (2).

(b) A situation in which one or more of such crimes appears to have been committed is referred to the Prosecutor by the Security Council acting under Chapter VII of the Charter of the United Nations; or

(c) The Prosecutor has initiated an investigation in respect of such a crime in accordance with article 15.

Each of these 'trigger' mechanisms merits detailed observations.

State Party referral

When the Rome Statute was being drafted, referral of a situation by a State Party was thought to have the least potential for making the Court operational, although it curiously appears first in the enumeration of Article 13. It was frequently pointed out that States were notoriously reluctant to complain against other States on a bilateral basis, unless they had vital interests at stake. They would not, however, be likely to act as international altruists, submitting petitions alleging that other States were committing international crimes. In support, the atrophied provisions of international human rights treaties establishing inter-State complaint mechanisms were cited. Most of these have never been used.[3]

The big exception is the European Convention on Human Rights, but even its inter-State complaint provision has rarely been invoked. The handful of major cases have involved Cyprus against Turkey and Ireland against the United Kingdom, and tend to confirm the observation that these remedies are only invoked when there is a genuine dispute between the two States concerned, generally about treatment accorded to the nationals or the property of the complaining State. States that desire the Court to take up a matter are more likely to lobby the Prosecutor than to launch the proceedings formally themselves. The result will be the same, but they will save the diplomatic discomforts that accompany public denunciation.

It was astonishing, therefore, and completely unexpected, when the State Party referral mechanism became the source of the first three situations to be 'triggered' before the Court. The mechanism did not, however, operate as most had expected. These were not inter-State complaints at all. Rather, the State in question referred a 'situation' within its own

---

[3] Daniel D. Ntanda Nsereko, 'The International Criminal Court: Jurisdictional and Related Issues', (1999) 10 *Criminal Law Forum* 87 at 109.

borders. These quickly became known as 'self-referrals',[4] although in reality the States concerned did not intend that prosecution be directed against themselves. Rather, they sought to induce the Court to prosecute rebel groups operating within their own borders.[5] Nor were they spontaneous initiatives taken by States. The Prosecutor had, in effect, solicited the 'self-referrals' pursuant to a 'policy of inviting and welcoming voluntary referrals by territorial states as a first step in triggering the jurisdiction of the Court'.[6]

The first referral was formulated by the Government of Uganda on 16 December 2003. The letter of referral made reference to the 'situation concerning the "Lord's Resistance Army" in northern and western Uganda'.[7] The Prosecutor responded to Uganda indicating his interpretation that 'the scope of the referral encompasses all crimes committed in Northern Uganda in the context of the ongoing conflict involving the [Lord's Resistance Army]'.[8] On 29 January 2004, the Prosecutor made a public announcement of the referral. The second referral, from the Democratic Republic of the Congo, came on 3 March 2004, when President Joseph Kabila wrote to Prosecutor Moreno-Ocampo:

> Au nom de la République Démocratique du Congo, Etat partie au Statut de la Court Pénale Internationale depuis le 1er juillet 2002, j'ai l'honneur de déférer devant votre juridiction, conformément aux article 13, alinéa a) et 14 du Statut, la situation qui se déroule dans mon pays depuis le 1er juillet 2002, dans laquelle il apparaît que des crimes relevant de la compétence de la Cour Pénale Internationale ont été commis, et de vous prier, en conséquence, d'enquêter sur cette situation, en vue de déterminer si une ou plusieurs personnes devraient être accusées de ses crimes. En raison de la situation particulière que connaît mon pays, les autorités compétentes ne sont malheureusement pas en mesure de mener des enquêtes sur les crimes mentionnées ci-dessus ni d'engager les poursuites nécessaires sans

---

[4] Paola Gaeta, 'Is the Practice of "Self-Referrals" a Sound Start for the ICC?', (2004) 2 *Journal of International Criminal Justice* 949.

[5] Concerns in this regard have been expressed by Antonio Cassese, 'Is the ICC Still Having Teething Problems?', (2006) 4 *Journal of International Criminal Justice* 434 at 436.

[6] Office of the Prosecutor, 'Report on the Activities Performed During the First Three Years (June 2003–June 2006)', 12 September 2006, p. 7.

[7] For the background to the conflict, see Mohamed El Zeidy, 'The Ugandan Government Triggers the First Test of the Complementarity Principle: An Assessment of the First State's Party Referral to the ICC', (2005) 5 *International Criminal Law Review* 83.

[8] See *Situation in Uganda* (ICC-02/04–01/05), Decision to Convene a Status Conference on the Investigation in the Situation in Uganda in Relation to the Application of Article 53, 2 December 2005, paras. 3–4.

la participation de la Cour Pénale Internationale. Cependant, les autorités de mon pays sont prêtes à coopérer avec cette dernière dans tout ce qu'elle entreprendra à la suite de la présente requête.[9]

Finally, on 7 January 2005, the Prosecutor announced publicly that the Central African Republic had made a similar referral to the Court on 22 December 2004. It covered crimes within the jurisdiction of the Court committed anywhere on the territory of the Central African Republic since 1 July 2002. There have been no subsequent referrals to the Court.

Article 14 of the Rome Statute sets out the terms for referral of a 'situation' by a State Party:

1. A State Party may refer to the Prosecutor a situation in which one or more crimes within the jurisdiction of the Court appear to have been committed requesting the Prosecutor to investigate the situation for the purpose of determining whether one or more specific persons should be charged with the commission of such crimes.
2. As far as possible, a referral shall specify the relevant circumstances and be accompanied by such supporting documentation as is available to the State referring the situation.

The referral must be in writing.[10]

The provision of the 1994 draft statute submitted to the General Assembly by the International Law Commission described the State Party making a referral as a 'complainant state'.[11] It said that a State Party could lodge a 'complaint'.[12] The Court was authorized to exercise its jurisdiction with respect to genocide if a State Party to the Statute that was also a contracting party to the 1948 Genocide Convention took the initiative to 'lodge a complaint' that genocide had been committed.[13] In the case of aggression, war crimes and crimes against humanity, the Court could proceed if a 'complaint' was lodged by the 'custodial state' (i.e. the State which had 'custody of the suspect with respect to the crime') and by 'the State on the territory of which the act or omission in question occurred'.[14] The language employed suggests that what was contemplated was a 'complainant State' 'lodg[ing] a complaint' against *another* State.

---

[9] ICC-01/04–01/06–32-AnxA1, 21 March 2004.
[10] Rules of Procedure and Evidence, ASP/1/3, pp. 10–107, Rule 45.
[11] Report of the International Law Commission on the Work of Its Forty-Sixth Session, 2 May–22 July 1994', Chapter II, UN Doc. A/49/10, para. 25(5).
[12] *Ibid.* [13] *Ibid.*, para. 21(1)(a). [14] *Ibid.*, para. 21(1)(b).

The reference to 'complaint' continued through the early drafts, and was still being used in the so-called 'Zutphen draft'[15] and in the final draft adopted by the Preparatory Committee that formed the basis of negotiations at the Rome Conference.[16] The nomenclature, though not the substance, was changed in a 'discussion paper' issued by the Bureau of the Rome Conference on 6 July 1998.[17] The title 'Complaint' was changed to 'Referral of a situation by a State', and the triggering of the jurisdiction of the Court by either the Security Council or a State Party was described as a 'referral'. The change in terminology was probably related to the fact that a complainant State was being prevented from submitting a specific case or crime to the Court. It could only refer a 'situation'. According to Philippe Kirsch, who chaired the Bureau at the Conference, 'the general approach of referring "situations" rather than "cases" seems a prudent one. This helps reduce the arguably unseemly prospect of States Parties referring complaints against specific individuals, which might create a perception of using the Court to "settle scores".'[18]

The famous Bureau draft was presented to a select group of delegations at a meeting held on a Sunday at the Canadian Embassy,[19] deeply irritating those delegations who were not invited, not to mention the NGOs, who were also excluded. But there is not a trace in the *travaux préparatoires* or in the various commentaries by participants in the drafting process to suggest that a State referring a case *against itself* was ever contemplated by this change in terminology. When Philippe Kirsch presented the Bureau draft for discussion, he did not draw the attention of delegates to the change from 'complaint' to 'referral', as would have been expected were some important modification being implied.[20]

---

[15] Report of the Inter-Sessional Meeting from 19 to 30 January 1998 in Zutphen, The Netherlands, UN Doc. A/AC.249/1998/L.13, Art. 45[25], p. 85.

[16] Report of the Preparatory Committee on the Establishment of an International Criminal Court, Draft Statute for the International Criminal Court, UN Doc. A/CONF.183/2/Add.1, Art. 11, pp. 35–6.

[17] Discussion Paper, Bureau, Part 2, Jurisdiction, Admissibility and Applicable Law, UN Doc. A/CONF.183/C.1/L.53, p. 16.

[18] Philippe Kirsch and Darryl Robinson, 'Referral by States Parties', in Antonio Cassese, Paola Gaeta and John R. W. D. Jones, eds., *The Rome Statute of the International Criminal Court: A Commentary*, vol. I, Oxford: Oxford University Press, 2002, pp. 619–25 at p. 623.

[19] Philippe Kirsch and Darryl Robinson, 'Reaching Agreement at the Rome Conference', in Antonio Cassese, Paola Gaeta and John R. W. D. Jones, eds., *The Rome Statute of the International Criminal Court: A Commentary*, vol. I, Oxford: Oxford University Press, 2002, pp. 67–91 at p. 74, n. 23.

[20] UN Doc. A/CONF.183/C.1/SR.25, para. 3.

When the coordinator responsible for the Bureau draft, Erkki Kourula, introduced the debate, he said: 'Article 11, entitled "Referral of a situation by a State", was a technical issue.'[21] The new terminology did not provoke a single comment, suggesting that the delegates to the Rome Conference considered 'referral' to be a synonym for 'complaint'.[22] The absence of any reference to self-referral in the main commentaries on the Statute, most of them authored by delegates to the Rome Conference, confirms this observation.[23] In other words, the drafting history of Article 14 of the Rome Statute tends to show that what was contemplated was a 'complaint' by a State Party against *another* State.

Although there had never been much suggestion, in the drafting history of the Statute, that a State might refer a case against itself, some early documents emerging from the Office of the Prosecutor had begun to hint at this novel construction. In his September 2003 Policy Paper, the Prosecutor wrote:

> Where the Prosecutor receives a referral from the State in which a crime has been committed, the Prosecutor has the advantage of knowing that that State has the political will to provide his Office with all the cooperation within the country that it is required to give under the Statute. Because the State, of its own volition, has requested the exercise of the Court's jurisdiction, the Prosecutor can be confident that the national authorities will assist the investigation, will accord the privileges and immunities necessary for the investigation, and will be anxious to provide if possible and appropriate the necessary level of protection to investigators and witnesses.[24]

Along somewhat the same lines, an expert consultation held by the Office of the Prosecutor in late 2003 said that '[t]here may also be situations where the Office of the Prosecutor (OTP) and the State concerned agree that a consensual division of labour is in the best interests of justice; for example, where a conflict-torn State is unable to carry out effective

---

[21] UN Doc. A/CONF.183/C.1/SR.29, para. 6.

[22] UN Doc. A/CONF.183/C.1/SR.29, paras. 11–187; UN Doc. A/CONF.183/C.1/SR.30, paras. 7–133; UN Doc. A/CONF.183/C.1/SR.31, paras. 1–44.

[23] Philippe Kirsch and Darryl Robinson, 'Referral by States Parties', in Antonio Cassese, Paola Gaeta and John R. W. D. Jones, eds., *The Rome Statute of the International Criminal Court: A Commentary*, vol. I, Oxford: Oxford University Press, 2002, pp. 619–25; Antonio Archesi, 'Article 14, in Otto Triffterer, ed., *Commentary on the Rome Statute of the International Criminal Court, Observers' Notes, Article by Article*, 2nd edn, Munich: C. H. Beck; Baden-Baden: Nomos; Oxford: Hart, 2008, pp. 701–12.

[24] Annex to the 'Paper on Some Policy Issues before the Office of the Prosecutor': Referrals and Communications, September 2003.

proceedings against persons most responsible'.[25] The expert paper did
not expressly consider a State Party referring a case against itself, but it
did contemplate what it called 'uncontested admissibility': 'There may
even be situations where the admissibility issue is further simplified,
because the State in question is prepared to expressly acknowledge that
it is not carrying out an investigation or prosecution.'[26] Two scenarios
were considered. In the first, the experts considered the case of a suspect
who had fled to a third state: 'All interested parties may agree that the
ICC has developed superior evidence, witnesses and expertise relating
to that situation, making the ICC the more effective forum. Where the
third State has not investigated, there is simply no obstacle to admissibility under Article 17, and no need to label the State as "unwilling" or
"unable" before it can co-operate with the Court by surrendering the
suspect.'[27] The second scenario envisaged a State 'incapacitated by mass
crimes' or alternatively 'groups bitterly divided by conflict' who feared
prosecution at each other's hands but would 'agree to leadership prosecution by a Court seen as neutral and impartial. In such cases, declining to exercise primary jurisdiction in order to facilitate international
jurisdiction is not a sign of apathy or lack of commitment.' The experts
were evidently troubled by the suggestion that such 'uncontested admissibility' might imply that States were shirking their duty to prosecute, an
obligation that is affirmed in the preamble to the Statute and which the
experts recalled was also a requirement under customary international
law. They wrote:

> In the types of situations described here, to decline to exercise jurisdic-
> tion in favour of prosecution before the ICC is a step taken to enhance the
> delivery of effective justice, and is thus consistent with both the letter and
> the spirit of the Rome Statute and other international obligations with
> respect to core crimes. This is distinguishable from a failure to prosecute
> out of apathy or a desire to protect perpetrators, which may properly be
> criticized as inconsistent with the fight against impunity.[28]

Self-referral and waiver of admissibility by a State have similarities,
but they are not identical concepts. A State may waive the debate about
admissibility no matter how the case is triggered.

'Self-referral' has been endorsed by one of the Pre-Trial Chambers.
When it confirmed the arrest warrant of Thomas Lubanga, Pre-Trial

---

[25] Informal Expert Paper: The Principle of Complementarity in Practice, p. 3.
[26] *Ibid.*, p. 18. Also p. 20.   [27] *Ibid.*, p. 19.   [28] *Ibid.*, p. 19, n. 24.

Chamber I said 'the self-referral of the Democratic Republic of the Congo appears consistent with the ultimate purpose of the complementarity regime'. Legal academics have also been enthusiastic. According to Claus Kreß, the concept of self-referral, or waiver, 'is firmly grounded in law and commendable as a matter of legal policy'.[29] Yet the utility of the State Party self-referral is not easy to comprehend. It is certainly superfluous. By ratifying or acceding to the Rome Statute, every State Party has in effect accepted the authority of the Prosecutor to investigate cases on its territory. The Prosecutor has suggested that an advantage of self-referral is indicating to the Prosecutor that the State in question had the 'political will' to cooperate with the investigation.[30] But all of the relevant obligations are already covered by the Rome Statute itself. Is ratification not a sufficient indication of 'political will' to cooperate with the Court and to facilitate its work? Several years since the three self-referrals, it seems that the claim these facilitate cooperation with the Court is hard to demonstrate in practice. As Paola Gaeta has observed, 'the government authorities may be prepared to cooperate where the crimes investigated have been allegedly committed by the opposing side; in contrast, it is unlikely that they will be fully cooperative in the investigation of crimes perpetrated by state agents.'[31]

When the arrest warrants against five leaders of the Lord's Resistance Army were unsealed, in October 2005, both Amnesty International and Human Rights Watch questioned the one-sided approach, and called upon the Prosecutor to proceed against the government forces as well.[32] The suspicion is inescapable that the Prosecutor has a tacit, if not an explicit, understanding with the Ugandan authorities that he will prosecute the rebel leaders only. Although the public record does not indicate this clearly, it seems apparent enough that the Prosecutor solicited Uganda's self-referral in December 2003. The self-referral cannot have been a spontaneous and unexpected development that emerged as a

---

[29] Claus Kreß, '"Self-Referrals" and "Waivers of Complementarity": Some Considerations in Law and Policy', (2004) 2 *Journal of International Criminal Justice* 944 at 945.

[30] See, e.g., Office of the Prosecutor, Annex to the 'Paper on Some Policy Issues before the Office of the Prosecutor, Referrals and Communications', undated (made public on 21 April 2004).

[31] Paula Gaeta, 'Is the Practice of "Self-Referrals" a Sound Start for the ICC?', (2004) 2 *Journal of International Criminal Justice* 949 at 952.

[32] Amnesty International, 'Uganda: First Ever Arrest Warrants by International Criminal Court – A First Step Towards Addressing Impunity', 14 October 2005, AI Index: AFR 59/008/2005; Human Rights Watch, 'ICC Takes Decisive Step for Justice in Uganda', 14 October 2005.

result of creative thinking by international lawyers within the Ugandan Foreign Ministry. Philosophically, it flowed from the ruminations within the Office of the Prosecutor in late 2003. The idea came from The Hague, not Kampala. To the extent that the Prosecutor believed his strategy of encouraging self-referral was a productive one, he surely had to reassure States that those who referred the case were not threatened. Indeed, if he intends for the strategy to continue, and to solicit more self-referrals, he will need to show a track record of one-sided investigations, directed against anti-government forces and entities.

Self-referral seems to have the interesting legal consequence of positioning the State Party at the top of the prosecutorial agenda. Without self-referral, Uganda would have been only one of more than 110 States within the territorial sights of the Prosecutor. Were he to contemplate prosecution in Uganda pursuant to his *proprio motu* powers, he would need to justify the choice with respect to the many competing alternatives. To the extent that he sought to justify arrest warrants based on the number of victims, as he has done with the Lord's Resistance Army, the Prosecutor would be required to look at killings throughout not only the territories of the 110 States Parties, but also those committed by nationals of States Parties elsewhere in the world, rather than those within a region of one sovereign state. This might lead him to Colombia, for example, or Burundi or Afghanistan, or even Iraq. In other words, by inciting Uganda to refer the situation in the north of the country against itself, so to speak, the Prosecutor allowed Uganda to jump the queue, where it might not otherwise belong if it was being treated as a *proprio motu* case.

One of the great flaws with 'self-referral' is that it encourages States to defer to the International Criminal Court rather than to assume their own responsibilities. Paragraph 6 of the Preamble to the Rome Statute declares that 'it is the duty of every State to exercise its criminal jurisdiction over those responsible for international crimes'. The Prosecutor has often invoked this principle, referring to what he calls 'positive complementarity'. In his September 2006 'Prosecutorial Strategy', he stated:

> With regard to *complementarity*, the Office emphasizes that according to the Statute national states have the primary responsibility for preventing and punishing atrocities in their own territories. In this design, intervention by the Office must be exceptional – it will only step in when States fail to conduct investigations and prosecutions, or where they purport to do so but in reality are unwilling or unable to genuinely carry out proceedings. A Court based on the principle of complementarity ensures the

international rule of law by creating an interdependent, mutually reinfor-
cing international system of justice. With this in mind, the Office has
adopted a *positive approach* to complementarity, meaning that it encourages genuine national proceedings where possible; relies on national and
international networks; and participates in a system of international
cooperation.[33]

When Uganda referred the situation of the Lord's Resistance Army, its
courts were fully functional and more than able to prosecute the alleged
offenders. Indeed, the Ugandan courts are among the most enlightened
in Africa. For example, in January 2009, the Supreme Court of Uganda
declared the country's mandatory death penalty legislation to be uncon-
stitutional.[34] The only reason Uganda was 'unable' to prosecute was its
inability to secure custody of the Lord's Resistance Army leaders. But in
this respect Uganda was no worse off than the Court itself. In fact, the
Court still depends upon Uganda in order to enforce the arrest warrants.
The self-referral sends the troubling message that States may decline to
assume their duty to prosecute, despite the terms of the preamble to the
Statute, not to mention obligations imposed by international human
rights law, by invoking the provisions of Article 14 and referring the
'situation' to The Hague. If the Prosecutor is sincere about his desire to
stimulate national systems, he might be better to send the case back, and
give the State in question a lecture about its responsibilities in addressing impunity.

The Statute does not contemplate the possibility of a State referring a
case and then withdrawing it. This question has arisen with respect to
the Uganda referral, because the sentiments of the government changed
with developments in the peace process. This is where the term 'trigger' is
a helpful metaphor. Once the jurisdiction has been 'triggered', it cannot
be 'untriggered'.[35] The decision not to proceed on a State Party referral
belongs to the Prosecutor and to the Pre-Trial Chamber, in accordance
with Article 53, or to the Security Council, pursuant to Article 16.

Note that special rules apply to triggering the jurisdiction in the case
of prosecutions for the crime of aggression, in accordance with Article
15*bis*. This is discussed in the previous chapter.

---

[33] 'Report on Prosecutorial Strategy', 14 September 2006 (emphasis in the original).
[34] *Attorney General* v. *Kigula et al.*, Supreme Court of Uganda, 21 January 2009.
[35] Mohamed El Zeidy, 'The Legitimacy of Withdrawing State Party Referrals and Ad
Hoc Declarations under the Statute of the International Criminal Court', in Carsten
Stahn and Goran Sluiter, *The Emerging Practice of the International Criminal Court*,
Leiden: Brill, 2009, pp. 55–78.

Security Council referral

The second means of triggering the exercise of jurisdiction by the Court is through a Security Council referral. Unlike the case of State Party referral, there is no detailed provision in the Statute concerning Security Council referral. Security Council referral is governed by Article 13(b), which authorizes the Court to exercise its jurisdiction over crimes within its jurisdiction in accordance with Article 5 if '[a] situation in which one or more of such crimes appears to have been committed is referred to the Prosecutor by the Security Council acting under Chapter VII of the Charter of the United Nations'. The provision governing Security Council referral was part of the 1994 International Law Commission draft, and did not undergo any significant change during the negotiating process.

The Security Council is one of the principal organs of the United Nations, and it has 'primary responsibility for the maintenance of international peace and security'.[36] In accordance with Article 23 of the Charter of the United Nations, the Security Council consists of five permanent members, China, France, Russia, the United Kingdom and the United States, and ten non-permanent members who are elected by the General Assembly from among the membership of the organization to two-year terms. Nine votes are required to adopt a resolution, but any permanent member may exercise a veto. Chapter VII of the Charter declares that '[t]he Security Council shall determine the existence of any threat to the peace, breach of the peace, or act of aggression and shall make recommendations, or decide what measures shall be taken in accordance with Articles 41 and 42, to maintain or restore international peace and security'. Acting in accordance with Chapter VII, the Security Council established the *ad hoc* tribunals for the former Yugoslavia and Rwanda.[37] Its authority under the Charter to act in this way was upheld in early rulings of the international tribunals,[38] and would now appear to be beyond dispute.

The Relationship Agreement between the United Nations and the Court makes specific provision for cooperation in the event of a Security Council referral.

---

[36] Charter of the United Nations, Art. 24.
[37] UN Doc. S/RES/827 (1993); UN Doc. S/RES/955 (1994).
[38] *Tadić* (IT-94-1-AR72), Decision on the Defence Motion for Interlocutory Appeal on Jurisdiction, 2 October 1995; *Kanyabashi* (ICTR-96-15-T), Decision on Jurisdiction, 18 June 1997, para. 20.

1. When the Security Council, acting under Chapter VII of the Charter of the United Nations, decides to refer to the Prosecutor pursuant to article 13, paragraph (b), of the Statute, a situation in which one or more of the crimes referred to in article 5 of the Statute appears to have been committed, the Secretary-General shall immediately transmit the written decision of the Security Council to the Prosecutor together with documents and other materials that may be pertinent to the decision of the Council. The Court undertakes to keep the Security Council informed in this regard in accordance with the Statute and the Rules of Procedure and Evidence. Such information shall be transmitted through the Secretary-General.

...

3. Where a matter has been referred to the Court by the Security Council and the Court makes a finding, pursuant to article 87, paragraph 5 (b) or paragraph 7, of the Statute, of a failure by a State to cooperate with the Court, the Court shall inform the Security Council or refer the matter to it, as the case may be, and the Registrar shall convey to the Security Council through the Secretary-General the decision of the Court, together with relevant information in the case. The Security Council, through the Secretary-General, shall inform the Court through the Registrar of action, if any, taken by it under the circumstances.[39]

If it triggers the Court, the Council should be prepared to live within the parameters of the Statute with respect to such matters as jurisdiction. For example, it could not request that the Court consider the atrocities committed by the Khmer Rouge in Cambodia during the late 1970s because Article 11 of the Statute clearly declares that the Court cannot judge crimes committed prior to the entry into force of the Statute. In such cases, the Council would be required to set up an additional *ad hoc* tribunal. For the same reason, the Council could not transfer the powers of the existing *ad hoc* tribunals to the new Court. It remains uncertain whether the Security Council must also meet the other admissibility criteria and respect the principle of complementarity, a matter that seems to have been intentionally left unresolved at the Rome Conference.[40] Some have also suggested that in the case of a Security Council referral, provisions that in principle are only applicable to States Parties because they depart from customary international

---

[39] Negotiated Relationship Agreement Between the International Criminal Court and the United Nations, Art. 17.

[40] Ruth B. Philips, 'The International Criminal Court Statute: Jurisdiction and Admissibility', (1999) 10 *Criminal Law Forum* 61 at 73; see also *ibid.*, p. 81.

law, such as Article 27 concerning the immunity of heads of State, do not apply.[41]

Referral to the International Criminal Court by the Security Council of the situation in Darfur, in western Sudan, was proposed by the International Commission of Inquiry in its January 2005 report. The Commission said that resort to the International Criminal Court would have at least six major merits. First, it said that the Court was established 'with an eye to crimes likely to threaten peace and security', and that this was 'the main reason why the Security Council may trigger the Court's jurisdiction under Article 13(b)'. Secondly, the Commission said that investigation and prosecution of crimes perpetrated in Darfur would 'be conducive, or contribute to, peace and stability in Darfur, by removing serious obstacles to national reconciliation and the restoration of peaceful relations'. The Commission said investigation and prosecution in the Sudan of persons with authority and prestige, who wielded control over the State apparatus, was difficult or even impossible. It said that holding trials in The Hague, 'far away from the community over which those persons still wield authority and where their followers live, might ensure a neutral atmosphere and prevent the trials from stirring up political, ideological or other passions'. Thirdly, it argued that only the authority of the Court, reinforced by that of the United Nations Security Council, 'might compel both leading personalities in the Sudanese Government and the heads of rebels to submit to investigation and possibly criminal proceedings'. Fourthly, the Commission said the Court was best suited to ensure a 'veritably fair trial'. Fifthly, the Court could be activated immediately, as opposed to alternative mechanisms such as mixed or internationalized courts. Finally, proceedings before the Court 'would not necessarily involve a significant financial burden for the international community'.[42] The Commission said that the Sudanese justice system was unable and unwilling to address the situation in Darfur.[43]

In March 2005, after several weeks of backroom discussions during which the United States proposed several other options in order to address impunity in Darfur, before ultimately conceding the referral, the Security Council sent the 'Situation in Darfur' to the Court. The

---

[41] Paola Gaeta, 'Does President Al Bashir Enjoy Immunity from Arrest?', (2009) 7 *Journal of International Criminal Justice* 315.

[42] Report of the International Commission of Inquiry on Darfur to the United Nations Secretary-General, Pursuant to Security Council Resolution 1564 of 18 September 2004, Geneva, 25 January 2005, paras. 571–2.

[43] *Ibid.*, para. 586.

United States abstained in the vote on the Resolution. Resolution 1593 reads as follows:

The Security Council,

Taking note of the report of the International Commission of Inquiry on violations of international humanitarian law and human rights law in Darfur (S/2005/60),

Recalling article 16 of the Rome Statute under which no investigation or prosecution may be commenced or proceeded with by the International Criminal Court for a period of 12 months after a Security Council request to that effect,

Also recalling articles 75 and 79 of the Rome Statute and encouraging States to contribute to the ICC Trust Fund for Victims,

Taking note of the existence of agreements referred to in Article 98–2 of the Rome Statute,

Determining that the situation in Sudan continues to constitute a threat to international peace and security,

Acting under Chapter VII of the Charter of the United Nations,

1. *Decides* to refer the situation in Darfur since 1 July 2002 to the Prosecutor of the International Criminal Court;
2. *Decides* that the Government of Sudan and all other parties to the conflict in Darfur shall cooperate fully with and provide any necessary assistance to the Court and the Prosecutor pursuant to this resolution and, while recognizing that States not party to the Rome Statute have no obligation under the Statute, urges all States and concerned regional and other international organizations to cooperate fully;
3. *Invites* the Court and the African Union to discuss practical arrangements that will facilitate the work of the Prosecutor and of the Court, including the possibility of conducting proceedings in the region, which would contribute to regional efforts in the fight against impunity;
4. *Also encourages* the Court, as appropriate and in accordance with the Rome Statute, to support international cooperation with domestic efforts to promote the rule of law, protect human rights and combat impunity in Darfur;
5. *Also emphasizes* the need to promote healing and reconciliation and encourages in this respect the creation of institutions, involving all sectors of Sudanese society, such as truth and/or reconciliation commissions, in order to complement judicial processes and thereby reinforce the efforts to restore long-lasting peace, with African Union and international support as necessary;
6. *Decides* that nationals, current or former officials or personnel from a contributing State outside Sudan which is not a party to the Rome

Statute of the International Criminal Court shall be subject to the exclusive jurisdiction of that contributing State for all alleged acts or omissions arising out of or related to operations in Sudan established or authorized by the Council or the African Union, unless such exclusive jurisdiction has been expressly waived by that contributing State;

7. *Recognizes* that none of the expenses incurred in connection with the referral including expenses related to investigations or prosecutions in connection with that referral, shall be borne by the United Nations and that such costs shall be borne by the parties to the Rome Statute and those States that wish to contribute voluntarily;

8. *Invites* the Prosecutor to address the Council within three months of the date of adoption of this resolution and every six months thereafter on actions taken pursuant to this resolution;

9. *Decides* to remain seized of the matter.

The Prosecutor has made bi-annual reports to the Security Council, beginning in June 2005, on the progress, or lack of it, in implementing the resolution.[44] He is under no obligation to do so pursuant to the Statute. The Security Council resolution 'invites' rather than 'orders' the Prosecutor to present such reports.

Although Resolution 1593 purports to exclude jurisdiction over 'nationals, current or former officials or personnel from a contributing State outside Sudan which is not a party to the Rome Statute of the International Criminal Court', it also does so with respect to all other jurisdictions except those of the State of nationality of the suspect. The provision is similar to one included in a 2003 Security Council resolution concerning Liberia.[45] It is a bit of legal poison injected into the resolution by John Bolton, who was then the United States representative in New York, and is quite plainly contrary to treaty provisions binding upon virtually all United Nations Member States, including the United States. It is well known that the four Geneva Conventions oblige a State Party 'to search for persons alleged to have committed, or to have ordered to be committed, such grave breaches, and [to] bring such persons, regardless of their nationality, before its own courts'.[46] Similar duties are imposed

---

[44] E.g. UN Doc. S/PV.6336.   [45] UN Doc. S/RES/1497 (2003), para. 7.

[46] Convention for the Amelioration of the Condition of the Wounded and Sick in Armed Forces in the Field, (1949) 75 UNTS 31, Art. 49; Convention for the Amelioration of the Condition of Wounded, Sick and Shipwrecked Members of Armed Forces at Sea, (1950) 75 UNTS 85, Art. 50; Convention Relative to the Treatment of Prisoners of War, (1950) 75 UNTS 135, Art. 129; Convention Relative to the Treatment of Civilian Persons in Time of War, (1950) 75 UNTS 287, Art. 146.

by the Convention Against Torture.[47] But Resolution 1593 tells them to do the opposite.

In a statement at the time the resolution was adopted, the French representative appeared to refer to this difficulty, noting that 'the jurisdictional immunity provided for in the text we have just adopted obviously cannot run counter to other international obligations of States and will be subject, where appropriate, to the interpretation of the courts of my country'.[48] The representative of Brazil described operative paragraph 6 as 'a legal exception that is inconsistent in international law'.[49] Denmark said:

> We also believe that the International Criminal Court (ICC) may be a casualty of resolution 1593 (2005). Operative paragraph 6 of the resolution is killing its credibility – softly, perhaps, but killing it nevertheless. We may ask whether the Security Council has the prerogative to mandate the limitation of the jurisdiction of the ICC under the Rome Statute once the exercise of its jurisdiction has advanced. Operative paragraph 6 subtly subsumed the independence of the ICC into the political and diplomatic vagaries of the Security Council. Nevertheless, that eventuality may well be worth the sacrifice if impunity is, indeed, ended in Darfur; if human rights are, indeed, finally protected and promoted; and if, indeed, the rule of law there is upheld.[50]

The answer to this apparent incompatibility may lie in Article 103 of the Charter of the United Nations: 'In the event of a conflict between the obligations of the Members of the United Nations under the present Charter and their obligations under any other international agreement, their obligations under the present Charter shall prevail.' If that is indeed the case, then the ability of the Security Council to in effect neutralize the grave breaches provisions of the Geneva Conventions puts in doubt the claims of many writers that these are norms of *jus cogens*.

Whatever the legality of paragraph 6 of the resolution, it is most certainly incompatible with the Rome Statute. It should be recalled that, when Uganda referred its conflict to the International Criminal Court in such a way as to exclude jurisdiction over certain individuals, the Prosecutor responded with his own interpretation by which no such

---

[47] Convention Against Torture and Other Cruel, Inhuman or Degrading Treatment or Punishment, (1987) 1465 UNTS 85, Art. 5.
[48] UN Doc. S/PV.5158, p. 8.
[49] *Ibid.*, p. 11. [50] *Ibid.*, p. 6.

exception *ratione personae* could be effective.[51] Indeed, this is why the concept of referral in the Rome Statute relates to 'situations' rather than to 'cases'. The language was adopted specifically to avoid the danger of one-sided referrals, which could undermine the legitimacy of the institution. But, when the Security Council performed a similar manoeuvre, the Prosecutor, and later the Pre-Trial Chambers, were silent. The Prosecutor might have sent the Resolution back, telling the Security Council that it was impossible to proceed on such a basis, and to reprise the adoption without paragraph 6.

Assuming that paragraph 6 of Resolution 1593 is illegal, the question of severability arises. If the impugned paragraph cannot be excised from the resolution, then the entire referral might be invalid. It seems necessary to resolve this question as a preliminary matter, before any prosecutions are undertaken. Certainly, a future scenario cannot be automatically excluded whereby the Prosecutor seeks authorization to proceed with a case against an individual in a peacekeeping force who is not a national of a State Party for acts committed in Sudan. How could the Prosecutor rule this out at the present time? Even if the current Prosecutor were to undertake not to take such an initiative, he could not bind his successor. And this leads to the possibility that the Court might rule on the legality of paragraph 6 – and the resolution as a whole – after a prosecution had already been undertaken and, perhaps, even, after one had been completed. Would the Court then declare the resolution and the referral to be valid notwithstanding the offending paragraph, which it would deem inoperative? Or would it refuse to sever paragraph 6 and conclude that the referral as a whole was fatally flawed?

The important question of funding arises with respect to the Darfur referral by the Security Council. In the case of tribunals formally created by the Council, it is normal that they be financed out of United Nations resources. The International Criminal Court is not a United Nations organ, and it seems unreasonable that its facilities be offered to the United Nations free of charge, so to speak. Article 115 of the Rome Statute contemplates two sources of funds for the Court, assessed contributions made by States Parties and '[f]unds provided by the United Nations, subject to the approval of the General Assembly, in particular in relation to the expenses incurred due to referrals by the Security

---

[51] *Situation in Uganda* (ICC-02/04–01/05), Decision to Convene a Status Conference on the Investigation in the Situation in Uganda in Relation to the Application of Article 53, 2 December 2005, paras. 3–4.

Council'. But paragraph 7 of Resolution 1593 states that 'none of the expenses incurred in connection with the referral including expenses related to investigations and prosecutions in connection with that referral, shall be borne by the United Nations'; rather, 'such costs shall be borne by the parties to the Rome Statute and those states that wish to contribute voluntarily'. When Resolution 1593 was adopted, the United States delegate said:

> We are pleased that the resolution recognizes that none of the expenses incurred in connection with the referral will be borne by the United Nations and that, instead, such costs will be borne by the parties to the Rome Statute and those that contribute voluntarily. That principle is extremely important and we want to be perfectly clear that any effort to retrench on that principle by this or other organizations to which we contribute could result in our withholding funding or taking other action in response. That is a situation that we must avoid.[52]

According to Professor Condorelli, '[t]he Security Council's unilateral ruling out of the provision of funds by the United Nations to the Court in connection with Darfur is thus at odds not only with the decision to refer, but also with the duty of good faith negotiations, which flows from the obligation mutually agreed upon between the ICC and the United Nations. The position of the United Nations is unlikely to be flexible on this point.'[53] However, during the debate on Resolution 1593, none of the members of the Security Council took exception to the provision in question. Like most initiatives in the Security Council, the resolution was a diplomatic compromise. Those States favouring referral to the Court must have felt they had the better of the Americans, and that the toxic paragraphs injected by the latter did not fatally compromise the referral itself.

Article 13(b) requires that the Security Council act under Chapter VII of the Charter of the United Nations. Resolution 1593, for example, specifically declares that the Council is acting under Chapter VII. There can be little doubt that the application of Chapter VII in the context of the Darfur conflict was consistent with the Charter. As the Appeals Chamber of the International Criminal Tribunal for the former

---

[52] UN Doc. S/PV.5158, pp. 3–4.
[53] Luigi Condorelli and Annalisa Ciampi, 'Comments on the Security Council Referral of the Situation in Darfur to the ICC', (2005) 3 *Journal of International Criminal Justice* 590 at 594. See also George Fletcher and Jens David Ohlin, 'The ICC – Two Courts in One?', (2006) 4 *Journal of International Criminal Justice* 428 at 429–30.

Yugoslavia has noted, 'there is a common understanding, manifested by the "subsequent practice" of the membership of the United Nations at large, that the "threat to the peace" of Article 39 [of the Charter of the United Nations] may include, as one of its species, internal armed conflicts'.[54] The Court is likely to show great deference for a determination by the Security Council that it is exercising its authority under Article 39, although a challenge based upon the claim that the Council might be acting irregularly or *ultra vires* (that is, outside of its powers) cannot be excluded. As the Yugoslav Tribunal Appeals Chamber noted, '[t]he Security Council is thus subjected to certain constitutional limitations, however broad its powers under the constitution may be'.[55] In other words, the Security Council cannot refer *any* situation to the Court.

The special rules for Security Council referral of prosecutions for the crime of aggression are discussed in the previous chapter.

Proprio motu authority of the Prosecutor

Louise Arbour, who was then Prosecutor of the International Criminal Tribunal for the former Yugoslavia, noted in a statement to the December 1997 session of the Preparatory Committee that there is a major distinction between domestic and international prosecution. It lies in the unfettered discretion of the prosecutor. In a domestic context, there is an assumption that all crimes that go beyond the trivial or *de minimis* range are to be prosecuted. But, before an international tribunal, particularly one based on complementarity, 'the discretion to prosecute is considerably larger, and the criteria upon which such Prosecutorial discretion is to be exercised are ill-defined, and complex. In my experience, based on the work of the two Tribunals to date, I believe that the real challenge posed to a Prosecutor is to choose from many meritorious complaints the appropriate ones for international intervention, rather than to weed out weak or frivolous ones.'[56]

One of the main inadequacies in the draft statute prepared by the International Law Commission, according to most non-governmental organizations and many States, was the failure to endow the Prosecutor with the independent authority to undertake prosecutions, in the

---

[54] *Tadić* (IT-94-1-AR72), Decision on the Defence Motion for Interlocutory Appeal on Jurisdiction, 2 October 1995, para. 30.

[55] *Ibid.*, para. 28.

[56] Statement by Justice Louise Arbour to the Preparatory Committee on the Establishment of an International Criminal Court, 8 December 1997, pp. 7–8.

absence of a complaint from a State Party or referral by the Security Council.[57] The principal argument was that the proposed court would be unlikely to have much work if it relied upon States Parties and the Security Council to trigger its jurisdiction. The caucus of 'like-minded' States made the independent or *proprio motu* prosecutor one of the main planks in its programme.[58] On the other side, the United States insisted that the independent or *proprio motu* prosecutor was one of the issues it could never abide.

Giving the prosecutor the power to initiate prosecution is the mechanism most analogous to domestic justice systems, but it was also the most controversial. The International Law Commission draft statute denied the prosecutor such power. The Commission conceived of the court as 'a facility available to States Parties to its Statute, and in certain cases to the Security Council', who alone were empowered to initiate a case.[59] During the drafting process, the 'like-minded countries' as well as the non-governmental organizations made the *proprio motu* prosecutor one of their battle cries. The concept of an independent prosecutor was an idea whose time had come, and it gained inexorable momentum as the drafting process unfolded.[60] The case for independent prosecutorial powers was immensely strengthened by the extremely positive model of responsible officials presented by Richard Goldstone and Louise Arbour, the *ad hoc* tribunals' prosecutors who held office while the Rome Statute was being drafted.

Some powerful States vigorously opposed the idea, fearful that the position might be occupied by an NGO-friendly litigator with an attitude. They used the expression 'Doctor Strangelove prosecutor', referring to a classic film in which a nutty American nuclear scientist loses his grip and personally initiates a nuclear war. During the Rome Conference, the United States declared that an independent prosecutor 'not only offers little by way of advancing the mandate of the Court and the principles of prosecutorial independence and effectiveness, but also will make

---

[57] Leila Nadya Sadat and S. Richard Carden, 'The New International Criminal Court: An Uneasy Revolution', (2000) 88 *Georgetown Law Journal* 381 at 400–1.

[58] See, e.g., Amnesty International, 'Challenges Ahead for the United Nations Preparatory Committee Drafting a Statute for a Permanent International Criminal Court', AI Index: IOR 40/003/1996, 1 February 1996.

[59] Report of the International Law Commission on the Work of Its Forty-Sixth Session, 2 May–22 July 1994, UN Doc. A/49/10, pp. 89–90.

[60] Silvia A. Fernández de Gurmendi, 'The Role of the International Prosecutor', in Roy Lee, ed., *The International Criminal Court: The Making of the Rome Statute: Issues, Negotiations, Results*, The Hague: Kluwer Law International, 1999, pp. 175–88.

much more difficult the prosecutor's central task of thoroughly and fairly investigating the most egregious of crimes'.[61] Department of State spokesman James Rubin had warned: 'If neither the Security Council nor any state endorses action by the Court, the prosecutor would act without a critical and essential base of international consensus.'[62] China[63] and Israel[64] were also openly critical of the *proprio motu* prosecutor.

The *proprio motu* prosecutor is recognized in Article 15 of the Statute. To allay fears of the opponents, the Prosecutor's independence is tempered by a degree of oversight from the Pre-Trial Chamber.[65] As Pre-Trial Chamber II has explained, both the proponents and the opponents of the *proprio motu* prosecutor were concerned about 'politicization'. It spoke of a 'balanced approach' reflected in the provision, noting that 'the sensitive nature and specific purpose of this procedure' was to be borne in mind by the Pre-Trial Chamber in the fulfilment of its duties under the Statute.[66]

Article 15 reads:

1. The Prosecutor may initiate investigations proprio motu on the basis of information on crimes within the jurisdiction of the Court.

2. The Prosecutor shall analyze the seriousness of the information received. For this purpose, he or she may seek additional information from States, organs of the United Nations, intergovernmental or non-governmental organizations, or other reliable sources that he or she deems appropriate, and may receive written or oral testimony at the seat of the Court.

3. If the Prosecutor concludes that there is a reasonable basis to proceed with an investigation, he or she shall submit to the Pre-Trial Chamber a request for authorization of an investigation, together with any

---

[61] The Concerns of the United States Regarding the Proposal for a Proprio Motu Prosecutor, 22 June 1998, p. 1.

[62] James P. Rubin, US Position on Self-Initiating Prosecutor at the Rome Conference on Establishment of an International Criminal Court, 23 June 1998.

[63] 'Permanent International Criminal Court Established', (1998) 35:2 *UN Chronicle Online Edition*.

[64] Views on International Criminal Court Put Forward in Sixth Committee, Press Release GA/L/2879, 2 November 1999.

[65] Silvia A. Fernandez de Gurmendi, 'The Role of the International Prosecutor', in Roy Lee, ed., *The International Criminal Court, The Making of the Rome Statute, Issues, Negotiations, Results*, The Hague: Kluwer Law International, 1999, pp. 175–88 at p. 181.

[66] *Situation in Kenya* (ICC-01/09), Decision Pursuant to Article 15 of the Rome Statute on the Authorization of an Investigation into the Situation in the Republic of Kenya, 31 March 2010, para. 18.

supporting material collected. Victims may make representations to the Pre-Trial Chamber, in accordance with the Rules of Procedure and Evidence.

4. If the Pre-Trial Chamber, upon examination of the request and the supporting material, considers that there is a reasonable basis to proceed with an investigation, and that the case appears to fall within the jurisdiction of the Court, it shall authorize the commencement of the investigation, without prejudice to subsequent determinations by the Court with regard to the jurisdiction and admissibility of a case.

5. The refusal of the Pre-Trial Chamber to authorize the investigation shall not preclude the presentation of a subsequent request by the Prosecutor based on new facts or evidence regarding the same situation.

6. If, after the preliminary examination referred to in paragraphs 1 and 2, the Prosecutor concludes that the information provided does not constitute a reasonable basis for an investigation, he or she shall inform those who provided the information. This shall not preclude the Prosecutor from considering further information submitted to him or her regarding the same situation in the light of new facts or evidence.

Also accompanying the *proprio motu* powers is a robust concept of complementarity, something that had barely been hinted at in the 1994 draft statute prepared by the International Law Commission. That the Court cannot proceed when a national jurisdiction is investigating or prosecuting is largely a response to the enhanced powers of the new independent prosecutor. But this was not enough to satisfy the United States.

When the Prosecutor concludes that there is a 'reasonable basis' for proceeding with an investigation, the Prosecutor must submit a request for authorization of an investigation to the Pre-Trial Chamber.[67] Supporting material is to be provided to the judges at this stage. Victims are specifically entitled to 'make representations' during this proceeding. The Pre-Trial Chamber must confirm that a 'reasonable basis' for investigation exists, in addition to making a preliminary determination that the case falls within the jurisdiction of the Court.[68] In establishing the 'reasonable basis', Pre-Trial Chamber II has said that reference must be made to the criteria set out in Article 53(1),[69] namely, admissibility,

---

[67] Rules of Procedure and Evidence, ASP/1/3, Rule 50.
[68] Rome Statute of the International Criminal Court, (2002) 2187 UNTS 90, Art. 15(4).
[69] *Situation in Kenya* (ICC-01/09), Decision Pursuant to Article 15 of the Rome Statute on the Authorization of an Investigation into the Situation in the Republic of Kenya, 31 March 2010, para. 24.

gravity and the interests of justice. The 'reasonable basis to believe' standard means that 'there exists a sensible or reasonable justification for a belief that a crime falling within the jurisdiction of the Court "has been or is being committed". A finding on whether there is a sensible justification should be made bearing in mind the specific purpose underlying this procedure.'[70] Determination by the Pre-Trial Chamber does not mean that issues of jurisdiction and admissibility are definitively settled, and the Court is not prevented from reversing its initial assessment at some subsequent stage. Should the Pre-Trial Chamber reject the Prosecutor's request, he or she can always return with a subsequent application for authorization based on new facts or evidence.

The Statute says the Prosecutor is to take action *proprio motu* 'on the basis of information'. Such information has to come from somewhere.[71] In fact, the Statute invites the Prosecutor to seek 'information' from States (it does not specify whether they must be parties or not), United Nations organs, intergovernmental or non-governmental organizations, 'and other reliable sources that he or she deems appropriate'.[72] This information is then considered during what is called 'preliminary examination'. It involves an initial cull of matters that manifestly fall outside the jurisdiction of the Court.[73] An acknowledgment must be sent to all information providers. The Prosecutor may decide to make public the fact that this preliminary examination is underway.[74] In its first three years of operation, the Office of the Prosecutor said it had received nearly 2,000 communications from individuals or groups in more than 100 countries. Some 63 per cent of these communications originated in three countries, the United States, Germany and France. They referred to crimes in 153 countries from all parts of the world. After initial review, approximately 80 per cent of them were determined to be manifestly outside of the Court's jurisdiction. An unsatisfied informant is without any further recourse and may not challenge or appeal the Prosecutor's decision, although the Statute explicitly contemplates the possibility of new facts being submitted.[75]

The Prosecutor is to consider the situation in light of several factors in deciding whether to exercise the proprio motu authority: the seriousness of the information, issues of jurisdiction, admissibility (including gravity), and the interests of justice. According to the Regulations of the

---

[70] *Ibid.*, para. 35.   [71] Rome Statute, Art. 15(1).   [72] *Ibid.*, Art. 15(2).
[73] Regulations of the Office of the Prosecutor, ICC-BD/05–01–09, Regulation 27.
[74] *Ibid.*, Regulation 28.   [75] Rome Statute, Art. 15(6).

Office of the Prosecutor, '[i]n order to assess the gravity of the crimes allegedly committed in the situation the Office shall consider various factors including their scale, nature, manner of commission, and impact'. These criteria, especially those of 'gravity' and 'interests of justice', provide enormous space for highly discretionary determinations.

The Office of the Prosecutor, in the 'Prosecutorial Strategy' published in September 2006, stated:

> Based on the Statute, the Office adopted a policy of focusing its efforts on the most serious crimes and on those who bear the greatest responsibility for these crimes. Determining which individuals bear the greatest responsibility for these crimes is done according to, and dependent on, the evidence that emerges in the course of an investigation. When the Court does not deal with a particular person, it does not mean that impunity is thereby granted – the Court is complementary to national efforts, and national measures against other offenders should still be encouraged. The Office also adopted a 'sequenced' approach to selection, whereby cases inside the situation are selected according to their gravity. Although any crime falling within the jurisdiction of the Court is a serious matter, the Statute clearly foresees and requires an additional consideration of 'gravity' whereby the Office must determine that a case is of sufficient gravity to justify further action by the Court. In the view of the Office, factors relevant in assessing gravity include: the scale of the crimes; the nature of the crimes; the manner of commission of the crimes; and the impact of the crimes. The policy also means that the Office selects a limited number of incidents and as few witnesses as possible are called to testify. This allows the Office to carry out short investigations and propose expeditious trials while aiming to represent the entire range of criminality. In principle, incidents will be selected to provide a sample that is reflective of the gravest incidents and the main types of victimization. Sometimes there are conflicting interests which force the Office to focus on only one part of the criminality in a particular conflict. The approach used in the selection of incidents and charges is one of the measures taken to address the security challenge and assists the Court in operating cost efficiently. Finally, it is part of this policy to request arrest warrants or summons to appear only when a case is nearly trial-ready in order to facilitate the expeditiousness of the judicial proceedings.[76]

Early in his mandate, the Prosecutor issued a statement on the 'communications' he had received in accordance with Article 15, informing

---

[76] 'Report on Prosecutorial Strategy', 14 September 2006, pp. 5–6 (reference omitted).

him of allegations that might lead to the exercise of his *proprio motu* authority. He indicated that his office had selected the situation in Ituri, Democratic Republic of the Congo, as the most urgent situation to be followed. In September 2003, in his report to the Assembly of States Parties, the Prosecutor confirmed that Ituri was the focus of his activity.[77] However, the situation benefited from a self-referral by the State concerned. The Prosecutor did not actually invoke Article 15 until November 2009, in an application to initiate an investigation with respect to the post-election violence in Kenya.[78]

In the selection of situations for prosecution, 'the interests of justice' is an important factor. Matthew Brubacher has written that 'the term "in the interests of justice" also requires the Prosecutor to take account of the broader interests of the international community, including the potential political ramifications of investigation on the political environment of the state over which he is exercising jurisdiction'.[79] Extremely difficult issues may present themselves where application of the 'interests of justice' concept may provide the Prosecutor with the possibility of declining to proceed in politically delicate situations, for example, in the context of peace negotiations. There is little unanimity on these matters among experts and practitioners. As a result, it is impossible to predict the individual choices that the Prosecutor might make 'in the interests of justice'.

A special regime applies to the exercise of *proprio motu* powers with respect to the crime of aggression. This is discussed in the previous chapter.

Security Council deferral

The Court may be prevented from exercising its jurisdiction when so directed by the Security Council, according to Article 16. This is called 'deferral'. The Statute says that the Security Council may adopt a resolution under Chapter VII of the Charter of the United Nations requesting

---

[77] Second Assembly of States Parties to the Rome Statute of the International Criminal Court Report of the Prosecutor of the ICC, Mr Luis Moreno-Ocampo, 8 September 2003.

[78] *Situation in Kenya* (ICC-01/09), Request for Authorization of an Investigation Pursuant to Article 15, 26 November 2009.

[79] Matthew R. Brubacher, 'Prosecutorial Discretion within the International Criminal Court', (2004) 2 *Journal of International Criminal Justice* 71 at 81. See also Luc Côté, 'International Justice: Tightening Up the Rules of the Game', (2006) 81 *International Review of the Red Cross* 133 at 142–3.

the Court to suspend prosecution, and that in such a case the Court may not proceed. The Relationship Agreement between the Court and the United Nations states:

> 2. When the Security Council adopts under Chapter VII of the Charter a resolution requesting the Court, pursuant to article 16 of the Statute, not to commence or proceed with an investigation or prosecution, this request shall immediately be transmitted by the Secretary-General to the President of the Court and the Prosecutor. The Court shall inform the Security Council through the Secretary-General of its receipt of the above request and, as appropriate, inform the Security Council through the Secretary-General of actions, if any, taken by the Court in this regard.[80]

Article 16 of the Rome Statute is a rather significant improvement upon a text in the original draft statute prepared by the International Law Commission. In that document, the Court was prohibited from prosecuting a case 'being dealt with by the Security Council as a threat to or breach of the peace or an act of aggression under Chapter VII of the Charter, unless the Security Council otherwise decides'.[81] Such a provision would have allowed a State that was a member of the Council to obstruct prosecution by placing a matter on the agenda, something that could only be overridden by a decision of the Council itself. And a decision of the Council itself can be blocked at any time by one of the five permanent members exercising its veto.

The International Law Commission proposal met with sharp criticism as interference with the independence and impartiality of the future court. By allowing political considerations to influence prosecution, many felt that the entire process could be discredited.[82] At the same time, it must be recognized that there may be times when difficult decisions must be taken about the wisdom of criminal prosecution when sensitive political negotiations are underway. Should the Court be in a position to trump the Security Council and possibly sabotage measures aimed at promoting international peace and security?

---

[80] Negotiated Relationship Agreement Between the International Criminal Court and the United Nations, Art. 17.

[81] Report of the International Law Commission on the Work of Its Forty-Sixth Session, 2 May–22 July 1994, UN Doc. A/49/10, Art. 23(3).

[82] For the debates, see Report of the Ad Hoc Committee on the Establishment of an International Criminal Court, UN Doc. A/50/22, paras. 124–5; Report of the Preparatory Committee on the Establishment of an International Criminal Court, UN Doc. A/51/22, paras. 140–4.

The debate in the Preparatory Committee and the Rome Conference itself about the International Law Commission proposal was in many respects a confrontation between the five permanent members and all other countries. The uninformed observer might have been given the impression that United Nations reform was being accomplished indirectly, in the creation of a new institution – the International Criminal Court – that would be involved in many of the same issues as the Security Council but where there would be no veto. A compromise, inspired by a draft submitted by Singapore, was ultimately worked out, allowing for the Council to suspend prosecution but only by positive resolution, subject to annual renewal.[83] But even the compromise was bitterly opposed by some delegates who saw it as a blemish on the independence and impartiality of the Court. In a statement issued on the night of the final vote in Rome, India said it was hard to understand or accept any power of the Security Council to block prosecution:

> On the one hand, it is argued that the ICC is being set up to try crimes of the gravest magnitude. On the other, it is argued that the maintenance of international peace and security might require that those who have committed these crimes should be permitted to escape justice, if the Council so decrees. The moment this argument is conceded, the Conference accepts the proposition that justice could undermine international peace and security.[84]

Nobody at Rome expected Article 16 to be invoked by the Security Council even before the Court was actually operational. After all, it was designed to block the activities of the Court. Prior to election of the judges and the Prosecutor, there could be no activities to block. But that is precisely what happened in July 2002, barely days after the entry into force of the Statute. In late June 2002, the United States announced that it would exercise its Security Council veto over all future peacekeeping missions unless the Council invoked Article 16 so as to shield United Nations-authorized missions from prosecution by the Court. The result was Resolution 1422, adopted by the Security Council on 12 July 2002, allegedly pursuant to Article 16 of the Statute. It 'requests' that, 'if a case arises involving current or former officials or personnel from a contributing State not a Party to the Rome Statute over acts or omissions

---

[83] See Lionel Yee, 'The International Criminal Court and the Security Council: Articles 13(b) and 16', in Lee, *The International Criminal Court*, pp. 143–52 at pp. 149–52.

[84] 'Explanation of Vote by India on the Adoption of the Statute of the International Criminal Court, Rome, July 17, 1998', p. 3.

relating to a United Nations established or authorized operation [the Court] shall for a twelve-month period starting 1 July 2002 not commence or proceed with investigation or prosecution of any such case, unless the Security Council decides otherwise'. It therefore extended deferral to such operations as the Stabilization Force (SFOR) in Bosnia and Herzegovina, whose role is authorized by a Security Council resolution although it is not at all under United Nations control. The resolution only applied to nationals of States that are not parties to the Statute.

Although adopted without opposition in the Council, the initiative was resoundingly condemned by several States during the debate, including such normally steadfast friends of the United States as Germany and Canada. Its legality is highly questionable, of course, because Article 16 contemplates a specific situation or investigation rather than some blanket exclusion of a category of persons. Moreover, Article 16 of the Statute says that the Council must be acting pursuant to Chapter VII of the Charter of the United Nations, applicable only when there is a threat to the peace, a breach of the peace or an act of aggression. Some United Nations-authorized missions are not even created pursuant to Chapter VII of the Charter.

Conceivably, the Court could assess whether or not the Council was validly acting pursuant to Chapter VII of the Charter of the United Nations (just as it might with respect to a Security Council referral, which must also be made pursuant to Chapter VII).[85] There has been much debate among international lawyers about whether or not Security Council resolutions can even have their legality reviewed by courts. The International Court of Justice has been hesitant to do this, because the International Court of Justice and the Council are both principal organs of the United Nations. The International Court of Justice has felt that the Charter does not establish a hierarchy in which one principal organ of the United Nations can review the decision of the other. This consideration does not apply to the International Criminal Court, which is not created by the Charter of the United Nations and, for that matter, is not an organ of the United Nations at all. The International Criminal Tribunal for the former Yugoslavia considered that it was entitled to review the legality of Resolution 827, which is in effect its constitutive

---

[85] This is discussed earlier in this chapter. See, e.g., Z. S. Deen-Racsmany, 'The ICC, Peacekeepers and Resolution 1422: Will the Court Defer to the Council?', (2002) 49 *Netherlands International Law Review* 378.

act.[86] In other words, to the extent that Resolution 1422 was an abuse of the powers of the Security Council, its legality, at least theoretically, could eventually be challenged in proceedings before the International Criminal Court.

Resolution 1422 expired after twelve months but was renewed for another year in 2003.[87] In 2004, the United States found itself dreadfully embarrassed by reports of torture carried out in prisons in Iraq and at its base in Guantanamo, Cuba. It did not pursue adoption of a third resolution based on Article 16. Resolutions 1422 and 1483 are ugly examples of bullying by the United States, and a considerable stain on the credibility of the Security Council. In practice, however, neither resolution posed an obstacle to the fulfilment of the Court's solemn mission.

Debates about the role of Article 16 returned in 2008, when the Prosecutor applied for an arrest warrant against the head of State of Sudan. Many African States, mainly through the African Union, objected that the Prosecutor was jeopardizing an ongoing peace process. They were frustrated to learn that the Prosecutor and many friends of the Court were holding out Article 16 as the sole mechanism to be employed when justice threatened peace. After all, the Security Council, at least in its present composition, is not always viewed as a friend of the global south. The African Union proposed an amendment to Article 16 by which deferral could also be imposed by the General Assembly of the United Nations.[88] Critics say this would 'further politicize' the mechanism, although it is hard to see how there could be anything more political than a monopoly in the hands of the Security Council. Explaining that the role of political considerations in decisions to defer prosecutions should be restricted as much as possible does not provide an adequate answer to the concerns of the African Union when the Rome Statute as it currently stands treats the matter as a monopoly of the Security Council.

---

[86] *Tadić* (IT-94-1-AR72), Decision on the Defence Motion for Interlocutory Appeal on Jurisdiction, 2 October 1995.
[87] UN Doc. S/RES/1483 (2003).
[88] 'Appendix VI, African Union States Parties to the Rome Statute', ICC-ASP/8/20, p. 70.

5

Admissibility

Whenever two legal systems or regimes can each exercise jurisdiction over the same issues, some mechanism will usually be developed in order to determine which one proceeds first. In the case of genocide, crimes against humanity, war crimes and the crime of aggression, the International Criminal Court operates in parallel with national justice systems, which are also positioned to prosecute the offences in question. The underlying premise of the Rome Statute is that, when national justice systems fail, the International Criminal Court steps in, as a last resort so to speak. The preamble to the Rome Statute recalls that 'it is the duty of every State to exercise its criminal jurisdiction over those responsible for international crimes'. Consequently, Article 17 of the Statute prescribes that the Court may take on a prosecution only when national justice systems are 'unwilling or unable genuinely' to proceed. The Statute addresses the issue under the rubric of 'admissibility'. The Court may well have jurisdiction over a case, in the sense that the alleged international crime was committed subsequent to 1 July 2002, on a territory of a State Party to the Statute, or by a national of a State Party, or where there has been a Security Council referral or a declaration accepting jurisdiction by a non-party State. But, if the case is being investigated or prosecuted by a State with jurisdiction over the crime, the Prosecutor must demonstrate that it is 'unwilling or unable genuinely'.

According to Article 17:

Issues of admissibility
1. Having regard to paragraph 10 of the Preamble and article 1, the Court shall determine that a case is inadmissible where:
   (a) The case is being investigated or prosecuted by a State which has jurisdiction over it, unless the State is unwilling or unable genuinely to carry out the investigation or prosecution;
   (b) The case has been investigated by a State which has jurisdiction over it and the State has decided not to prosecute the person

concerned, unless the decision resulted from the unwillingness or inability of the State genuinely to prosecute;

   (c) The person concerned has already been tried for conduct which is the subject of the complaint, and a trial by the Court is not permitted under article 20, paragraph 3;

   (d) The case is not of sufficient gravity to justify further action by the Court.

2. In order to determine unwillingness in a particular case, the Court shall consider, having regard to the principles of due process recognized by international law, whether one or more of the following exist, as applicable:

   (a) The proceedings were or are being undertaken or the national decision was made for the purpose of shielding the person concerned from criminal responsibility for crimes within the jurisdiction of the Court referred to in article 5;

   (b) There has been an unjustified delay in the proceedings which in the circumstances is inconsistent with an intent to bring the person concerned to justice;

   (c) The proceedings were not or are not being conducted independently or impartially, and they were or are being conducted in a manner which, in the circumstances, is inconsistent with an intent to bring the person concerned to justice.

3. In order to determine inability in a particular case, the Court shall consider whether, due to a total or substantial collapse or unavailability of its national judicial system, the State is unable to obtain the accused or the necessary evidence and testimony or otherwise unable to carry out its proceedings.

The Rome Statute distinguishes between two related concepts, jurisdiction and admissibility. Jurisdiction refers to the legal parameters of the Court's operations, in terms of subject matter (jurisdiction *ratione materiae*), time (jurisdiction *ratione temporis*) and space (jurisdiction *ratione loci*) as well as over individuals (jurisdiction *ratione personae*).[1] The question of admissibility concerns whether matters over which the Court properly has jurisdiction should be litigated before it. The Court may have jurisdiction over a 'situation', because it arises within the territory of a State Party or involves its nationals as perpetrators, yet it will be inadmissible because prosecutions are underway or are not of sufficient gravity to justify intervention by the international tribunal. 'Admissibility' suggests a degree of discretion, whereas the Court cannot

---

[1] See Chapter 3, 'Jurisdiction', above.

act where it is without jurisdiction. It may even be possible for a State to acquiesce to the exercise of the jurisdiction of the Court, in effect waiving any claim that it might legitimately make to the effect that the case is inadmissible. The Court must always satisfy itself that it has jurisdiction over a case, whether or not the parties raise the issue, whereas its consideration of admissibility appears to be only permissive. Nevertheless, the Court may decide to examine the admissibility of a case on its own initiative, even if the issue is not raised by one of the parties.[2] According to John Holmes, '[a]dmissibility, on the other hand, was less the duty of the Court to establish than a bar to the Court's consideration of a case'.[3]

The line between jurisdiction and admissibility is not always easy to discern, and provisions in the Statute that seem to address one or the other concept appear to overlap. For example, in a clearly jurisdictional provision, the Statute declares that the Court has jurisdiction over war crimes 'in particular when committed as a part of a plan or policy or as part of a large-scale commission of such crimes'.[4] Yet, in a provision dealing with admissibility, the Court is empowered to refuse to hear a case that 'is not of sufficient gravity'.[5] In practice, the implications of the two provisions, one addressing jurisdiction while the other addresses admissibility, may be rather comparable, in that the Court will decline to prosecute less serious or relatively minor crimes.

The admissibility procedure applies to all cases that come before the Court, even those resulting from referral by the Security Council. It might be thought that, in the case of a Security Council referral, where the Court is operating essentially like a permanent version of the *ad hoc* international criminal tribunals, no admissibility test would arise. In fact, in recent years even the *ad hoc* tribunals have developed forms of admissibility tests to ensure that they do not waste their resources on less serious crimes.[6] Article 18 seems to imply this, because it contemplates challenges based on admissibility only in the case of a State Party referral or a case based upon the Prosecutor's *proprio motu* authority.

---

[2] Rome Statute of the International Criminal Court, (2002) 2187 UNTS 90, Art. 19(1).

[3] John T. Holmes, 'The Principle of Complementarity', in Roy Lee, ed., *The International Criminal Court: The Making of the Rome Statute: Issues, Negotiations, Results*, The Hague: Kluwer Law International, 1999, pp. 41–78 at p. 61.

[4] Rome Statute, Art. 8(1).   [5] *Ibid.*, Art. 17(1)(d).

[6] See, e.g., Rule 28(A) of the Rules of Procedure and Evidence of the International Criminal Tribunal for the former Yugoslavia, as amended on 6 April 2004, which requires the judges comprising the Bureau to determine whether an indictment, 'prima facie, concentrates on one or more of the most senior leaders suspected of being most responsible for crimes within the jurisdiction of the Tribunal'.

However, the Prosecutor has made it abundantly clear, in his reports to the Security Council with respect to the *Situation in Darfur*, that he is required to determine whether the case is admissible pursuant to the provisions of Article 17.[7] There have been no objections from members of the Council.

There are three components to the admissibility determination. The most important is complementarity, by which the Court is not to proceed if the case is being addressed by the domestic jurisdiction. The second, gravity, has been held to have a relatively insignificant function. The third is *non bis in idem*: the Court should not proceed if the accused has already been prosecuted for the crime.

Complementarity

The Statute provides a framework for determining whether the national justice system is 'unwilling or unable genuinely' to proceed with a case. With respect to inability, Article 17(2) declares that 'having regard to the principles of due process recognized by international law', the Court is to consider whether the purpose of the national proceedings was to shelter an offender, whether they have been unjustifiably delayed, and whether they were not conducted independently or impartially, 'and they were or are being conducted in a manner which, in the circumstances, is inconsistent with an intent to bring the person concerned to justice'. Article 17(3) says that, in ruling on inability, the Court is to consider 'whether, due to a total or substantial collapse or unavailability of its national judicial system, the State is unable to obtain the accused or the necessary evidence and testimony or otherwise unable to carry out its proceedings'. In their description of the elements of the admissibility determination, judges have added an additional component, namely, whether the national system has 'remained inactive'.

The key word here is 'complementarity', a term that does not in fact appear anywhere in the Statute. However, paragraph 10 of the preamble says that 'the International Criminal Court established under this Statute shall be complementary to national criminal jurisdictions', and Article 1 reiterates this. Article 17(1) makes an explicit reference to paragraph 10 of the preamble and to Article 1.[8] As originally conceived, the

---

[7] UN Doc. S/PV.5216, p. 2; UN Doc. S/PV.5321, p. 3; UN Doc. S/PV.5459, p. 4; UN Doc. S/PV.5589, p. 2.

[8] See John T. Holmes, 'The Principle of Complementarity', in Lee, *The International Criminal Court*, pp. 41–78.

term 'complementarity' may be somewhat of a misnomer, because what is established is a relationship between international justice and national justice that is far from 'complementary'. Rather, the two systems function in opposition and to some extent with hostility *vis-à-vis* each other. The concept is very much the contrary of the scheme established for the *ad hoc* tribunals, referred to as 'primacy', whereby the *ad hoc* tribunals can assume jurisdiction as of right, without having to demonstrate the failure or inadequacy of the domestic system.[9] It is more analogous with the approach taken by international human rights bodies, which require a petitioner or complainant to demonstrate that domestic remedies have been exhausted. National systems are given priority in terms of resolving their own human rights problems, and only when they fail to do so may the international bodies proceed. Probably most international human rights petitions are dismissed at this stage, for failure to exhaust domestic remedies. A concept described as 'positive complementarity' has emerged, by which a more benign relationship with national justice systems is encouraged. The Court, and other States Parties not involved in the prosecution itself, are to cooperate with the State concerned in provision of technical assistance.[10]

The concept of complementarity emerged as early as the International Law Commission draft in 1994.[11] Its preamble said: 'Emphasizing further that such a court is intended to be complementary to national criminal justice systems in cases where such trial procedures may not be available or may be ineffective.' Under a provision entitled 'Issues of admissibility', the International Law Commission draft allowed challenges to a case where, 'having regard to the purposes of this Statute set out in the preamble', it had 'been duly investigated by a State with jurisdiction over it, and the decision of that State not to proceed to a

---

[9] Bartram S. Brown, 'Primacy or Complementarity: Reconciling the Jurisdiction of National Courts and International Criminal Tribunals', (1998) 23 *Yale Journal of International Law* 383; Adolphus G. Karibi-Whyte, 'The Twin Ad Hoc Tribunals and Primacy over National Courts', (1998–9) 9 *Criminal Law Forum* 55; Flavia Lattanzi, 'The Complementary Character of the Jurisdiction of the Court with Respect to National Jurisdictions', in Flavia Lattanzi, ed., *The International Criminal Court: Comments on the Draft Statute*, Naples: Editoriale Scientifica, 1998, pp. 1–18; Paolo Benvenuti, 'Complementarity of the International Criminal Court to National Criminal Jurisdictions', in Lattanzi and Schabas, *Essays on the Rome Statute*, pp. 21–50.

[10] See e.g. Assembly of States Parties to the Rome Statute of the International Criminal Court, Resumed Eighth Session, New York, 22–25 March 2010, Official Records, paras. 35–6; Complementarity, Resolution RC/Res.1.

[11] Report of the International Law Commission on the Work of Its Forty-Sixth Session, 2 May–22 July 1994, UN Doc. A/49/10, Art. 35.

prosecution is apparently well-founded', or 'is under investigation by a State which has or may have jurisdiction over it, and there is no reason for the Court to take any further action for the time being with respect to the crime', or 'is not of such gravity to justify further action by the Court'. In the course of the negotiations subsequent to 1994, the admissibility test became immensely more complex and considerably more rigorous. This evolved in parallel with the development of the concept of an independent prosecutor who would have the authority to undertake a case *proprio motu*, and with the weakening of the power of the Security Council to block a prosecution. In other words, as long as the court was conceived of as subordinate to the Security Council, which could control the prosecutorial agenda, States were relatively relaxed about the rules involved in determining whether the international tribunal could proceed. Once they had unleashed an independent prosecutor who might be in a position to act in spite of the views of the permanent members of the Security Council, a strict procedure and mechanisms for determining admissibility became essential.

The complementarity assessment has not proven to be very significant in the work of the Court to date. This may seem surprising, given the importance attached to the issue at the Rome Conference and in much of the academic writing. It was always assumed that States would resist the Court's involvement, arguing the merits of their own justice systems. But, with the exception of the *Situation in Darfur*, all of the prosecutions have involved self-referrals, where such challenges seem improbable because the State concerned has, in effect, invited the Court to intervene. As for Sudan, its policy to date has been to ignore the Court altogether. The only significant ruling on admissibility has come from one of the defendants, Germain Katanga, who was unsuccessful in his motion based upon complementarity.[12]

The Court has made a gloss on Article 17 by which a third condition, not explicitly discussed in the provision, is applied. In effect, where a State is 'inactive', the Court has taken the view that an examination of the issues of inability or unwillingness is not necessary. This approach has the advantage of accommodating cases that arrive at the Court through self-referrals, where it might otherwise be argued that by its cooperation

---

[12] *Katanga et al.* (ICC-01/04–01/07), Reasons for the Oral Decision on the Motion Challenging the Admissibility of the Case (Article 19 of the Statute), 16 June 2009; *Katanga et al.* (ICC-01/04–01/07 OA 8), Judgment on the Appeal of Mr Germain Katanga Against the Oral Decision of Trial by Chamber II of 12 June 2009 on the Admissibility of the Case, 25 September 2009.

the State Party is in fact demonstrating its willingness to investigate and prosecute. Although the Rome Statute appears to suggest a presumption that cases should be tried by national courts, Article 17 has been read in to suggest the opposite: there is a presumption of admissibility unless one of the conditions set out in Article 17 is present. Instead of insisting that States assume their responsibilities, judges have been content to view cases as admissible where the State, by doing nothing, in effect defers the matter to the Court. They have embraced a theory whereby the analysis proposed in Article 17 is unnecessary, to the extent that the State Party chooses to designate cases for prosecution at the Court by declining to prosecute. According to the Appeals Chamber:

> [I]n considering whether a case is inadmissible under article 17(1)(a) and (b) of the Statute, the initial questions to ask are (1) whether there are ongoing investigations or prosecutions, or (2) whether there have been investigations in the past, and the State having jurisdiction has decided not to prosecute the person concerned. It is only when the answers to these questions are in the affirmative that one has to look to the second halves of sub-paragraphs (a) and (b) and to examine the question of unwillingness and inability. To do otherwise would be to put the cart before the horse. It follows that in case of inaction, the question of unwillingness or inability does not arise; inaction on the part of a State having jurisdiction (that is, the fact that a State is not investigating or prosecuting, or has not done so) renders a case admissible before the Court, subject to article 17(1)(d) of the Statute.[13]

In order to determine unwillingness, three factors are enumerated in paragraph 17(2): the proceedings or the decision not to prosecute were made to shield the person concerned from criminal responsibility for crimes within the jurisdiction of the Court; unjustified delay in the proceedings which in the circumstances is inconsistent with an intent to bring the person concerned to justice; proceedings were not or are not being conducted independently or impartially, and they were or are being conducted in a manner which, in the circumstances, is inconsistent with an intent to bring the person concerned to justice. Trial Chamber II has spoken about different forms of unwillingness, noting that the sub-paragraphs in Article 17(2) are addressed to 'the absence of intent on the part of the State concerned to bring the person concerned

---

[13] *Katanga et al.* (ICC-01/04–01/07 OA 8), Judgment on the Appeal of Mr Germain Katanga against the Oral Decision of Trial by Chamber II of 12 June 2009 on the Admissibility of the Case, 25 September 2009, para. 78.

to justice'. It specifically referred to the intent to shield the person from criminal responsibility, which is 'unwillingness motivated by the desire to obstruct the course of justice'. There is also the case of a State which may not want to prosecute an individual before its own national system, but which is willing to cooperate with the Court. It explained:

> The Chamber is not in a position to ascertain the real motives of a State which expresses its unwillingness to prosecute a particular case. A State may, without breaching the complementarity principle, refer a situation concerning its territory to the Court if it considers it opportune to do so, just as it may decide not to carry out an investigation or prosecution of a particular case. The reasons for such a decision may be because the State considers itself unable to hold a fair and expeditious trial or because it considers that circumstances are not conducive to conducting effective investigations or holding a fair trial.[14]

The Trial Chamber said this second form of unwillingness is not explicitly provided for in Article 17, but that it is 'in line with the object and purpose of the Statute, in that it fully respects the drafters' intention "to put an end to impunity", while at the same time adhering to the principle of complementarity. This principle is designed to protect the sovereign right of States to exercise their jurisdiction in good faith when they wish to do so.'[15] Time will only tell how important this interpretation of Article 17 proves to be. For the time being, it facilitates the admissibility of cases resulting from self-referrals. As the Court matures, however, self-referrals may increasingly appear to be a youthful aberration, designed to bring work to an institution in its early years.

Inability is assessed with reference to 'whether, due to a total or substantial collapse or unavailability of its national judicial system, the State is unable to obtain the accused or the necessary evidence and testimony or otherwise unable to carry out its proceedings'. Pre-Trial Chamber I considered the 'inability' criterion when it issued the arrest warrant against Thomas Lubanga in February 2006. In referring the *Situation in the Democratic Republic of Congo*, in March 2004, President Joseph Kabila had said:

> En raison de la situation particulière que connaît mon pays, les autorités compétentes ne sont malheureusement pas en mesure de mener des

---

[14] *Katanga et al.* (ICC-01/04–01/07), Reasons for the Oral Decision on the Motion Challenging the Admissibility of the Case (Article 19 of the Statute), 16 June 2009, para. 80.

[15] *Ibid.*, para. 79.

enquêtes sur les crimes mentionnées ci-dessus ni d'engager les poursuites nécessaires sans la participation de la Cour Pénale Internationale.
Cependant, les autorités de mon pays sont prêtes à coopérer avec cette
dernière dans tout ce qu'elle entreprendra à la suite de la présente
requête.[16]

Kabila did not use the language of the Statute, and speak of 'collapse', but
the implied reference to Article 17(3) seems clear enough. Nevertheless, by
February 2006, when the Prosecutor applied for an arrest warrant in the
case of Thomas Lubanga, the Pre-Trial Chamber said that, since President
Kabila had referred the situation, the justice system in the Democratic
Republic of the Congo had improved. The *Tribunal de grande instance*
had reopened in Bunia, in the Ituri region. The Pre-Trial Chamber noted
that the Prosecutor's position 'that the DRC national justice system continues to be unable in the sense of Article 17(1)(a) to (c) and (3), of the
Statute does not wholly correspond to the reality any longer'.[17]

In *Situation in Central African Republic*, the Prosecutor justified
a rather lengthy delay between referral and his decision to initiate an
investigation by uncertainty about whether or not the State concerned
was able to prosecute. In May 2007, the Prosecutor explained that the
Cour de Cassation, the country's highest judicial body, had confirmed
that the national justice system was unable to carry out the complex proceedings necessary to investigate and prosecute the alleged crimes, and
that this was important in his own decision to proceed.[18]

In one of the bi-annual reports to the Security Council on the *Situation
in Darfur*, in accordance with Security Council Resolution 1593 (2005),
the Prosecutor explained that decrees had established a 'special court
for Darfur', as well as for Geneina and Nyala. But, said the Prosecutor,
these courts remain 'relatively inaccessible', and suffer from limited
resources, a lack of expertise and security issues.[19] In December 2006,
the Prosecutor told the Security Council that these efforts had not been
sufficient to render inadmissible the cases that he was preparing.[20]

[16] ICC-01/04–01/06–32-AnxA1, 21 March 2004.
[17] *Lubanga* (ICC-01/04–01/06–8), Decision on the Prosecutor's Application for a Warrant
of Arrest, 10 February 2006, para. 36.
[18] Prosecutor Opens Investigation in the Central African Republic, ICC-OTP-PR-
20070522-220_EN, 22 May 2007. Also: *Situation in Central African Republic* (ICC-
01/05), Prosecution's Report Pursuant to Pre-Trial Chamber III's 30 November 2006
Decision Requesting Information on the Status of the Preliminary Examination of the
Situation in the Central African Republic, 15 December 2006, paras. 9, 12–20.
[19] UN Doc. S/PV.5450, pp. 3–4.
[20] UN Doc. S/PV.5589, p. 2.

When the Rome Statute was being drafted, the proposed complementarity mechanism was harshly criticized by such experienced
international criminal law personalities as the Prosecutor of the *ad
hoc* tribunals. Louise Arbour argued essentially that the regime would
work in favour of rich, developed countries and against poor countries. Although the Court's Prosecutor might easily make the claim
that a justice system in an underdeveloped country was ineffective and
therefore 'unable' to proceed, essentially for reasons of poverty, the difficulties involved in challenging a State with a sophisticated and functional justice system would be virtually insurmountable. Certainly,
there is a danger that the provisions of Article 17 will become a tool
for overly harsh assessments of the judicial machinery in developing countries. Trial Chamber I's acknowledgment of the revival of
the justice system in Ituri in 2005 is a welcome development in this
respect.[21]

This issue of concordance between infractions in national criminal
justice and the Rome Statute had been much debated when the Court
was being established, and has important consequences in terms of legislative implementation.[22] Pre-Trial Chamber I has implied that States

---

[21] *Lubanga* (ICC-01/04–01/06–8), Decision on the Prosecutor's Application for a Warrant
of Arrest, 10 February 2006, para. 36.

[22] There is now a substantial literature on the subject of implementation of the Rome
Statute in national law: Ben Brandon and Max Du Plessis, eds., *The Prosecution of
International Crimes, A Guide to Prosecuting ICC Crimes in Commonwealth States*,
London: Commonwealth Secretariat, 2005; Gideon Boas, 'Implementation by Australia
of the Statute of the International Criminal Court', (2004) 2 *Journal of International
Criminal Justice* 179; Robert Cryer, 'Implementation of the International Criminal Court
Statute in England and Wales', (2002) 51 *International and Comparative Law Quarterly*
733; Claus Kreß and Flavia Lattanzi, eds., *The Rome Statute and Domestic Legal Orders*,
vol. I, *General Aspects and Constitutional Issues*, Baden-Baden: Nomos, 2000; Claus
Kreß, Bruce Broomhall, Flavia Lattanzi and Valeria Santori, eds., *The Rome Statute
and Domestic Legal Orders*, vol. II, *Constitutional Issues, Cooperation and Enforcement*,
Baden-Baden: Nomos, 2005; Hugo Relva, 'The Implementation of the Rome Statute
in Latin American States', (2003) 16 *Leiden Journal of International Law* 331; Goran
Sluiter, 'Implementation of the ICC Statute in the Dutch Legal Order', (2004) 2 *Journal
of International Criminal Justice* 158; David Turns, 'Aspects of National Implementation
of the Rome Statute', in Dominic McGoldrick, Peter Rowe and Eric Donnelly, eds., *The
Permanent International Criminal Court: Legal and Policy Issues*, Oxford and Portland,
OR: Hart Publishing, 2004, pp. 337–88; Bakhtiyar Tuzmukhamedov, 'The ICC and
Russian Constitutional Problems', (2005) 3 *Journal of International Criminal Justice* 621;
Julio Bacio Terracino, 'National Implementation of ICC Crimes: Impact on National
Jurisdictions and the ICC', (2007) 5 *Journal of International Criminal Justice* 421;
M. Roscini, 'Great Expectations: The Implementation of the Rome Statute into Italy',
(2007) 5 *Journal of International Criminal Justice* 512.

must implement the crimes as they are spelled out in the Rome Statute. It will not be enough for a State to prosecute the underlying 'ordinary' crimes, such as murder or rape. Strictly speaking, the issue in *Lubanga* was whether the national courts could prosecute the specific offence of enlistment of child soldiers, when they were actually proceeding to deal with two other categories of offence within the jurisdiction of the International Criminal Court, genocide and crimes against humanity.[23] Arguably, genocide and crimes against humanity are more serious than the enlistment of child soldiers, a crime that was not even prosecuted until relatively recently. It was always unlikely that Lubanga would contest admissibility on this ground, because he appeared to be far better off in The Hague, facing the relatively less important charge of enlistment of child soldiers, rather than in Bunia, where he was charged with crimes of the greatest seriousness.

In such a context, where an accused person is also being prosecuted by national authorities, it seems improper to reduce the determination of admissibility to a mechanistic comparison of charges in the national and the international jurisdictions, in order to see whether a crime contemplated by the Rome Statute is being prosecuted directly or even indirectly. It must involve an assessment of the relative gravity of the offences tried by the national jurisdiction put alongside those of the international jurisdiction. Recruitment of child soldiers is serious enough, but maybe Lubanga was being prosecuted in Congo for large-scale rape and murder. We were simply not given this information in the Court's ruling, and it seems important.

A related issue presented itself to the International Criminal Tribunal for Rwanda in the context of its attempts to transfer cases to national courts as part of its completion strategy. Norway had offered to prosecute the case of an accused who was also an informer and who was being held in protective custody. The Trial Chamber rejected the application, holding that, although Norway could prosecute murder, it was unable to deal expressly with the crime of genocide, because this offence

---

[23] According to documents filed with the International Criminal Court, an arrest warrant was issued by the Congolese authorities for Lubanga on 19 March 2005, charging him with 'atteinte à la sûreté de l'Etat'. A second warrant was issued ten days later charging him with 'assassinat' and 'arrestation et détention illégale suivie de tortures corporelles'. His preventive detention was ordered on 7 April 2005 for 'atteinte à la sûreté de l'Etat' But preventive detention was also authorized on 2 April 2005 for 'crimes de génocide' and 'crimes contre l'humanité'.

had never been implemented in national law.[24] The ruling was upheld by the Appeals Chamber.[25]

There are good arguments as to why this approach is excessively exacting. If the object of the exercise is to address impunity, the fact that an offender is being held accountable for serious crimes should satisfy the requirements of international law. This is not to excuse the lethargy of legislators within States Parties, but the Court ought to take a realistic approach to the subject. Even where States have actually incorporated the Rome Statute crimes within national law, they will not always proceed against alleged offenders under the international criminal law provisions, if only for reasons of expediency. Why would a national prosecutor complicate matters by attempting to establish the complex threshold requirements of genocide or crimes against humanity when he or she can more easily obtain a conviction for murder and the severe penalty likely to accompany it?

For victims, a conviction for murder or rape of their loved ones ought to be enough to quench their thirst for justice. Historically, crimes of murder and rape were qualified as genocide, crimes against humanity and war crimes principally in order to put them outside of the general rule by which States have exclusive sovereignty over crimes committed on their territory or by their nationals. Only by establishing that killing had taken place in a qualitatively distinct context, generally one of State complicity and organization, was an exception to this principle allowed, thereby opening the door to prosecution by international tribunals, or to prosecution by national courts under the notion of universal jurisdiction. There was no inherent virtue in prosecuting international crimes; rather, they were required in order to justify the exercise of jurisdiction, a problem that does not generally arise when the offence is being dealt with by the courts of the territory where it was committed.

There was also great debate about the attitude that the Court should take to alternative methods of accountability. The South Africans were the most insistent on this point, concerned that approaches like their Truth and Reconciliation Commission, which offered amnesty in return for truthful confession, would be dismissed as evidence of a State's unwillingness to prosecute. While there was widespread sympathy

---

[24] *Bagaragaza* (ICTR-2005-86-R11*bis*), Decision on the Prosecution's Motion for Referral to the Kingdom of Norway, 19 May 2006.
[25] *Bagaragaza* (ICTR-05-86-AR11*bis*), Decision on Rule 11*bis* Appeal, 30 August 2006.

with the South African model, many delegations recalled the disgraceful amnesties accorded by South American dictators to themselves, the most poignant being that of former Chilean president Augusto Pinochet. But drafting a provision that would legitimize the South African experiment yet condemn the Chilean one proved elusive. It has been suggested that genuine but non-judicial efforts at accountability that fall short of criminal prosecution might have the practical effect of convincing the Prosecutor to set priorities elsewhere.[26] In his reports to the Security Council on Darfur, he has acknowledged the significance of such alternative approaches to accountability, suggesting that these are relevant to the exercise of his discretion, but without, however, indicating that they may pose an obstacle to the admissibility of a case.[27] Speaking of traditional tribal reconciliation mechanisms in Darfur, he said: 'These are not criminal proceedings as such for the purpose of assessing the admissibility of cases before the International Criminal Court, but they are an important part of the fabric of reconciliation for Darfur, as recognized in resolution 1593 (2005).'[28]

Judges of the Court might well consider that a sincere truth commission project amounts to a form of investigation that does not suggest 'genuine unwillingness' on the part of the State to administer justice, thereby meeting the terms of Article 17(1)(a) and (b). Should that not be enough, the Statute also declares inadmissible a case that is not 'of sufficient gravity to justify further action by the Court'.[29] Moreover, the Prosecutor is invited to consider, in determining whether or not to investigate a case, whether '[t]aking into account the gravity of the crime and the interests of victims, there are nonetheless substantial reasons to believe that an investigation would not serve the interests of justice'.[30] Yet judicial attitudes are impossible to predict, and judges or prosecutors might well decide that it is precisely in cases like the South African one where a line must be drawn establishing that amnesty for such crimes is unacceptable.[31]

---

[26] For a comprehensive discussion of these issues, see Carsten Stahn, 'Complementarity, Amnesties and Alternative Forms of Justice: Some Interpretative Guidelines for the International Criminal Court', (2005) 3 *Journal of International Criminal Justice* 695.

[27] UN Doc. S/PV.5321, p. 3.   [28] UN Doc. S/PV.5459, p. 3.

[29] Rome Statute, Art. 17(1)(d).   [30] *Ibid.*, Art. 53(1)(c).

[31] Nsereko, 'The International Criminal Court', pp. 119–20; Michael P. Scharf, 'The Amnesty Exception to the Jurisdiction of the International Criminal Court', (1999) 32 *Cornell International Law Journal* 507; John Dugard, 'Possible Conflicts of Jurisdiction with Truth Commissions', in Antonio Cassese, Paola Gaeta and John R. W. D. Jones, eds., *The Rome Statute of the International Criminal Court: A Commentary*, vol. I, Oxford: Oxford University Press, 2002, pp. 693–704.

Gravity

Article 17(1)(d) of the Rome Statute states that a case may be declared inadmissible when it 'is not of sufficient gravity to justify further action by the Court'.[32] These words are essentially similar to a paragraph in the 1994 draft of the International Law Commission, the only real change being the replacement of 'such' with 'sufficient'. Introducing the proposal, in the Commission, Special Rapporteur James Crawford said that grounds for admissibility 'might include, say ... the fact that the acts alleged were not of sufficient gravity to warrant trial at the international level. Failing such power, the court might be swamped by peripheral complaints involving minor offenders, possibly in situations where the major offenders were going free.'[33] At the time, there was as yet no clarity about the subject-matter jurisdiction of the Court, and some members probably thought it wise to avoid creating an institution that might be required to prosecute any violation of international criminal law, no matter how slight. There was to be a list of applicable treaties appended to the draft statute from which the Court could identify relevant crimes; some of these might not be serious enough, however, to justify the intervention of an international institution.

In the course of the drafting of the Rome Statute, only the most perfunctory consideration of the gravity criterion for admissibility was given. That this attracted virtually no attention can be seen in the first academic studies of the Statute, which essentially ignored the provision.[34] Eventually, as the negotiations evolved, the Prosecutor was given discretion to decide not to proceed with a situation or a case that is not of sufficient gravity.[35] Indeed, prosecutorial discretion should provide an adequate bulwark against the concerns expressed by Professor Crawford in 1994, obviating the need for the chambers to apply Article 17(1)(d).

The insignificance of Article 17(1)(d) was confirmed by the Appeals Chamber, overturning an early ruling on issuance of an arrest warrant.

---

[32] See, generally, Ray Murphy, 'Gravity Issues and the International Criminal Court', (2006) 17 *Criminal Law Forum* 281.

[33] UN Doc. A/CN.4/SR.2330, para. 9.

[34] Sharon A. Williams, 'Article 17', in Otto Triffterer, ed., *Commentary on the Rome Statute of the International Criminal Court*, Baden Baden: Nomos, 1999, pp. 383–94 at p. 393; Morten Bergsmo and Pieter Kruger, 'Article 53', in *ibid.*, pp. 701–14 at pp. 708–9; John T. Holmes, 'Complementarity: National Courts Versus the ICC', in Cassese, *Rome Statute*, pp. 667–86; Giuliano Turone, 'Powers and Duties of the Prosecutor', in *ibid.*, pp. 1137–80 at p. 1153–4; Eric David, 'La Cour pénale internationale', (2005) 313 *Recueil des cours* 325 at 248–51.

[35] Rome Statute, Art. 53.

A Pre-Trial Chamber had held that, because all crimes within the jurisdiction of the Court were in principle serious, there was an additional gravity dimension to be assessed in determinations of admissibility. The Pre-Trial Chamber required that conduct be either systematic or large scale, and provoke what it labelled 'social alarm'.[36] The Appeals Chamber said such a requirement blurred the distinction between the jurisdictional requirements for war crimes and crimes against humanity.[37] The Appeals Chamber considered that a criterion of 'social alarm' depended upon 'subjective and contingent reactions to crimes rather than upon their objective gravity'.[38] Referring to the preamble to, and to Articles 1 and 5 of, the Statute, the Appeals Chamber said that crimes within the jurisdiction of the Court are considered the 'most serious crimes of international concern', and that 'the subjective criterion of social alarm therefore is not a consideration that is necessarily appropriate for the determination of the admissibility of a case'.[39]

The Pre-Trial Chamber had also opined that the deterrent effect of the Court would be greatest if it focused only on the highest-ranking perpetrators. It said persons at the top of the hierarchy who play a major role 'are the ones who can most effectively prevent or stop the commission of such crimes' and that 'only by concentrating on this type of individual can the deterrent effects of the Court be maximised'.[40] The Appeals Chamber said this was 'questionable', explaining that it was difficult to understand how the deterrent effect could be greatest if perpetrators other than leaders could not be brought before the Court. 'It seems more logical to assume that the deterrent effect of the Court is highest if no category of perpetrators is *per se* excluded from potentially being brought before the Court'.[41] The Appeals Chamber continued:

> The imposition of rigid standards primarily based on top seniority may result in neither retribution nor prevention being achieved. Also the

---

[36] *Lubanga* (ICC-01/04–01/06–8), Decision on the Prosecutor's Application for a Warrant of Arrest, 10 February 2006, paras. 42–64.

[37] *Situation in the Democratic Republic of the Congo* (ICC-01/04), Judgment on the Prosecutor's Appeal Against the Decision of Pre-Trial Chamber I Entitled 'Decision on the Prosecutor's Application for Warrants of Arrest, Article 58', 13 July 2006, para. 70.

[38] *Ibid.*, para. 72.   [39] *Ibid.*, para. 72.

[40] *Lubanga* (ICC-01/04–01/06–8), Decision on the Prosecutor's Application for a Warrant of Arrest, 10 February 2006, paras. 54–5.

[41] *Situation in the Democratic Republic of the Congo* (ICC-01/04), Judgment on the Prosecutor's Appeal Against the Decision of Pre-Trial Chamber I Entitled 'Decision on the Prosecutor's Application for Warrants of Arrest, Article 58', 13 July 2006, para. 73.

capacity of individuals to prevent crimes in the field should not be implicitly or inadvertently assimilated to the preventive role of the Court more
generally. Whether prevention is interpreted as a long-term objective,
i.e., the overall result of the Court's activities generally, or as a factor
in a specific situation, the preventive role of the Court may depend on
many factors, much broader than the capacity of an individual to prevent
crimes. The predictable exclusion of many perpetrators on the grounds
proposed by the Pre-Trial Chamber could severely harm the preventive,
or deterrent, role of the Court which is a cornerstone of the creation of
the International Criminal Court, but announcing that any perpetrators
other than those at the very top are automatically excluded from the exercise of the jurisdiction of the Court.[42]

The Appeals Chamber noted that the *travaux préparatoires* of the Statute
contradict the interpretation of the gravity requirement developed by
the Pre-Trial Chamber in *Lubanga*. It explained that the formulation in
Article 17(1)(d) is derived from the draft prepared by the International
Law Commission in 1994. During the Preparatory Committee sessions,
an amendment aimed at changing the term to 'exceptional gravity' was
not accepted.[43]

In the same ruling, Judge Pikis of the Appeals Chamber attempted his
own interpretation of 'sufficient gravity':

> Which cases are unworthy of consideration by the International Criminal
> Court? The answer is cases insignificant in themselves; where the crim-
> inality on the part of the culprit is wholly marginal; borderline cases. A
> crime is insignificant in itself if, notwithstanding the fact that it satisfies
> the formalities of the law, i.e., the insignia of the crime, bound up with the
> mens rea and the actus reus, the acts constituting the crime are wholly
> peripheral to the objects of the law in criminalizing the conduct. Both,
> the conception and the consequences of the crime must be negligible. In
> those circumstances, the Court need not concern itself with the crime nor
> will it assume jurisdiction for the trial of such an offence, when national
> courts fail to do so.[44]

When the Appeals Chamber overturned the Pre-Trial Chamber, it left
virtually no guidance as to the scope that Article 17(1)(d) should be
given. Some subsequent decisions of Pre-Trial Chambers have described

[42] *Ibid.*, paras. 73–4.   [43] *Ibid.*, para. 81.
[44] *Situation in the Democratic Republic of the Congo* (ICC-01/04), Separate and Partly
Dissenting Opinion of Judge Georghios M. Pikis, 13 July 2006, para. 40.

the ruling as an 'obiter dictum',[45] thereby casting doubt on the binding authority of the position taken by the Appeals Chamber. Ruling on the Prosecutor's application to initiate an investigation in Kenya, Pre-Trial Chamber II referred to the 1996 decision, since overturned by the Appeals Chamber. It suggested that one factor to be considered in assessing the gravity of a situation was whether it captured 'those who may bear the greatest responsibility for the alleged crimes committed'.[46] It said that 'gravity may be examined following a quantitative as well as a qualitative approach'.[47] The Chamber also drew upon the sentencing factors considered in Rule 145 of the Rules of Procedure and Evidence, saying they could provide useful guidance in assessing gravity. These include: the scale of the alleged crimes (including assessment of geographical and temporal intensity); the nature of the unlawful behaviour or of the crimes allegedly committed; the means employed for the execution of the crime (i.e., the manner of their commission); and the impact of the crimes and the harm caused to victims and their families.[48]

Ne bis in idem

When a case has already been tried by a domestic justice system, the admissibility provisions in the Statute point to another Article where the prohibition of double jeopardy or *ne bis in idem* is set out. Article 20 of the Rome Statute reaffirms a norm that is codified in important human rights treaties such as the International Covenant on Civil and Political Rights.[49] The test as to whether the national trial proceedings were legitimate is slightly different from the 'unable or unwilling genuinely' standard of Article 17, which applies with respect to pending or completed investigations and pending prosecutions. If a domestic trial has already been completed, the judgment is a bar to prosecution by the Court except in the case of sham proceedings. These are defined as trials

---

[45] *Bashir* (ICC-02/05–01/09), Decision on the Prosecution's Application for a Warrant of Arrest Against Omar Hassan Ahmad Al Bashir, 4 March 2009, para. 48, n. 51. In an earlier decision, *Situation in Darfur, Sudan* (ICC-02/05), Decision on Application under Rule 103, 4 February 2009, para. 25, n. 24, the same Pre-Trial Chamber used the term 'opinio juris', but this was obviously a mistake, and it must have meant *obiter dictum*, as the subsequent ruling makes clear.

[46] *Situation in Kenya* (ICC-01/09), Decision Pursuant to Article 15 of the Rome Statute on the Authorization of an Investigation into the Situation in the Republic of Kenya, 31 March 2010, para. 60.

[47] *Ibid.*, para. 62.   [48] *Ibid.*

[49] International Covenant on Civil and Political Rights, (1966) 999 UNTS 171, Art. 14(7).

held to shield an offender from criminal responsibility, or that were otherwise not conducted independently or impartially and were held in a manner which 'in the circumstances, was inconsistent with an intent to bring the person concerned to justice'.[50]

In a case where an individual is properly tried and convicted, but is subsequently pardoned, the Court would seem to be permanently barred from intervening. The case is far from hypothetical. In the early 1970s, William Calley was convicted of war crimes for an atrocious massacre in My Lai village in Vietnam. Justice had done its job and he was duly sentenced to a term of life imprisonment. Then the United States President, Richard Nixon, intervened and granted him a pardon after only a brief term of detention had been served.

There is some doubt about the application of complementarity and the *ne bis in idem* rule to situations where an individual has already been tried by a national justice system, but for a crime under ordinary criminal law such as murder, rather than for the truly international offences of genocide, crimes against humanity and war crimes. The arguments are broadly similar to those of the debate concerning whether or not national courts must prosecute for crimes that are the same as those enumerated in the Rome Statute in order to demonstrate that they are willing and able, for the purposes of the complementary determination.[51] It will be argued that trial for an underlying offence tends to trivialize the crime and contribute to revisionism and denial. Many who violate human rights may be willing to accept the fact that they have committed murder or assault, but will refuse to admit the more grievous crimes of genocide or crimes against humanity. Yet murder is a very serious crime in all justice systems and is generally sanctioned by the most severe penalties. Article 20(3) seems to suggest this, when it declares that such subsequent proceedings before the International Criminal Court when there has already been a trial 'for conduct also proscribed under Articles 6, 7, 8 and 8*bis*' is prohibited. In the alternative, the Statute ought to have said 'for a crime referred to in Article 5', as it does in Article 20(2).

The Statute also prohibits domestic justice systems from trying an individual for one of the crimes listed in the Statute if that person has already been convicted or acquitted by the Court. This rule is somewhat narrower, in that it only excludes prosecution before national courts for genocide, crimes against humanity, war crimes and the crime of aggression. Accordingly, someone acquitted of genocide by the International

---

[50] Rome Statute, Art. 20(3).   [51] This issue is discussed earlier in this chapter.

Criminal Court, for lack of evidence of intent, could subsequently be tried by national courts for the crime of murder without violating the Statute. This rule in the Statute goes somewhat further than the prohibition of double jeopardy in international human rights law, because international courts and tribunals have generally considered that the norm only applies within the same jurisdiction, and does not prevent a subsequent trial in another jurisdiction.[52]

What about the relationship between the International Criminal Court and the activities of other international criminal tribunals? When the Rome Statute entered into force, there were two such institutions whose jurisdiction might be competitive with that of the International Criminal Court, namely, the International Criminal Tribunal for the former Yugoslavia and the Special Court for Sierra Leone. Both of these bodies are creatures of international law, the former established by a Security Council resolution, the latter by an agreement between the United Nations and the Government of Sierra Leone, and both have jurisdiction over crimes committed on territories that are also subject to prosecution by the International Criminal Court. Moreover, in both territories there was an ongoing situation of political instability making further outbreaks of conflict not at all impossible. The Rome Statute, whose admissibility provisions are focused on national legal systems, does not address this matter directly. A solution recognizing the authority of the first to obtain physical custody of the accused is only part of the answer, because situations of competing requests to a State Party for transfer to one or the other body cannot be excluded.

---

[52] *AP* v. *Italy* (No. 204/1986), UN Doc. A/4340, Annex VIII.A, para. 7.3.

6

General principles of criminal law

The statutes of the Nuremberg and Tokyo tribunals, as well as those of the *ad hoc* tribunals for the former Yugoslavia and Rwanda, are very thin when it comes to what criminal lawyers call 'general principles'. Once the crimes were defined, the drafters of these earlier models left issues such as the appreciation of the evidence or the assessment of responsibility for accomplices and other 'secondary' offenders to the discretion of the judges. After all, those appointed to preside over these tribunals were eminent jurists in their own countries and could draw on a rich, multicultural resource of domestic criminal law practice. The Rome Statute is far less generous to the judges. It seeks to delimit in great detail any possible exercise of judicial discretion. Part 3 of the Statute, consisting of Articles 22–33, is entitled 'General principles of criminal law'.[1] It directs the Court on such issues as criminal participation, the mental element of crimes and the availability of various defences. But elsewhere in the Statute can be found other provisions that are also germane to the issue of general principles. They present a fascinating experiment in comparative criminal law, drawing upon elements from the common law, the Romano-Germanic system, *Sharia* law and other regimes of penal justice.

Sources of law

Article 21 of the Rome Statute, entitled 'Applicable law', sets out the legal sources upon which the International Criminal Court may draw. The

[1] On the general principles, see Per Saland, 'International Criminal Law Principles', in Roy Lee, ed., *The International Criminal Court: The Making of the Rome Statute: Issues, Negotiations, Results*, The Hague: Kluwer Law International, 1999, pp. 189–216; William A. Schabas, 'General Principles of Criminal Law in the International Criminal Court Statute (Part III)', (1998) 6 *European Journal of Crime, Criminal Law and Criminal Justice* 84; Kai Ambos, 'General Principles of Law in the Rome Statute', (1999) 10 *Criminal Law Forum* 1; Robert Cryer, 'General Principles of Liability in International Criminal Law', in

Statute itself cannot provide answers to every question likely to arise before the Court, and judges will have to seek guidance elsewhere, just as they do under domestic law when criminal codes leave questions ambiguous or simply unanswered.[2]

International law already has a general response to this problem in Article 38 of the Statute of the International Court of Justice, the international judicial organ created as part of the United Nations in 1945 with jurisdiction over disputes between sovereign States. The Statute of the International Court of Justice defines three primary sources of international law: international treaties; international custom; and general principles of law recognized by civilized nations. It is accepted that the three sources are of equal value and that there is no hierarchy among them, although case law has tended to give the third source, general principles of law, a rather marginal significance. According to the Statute of the International Court of Justice, subsidiary means for determining the rules of law are judicial decisions and academic writings. Besides these enumerated sources, international legal rules can also be created by unilateral acts, such as a declaration or a reservation.

The Rome Statute creates a special regime as far as sources of law are concerned. The Statute proposes a three-tiered hierarchy. At the top is the Statute itself, accompanied by the Elements of Crimes and the Rules of Procedure and Evidence. The Rome Statute was adopted at the 1998 Rome Diplomatic Conference, whereas the Elements and the Rules were drafted by the subsequent Preparatory Commission sessions, in 1999 and 2000, and then confirmed by the Assembly of States Parties at its first session in September 2002.[3] Although Article 21 suggests that the Statute, the Elements and the Rules are all of equal importance, provisions elsewhere in the Statute make it clear that, in case of conflict, the Elements (Art. 9) and the Rules (Art. 51) are overridden by the Statute itself.[4]

Dominic McGoldrick, Peter Rowe and Eric Donnelly, eds., *The Permanent International Criminal Court: Legal and Policy Issues*, Oxford and Portland, OR: Hart Publishing, 2004, pp. 233–62.

[2] Ida Caracciolo, 'Applicable Law', in Flavia Lattanzi and William A. Schabas, eds., *Essays on the Rome Statute of the International Criminal Court*, Rome: Editrice il Sirente, 2000, pp. 211–32.

[3] Elements of Crimes, ASP/1/3, pp. 108–55; Rules of Procedure and Evidence, ASP/1/3, pp. 10–107.

[4] Herman von Hebel and Darryl Robinson, 'Crimes within the Jurisdiction of the Court', in Lee, *The International Criminal Court*, pp. 79–126 at p. 88.

The second tier in the hierarchy of sources consists of 'applicable treaties and the principles and rules of international law, including the established principles of the international law of armed conflict'. This category rather generally corresponds to the sources of international law set out in Article 38 of the Statute of the International Court of Justice, although the wording is quite original. There is no express mention of customary international law, but it is surely covered by the reference to 'principles and rules of international law'. Moreover, the third source in the enumeration of the Statute of the International Court of Justice, general principles of law, is excluded from this second tier of sources. The reference to the 'international law of armed conflict' provides an opening for a detailed and increasingly sophisticated body of law of which the Hague Conventions of 1899 and 1907, together with the Geneva Conventions of 1949 and their two Additional Protocols of 1977, are the centrepiece. It may, for example, invite recognition by the Court of certain defences, such as reprisal and military necessity, not codified elsewhere in the Statute. But it is perhaps significant that the Rome Conference referred to the 'international law of armed conflict' rather than to 'international humanitarian law'.[5] The Appeals Chamber of the International Criminal Tribunal for the former Yugoslavia has suggested that 'international humanitarian law' is a more modern terminology than the more archaic 'laws of armed conflict', one that has emerged as a result of the influence of human rights doctrines.[6]

In the context of Article 21, judges of the International Criminal Court have cautioned against mechanistic application of the case law of the *ad hoc* tribunals:

> As to the relevance of the case law of the ad hoc tribunals, the matter must be assessed against the provisions governing the law applicable before the Court. Article 21, paragraph 1, of the Statute mandates the Court to apply its Statute, Elements of Crimes and Rules of Procedure and Evidence 'in the first place' and only 'in the second place' and 'where appropriate', 'applicable treaties and the principles and rules of international law, including the established principles of the international law of aimed conflict'. Accordingly, the rules and practice of other jurisdictions, whether

---

[5] Several delegates indicated a preference for the term 'international humanitarian law': UN Doc. A/CONF.183/C.1/SR.12, para. 54 (Syria), para. 63 (Chile), para. 64 (Afghanistan), para. 72 (Greece); UN Doc. A/CONF.183/C.1/SR.13, para. 10 (Venezuela), para. 12 (Guinea), para. 18 (Saudi Arabia).

[6] *Tadić* (IT-94-1-AR72), Decision on the Defence Motion for Interlocutory Appeal on Jurisdiction, 2 October 1995, para. 87.

national or international, are not as such 'applicable law' before the Court beyond the scope of article 21 of the Statute. More specifically, the law and practice of the ad hoc tribunals, which the Prosecutor refers to, cannot per se form a sufficient basis for importing into the Court's procedural framework remedies other than those enshrined in the Statute.[7]

The third tier in the hierarchy is pointed towards domestic law. Article 21 invites the Court, should it fail to resolve questions applying the first two sources, to resort to general principles of law derived from national laws of legal systems of the world including, as appropriate, 'the national laws of States that would normally exercise jurisdiction over the crime'. The reference to general principles enhances the role of comparative criminal law and corresponds, in practice, to what international judges do already before the *ad hoc* tribunals. The special attention given to national laws of States that would normally exercise jurisdiction is intriguing because it suggests that the law applied by the Court might vary slightly depending on the place of the crime or the nationality of the offender. As Per Saland has noted, '[t]here is of course a certain contradiction between the idea of deriving general principles, which indicates that this process could take place before a certain case is adjudicated, and that of looking also to particular national laws of relevance to a certain case; but that price had to be paid in order to reach a compromise'.[8] In its limited case law, the International Criminal Court has already resorted to general principles of law derived from national systems. For example, in its discussion of 'witness proofing', Pre-Trial Chamber I observed a broad variety of approaches in national justice systems.[9]

Generally, the Court has been quite resistant to arguments based upon national practice as a source of general principles. It has recalled that it

[7] *Situation in Uganda* (ICC-02/04–01/05), Decision on the Prosecutor's Position on the Decision of Pre-Trial Chamber II to Redact Factual Descriptions of Crimes from the Warrant of Arrest, Motion for Reconsideration, and Motion for Clarification, 28 October 2005, para. 19. Also *Situation in Kenya* (ICC-01/09), Dissenting Opinion of Judge Hans-Peter Kaul, 31 March 2010, paras. 28–32; *Bashir* (ICC-02/05–01/09), Decision on the Prosecution's Application for a Warrant of Arrest Against Omar Hassan Ahmad Al Bashir, 4 March 2009, paras. 118–20.

[8] Saland, 'International Criminal Law Principles', p. 215. See also Margaret McAuliffe DeGuzman, 'Article 21', in Otto Triffterer, ed., *Commentary on the Rome Statute of the International Criminal Court, Observers' Notes, Article by Article*, 2nd edn, Munich: C. H. Beck; Baden-Baden: Nomos; Oxford: Hart, 2008, pp. 702–4.

[9] *Lubanga* (ICC-01/04–01/06), Decision on the Practices of Witness Familiarisation and Witness Proofing, 8 November 2006, para. 35–7.

is not bound by national law in any respect.[10] In response to arguments from the Prosecutor that 'witness proofing' was an established practice in national legal systems, Trial Chamber I stated:

> However, the Trial Chamber does not consider that a general principle of law allowing the substantive preparation of witnesses prior to testimony can be derived from national legal systems worldwide, pursuant to Article 21(1)(c) of the Statute. Although this practice is accepted to an extent in two legal systems, both of which are founded upon common law traditions, this does not provide a sufficient basis for any conclusion that a general principle based on established practice of national legal systems exists. The Trial Chamber notes that the prosecution's submissions with regard to national jurisprudence did not include any citations from the Romano-Germanic legal system.[11]

This is the only explicit application of Article 21(1)(c) in the case law of the Court.

As sources of law, the Statute does not formally recognize the important body of international human rights treaties and declarations that has developed since the Universal Declaration of Human Rights in 1948, although arguably this is included in the general reference to applicable treaties and principles and rules found in Article 21(1)(b). However, Article 21(3) states that the application and interpretation of law 'must be consistent with internationally recognized human rights'. There are obvious implications of this principle with respect to the rights of the accused. With reference to Article 21(3), the Appeals Chamber of the Court has written:

> Human rights underpin the Statute; every aspect of it, including the exercise of the jurisdiction of the Court. Its provisions must be interpreted and more importantly applied in accordance with internationally recognized human rights; first and foremost, in the context of the Statute, the right to a fair trial, a concept broadly perceived and applied, embracing the judicial process in its entirety. The Statute itself makes evidence obtained in breach of internationally recognized human rights inadmissible in the circumstances specified by article 69(7) of the Statute. Where fair trial becomes impossible because of breaches of the fundamental rights of the

---

[10] *Lubanga* (ICC-01/04–01/06), Decision on the Confirmation of the Charges, 29 January 2007, para. 69; *Katanga et al.* (ICC-01/04–01/07), Decision on the Confirmation of Charges, 30 September 2008, para. 91.

[11] *Lubanga* (ICC-01/04–01/06), Decision Regarding the Practices Used to Prepare and Familiarise Witnesses for Giving Testimony at Trial, 30 November 2007, para. 41.

suspect or the accused by his/her accusers, it would be a contradiction in terms to put the person on trial. Justice could not be done. A fair trial is the only means to do justice. If no fair trial can be held, the object of the judicial process is frustrated and the process must be stopped.[12]

In setting out the conditions for disclosure of evidence in preparation of the confirmation hearing in the *Lubanga* case, Judge Steiner cited Article 21(3) and made particular reference to a range of human rights treaties.[13] She used the reference to reject the arguments of the defence, noting that its demand for full access to materials in the possession of the Prosecutor was unsupported by any authority from the main international human rights tribunals.[14] Judges have also held that there is a right of the accused to disclosure with respect to the grounds relied upon in a ruling on detention at the stage of issuance of the arrest warrant.[15] According to the Appeals Chamber, '[t]he Regulations of the Court must be read subject to the fundamental right of the accused to legal representation'.[16] The role of Article 21(3) may well extend into other areas, such as the rights of victims. Human rights law sources have been used to interpret the reference to 'reasonable grounds to believe' found in Article 58.[17] The provision also means that the Statute is not locked into the prevailing values at the time of its adoption. International human rights law continues to evolve inexorably, and the

[12] *Lubanga* (ICC-01/04–01/06), Judgment on the Appeal of Mr Thomas Lubanga Dyilo Against the Decision on the Defence Challenge to the Jurisdiction of the Court Pursuant to Article 19(2)(a) of the Statute of 3 October 2006, 14 December 2006, para. 37 (references omitted).
[13] *Lubanga* (ICC-01/04–01/06), Décision relative au système définitif de divulgation et à l'établissment d'un échéancier, Annexe I, Analyse de la décisions relative au système définitif de divulgation, 15 May 2006, para. 3.
[14] *Ibid.*, para. 14.
[15] *Bemba* (ICC-01/05–01/08 OA), Judgment on the Appeal of Mr Jean-Pierre Bemba Gombo Against the Decision of Pre-Trial Chamber III Entitled 'Decision on Application for Interim Release', 16 December 2008, paras. 28–34.
[16] *Lubanga* (ICC-01/04–01/06 OA 8), Reasons for 'Decision of the Appeals Chamber on the Defence Application "Demande de suspension de toute action ou procédure afin de permettre la désignation d'un nouveau Conseil de la Défense" Filed on 20 February 2007' Issued on 23 February 2007, 9 March 2007, para. 13.
[17] *Harun et al.* (ICC-02/05–01/07), Decision on the Prosecution Application under Article 58(7) of the Statute, 27 April 2007, para. 27; *Situation in the Democratic Republic of the Congo* (ICC-01/04–01/07), Decision on the Prosecutor's Application for Warrants of Arrest, Article 58, 10 February 2006, para. 12. See Göran Sluiter, 'Human Rights Protection in the ICC Pre-Trial Phase', in Carsten Stahn and Goran Sluiter, *The Emerging Practice of the International Criminal Court*, Leiden: Brill, 2009, pp. 459–75 at pp. 460–7.

reference to it in the Statute is full of promise for innovative interpretation in future years.

The reference to internationally recognized human rights was only won after considerable controversy. Ostensibly, the debate focused on use of the word 'gender' instead of 'sex' as a prohibited ground for discrimination. Several States, led by the Holy See, were opposed to such contemporary terminology, apparently out of concerns that it somehow condoned homosexuality, although the word was never mentioned in the discussion.[18] But underlying the dispute was also a malaise with the reference to human rights, and for a time at Rome the entire provision seemed in jeopardy. There was a proposal to truncate the text after the words 'human rights', thereby eliminating the troublesome term 'gender'. Another attempt at compromise envisaged a statement by the President of the Conference referring to the use of the term 'gender' in the 1995 Beijing Declaration. Ultimately, the term 'gender' survived, but was accompanied by a definition: 'For the purpose of this Statute it is understood that the term "gender" refers to the two sexes, male and female, within the context of society. The term "gender" does not indicate any meaning different from the above.'[19]

In addition to the Statute, the Rules of Procedure and the Elements of Crimes, several other legal instruments have been adopted by the various institutions of the International Criminal Court. Four of these are required by the Statute itself: the 'relationship agreement' with the United Nations,[20] the 'headquarters agreement' with the Netherlands,[21] the Staff Regulations,[22] and the Regulations of the Court which are 'necessary for its routine functioning'.

Other instruments adopted by various organs of the Court include the Regulations of the Office of the Prosecutor, the Regulations of the Registry, the Code of Professional Conduct for Counsel, the Code of Judicial Ethics, and the Financial Regulations and Rules. Collectively, all of these texts, together with the Statute itself, the Rules of Procedure and Evidence and the Elements of Crimes, comprise the Official Journal.[23]

---

[18] Saland, 'International Criminal Law Principles', p. 216.

[19] See Barbara C. Bedont, 'Gender-Specific Provisions in the Statute of the ICC', in Lattanzi and Schabas, *Essays on the Rome Statute*, pp. 183–210 at pp. 186–8.

[20] Rome Statute of the International Criminal Court, (2002) 2187 UNTS 90, Art. 2.

[21] *Ibid.*, Art. 3(2).   [22] *Ibid.*, Art. 44(3).

[23] Regulations of the Court, Regulation 7. In conformity with Regulation 8, the *Official Journal* is published on the website of the Court.

Interpreting the Rome Statute

The Rome Statute provides little in the way of guidance as to the rules of legal interpretation that ought to be followed. As an international treaty, the governing principles are those contained in Articles 31 and 32 of the 1969 Vienna Convention on the Law of Treaties.[24] According to the Appeals Chamber, in the interpretation of the Rome Statute the Court should be guided by the Vienna Convention, and especially by Articles 31 and 32.[25] These provisions establish, as a general rule of interpretation, that a treaty is to be interpreted in good faith in accordance with the ordinary meaning to be given to the terms of the treaty in their context and in the light of its object and purpose. According to the Appeals Chamber:

> The principal rule of interpretation is set out in article 31(1) that reads: 'A treaty shall be interpreted in good faith in accordance with the ordinary meaning to be given to the terms of the treaty in their context and in the light of its object and purpose.' The Appeals Chamber shall not advert to the definition of good faith, save to mention that it is linked to what follows and that is the wording of the Statute. The rule governing the interpretation of a section of the law is its wording read in context and in light of its object and purpose. The context of a given legislative provision is defined by the particular sub-section of the law read as a whole in conjunction with the section of an enactment in its entirety. Its object may be gathered from the chapter of the law in which the particular section is included and its purposes from the wider aims

---

[24] Vienna Convention on the Law of Treaties, (1979) 1155 UNTS 331.

[25] *Situation in the Democratic Republic of the Congo* (ICC-01/04), Judgment on the Prosecutor's Application for Extraordinary Review of Pre-Trial Chamber I's 31 March 2006 Decision Denying Leave to Appeal, para. 5. Also *Lubanga* (ICC-01/04–01/06 OA 8), Separate Opinion of Judge Georghios M. Pikis, 13 June 2007, para. 12; *Katanga et al.* (ICC-01/04–01/07 OA 7), Judgment on the Appeal of the Prosecutor Against the 'Decision on Evidentiary Scope of the Confirmation Hearing, Preventive Relocation and Disclosure under Article 67(2) of the Statute and Rule 77 of the Rules' of Pre-Trial Chamber I, 26 November 2008, para. 82; *Katanga et al.* (ICC-01/04–01/07 OA 7), Dissenting Opinion of Judge Georghios M. Pikis and Judge Daniel David Ntanda Nsereko, 26 November 2008, para. 13; *Situation in Darfur, Sudan* (ICC-02/05), Decision on Application under Rule 103, 4 February 2009, para 18; *Bashir* (ICC-02/05–01/09), Decision on the Prosecution's Application for a Warrant of Arrest Against Omar Hassan Ahmad Al Bashir, 4 March 2009, para. 44; *Bemba* (ICC-01/05–01/08), Decision Pursuant to Article 61(7)(a) and (b) of the Rome Statute on the Charges of the Prosecutor Against Jean-Pierre Bemba Gombo, 15 June 2009, para. 361.

of the law as may be gathered from its preamble and general tenor of the treaty.[26]

In accordance with Article 31 of the Vienna Convention, the context includes the preamble to the Rome Statute, as well as the Final Act adopted on 17 July 1998. In addition, subsequent agreements, such as the Rules of Procedure and Evidence and the Elements of Crimes, are germane to interpretation. Similarly, the 'understandings' that were reached at the 2010 Review Conference concerning the interpretation of the amendments to Article 8 and the new Article 8*bis* will be germane in this respect.

As supplementary means of interpretation, the Vienna Convention points to the drafting history or *travaux préparatoires* of the Statute, in order to confirm the meaning determined in application of Article 31, or when the meaning is ambiguous or obscure, or if the general rule of interpretation leads to an absurd or unreasonable result. Dismissing the Prosecutor's argument that there was a lacuna in the Rome Statute, and that there was an inherent right to appeal a ruling of a Pre-Trial Chamber denying leave to appeal, the Appeals Chamber said:

> The *travaux préparatoires* reveal that a specific suggestion made by the Kenyan delegation to the Committee of the Whole at the 1998 United Nations Diplomatic Conference of Plenipotentiaries designed in essence to give effect to the right claimed by the Prosecutor was turned down. The suggestion was: 'Other decisions may be appealed with the leave of the Chamber concerned and in the event of refusal such refusal may be appealed.' The dismissal of the suggestion rules out any possibility that the content of article 82(1)(d) of the Statute was anything other than deliberate. The *travaux préparatoires* confirm that article 82(1)(d) of the Statute reflects what was intended by its makers.[27]

Many of the judges of the Court were delegates to the Rome Conference. There has been some concern that they may confound their own personal recollections of what was intended by the drafters with what is reflected in the record itself. There is no evidence of this problem in the rulings to

---

[26] *Situation in the Democratic Republic of the Congo* (ICC-01/04), Judgment on the Prosecutor's Application for Extraordinary Review of Pre-Trial Chamber I's 31 March 2006 Decision Denying Leave to Appeal, 13 July 2006, para. 33 (references omitted).

[27] *Situation in the Democratic Republic of the Congo* (ICC-01/04), Judgment on the Prosecutor's Application for Extraordinary Review of Pre-Trial Chamber I's 31 March 2006 Decision Denying Leave to Appeal, paras. 40–1 (references omitted).

date. Some of the academic commentary on the Statute was also written by participants in the Rome Conference, and their memories of the process and personal experiences colour their own analysis of the Statute (the present author is no exception). For the purposes of judicial interpretation, however, it is preferable to confine analysis of the *travaux* to what appears in the official documents.[28]

Some may argue that, as a source of criminal law, the Rome Statute should be subject to the rule of 'strict construction', or that, in the event of ambiguity or uncertainty, the result more favourable to the accused should be endorsed. Such a rule is drawn from national criminal law practice. It is confirmed, at least with respect to the definitions of crimes, in Article 22(2) of the Rome Statute: 'The definition of a crime shall be strictly construed and shall not be extended by analogy. In case of ambiguity, the definition shall be interpreted in favour of the person being investigated, prosecuted or convicted.' Article 22(2) is in many respects a reaction to the large and liberal approach to construction taken by the judges of the International Criminal Tribunal for the former Yugoslavia. The approach to the definitions of crimes in such cases as the *Tadić* jurisdiction decision, which quite dramatically opened up the category of war crimes to include offences committed in non-international armed conflict, was not within the spirit of strict construction.[29] Frequently, the judges of the Yugoslav Tribunal have invoked the principles of interpretation in the Vienna Convention on the Law of Treaties, which are essentially contextual and purposive in scope.[30]

---

[28] The documentary record of the Rome Conference is now available in an official United Nations publication, consisting of three volumes: United Nations Diplomatic Conference of Plenipotentiaries on the Establishment of an International Criminal Court, 15 June–17 July 1998, UN Doc. A/CONF.183/13. Also M. Cherif Bassiouni, ed., *The Statute of the International Criminal Court: A Documentary History*, Ardsley, NY: Transnational Publishers, 1998; M. Cherif Bassiouni, ed., *The Legislative History of the International Criminal Court: Introduction, Analysis and Integrated Text*, Ardsley, NY: Transnational Publishers, 2005.

[29] *Tadić* (IT-94-1-AR72), Decision on the Defence Motion for Interlocutory Appeal on Jurisdiction, 2 October 1995.

[30] *Erdemović* (IT-96-22-A), Joint Separate Opinion of Judge McDonald and Judge Vohrah, 7 October 1997, para. 3; *Bagosora and 28 Others* (ICTR-98-37-A), Decision on the Admissibility of the Prosecutor's Appeal from the Decision of a Confirming Judge Dismissing an Indictment Against Théoneste Bagosora and 28 Others, 8 June 1998, para. 28; *Delalić et al.* (IT-96-21-T), Judgment, 16 November 1998, para. 1161. In contrast, the references to strict construction have been perfunctory at best: *Tadić* (IT-94-1-A), Decision on Appellant's Motion for the Extension of the Time-Limit and Admission of Additional Evidence, 15 October 1998, para. 73; *Erdemović* (IT-96-22-A), Separate and Dissenting Opinion of Judge Cassese, 7 October 1997, para. 49.

The Rome Conference was obviously unsettled by such judicial licence, and Article 22(2) is the result.

The wording of Article 22(2) is precise enough to leave open the question of whether or not strict construction applies to provisions of the Statute other than those that define the offences themselves. When problems of interpretation arise, the 'contextual rule' of the Vienna Convention and the principle of strict construction drawn from national legal practice, as well as from Article 22, may lead to very different results. The judges of the Court will have to resolve this without any substantial assistance from the Statute. Perhaps the judges recruited from the public international law field will lean towards the Vienna Convention while those who are criminal law practitioners in national legal systems will favour strict construction. To date, strict construction has rarely figured in the jurisprudence of the Court, which has regularly invoked the provisions of the Vienna Convention as the authoritative source of interpretative principles. Article 22(2) was relied upon by Pre-Trial Chamber II in its construction of Article 30, by which it excluded *dolus eventualis* or recklessness from the scope of the Rome Statute.[31]

Presumption of innocence

The presumption of innocence, recognized in Article 66 of the Statute, imposes the burden upon the prosecution to prove guilt beyond a reasonable doubt, a specialized application in criminal law of a general rule common to most forms of litigation, namely, that the plaintiff has the burden of proof. According to Pre-Trial Chamber II, 'it is guided by the principle *in dubio pro reo* as a component of the presumption of innocence, which as a general principle in criminal procedure applies, *mutatis mutandis*, to all stages of the proceedings, including the pre-trial stage'.[32] But the presumption of innocence has other manifestations, for example in the right of an accused person to interim release pending trial, subject to exceptional circumstances in which preventive detention may be ordered, the right of the accused person to be detained separately from those who have been convicted, and the right of the accused to remain silent during the investigation and during trial. Several of the rules that reflect the presumption of innocence are incorporated within

---

[31] *Bemba* (ICC-01/05–01/08), Decision Pursuant to Article 61(7)(a) and (b) of the Rome Statute on the Charges of the Prosecutor Against Jean-Pierre Bemba Gombo, 15 June 2009, para. 369.

[32] *Ibid.*, para. 31.

the Statute. For example, during an investigation, there is a right '[t]o remain silent, without such silence being a consideration in the determination of guilt or innocence';[33] there is a right to interim release;[34] and there are grounds for appeal which are wider in scope for the defence than for the prosecution.[35] Nevertheless, it was also felt necessary to affirm the principle generally and explicitly. Professor Cherif Bassiouni, who chaired the Drafting Committee at the Rome Conference, has argued that it was a mistake not to include the provision ensuring the presumption of innocence within Part 3 of the Statute:

> [T]here is no valid methodological explanation for the separation and placement of the provision concerning the presumption of innocence (Article 66) in Part 6 and the provisions concerning ne bis in idem (Article 20) and applicable law (Article 21) in Part 2. All of these provisions properly belong in Part 3 of the Statute, which deals with general principles of criminal responsibility.[36]

He has added, in a footnote to his comment: 'While Articles 20 and 21 were included in Part 2 as a result of political considerations, the location of Article 66 in Part 6 reflects an insufficient appreciation of traditional legal methods of criminal law.'[37]

The European Court of Human Rights has defined the presumption of innocence as follows:

> It requires, *inter alia*, that when carrying out their duties, the members of a court should not start with the preconceived idea that the accused has committed the offence charged; the burden of proof is on the prosecution, and any doubt should benefit the accused. It also follows that it is for the prosecution to inform the accused of the case that will be made against him, so that he may prepare and present his defence accordingly, and to adduce evidence sufficient to convict him.[38]

In its 'General Comment' on Article 14 of the International Covenant on Civil and Political Rights, the UN Human Rights Committee has

[33] Rome Statute, Art. 55(2)(b).   [34] *Ibid.*, Arts. 59(3)–(6) and 60(2)–(4).
[35] *Ibid.*, Art. 81(1). See M. Cherif Bassiouni and Peter Manikas, *The Law of the International Criminal Tribunal for the former Yugoslavia*, New York: Transnational Publishers, 1995, p. 961, for a similar observation on the Statute of the International Criminal Tribunal for the former Yugoslavia, UN Doc. S/RES/827, Annex, and its Rules of Procedure and Evidence, UN Doc. IT/32.
[36] M. Cherif Bassiouni, 'Negotiating the Treaty of Rome on the Establishment of an International Criminal Court', (1999) 32 *Cornell International Law Journal* 443 at 454.
[37] *Ibid.*, n. 48.
[38] *Barberà, Messegué and Jabardo* v. *Spain*, Series A, No. 146, 6 December 1988, para. 77.

insisted that the presumption of innocence imposes a duty on all public authorities to 'refrain from prejudging the outcome of a trial'.[39] According to the European Commission of Human Rights:

> It is a fundamental principle embodied in [the presumption of innocence] which protects everybody against being treated by public officials as being guilty of an offence before this is established according to law by a competent court. Article 6, paragraph 2 [of the European Convention on Human Rights], therefore, may be violated by public officials if they declare that somebody is responsible for criminal acts without a court having found so. This does not mean, of course, that the authorities may not inform the public about criminal investigations. They do not violate Article 6, paragraph 2, if they state that a suspicion exists, that people have been arrested, that they have confessed, etc. What is excluded, however, is a formal declaration that somebody is guilty.[40]

Transposing these notions, derived from domestic prosecutions, to the international context gives some intriguing results. The 'authorities' on the international scene will be such bodies as the Human Rights Council, the High Commissioner for Human Rights, the Security Council, the General Assembly and the Secretary-General. If, for example, the General Assembly charges that genocide has been committed by the leaders of a given regime, can the latter invoke this essentially political accusation before the International Criminal Court in claiming that the presumption of innocence has been denied?[41] One answer is that there may well be a denial of the presumption of innocence but that it will not have been committed by the Court itself. But the Appeals Chamber of the International Criminal Tribunal for Rwanda has already judged it appropriate to grant a stay of proceedings

---

[39] General Comment 13/21, UN Doc. A/39/40, pp. 143–7.

[40] *Krause* v. *Switzerland* (App. No. 7986/77), (1978) 13 DR 73. Also, from the Court, see *Allenet de Ribemont* v. *France*, Series A, No. 308, 10 February 1995, paras. 37 and 41. See Francis G. Jacobs and Robin C. A. White, *The European Convention on Human Rights*, 2nd edn, Oxford: Clarendon Press, 1996, p. 150.

[41] A Security Council resolution denouncing the atrocities in Srebrenica, UN Doc. S/RES/1034 (1995), singled out for special mention the Bosnian Serb leaders Radovan Karadžić and Ratko Mladić, noting that they had been indicted by the International Criminal Tribunal for the former Yugoslavia for their responsibilities in the massacre. The word 'alleged' did not accompany the reference to their responsibilities. The resolution '[c]ondemn[ed] in particular in the strongest possible terms the violations of international humanitarian law and of human rights by Bosnian Serb and paramilitary forces in the areas of Srebrenica'.

in a case where the rights of an accused were violated by a national justice system and not by the authorities of the tribunals themselves.[42]

Arguably, the presumption of innocence may require that decisions by the Court, particularly given the seriousness of the charges and of the available sentences, be unanimous. Certainly, where questions of fact are at issue, is it not logical to conclude that, where one member of the Court has a reasonable doubt, this should be enough to create a reasonable doubt in the minds of the tribunal as a whole?[43] Compelling as the suggestion may be – and it was argued by some delegates at the Rome Conference – the Statute provides clearly that, in case of division, a majority of the Court will suffice for a finding of guilt.[44]

Rights of the accused

During World War II, Churchill and other Allied leaders flirted with the idea of some form of summary justice for major war criminals.[45] But, speaking of the Nuremberg trial, prosecutor Robert Jackson said that history would assess the proceedings in light of the fairness with which the defendants were treated. Only a few years later, one of the 'successor' military tribunals at Nuremberg held that Nazi prosecutors and judges involved in a trial lacking the fundamental guarantees of fairness could be held responsible for crimes against humanity.[46] Such guarantees include the presumption of innocence, the right of the accused to introduce evidence, to confront witnesses, to present evidence, to be tried in public, to have counsel of choice, and to be informed of the nature of the charges.[47] And, more recently, the judges of the International Criminal Tribunal for the former Yugoslavia, in the first major ruling of the

---

[42] *Barayagwiza* (ICTR-97-19-AR72), Decision of 3 November 1999. Also *Kajelijeli* (ICTR-98-44A-A), Judgment, 23 May 2005, paras. 197–255.

[43] For such a suggestion, see Lawyers Committee for Human Rights, 'Fairness to Defendants at the International Criminal Court', August 1996, pp. 12–13.

[44] Rome Statute, Art. 74(3).

[45] Arieh J. Kochavi, *Prelude to Nuremberg: Allied War Crimes Policy and the Question of Punishment*, Chapel Hill, NC, and London: University of North Carolina Press, 1998, pp. 63–91.

[46] *United States of America* v. *Alstötter et al.* ('Justice trial'), (1948) 3 TWC 1; 6 LRTWC 1; 14 ILR 274. A recent and ironic echo is the trial of Saddam Hussein, who was convicted of crimes against humanity for his role in unfair trials leading to the death penalty. The judgment would have been a nice contemporary precedent, except that the Hussein trial was itself deeply flawed, and it too led to the death penalty.

[47] *Ibid.*

Appeals Chamber, said: 'For a Tribunal such as this one to be established according to the rule of law, it must be established in accordance with the proper international standards; it must provide all the guarantees of fairness, justice and even-handedness, in full conformity with internationally recognized human rights instruments.'[48] As if there could be any doubt, the Rome Statute ensures the protection of the rights of the accused with a detailed codification of procedural guarantees.

Article 67 of the Rome Statute, entitled 'Rights of the accused', is modelled on Article 14(3) of the International Covenant on Civil and Political Rights, one of the principal human rights treaties.[49] The right to a fair trial is also enshrined in the Universal Declaration of Human Rights,[50] the regional human rights conventions,[51] as well as in humanitarian law instruments.[52] The general right to a 'fair hearing' established in the *chapeau* of Article 67 of the Statute provides defendants with a powerful tool to go beyond the text of the Statute, and to require that the Court's respect for the rights of an accused keep pace with the progressive development of human rights law. Although Article 67 is placed with the provisions dealing with the trial itself, the right to a fair hearing applies at all stages of the proceedings, and even during the investigation, when no defendant has even been identified.[53] The case law of the

[48] *Tadić* (IT-94-1-AR72), Decision on the Defence Motion for Interlocutory Appeal on Jurisdiction, 2 October 1995, para. 45.

[49] International Covenant on Civil and Political Rights, (1966) 999 UNTS 171.

[50] GA Res. 217 A (III), UN Doc. A/810 (1948). Art. 10: 'Everyone is entitled in full equality to a fair and public hearing by an independent and impartial tribunal, in the determination of his rights and obligations and of any criminal charge against him.' Art. 11(3): 'Everyone charged with a penal offence has the right to be presumed innocent until proved guilty according to law in a public trial at which he has had all the guarantees necessary for his defence.'

[51] American Convention on Human Rights, (1978) 1144 UNTS 123, Art. 8; European Convention on Human Rights, (1955) 213 UNTS 221, Art. 6; African Charter on Human and Peoples' Rights, (1986) 1520 UNTS 217, Art. 7; Convention on the Rights of the Child, (1990) 1577 UNTS 3, Art. 40, para. 2.

[52] Geneva Convention (III) Relative to the Treatment of Prisoners of War, (1950) 75 UNTS 135, Arts. 84–87 and 99–108; Geneva Convention (IV) Relative to the Protection of Civilians, (1950) 75 UNTS 287, Arts. 5 and 64–76; Protocol Additional I to the 1949 Geneva Conventions and Relating to the Protection of Victims of International Armed Conflicts, (1979) 1125 UNTS 3, Art. 75; Protocol Additional II to the 1949 Geneva Conventions and Relating to the Protection of Victims of Non-International Armed Conflicts, (1979) 1125 UNTS 3, Art. 6.

[53] *Situation in the Democratic Republic of the Congo* (ICC-01/04), Decision on the Prosecution's Application for Leave to Appeal the Chamber's Decision of 17 January 2006 on the Applications for Participation in the Proceedings of VPRS 1, VPRS 2, VPRS 3, VPRS 4, VPRS 5 and VPRS 6, 31 March 2006, para. 35.

Strasbourg organs, established to implement the European Convention on Human Rights, has used this residual right to a fair hearing to fill in some of the gaps in the more specific provisions.[54] That the term 'fair hearing' invites the Court to exceed the precise terms of Article 67 in appropriate circumstances is confirmed by the reference within the *chapeau* to 'minimum guarantees'. As Judge Steiner, sitting as a single judge of Pre-Trial Chamber I, has noted, the reference to 'minimum guarantees' in Article 67(1) means that sometimes the competent Chamber will need to go beyond the terms of Article 67 itself. She cited the case law of the European Court of Human Rights in support.[55] The term 'fair hearing' also suggests that, where individual problems with specific rights set out in Article 67 do not, on their own, amount to a violation, the requirement of a fair hearing may allow a cumulative view and lead to the conclusion that there is a breach where there have been a number of apparently minor or less significant encroachments on Article 67.[56]

The case law of international human rights tribunals has developed the notion of 'equality of arms' within the concept of the right to a fair trial.[57] The concept has been readily embraced by judges at the International Criminal Court.[58] According to Pre-Trial Chamber II,

---

[54] D. J. Harris, M. O'Boyle and C. Warbrick, *Law of the European Convention on Human Rights*, London: Butterworths, 1995, pp. 202–3.

[55] *Lubanga* (ICC-01/04–01/06), Décision relative au système définitif de divulgation et à l'établissment d'un échéancier, Annexe I, Analyse de la décisions relative au système définitif de divulgation, 15 May 2006, para. 97. Judge Steiner also referred to the previous edition of this book as authority for such a view.

[56] *Stanford* v. *United Kingdom*, Series A, No. 182-À, 30 August 1990, para. 24.

[57] *Neumeister* v. *Austria*, Series A, No. 8, 11 *Yearbook* 822, 27 June 1968; *Morael* v. *France* (No. 207/1986), UN Doc. CCPR/8/Add/1, p. 416; Manfred Novak, *CCPR Commentary*, Kehl, Germany: N. P. Engel, 1993. For recognition of the principle of 'equality of arms' by the International Criminal Tribunal for the former Yugoslavia, see *Tadić* (IT-94-1-T), Separate Opinion of Judge Vohrah on Prosecution Motion for Production of Defence Witness Statements, 27 November 1996, pp. 4 and 7.

[58] *Bemba* (ICC-01/05–01/08 OA), Judgment on the Appeal of Mr Jean-Pierre Bemba Gombo Against the Decision of Pre-Trial Chamber III Entitled 'Decision on Application for Interim Release', 16 December 2008, para. 32; *Katanga* (ICC-01/04–01/07 OA), Judgment on the Appeal of the Prosecutor Against the Decision of Pre-Trial Chamber I Entitled 'First Decision on the Prosecution Request for Authorization to Redact Witness Statements', 13 May 2008, para. 73; *Katanga* (ICC-01/04–01/07 OA 2), Judgment on the Appeal of Mr Germain Katanga Against the Decision of Pre-Trial Chamber I Entitled 'First Decision on the Prosecution Request for Authorization to Redact Witness Statements', 13 May 2008, para. 63; *Situation in Darfur, Sudan* (ICC-02/05), Decision on the Request for Leave to Appeal to the Decision Issued on 23 September 2007, 31 October 2007, p. 6; *Lubanga* (ICC-01/04–01/06), Decision on the Consequences of Non-Disclosure of Exculpatory Materials Covered by Article 54(3)(e) Agreements and the

'[f]airness is closely linked to the concept of "equality of arms", or of balance between the parties during the proceedings. As commonly understood, it concerns the ability of a party to a proceeding to adequately make its case, with a view to influencing the outcome of the proceedings in its favour.'[59] The Appeals Chamber of the International Criminal Tribunal for the former Yugoslavia has noted that, when international tribunals are concerned, the scope given to the defence under the principle of 'equality of arms' deserves a more liberal interpretation. According to the Appeals Chamber, '[i]t follows that the Chamber shall provide every practicable facility it is capable of granting under the Rules and Statute when faced with a request by a party for assistance in presenting its case. The Trial Chambers are mindful of the difficulties encountered by the parties in tracing and gaining access to evidence in the territory of the former Yugoslavia where some States have not been forthcoming in complying with their legal obligation to cooperate with the Tribunal.'[60] The International Criminal Tribunal for the former Yugoslavia has considered it 'important and inherent in the concept of equality of arms that each party be afforded a reasonable opportunity to present his or her case under conditions that do not place him at an appreciable disadvantage *vis-à-vis* his opponent'. Moreover, 'the concept of equality of arms could be exemplified having regard to the right to call witnesses as between the Prosecution and the Defence, as well as the duty of the Prosecution to disclose relevant material to the Defence'.[61]

The Rome Statute states that the hearing must be 'conducted impartially'. According to the European Court of Human Rights, 'impartiality' means lack of 'prejudice or bias'.[62] It comprises both a subjective and an objective dimension: '[t]he existence of impartiality ... must be determined according to a subjective test, that is, on the basis of the personal conviction of a particular judge in a given case, and also according to

Application to Stay the Prosecution of the Accused, Together with Certain Other Issues Raised at the Status Conference on 10 June 2008, 13 June 2008, para. 79.

[59] *Situation in Uganda* (ICC-02/04–01/05), Decision on Prosecutor's Application for Leave to Appeal in Part Pre-Trial Chamber II's Decision on the Prosecutor's Applications for Warrants of Arrest under Article 58, 19 August 2005, para. 30. Also *Lubanga* (ICC-01/04–01/06), Décision sur la demande d'autorisation d'appel de la Défense relative à la transmission des Demandes de participation des victimes, 6 November 2006, p. 7.

[60] *Tadić* (IT-94-1-A), Judgment, 15 July 1999, para. 52.

[61] *Brdjanin and Talić* (IT-99-36-PT), Public Version of the Confidential Decision on the Alleged Illegality of Rule 70 of 6 May 2002, 23 May 2002. See also *Krajisnik and Plavšić* (IT-00-39 and 40-PT), Decision on Prosecution Motion for Clarification in Respect of Application of Rules 65*ter*, 66(B) and 67(C), 1 August 2001.

[62] *Piersack v. Belgium*, Series A, No. 53, 1 October 1982.

an objective test, namely, ascertaining whether the judge offered guarantees sufficient to exclude any legitimate doubt in this respect'.[63] Here, too, the case law of the *ad hoc* tribunals provides guidance as to how such provisions are applied in a context of international criminal justice. In one case, defendants challenged the impartiality of a judge who had, during the proceedings, been elected vice-president of her country. Dismissing the argument, the Appeals Chamber noted that she had not exercised any executive functions while the trial was underway. It said the test to be applied was 'whether the reaction of the hypothetical fair-minded observer (with sufficient knowledge of the circumstances to make a reasonable judgment) would be that [the judge] might not bring an impartial and unprejudiced mind to the issues arising in the case'.[64]

There is a right to a speedy trial. This has proven to be one of the great challenges to international criminal justice. The trial of the International Military Tribunal at Nuremberg took less than a year from the time the indictments were served, in mid-October 1945, until the final judgment, on 30 September–1 October 1946. Since then, proceedings have become considerably longer. This is often explained by the heightened concern for procedural fairness dictated by international human rights standards, the implication being that Nuremberg was perhaps a bit too quick. But some recent trials of the *ad hoc* tribunals have been quite stunning in their length. The 'Butare case', which is being heard by the International Criminal Tribunal for Rwanda, began in 2001 and is expected to finish in 2010. Its six defendants have been in custody since 1996 and 1997.[65] The most important trial of the International Criminal Tribunal for the former Yugoslavia, of former Yugoslav president Slobodan Milošević, was well into its fourth year when the defendant died of natural causes, depriving the victims of a final judgment and squandering the precious resources of the Tribunal. There are suspicions that some judges at the international tribunals have been dragging their feet so that their employment by the tribunals at lucrative international salaries by comparison with what they might otherwise earn will continue as long as possible.

If anything, the chronic problems of lengthy proceedings at international criminal tribunals have only become aggravated at the

---

[63] *Hauschildt* v. *Denmark*, Series A, No. 154, 24 December 1989, para. 46.

[64] *Delalić* (IT-96-21-A), Judgment, 20 February 2001, para. 683. Judge Odio Benito was elected to the International Criminal Court in 2003. She served as one of its two vice-presidents from 2003 until 2006.

[65] Completion Strategy of the International Criminal Tribunal for Rwanda, UN Doc. S/2005/782, enclosure, p. 19.

International Criminal Court. Additional procedural stages, like the confirmation hearing required by Article 61, have contributed. There has also been an obsession with the writing of lengthy judgments, even for rather minor matters, and this has added to the delays. Interlocutory appeals, which are almost unknown in domestic criminal trials, also make their contribution to the duration of the proceedings at the International Criminal Court.

Among the other guarantees to the defendant set out in Article 67 are the right to be informed in detail of the nature, cause and content of the charge, to have adequate time and facilities for the preparation of the defence, to communicate freely with counsel of one's choosing, to be tried without undue delay, to be present at trial, to examine witnesses, and to benefit from the services of an interpreter if required. The International Covenant on Civil and Political Rights is forty-five years old. Reflecting evolving contemporary standards of procedural fairness, the Rome Statute goes somewhat beyond the minimum requirements found in Article 14(3) of the Covenant. Thus, Article 67 of the Statute ensures the right to silence, the right to make an unsworn statement, and a protection against any reversal of the burden of proof or an onus of rebuttal. In addition to persons charged with an offence, the Statute also enumerates rights that accrue to 'persons during an investigation'[66] and to persons about to be questioned by the Prosecutor or even national authorities for crimes within the jurisdiction of the Court.[67]

Individual criminal responsibility

The International Criminal Court is concerned with trying and punishing individuals, not States. 'Crimes against international law are committed by men, not by abstract entities, and only by punishing individuals who commit such crimes can the provisions of international law be enforced', wrote the Nuremberg Tribunal in 1946.[68] This is reflected in Article 25 of the Rome Statute. Proposals that the Court also exercise jurisdiction over corporate bodies in addition to individuals were seriously considered at the Rome Conference. While all national legal systems provide for individual criminal responsibility, their approaches to corporate criminal liability vary considerably. With a Court predicated

---

[66] Rome Statute, Art. 55(1).   [67] *Ibid.*, Art. 55(2).
[68] *France et al.* v. *Goering et al.*, (1946) 22 IMT 203; (1946) 13 ILR 203; (1946) 41 *American Journal of International Law* 172, p. 221 (AJIL).

on the principle of complementarity, it would have been unfair to establish a form of jurisdiction that would in effect be inapplicable to those States that do not punish corporate bodies under criminal law. During negotiations, attempts at encompassing some form of corporate liability made considerable progress. But time was simply too short for the delegates to reach a consensus and ultimately the concept had to be abandoned.[69]

The 2010 amendments to the Rome Statute add the following paragraph to Article 25: 'In respect of the crime of aggression, the provisions of this article shall apply only to persons in a position effectively to exercise control over or to direct the political or military action of a State.'[70] The post-Second World War cases are authority for this limitation *ratione personae* on the scope of prosecutions for the crime of aggression.[71] This is in rather stark contrast with the other crimes within the jurisdiction of the Court, where not only is no such limitation contemplated but lower-ranking suspects are denied the defence that they were only following orders.[72] Jeff McMahan has written that 'if people generally believed that participation in an unjust or morally unjustified war is wrong – that could make a significant practical difference to the practice of war ... Many people, including active-duty soldiers, would be more reluctant to fight in wars they believed to be unjust.'[73]

The International Criminal Court, like its earlier models at Nuremberg, The Hague and Arusha, is targeted at the major criminals responsible for large-scale atrocities. Most of its 'clientele' will not be the actual perpetrators of the crimes, soiling their hands with flesh and blood. Rather, they will be 'accomplices', those who organize, plan and incite genocide, crimes against humanity and war crimes. Case law of the International Criminal Court supports a broad approach to the concept of commission, so as to encompass leaders and organizers who do not physically perpetrate the criminal acts. Under this 'control over the crime' paradigm, an individual is deemed a co-perpetrator if he or she has 'joint control' as a result of an 'essential contribution' to its

---

[69] Saland, 'International Criminal Law Principles', p. 199; Ambos, 'General Principles', p. 7. For the debates in the Committee of the Whole at the Rome Conference, see UN Doc. A/CONF.183/C.1/SR.1, paras. 32–66; UN Doc. A/CONF.183/C.1/SR.23, para. 3.

[70] The Crime of Aggression, RC/Res.4, Annex I, para. 5.

[71] *United States of America* v. *von Leeb et al.* ('High Command Case'), (1948) 11 TWC 462 at 488–9; *United States of America* v. *Krauch et al.* ('I. G. Farben Trial'), (1948) 8 TWC 1081 at 1125.

[72] Rome Statute, Art. 33.

[73] Jeff McMahan, *Killing in War*, Oxford: Oxford University Press, 2009, p. 7.

commission. Decisions of the Pre-Trial Chambers have used literal and contextual approaches to interpretation in order to reach this result.[74] As a result, and because the concept is rooted in interpretation of the provisions of the Rome Statute, Pre-Trial Chambers have distinguished 'co-perpetration' from the joint criminal enterprise approach to liability that has become firmly entrenched in the case law of the *ad hoc* tribunals. The International Criminal Court has characterized the approach of the *ad hoc* tribunals as subjective, in that it focuses on the individual state of mind of the accused rather than on his or her actual control over the commission of the offence.[75] Accordingly, 'principals to a crime are not limited to those who physically carry out the objective elements of the offence, but also include those who, in spite of being removed from the scene of the crime, control or mastermind its commission, because they decide whether and how the offence will be committed'.[76]

In his dissenting opinions, Judge Wolfgang Schomburg of the Appeals Chamber of the International Criminal Tribunal for Rwanda stressed the importance of 'co-perpetratorship' with reference to Article 25(3)(a), noting: 'Given the wide acknowledgment of co-perpetratorship and indirect perpetratorship, the ICC Statute does not create new law in this respect, but reflects existing law.'[77] But his colleagues continued to reject the concept of 'co-perpetration', opting instead for that of 'joint criminal enterprise'.[78] Ironically, the introduction of the concept of 'joint

---

[74] *Lubanga* (ICC-01/04–01/06), Decision on the Confirmation of Charges, 29 January 2007, paras. 334–5. Also *Bashir* (ICC-02/05–01/09), Decision on the Prosecution's Application for a Warrant of Arrest Against Omar Hassan Ahmad Al Bashir, 4 March 2009, para. 210.

[75] *Ibid.*, para. 329; also para. 335. Also *Katanga et al.* (ICC-01/04–01/07), Decision on the Confirmation of the Charges, 30 September 2008, paras. 506–8. Recognition of the concept of co-perpetration by the Pre-Trial Chamber was welcomed by a judge of the Appeals Chamber of the International Criminal Tribunal for Rwanda (*Gacumbitsi* (ICTR-2001-64-A), Separate Opinion of Judge Schomburg on the Criminal Responsibility of the Appellant for Committing Genocide, 7 July 2006, para. 21, n. 609). However, the case law of the *ad hoc* tribunals has not been influenced by the positions taken at the International Criminal Court, where the divergence is explained either as a result of differences in the applicable legal texts (see e.g. *Seromba* (ICTR-2001-66-A), Dissenting Opinion of Judge Liu, 10 March 2008, para. 10) or the questionable notion that the *ad hoc* tribunals apply customary international law whereas the International Criminal Court applies its Statute.

[76] *Ibid.*, para. 332. Also *Katanga et al.* (ICC-01/04–01/07), Decision on the Confirmation of the Charges, 30 September 2008, para. 485.

[77] *Gacumbitsi* (ICTR-2001-64-A), Separate Opinion of Judge Schomburg on the Criminal Responsibility of the Appellant for Committing Genocide, 7 July 2006, para. 21.

[78] *Stakić* (IT-97-24-A), Judgment, 22 March 2006.

criminal enterprise' into the case law of the International Criminal Tribunal for the former Yugoslavia was justified with reference to Article 25(3)(d) of the Rome Statute.[79]

According to the case law of the International Criminal Court, perpetration within the meaning of Article 25(3)(a) covers three categories of offenders: those who physically commit the crime (commission of the crime in person or direct perpetration); those who control the will of the physical perpetrators (commission through another person or indirect perpetration); those who control the offence because of essential tasks assigned to them (commission of the crime jointly, or co-perpetration).[80] According to Pre-Trial Chamber I, 'the concept of co-perpetration is originally rooted in the idea that when the sum of the co-ordinated individual contributions of a plurality of persons results in the realization of all the objective elements of a crime, any person making a contribution can be held vicariously responsible for the contributions of all the others and, as a result, can be considered as a principal to the whole crime'.[81] It does not seem to be substantially different from the vision of the District Court of Jerusalem which condemned Eichmann: 'His responsibility is that of a "principal offender" who has committed the entire crime in conjunction with the others.'[82] Pre-Trial Chamber I has explained that, under the co-perpetration theory, 'none of the participants has overall control over the offence because they all depend on one another for its commission, they all share control because each of them could frustrate the commission of the crime by not carrying out his or her task'.[83] There must be an agreement or common plan between two or more persons, although its existence need not be explicit and may be inferred.[84] According to Pre-Trial Chamber III, 'criminal responsibility under the concept of co-perpetration requires the proof of two objective elements: (i) the suspect must be

[79] *Tadić* (IT-94-1-A), Judgment, 15 July 1999, para. 222.
[80] *Ibid.*, para. 332. Also *Katanga et al.* (ICC-01/04–01/07), Decision on the Confirmation of the Charges, 30 September 2008, para. 488; *Bashir* (ICC-02/05–01/09), Decision on the Prosecution's Application for a Warrant of Arrest Against Omar Hassan Ahmad Al Bashir, 4 March 2009, para. 210.
[81] *Ibid.*, para. 326. Cited in *Katanga et al.* (ICC-01/04–01/07), Decision on the Confirmation of the Charges, 30 September 2008, para. 520.
[82] *A-G Israel* v. *Eichmann*, (1968) 36 ILR 18 (District Court, Jerusalem), para. 194.
[83] *Lubanga* (ICC-01/04–01/06), Decision on the Confirmation of Charges, 29 January 2007, para. 342; also paras. 346–8. Cited in *Bashir* (ICC-02/05–01/09), Decision on the Prosecution's Application for a Warrant of Arrest Against Omar Hassan Ahmad Al Bashir, 4 March 2009, para. 212.
[84] *Ibid.*, paras. 344–5. Also *Katanga et al.* (ICC-01/04–01/07), Decision on the Confirmation of the Charges, 30 September 2008, paras. 522–3.

part of a common plan or an agreement with one or more persons; and (ii) the suspect and the other co-perpetrator must carry out essential contributions in a coordinated manner which result in the fulfilment of the material elements of the crime.'[85]

Complicity is specifically addressed in the Rome Statute in subparagraphs (b) and (c) of Article 25(3). The former covers the individual who 'orders, solicits or induces' the crime, while the latter deals with the person who 'aids, abets or otherwise assists'. There is a certain redundancy about these two paragraphs, perhaps because of an unfamiliarity of the drafters with the common law term 'abets' which, while it appears in paragraph (c), in reality covers everything described in paragraph (b). The Rome Statute does not indicate whether there is some quantitative degree of aiding and abetting required to constitute the material acts involved in complicity. Here, it departs from a model that was familiar to the drafters, the 1996 'Code of Crimes' of the International Law Commission, which specifies that complicity must be 'direct and substantial'.[86] The judges of the *ad hoc* tribunals have read this requirement into the complicity provisions of their statutes, despite the silence of their statutes.[87] The absence of words like 'substantial' in the Rome Statute, and the failure to follow the International Law Commission draft, may suggest that the Diplomatic Conference meant to reject the higher threshold of the case law of The Hague and Arusha.[88] It is clear that mere presence at the scene of a crime, in the absence of a material act or omission, does not constitute complicity. But, where the accused has a legal duty to intervene, because of a hierarchically superior position for example, presence without any other overt act may amount to a form of participation; the failure to intervene constitutes encouragement or incitement.[89] However, aside from the specific provision dealing with responsibility of commanders and other superiors, there is no criminal liability established in the Statute for mere failure to act.

---

[85] *Bemba* (ICC-01/05–01/08), Decision Pursuant to Article 61(7)(a) and (b) of the Rome Statute on the Charges of the Prosecutor Against Jean-Pierre Bemba Gombo, 15 June 2009, para. 350.

[86] Report of the International Law Commission on the Work of Its Forty-Eighth Session, 6 May–26 July 1996, UN Doc. A/51/10, p. 24.

[87] *Orić* (IT-03-68-T), Judgment, 30 June 2006, para. 284; *Kajelijeli* (ICTR-98-44A-T), Judgment and Sentence, 1 December 2003, para. 766.

[88] *Tadić* (IT-94-1-T), Opinion and Judgment, 7 May 1997, paras. 691 and 692. See also *Aleksovski* (IT-95-14/1-T), Judgment, 25 June 1999, para. 61.

[89] *Tadić* (IT-94-1-T), Opinion and Judgment, 7 May 1997, paras. 678 and 691; *Orić* (IT-03-68-T), Judgment, 30 June 2006, para. 283.

The Rome Statute also specifically provides for the incomplete or 'inchoate' crime of direct and public incitement to commit genocide, an offence that takes place even if there is no result.[90] The text is derived from Article III(c) of the Genocide Convention, a provision which was controversial in 1948 and which remains so today.[91] When the Genocide Convention was being drafted, the terms 'direct and public' were added, mainly at the request of the United States, in order to limit the scope of the provision. The United States was concerned that this might encroach upon the right of free speech. There were unsuccessful efforts during the drafting of the Rome Statute to enlarge the inchoate offence of incitement so as to cover the other core crimes but the same arguments that had been made in 1948, essentially based on freedom of expression, resurfaced.[92]

The issue of conspiracy has vexed international criminal law since Nuremberg. Under the common law system, a conspiracy is committed once two or more persons agree to commit a crime, whether or not the crime itself is committed, whereas in continental systems inspired by the Napoleonic tradition, conspiracy is generally viewed as a form of complicity or participation in an actual crime or attempt. Here, the Rome Statute strikes a compromise, requiring the commission of some overt act as evidence of the conspiracy but imposing no requirement that the crime itself actually be committed. The solution was borrowed from the 1997 Convention for the Suppression of Terrorist Bombings, where an acceptable formula had been adopted by consensus.[93] One unfortunate consequence is that the Rome Statute does not fully reflect the provisions of the Genocide Convention which, in Article III(b), defines 'conspiracy' as an act of genocide. The drafting history of the Genocide Convention indicates the intent to cover the common law notion of conspiracy, that is, a truly inchoate offence.[94]

Under the concept of common purpose complicity, those who participate in a criminal enterprise are liable for acts committed by their

[90] Rome Statute, Art. 25(3)(e).
[91] See William A. Schabas, *Genocide in International Law: The Crime of Crimes*, 2nd edn, Cambridge: Cambridge University Press, 2009, pp. 319–34. The Appeals Chamber of the International Criminal Tribunal for Rwanda has issued an important judgment on the subject: *Nahimana et al.* (ICTR-99-52-A), Judgment and Sentence, 28 November 2007.
[92] Saland, 'International Criminal Law Principles', p. 200; Ambos, 'General Principles', pp. 13–14.
[93] GA Res. 52/164, Annex. See also Saland, 'International Criminal Law Principles', pp. 199–200.
[94] Schabas, *Genocide in International Law*, pp. 310–17.

colleagues. Paragraph (3)(d) of Article 25 describes this as contributing 'to the commission or attempted commission of such a crime by a group of persons acting with a common purpose'. The text of paragraph 25(3)(d) reads:

> 3. In accordance with this Statute, a person shall be criminally responsible and liable for punishment for a crime within the jurisdiction of the Court if that person:
>
> ...
>
> (d) In any other way contributes to the commission or attempted commission of such a crime by a group of persons acting with a common purpose. Such contribution shall be intentional and shall either:
>
>   (i) Be made with the aim of furthering the criminal activity or criminal purpose of the group, where such activity or purpose involves the commission of a crime within the jurisdiction of the Court; or
>
>   (ii) Be made in the knowledge of the intention of the group to commit the crime.

In other words, a person can be held responsible for contributing to the commission of a crime within the jurisdiction of the Court to the extent it is made with the aim of furthering the criminal activity or criminal purpose of the group, 'where such activity or purpose involves the commission of a crime within the jurisdiction of the Court'. Article 25 of the Rome Statute makes it quite clear that the common purpose must be to commit a crime within the jurisdiction of the court. In other words, the enterprise cannot be one to commit any crime, or any act, but only one to commit a crime that is already within the jurisdiction of the court.

The Rome Statute provisions on criminal participation also contemplate liability in the case of an attempted crime.[95] If the ultimate goal of the Court is to prevent human rights abuses and atrocities, prosecution for attempts ought to be of considerable significance. But the history of war crimes prosecutions yields few examples, probably because the very idea of criminal repression has arisen after the commission of the crimes. Starting from the premise that guilty thoughts, in and of themselves, should not be subject to criminal liability, the theoretical problem with attempts is determining at what point prior to committing the actual act should prosecution be permitted. Domestic justice

---

[95] Rome Statute, Art. 25(3)(f).

systems have devised a variety of tests to distinguish between genuine attempts and 'mere preparatory acts'. The Rome Statute speaks of 'action that commences [the crime's] execution by means of a substantial step', a hybrid and internally contradictory formulation drawn from French and American law that sets a relatively low threshold. The Statute allows a defendant to plead that an attempt was voluntarily abandoned.[96] In the *Katanga* Confirmation Decision, Pre-Trial Chamber I suggested that attempt might have been included in the charges. It referred to attacks on civilians that involved indiscriminate use of machetes, firearms and heavy weapons. Thus, concluded the Chamber, the perpetrators had the specific intent to kill civilians rather than cause severe injuries:

> They commenced the execution of the conduct of killing civilians by means of a substantial step toward the killing of one or more persons, but did not achieve the act because of circumstances independent of the perpetrator's intent. In the view of the majority of the Chamber, the intent to perpetrate a specific act necessarily precedes the decision to further the act. In other words, the subjective elements, or the mens rea, is to be inferred from the moment in which the perpetrator takes the action that commences its execution by means of a substantial step, according to the language of article 25(3)(f) of the Statute. The majority of the Chamber endorses the doctrine that establishes that the attempt to commit a crime is a crime in which the objective elements are incomplete, while the subjective elements are complete. Therefore, the dolus that embodies the attempt is the same than the one that embodies the consummated act. As a consequence, in order for an attempt to commit a crime to be punished, it is necessary to infer the intent to further an action that would cause the result intended by the perpetrator, and the commencement of the execution of the act.[97]

Attempt is also charged in two of the Ugandan arrest warrants.[98]

Responsibility of commanders and other superiors

One of the dilemmas of war crimes prosecution is the difficulty of linking commanders to the crimes committed by their subordinates. The Rome

---

[96] Ambos, 'General Principles', pp. 12–13; Kai Ambos, 'Article 25', in Triffterer, ed., *Commentary*, pp. 743–70.

[97] *Katanga et al.* (ICC-01/04–01/07), Decision on the Confirmation of the Charges, 30 September 2008, paras. 458–60 (references omitted).

[98] *Kony* (ICC-02/04–53), Warrant of Arrest for Joseph Kony Issued on 8 July 2005 as Amended on 27 September 2005, pp. 12, 13; *Otti* (ICC-02/04–54), Warrant of Arrest for Vincent Otti, 8 July 2005, pp. 12, 13.

Statute requires proof of guilt beyond a reasonable doubt. In cases where this is forthcoming, the commanding superior's guilt sits on a plane that is much higher than that of the underling who follows orders. As a Trial Chamber of the Yugoslav Tribunal has noted, '[t]he Tribunal has particularly valid grounds for exercising its jurisdiction over persons who, through their position of political or military authority, are able to order the commission of crimes falling within its competence *ratione materiae* or who knowingly refrain from preventing or punishing the perpetrators of such crimes'.[99] But, while the responsibility of a commander, in the absence of actual proof that orders were given, might seem probable, judges may be reluctant to convict based solely on such circumstantial evidence. This probably explains why Louise Arbour, Prosecutor of the Yugoslav Tribunal, waited for many weeks before indicting President Milošević for crimes against humanity. She must have been unsatisfied with the circumstantial evidence of atrocities in Kosovo for which he had been condemned in the international press, and she was awaiting more concrete evidence that he had ordered them before proceeding.

There are two possible solutions to the dilemma of prosecuting commanders when direct evidence is lacking that they ordered crimes or knowingly ignored their perpetration. The first is to create a presumption by which commanders are deemed to have ordered the crimes committed by their subordinates, leaving it to the commander to answer the charges by establishing that no such orders were given. This technique is common in domestic criminal systems where it is difficult to prove that certain crimes were committed knowingly, such as environmental damage, false advertising and driving while intoxicated. This simplifies considerably the task of prosecutors, but it runs up against the principle of the presumption of innocence.[100] Moreover, Article 67 of the Rome Statute expressly excludes any mechanism by which the burden of proof is shifted onto the accused. The other solution is to prosecute the commander not for ordering the crime itself, but for being negligent in preventing it. This second approach has some precedents to support it and is enshrined in Article 28 of the Rome Statute.

The notion that military commanders are criminally liable for the acts of their subordinates, even where it cannot be proven that they had knowledge of these acts, was established in controversial rulings of

<hr>

[99] *Martić* (IT-95-11), Rule 61 Decision, 6 March 1996, para. 21.
[100] Nevertheless, the European Court of Human Rights has tolerated such provisions in some circumstances: *Salabiaku v. France*, Series A, No. 141-A, 7 October 1988, para. 28; *Pham Hoang v. France*, Series A, No. 243, 25 September 1992.

the post-World War II trials.[101] It is important to distinguish this from liability under criminal or disciplinary law for negligent supervision of troops, which has always featured in the law concerning military commanders. Under command responsibility, the commander is prosecuted for the crime committed by the subordinate, and not just for the distinct offence of negligence while in a position of authority. After the World War II precedents, the concept of command responsibility was recognized as a positive legal norm in prosecutions for grave breaches of Additional Protocol I to the Geneva Conventions, adopted in 1977.[102] In the case of the Yugoslav, Rwanda and Sierra Leone Tribunals, the fact that a crime within the jurisdiction of the Tribunals was committed by a subordinate 'does not relieve his or her superior of criminal responsibility if he or she knew or had reason to know that the subordinate was about to commit such acts or had done so and the superior failed to take the necessary and reasonable measures to prevent such acts or to punish the perpetrators thereof'.[103]

There was no real controversy about including the concept of command responsibility within the Statute. Extending it to include civilian superiors gained widespread support, although China continued to oppose such a development.[104] The compromise, brokered by the United States, was to adopt different rules on command responsibility depending on whether military commanders or civilian superiors are involved.[105] In order to incur liability, a military commander must know or 'should have known', whilst a civilian superior must either have known or 'consciously disregarded information which clearly indicated' that subordinates were committing or were about to commit crimes. The military commander can be prosecuted for what amounts to negligence ('should have known'). Guilt of a civilian superior under this provision, however, must meet a higher standard. It is necessary to establish

---

[101] *United States of America* v. *Yamashita*, (1948) 4 LRTWC 1, pp. 36–7; *In re Yamashita*, 327 US 1 (1945); *Canada* v. *Meyer*, (1948) 4 LRTWC 98 (Canadian Military Court).

[102] Additional Protocol I, Art. 86(2).

[103] Statute of the International Criminal Tribunal for the former Yugoslavia, UN Doc. S/RES/827, Annex, Art. 7(3); Statute of the International Criminal Tribunal for Rwanda, UN Doc. S/RES/955, Annex, Art. 6(3); Statute of the Special Court for Sierra Leone, Art. 6(3).

[104] Civilian responsibility on this basis is now recognized at customary law: *Delalić et al.* (IT-96-21-T), Judgment, 16 November 1998, paras. 355–63.

[105] Saland, 'International Criminal Law Principles', pp. 202–3. See UN Doc. A/CONF.183/C.1/SR.1, paras. 67–83. Also Mohamed Elewa Badar, *Mens Rea in International Criminal Law*, Oxford: Hart Publishing, 2009.

that the civilian superior had actual or 'constructive' knowledge of the crimes being committed.[106]

Judges of the *ad hoc* tribunals have been wary of extending the doctrine to cases of what might be deemed pure negligence.[107] In the Čelebići case, the Appeals Chamber of the International Criminal Tribunal for the former Yugoslavia dismissed an argument by the Prosecutor aimed at expanding the concept, noting that 'a superior will be criminally responsible through the principles of superior responsibility only if information was available to him which would have put him on notice of offences committed by subordinates'.[108] Obviously sensitive to the charges of abuse that could result from an overly large construction, the Appeals Chamber said it 'would not describe superior responsibility as a vicarious liability doctrine, insofar as vicarious liability may suggest a form of strict imputed liability'.[109] Several of the judgments testify to this judicial discomfort with respect to the outer limits of superior responsibility, and reveal concerns among the judges that a liberal interpretation may offend the *nullum crimen sine lege* principle.[110]

In the early years of the tribunals, superior responsibility was presented as the silver bullet of the prosecution. It was an endless source of fascination for commentators and postgraduate students. Its practical results have been relatively inconsequential. Several convictions on the basis of superior responsibility have been recorded by both the Yugoslavia and the Rwanda Tribunals, but with only a few exceptions these also involved offenders convicted as perpetrators or accomplices. One Trial Chamber of the International Criminal Tribunal for the former Yugoslavia described the superior responsibility inquiry as 'a waste of judicial resources' in cases where liability as a principal perpetrator or accomplice has already been established.[111] Eventually, the Appeals

---

[106] Roberta Arnold and Otto Triffterer, 'Article 28', in Triffterer, ed., *Commentary*, pp. 795–843.

[107] *Bagilishema* (ICTR-95-1A-A), Judgment, 3 July 2002, para. 35; *Blaškić* (IT-95-14-A), Judgment, 29 July 2004, para. 63.

[108] *Delalić* (IT-96-21-A), Judgment, 20 February 2001, para. 241 (reference omitted). See also *Galić* (IT-98-29-AR73.2), Decision on Interlocutory Appeal Concerning Rule 92*bis*(c), 7 June 2002.

[109] *Delalić* (IT-96-21-A), Judgment, 20 February 2001, para. 239.

[110] See, e.g., the views of Judge Bennouna, in *Krajisnik* (IT-00-39), Separate Opinion of Judge Bennouna, 22 September 2000; see also *Stakić* (IT-97-24-T), Decision on Rules 98*bis* Motion for Judgment of Acquittal, 31 October 2002, para. 116. But, for a recent discussion on this point, see *Hadžihasanović et al.* (IT-01-47-PT), Decision on Joint Challenge to Jurisdiction, 12 November 2002.

[111] *Stakić* (IT-97-24-T), Judgment, 31 July 2003, para. 466.

Chamber said that it was wrong to convict an individual on the basis of command responsibility if he or she was also guilty as a perpetrator.[112] The handful of convictions by the *ad hoc* tribunals that have depended upon superior responsibility alone have, with few exceptions,[113] resulted in short sentences,[114] reflecting an assessment that they do not belong in the category of the most serious crimes committed by the most serious perpetrators.

In its ruling on the confirmation of charges in *Bemba*, Pre-Trial Chamber II reframed the charges as command responsibility.[115]

Mens rea or mental element

Criminal law sets itself apart from other areas of law in that, as a general rule, it is concerned with intentional and knowing behaviour. An individual who causes accidental harm to another may be liable before some other body but will by and large not be held responsible before the criminal courts. Intent is often described using the Latin expression *mens rea* ('guilty mind'), taken from the phrase *actus non facit reum nisi mens sit rea*. But, even if it is understood that a criminal act must be intentional and knowing, there are degrees of intention ranging from mere negligence to recklessness and full-blown intent with premeditation.[116] In keeping with the seriousness of the offences over which the Court has jurisdiction, the Rome Statute sets a high standard for the mental element. It requires, in paragraph (1) of Article 30, that '[u]nless otherwise provided' the material elements of the offence must be committed 'with intent and knowledge'.[117] In two subsequent paragraphs, the Statute defines these concepts. A person has intent with respect to

---

[112] *Kvoèka et al.* (IT-98-30/1-A), Judgment, 28 February 2005, para. 104. See also *Brdjanin* (IT-99-36-T), Judgment, 1 September 2004, para. 285.

[113] *Nahimana et al.* (ICTR-99-52-A), Judgment, 28 November 2007; *Šlijivanèanin* (IT-95-13/1-A), Judgment, 5 May 2009.

[114] *Strugar* (IT-01-42), Judgment, 31 January 2005 (eight years); *Hadžihasanović et al.* (IT-01-47-T), Judgment, 15 March 2006 (Hadžihasanović, five years; Kubura, thirty months); *Orić* (IT-03-68-T), Judgment, 30 June 2006 (four years).

[115] *Bemba* (ICC-01/05–01/08), Decision Pursuant to Article 61(7)(a) and (b) of the Rome Statute on the Charges of the Prosecutor Against Jean-Pierre Bemba Gombo, 15 June 2009.

[116] Jean Pradel, *Droit pénal comparé*, Paris: Dalloz, 1995, p. 251.

[117] UN Doc. A/CONF.183/C.1/L.76/Add.3, p. 4. See Gerhard Werle and Florian Jessberger, '"Unless Otherwise Provided": Article 30 of the ICC Statute and the Mental Element of Crimes under International Criminal Law', (2005) 3 *Journal of International Criminal Justice* 3.

conduct when that person means to engage in the conduct. A person has intent with respect to a consequence when that person means to cause that consequence or is aware that it will occur in the ordinary course of events. Knowledge is defined as 'awareness that a circumstance exists or a consequence will occur in the ordinary course of events'. Article 30 defines 'knowledge', adding that 'know and knowingly' shall be construed accordingly.[118]

The general rule requiring intent or knowledge is hardly necessary for most of the crimes listed in the Rome Statute, because the definitions have their own built-in mental requirement. Thus, genocide is defined as a punishable act committed 'with the intent to destroy' a protected group.[119] Crimes against humanity involve a widespread or systematic attack directed against a civilian population 'with knowledge of the attack'.[120] Many of the war crimes listed in Article 8 include the adjectives 'wilfully', 'wantonly' or 'treacherously'. Indeed, it is at least partly for this reason that Article 30 begins with the words '[u]nless otherwise provided'.[121] During the drafting of the Statute, difficulties arose when attempting to lower the *mens rea* threshold to such concepts as recklessness and gross negligence.[122] A square bracketed text on recklessness[123] was ultimately dropped by the Working Group.[124] There was really little reason to define recklessness, as it is not an element in the definition of any of the offences within the jurisdiction of the Court.[125] Judges of the International Criminal Court are sure to exercise their minds as they attempt to reconcile the general principles expressed in Article 30 dealing with intent and the specific definitions of crimes that speak to the same subject.[126]

---

[118] But 'know' and 'knowingly' are not used in Art. 30 or, for that matter, elsewhere in the Rome Statute. The word 'known' appears in the command responsibility provision (Art. 28). The word 'knowledge' is in the *chapeau* of Art. 7, crimes against humanity.

[119] Rome Statute, Art. 6.

[120] *Ibid.*, Art. 7.

[121] Donald K. Piragoff and Darryl Robinson, 'Article 30', in Triffterer, ed., *Commentary*, pp. 849–61 at pp. 856–8.

[122] Saland, 'International Criminal Law Principles', pp. 205–6.

[123] UN Doc. A/CONF.183/C.1/WGGP/L.4, p. 1.

[124] UN Doc. A/CONF.183/C.1/WGGP/L.4/Corr.1; UN Doc. A/CONF.183/C.1/L.76/Add.3, p. 4.

[125] 'Commentary on Parts 2 and 3 of the Zutphen Intersessional Draft: General Principles of Criminal Law', (1998) 13*bis Nouvelles études pénales* 43 at 52.

[126] On this, see the very thoughtful piece by Professor Roger Clark, 'The Mental Element in International Criminal Law: The Rome Statute of the International Criminal Court and the Elements of the Offences', (2001) 12 *Criminal Law Forum* 291.

The words '[u]nless otherwise provided' protect Article 28, which sets a negligence standard for guilt by command responsibility that clearly falls below the knowledge and intent requirements of Article 30. They also shelter Article 25(3)(d)(ii), which establishes criminal liability for acts committed by participants in a 'common purpose' even if they lack knowledge of the specific criminal intent of their colleagues. Whether these words mean, in practice, '[u]nless otherwise provided *by the Statute*' is somewhat of an open question. It would seem to be going too far to suggest that the Article 30 standard in the Statute could be amended if an exception is provided for in the Elements of Crimes, yet this is precisely what is done when the Elements refer to a crime committed against a person whom the offender 'should have known' was under age,[127] or in cases where he or she 'should have known' of the prohibited use of a flag of truce or the Red Cross emblem and similar insignia.[128] The general introduction to the Elements states that they include exceptions to Article 30 that are based on both the Article 30 standard and 'applicable law'.

There is no equivalent provision for the material element of the offence, the *actus reus*.[129] The final Preparatory Committee draft contained an *actus reus* Article, but the Working Group was unable to reach consensus on its content,[130] essentially because of problems in defining the notion of omission. During the debates, the Chair of the Working Group noted that Article 22(2) prohibiting analogies would ensure that judicial discretion on the subject of omissions was never abusive. A footnote to the Working Group's report stated: 'Some delegations were of the view that the deletion of article 28 [on omission] required further consideration and reserved their right to reopen the

---

[127] Elements of Crimes, Art. 6(e), para. 6 and Arts. 8(2)(b)(xxvi), para. 3 and 8(2)(e)(vii), para. 3. Note, also, in the Introduction to the Elements for genocide, the words '[n]otwithstanding the normal requirement for a mental element provided for in article 30 …', suggesting that the drafters of the Elements believed they could modify the Art. 30 *mens rea* requirement.

[128] Elements of Crimes, Art. 8(2)(b)(vii).

[129] Saland, 'International Criminal Law Principles', pp. 212–13.

[130] Report of the Ad Hoc Committee on the Establishment of an International Criminal Court, UN Doc. A/50/22, Annex II, p. 58; Report of the Preparatory Committee on the Establishment of an International Criminal Court, UN Doc. A/51/22, vol. I, p. 45; Report of the Preparatory Committee on the Establishment of an International Criminal Court, UN Doc. A/51/22, vol. II, pp. 90–1; UN Doc. A/AC.249/1997/L.5, pp. 26–7; UN Doc. A/AC.249/1997/WG.2/CRP.5; UN Doc. A/AC.249/1998/L.13, pp. 58–9; UN Doc. A/CONF.183/2/Add.1, pp. 54–5.

issue at an appropriate time.'[131] However, nothing more was heard of the subject.[132]

Defences

A defence is an answer to a criminal charge. It is used to denote 'all grounds which, for one reason or another, hinder the sanctioning of an offence – despite the fact that the offence has fulfilled all definitional elements of a crime'.[133] But the Rome Statute opts for another term, 'grounds for excluding criminal responsibility', rather than defence.[134] This was an attempt to address conceptual differences to the issue in national criminal justice systems.[135] Previous international criminal law instruments have made no real attempt at even a partial codification of defences, confining themselves to rather limited issues such as the inadmissibility of the defences of superior orders or of official capacity. Case law on war crimes prosecutions suggests that the main pleas invoked by the accused are superior orders, official capacity, duress, military necessity, self-defence, reprisal, mistake of law or fact, and insanity.

The Rome Statute partially codifies available defences in Articles 31, 32 and 33. Article 31, entitled 'Grounds for excluding criminal responsibility',[136] deals specifically with insanity, intoxication, self-defence, duress and necessity. Article 32 addresses mistake of fact and law, and Article 33 concerns superior orders and prescription of law. The Statute allows the Court to accept other defences,[137] relying on the sources set out in Article 21(1). Indeed, it affirms a general right of the accused to raise defences.[138] Obvious candidates for uncodified defences

---

[131] UN Doc. A/CONF.183/C.1/WGGP/L.4/Add.1/Rev.1, p. 3, n. 3.
[132] One writer has argued that, despite the lack of such a general provision on omission in the Rome Statute, the International Criminal Court is in a position to apply the concept of liability by omission: Michael Duttwiller, 'Liability for Omission in International Criminal Law', (2006) 6 *International Criminal Law Review* 1.
[133] Albin Eser, '"Defences" in War Crimes Trials', in Yoram Dinstein and Mala Tabory, eds., *War Crimes in International Law*, The Hague, Boston and London: Kluwer Law International, 1996, pp. 251–73 at p. 251. Also Ilias Bantekas, 'Defences in International Criminal Law', in Dominic McGoldrick, Peter Rowe and Eric Donnelly, eds., *The Permanent International Criminal Court: Legal and Policy Issues*, Oxford and Portland, OR: Hart Publishing, 2004, pp. 263–85.
[134] Rome Statute, Art. 31.   [135] UN Doc. A/CONF.183/C.1/SR.1, para. 26.
[136] Albin Eser, 'Article 31', in Triffterer, ed., *Commentary*, pp. 863–93.
[137] Rome Statute, Art. 31(3).   [138] *Ibid.*, Art. 67(1)(e).

would include alibi, military necessity, abuse of process,[139] consent and reprisal.[140]

Where the defence intends to raise an uncodified defence, it is required by the Rules of Procedure and Evidence to give notice to the Prosecutor prior to trial, and to obtain a preliminary ruling on the admissibility of the defence from the Trial Chamber.[141] Other defences are formally excluded, either by the terms of the Statute itself – defence of official capacity and immunity,[142] lack of knowledge (in the case of command responsibility)[143] and superior orders (in cases of genocide and crimes against humanity)[144] – or by international case law – for example, *tu quoque* (literally, I can do to you what you have done to me).[145]

Reprisal against prisoners of war and civilians is prohibited by modern treaties, and a Trial Chamber of the Yugoslavia Tribunal has said that reprisals usually attract 'universal revulsion' because they are arbitrary, and are generally not directed against the person responsible for the violation of humanitarian law that provoked the reprisal. The Trial Chamber said reprisals against civilians are inherently a barbarous means of seeking compliance with international law.[146] But the United Kingdom *Manual of the Law of Armed Conflict* says 'the court's reasoning [in *Kupreškić*] is unconvincing and the assertion that there is a prohibition in customary law flies in the face of most of the state practice that exists. The UK does not accept the position as stated in this judgment.'[147] When the United Kingdom ratified the Rome Statute, it

---

[139] A challenge to jurisdiction based upon alleged abuse of process prior to the transfer of Thomas Lubanga to the Court in The Hague was dismissed by the Pre-Trial Chamber: *Lubanga* (ICC-01/04–01/0), Decision on the Defence Challenge to the Jurisdiction of the Court Pursuant to Article 19(2)(a) of the Statute, 3 October 2006. The ruling was upheld by the Appeals Chamber: *Lubanga* (ICC-01/04–01/06), Judgment on the Appeal of Mr Thomas Lubanga Dyilo against the Decision on the Defence Challenge to the Jurisdiction of the Court Pursuant to Article 19(2)(a) of the Statute of 3 October 2006, 14 December 2006.

[140] Eser, '"Defences"', pp. 266–7. Note, however, attempts in the Elements of Crimes, Arts. 8(2)(b)(x), n. 46, and 8(2)(e)(xi), n. 68, and the Rules of Procedure and Evidence, Rule 70, to limit the defence of consent.

[141] Rules of Procedure and Evidence, Rule 80.

[142] Rome Statute, Art. 27.   [143] *Ibid.*, Art. 28.   [144] *Ibid.*, Art. 33.

[145] *Kupreškić et al.* (IT-95-16), Decision on Defence Motion to Summon Witness, 3 February 1999; *Kupreškić et al.* (IT-95-16), Decision on Evidence of the Good Character of the Accused and the Defence of Tu Quoque, 17 February 1999.

[146] *Kupreškić et al.* (IT-95-16-T), Judgment, 14 January 2000, para. 527.

[147] United Kingdom Ministry of Defence, *The Manual of Law of Armed Conflict*, Oxford and New York: Oxford University Press, 2004, p. 421, n. 62.

formulated a declaration aimed at preserving the right to practise reprisals, even against civilians.

Insanity as a defence has arisen only rarely in the case law of major war crimes prosecutions. Rudolf Hess and Julius Streicher unsuccessfully raised it at Nuremberg. The text of Article 31(1)(a) echoes the so-called *M'Naghten* rules derived from the common law,[148] but would also seem to be generally consistent with the approach taken in Romano-Germanic and *Sharia* systems. An individual who succeeds with a plea of insanity is entitled to a declaration that he or she is not criminally responsible. The Statute does not speak directly to the burden of proof in cases of the defence of insanity. Is a defendant required only to raise a doubt about mental capacity, or must he or she actually prove such an exception based on a preponderance of evidence? Domestic justice systems take different views of this matter. The International Criminal Tribunal for the former Yugoslavia has opted for the preponderance of evidence standard, making proof of insanity more difficult for the accused.[149] Yet Article 67 of the Statute, which shields the accused from 'any reversal of the burden of proof or any onus of rebuttal', may compel the less onerous requirement that the accused only raise a reasonable doubt.

If the codification of an uncontroversial definition of the insanity defence appears somewhat unnecessary, given the rare cases where this will arise in practice, the provision that follows, concerning intoxication, seems to go from the sublime to the ridiculous. Drafting of the text was troublesome, and the final result 'had the benefit of not satisfying anyone'.[150] Many individual war crimes may be committed by soldiers and thugs under the influence of drugs and alcohol, but the Court is surely not intended to deal with such 'small fry'. This is a Court established for 'big fish', a relatively small number of leaders, organizers and planners, in cases of genocide, crimes against humanity and large-scale war crimes, something confirmed by the early case law of the Court establishing a daunting gravity threshold for admissibility.[151] The nature

---

[148] *M'Naghten's Case* (1843) 10 Cl. and Fin. 200; 8 ER 718.

[149] *Delalić et al.* (IT-96-21-T), Order on Esad Landzo's Submission Regarding Diminished or Lack of Mental Capacity, 18 June 1998; *Delalić et al.* (IT-96-21-T), Order on Landzo's Request for Definition of Diminished or Lack of Mental Capacity, 15 July 1998; *Delalić et al.* (IT-96-21-T), Judgment, 16 November 1998, (1999) 38 ILM 57, para. 1160; *Delalić* (IT-96-21-A), Judgment, 20 February 2001, para. 582.

[150] Saland, 'International Criminal Law Principles', p. 207.

[151] E.g., *Lubanga* (ICC-01/04–01/06–8), Decision on the Prosecutor's Application for a Warrant of Arrest, 10 February 2006.

of such crimes, involving planning and preparation, is virtually inconsistent with a plea of voluntary intoxication. A footnote in the text prepared by the Drafting Committee said: 'It was the understanding that voluntary intoxication as a ground for excluding criminal responsibility would generally not apply in cases of genocide or crimes against humanity, but might apply to isolated acts constituting war crimes.'[152]

In practice, examples of voluntary intoxication in case law, even for mere war crimes, are as infrequent as in the case of insanity. The Rome Statute admits the defence of intoxication if it has destroyed the accused's capacity to appreciate the unlawfulness or the nature of his or her conduct, or the capacity to control his or her conduct to conform to the requirements of law. But the defence cannot be invoked if the person became voluntarily intoxicated knowing of the likelihood that he or she would engage in such terrible crimes. This is the case of somebody who drinks in order to get up courage to commit an atrocity.

The Statute allows a defence of self-defence or defence of another person where an accused acts 'reasonably' and in a manner that is 'proportionate' to the degree of danger. These terms are common in national legal norms that deal with the use of force, and there will be no shortage of authority to guide the Court.[153] A judgment of the *ad hoc* tribunals has noted that the principle of self-defence enshrined in Article 31(1)(c) corresponds to provisions found in most national criminal codes and may be regarded as constituting a rule of customary international law.[154] But a disturbing compromise during the Rome Conference resulted in recognition of the defence of property, although it is confined to cases of war crimes. The property defended must be 'essential for the survival of the person or another person' or 'essential for accomplishing a military mission, against an imminent and unlawful use of force'. In practice, these terms are narrow enough that the troublesome recognition of defence of property in the Statute is unlikely to have much in the way of practical consequences. But they have provoked sharp criticism from some quarters. The Belgian scholar Eric David calls the exception 'a Pandora's box that is rigorously incompatible with the law of armed conflict'. Professor David goes as far as to call this provision a violation of *jus cogens*, concluding that it is, consequently, null and void pursuant

---

[152] UN Doc. A/CONF.183/C.1/WGGP/L.4/Add.1/Rev.1 and Corr.1, n. 8.

[153] One interesting source may be the case law of the European Court of Human Rights in the interpretation of Art. 2(2) of the European Convention on Human Rights, allowing for self-defence as an exception to the right to life.

[154] *Kordić et al.* (IT-95-14/2-T), Judgment, 26 February 2001, para. 451.

to the Vienna Convention on the Law of Treaties.[155] When Belgium ratified the Statute, it appended a declaration stating that it considered that Article 31(1)(c) could only be applied and interpreted 'having regard to the rules of international humanitarian law which may not be derogated from'.

Article 31 also codifies the defences of duress and necessity. The defence of duress is often confounded with that of superior orders, but the two are quite distinct. A person acting under duress is someone who is compelled to commit the crime by a threat to his or her life, or to that of another person. In the related defence of necessity, this inexorable threat is the result of natural circumstances rather than that of other persons. But, in either case, the defendant is deemed to have no viable moral choice in the matter. An exhaustive judgment of the Appeals Chamber of the International Criminal Tribunal for the former Yugoslavia, in 1997, determined, by a majority of three to two, that duress is not admissible as a defence to crimes against humanity.[156] The consequence of the provision in the Rome Statute is to set aside the precedent established by the Yugoslav Tribunal and to reinstate the defence of duress.

The defences of mistake of fact and mistake of law are defined in a distinct provision.[157] An offender who lacks knowledge of an essential fact does not possess the guilty mind or *mens rea* necessary for conviction. This is actually what the Rome Statute declares, admitting mistake only if it 'negates the mental element'. Mistake of fact as a defence is not controversial, and it is a simple matter to conceive of examples where it might be invoked. A military recruiter charged with conscripting children under fifteen might argue a mistaken belief that the victim was older than he or she appeared. Of course, the Court will need to assess the credibility of such a claim in the light of the circumstances, and would be unlikely even to consider a defence of mistake of fact that did not have an air of reality to it.

Most national legal systems refuse to admit the defence of mistake of law on public policy grounds, although war crimes jurisprudence has tended to be more flexible, probably because international humanitarian law is considered to be quite specialized and rather technical. This is not always easy to understand, however, given that most basic norms

---

[155] Eric David, *Principes de droit des conflits armés*, 2nd edn, Brussels: Bruylant, 1999, p. 693.

[156] *Erdemović* (IT-96-22-A), Sentencing Appeal, 7 October 1997, (1998) 111 ILR 298.

[157] Rome Statute, Art. 32. See Otto Triffterer, 'Article 32', in Triffterer, ed., *Commentary*, pp. 895–914.

of humanitarian law constitute a common denominator of humane behaviour, and ought to be within the grasp of everyone. In *Lubanga*, the defence argued that, because the Rome Statute is so new, and because the suspect's own country had not enacted an offence of enlistment of child soldiers, the law was not 'accessible' or 'foreseeable'; in effect, although the argument was framed as one of retroactivity, it looks more like a claim of ignorance of the law.[158] The wording of Article 30 is somewhat enigmatic, and arguments continue as to whether it authorizes or forbids the defence of mistake of law. That it was the intent of the Rome Conference to *include* mistake of law appears rather clearly in the report of the Working Group on General Principles. In effect, a footnote to draft Article 30 says that '[s]ome delegations were of the view that mistake of fact or mistake of law does not relieve an individual of criminal responsibility for the crimes within the jurisdiction of the Court';[159] this would have been superfluous if mistake of law was actually excluded.

Mistake of law is particularly relevant to the final defence set out in the Rome Statute, that of superior orders and prescription of law. Indeed, the relationship is provided for in the text itself, which admits the defence of mistake of law 'as provided for in article 33'. Although the defence of superior orders is ruled out in some international criminal law instruments, such as the Charter of the Nuremberg Tribunal and the statutes of the *ad hoc* tribunals, other treaties such as the Genocide Convention stopped short of proscribing it entirely, and the same is the case for the Rome Statute. Article 33 allows the defence under three conditions: the accused must be under a legal obligation to obey orders; the accused must not know that the order was unlawful; and the order must not be manifestly unlawful. The text corresponds to case law on the subject.[160] With respect, then, to mistake of law, the accused may be excused for ignorance of the illegality of the order but not for ignorance of the manifest illegality of the order. But the Rome Statute subjects this to an exception: 'For the purposes of this article, orders to commit genocide or crimes against humanity are manifestly unlawful.'[161]

---

[158] *Lubanga* (ICC-01/04–01/06), Decision on the Confirmation of the Charges, 29 January 2007, para. 301. For the defence arguments, see *Lubanga* (ICC-01/04–01/06), Transcript, 26 November 2006.

[159] UN Doc. A/CONF.183/C.1/WGGP/L.4/Add.1/Rev.1 and Corr.1, n. 5. Also UN Doc. A/CONF.183/C.1/SR.23, para. 4.

[160] *Llandovery Castle Case* (1923–4) 2 Ann. Dig. 436 (German *Reichsgericht* of Leipzig); *United States* v. *Calley*, 22 USMCA 534 (1973).

[161] Paola Gaeta, 'The Defence of Superior Orders: The Statute of the International Criminal Court Versus Customary International Law', (1999) 10 *European Journal of*

The Rome Statute also declares official capacity as Head of State or Government or some other form to be irrelevant to the issue of criminal responsibility and, furthermore, to the issue of mitigation of sentence.[162] Similar provisions can be found in the applicable law of the Nuremberg, Tokyo, Yugoslavia, Rwanda and Sierra Leone tribunals. The issue was uncontested during negotiations and there were no problems reaching agreement on an acceptable text.[163] The earlier models did not, however, include a provision equivalent to what appears in Article 27(2): 'Immunities or special procedural rules which may attach to the official capacity of a person, whether under national or international law, shall not bar the Court from exercising its jurisdiction over such a person.' Unlike 'official capacity', which may be a defence admitted in some national justice systems but which has no real basis in international law, 'immunity' attaching to a person's capacity is an important concept in public international law. The two notions tend to become confused, and it is not exactly helpful that Article 27 bears the title 'Irrelevance of official capacity' when in fact it deals with two distinct issues.

Immunity of Heads of State, other senior government officials, diplomatic personnel and functionaries and experts of international organizations, exists by virtue of customary international law. It is codified in various treaties, and has been applied by the International Court of Justice in an important ruling dealing with a prosecution for international crimes under universal jurisdiction. The International Court of Justice may have contributed to misunderstanding here in its rather laconic discussion of immunities before international criminal tribunals. In its judgment in the so-called *Yerodia* case, the Court said:

> [A]n incumbent or former Minister for Foreign Affairs may be subject to criminal proceedings before certain international criminal courts, where they have jurisdiction. Examples include the International Criminal Tribunal for the former Yugoslavia, and the International Criminal Tribunal for Rwanda, established pursuant to Security Council resolutions under Chapter VII of the United Nations Charter, and the future International Criminal Court created by the 1998 Rome Convention. The latter's Statute expressly provides, in Article 27, paragraph 2, that

---

International Law 172; Hilaire McCoubrey, 'From Nuremberg to Rome: Restoring the Defence of Superior Orders', (2001) 50 *International and Comparative Law Quarterly* 386.

[162] Rome Statute, Art. 27.

[163] Saland, 'International Criminal Law Principles', p. 202; Roberta Arnold and Otto Triffterer, 'Article 28', in Triffterer, ed., *Commentary*, pp. 795–843.

'[i]mmunities or special procedural rules which may attach to the official capacity of a person, whether under national or international law, shall not bar the Court from exercising its jurisdiction over such a person'.[164]

A literal reading of Article 27(2) suggests that immunity cannot be invoked under any circumstances. But it does not make sense that the Court can ignore the claim to immunity of a Head of State or senior official from a non-party State. States Parties to the Rome Statute have agreed, by treaty, not to invoke the immunity of their own leaders before the International Criminal Court. But this surely cannot affect the situation with respect to those States that have not yet taken this step. The analogy made by the International Court of Justice between the *ad hoc* tribunals created by the Security Council and the International Criminal Court is imprecise. The Security Council can withdraw immunity from anyone, and this is arguably what it has done in establishing the *ad hoc* tribunals.[165] Another explanation is that immunity is only an issue between sovereign States, so the logic of respect for sovereignty is without consequence in the case of an institution established by the United Nations. But can a group of States, acting collectively, withdraw an immunity that exists under international law, when they cannot do this individually?

During the negotiations of the Relationship Agreement between the International Criminal Court and the United Nations, Belgium proposed the following provision: 'Paragraph 1 of this article shall be without prejudice to the relevant norms of international law, particularly article 6 of the Convention on the Prevention and Punishment of the Crime of Genocide and article 27 of the Statute, in respect of the crimes that come under the jurisdiction of the Court.' Belgium's provision was rejected during the drafting, and the final version of the Agreement confirms the immunities to which officials of the United Nations are entitled. According to Article 19 of the Relationship Agreement, the United Nations agrees to waive these immunities. But, if Article 27(2) removed such immunity, there would be no need for any such provision, and this was precisely the point that Belgium unsuccessfully tried to confirm.

---

[164] *Case Concerning the Arrest Warrant of 11 April 2000* (*Democratic Republic of the Congo v. Belgium*), 15 February 2002, para. 61.

[165] *Milošević* (IT-02-54-PT), Decision on Preliminary Motions, 8 November 2001, paras. 26–34; *Taylor* (SCSL-2003-01-I), Decision on Immunity from Jurisdiction, 31 May 2004, para. 41.

Pre-Trial Chamber I, in *Bashir*, held that the position of the accused person as head of State of a non-party State 'has no effect on the Court's jurisdiction over the present case'.[166] It said this conclusion was based upon four considerations.[167] The first is a rather gratuitous and unhelpful reference in the preamble to the core goals of the Statute, which are 'to put an end to impunity for the perpetrators of the most serious crimes of concern to the international community as a whole, which "must not go unpunished"'.[168] The second consists of an equally gratuitous and unhelpful recital of the terms of Article 27.[169] The third is more compelling: a reference to Article 21 of the Statute, and the observation that unless there is a lacuna in the Statute the Court is not to apply other sources of law.[170] The message is that, even if general public international law provides for head of State immunity, it is not formally contemplated by Article 27 and therefore cannot be invoked in proceedings before the Court. Finally, the Pre-Trial Chamber said that, by referring the Darfur situation to the Court in accordance with Article 13(b) of the Statute, the Security Council 'accepted that the investigation into the said situation, as well as any prosecution arising therefrom, will take place in accordance with the statutory framework provided for in the Statute, the Elements of Crimes and the Rules as a whole'.[171]

Immunities are also considered in Article 98 of the Statute. Article 98 concerns obligations that States Parties assume under the Statute with respect to surrender of accused persons and other forms of cooperation. Paragraph 1 grants an exemption from these undertakings to the extent they may conflict with immunities granted under 'international law with respect to the State or diplomatic immunity'. Paragraph 2 gives an exemption from surrender obligations where these conflict with 'international agreements', of which so-called 'status of forces agreements' governing foreign military personnel are the classic example. Professor Bassiouni, who chaired the Drafting Committee at the Rome Conference, has written that Article 98 and Article 27 should have been

---

[166] *Bashir* (ICC-02/05–01/09), Decision on the Prosecution's Application for a Warrant of Arrest Against Omar Hassan Ahmad Al Bashir, 4 March 2009, para. 41.

[167] For academic critique of this aspect of the decision, see Paola Gaeta, 'Does President Al Bashir Enjoy Immunity from Arrest?', (2009) 7 *Journal of International. Criminal Justice* 315 at 323–5.

[168] *Bashir* (ICC-02/05–01/09), Decision on the Prosecution's Application for a Warrant of Arrest Against Omar Hassan Ahmad Al Bashir, 4 March 2009, para. 42.

[169] *Ibid.*, para. 43.   [170] *Ibid.*, para. 44.   [171] *Ibid.*, para. 45.

joined in a single provision, so as to avoid problems of interpretation.[172] But there is no incompatibility or inconsistency between the two provisions, given that Article 27 governs the exercise of jurisdiction over an accused before the Court whereas Article 98 applies solely to obligations of cooperation.

Statutory limitation

The Rome Statute declares that crimes within the jurisdiction of the Court shall not be subject to any statute of limitations.[173] Why such a provision is even necessary is unclear. It would seem that a statutory limitation requires an affirmative provision, not one declaring that they do not exist. This was really a way to resolve a debate, as some States argued that statutory limitations might be allowed for war crimes.[174] Nobody contended that they might exist in the case of crimes against humanity and genocide. Statutory limitations were also considered in the context of a discussion about whether to include 'treaty crimes' within the subject-matter jurisdiction of the Court.[175]

Because there is no statutory limitation provided within the Statute itself, it seems that Article 29 is directed more at national legislation. Many domestic criminal law systems provide for the statutory limitation of crimes, even the most serious.[176] Under French law, for example, prosecutions for murder are time-barred after ten years.[177] Codes derived from the Napoleonic model generally have similar provisions. At his trial in Israel in 1961, Nazi war criminal Adolf Eichmann invoked a fifteen-year limitation period in force in Argentina, from where he had been kidnapped. The District Court of Jerusalem ruled that Argentine norms could not apply, adding a reference to applicable Israeli legislation declaring that 'the rules of prescription ... shall not apply to offences under this Law'.[178]

---

[172] M. Cherif Bassiouni, 'International Criminal Justice in Historical Perspective', in M. Cherif Bassiouni, *The Legislative History of the International Criminal Court: Introduction, Analysis and Integrated Text*, vol. I, Ardsley, New York: Transnational, 2005, p. 84.

[173] Rome Statute, Art. 29.

[174] UN Doc. A/CONF.183/C.1/SR.2, para. 47 (France) and para. 70 (China).

[175] *Ibid.*, para. 45.

[176] See Anne-Marie Larosa, *Dictionnaire de droit international pénal, Termes choisis*, Paris: Presses universitaires de France, 1998, pp. 50–2.

[177] Penal Code (France), Art. 7.

[178] *A-G Israel* v. *Eichmann*, (1968) 36 ILR 18 (District Court, Jerusalem), para. 53.

International opposition to statutory limitation for war crimes, crimes against humanity and genocide has taken the form of General Assembly resolutions,[179] and treaties within both the United Nations system[180] and that of the Council of Europe.[181] The low rate of adhesion to the United Nations Convention has led some academics to contest the suggestion that this is a customary norm.[182] Nevertheless, in the *Barbie* case, the French *Cour de cassation* ruled that the prohibition on statutory limitations for crimes against humanity is now part of customary law.[183]

---

[179] GA Res. 3 (I); GA Res. 170 (II); GA Res. 2583 (XXIV); GA Res. 2712 (XXV); GA Res. 2840 (XXVI); GA Res. 3020 (XXVII); GA Res. 3074 (XXVIII).

[180] Convention on the Nonapplicability of Statutory Limitations to War Crimes and Crimes Against Humanity, (1970) 754 UNTS 73. See Robert H. Miller, 'The Convention on the Non-Applicability of Statutory Limitations to War Crimes and Crimes Against Humanity', (1971) 65 *American Journal of International Law* 476.

[181] European Convention on the Non-Applicability of Statutory Limitation to Crimes Against Humanity and War Crimes, 25 January 1974, ETS No. 82.

[182] Steven R. Ratner and Jason S. Abrams, *Accountability for Human Rights Atrocities in International Law: Beyond the Nuremberg Legacy*, Oxford: Clarendon Press, 1997, p. 126.

[183] *Fédération nationale des déportés et internés résistants et patriotes et al. v. Barbie*, (1984) 78 ILR 125 at 135.

7

Investigation and pre-trial procedure

Many of the States involved in drafting the Rome Statute initially treated debates about the procedural regime to be followed by the Court as an opportunity to affirm the merits of their own justice systems within an international forum. Often, they were simply unable, because of training or prejudice, to conceive of the possibility that other judicial models from different cultures could offer alternative and perhaps better solutions to procedural issues. Describing debates in the International Law Commission, James Crawford noted 'the tendency of each duly socialized lawyer to prefer his own criminal justice system's values and institutions'.[1] But, over time, the drafters came to appreciate that there was much to be learned from different legal systems. Of course, they also recognized that compromise was essential if agreement was to be reached. As one observer of the Rome Conference said so eloquently: 'the fight between common law and civil law has been replaced by an agreement on common principles and civil behaviour.'[2] In this regard, the ongoing work of the *ad hoc* international criminal tribunals was of great value. Since their establishment in 1993 and 1994, the tribunals in The Hague and Arusha have been engaged in a fascinating exercise in comparative criminal procedure, borrowing the best from different national legal systems and in some cases simply devising innovative and original rules.

The procedural regime of the International Criminal Court is largely a hybrid of two different systems: the adversarial approach of the English common law and the inquisitorial approach of the Napoleonic code and other European legislations of the Romano-Germanic tradition (often

---

[1] James Crawford, 'The ILC Adopts a Statute for an International Criminal Court', (1995) 89 *American Journal of International Law* 404.

[2] Hans-Jörg Behrens, 'Investigation, Trial and Appeal in the International Criminal Court Statute (Parts V, VI, VIII)', (1998) 6 *European Journal of Crime, Criminal Law and Criminal Justice* 113 at 113, n. 2.

described, somewhat erroneously, as the 'civil law' system).[3] This is perhaps an oversimplification, because within the English and continental models there is enormous variation from one country to another. Some States have rethought their approach to criminal procedure, largely in reaction to judgments of the European Court of Human Rights.[4]

Under the adversarial procedure, which is the general rule in common law countries, the authorities responsible for prosecution prepare a criminal charge inspired either by a private complaint or on their own initiative. Although generally bound to respect standards of fairness and the presumption of innocence, their efforts focus on building a case against the accused. When the trial begins, there is no evidence before the judge. Evidence is admitted in accordance with specific and often quite restrictive rules, and its admission may be contested by the defence. Many of these strict rules exist because in trials for the most serious crimes questions of fact will be decided by lay jurors who lack the training and instincts of professional judges in the assessment of the probity of different types of evidence. For example, the lay juror may have difficulty determining the value of indirect or 'hearsay' evidence, whereas the professional judge knows that it is often quite unreliable. At trial, the prosecution will attempt to lead incriminating evidence, and will simply ignore exculpatory evidence, as this is counterproductive to its own case. Under certain national systems, the prosecution must provide the defence with any favourable evidence that is in its possession, but the obligation rarely goes any further. When the prosecution's case is complete, if the evidence is insufficient to establish guilt, the defence may move to dismiss the charges. Where the evidence appears sufficient, the defence may then decide to reply with its own materials and testimony, whose admissibility is subject to the same rules as for the prosecution.

Under the inquisitorial system, instructing magistrates prepare the case by collecting evidence and interviewing witnesses, often unbeknownst to the accused. The instructing magistrate is a judicial official, who is bound to complete the job with neutrality and impartiality, and who must collect evidence of both guilt and innocence. The evidence compiled, including witness statements, is then filed in court prior to the start of the trial itself. Usually, the trial becomes more adversarial at this point, because the prosecution and the defence each participate

---

[3] Claus Kreß, 'The Procedural Law of the International Criminal Court in Outline: Anatomy of a Unique Compromise', (2003) 1 *Journal of International Criminal Justice* 60.

[4] Mireille Delmas-Marty, *Pour un droit commun*, Paris: Editions du Seuil, 1994.

in the judicial debates. The trial judges may then assess the evidence in the case file, or, at the request of one or other of the parties or on their own initiative, require that additional evidence be presented. Rules of evidence are not nearly as technical under the inquisitorial as under the adversarial system, mainly because the evidence is being assessed exclusively by professional judges rather than, in the case of the common law system, by lay jurors.

Trials under the inquisitorial system are generally much shorter than their common law counterparts because most of the evidence has already been produced in the court record before the trial begins. Common law trials tend to be considerably longer and probably more thorough, although there are fewer of them. Because common law proceedings are so complex, in many systems only a minority of cases actually get to trial. Cases are resolved by agreement between prosecutor and defence counsel, who can usually reach a reasonable compromise as to the likely outcome of a trial based on their own experience. The accused pleads guilty to a charge that is agreed to by both lawyers, and after a summary verification the plea is simply endorsed by a trial judge who imposes a sentence, again usually following a recommendation from both counsel. The inquisitorial system does not allow for such 'plea bargaining', and a conviction is impossible until the instructing magistrate has prepared evidence that satisfies the trial judges of guilt.

There are also important differences in terms of the culture of the courtroom. Under some systems, especially adversarial ones, there are often quite intense exchanges between counsel for the defence and the prosecution, with aggressive cross-examination of witnesses by both sides. The courtroom is a battleground, out of which the truth is expected to emerge. The presiding judge's role can be relatively passive, rather like that of a referee during a football game. In other systems, notably the continental or Romano-Germanic ones, the judge plays a much more central role. Counsel for the two parties are more subdued, and there is little if any cross-examination. Questions to witnesses are asked through the judge, removing much of the drama and any element of surprise that might trap an unsure or dishonest individual.

Drawing on both systems, the Rome Statute provides for an adversarial approach, but one where the Court has dramatic powers to intervene and control the procedure. Although the inquisitorial system is often criticized by lawyers of the common law for its inadequate protection of the rights of the defence, in an international context, where the defence may have insurmountable obstacles to obtaining evidence and interviewing witnesses within uncooperative States, the inquisitorial system may ultimately prove the better approach. Accordingly, the International Criminal Court has wide authority under the Statute to supervise matters at the investigation stage. Both the Prosecutor and the Pre-Trial Chamber are particularly important in this respect, and they have special responsibilities in terms of identifying and securing exculpatory evidence to assist in preparation of the defence.[5]

At the beginning of its activities, the International Criminal Tribunal for the former Yugoslavia probably leaned more towards the common law adversarial approach, and only gradually came to embrace paradigms drawn from the inquisitorial model. This may be explained, at least partially, by the individuals who were engaged in the process. Common law-trained jurists tended to predominate in the early days of the Yugoslav Tribunal, particularly in the Office of the Prosecutor. The International Criminal Tribunal for Rwanda seemed to lean in somewhat of the other direction, again perhaps because of the personalities who were involved. The initial procedural decisions of the International Criminal Court have seemed to be strongly influenced by the inquisitorial regime, with pro-active and interventionist judges attempting to dominate the proceedings at every step. They find support, of course, in the provisions of the Statute and the Rules of Procedure and Evidence, which are more conducive to inquisitorial procedure than the counterparts in the *ad hoc* tribunals established by the Security Council.

Initiation of an investigation

The jurisdiction of the Court may be triggered by one of three sources: a State Party, the Security Council or the Prosecutor.[6] If the jurisdiction is triggered by the Security Council or by a State Party, the Prosecutor analyses the information in order to determine whether or not to 'initiate an investigation'. This first stage in the proceedings is termed 'preliminary examination' when the Prosecutor is acting pursuant to his *proprio motu* powers.[7] and a 'pre-investigative phase ("analysis of information")'

---

[5] Leila Nadya Sadat and S. Richard Carden, 'The New International Criminal Court: An Uneasy Revolution', (2000) 88 *Georgetown Law Journal* 381 at 399–400.

[6] Rome Statute of the International Criminal Court, (2002) 2187 UNTS 90, Art. 13. See Chapter 4, 'Triggering the jurisdiction', above.

[7] Rome Statute, Art. 15(6), when the Prosecutor is acting pursuant to his *proprio motu* powers. In the case of a referral, see *Situation in the Central African Republic* (ICC-01/05), Decision Requesting Information on the Status of the Preliminary Examination of the Situation in the Central African Republic, 30 November 2006, p. 4.

when the matter is the result of a referral by the Security Council or a State Party.[8]

The terms of the Rome Statute are mandatory. According to Article 53(1), the Prosecutor *shall* initiate an investigation after evaluating information submitted to him unless he determines that there is 'no reasonable basis to proceed under the Statute'. The mandatory nature is obvious enough when the situation is referred by a State Party or the Security Council. When it comes from the Prosecutor exercising his *proprio motu* powers, the term 'shall' is confusing, because the source of the legal requirement to investigate is the Prosecutor himself. In other words, he *shall* proceed, but only after he has decided to do so in the exercise of his discretion under Article 15. Mireille Delmas-Marty has described Article 53 as a compromise between the choice of strict legality and prosecutorial discretion.[9]

In determining whether there is 'a reasonable basis' to proceed, the Prosecutor is to consider the factors listed in article 53(1)(a)–(c), namely whether the information available provides a reasonable basis to believe that a crime within the jurisdiction of the Court has been or is being committed; whether the case would be admissible, and whether, taking into account the gravity of the crime and the interests of victims, there are nonetheless substantial reasons to believe that an investigation would not serve the interests of justice.[10] The Prosecutor has described the process of 'preliminary examination':

> The OTP first submits that the preliminary examination by the Prosecutor of available information in respect of a situation under Article 53(1) must be performed in a comprehensive and thorough manner. The Prosecutor must make an informed and well-reasoned decision on whether the requirements of Article 53(1) have been satisfied. Consequently it must be for him to determine the breadth and scope of this preliminary assessment. Further, the breadth and scope of an examination under Article 53(1) is situation specific: it depends on the particular features of each situation, including, inter alia, the availability of information, the nature

---

[8] Office of the Prosecutor, Annex to the 'Paper on Some Policy Issues Before the Office of the Prosecutor; Referrals and Communications', undated (made public on 21 April 2004).

[9] Mireille Delmas-Marty, 'Interactions Between National and International Criminal Law in the Preliminary Phase of Trial at the ICC', (2006) 4 *Journal of International Criminal Justice* 2 at 4.

[10] Rules of Procedure and Evidence, ASP/1/3, Rule 48.

and scale of the crimes, and the existence of national responses in respect of alleged crimes.[11]

The Prosecutor has explained that he may also take into consideration other factors in deciding not to invoke his *proprio motu* powers, including 'the published prosecutorial policy and the likelihood of any effective investigation being possible, having regard to the circumstances in the country concerned'. Resource issues are also highly relevant.[12]

The first two criteria listed in Article 53(1) and (2) that the Prosecutor is to consider, jurisdiction and admissibility, are discussed in distinct chapters of this book. The Prosecutor has attempted to set out his approach to the third criterion, 'interests of justice', in a policy paper issued in 2007.[13] The two provisions dealing with the interests of justice, Article 53(1)(c) and (2)(c), are worded slightly differently. Because Article 53(1)(c) refers to a 'situation', whereas Article 53(2)(c) refers to a 'case', only in the latter is the defendant identifiable.[14] This explains the reference in Article 53(2)(c) to the 'age or infirmity of the alleged perpetrator, and his or her role in the alleged crime'.

When the Prosecutor is acting *proprio motu*, he is to base himself upon information obtained from various sources, as Article 15(2) declares:

> The Prosecutor shall analyze the seriousness of the information received. For this purpose, he or she may seek additional information from States, organs of the United Nations, intergovernmental or non-governmental organizations, or other reliable sources that he or she deems appropriate, and may receive written or oral testimony at the seat of the Court.

Rule 47(2) provides a procedural framework for the taking of testimony pursuant to Article 15(2):

> When the Prosecutor considers that there is a serious risk that it might not be possible for the testimony to be taken subsequently, he or she may

---

[11] *Situation in the Central African Republic* (ICC-01/05–1), Prosecution's Report Pursuant to Pre-Trial Chamber III's 30 November 2006 Decision Requesting Information on the Status of the Preliminary Examination of the Situation in the Central African Republic, 15 December 2006, paras. 7–8.

[12] Office of the Prosecutor, Annex to the 'Paper on Some Policy Issues Before the Office of the Prosecutor: Referrals and Communications', undated (made public on 21 April 2004).

[13] Office of the Prosecutor, Policy Paper on the Interests of Justice, September 2007.

[14] Morten Bergsmo and Pieter Kruger, 'Article 53', in Otto Triffterer, ed., *Commentary on the Rome Statute of the International Criminal Court, Observers' Notes, Article by Article*, 2nd edn, Munich: C. H. Beck; Baden-Baden: Nomos; Oxford: Hart, 2008, pp. 1065–76 at pp. 1071–4.

request the Pre-Trial Chamber to take such measures as may be necessary to ensure the efficiency and integrity of the proceedings and, in particular, to appoint a counsel or a judge from the Pre-Trial Chamber to be present during the taking of the testimony in order to protect the rights of the defence. If the testimony is subsequently presented in the proceedings, its admissibility shall be governed by article 69, paragraph 4, and given such weight as determined by the relevant Chamber.

If the Prosecutor decides not to seek permission to initiate an investigation, he is to inform those who provided the information.[15] The procedure is formalized in Rule 49 ('Decision and notice under article 15, paragraph 6'):

1. Where a decision under article 15, paragraph 6, is taken, the Prosecutor shall promptly ensure that notice is provided, including reasons for his or her decision, in a manner that prevents any danger to the safety, well-being and privacy of those who provided information to him or her under article 15, paragraphs 1 and 2, or the integrity of investigations or proceedings.
2. The notice shall also advise of the possibility of submitting further information regarding the same situation in the light of new facts and evidence.

The Prosecutor has provided a general response with respect to communications submitted to him in 2002 and early 2003.[16] In February 2006, he issued a second general response, and two specific ones, dealing with the situations in Iraq and Venezuela.[17]

If the Prosecutor decides to proceed pursuant to his *proprio motu* powers, as set out in Article 15, once he has determined that a 'reasonable basis' exists for proceeding, the authorization of the Pre-Trial Chamber must be obtained in order to 'initiate an investigation'. In the case of a prosecution for the crime of aggression, permission must be obtained from the Pre-Trial Division.[18] According to Article 15:

3. If the Prosecutor concludes that there is a reasonable basis to proceed with an investigation, he or she shall submit to the Pre-Trial Chamber

---

[15] Rome Statute, Art. 15(6).
[16] Office of the Prosecutor, Communications Received by the Office of the Prosecutor of the ICC, 16 July 2003; Office of the Prosecutor, Update on Communications Received by the Office of the Prosecutor of the ICC, undated (issued in February 2006).
[17] Letter of Prosecutor dated 9 February 2006 (Venezuela); Letter of Prosecutor dated 9 February 2006 (Iraq).
[18] Rome Statute, Art. 15*bis*(8).

a request for authorization of an investigation, together with any supporting material collected. Victims may make representations to the Pre-Trial Chamber, in accordance with the Rules of Procedure and Evidence.

4. If the Pre-Trial Chamber, upon examination of the request and the supporting material, considers that there is a reasonable basis to proceed with an investigation, and that the case appears to fall within the jurisdiction of the Court, it shall authorize the commencement of the investigation, without prejudice to subsequent determinations by the Court with regard to the jurisdiction and admissibility of a case.

5. The refusal of the Pre-Trial Chamber to authorize the investigation shall not preclude the presentation of a subsequent request by the Prosecutor based on new facts or evidence regarding the same situation.

Rule 50 sets out the details of the procedure for authorization:

1. When the Prosecutor intends to seek authorization from the Pre-Trial Chamber to initiate an investigation pursuant to article 15, paragraph 3, the Prosecutor shall inform victims, known to him or her or to the Victims and Witnesses Unit, or their legal representatives, unless the Prosecutor decides that doing so would pose a danger to the integrity of the investigation or the life or well-being of victims and witnesses. The Prosecutor may also give notice by general means in order to reach groups of victims if he or she determines in the particular circumstances of the case that such notice could not pose a danger to the integrity and effective conduct of the investigation or to the security and well-being of victims and witnesses. In performing these functions, the Prosecutor may seek the assistance of the Victims and Witnesses Unit as appropriate.

2. A request for authorization by the Prosecutor shall be in writing.

3. Following information given in accordance with sub-rule 1, victims may make representations in writing to the Pre-Trial Chamber within such time limit as set forth in the Regulations.

4. The Pre-Trial Chamber, in deciding on the procedure to be followed, may request additional information from the Prosecutor and from any of the victims who have made representations, and, if it considers it appropriate, may hold a hearing.

5. The Pre-Trial Chamber shall issue its decision, including its reasons, as to whether to authorize the commencement of the investigation in accordance with article 15, paragraph 4, with respect to all or any part of the request by the Prosecutor. The Chamber shall give notice of the decision to victims who have made representations.

6. The above procedure shall also apply to a new request to the Pre-Trial Chamber pursuant to article 15, paragraph 5.

In November 2009, the Prosecutor made his first application to a Pre-Trial Chamber. Ruling on the application, Pre-Trial Chamber II decided to make its assessment in light of the criteria listed in Article 53, namely, whether the case would be admissible under Article 17 and, 'taking into account the gravity of the crime and the interests of victims, there are nonetheless substantial reasons to believe that an investigation would not serve the interests of justice'.[19]

The Prosecutor is not required to obtain authorization to 'initiate an investigation' when a State Party or the Security Council is the trigger, although he still determines at a preliminary stage whether there is a 'reasonable basis' to proceed.[20] Because no authorization is required from the Pre-Trial Chamber, in the case of referrals there is a blurring between the preliminary analysis undertaken by the Prosecutor and the decision to 'initiate an investigation'. Nevertheless, the Prosecutor has insisted upon the distinction, noting in the case of each of three referrals before the Court, namely Uganda, Congo and Sudan, the date on which he took the decision to begin the investigation.[21] With respect to the fourth situation, Central African Republic, he made it quite clear that, despite a referral in December 2004, as of 15 December 2006 no decision to initiate an investigation had yet been taken.[22] On 7 May 2007, he announced his decision to open an investigation in the Central African Republic.[23]

A decision by the Prosecutor not to seek authorization by the Pre-Trial Chamber to 'initiate an investigation' appears to be entirely discretionary and not subject to any form of judicial review, if the

[19] *Situation in Kenya* (ICC-01/09), Decision Pursuant to Article 15 of the Rome Statute on the Authorization of an Investigation into the Situation in the Republic of Kenya, 31 March 2010, para. 21.

[20] There appears to be an exception in the case of the crime of aggression, where authorization of the Pre-Trial Division is required even when a State Party has referred the situation. See Rome Statute, Art. 15*bis*(8).

[21] Democratic Republic of the Congo: 21 June 2004; Uganda: 28 July 2004; Sudan: 6 June 2005.

[22] *Situation in the Central African Republic* (ICC-01/05–1), Prosecution's Report Pursuant to Pre-Trial Chamber III's 30 November 2006 Decision Requesting Information on the Status of the Preliminary Examination of the Situation in the Central African Republic, 15 December 2006.

[23] 'Prosecutor Opens Investigation in the Central African Republic', ICC-OTP-20070522-220.

preliminary examination is the result of the exercise of his *proprio motu* powers and the decision is based upon either jurisdiction or admissibility. The only requirement is that he inform those who provided the information.[24] The circumstances are different when the trigger of the investigation is a referral by a State Party or by the Security Council. Then, the Prosecutor's determination that there is no 'reasonable basis' to proceed may be reviewed by the Pre-Trial Chamber. The Pre-Trial Chamber may intervene at the request of the Security Council or the State Party, depending upon the source of the referral. If the Prosecutor decides not to 'initiate an investigation', he is to notify the source of the referral, either the State Party or the Security Council, as the case may be:[25] Rule 49, cited above, is deemed to apply to the notification.[26] If the Prosecutor decides that there is no 'reasonable basis' because of the third criterion, 'the interests of justice', then the Pre-Trial Chamber may intervene on its own initiative and without any application having been made.[27]

The available remedy should the Pre-Trial Chamber disagree with the Prosecutor's decision not to proceed remains completely unclear. The idea seems to be that it could order the Prosecutor to proceed. But, since the Prosecutor makes determinations about the use of resources, especially human resources in his Office, it would seem that if ordered to do so he could proceed with an investigation in a perfunctory and superficial manner, assigning the international equivalent of an Inspector Clouseau to handle the case. Perhaps faced with such defiance, a Pre-Trial Chamber might countenance a citation for contempt. Alternatively, the Assembly of States Parties might threaten removal of the Prosecutor for 'misconduct or a serious breach of his or her duties', as authorized by Article 46(1). It is to be hoped that tensions between the Prosecutor and the Pre-Trial Chamber about where to target the energies of the Court will never become so aggravated.

Already, however, there have been signs of conflict. The Statute sets no time limit for the Prosecutor to decide that there is no reasonable basis to proceed, following a referral. No specific procedure is provided in the event of prosecutorial inertia, but presumably the source of the referral, whether it be the Security Council or a State Party, could take measures to stimulate the Prosecutor to make a determination. In the case of the

---

[24] Rome Statute, Art. 15(6).
[25] Rules of Procedure and Evidence, pp. 10–107, Rule 105(1).
[26] *Ibid.*, Rule 105(2).   [27] Rome Statute, Art. 53(3)(b).

Security Council, although a forum is not provided by the Rome Statute, the only resolution referring a case to date has required the Prosecutor to make bi-annual reports to the Council on his progress.[28] With respect to State Party referrals, the Pre-Trial Chambers have seized the initiative, convening status conferences to inquire from the Prosecutor about his progress (or lack of it). The authority given by the Pre-Trial Chambers is Regulation 30 of the Regulations of the Court, a vague provision that sets out the modalities of such meetings but says nothing about the circumstances of their convocation.

Pre-Trial Chamber II was the first off the mark, ordering a status conference following the unsealing of the five Lord's Resistance Army arrest warrants in order to obtain clarifications from the Prosecutor about some of his public statements concerning future investigations and charges. He had suggested that there would be no further investigation of past crimes attributable to the rebel group.[29] The Prosecutor responded that his Office did not intend to seek further warrants for past crimes with respect to the Lord's Resistance Army, but he confirmed that inquiries and analysis was ongoing about other groups, notably the Ugandan Defence Forces.[30] He said that no application had been made pursuant to Article 53(2) because no decision had been reached yet that there was not a sufficient basis for prosecution.[31]

In September 2006, some twenty-one months after its referral to the Court, the Central African Republic inquired as to the intentions of the Prosecutor.[32] Pre-Trial Chamber III reacted by requesting the Prosecutor 'to provide the Chamber and the Government of the Central African Republic, no later than 15 December 2006, with a report containing information on the current status of the preliminary examination of the CAR situation, including an estimate of when the preliminary examination of the CAR situation will be concluded and when a decision pursuant to article 53(1) of the Statute will be

---

[28] UN Doc. S/RES/1593 (2005), para. 8.
[29] *Situation in Uganda* (ICC 01/05), Decision to Convene a Status Conference on the Investigation in the Situation in Uganda in Relation to the Application of Article 53, 2 December 2005.
[30] *Situation in Uganda* (ICC 02/04–01/05), OTP Submission Providing Information on Status of the Investigation in Anticipation of the Status Conference to Be Held on 13 January 2006, 11 January 2006, paras. 6–7.
[31] *Ibid.*, para. 8.
[32] *Situation in Central African Republic* (ICC-01/05), Transmission par le Greffier d'une Requête aux fins de Saisine de la Chambre Préliminaire de la Cour Pénale Internationale et Annexes Jointes, 27 September 2006.

taken'.[33] Despite the silence of the Statute and the Rules of Procedure and Evidence concerning the time allowed to the Prosecutor to make his decision, the Pre-Trial Chamber reasoned by analogy with other provisions of these instruments and said: 'the preliminary examination of a situation pursuant to article 53(1) of the Statute and rule 104 of the Rules must be completed within a reasonable time from the reception of a referral by a State Party under articles 13(a) and 14 of the Statute, regardless of its complexity.' The Chamber noted that, in the two other State Party referrals, the decision to initiate an investigation had been taken within two to six months.[34]

The Prosecutor has taken the position that, until he makes a decision not to proceed following a referral, the Pre-Trial Chamber is without authority to review or control his activities. Nor does he have any duty to inform the referring State until the decision has been reached. According to the Prosecutor:

> The Rome Statute, in Article 53(1), grants to the Prosecutor the prerogative to determine when to initiate an investigation. The Pre-Trial Chamber's supervisory role, under Article 53(3), only applies to the review of a decision under Article 53(1) and (2) by the Prosecutor not to proceed with an investigation or a prosecution. The OTP submits that to date no decision under Article 53(1) has been made, and that accordingly there is no exercise of prosecutorial discretion susceptible to judicial review by the Chamber.[35]

The Prosecutor's position may amount to saying he can do indirectly what he cannot do directly. If the Statute requires him to obtain the authorization of a Pre-Trial Chamber if he decides not to proceed with an investigation following a referral by the Security Council or a State Party, can he avoid this supervision by simply declining to ask for such permission? Probably aware of how flimsy his position was, the Prosecutor proceeded to provide Pre-Trial Chamber III with an account of his activities since the referral in December 2004.

---

[33] *Situation in Central African Republic* (ICC-01/05), Decision Requesting Information on the Status of the Preliminary Examination of the Situation in the Central African Republic, 30 November 2006, p. 5.

[34] *Ibid.*, p. 4.

[35] *Situation in Central African Republic* (ICC-01/05), Prosecution's Report Pursuant to Pre-Trial Chamber III's 30 November 2006 Decision Requesting Information on the Status of the Preliminary Examination of the Situation in the Central African Republic, 30 November 2006, paras. 1 and 10.

Investigation

The Prosecutor has both 'duties' and 'powers' with respect to an investigation.[36] He is required 'to cover all facts and evidence relevant to an assessment of whether there is criminal responsibility under this Statute, and, in doing so, investigate incriminating and exonerating circumstances equally'.[37] The wording suggests a Prosecutor with a high level of neutrality and impartiality. Such a Prosecutor is rather more like the investigating magistrate or *juge d'instruction* of the continental legal system than the adversarial prosecuting attorney of the common law. This provision is one of many examples of the efforts of the drafters to seek some balance between common law and Romano-Germanic procedural models.[38] Other language in the same provision recalls the often delicate and highly sensitive nature of investigations into war crimes, crimes against humanity and genocide. The Prosecutor is to respect the interests and personal circumstances of victims and witnesses, and to be especially thoughtful in matters involving sexual violence, gender violence or violence against children.[39]

It is at the investigation stage that major differences between national and international justice are highlighted. Under a national justice system, the prosecuting authority has more or less unfettered access to witnesses and material evidence, subject to judicial authorization where search or seizure are involved. The matter is not nearly as simple for an international court, because the Prosecutor must conduct investigations on the territory of sovereign States. The investigation depends on the receptivity of the domestic legal system to initiatives from the Prosecutor's office. This will be especially difficult in the case of States that are not parties to the Statute or States that find themselves threatened by such an investigation, both of them rather probable scenarios.

The Prosecutor's powers during an investigation consist of collection and examination of evidence and attendance and questioning of suspects, victims and witnesses. Here, the Prosecutor may seek the cooperation of States or intergovernmental organizations, and even enter into arrangements or agreements necessary to facilitate such cooperation. He or she may also agree to the non-disclosure of materials that are obtained under the condition of confidentiality and solely for the purpose of

---

[36] Rome Statute, Art. 54, title. [37] *Ibid.*, Art. 54(1).

[38] Morten Bergsmo and Pieter Kruger, 'Article 53', in Triffterer, ed., *Commentary*, pp. 1065–76 at pp. 1071–4.

[39] Rome Statute, Art. 54(1)(b).

generating new evidence.[40] Similar norms exist at the *ad hoc* tribunals,[41] as well as in many national legal systems. But this may conflict with the duty to 'disclose to the defence evidence in the Prosecutor's possession or control which he or she believes shows or tends to show the innocence of the accused, or to mitigate the guilt of the accused, or which may affect the credibility of prosecution evidence'.[42] The prosecution 'has a duty to conduct itself with extreme care in gathering documents pursuant to article 54(3)(e) of the Statute'.[43] It has been held that the reference to 'proceedings' in article 54(3)(e) refers to the 'investigation stage'.[44]

Article 54(3)(e) empowers the Prosecutor; it does not act as a bar to the production of evidence.[45] Rule 82 of the Rules of Procedure and Evidence completes this provision. It prohibits the Prosecutor from introducing any material that has been obtained on the basis of a pledge of confidentiality in accordance with Article 54(3)(e) without the consent of the provider and adequate disclosure to the accused.[46] However, it also facilitates the work of the Prosecutor by authorizing the production of such evidence, assuming consent has been obtained and disclosure provided, while at the same time sheltering witnesses from cross-examination about the source of the information and protecting the Prosecutor from submission of any related evidence. Article 18(3) of the Negotiated Relationship Agreement with the United Nations essentially repeats the terms of Article 54(3)(e), but adds that any documents or information provided on a confidential basis 'shall not be disclosed to other organs of the Court or to third parties, at any stage of the proceedings or thereafter, without the consent of the United Nations'.

---

[40] *Ibid.*, Art. 54(3)(e).
[41] Rules of Procedure and Evidence [of the International Criminal Tribunal for the former Yugoslavia], UN Doc. IT/32, Rule 70.
[42] Rome Statute, Art. 67(2). On disclosure obligations more generally, see Rules of Procedure and Evidence, Rules 76–84.
[43] *Katanga et al.* (ICC-01/04–01/07), Decision on Article 54(3)(e) Documents Identified as Potentially Exculpatory or Otherwise Material to the Defence's Preparation for the Confirmation Hearing, 20 June 2008, para. 36.
[44] *Situation in the Democratic Republic of the Congo* (ICC-01/04–01/06), Decision on the Applications for Participation in the Proceedings of a/0001/06, a/0002/06 and a/0003/06 in the Case of the Thomas Lubanga Dyilo and of the Investigation in the Democratic of the Congo, 28 July 2007, para. 33.
[45] But, for the contrary view, see *Lubanga* (ICC-01/04–01/06 OA 6), Separate Opinion by Judge Georghios M. Pikis, 14 December 2006, para. 12.
[46] *Katanga et al.* (ICC-01/04–01/07), Decision Requesting Observations Concerning Article 54(3)(e) Documents Identified as Potentially Exculpatory or Otherwise Material for the Defence's Preparation for the Confirmation Hearing, 2 June 2008, para. 20.

In *Lubanga*, the Prosecutor invoked Article 18(3) of the Negotiated Relationship Agreement in refusing to show documents to the judges of the Trial Chamber.[47] The Trial Chamber in that case implied, at the very least, that this was an invalid clause, because it concluded that the consequence was to impede the Chamber in exercising its jurisdiction in accordance with Articles 64 and 67, in that it could not determine whether non-disclosure of potentially exculpatory material constituted a breach of the right to a fair trial.[48] A Pre-Trial Chamber has held that '[i]f all or part of such agreements are found to be contrary to the statutory framework provided for by the Statute and the Rules, some of their confidentiality clauses may be declared null and void'.[49] This wording is imprecise. Chambers of the Court do not have the authority to declare international agreements to be null and void. Rather, they can refuse to give effect to them in proceedings before the Court.

Application of Article 54(3)(e) by the Prosecutor provoked a crisis that almost scuttled the first trial at the Court. The Prosecutor had obtained information from the United Nations mission in the Democratic Republic of the Congo, as well as from several non-governmental organizations, promising that it would remain confidential. According to the Prosecutor, as much as 50 per cent of the material obtained during investigations in the Democratic Republic of the Congo was subject to confidentiality pledges.[50] This approach was described by one judge as 'reckless', given the potential for conflict with the obligation to disclose, especially when this concerned exculpatory evidence.[51] The Prosecutor

---

[47] *Lubanga* (ICC-01/04–01/06), Decision on the Consequences of Non-Disclosure of Exculpatory Materials Covered by Article 54(3)(e) Agreements and the Application to Stay the Prosecution of the Accused, Together with Certain Other Issues Raised at the Status Conference on 10 June 2008, 13 June 2008, para. 44.

[48] *Ibid.*, para. 92. Approved: *Lubanga* (ICC-01/04–01/06 OA 13), Judgment on the Appeal of the Prosecutor Against the Decision of Trial Chamber I Entitled 'Decision on the Consequences of Non-Disclosure of Exculpatory Materials Covered by Article 54(3)(e) Agreements and the Application to Stay the Prosecution of the Accused, Together with Certain Other Issues Raised at the Status Conference on 10 June 2008', 21 October 2008, para. 45; also para. 48.

[49] *Katanga et al.* (ICC-01/04–01/07), Decision on Article 54(3)(e) Documents Identified as Potentially Exculpatory or Otherwise Material to the Defence's Preparation for the Confirmation Hearing, 20 June 2008, para. 63.

[50] *Lubanga* (ICC-01/04–01/06), Transcript, 1 October 2007, p. 13, lines 17–22.

[51] *Katanga et al.* (ICC-01/04–01/07), Decision on Article 54(3)(e) Documents Identified as Potentially Exculpatory or Otherwise Material to the Defence's Preparation for the Confirmation Hearing, 20 June 2008, para. 56.

conceded that this was 'excessive',[52] and stated that corrective measures have since been taken.[53]

In the *Lubanga* proceedings, the Trial Chamber first postponed the date at which the trial was scheduled to begin, and then imposed a stay of proceedings as a result of the Prosecutor's failure to provide disclosure of exculpatory evidence which he claimed was subject to a promise of confidentiality under Article 54(3)(e).[54] The Trial Chamber concluded that, as a result of the failure to disclose exculpatory evidence, which flowed from the Prosecutor's undertakings, there was no prospect that a fair trial could be held.[55] Its finding in this respect was upheld by the Appeals Chamber.[56] However, the Prosecutor was able to obtain the consent of the United Nations and the other information providers to the disclosure of the hitherto confidential evidence,[57] thereby rectifying the situation and allowing the trial to proceed.

The Appeals Chamber set out the methodology for dealing with conflicts between Article 67(2) and Article 54(3)(e). It recalled that agreements by the Prosecutor would have to be respected, and that a chamber could not order disclosure if confidentiality had been promised. It said that the issue would be litigated before the Chamber in *ex parte* proceedings with only the Prosecutor present. The Appeals Chamber left unclear whether a chamber could order the Prosecutor to show it the material in question, and whether agreements requiring the Prosecutor not to reveal such materials, even to the judges, were contrary to the Statute. If disclosure to the defence of the material is deemed necessary, the Appeals Chamber said that, failing consent by the information provider, the Chamber would have to determine 'whether and, if so, which counter-balancing measures can be taken to ensure that the rights of the

---

[52] *Lubanga* (ICC-01/04–01/06), Transcript, 2 October 2007, p. 2, lines 6–9.

[53] *Katanga et al.* (ICC-01/04–01/07), Transcript, 3 June 2008, p. 26, lines 5–8.

[54] For the lengthy background to the decision granting a stay, see *Lubanga* (ICC-01/04–01/06), Decision on the Consequences of Non-Disclosure of Exculpatory Materials Covered by Article 54(3)(e) Agreements and the Application to Stay the Prosecution of the Accused, Together with Certain Other Issues Raised at the Status Conference on 10 June 2008, 13 June 2008, paras. 3–6.

[55] *Ibid.*

[56] *Lubanga* (ICC-01/04–01/06 OA 13), Judgment on the Appeal of the Prosecutor Against the Decision of Trial Chamber I Entitled 'Decision on the Consequences of non-Disclosure of Exculpatory Materials Covered by Article 54(3)(e) Agreements and the Application to Stay the Prosecution of the Accused, Together with Certain Other Issues Raised at the Status Conference on 10 June 2008', 21 October 2008, paras. 37ff.

[57] See generally *Lubanga* (ICC-01/04–01/06), Reasons for Oral Decision Lifting the Stay of Proceedings, 23 January 2009.

accused are protected and that the trial is fair, in spite of the nondisclo-sure of the information'.[58]

The Prosecutor's ability to conduct 'on site investigations', as they were referred to during the drafting, was highly controversial. Some del-egations were unambiguously opposed, taking the view that investiga-tion was solely the prerogative of the State in question, as it would be in the case of inter-State judicial cooperation. Ultimately, the Prosecutor is allowed under the Statute to undertake specific investigative steps in the territory of a State *without* having previously obtained its consent and cooperation. But any such investigation is contingent upon judicial leave. Thus, the Pre-Trial Chamber must authorize any such measures, and it can only do so after determining that the State is clearly unable to execute a request for cooperation due to the unavailability of any appro-priate authority within its judicial system.[59] In practice, such a power 'is not practicable and cannot be effectively utilized', as Fabricio Guariglia has pointed out.[60] Elsewhere, the Statute allows the Prosecutor to take evidence and interview witnesses within a State and without its consent, but all of this must be carried out on a voluntary basis and after seeking permission from the State.[61]

Cases may arise where a State Party is 'clearly unable to execute a request for cooperation due to the unavailability of any authority or any component of its judicial system competent to execute the request for cooperation'. In such situations, the Pre-Trial Chamber may enable the Prosecutor to take specific investigative steps within that State's territory without its consent, although the Statute urges that this be done 'whenever possible having regard to the views of the State concerned'.[62]

States Parties are under a general obligation to cooperate with the Court in its investigation of crimes.[63] They must ensure that they have domestic legal provisions in effect in order to provide such

---

[58] *Lubanga* (ICC-01/04–01/06 OA 13), Judgment on the Appeal of the Prosecutor Against the Decision of Trial Chamber I Entitled 'Decision on the Consequences of Non-Disclosure of Exculpatory Materials Covered by Article 54(3)(e) Agreements and the Application to Stay the Prosecution of the Accused, Together with Certain Other Issues Raised at the Status Conference on 10 June 2008', 21 October 2008, para. 48.

[59] Rome Statute, Art. 57(3)(d).

[60] Fabricio Guariglia, 'Investigation and Prosecution', in Lee, *The International Criminal Court*, pp. 227–38.

[61] Rome Statute, Art. 99(4). See Kimberly Prost, 'Article 99', in Triffterer, ed., *Commentary*, pp. 1621–9.

[62] Rome Statute, Art. 57(3)(d).   [63] *Ibid.*, Art. 86.

cooperation.[64] But the formulation of this obligation, which would seem obvious enough for States Parties to the Statute, proved difficult at Rome. According to Phakiso Mochochoko, '[d]elegations were divided on the issue of whether cooperation should be defined as a matter of legal obligation that the Court can rely upon, or whether such cooperation should remain an uncertain variable, subject to the will or circumstances of a particular State'.[65] The resulting compromise specifies precise obligations with respect to cooperation, but also requires more generally that States Parties 'cooperate fully' with the Court.

The mechanisms established by the Court will be largely familiar to States, in that they closely resemble those that already exist in the form of bilateral or multilateral treaties on judicial assistance. Requests for cooperation are to be transmitted through the diplomatic channel or any other appropriate mechanism designated by each State Party.[66] The request is to be formulated in an official language of the State, or in a language designated by the State. States are required to safeguard the confidentiality of the request, except to the extent necessary for its fulfilment.[67] Requests may also be transmitted through Interpol or an appropriate regional police organization. Applications for assistance are to be made in writing, as a general rule, and are to include a concise statement of the purpose of the request, including its legal basis and the grounds for it.[68]

The specific forms of cooperation to which the Court is entitled are listed in Article 93 of the Statute, although there is a more general obligation to provide any type of assistance not prohibited by the law of the requested State, with a view to facilitating investigation. States Parties are required to provide assistance in: identifying and determining the whereabouts of persons or the location of items; the taking of evidence, including testimony under oath, and the production of evidence, including expert opinions and reports necessary to the Court; the questioning of suspects; the service of documents; facilitating the voluntary

---

[64] *Ibid.*, Art. 88. See Claus Kreß, Bruce Broomhall, Flavia Lattanzi and Valeria Santori, eds., *The Rome Statute and Domestic Legal Orders*, vol. II, *Constitutional Issues, Cooperation and Enforcement*, Baden-Baden: Nomos, 2005.

[65] Phakiso Mochochoko, 'International Cooperation and Judicial Assistance', in Lee, *The International Criminal Court*, pp. 305–17 at p. 306.

[66] Rome Statute, Art. 87(1)(a); Rules of Procedure and Evidence, Rules 176–180. Several States have made declarations specifying diplomatic channels, the Department of Justice or the Public Prosecutor's Office.

[67] Rome Statute, Art. 87(3).   [68] *Ibid.*, Art. 96(2).

appearance of persons as witnesses or experts before the Court; the examination of places or sites, including the exhumation and examination of grave sites; the execution of searches and seizures; the provision of records and documents, including official records and documents; the protection of victims and witnesses and the preservation of evidence; and identifying, tracing and freezing or seizing proceeds, property and assets and instrumentalities of crimes for the purpose of eventual forfeiture.[69] States are only entitled to deny requests for production of documents or disclosure of evidence relating to 'national security', a matter of which they seem to be the sole arbiters.[70] Incidentally, there is a certain reciprocity to the cooperation procedures, in that the Court may also provide assistance to States Parties that are conducting their own investigations into serious crimes.[71]

In most States, specific implementing legislation is necessary in order to authorize cooperation with the Court. Some have had to address complex constitutional issues, such as prohibitions on the extradition of nationals or of extradition to States where life imprisonment may be imposed.[72] For most, however, it has been a relatively straightforward matter, though one that is usually technically of considerable complexity. Although there are some exemplary cases, most States Parties to the Rome Statute have not insisted upon having such implementing legislation in place and operational before ratifying the Statute.

But what can be done when States Parties, who are bound by the Statute to cooperate with the Court, refuse perfectly legal requests for assistance? Article 87(7) states that the Court may make a finding of non-compliance and then refer the matter to the Assembly of States Parties. Where the Security Council has referred the matter to the Court, the Court may send the matter to the Security Council, although this would hardly seem necessary as the Security Council could certainly take action in any case, pursuant to its powers under the Charter of the United Nations. In its carefully worded resolution referring the Darfur situation to the Court, the Security Council '[d]ecides that the Government of Sudan and all other parties to the conflict in Darfur, shall cooperate fully with and provide any necessary assistance to the

---

[69] Ibid., Art. 93(1). See also ibid., Art. 72.
[70] Ibid., Arts. 93(4) and 72.   [71] Ibid., Art. 93(10).
[72] See generally Claus Kreß, Bruce Broomhall, Flavia Lattanzi and Valeria Santori, eds., *The Rome Statute and Domestic Legal Orders*, vol. II, *Constitutional Issues, Cooperation and Enforcement*, Baden-Baden: Nomos, 2005.

Court and the Prosecutor pursuant to this resolution and, while recognizing that States not party to the Rome Statute have no obligation
under the Statute, urges all States and concerned regional and other
international organizations to cooperate fully'.[73] If non-party States
have no obligation to cooperate under the Statute, why did the Security
Council decide that Sudan, which is a non-party State, 'shall cooperate'?
The answer can only be that the Security Council can order States to
cooperate with the Court pursuant to Chapter VII of the Charter of the
United Nations, regardless of whether obligation exists under the Rome
Statute. Presumably, the Council could even order forms of cooperation
that are not contemplated by the Rome Statute. And it can certainly
order sanctions where a State does not cooperate. As for the Assembly of
States Parties, its powers, in the case of non-compliance, would seem to
be limited to 'naming and shaming'.

Although in practice most of the investigation will take place under
the provisions of a State's national law, with respect to questioning,
search, seizure and similar processes, the rights of individuals during
investigations are subject to special protection by the Statute. National
law varies considerably in this area, and it would be unconscionable for
the Court to implicate itself in domestic judicial proceedings that breach
fundamental rights. In fact, the Statute almost seems to be saying that it
cannot trust domestic justice systems to provide adequate respect for the
rights of the individual. The provisions in the Statute set a high standard and offer a good model for national systems. According to Article
55, during investigation a person shall not be compelled to incriminate himself or herself or to confess guilt; shall not be subjected to any
form of coercion, duress or threat, to torture or to any other form of
cruel, inhuman or degrading treatment or punishment; shall, if questioned in a language other than a language the person fully understands
and speaks, have, free of any cost, the assistance of a competent interpreter and such translations as are necessary to meet the requirements
of fairness; shall not be subjected to arbitrary arrest or detention; and
shall not be deprived of his or her liberty except on such grounds and
in accordance with such procedures as are established in the Statute. If
such standards were universally respected, there would probably be no
need for an international criminal court!

A person suspected of having committed a crime subject to the jurisdiction of the Court is entitled to be informed of other specific rights

---

[73] UN Doc. S/RES/1593 (2005), para. 2.

prior to being questioned.[74] The person shall be informed that he or she is indeed suspected of having committed a crime, that he or she may remain silent without such silence being a consideration in determining guilt or innocence at trial, to have legal assistance, if necessary provided for them in cases of indigence and where the interests of justice so require, and to be questioned in the presence of counsel unless this right has been voluntarily waived. These rights go well beyond the requirements of international human rights norms set out in such instruments as the International Covenant on Civil and Political Rights,[75] and as a general rule surpass the rights recognized in even the most advanced and progressive justice systems.[76] But the Statute insists that these norms be honoured, even if the questioning is being carried out by officials of national justice systems pursuant to a request from the Court. If these rules are violated, the Court is entitled to exclude any evidence obtained, such as a confession.[77] However, before excluding evidence the Court must also satisfy itself that the violation 'raises substantial doubt on the reliability of the evidence' or that 'the admission of the evidence would be antithetical to and would seriously damage the integrity of the proceedings'. In any event, given these elaborate provisions, it is hard to imagine why any suspect would ever agree to talk to investigators from the Office of the Prosecutor. Certainly, competent defence counsel will almost invariably advise against any cooperation, except in exceptional circumstances, such as a declaration that an alibi defence will be invoked at trial.

The Statute makes allowance for testimony or evidence that may not be available at trial. An example would be testimony of a victim who will die before trial. While the interests of justice require that special provision be made to facilitate the admissibility of such evidence, or rather a record of it, there is also the need to protect the rights of the defence. Article 56 entitles the Prosecutor, when there is a 'unique investigative opportunity' with respect to testimony or evidence that may subsequently be unavailable, to request authorization to record the testimony or to collect and test the evidence. The Pre-Trial Chamber is to ensure that measures are taken to guarantee the efficiency and integrity of the proceedings and, in particular, that the rights of the defendant are

---

[74] See on this point *Mucić* (IT-96-21-T), Decision on Mucić's Motion for Exclusion of Evidence, 2 September 1997.
[75] International Covenant on Civil and Political Rights, (1966) 999 UNTS 171, Art. 9.
[76] Rome Statute, Art. 55(2).   [77] *Ibid.*, Art. 69(7).

protected. The Pre-Trial Chamber is to name one of its judges to attend proceedings in this respect. The Prosecutor is expected to seek such measures, even when the evidence is favourable to the defence, in keeping with the duty of neutrality and impartiality.[78] The Pre-Trial Chamber has a certain role in supervising the Prosecutor, and may challenge the latter if measures to preserve testimony or evidence in such cases are not sought. If the Prosecutor's failure to do so is deemed unjustifiable, the Pre-Trial Chamber may take such measures on its own initiative. Here, too, the Statute departs from a purely adversarial model in favour of the more neutral prosecution of the continental or Romano-Germanic system of criminal procedure. As Claus Kreß has observed, '[t]he interplay between the Prosecutor and the Pre-Trial Chamber at the early stages of the proceedings constitutes one of the most striking examples of the uniqueness of the ICC procedural law'.[79]

In the first cases before the Court, one of the Pre-Trial Chambers took a very expansive approach to its role at the investigation stage. Article 57(3) of the Statute sets out the powers of a Pre-Trial Chamber to intervene during the investigation:

> (a) At the request of the Prosecutor, issue such orders and warrants as may be required for the purposes of an investigation;
>
> ...
>
> (c) Where necessary, provide for the protection and privacy of victims and witnesses, the preservation of evidence, the protection of persons who have been arrested or appeared in response to a summons, and the protection of national security information;
>
> (d) Authorize the Prosecutor to take specific investigative steps within the territory of a State Party without having secured the cooperation of that State under Part 9 if, whenever possible having regard to the views of the State concerned, the Pre-Trial Chamber has determined in that case that the State is clearly unable to execute a request for cooperation due to the unavailability of any authority or any component of its judicial system competent to execute the request for cooperation under Part 9.

After the investigation in the Democratic Republic of the Congo situation had been initiated, but before a request for an arrest warrant

---

[78] Behrens, 'Investigation, Trial and Appeal', pp. 122–3.

[79] Claus Kreß, 'The Procedural Law of the International Criminal Court in Outline: Anatomy of a Unique Compromise', (2003) 1 *Journal of International Criminal Justice* 606. Cited in *Situation in Uganda* (ICC 02/-4-01/05), Decision on the Prosecutor's Application That the Pre-Trial Chamber Disregard as Irrelevant the Submission Filed by the Registry on 5 December 2005, 9 March 2006, para. 19.

had been submitted, Pre-Trial Chamber I issued a decision to convene a status conference.[80] The Pre-Trial Chamber said it wished to consider matters that had arisen concerning the protection of witnesses and the preservation of evidence. This provoked a serious controversy with the Prosecutor, one that highlighted the issues involved in the creation of this unique new procedural regime built on concepts derived from very different systems. The Prosecutor reacted thus:

> It is submitted that the interplay between Pre-Trial Chamber and Prosecution is a sensitive matter that lies at the heart of the compromises reached in Rome between different legal traditions and values, and must be approached with the utmost caution. In relation to the investigative activities undertaken by the Court, this compromise between different legal cultures is represented by two main features of the Statute: the independence and autonomy of the Prosecutor in conducting investigations, always under strict application of the principle of objectivity enshrined in Article 54(1)(a), and the specific supervisory powers of the Pre-Trial Chamber. The system enshrined in the Statute is one where the investigation is not performed or shared with a judicial body, but rather entrusted to the Prosecution, as expressly provided for in Article 42(1) of the Statute: the Office of the Prosecutor 'shall be responsible for conducting investigations ... before the Court'. At the same time, the system also includes a closed number of provisions empowering the Pre-Trial Chamber to engage in specific instances of judicial supervision over the Prosecution's investigative activities. The Prosecution submits that this delicate balance between both organs must be preserved at all times in order to honour the Statute, and to enable the Court to function in a fair and efficient manner.[81]

The Prosecutor took the position that the Pre-Trial Chamber was without any authority to convene a status conference.[82] The Prosecutor argued that excessive involvement of the Pre-Trial Chamber at the investigation stage would lead to charges of a lack of impartiality. The Pre-Trial Chamber responded a day later with a ruling dismissing the Prosecutor's

---

[80] *Situation in the Democratic Republic of Congo* (ICC-01/04–9-t), Décision de convoquer une conférence de mise en état, 17 February 2005. See Michela Miraglia, 'The First Decision of the ICC Pre-Trial Chamber, International Criminal Procedure under Construction', (2006) 4 *Journal of International Criminal Justice* 188.

[81] *Situation in the Democratic Republic of Congo* (ICC-01/04), Prosecutor's Position on Pre-Trial Chamber I's 17 February 2005 Decision to Convene a Status Conference, 8 March 2005, para. 3.

[82] *Ibid.*, paras. 12–19.

objections, on purely procedural grounds, and confirming that the status conference was to take place.[83] The whole controversy was part of an ongoing struggle between the Office of the Prosecutor and the judges, one that is underpinned by the great cultural debates in comparative criminal procedure. Late in 2005, Pre-Trial Chamber II convened a status conference to inquire about issues concerning security in Uganda.[84] This time, there was no apparent protest from the Prosecutor.

Arrest and surrender

At any time after the initiation of an investigation, the Prosecutor may seek from the Pre-Trial Chamber a warrant of arrest or a summons to appear.[85] Later, if and when the suspect is brought before the Court, a 'document containing the charges' is issued.[86] The terminology is somewhat different from that employed at the *ad hoc* tribunals, which speak of indictment. The term 'indictment' is unknown to the International Criminal Court.

If it issues an arrest warrant, the Pre-Trial Chamber must be satisfied that there are reasonable grounds to believe the person has committed a crime within the Court's jurisdiction, and that the arrest of the person is necessary. Summons is offered as an alternative to arrest, where it will be sufficient to ensure a person's appearance before the Court.[87] Arrest is considered necessary in order to ensure appearance at trial, to prevent obstruction of the investigation, or to prevent the person from undertaking any further activity prohibited by the Statute.[88]

The language of Article 58 of the Statute suggests that arrest is the exception,[89] in that the grounds for it need be specifically alleged, and

---

[83] *Situation in the Democratic Republic of Congo* (ICC-01/04), Decision on the Prosecutor's Position on Pre-Trial Chamber I's 17 February 2005 Decision to Convene a Status Conference, 9 March 2005.

[84] *Situation in Uganda* (ICC-02/04–01/05), Decision to Convene a Status Conference on Matters Related to Safety and Security in Uganda, 25 November 2005.

[85] Rome Statute, Art. 58.

[86] *Ibid.*, Art. 61(3)(a); Regulations of the Court, ICC-BD/01–01–04, Regulation 52.

[87] Rome Statute, Art. 58(7).

[88] *Ibid.*, Art. 58(1); Rules of Procedure and Evidence, Rule 117.

[89] For statements to this effect, see: *Katanga et al.* (ICC-01/04–01/07), Decision on the Powers of the Pre-Trial Chamber to Review *Proprio Motu* the Pre-Trial Detention of Germain Katanga, 18 March 2008, p. 6; *Katanga et al.* (ICC-01/04–01/07), Decision on the Application for Interim Release of Mathieu Ngudjolo Chui, 27 March 2008, p. 6; *Katanga et al.* (ICC-01/04–01/07), Decision on the Conditions of the Pre-Trial Detention of Germain Katanga, 21 April 2008, p. 6.

that summons to appear is the general rule. But, in practice, the Pre-Trial Chamber has reversed this, requiring the Prosecutor to satisfy the Court that a summons will be adequate, and issuing a warrant of arrest if this is not accomplished. In two applications in the *Situation in Darfur*, the Prosecutor requested summonses to appear but was overruled by the Pre-Trial Chamber. The Chamber noted the terms of Article 58(7), which require it to be 'satisfied … that a summons is sufficient to ensure the person's appearance'. In applying the provision, it said it would be 'satisfied that a summons to appear would be equally effective as a warrant of arrest to ensure the person's appearance before the Court'.[90] The Chamber treated Article 58(7) as an exceptional provision, whose application 'is restricted to cases in which the person can and will appear voluntarily before the Court without the necessity of presenting a request for arrest and surrender'.[91]

The process itself seems to have involved some vigorous exchanges between Prosecutor and Pre-Trial Chamber, characteristic of the interventionist approach taken by the judges in this case and the corresponding resistance of the Prosecutor. Article 58(2) of the Rome Statute requires the Prosecutor to submit a 'concise statement of the facts' and 'a summary of the evidence' as part of an application for an arrest warrant. But apparently Pre-Trial Chamber I answered the request for the warrant with an 'invitation' that the Prosecutor provide additional 'supporting materials'. The Prosecutor seems to have bristled at the suggestion, although he eventually cooperated, noting that he was not required by the Statute to comply with such an 'invitation'. The Prosecutor insisted that the terms of the Statute indicate that 'the legislator has deliberately chosen, at the stage of the arrest warrant application, to require the Pre-Trial Chamber to trust the Prosecutor's summary' and that 'the Prosecutor has a choice in what to present to the Pre-Trial Chamber'.[92]

The Pre-Trial Chamber conceded that the Prosecutor was under no procedural obligation to submit further materials, but said that, if the judges were not satisfied with the materials presented to them, they could decline to issue an arrest warrant.[93]

---

[90] *Situation in Darfur, Sudan* (ICC-02/05-01/07), Decision on the Prosecution Application under Article 58(7) of the Statute, 27 April 2007, para. 116.

[91] *Ibid.*, para. 117.

[92] *Lubanga* (ICC-01/04-01/06), Prosecutor's Further Submission, cited *in extenso* in *Lubanga* (ICC-01/04-01/06-8), Decision on the Prosecutor's Application for a Warrant of Arrest, 10 February 2006.

[93] *Ibid.*, para. 9.

Pre-Trial Chamber I invoked the rights of the accused in this respect, in effect disagreeing that it should 'trust' the Prosecutor. It referred to the 'reasonable suspicion' standard established in the case law of the European Court of Human Rights[94] and the Inter-American Court of Human Rights.[95] Supporting its reference to international human rights law, the Pre-Trial Chamber invoked Article 21(3) of the Rome Statute, the provision on applicable law, which states: 'The application and interpretation of law pursuant to this article must be consistent with internationally recognized human rights, and be without any adverse distinction founded on grounds such as gender, as defined in article 7, paragraph 3, age, race, colour, language, religion or belief, political or other opinion, national, ethnic or social origin, wealth, birth or other status.' This resort to international human rights sources in an early ruling of the International Criminal Court presents a nice contrast with the first decisions of the International Criminal Tribunal for the former Yugoslavia, slightly more than a decade earlier. In its initial ruling on an application to allow anonymous witnesses, a Trial Chamber of the Yugoslav Tribunal dismissed the relevance of European Court of Human Rights precedents, saying that the international criminal tribunal was 'in certain respects, comparable to a military tribunal, which often has limited rights of due process and more lenient rules of evidence'.[96]

Assessing whether the arrest of Lubanga was necessary, Pre-Trial Chamber I noted that he had been in prison since March 2005 but that there was information that he might be released within the next three to four weeks and that, 'due to the wide variety of his national and international contacts, including, *inter alia*, to Uganda and Rwanda, [h]e will easily be in a position to flee and disappear'. The Chamber referred to recent reports of Human Rights Watch, which supported the claim that Lubanga would be released from custody.[97]

---

[94] *Ibid.*, para. 12, citing: *Fox, Campbell and Hartley* v. *United Kingdom*, Series A, No. 182, 30 August 1990, paras. 31–6; *K.F.* v. *Germany*, Reports 1997-VII, 27 November 1997, para. 57; *Labita* v. *Italy* (App. No. 26772/95), 6 April 2000, paras. 155–61; *Berktay* v. *Turkey* (App. No. 22493/93), 1 March 2001, para. 199; *O'Hara* v. *United Kingdom* (App. No. 37995/57), 16 October 2001, paras. 34–44.

[95] *Ibid.*, citing: *Barnaca Velasquez* v. *Guatemala*, Series C, No. 70, 25 November 2000, paras. 138–44; *Lorryza-Tarniyo* v. *Peru*, Series C, No. 33, 17 September 1997, paras. 49–55; *Gangaram Panday* v. *Suriname*, Series C, No. 16, 21 January 1994, paras. 46–51.

[96] *Tadić* (IT-94-1-T), Decision on the Prosecutor's Motion Requesting Protective Measures for Victims and Witnesses, 10 August 1995, para. 28.

[97] *Lubanga* (ICC-01/04–01/06–8), Decision on the Prosecutor's Application for a Warrant of Arrest, 10 February 2006, paras. 98–102.

The warrant of arrest should contain a concise statement of the facts but does not need to indicate the evidence that supports this. The Court communicates its request for arrest to the State concerned, which is then required to take immediate steps to arrest the person.[98]

As a general rule, all arrest warrants have been issued 'under seal'. For example, in *Lubanga*, Pre-Trial Chamber I issued a sealed warrant. Because the suspect was already in custody, there was nothing to be gained in terms of obtaining physical custody. However, the Chamber suggested that the element of surprise would facilitate locating and freezing his assets.[99] The warrant was unsealed upon an application from the Prosecutor once the transfer of Lubanga had been organized and he had left Congolese airspace on board a French military plane bound for The Hague.[100] A request was eventually issued by Judge Steiner, acting pursuant to the earlier decision but without any request having been made by the Prosecutor or the victims, to all States Parties for them to take all necessary measures to identify and seize Lubanga's assets.[101] In the Uganda situation, Pre-Trial Chamber II ruled that the warrant issued for Joseph Kony was to be made available and disclosed to persons or entities designated by the national authorities 'only for the purposes of the execution of the warrant', but that it should 'in all other respects, be kept under seal until further order by the Chamber'.[102] The Prosecutor had sought the sealing of the arrest warrants on the grounds that immediate disclosure could subject vulnerable groups in Uganda to the risk of retaliatory attacks by the Lord's Resistance Army and undermine continuing investigative efforts. Months later, he applied to have them unsealed, explaining that his Office together with the Victims and Witnesses Unit had nearly completed an overall plan for the security of witnesses and victims, and that unsealing of the warrants would be 'a feasible and powerful means of garnering international attention and support for arrest efforts, thus further ensuring the protection of

---

[98] *Ibid.*, Art. 59(1).   [99] *Ibid.*, para. 140.

[100] *Lubanga* (ICC-01/04–01/06), Decision to Unseal the Warrant of Arrest Against Mr Thomas Lubanga Dyilo and Related Documents, 17 March 2006.

[101] *Lubanga* (ICC-01/04–01/06), Demande adressée aux Etats parties au Statut de Rome en vue d'obtenir 'l'identification, la localisation et la saisie des biens et avoirs de M. Thomas Lubanga Dyilo', 31 March 2006.

[102] *Situation in Uganda* (ICC-02/04–53), Warrant of Arrest for Joseph Kony Issued on 8 July 2005 as Amended on 27 September 2005; *Situation in Uganda* (ICC-02/04–01/05–1-US-Exp.), Decision on the Prosecution's Application for Warrants of Arrest under Article 58, 12 July 2005, p. 7.

victims, potential witnesses and their families'.[103] The Prosecutor further explained that keeping the warrants under seal was actually impairing arrest efforts.[104] On 13 October 2005, the arrest warrants of Kony and the other leaders of the Lord's Resistance Army were unsealed.[105]

There is no explicit authorization in the Statute or the Rules for issuance of sealed warrants, and in making the rulings the Pre-Trial Chambers have cited no basis for this. In principle, the arrest warrant and the document containing the charges are public documents, and can be readily consulted on the website of the Court.[106] At the International Criminal Tribunal for the former Yugoslavia, the practice of issuing sealed indictments was controversial. A policy of sealing indictments until arrest of the suspect became relatively systematic in the mid-1990s.[107] The practice was abandoned in 2002, when it became apparent that publicizing indictments seemed to prompt accused persons to surrender.[108] At the Special Court for Sierra Leone, Liberian President Charles Taylor was the subject of a sealed indictment, whose existence was only made public by the Prosecutor himself, when he publicly but unsuccessfully called upon Ghana to arrest the accused. By then, the cat was out of the bag. The sealed indictment never helped to arrest Charles Taylor, and the utility of the practice would seem marginal, at best.

The Pre-Trial Chamber retains a degree of control over the procedure once arrest warrants have been issued. In the Uganda cases, more than a year after the warrants were issued but before any of them had been successfully executed, Pre-Trial Chamber II convened a status conference. Its order 'reiterat[ed] the need for the Chamber to receive a complete update on the status of the execution of the Warrants and of the ongoing cooperation with the relevant States with a view to exercising its powers and fulfilling its duties, in particular under Part 9 of the Statute'.[109] The Chamber seemed particularly concerned about the extent to which 'the peace negotiations and recent events in the region have affected the level

---

[103] *Situation in Uganda* (ICC-02/04–01/05), Decision on the Prosecutor's Application for Unsealing of the Warrants of Arrest, 13 October 2005, para. 14.

[104] *Ibid.*, para. 16.   [105] *Ibid.*

[106] Regulations of the Court, Regulation 8(c).

[107] Sean D. Murphy, 'Progress and Jurisprudence of the International Criminal Tribunal for the former Yugoslavia', (1999) 93 *American Journal of International Law* 57 at p. 74.

[108] Seventh Annual Report of the International Criminal Tribunal for Rwanda, UN Doc. A/57/163-S/2002/733, Annex, para. 216.

[109] *Situation in Uganda* (ICC-02/04–01/05), Order to the Prosecutor for the Submission of Additional Information on the Status of the Execution of the Warrants of Arrest in the Situation in Uganda, 30 November 2006, p. 3.

of cooperation by the relevant governments'.[110] The judges also inquired about 'recent events and reported meetings of UN officials with Joseph Kony', and asked the Prosecutor to report on whether he had requested or intended to request cooperation from the United Nations for the purpose of supporting the execution of the warrants.[111]

For the purpose of the provisions concerning arrest warrants, the State is called the 'custodial State' in the Statute. The warrant of arrest must be personally served upon the accused.[112] The arrested person is to be brought promptly before the competent judicial authority in the custodial State which is to determine that the warrant applies to that person, that proper process has been followed and that the person's rights have been respected 'in accordance with the law of that State'. A Pre-Trial Chamber, in *Lubanga*, held that the words 'in accordance with the law of the State' means 'that it is for national authorities to have primary jurisdiction for interpreting and applying national law ... although this does not prevent the Chamber from retaining a degree of jurisdiction over how the national authorities interpret and apply national law when such an interpretation and application relates to matters which ... are referred directly back to the national law by the Statute'.[113] Mohamed El Zeidy has described Article 59, which governs the arrest process within the custodial State, as 'one of the most delicate provisions of the Statute'. He has explained how some of its provisions interfere with the core idea of the primacy of national courts, because certain proceedings are no longer under the control of the domestic jurisdiction.[114]

In urgent cases, the Court may request the provisional arrest of the person, pending presentation of the request for surrender together with the supporting documents.[115] The request for provisional arrest may be delivered 'by any medium capable of delivering a written record'. A person arrested provisionally is entitled to be released if the formal request for surrender and the supporting documents are not produced within sixty days.[116] However, a suspect may consent to surrender even prior to the expiry of the period if the laws of the custodial State permit this.

---

[110] *Ibid.*, p. 5.   [111] *Ibid.*
[112] Regulations of the Court, ICC-BD/01–01–04, Regulation 31(2).
[113] *Lubanga* (ICC-01/04–01/06), Decision on the Defence Challenge to the Jurisdiction of the Court Pursuant to Article 19(2)(a) of the Statute, 3 October 2006, p. 6.
[114] Mohamed El Zeidy, 'Critical Thoughts on Article 59(2) of the ICC Statute', (2006) 4 *Journal of International Criminal Justice* 449.
[115] Rome Statute, Art. 59(2); Rules of Procedure and Evidence, Rule 119.
[116] Rules of Procedure and Evidence, Rule 188.

The arrested person is entitled to apply to the authorities of the custodial State for interim release pending surrender. However, the Statute creates a presumption in favour of detention.[117] The authorities of the custodial State are to grant interim release only when justified by 'urgent and exceptional circumstances' and where the necessary safeguards exist to ensure the surrender of the person to the Court. The Pre-Trial Chamber has a supervisory role in the area of interim release. It is to be informed by the custodial State of any application for interim release, and may make recommendations to the competent authorities of the custodial State. These recommendations are to be given 'full consideration'. If interim release is authorized, the Pre-Trial Chamber may request periodic reports on its status.

The competent authorities of the custodial State are expressly forbidden by the Statute from questioning whether the warrant has been properly issued by the Pre-Trial Chamber. However, the Statute contemplates other forms of contestation by the accused. For example, an accused may challenge arrest on the grounds of double jeopardy, in which case the custodial State is to consult with the Court to determine whether there has been a ruling on admissibility.[118] If the Court is considering the issue of admissibility, then the custodial State may postpone execution of the request for surrender.

The fact that Lubanga was detained for a prolonged period in the Democratic Republic of the Congo before issuance of the arrest warrant raises questions of arbitrary detention for which the Court itself may be responsible. Lubanga had been in detention for approximately one year, and possibly longer. His detention was well known to international NGOs, so it seems reasonable to presume that the Prosecutor was also aware of the situation. The Prosecutor only proceeded to seek an arrest warrant when it appeared that the detention was coming to an end, and that there was the possibility Lubanga would be released. This was specifically invoked in the application for the arrest warrant, and helped to persuade the Pre Trial Chamber.[119] Thus, it would appear that the Prosecutor may have been content, for a protracted period, to let Lubanga remain in the Congolese prison while he proceeded to prepare

---

[117] The International Covenant on Civil and Political Rights, (1966) 999 UNTS 171, Art. 9(3), states that '[i]t shall not be the general rule that persons awaiting trial shall be detained in custody'.

[118] Rome Statute, Art. 89(2).

[119] *Lubanga* (ICC-01/04–01/06–8), Decision on the Prosecutor's Application for a Warrant of Arrest, 10 February 2006, paras. 98–102.

his case, and that implies a degree of complicity with the detention within the Democratic Republic of the Congo prior to issuance of the arrest warrant. Similar issues have been raised before the International Criminal Tribunal for Rwanda, where the Appeals Chamber has manifested considerable unease when suspects have been held in African prisons under dubious legal pretexts while the Prosecutor continued to investigate.[120]

The Statute does not use the term 'extradition' to describe the rendition of a suspect from a State Party to the Court. This is consistent with an approach to this issue already adopted in the statutes of the *ad hoc* tribunals, which speak of 'surrender or transfer' (*le transfert ou la traduction*).[121] So that there is no doubt about the point, the Rome Statute includes a rather exceptional definitional provision that declares extradition to be 'the delivering up of a person by one State to another as provided by treaty, convention or national legislation' and surrender to be 'the delivering up of a person by a State to the Court, pursuant to this Statute'.[122] But the international court is really only the sum of its parts, and 'transfer' or 'surrender' is in a sense the 'extradition' to an ensemble of States, acting collectively. The reason for what at first blush seems obtuse terminology is to respond to objections from States that have legislation, and sometimes even constitutional provisions, prohibiting the *extradition* of their own nationals. Obviously, a refusal to extradite citizens would be totally incompatible with a State's obligations under the Statute. But early drafts of the Statute had allowed States to refuse surrender of their nationals, and the matter remained controversial through to the final days of the Rome Conference.[123] The issue of non-extradition of nationals was a problem for several States in the adjustment of their legislation, and even their constitutions, as a preliminary to ratification of the Statute.[124]

---

[120] *Barayagwiza* (ICTR-97-19-AR72), Decision, 3 November 1999; *Barayagwiza* (ICTR-97-19-AR72), Decision (Prosecutor's Request for Review or Reconsideration), 31 March 2000; *Kajelijeli* (ICTR-98-44A-A), Judgment, 23 May 2005, paras. 197–255.

[121] Statute of the International Criminal Tribunal for the former Yugoslavia, UN Doc. S/RES/827, Annex, Art. 29(2)(e); Statute of the International Criminal Tribunal for Rwanda, UN Doc. S/RES/955, Annex, Art. 28(2)(e). See also Rules of Procedure and Evidence, UN Doc. IT/32, Rule 58.

[122] Rome Statute, Art. 102.

[123] Phakiso Mochochoko, 'International Cooperation and Judicial Assistance', in Lee, *The International Criminal Court*, pp. 305–17 at pp. 311–12.

[124] UN Doc. A/CONF.183/SR.9, para. 32 (Brazil); UN Doc. A/CONF.183/C.1/SR.38, para. 21 (Israel) and para. 27 (Algeria).

It is difficult to predict how national courts will take to these distinctions, and there are few precedents. Three rationales have been advanced by academic writers for the prohibitions on extradition of nationals that are relatively common in domestic laws: national judges are the natural judges of the offence; a State must protect its own nationals; and a foreigner would be subject to prejudice.[125] None of these applies to the International Criminal Court, especially given that States Parties have the first bite at the apple, in accordance with the principle of complementarity. Yet some national judges seem to have a visceral hostility to international justice, as can be seen in the embarrassingly tardy efforts of the United States to secure the transfer of a Rwandan suspect to the Arusha tribunal.[126] Accordingly, that a national judge would consider a distinction between 'transfer or surrender' and 'extradition' to be little more than legal sophistry cannot be ruled out, despite the clear words of Article 102.[127]

Penalties may also pose problems for some States with regard to transfer and surrender. The issue was raised at Rome during the debates on the death penalty and life imprisonment, with some delegations noting their constitutional prohibition on extradition in the case of such severe penalties. For example, the Colombian Constitution forbids life imprisonment. Presumably, a Colombian accused could argue before domestic courts in proceedings to effect transfer to the International Criminal Court that eligibility for parole, as set out in Article 77 of the Statute, does not exclude the possibility of such a sentence.[128] Colombian courts might hold, by analogy with a decision of the Italian Constitutional Court,[129] that, because they cannot or should not speculate upon whether parole might be granted, transfer or surrender must

---

[125] Geoff Gilbert, *Aspects of Extradition Law*, Boston, Dordrecht and London: Martinus Nijhoff, 1991, p. 96.

[126] Robert Kushen and Kenneth J. Harris, 'Surrender of Fugitives by the United States to the War Crimes Tribunals for Yugoslavia and Rwanda', (1996) 90 *American Journal of International Law* 254.

[127] According to Cherif Bassiouni, 'in most States, surrender is equivalent to extradition': M. Cherif Bassiouni and Peter Manikas, *The Law of the International Criminal Tribunal for the former Yugoslavia*, Irvington-on-Hudson, NY: Transnational Publishers, 1995, p. 787.

[128] Gisbert H. Flanz, 'Colombia', translated by Peter B. Heller and Marcia W. Coward, in Gisbert H. Flanz, ed., *Constitutions of the Countries of the World*, Dobbs Ferry, NY: Oceana Publications, 1995, Art. 34.

[129] *Venezia v. United States of America*, Decision No. 223, 25 June 1996 (Constitutional Court of Italy).

be denied. Portugal finessed the issue at the time of ratification, making the following declaration: 'The Portuguese Republic declares the intention to exercise its jurisdictional powers over every person found in the Portuguese territory, that is being prosecuted for the crimes set forth in Article 5, paragraph 1 of the Rome Statute of the International Criminal Court, within the respect for the Portuguese criminal legislation.' Nor should the prospect be gainsaid that, some time in the future, regional or universal human rights bodies might determine that the sentences allowed by the Rome Statute, specifically life imprisonment without the possibility of parole before twenty-five years, are in breach of international human rights norms.[130] States preoccupied by their compliance with the Rome Statute might be led to contemplate reservations to human rights treaties on this basis, although the compatibility of such reservations with the object and purpose of human rights instruments would be debatable.

There may be competing requests for the same individual, one from the Court and the other from another State seeking extradition. This of course raises the issue of complementarity, because the application by the State for extradition indicates that there is in fact a national justice system seeking to exercise its jurisdiction over the offender and the offence. In such cases, the custodial State may not extradite the person until the Court has ruled that the case is inadmissible.[131] It may also confront a State with two incompatible legal obligations, that of extradition pursuant to the applicable extradition treaty and that of surrender in accordance with the Statute. Here, the Statute does not impose an affirmative duty on the custodial State to proceed with surrender to the Court. Rather, the custodial State is entitled to assess a number of relevant factors, including the respective dates of the requests, whether the requesting State may have territorial or personal jurisdiction over the offender, and the possibility of subsequent surrender from the Court to the requesting State.[132]

A person who has been unlawfully arrested or detained is entitled to compensation.[133] This right goes beyond existing international human rights obligations, which generally provide for some form of indemnification only when there has been a genuine miscarriage of justice. The

---

[130] See, e.g., Dirk Van Zyl Smit, 'Life Imprisonment as the Ultimate Penalty in International Law: A Human Rights Perspective', (1998) 9 *Criminal Law Forum* 1.

[131] Rome Statute, Art. 90.   [132] *Ibid.*, Art. 90(6).

[133] *Ibid.*, Art. 85(1); Rules of Procedure and Evidence, Rules 173–175.

Appeals Chamber of the International Criminal Tribunal for Rwanda has ruled that a person unlawfully detained may be entitled to a stay of proceedings and release, in extreme cases. Alternatively, in less severe situations, if the individual is acquitted, then financial compensation is in order, and if the individual is convicted he or she should receive a reduction in sentence.[134]

The Pre-Trial Chamber is given specific powers with respect to an arrest. These are set out in Article 57(3):

> In addition to its other functions under this Statute, the Pre-Trial Chamber may:
>
> ...
>
> (b) Upon the request of a person who has been arrested or has appeared pursuant to a summons under article 58, issue such orders, including measures such as those described in article 56, or seek such cooperation pursuant to Part 9 as may be necessary to assist the person in the preparation of his or her defence;
>
> ...
>
> (e) Where a warrant of arrest or a summons has been issued under article 58, and having due regard to the strength of the evidence and the rights of the parties concerned, as provided for in this Statute and the Rules of Procedure and Evidence, seek the cooperation of States pursuant to article 93, paragraph 1(j), to take protective measures for the purpose of forfeiture in particular for the ultimate benefit of victims.

When it issued the arrest warrant in *Lubanga*, Pre-Trial Chamber I considered the scope of Article 57(3)(e). It said that, while a first reading of the provision might suggest that cooperation requests for protective measures can be aimed only at guaranteeing the enforcement of a future penalty of forfeiture, as provided for by Article 77(2) of the Statute, 'the literal interpretation of the scope of such provision is not clear, because of the reference to the "ultimate benefit of the victims"'.[135] The Chamber said that a contextual and teleological interpretation suggested that it could seek the cooperation of States to take protective measures for the purpose of securing the enforcement of a future reparation award. 'As the power conferred on the Court to grant reparations to victims is one of the distinctive features of the Court, intended to alleviate, as much

---

[134] *Barayagwiza* (ICTR-97-19-AR72), Decisions of 3 November 1999 and 31 March 2000; *Kajelijeli* (ICTR-98-44A-A), Judgment, 23 May 2005, paras. 197–255.

[135] *Lubanga* (ICC-01/04–01/06–8), Decision on the Prosecutor's Application for a Warrant of Arrest, 10 February 2006, para. 132.

as possible, the negative consequences of their victimization, it will be in the "ultimate interest of victims" if, pursuant to article 57(3)(e), the cooperation of States Parties can be sought in order to take protective measures for the purpose of securing the enforcement of a future reparation award', wrote the Pre-Trial Chamber.[136] Here, Pre-Trial Chamber I referred to the order issued by the International Criminal Tribunal for the former Yugoslavia to freeze the assets of former president Slobodan Milošević.[137] But the order in that case was not premised on reparations to victims, something for which the Yugoslav Tribunal has no power, as the Pre-Trial Chamber pointed out.

Affirming its view that the reparation scheme was not only one of the unique features of the Rome Statute but also among its 'key features', the Pre-Trial Chamber continued:

> In the Chamber's opinion, the success of the Court is, to some extent, linked to the success of its reparation system. In this context, the Chamber considers that early tracing, identification and freezing or seizure of the property and assets of the person against whom a case is launched through the issuance of a warrant of arrest or a summons to appear is a necessary tool to ensure that, if that person is finally convicted, individual or collective reparation awards ordered in favour of victims will be enforced. Should this not happen, the Chamber finds that by the time an accused person is convicted and a reparation award ordered, there will be no property or assets available to enforce the award. In the Chamber's view, existing technology makes it possible for a person to place most of his assets and moveable property beyond the Court's reach in only a few days. Therefore, if assets and property are not seized or frozen at the time of the execution of a cooperation request for arrest and surrender, or very soon thereafter, it is likely that the subsequent efforts of the Pre-Trial Chamber, the Prosecution or the victims participating in the case will be fruitless.[138]

Noting that the Prosecutor had made no request for an order concerning the assets of Lubanga, Pre-Trial Chamber I said it would act *proprio motu* (that is, on its own initiative). It pointed out that this was specifically authorized by Rule 99(1) of the Rules of Procedure and Evidence. The Pre-Trial Chamber decided to prepare requests to all States Parties

[136] *Ibid.*, para. 135.
[137] *Milošević et al.* (IT-99-37-I), Decision on Review of Indictment and Application for Consequential Orders, 24 May 1999, para. 29.
[138] *Ibid.*, paras. 136–7.

to identify, trace and freeze or seize the property and assets of Lubanga at the earliest opportunity. The request was to be sent by the Registrar to the Democratic Republic of the Congo with the arrest warrant, but the Pre-Trial Chamber said that the Registrar should await its further instructions before communicating the requests to the other States Parties. It said that, in the future, the Prosecutor should take the matter into consideration with respect to applications for a warrant of arrest or summons to appear.

Appearance before the Court and interim release

An accused may appear before the Court in one of two ways: by surrender from a State where he or she has been apprehended; or by voluntarily presenting him or herself pursuant to a summons to appear. There have been three such voluntary appearances.[139] Rule 121(1) declares:

> A person subject to a warrant of arrest or a summons to appear under article 58 shall appear before the Pre-Trial Chamber, in the presence of the Prosecutor, promptly upon arriving at the Court. Subject to the provisions of articles 60 and 61, the person shall enjoy the rights set forth in article 67. At this first appearance, the Pre-Trial Chamber shall set the date on which it intends to hold a hearing to confirm the charges. It shall ensure that this date, and any postponements under sub-rule 7, are made public.

At the initial appearance, the Pre-Trial Chamber must satisfy itself that the accused has been informed of the crimes alleged and of his or her rights under the Statute, including the right to apply for interim release pending trial.[140]

Defendants who have been transferred to the Court may use the initial appearance to raise issues concerning their treatment in the sending State. Thomas Lubanga, argued that he had been the victim of abusive detention in the Democratic Republic of the Congo, where he had been held for as long as two-and-a-half years without being informed of the charges against him. Lubanga invoked the doctrine of 'abuse of process', claiming that there was a continuing violation of his rights for which the Court bore some responsibility. He said that, by transferring him

---

[139] Confirmation of Charges Hearing in the Case of The Prosecutor v. Bahr Idriss Abu Garda Scheduled to Start on Monday, 12 October 2009, ICC-CPI-20090519-PR414, 19 May 2009; As Darfur rebel Commanders Surrender to the Court, ICC Prosecutor 'Welcomes Compliance with the Court's Decisions and with Resolution 1593 (2005) of the Security Council', ICC-OTP-20100616-PR548, 13 June 2010.

[140] Rome Statute, Art. 60(1).

to The Hague, the Court had deprived him of a remedy for his abusive detention, which might be exercised before the courts of the Democratic Republic of the Congo, or at the international level, before the African Commission and Court of Human and Peoples' Rights. Pre-Trial Chamber I dismissed the challenge, ruling that the doctrine of 'abuse of process' did not apply unless 'it has been established that there has been concerted action between the Court and the authorities' of the Democratic Republic of the Congo or if the violation was in 'some way related to the process of arrest and transfer of the person to the relevant international criminal tribunal' and the violation amounted to 'torture or serious mistreatment'.[141]

In the case of individuals who present themselves pursuant to a summons, the Statute presumes that they will be allowed to remain at liberty during trial. For those arrested and surrendered, detention would seem to be the rule. Basically, the Prosecutor must *satisfy* the Pre-Trial Chamber that the same reasons that justified arrest continue to exist, namely, that detention is necessary to ensure attendance at trial, to prevent obstruction of the investigation or court proceedings, or to prevent continued criminal behaviour.[142]

International human rights law favours release during trial, a corollary of the presumption of innocence. A Pre-Trial Chamber has already noted that the interim release provisions must be applied in a manner consistent with internationally recognized human rights, as required by Article 21(3) of the Rome Statute.[143] But it seems appropriate that the rule be somewhat attenuated in the case of the International Criminal Court. Several reasons justify this. First, because the crimes – and the penalties – are so serious, it seems logical to expect an accused to try to avoid trial by any means possible. In *Lubanga*, the Pre-Trial Chamber said that the gravity of the crimes charged meant there was 'a substantial

[141] *Lubanga* (ICC-01/04–01/06), Decision on the Defence Challenge to the Jurisdiction of the Court Pursuant to Article 19(2)(a) of the Statute, 3 October 2006, pp. 9–10. Confirmed in *Lubanga* (ICC-01/04–01/06), Judgment on the Appeal of Mr Thomas Lubanga Dyilo against the Decision on the Defence Challenge to the Jurisdiction of the Court Pursuant to Article 19(2)(a) of the Statute of 3 October 2006, 14 December 2006.

[142] *Ibid.*, Art. 60(2). This provision was briefly considered by the Appeals Chamber of the International Criminal Tribunal for the former Yugoslavia in *Bala* (IT-03-66-AR65.2), Decision on Haradin Bala's Request for Provisional Release, 31 October 2003, paras. 15–18; *Limaj et al.* (IT-03-66-AR65), Decision on Fatmir Limaj's Request for Provisional Release, 31 October 2003, paras. 15–18.

[143] *Lubanga* (ICC-01/04–01/06), Decision on the Application for the Interim Release of Thomas Lubanga Dyilo, 18 October 2006, p. 5.

risk that he may wish to abscond from the jurisdiction of the Court'. Judgments of the European Court of Human Rights were cited in support of this proposition.[144] Secondly, release during trial as a general rule might well trivialize the role of the Court in the public eye and, more particularly, outrage victims of the crimes in question. Thirdly, the Court has no enforcement mechanisms of its own, such as a police force, and is therefore bereft of its own effective mechanisms to monitor interim release.[145] The *Lubanga* Pre-Trial Chamber also noted that the accused had established networks of contacts, both within his home country and internationally, that would facilitate absconding. Moreover, Lubanga 'now knows the identities of certain witnesses ... [I]f Thomas Lubanga Dyilo were to be released and were thus to be in a position to have completely unmonitored communications with the outside world, there would be a risk that he would, directly, or indirectly with the help of others, exert pressure on the witnesses, thus obstructing or endangering the court proceedings.' The Pre-Trial Chamber said there was evidence that witnesses who had appeared in proceedings before the courts of the Democratic Republic of the Congo in cases concerning Lubanga's organization had been killed or threatened.[146]

Criticizing 'a culture of detention that is wholly at variance with the customary norm that detention shall not be the general rule', some judges at the International Criminal Tribunal for the former Yugoslavia have noted that, '[w]hile the Tribunal's lack of a police force, its inability to execute its arrest warrants in States and its corresponding reliance on States for such execution may be relevant in considering an application for provisional release, on no account can that feature of the Tribunal's regime justify either imposing a burden on the accused in respect of an application ... or rendering more substantial such a burden, or warranting a detention of the accused for a period longer than would be justified having regard to the requirement of public interest, the presumption of innocence and the rule of respect for individual liberty'.[147] The same

---

[144] *Ibid.*, pp. 5–6. The Pre-Trial Chamber referred to: *Tomasi v. France* App. No. 12850/87, 27 August 1992, para. 89; *Mansur v. Turkey* (App. No. 16026/90), 8 June 1995, para. 52.

[145] *Krajisnik and Plavšić* (IT-00-39 and 40-AR73.2), Decision on Interlocutory Appeal by Momcilo Krajisnik, 26 February 2002, para. 22; *Jokić, Ademi* (IT-01-42-PT and IT-01-46-PT), Orders on Motions for Provisional Release, 22 February 2002.

[146] *Lubanga* (ICC-01/04–01/06), Decision on the Application for the Interim Release of Thomas Lubanga Dyilo, 18 October 2006, p. 6.

[147] *Krajisnik and Plavšić* (IT-00-39 and 40-PT), Decision on Momcilo Krajisnik's Notice of Motion for Provisional Release, Dissenting Opinion of Judge Patrick Robinson, 8 October 2001, para. 11. See also *Hadžihasanović, Alagic and Kubura* (IT-01-47-PT),

judge said that Article 9(3) of the International Covenant on Civil and Political Rights, stating that 'it shall not be the general rule that persons awaiting trial shall be detained in custody', reflects a customary norm. Even international courts would be 'wholly wrong to employ a peculiarity in the Tribunal system, namely, its lack of a police force and its inability to execute its warrants in other countries, as a justification for derogating from that customary norm'.[148] Following the confirmation hearing, at which charges based upon command responsibility for war crimes and crimes against humanity were confirmed, the Pre-Trial Chamber granted interim release, subject to finding a State prepared to accept the accused pending trial.[149] The decision was later overturned by the Appeals Chamber, which said that 'the Pre-Trial Chamber erred in granting conditional release without specifying the appropriate conditions that make conditional release feasible, identifying the State to which Mr Bemba would be released and whether that State would be able to enforce the conditions imposed by the Court'.[150]

The Pre-Trial Chamber must ensure that individuals are not detained 'for an unreasonable period' prior to trial where this is due to 'inexcusable delay' by the Prosecutor. In such cases, the Court is to consider releasing the person, with or without conditions. The Appeals Chamber of the International Criminal Tribunal for Rwanda has considered that inexcusable delay attributable to the Prosecutor, in extreme circumstances, entitles the accused to have the charges dropped 'with prejudice' to the Prosecutor, that is, without the possibility of retrial.[151] But the Statute of the Rwanda Tribunal is silent as to an appropriate remedy in such cases. That the Rome Statute establishes a specific remedy, namely, release from custody (but not a stay of the proceedings), would seem to rule out the more radical solution adopted by the Appeals Chamber of the Rwanda Tribunal.

Decisions Granting Provisional Release to Enver *Hadžihasanović*, Mehmed Alagic and Amir Kubura, 9 December 2001.

[148] *Ibid.*, para. 12.

[149] *Bemba* (ICC-01/05–01/08), Decision on the Interim Release of Jean-Pierre Bemba Gombo and Convening Hearings with the Kingdom of Belgium, the Republic of Portugal, the Republic of France, the Federal Republic of Germany, the Italian Republic, and the Republic of South Africa, 14 August 2009.

[150] *Bemba* (ICC-01/05–01/08 OA 2), Judgment on the Appeal of the Prosecutor Against Pre-Trial Chamber II's 'Decision on the Interim Release of Jean-Pierre Bemba Gombo and Convening Hearings with the Kingdom of Belgium, the Republic of Portugal, the Republic of France, the Federal Republic of Germany, the Italian Republic, and the Republic of South Africa', 2 December 2009, para. 109.

[151] *Barayagwiza* (ICTR-97-19-AR72), Decisions of 3 November 1999 and 31 March 2000.

The issue of interim release can be revisited by both Prosecutor and defendant at any time on the basis of changed circumstances. In the case of a person who is at liberty, the Pre-Trial Chamber may issue an arrest warrant.

Confirmation hearing

The Pre-Trial Chamber is to hold a hearing to confirm the charges on which the Prosecutor intends to go to trial.[152] The confirmation hearing is an innovation in the procedure of international criminal courts. No equivalent mechanism exists at the *ad hoc* tribunals. It has proven to add significant length to the trial proceedings overall. Judges have used the confirmation hearing to recharacterize the crimes in light of the evidence presented. The professed purpose of the confirmation hearing is to protect the defendant against abusive and unfounded accusations.[153] The confirmation hearing seems to resemble preliminary hearings held under common law procedure, allowing the Court to ensure that a prosecution is not frivolous and that there is sufficient evidence for a finding of guilt. From the standpoint of the defendant, it also provides a useful opportunity to be informed of important evidence in the possession of the prosecution and even to test the value of such evidence, at least in a superficial way, during a judicial proceeding. At the confirmation hearing, the Prosecutor is required to support each charge with sufficient evidence to establish substantial grounds to believe that the person committed the crime charged. The Prosecutor is entitled to rely on documentary or summary evidence and need not call the witnesses expected to testify at the trial.[154]

The pre-trial confirmation has analogies with the 'Rule 61 Procedure' adopted by the *ad hoc* tribunals. In the early days, when there was little real trial work because few accused had been apprehended, the judges of the International Criminal Tribunal for the former Yugoslavia developed an original technique of *ex parte* hearings, pursuant to Rule 61 of their Rules of Procedure and Evidence, at which prosecution evidence was led and the Tribunal ruled on the sufficiency of the evidence.[155] Despite

---

[152] Rome Statute, Art. 61(1).
[153] *Lubanga* (ICC-01/04–01/06), Decision on the Confirmation of the Charges, 29 January 2007, para. 37.
[154] Rome Statute, Art. 61(5).
[155] Pursuant to Rule 61 of the Rules of Procedure and Evidence, UN Doc. IT/32. See Faiza Patel King, 'Public Disclosure in Rule 61 Proceedings Before the International Criminal Tribunal for the Former Yugoslavia', (1997) 29 *New York University Journal of*

persistent denials,[156] it had similarities with an *in absentia* procedure and was, in many respects, an honourable compromise between the different views of the Romano-Germanic and common law systems with respect to such proceedings.[157] The Tribunal has used the *ex parte* hearing procedure when frustrated with attempts to arrest a defendant. The situation is rather different with the pre-trial confirmation hearing of the International Criminal Court, as this will only take place with an absent accused in the case of an individual who was arrested or summoned, who appeared before the Pre-Trial Chamber and was granted interim release, and who subsequently absconded, or an accused who refuses to appear.

Within a reasonable time prior to the hearing, the 'person' – note that the Rome Statute avoids using the term 'accused' until after the confirmation hearing[158] – is entitled to be provided with a copy of the 'document containing the charges'.[159] This is innovative terminology; the Rome Statute avoids using the word 'indictment', although colloquially this is often how observers speak about the 'arrest warrant' and the 'document containing the charges'. The contents of the document containing the charges are set out in the Regulations of the Court:

Regulation 52. Document containing the charges

The document containing the charges referred to in article 61 shall include:

(a) The full name of the person and any other relevant identifying information;

(b) A statement of the facts, including the time and place of the alleged crimes, which provides a sufficient legal and factual basis to bring the

---

International Law and Policy 523; Mark Thieroff and Edward A. Amley Jr, 'Proceeding to Justice and Accountability in the Balkans: The International Criminal Tribunal for the Former Yugoslavia and Rule 61', (1998) 23 *Yale Journal of International Law* 231.

[156] *Rajić* (IT-95-12-R61), Review of the Indictment Pursuant to Rule 61 of the Rules of Procedure and Evidence, 13 September 1996: 'A Rule 61 proceeding is not a trial in absentia. There is no finding of guilt in this proceeding.' *Nikolić* (IT-95-2-R61), Review of Indictment Pursuant to Rule 61, 20 October 1995, (1998) 108 ILR 21: 'The Rule 61 procedure ... cannot be considered a trial in absentia: it does not culminate in a verdict nor does it deprive the accused of the right to contest in person the charges brought against him before the Tribunal.'

[157] The Special Tribunal for Lebanon can hold *in absentia* trials: Statute of the Special Tribunal for Lebanon, UN Doc. S/2006/893, Attachment, Art. 22.

[158] During the first confirmation hearing, Pre-Trial Chamber I reprimanded the Registry for referring to Charles Lubanga as the 'accused' in one of its publications. Judge Jorda ordered the Registry to draft a correction and circulate it to the public: *Lubanga* (ICC-01/04–01/06), Transcript, 10 November 2006.

[159] Rome Statute, Art. 61(3)(a).

person or persons to trial, including relevant facts for the exercise of jurisdiction by the Court;

(c) A legal characterisation of the facts to accord both with the crimes under articles 6, 7 or 8 and the precise form of participation under articles 25 and 28.

Confirming the charges against Charles Lubanga, Pre-Trial Chamber I criticized the Prosecutor's first such document, saying it 'ne peut d'ailleurs que regretter que l'Accusation n'ait pas jugé utile d'exposer de façon plus détaillée le contexte dans lequel se sont déroulés les faits reprochés à Thomas Lubanga Dyilo'.[160]

Prior to the confirmation hearing, in addition to the document containing the charges the accused is to be informed of the evidence on which the Prosecutor intends to rely at the hearing. The Pre-Trial Chamber may make orders concerning disclosure of information for the purposes of the hearing.[161] According to Rule 121(2):

> In accordance with article 61, paragraph 3, the Pre-Trial Chamber shall take the necessary decisions regarding disclosure between the Prosecutor and the person in respect of whom a warrant of arrest or a summons to appear has been issued. During disclosure:
>
> (a) The person concerned may be assisted or represented by the counsel of his or her choice or by a counsel assigned to him or her;
>
> (b) The Pre-Trial Chamber shall hold status conferences to ensure that disclosure takes place under satisfactory conditions. For each case, a judge of the Pre-Trial Chamber shall be appointed to organize such status conferences, on his or her own motion, or at the request of the Prosecutor or the person;
>
> (c) All evidence disclosed between the Prosecutor and the person for the purposes of the confirmation hearing shall be communicated to the Pre-Trial Chamber.

At this stage, the defence has no general and unlimited right to inspect documents that are in the possession of the Prosecutor and that may be relevant to the case,[162] subject to the exceptions set out in

---

[160] *Lubanga* (ICC-01/04–01/06), Decision on the Confirmation of the Charges, 29 January 2007, para. 153.

[161] E.g. *Lubanga* (ICC-01/04–01/06), Decision on the Defence Request for Order to Disclose Exculpatory Materials, 2 November 2006.

[162] *Lubanga* (ICC-01/04–01/06), Décision relative au système définitif de divulgation et à l'établissement d'un échéancier, Annexe I, Analyse de la décisions relative au système définitif de divulgation, 15 May 2006, para. 14.

Rule 81.[163] For the purposes of disclosure, most of the material is exchanged *inter partes*, a process involving only Prosecutor and defence counsel, and where the Registry is largely absent.[164]

In principle, the confirmation hearing is held in public,[165] but parts of it may take place in closed session (*in camera*) in order to protect witnesses.[166] Normally, the hearing is to be held in the presence of the accused as well as his or her counsel. Exceptionally, however, the Pre-Trial Chamber may hold this confirmation hearing in the absence of the accused, either at the Prosecutor's request or at its own initiative. Such an *ex parte* (i.e. with one of the parties being absent) hearing will be justified where the accused has waived the right to be present, or where the accused has fled or cannot be found. In such cases, the Chamber is to satisfy itself that all reasonable steps have been taken to secure the person's appearance and to inform him or her of the charges and the fact that such a confirmation hearing is to be held. The Pre-Trial Chamber may allow an absent accused to be represented by counsel when this is in 'the interests of justice'.[167] Whether a confirmation hearing can be held when the accused has not yet been taken into custody remains an open question.

At the confirmation hearing itself, the Prosecutor is required to support each specific charge with 'sufficient evidence to establish substantial grounds to believe that the person committed the crime charged'.[168] The Prosecutor can do this by means of documentary or summary evidence, and is not required to call the witnesses expected to testify at the trial itself. The accused may challenge the Prosecutor's evidence and present evidence. According to Judge Pikis:

> Confirmation of charges is neither automatic nor free from an evaluation of the evidence adduced, with a direct bearing on the decision of the

---

[163] *Lubanga* (ICC-01/04–01/06), Judgment on the Prosecutor's Appeal Against the Decision of Pre-Trial Chamber I Entitled 'Decision Establishing General Principles Governing Applications to Restrict Disclosure Pursuant to Rule 81(2) and (4) of the Rules of Procedure and Evidence', 13 October 2006; *Lubanga* (ICC-01/04–01/06), Judgment on the Prosecutor's Appeal Against the Decision of Pre-Trial Chamber I Entitled 'Second Decision on the Prosecution Requests and Amended Requests for Redactions under Rule 81', 14 December 2006.

[164] *Ibid.*, paras. 66–7.

[165] *Lubanga* (ICC-01/04–01/06), Ordonnance autorisant la prise de photographies à l'audience du 9 novembre 2006, 6 November 2006.

[166] *Lubanga* (ICC-01/04–01/06), Decision on the Schedule and Conduct of the Confirmation Hearing, 7 November 2006.

[167] Rome Statute, Art. 61(2); Rules of Procedure and Evidence, Rules 121–126.

[168] *Ibid.*, Art. 61(5).

PTC whether to confirm the charges or not ... At the confirmation hearing the person under investigation is entitled to challenge not only the charges but the evidence presented by the Prosecutor ... Evidence tending to exonerate a person of the charges levied against him/her could have a bearing on the sufficiency of evidence before the PTC for the purpose of determining whether the standard for the confirmation of charges has been satisfied.[169]

If it elects to lead evidence, Rule 121 requires the defence to provide the Pre-Trial Chamber with a list of what it intends to produce at the confirmation hearing.[170] A more general disclosure obligation, applicable not only to the trial but also to the confirmation hearing, is imposed by Rule 78. In *Lubanga*, a judge of the Pre-Trial Chamber spoke of the duty of 'the parties', and clearly considered that both Prosecutor and defendant were required to participate in disclosure.[171] At the first of the Court's confirmation hearings, in *Lubanga*, the defence chose to submit evidence. Then, after presenting it, the defence lawyer attempted to withdraw some of the evidence that had been produced.[172]

The written decision of the Pre-Trial Chamber setting out its findings on each of the charges shall be delivered within sixty days from the end of the confirmation hearing.[173] Applying the test of 'substantial grounds', the Pre-Trial Chamber may confirm or deny the charges.[174] If charges are denied, any previously issued arrest warrant ceases to be enforceable.[175] The Pre-Trial Chamber may also adjourn the hearing and request the Prosecutor to consider providing further evidence, in circumstances where the evidence presented 'is not irrelevant and insufficient to a degree that merits declining to confirm the charges'.[176] To date,

---

[169] *Lubanga* (ICC-01/04–01/06 OA 13), Separate Opinion of Judge Georghios M. Pikis, 21 October 2008, para. 43.

[170] Rules of Procedure and Evidence, Rule 121(6).

[171] *Lubanga* (ICC-01/04–01/06), Décision relative au système définitif de divulgation et à l'établissement d'un échéancier, Annexe I, Analyse de la décisions relative au système définitif de divulgation, 15 May 2006, paras. 37, 42. Also *Lubanga* (ICC-01/04–01/06), Decision to Give Access to the Prosecution to the Evidence Included in the Defence List of Evidence Filed on 2 November 2006, 8 November 2006.

[172] See *Lubanga* (ICC-01/04–01/06), Transcript, 27 November 2006.

[173] Regulations of the Court, Regulation 53.

[174] See Rule 127 of the Rules of Procedure and Evidence for the procedure in the event of different decisions on multiple charges.

[175] Rome Statute, Art. 61(10). The norm also applies if they have been withdrawn by the Prosecutor.

[176] *Bemba* (ICC-01/05–01/08), Decision Adjourning the Hearing Pursuant to Article 61(7)(c)(ii) of the Rome Statute, 3 March 2009, para. 16.

the Pre-Trial Chambers have not adjourned confirmation hearings with a request for further evidence.[177] Adjournment is also authorized, under Article 61(7)(c)(ii), to allow the Prosecutor to amend a charge because the evidence submitted appears to establish a different crime within the jurisdiction of the Court.[178] The purpose of the provision is 'to prevent the Chamber from committing a person for trial for crimes which would be materially different from those set out in the Document Containing the Charges and for which the Defence would not have had the opportunity to submit observations at the confirmation hearing'.[179] In deciding to adjourn the confirmation hearing, the Chamber does not make a definitive ruling on the sufficiency of evidence but rather 'a prima facie finding that it has doubts as to the legal characterisation of the facts as reflected in the document containing the charges'.[180] The expression 'different crime' in Article 61(7)(c)(ii) refers not only to the definition but also to the mode of liability.[181]

Rather than adjourn the hearing, Pre-Trial Chamber I, in *Lubanga*, recharacterized the crimes in its confirmation decision. Lubanga had been charged with enlistment, conscription and active use of child soldiers during an internal armed conflict, in accordance with Article 8(2)(e)(vii). Initially, the Prosecutor had requested and obtained an arrest warrant for such offences committed in both international and internal armed conflict.[182] The two provisions concerning child soldiers, in international and internal armed conflict, are very similar. But, subsequently, the Prosecutor issued a document containing the charges that referred only to the offence when committed in internal armed conflict. Pre-Trial Chamber I considered that the conflict might well be qualified as international in nature, and added a charge based upon Article 8(2)(b)(xxvi).[183] The Prosecutor sought leave to appeal the ruling,

---

[177] See, however, *Katanga et al.* (ICC-01/04–01/07), Partly Dissenting Opinion of Judge Anita Ušacka, 30 September 2008, para. 29.

[178] *Ibid.*, paras. 16–18.

[179] *Lubanga* (ICC-01/04–01/06), Decision on the Confirmation of the Charges, 29 January 2007, para. 203. Also *Bemba* (ICC-01/05–01/08), Decision Adjourning the Hearing Pursuant to Article 61(7)(c)(ii) of the Rome Statute, 3 March 2009, para. 23.

[180] *Bemba* (ICC-01/05–01/08), Decision Adjourning the Hearing Pursuant to Article 61(7)(c)(ii) of the Rome Statute, 3 March 2009, para. 25.

[181] *Ibid.*, para. 26.

[182] *Lubanga* (ICC-01/04–01/06), Decision on the Prosecutor's Application for a Warrant of Arrest, 10 February 2006.

[183] *Lubanga* (ICC-01/04–01/06), Decision on the Confirmation of the Charges, 29 January 2007, paras. 200–37.

challenging the authority of the Pre-Trial Chamber to add charges in its decision following the confirmation hearing.[184] He argued that the text of Article 61 simply did not contemplate such a possibility. Moreover, he said proving the additional charges would impose an onerous and undesired burden on the Prosecutor, and that the ruling interfered with the exercise of his independence. Of course, the Pre-Trial Chamber has no subsequent control over the Prosecutor, and it would seem that he cannot be under an obligation to investigate and prove certain charges simply because the confirmation decision has added them.

Rulings on jurisdiction and admissibility

Issues of jurisdiction and admissibility arise at several stages in the work of the Court. The Prosecutor needs to make an initial assessment with respect to both matters before deciding that there is a 'reasonable basis' to initiate an investigation.[185] The Pre-Trial Chamber must assess jurisdiction and admissibility in authorizing the Prosecutor to initiate an investigation in accordance with his *proprio motu* powers.[186] It is also required to make a determination of these issues prior to issuance of an arrest warrant.[187] But these decisions are all *ex parte*. The Rome Statute envisages special procedures for contestation of the issue that may involve the accused person, the referring State or the Security Council, as the case may be, and the victims. Two distinct preliminary proceedings are envisaged in the Statute allowing for contestation on either jurisdictional or admissibility grounds. The first, set out in Article 18, is entitled 'Preliminary rulings regarding admissibility', and applies only to investigations initiated by a State Party referral or at the initiative of the Prosecutor. The second, set out in Article 19, is described as 'Challenges to the jurisdiction of the Court or the admissibility of a case', and applies generally to cases before the Court, including those resulting from situations referred by the Security Council. Article 18 applies to 'situations' whereas Article 19 applies to 'cases'.

---

[184] *Lubanga* ICC-01/04–01/06, Application for Leave to Appeal Pre-Trial Chamber I's 29 January 2007 Decision on the Confirmation of the Charges, 5 February 2007.

[185] Rome Statute, Art. 53(1)(a)–(b).

[186] *Ibid.*, Art. 15(3); *Situation in Kenya* (ICC-01/09), Decision Pursuant to Article 15 of the Rome Statute on the Authorization of an Investigation into the Situation in the Republic of Kenya, 31 March 2010.

[187] *Ibid.*, Art. 58(1)(a).

Pursuant to Article 18, which applies to all situations except those referred by the Security Council, the Prosecutor is required to publicize his or her intention to proceed with an investigation. Notice must be sent to all States Parties to the Statute as well as to any and all States that would normally exercise jurisdiction over the crimes concerned. In practice, this means that the State where the crime has been committed as well as the State of nationality of the alleged offender will normally be informed. Indeed, on a generous interpretation of the requirement, it could be argued that all States in the world should be informed as they may normally exercise jurisdiction over the crimes pursuant to the concept of universal jurisdiction. The Statute entitles the Prosecutor to give such notice on a confidential basis, and to limit the scope of information provided so as to protect persons, prevent destruction of evidence or prevent absconding of suspects.[188] But, because at least one State with jurisdiction over the situation is likely to be complicit with the suspects, the Prosecutor will probably lose all element of surprise. Perhaps it is too soon, however, to be overly pessimistic about the consequences of this requirement. The *ad hoc* tribunals have, after all, been able to arrest suspects, obtain evidence and protect witnesses despite the fact that the same kind of information as that which must be communicated by the International Criminal Court's Prosecutor is common knowledge.

States have one month from receipt of the notice from the Prosecutor in which to inform him that they are investigating or have investigated the crimes in question. In effect, they are putting the Prosecutor on notice that they consider the situation to be inadmissible under the principles of complementarity, as set out in Article 17. Upon receipt of such notice, the Prosecutor cannot proceed further until authorization from the Pre-Trial Chamber has been obtained.[189] Thus, should he receive such a notice, it is the Prosecutor who applies to the Pre-Trial Chamber for a 'preliminary ruling on admissibility'. If authorization is refused by the Pre-Trial Chamber, the Prosecutor can make a new application for a preliminary ruling after six months have passed, or at any time with new facts or evidence indicating a significant change in circumstances. Both sides can appeal a determination by the Pre-Trial Chamber to the Appeals Chamber. The Prosecutor can apply for provisional measures in order to preserve evidence while the Article 18 proceedings are underway.

---

[188] *Ibid.*, Art. 18(1).   [189] *Ibid.*

A second assessment of the admissibility of cases is envisaged by Article 19. The Article 19 procedure applies to all cases before the Court, including those resulting from a situation referred by the Security Council. It is much broader than the Article 18 inquiry, because it concerns all issues arising from both jurisdiction and admissibility, but also narrower, because it covers only 'cases' and not 'situations'. The Rules of Procedure and Evidence refer to a 'challenge or question' to jurisdiction or admissibility under Article 19 in order to distinguish where this arises at the request of a Party ('challenge'), or on the Court's own initiative ('question'). Thus, Article 19(1) says that the Court is required to satisfy itself that it has jurisdiction over a case, regardless of whether this is actually challenged. This is a power that must be inherent in any event, because a judicial institution should not operate with the consent or acquiescence of the parties if it is without jurisdiction.[190] In addition, the Court *may* determine, on its own initiative, the admissibility of a case according to the criteria of Article 17, namely, both lack of complementarity with national proceedings and gravity. In other words, the Court is to rule first on jurisdiction and second on admissibility.[191] The first inquiry is mandatory, while the second is not.

Whatever the result of the Court's own assessment, Article 19 also allows challenges to the Court's jurisdiction or to the admissibility of a case by the accused, or by a State with jurisdiction over the case, or a non-party State whose consent is required under Article 12(3), and even by the Prosecutor. Victims cannot formally file challenges, although they are most certainly entitled to be present and to participate in the debate.[192] Lack of recognition of their right to challenge jurisdiction or admissibility is probably not all that significant, given that the Court is authorized by Article 19 to rule on its own initiative, and without a challenge from one of the parties. Thus, victims can make representations and the Court can act upon them. The same applies where a case is triggered under Article 13. Depending on the trigger, either the referring State or the Security Council is entitled to participate in the debate about admissibility.

Because Article 19 applies to a 'case', its provisions cannot apply prior to issuance of a warrant of arrest or a summons to appear. Until the

---

[190] Christopher K. Hall, 'Article 19', in Triffterer, ed., *Commentary*, pp. 637–67 at pp. 640–4.
[191] Rules of Procedure and Evidence, Rule 58(4).
[192] Rome Statute, Art. 19(3); Rules of Procedure and Evidence, Rule 59(1)(b).

warrant or summons is issued, there is only a 'situation', and not a 'case'. 'Article 19 of the Statute regulates the context within which challenges to jurisdiction and admissibility may be raised by a party having an interest in the matter', according to the Appeals Chamber.[193] Motions attacking jurisdiction and admissibility have been filed by the *ad hoc* counsel appointed to protect the general rights of the defence at the investigation stage. In the *Situation in the Democratic Republic of Congo* dossier, *ad hoc* counsel raised these issues when he contested the assertion of the Prosecutor about the existence of a unique investigative opportunity.[194] Dismissing the application, Pre-Trial Chamber I ruled as follows:

> [C]hallenges to the jurisdiction of the Court or the admissibility of a case pursuant to article 19(2)(a) of the Statute may only be made by an accused person or a person for whom a warrant of arrest or a summons to appear has been issued under article 58 ... [A]t this stage of the proceedings no warrant of arrest or summons to appear has been issued and thus no case has arisen ... [T]he *Ad hoc* Counsel for the Defence has no procedural standing to make a challenge under article 19(2)(a) of the Statute.[195]

Similarly, the *ad hoc* counsel for the defence in *Situation in Darfur* also raised a challenge to jurisdiction and admissibility.[196] The motion itself bordered on the incoherent. Without discussing the merits of the challenge, Pre-Trial Chamber III ruled in the same manner as Pre-Trial Chamber I.[197]

A referring State or a non-party State whose consent is required under Article 12(3) must file its challenge 'at the earliest opportunity'.[198]

---

[193] *Lubanga* (ICC-01/04–01/06 OA 4), Judgment on the Appeal of Mr Thomas Lubanga Dyilo Against the Decision on the Defence Challenge to the Jurisdiction of the Court Pursuant to Article 19(2)(a) of the Statute of 3 October 2006, 14 December 2006, para. 24.

[194] *Situation in the Democratic Republic of Congo* (ICC-01/04–86-Conf), Ad Hoc Counsel for the Defence's Submissions, 22 August 2005. Also *Situation in the Democratic Republic of Congo* (ICC-01/04), Submissions on Jurisdiction and Admissibility, 11 October 2005.

[195] *Situation in the Democratic Republic of Congo* (ICC-01/04–93), Decision Following the Consultation Held on 11 October 2005 and the Prosecution's Submission on Jurisdiction and Admissibility Filed on 31 October 2005, 9 November 2005.

[196] *Situation in Darfur, Sudan* (ICC-02/05), Conclusions aux fins d'exception d'incompétence et d'irrecevabilité, 9 October 2006.

[197] *Situation in Darfur, Sudan* (ICC-02/05), Décision relative aux conclusions aux fins d'exception d'incompétence et d'irrecevabilité, 22 November 2006. Application for leave to appeal denied in *Situation in Darfur, Sudan* (ICC-02/05), Décision sur la requête du conseil ad hoc de la Défense sollicitant l'autorisation d'interjeter appel, 8 December 2006.

[198] Rome Statute, Art. 19(5).

Questions of jurisdiction and admissibility may be raised before confirmation of the charges, in which case they are heard by the Pre-Trial
Chamber, or later, before the Trial Chamber. In exceptional circumstances, the Court may grant leave for a challenge to be brought more
than once or at a time later than the commencement of the trial.
Challenges to the admissibility of a case made at the commencement of
a trial, or subsequently with the leave of the Court, may only be based on
the fact that the accused has already been tried for conduct which is the
subject of the complaint, thereby barring prosecution on the ground of
double jeopardy (*ne bis in idem*).[199]

Article 19 of the Statute clearly envisages a hearing before the Court
in which Prosecutor and State participate, along with the accused, and
all sides are entitled to appeal the decision to the Appeals Chamber.
Fears, no doubt well founded, that precious time would elapse during
this tedious procedure led the drafters of the Rome Statute to make special allowance for interim investigative steps being authorized by the
Court. Thus, pending a ruling by the Pre-Trial Chamber, the Prosecutor
may seek leave to investigate with a view to preserving evidence 'where
there is a unique opportunity to obtain important evidence or there is a
significant risk that such evidence may not be subsequently available'.[200]
If the Prosecutor decides not to challenge the State's claim that it is investigating the matter, he may review this determination six months later,
or at any time when there has been a significant change of circumstances
with respect to the State's unwillingness or inability to investigate. The
Prosecutor is entitled to request the State to provide periodic updates on
the progress of investigations and subsequent prosecutions with a view
to ongoing monitoring of the State's 'willingness'.[201]

Preparation for trial

Once the Pre-Trial Chamber has determined 'there is sufficient evidence
to establish substantial grounds to believe that the person committed
each of the crimes charged', in accordance with Article 61, the accused
is then committed for trial.[202] The Pre-Trial Chamber's work is complete.
The Presidency is required to constitute a Trial Chamber, and to refer the

---

[199] *Ibid.*, Art. 19(4).   [200] *Ibid.*, Art. 19(8). See also *ibid.*, Art. 95.
[201] *Ibid.*, Art. 18(5).
[202] Also, Regulation 53 of the Regulations of the Court, requiring that the decision of the
Pre-Trial Chamber be issued within sixty days of the end of the confirmation hearing.

case to it.[203] The Trial Chamber convenes a status conference 'promptly', in order to set the date for trial.[204] The Trial Chamber is also required to confer with the parties so as to adopt procedures to facilitate the fair and expeditious conduct of the proceedings and to determine the language or languages to be used at trial.[205] Subsequent status conferences are convened for this purpose. Regulation 54 of the Regulations of the Court enumerates a broad range of issues that may be considered during these status conferences:

> At a status conference, the Trial Chamber may, in accordance with the Statute and the Rules, issue any order in the interests of justice for the purposes of the proceedings on, *inter alia*, the following issues:
> (a) The length and content of legal arguments and the opening and closing statements;
> (b) A summary of the evidence the participants intend to rely on;
> (c) The length of the evidence to be relied on;
> (d) The length of questioning of the witnesses;
> (e) The number and identity (including any pseudonym) of the witnesses to be called;
> (f) The production and disclosure of the statements of the witnesses on which the participants propose to rely;
> (g) The number of documents as referred to in article 69, paragraph 2, or exhibits to be introduced together with their length and size;
> (h) The issues the participants propose to raise during the trial;
> (i) The extent to which a participant can rely on recorded evidence, including the transcripts and the audio- and video-record of evidence previously given;
> (j) The presentation of evidence in summary form;
> (k) The extent to which evidence is to be given by an audio- or videolink;
> (l) The disclosure of evidence;
> (m) The joint or separate instruction by the participants of expert witnesses;
> (n) Evidence to be introduced under rule 69 as regards agreed facts;
> (o) The conditions under which victims shall participate in the proceedings;
> (p) The defences, if any, to be advanced by the accused.

Other interlocutory issues may also be addressed at this stage, including the amendment of the charges, and decisions on joinder and severance of the charges in cases where there are multiple accused.

---

[203] Rome Statute, Art. 61(11); Rules of Procedure and Evidence, Rule 130.
[204] Rules of Procedure and Evidence, Rule 132.   [205] Rome Statute, Art. 64(3).

International human rights law is somewhat uncertain as to the scope of the obligation on the prosecution to disclose evidence to the defence prior to trial. Although the instruments impose no clear duty in this respect,[206] the European Court of Human Rights has declared that 'it is a requirement of fairness ... that the prosecution authorities disclose to the defence all material evidence for or against the accused'.[207] The Rules of the *ad hoc* tribunals make detailed provision for disclosure of both the prosecution and the defence case.[208] A duty on the prosecution to disclose its evidence, both exculpatory and inculpatory, is now recognized in many legal systems.[209] The existence of a reciprocal duty on the defence is less common although in some cases, such as alibi, the credibility of the plea will depend on prompt disclosure of material facts.[210] In an interlocutory decision in the *Tadić* case, Judge Stephen of the Yugoslav Tribunal said that the defence has 'no disclosure obligation at all unless an alibi or a special defence is sought to be relied upon and then only to a quite limited extent'.[211] But what was perhaps the traditional position in international criminal law in that respect has now changed.

The Rules of Procedure and Evidence adopted by the Assembly of States Parties establish a far more thorough regime of disclosure, applicable to both Prosecutor and defence. The prosecution is required to provide the defence with the names of witnesses it intends to call at trial together with copies of their statements, subject to certain exceptions relating to the protection of the witnesses themselves.[212] The defence has a corresponding obligation with respect to witnesses, although this is worded slightly more narrowly, applying only to those expected to support specific defences.[213] Each side is required to allow the other to

---

[206] The closest is Principle 21 of the United Nations Basic Principles on the Role of Lawyers, UN Doc. A/CONF.144/28/Rev.1 (1990): 'It is the duty of the competent authorities to ensure lawyers access to appropriate information, files and documents in their possession or control in sufficient time to enable lawyers to provide effective legal assistance to their clients.'

[207] *Edwards* v. *United Kingdom*, Series A, No. 247-B, 16 December 1992.

[208] Rules of Procedure and Evidence, UN Doc. IT/32, Rules 65*ter*, 66, 67 and 68. See Anne-Marie La Rosa, 'Réflexions sur l'apport du Tribunal pénal international pour l'ex-Yougoslavie au droit à; un procès équitable', (1997) *Revue générale de droit international public* 945 at 974.

[209] Jean Pradel, *Droit pénal comparé*, Paris: Dalloz, 1995, pp. 414–20.

[210] *Williams* v. *Florida*, 399 US 78 (1970).

[211] *Tadić* (IT-94-1-T), Separate Opinion of Judge Stephen on Prosecution Motion for Production of Defence Witness Statements, 27 November 1996.

[212] Rules of Procedure and Evidence, Rule 76.   [213] *Ibid.*, Rule 79.

inspect books, documents, photographs and other tangible objects in their possession or control which they intend to use as evidence. The Prosecutor must also disclose any such items that may assist the defence, although a comparable duty is not imposed upon the defence to disclose items that might assist the prosecution.[214] These provisions should have the effect of reducing cases of 'trial by ambush', enhancing fairness and also contributing to expeditious hearings.

[214] *Ibid.*, Rules 77–78. See the discussion of the debates around disclosure in the *Lubanga* case, at pp. 263–5 above.

8

Trial and appeal

Although much of the procedure of the Court is a hybrid of different judicial systems, it seems clear that there is a definite tilt towards the common law approach of an adversarial trial hearing. However, the exact colouring that the Court may take will ultimately be determined by its judges. The terms of the Statute are large enough to provide for considerable divergence in judicial approaches. For example, Article 64(6)(d) entitles the Trial Chamber to '[o]rder the production of evidence in addition to that already collected prior to the trial or presented during the trial by the parties'. A traditional common law judge would view this as a power to be exercised only rarely, because an aggressively interventionist approach might distort the balance between the two adversaries at trial. A judge favouring the continental system could interpret the provision as a licence for major judicial involvement in the production of evidence, something that would seem most normal under his or her system. Initial rulings of the Court suggest that the debate about the procedural orientation is still very much underway, and it would appear premature to attempt to draw conclusions at this early stage.

Judges in the continental system expect most of the evidence to form part of the court record even prior to trial. The evidence already on the record will have been prepared beforehand by the investigating magistrate as part of the pre-trial proceedings. Common law judges, on the other hand, consider that they begin the trial as a blank sheet; indeed, they believe that any prior knowledge of the facts is likely to prejudice their judgment. Under the common law system, prosecutor and defence submit the evidence that makes up the record in accordance with strict technical rules. Here, too, the Statute leaves considerable ambiguity on this point. Nothing, for example, would seem to prevent a judge from ordering the production of the Prosecutor's record as evidence at the outset of the trial, in much the same way as an investigating magistrate's file would be used by the trial court. The International Criminal Tribunal for Rwanda, under the presidency of a judge trained in the Romano-Germanic system, took this approach in the *Akayesu* case, requiring that the prosecutor's file be submitted as part of the record.

The trial is to take place at the seat of the Court, in The Hague, unless otherwise decided.[1] Trial Chamber I considered holding part of the proceedings in the *Lubanga* case in the Democratic Republic of the Congo, where the alleged crimes were committed.[2] Legal representatives of victims were supportive because they felt it would make the proceedings more visible, although they expressed concerns about security.[3] The majority of witnesses who were canvassed did not want to testify in the Democratic Republic of the Congo. The defence expressed concerns that holding the trial outside The Hague would also limit the right of the accused to be present.[4] A feasibility study was conducted, and the Court was informed by the Democratic Republic of the Congo that 'the location identified by the Chamber for a hearing in the Democratic Republic of the Congo was inappropriate as it could lead to ethnic tensions in an area that had been recently pacified and is potentially unstable'.[5] Failing the consent of the government, the Trial Chamber concluded that holding the trial outside The Hague was not an option.[6] When it referred the *Situation in Darfur* to the Court, the United Nations Security Council '[i]nvite[d] the Court and the African Union to discuss practical arrangements that will facilitate the work of the Prosecutor and of the Court, including the possibility of conducting proceedings in the region, which would contribute to regional efforts in the fight against impunity'.[7]

The trial shall be held in public, something that is expressed both as a duty of the Trial Chamber and as a right of the accused.[8] Pre-Trial Chamber I has explained that '[t]he legal regime of the ICC presumes the public nature of court proceedings and documents'.[9] Nevertheless, the Trial Chamber may depart from the general principle of a public hearing. Visitors to the Court are often taken aback by how little they can actually see of the proceedings. Often, the sessions are closed to the public

---

[1] Rome Statute of the International Criminal Court, (2002) 2187 UNTS 90, Art. 62; Rules of Procedure and Evidence, ASP/1/3, pp. 10–107, Rule 100; Strategic Plan of the International Criminal Court, ASP/5/6, para. 34.
[2] *Lubanga* (ICC-01/04–01/06), Decision on Disclosure Issues, for Protective Measures and Other Procedural Matters, 24 April 2008, para. 68.
[3] *Ibid.*, para. 69.   [4] *Ibid.*, para. 69.   [5] *Ibid.* para. 105.   [6] *Ibid.*
[7] UN Doc. S/RES/1593 (2005), para. 3.
[8] Also Regulations of the Court, ICC-BD/01–01–04, Regulations 20 and 21.
[9] *Situation in Darfur, Sudan* (ICC-02/05), Prosecutor's Application under Article 58(7), 27 February 2007, para. 17.

entirely; other limitations are also frequent, such as witnesses testifying behind screens. A detailed enumeration of exceptions to the public hearing principle had been proposed but was rejected by the Preparatory Committee. Article 64(7) explicitly allows *in camera* proceedings for the protection of victims and witnesses, or to protect confidential or sensitive information to be given in evidence. Furthermore, Article 68(2) provides:

> As an exception to the principle of public hearings provided for in article 67, the Chambers of the Court may, to protect victims and witnesses or an accused, conduct any part of the proceedings *in camera* or allow the presentation of evidence by electronic or other special means. In particular, such measures shall be implemented in the case of a victim of sexual violence or a child who is a victim or a witness, unless otherwise ordered by the Court, having regard to all the circumstances, particularly the views of the victim or witness.

The already elaborate case law of the *ad hoc* tribunals in this matter should guide the Court in this difficult area.[10]

Limitations on the public nature of the proceedings are also justified in order to protect confidential or sensitive information. There may also be claims to confidentiality based on privilege, and the Court is to respect this pursuant to Article 69(5), as provided for in the Rules of Procedure and Evidence. But the major source of problems with this exception will be information derived from sovereign States. The Statute allows a State to apply 'for necessary measures' to respect 'confidential or sensitive information'.[11]

Presence at trial

The accused must be present at trial,[12] even those parts of it that are held *in camera*.[13] During the drafting of the Statute, there was considerable

---

[10] For example, *Tadić* (IT-94-1-T), Decision on the Prosecutor's Motion Requesting Protective Measures for Victims and Witnesses, 10 August 1995; *Rutaganda* (ICTR-96-3-T), Decision on the Preliminary Motion Submitted by the Prosecutor for Protective Measures for Witnesses, 26 September 1996. See Anne-Marie La Rosa, 'Réflexions sur l'apport du Tribunal pénal international pour l'ex-Yougoslavie au droit à un procès équitable', (1997) *Revue générale de droit international public* 945 at 962–70.

[11] Rome Statute, Art. 68(6).

[12] *Ibid.*, Art. 63. Art. 67(1)(d), concerning the rights of the accused, also declares: 'Subject to article 63, paragraph 2, [the accused has the right] to be present at the trial.'

[13] Rome Statute, Art. 72(7), allows for a hearing concerning the protection of national security information to take place *ex parte*, that is, in the absence of one or both of the parties.

debate about whether or not to permit *in absentia* trials,[14] which are widely held under the continental procedural model. It was argued that *in absentia* trials were particularly important in the context of international justice because of the didactic effect as well as the extreme practical difficulties involved in compelling attendance at trial.[15] The accused's right to be present at trial is recognized in the principal international human rights instruments,[16] but international tribunals and monitoring bodies have not viewed presence at trial as indispensable. The practice of domestic justice systems that derive from the Romano-Germanic models, where *in absentia* proceedings are well accepted, is considered compatible with the right to presence at trial, as long as the accused has been duly served with appropriate notice of the hearing.[17] During the drafting of the Rome Statute, the issue was often presented, erroneously, as one of principled difference with the common law system, which does not allow for *in absentia* trials as a general rule. But the fact that common law jurisdictions make a number of exceptions, and allow for such proceedings where appropriate, shows that this is not an issue of fundamental values so much as one of different practice. At Nuremberg, one of the major war criminals, Martin Bormann, was tried in his absence, pursuant to Article 12 of the Charter of the International Military Tribunal.[18] Because of the devotion of negotiators to their own domestic models, it proved impossible to reach consensus on this question. As one observer has noted, '[n]o compromise could be

---

[14] Daniel J. Brown, 'The International Criminal Court and Trial in Absentia', (1999) 24 *Brooklyn Journal of International Law* 763; Hans-Jörg Behrens, 'Investigation, Trial and Appeal in the International Criminal Court Statute (Parts V, VI, VIII)', (1998) 6 *European Journal of Crime, Criminal Law and Criminal Justice* 113 at 123; Hakan Friman, 'Rights of Persons Suspected or Accused of a Crime', in Roy Lee, ed., *The International Criminal Court: The Making of the Rome Statute: Issues, Negotiations, Results*, The Hague: Kluwer Law International, 1999, pp. 247–62 at pp. 255–61.

[15] Report of the Preparatory Committee on the Establishment of an International Criminal Court, UN Doc. A/51/10, vol. I, para. 254, pp. 54–5; also para. 259, p. 55. See also Eric David, 'Le Tribunal international pénal pour l'ex-Yougoslavie', (1992) 25 *Revue belge de droit international* 565; Alain Pellet, 'Le Tribunal criminel international pour l'ex-Yougoslavie: Poudre aux yeux ou avancée décisive?', (1994) 98 *Revue générale de droit international public* 7.

[16] International Covenant on Civil and Political Rights, (1966) 999 UNTS 171, Art. 14; American Convention on Human Rights, (1978) 1144 UNTS 123, Art. 8; European Convention on Human Rights, (1955) 213 UNTS 221, Art. 6.

[17] *Mbenge* v. *Zaire* (No. 16/1977), UN Doc. A/34/40, p. 134; General Comment No. 13 (21), UN Doc. A/36/40, para. 11; *Colozza and Rubinat* v. *Italy*, Series A, No. 89, 12 February 1985, para. 29; *Stamoulakatos* v. *Greece*, Series A, No. 271, 26 October 1993.

[18] *France et al.* v. *Goering et al.*, (1946) 22 IMT 203. It has since been established that Bormann was already dead when the trial took place.

found and the time constraint ruled in favour of a straightforward solution – trials *in absentia* are not provided for under any circumstances in
the Statute'.[19]

Presence at trial should imply more than mere physical presence. The
accused should be in a position to understand the proceedings, and this
may require interpretation in cases where the two official languages of
the Court are not available to the accused.[20] The Statute is silent with
respect to cases of an accused who is unfit to stand trial because of mental disorder, although this lacuna is corrected in the Rules, which direct
the Trial Chamber to adjourn the proceedings when it 'is satisfied that
the accused is unfit to stand trial'.[21] The problem of fitness to stand trial
should not be confused with the defence of insanity, allowed by Article
31(1)(a) of the Statute, where the issue is the accused's mental condition
at the time of the crime. An accused who is unfit to stand trial is not
'present' within the meaning of Article 63 and therefore the hearing
cannot proceed. In many national justice systems, an accused may be
held in detention pending a change in his or her condition permitting
the court to determine fitness. The suggestion in the International Law
Commission draft statute that the Court be permitted to continue proceedings in the case of 'ill health' of an accused, a provision that might
possibly have allowed the Court to address such situations, was rejected
by the Diplomatic Conference.

The situation of an accused who is unfit to stand trial is far from
an idle hypothesis. In the *Erdemović* case, the International Criminal
Tribunal for the former Yugoslavia remanded the accused for psychiatric examination so as to determine whether the plea of guilty had
been made by a man who was 'present' in all senses of the word. A panel
of experts concluded that he was suffering from post-traumatic stress
disorder and that his mental condition at the time did not permit his
trial before the Trial Chamber.[22] The Trial Chamber postponed the pre-
sentencing hearing and ordered a second evaluation of the appellant to
be submitted in three months' time.[23] A subsequent report concluded
that Erdemović's condition had improved such that he was 'sufficiently
able to stand trial'.[24] At Nuremberg, the International Military Tribunal

---

[19] Friman, 'Rights of Persons', pp. 255–61 at p. 262.
[20] See also Rome Statute, Art. 67(1)(f).
[21] Rules of Procedure and Evidence, Rule 135(4).
[22] *Erdemović* (IT-96-22-T), Sentencing Judgment, 29 November 1996, para. 5.
[23] *Erdemović* (IT-96-22-A), Appeal Judgment, 7 October 1997, para. 5.
[24] *Ibid.*, para. 8.

rejected suggestions that defendants Rudolf Hess and Julius Streicher were not fit to stand trial.[25]

The trial may proceed in the absence of the accused where he or she disrupts the proceedings. The Statute indicates that the accused must 'continue' to disrupt the trial, indicating that the trouble must be repetitive and persistent.[26] It is, of course, difficult to codify in any detail how judges are to administer such a power. The problem is a familiar one in domestic justice systems, and the Court will surely rely on national practices in developing its own jurisprudence on this point. It must bear in mind, however, that its case load will be, by its very nature, quite politicized, and that this will increase the likelihood that defendants mount vigorous, energetic and original challenges to the charges. The Court's definition of 'disruption' should not become a tool to muzzle defendants in such circumstances.[27] This is why the Statute also specifies that such measures shall be taken only in exceptional circumstances, after other reasonable alternatives have proved inadequate. Also, exclusion from the hearing is only allowed for such duration as is strictly required. The Court must review periodically whether the accused may be permitted to return to the hearing. Where the accused has been excluded from the hearing, the Statute requires the Trial Chamber to make provision for the accused to observe the trial and instruct counsel from outside the courtroom, through the use of communications technology, if required.

The Statute recognizes a right to an interpreter. An accused who does not understand the proceedings is not 'present' at trial. Thus, the right to an interpreter seems axiomatic. Although the requirement that documents be translated may be cumbersome, time-consuming and costly, it has been recognized by the European Court of Human Rights as a corollary of the right to an interpreter.[28] The provision does not require interpretation into the accused's mother tongue, or into a language of the accused's choice.[29] In an interlocutory ruling, the International Criminal Tribunal for the former Yugoslavia denied an accused's request

---

[25] *France et al. v. Goering et al.*, (1946) 22 IMT 203.

[26] Rome Statute, Art. 63(2); Rules of Procedure and Evidence, Rule 170.

[27] *Milošević* (IT-02-54-AR73.7), Decision on Interlocutory Appeal of the Trial Chamber's Decision on the Assignment of Defence Counsel, 1 November 2004.

[28] *Luedicke, Belkacem and Koc v. Germany*, Series A, No. 29, 28 November 1978, para. 48; *Kamasinski v. Federal Republic of Germany*, Series A, No. 168, 19 December 1989, para. 74.

[29] *Guesdon v. France* (No. 219/1986), UN Doc. A/44/40, p. 222, paras. 10.2 and 10.3.

for a 'Croatian' interpreter, given that there was regular translation of Serbo-Croatian, a sufficiently similar language.[30]

Defence and right to counsel

The accused is entitled to defend himself or herself in person. There are several precedents at the *ad hoc* tribunals, including the case of Jean-Paul Akayesu before the International Criminal Tribunal for Rwanda, who fired his counsel after being convicted and acted on his own at the sentencing phase of his trial, and that of Slobodan Milošević. Another defendant, Vojislav Šešelj, went on a hunger strike when his wish to act in his own defence was denied. After he had been without food for many days, the Appeals Chamber overruled the Trial Chamber.[31] According to the Strasbourg jurisprudence, the accused may be required to be assisted by a lawyer under certain circumstances, where this may affect the fairness of the trial.[32] Furthermore, a defendant who acts without legal assistance may be held responsible for a lack of due diligence in the proceedings, and may not always be able to rely on claims of inexperience, although he or she is entitled to some degree of indulgence.[33] In rare cases of a stubborn defendant who refuses all assistance by counsel, the Court might opt to appoint an *amicus curiae* (literally, 'friend of the court') in order to ensure that justice is not offended.[34] However, Rule 103 seems to limit the role of *amici curiae* to the submission of observations rather than an active participant in proceedings. In the *Situation in Darfur*, the Pre-Trial Chamber made an order pursuant to Rule 103 inviting submissions from Professor Antonio Cassese and the United Nations High Commissioner for Human Rights Louise Arbour on matters relating to the protection of witnesses and the preservation of evidence.[35] In *Lubanga*, it denied leave to intervene to the Women's Initiatives for Gender Justice.[36] It is more likely, where the right to an

---

[30] *Delalić et al.* (IT-96-21-T), Order on Zdravko Mucic's Oral Request for Croatian Interpretation, 23 June 1997.

[31] *Šešelj* (IT-03-67-AR73.3), Decision on Appeal Against the Trial Chamber's Decision on Assignment of Counsel, 20 October 2006.

[32] *Croissant v. Germany*, Series A, No. 237-B, 25 September 1992; *Philis v. Greece* (App. No. 16598/90), (1990) 66 DR 260.

[33] *Melin v. France*, Series A, No. 261-A, 22 June 1993, para. 25.

[34] Rules of Procedure and Evidence, Rule 103.

[35] *Situation in Darfur, Sudan* (ICC-02/05), Decision Inviting Observations in Application of Rule 103 of the Rules of Procedure and Evidence, 24 July 2006.

[36] *Lubanga* (ICC-01/04–01/06–480), Decision on Request Pursuant to Rule 103(1) of the Statute, 26 September 2006.

adequate defence seems threatened, that the Court would appoint stand-by counsel. This is not contemplated by the Statute or the Rules of the International Criminal Court, but it is now well entrenched in the practice of the *ad hoc* tribunals.

Although the accused is entitled to choice of counsel, this right cannot be unlimited. The *ad hoc* tribunals have adopted a rule requiring that counsel be either admitted to the practice of law in a State or be a university professor of law.[37] The Rules of Procedure and Evidence of the International Criminal Court are somewhat different, and focus on substance rather than form, requiring that 'counsel for the defence shall have established competence in international or criminal law and procedure, as well as the necessary relevant experience, whether as judge, prosecutor, advocate or in other similar capacity, in criminal proceedings'. Defence counsel must also have 'an excellent knowledge of and be fluent in at least one of the working languages of the Court'.[38] In the *Situation in Darfur*, the Pre-Trial Chamber instructed the Registrar to appoint *ad hoc* counsel for the defence who was not only fluent in one of the working languages, but who was also capable of working in Arabic.[39] The European Commission on Human Rights has dismissed claims alleging a violation of the right to counsel on the basis of failure to respect professional ethics,[40] where counsel was also a defence witness,[41] and even for a refusal to wear a gown.[42] But it is unclear who is to evaluate whether in fact counsel meet these requirements. In one case of Court-appointed counsel, the Registrar appeared to make only the most perfunctory of verifications as to the experience and competence of the candidates.[43] Moreover, there is a potential conflict between these rather rigorous requirements in the Rules and Article 67(1)(d) of the Statute itself, which recognizes the defendant's right 'to conduct the defence in person or through legal assistance of the accused's choosing'.

Under the International Covenant on Civil and Political Rights, the right to funded counsel for indigent defendants is subject to the

---

[37] Rules of Procedure and Evidence, Rule 44. [38] *Ibid.*, Rule 22.

[39] *Situation in Darfur* (ICC-02/05), Décision du Greffier relative à la nomination de Me Hadi Shalluf en qualité de conseil ad hoc de la Défense, 25 August 2006, p. 2.

[40] *Ensslin, Baader and Raspe v. Federal Republic of Germany* (App. Nos. 7572/76, 7586/76 and 7587/76), (1978) 14 DR 64.

[41] *K v. Denmark* (App. No. 19524/92), unreported.

[42] *X and Y v. Federal Republic of Germany* (App. Nos. 5217/71 and 5367/72), (1972) 42 Coll. 139.

[43] *Situation in Darfur, Sudan* (ICC-02/05), Décision du Greffier relative à la nomination de Me Hadi Shalluf en qualité de conseil ad hoc de la Défense, 25 August 2006.

requirement that this be in cases 'where the interests of justice so require',[44] a provision echoed in Article 67 of the Rome Statute. Arguably, this will be the situation in all matters before the International Criminal Court. Probably for this reason, the International Law Commission removed the 'interests of justice' condition in its draft statute,[45] only to have it introduced again by the Preparatory Committee.[46] With rare exceptions, counsel for all defendants before the *ad hoc* tribunals have been funded by the institution. Administration of the system of legal aid for indigent defendants is the responsibility of the Registrar.[47]

Guilty plea procedure

The trial is to begin with the accused being read all charges previously confirmed by the Pre-Trial Chamber. The Trial Chamber is to satisfy itself that the accused understands the nature of the charges. The accused is asked to plead guilty or not guilty.[48] The practice of the *ad hoc* tribunals has shown that it is not at all unusual for an accused to offer to plead guilty,[49] although there have as yet been none at the International Criminal Court. A guilty plea may be motivated by a number of factors, including a genuine feeling of remorse and contrition in the more sincere cases, and a hope that admission of guilt when conviction seems certain may result in a reduced sentence and better treatment in the more cynical cases. In the drafting of the Rome Statute, there were difficulties in circumscribing the rules applicable to guilty pleas because of differing philosophical approaches to the matter in the main judicial systems of national law. Under common law, a guilty plea is often the norm, obtained from an accused in exchange for commitments from the prosecutor as to the severity of the sentence and the nature of the

---

[44] International Covenant on Civil and Political Rights, (1966) 999 UNTS 171, Art. 14(3)(d).

[45] Report of the International Law Commission on the Work of Its Forty-Sixth Session, 2 May–22 July 1994, UN Doc. A/49/10, p. 116. See also Code of Crimes Against the Peace and Security of Mankind, UN Doc. A/51/332, Art. 11(e).

[46] Decisions Taken by the Preparatory Committee at Its Session Held 4 to 15 August 1997, UN Doc. A/AC.249/1997/L.8/Rev.1.

[47] Rules of Procedure and Evidence, Rule 21.

[48] Rome Statute, Art. 64(8)(a).

[49] *Erdemović* (IT-96-22-S), Sentencing Judgment, 5 March 1998, (1998) 37 ILM 1182; *Kambanda* (ICTR-97-23-S), Judgment and Sentence, 4 September 1998, (1998) 37 ILM 1411; *Nikolić* (IT-94-2-S), Sentencing Judgment, 18 December 2003; *Plavšić* (IT-00-39 and 40/1), Sentencing Judgment, 27 February 2003; *Rutaganira* (ICTR-95-1C-0022), Jugement portant condamnation, 14 March 2005; *Nikolić* (IT-02-60/1-A), Judgment on Sentencing Appeal, 4 February 2005.

charges. Under continental law, confession of guilt is viewed with deep suspicion and courts are expected to rule on guilt and innocence based on the evidence, irrespective of such a plea.[50] But, on a practical level, the differences may not be so great, although there are many misconceptions on both sides about the other system's approach to admissions of guilt. At common law, undertakings by the prosecutor do not bind the judge, who must be satisfied that there is sufficient evidence and that there is no charade or fraud on the court. But erroneous notions by some European lawyers about common law procedure resulted in the addition of a totally superfluous provision, Article 65(5), to reassure them that plea negotiations could not bind the Court. In continental systems, an admission of guilt will be a compelling factor and will almost certainly simplify the process.[51] Thus, it is not correct to say that continental judges are indifferent to admissions of guilt and that this does not accelerate the trial.

Under the Rome Statute, a 'healthy balance' has been struck between the two approaches.[52] When an accused makes an admission of guilt, the Trial Chamber is to ensure that he or she understands its nature and consequences, that the admission has been made voluntarily after sufficient consultation with counsel, and that it is supported by the facts of the case.[53] If the Trial Chamber is not satisfied that these conditions have been met, it deems the admission not to have been made and orders that the trial proceed. It may even order that the trial take place before another Trial Chamber. Alternatively, the Trial Chamber may consider that 'a more complete presentation of the facts of the case is required in the interests of justice, in particular the interests of the victims', and request additional evidence to be adduced.

Evidence

Unlike the common law system, with its complex and technical rules of evidence, the Statute follows the tradition of international criminal tribunals by allowing the admission of all relevant and necessary evidence.[54]

---

[50] See Henri-D. Bosly, 'Admission of Guilt before the ICC and in Continental Legal Systems', (2004) 2 *Journal of International Criminal Justice* 1040.

[51] Behrens, 'Investigation, Trial and Appeal', pp. 123–4.

[52] Silvia A. Fernández de Gurmendi, 'International Criminal Law Procedures', in Lee, *The International Criminal Court*, pp. 217–27 at p. 223.

[53] Rome Statute, Art. 65(1).

[54] Two volumes fill a gap in the literature, providing general overviews on the issue of evidence before international criminal tribunals, including the International Criminal

Probably the biggest surprise here, for lawyers trained in common law systems, is that there is no general rule excluding hearsay or indirect evidence,[55] although it seems likely that in ruling on the admissibility of such evidence the Court will be guided by 'hearsay exceptions generally recognized by some national legal systems, as well as the truthfulness, voluntariness and trustworthiness of the evidence, as appropriate'.[56] As Helen Brady has explained, '[d]ebates in the Ad Hoc Committee and the Preparatory Committee revealed a deep chasm between the civil law and the common law traditions on the scope and nature of the ICC's rules of evidence. However, a compromise was finally attained [that] is a delicate combination of civil and common-law concepts of fair trial and due process.'[57]

To be admissible, evidence must be relevant and necessary.[58] This general rule is similar to a provision in the Rules of Procedure and Evidence adopted by the International Criminal Tribunal for the former Yugoslavia.[59] Interpreting the provision, the Tribunal has considered whether or not to read into the text a requirement of reliability. National practice on this point varies considerably. The Trial Chamber described reliability as 'the invisible golden thread which runs through all the components of admissibility', but stopped short of adding it as a requirement to the extent that it was not specifically set out in the provision.[60] Thus, points out Helen Brady, although Article 69 does not actually refer to reliability as a condition of admissibility of evidence, it would seem that reliability is an implicit component of relevance and probative value. 'Any assessment of relevance and probative value must involve some consideration of the reliability of the evidence – it must be *prima facie* credible. Evidence which does not have sufficient indicia

---

Court: Richard May and Marieka Wierda, *International Criminal Evidence*, Ardsley, NY: Transnational Publishers, 2002; Rodney Dixon and Karim Khan, *Archbold: Practice, Procedure and Evidence: International Criminal Courts*, 2nd edn, London: Sweet & Maxwell, 2005. Also Kevin R. Gray, 'Evidence Before the ICC', in Dominic McGoldrick, Peter Rowe and Eric Donnelly, eds., *The Permanent International Criminal Court: Legal and Policy Issues*, Oxford and Portland, OR: Hart Publishing, 2004, pp. 287–314.

[55] See *Tadić* (IT-94-1-T), Opinion and Judgment, 7 May 1997, para. 555.

[56] *Tadić* (IT-94-1-T), Decision on Defence Motion on Hearsay, 5 August 1996, paras. 7–19.

[57] Helen Brady, 'The System of Evidence in the Statute of the International Criminal Court', in Flavia Lattanzi and William A. Schabas, eds., *Essays on the Rome Statute of the International Criminal Court*, Rome: Editrice il Sirente, 2000, pp. 279–302 at p. 286.

[58] Rome Statute, Art. 69(3).

[59] Rules of Procedure and Evidence, UN Doc. IT/32, Rule 89(C).

[60] *Delalić et al.* (IT-98-21-T), Decision on the Admissibility of Exhibit 155, 19 January 1998, para. 32.

of reliability cannot be said to be either relevant or probative to the issues to be decided.'[61] No corroboration is required for evidence to be admissible.[62]

Evidence may be called by either party. Moreover, the Court may, on its own initiative, require that evidence become part of the record, and even summon its own witnesses.[63] This is not so extraordinary, but in adversarial criminal justice systems it is exercised infrequently. At the International Criminal Court, current indications suggest judges may make wide use of the power. During the *Lubanga* confirmation hearing, the defence objected when the Prosecutor presented an NGO report that had not been part of the pre-hearing disclosure. Presiding Judge Claude Jorda dismissed the objection, telling defence counsel that '[t]he Chamber, in any case, has one remit – and only one remit – and that is to establish the truth[,] and the objective of this confirmation hearing is to supplement the adversarial debate between the parties'. In effect, he was saying that, when the Court was interested in receiving evidence, it would be admitted whatever the situation resulting from disclosure between the parties. After all, according to Judge Jorda the objective was to determine the truth, not to ensure that the two sides had been treated fairly. He warned that the defence should not always base its arguments 'on fairness or injustice'.[64] Judges with a background in an adversarial system would probably have expressed themselves differently.

The defence has the right to examine witnesses on the same basis as the Prosecutor.[65] There is no explicit provision for a full right to cross-examination, as it is understood in the common law. Under continental or Romano-Germanic legal systems, questions may be posed by the judge at the request of counsel. At trial, the presiding judge may issue directions as to the conduct of the proceedings,[66] failing which the Prosecutor and the defence are to agree on the order and the manner in which evidence is to be presented.[67] Witnesses are questioned by the party that presents them, followed by questioning by the other party and

---

[61] Brady, 'The System of Evidence', p. 290.

[62] *Lubanga* (ICC-01/04–01/06), Decision on the Confirmation of the Charges, 29 January 2007, paras. 121–2.

[63] Rome Statute, Art. 64(6)(d).

[64] *Lubanga* (ICC-01/04–01/06), Transcript, 27 November 2006. On another occasion, Pre-Trial Chamber I appeared to admit a defence exhibit that had not been previously identified or authorized, on the same basis: *Lubanga* (ICC-01/04–01/06), Transcript, 26 November 2006.

[65] Rome Statute, Art. 67(1)(e).   [66] *Ibid.*, Art. 64(8)(b).

[67] Rules of Procedure and Evidence, Rule 140(1).

by the Court. The defence has the right to be the last to examine a wit-ness.[68] The defence is also the last to make closing arguments.[69]

There are limits to the right to examine witnesses. The formal pro-visions governing the testimony of victims of sexual crimes are an example. The Statute permits the Court to allow the presentation of evi-dence by electronic or other special means.[70] Some questions are out of bounds: the Rules of Procedure and Evidence state that evidence of the prior or subsequent sexual conduct of a victim or witness is not to be admitted.[71] It may also disallow questions because they are abusive or repetitive. What is important is that the parties, prosecution and defence, be treated equally and that the trial be fundamentally fair.

The Statute also allows the Court to recognize witness privileges. The Assembly of States Parties agreed to confirm a principle already recog-nized by the International Criminal Tribunal for the former Yugoslavia, by which the International Committee of the Red Cross has a right to non-disclosure of evidence obtained by a former employee in the course of official duties.[72] The Tribunal relied on customary international law in reaching its decision.[73] Rule 73 of the Rules of Procedure and Evidence also acknowledge attorney–client privilege, and enable the Court to extend privilege to other categories of witnesses:

1. Without prejudice to article 67, paragraph 1(b), communications made in the context of the professional relationship between a person and his or her legal counsel shall be regarded as privileged, and consequently not subject to disclosure, unless:
    (a) The person consents in writing to such disclosure; or
    (b) The person voluntarily disclosed the content of the communica-tion to a third party, and that third party then gives evidence of that disclosure.
2. Having regard to rule 63, sub-rule 5, communications made in the con-text of a class of professional or other confidential relationships shall be regarded as privileged, and consequently not subject to disclosure, under the same terms as in sub-rules 1(a) and 1(b) if a Chamber decides in respect of that class that:
    (a) Communications occurring within that class of relationship are made in the course of a confidential relationship producing a rea-sonable expectation of privacy and non-disclosure;

[68] *Ibid.*, Rule 140(2).   [69] *Ibid.*, Rule 141.   [70] Rome Statute, Art. 68(2).
[71] Rules of Procedure and Evidence, Rule 71.   [72] *Ibid.*, Rule 73(3), (4) and (5).
[73] *Simić et al.* (IT-95-9-PT), Decision on the Prosecution Motion under Rule 73 for a Ruling Concerning the Testimony of a Witness, 27 July 1999.

    (b) Confidentiality is essential to the nature and type of relationship between the person and the confidant; and

    (c) Recognition of the privilege would further the objectives of the Statute and the Rules.

  3. In making a decision under sub-rule 2, the Court shall give particular regard to recognizing as privileged those communications made in the context of the professional relationship between a person and his or her medical doctor, psychiatrist, psychologist or counsellor, in particular those related to or involving victims, or between a person and a member of a religious clergy; and in the latter case, the Court shall recognize as privileged those communications made in the context of a sacred confession where it is an integral part of the practice of that religion.

It has been suggested that on this basis privilege might be extended to other non-governmental organizations with humanitarian purposes, and bodies such as a truth and reconciliation commission. Witnesses may also refuse to make statements that might tend to incriminate a spouse, child or parent.[74] The practice of 'witness proofing' has been common at the *ad hoc* tribunals. There is a benign dimension of preparation of witnesses, involving familiarization with the layout and potential theatrics of the courtroom so that they are not taken by surprise or disconcerted. More controversial is the rehearsal or coaching of them to respond to questions in the manner desired by the party that calls the witness. As authority for the legitimacy of the practice, the Prosecutor has invoked a decision of the International Criminal Tribunal for the former Yugoslavia.[75] Condemning the practice of witness proofing, Pre-Trial Chamber I endorsed defence submissions to the effect that it was not widely accepted at the *ad hoc* tribunals, contrary to what the Prosecutor had argued. Rather, 'the prevalence of the practice of proofing should be more accurately attributed to the geographical makeup and hierarchy of the Prosecution sections of the ICTY'.[76] The Chamber ordered the Prosecutor not to engage in witness proofing, and 'to refrain from all contact with the witness outside the courtroom from the moment the witness takes the stand'.[77]

---

[74] Rules of Procedure and Evidence, Rule 75.

[75] *Limaj et al.* (IT-03-66-T), Decision on the Defence Motion on Prosecution Practice of 'Proofing Witnesses', 10 December 2004.

[76] *Lubanga* (ICC-01/04–01/06), Decision on the Practices of Witness Familiarisation and Witness Proofing, 8 November 2006, para. 34.

[77] *Ibid.*, p. 22. Also *Lubanga* (ICC-01/04–01/06), Decision Regarding the Practices Used to Prepare and Familiarise Witnesses for Giving Testimony at Trial, 30 November 2007;

Nothing in the Statute provides for compellability of witnesses, for example by issuance of *subpoenae* or similar orders to appear before the Court. Witnesses are to appear voluntarily. Some are shocked by this, and think it inconceivable that a criminal tribunal operate without the power to compel testimony. In fact, witnesses are rarely forced to testify in criminal (or other) trials. Unhappy witnesses who are in court against their will rarely deliver the testimony that those who have brought them are expecting. Occasionally, a witness will insist upon a *subpoena* in order to prove to an employer, or to acquaintances, that he or she had no choice. But it would be a mistake to exaggerate the constraints that the absence of *subpoena* power may impose. Nor can this be claimed to be unfair to the defence, because the same principle applies to both sides in the trial.

Once a person is before the Court, Article 71 gives the Court a degree of control over the recalcitrant witness, and allows for the imposition of a fine.[78] Testimony given by witnesses must be accompanied by an undertaking: 'I solemnly declare that I will speak the truth, the whole truth and nothing but the truth.'[79] Witnesses testify before the Court in person, subject to the possibility of testimony being delivered by electronic or other special means in order to protect victims, witnesses or an accused. Such measures should particularly be considered in the case of victims of sexual violence or children.[80] There is one witness who can never be compelled to testify, however: the defendant. The right-to-silence provision in the Statute is based on the International Covenant on Civil and Political Rights, but goes considerably further. The Covenant says that an accused has the right '[n]ot to be compelled to testify against himself or to confess guilt'.[81] The Statute removes the qualification 'against himself', and adds an additional norm that is not at all implicit in the Covenant, namely, that the silence of an accused cannot be a consideration in the determination of guilt or innocence. The text clarifies the fact that an accused may refuse to testify altogether, and not merely to testify when the evidence is 'against himself'. The provision reflects concerns with encroachments upon the right to silence

---

Katanga et al. (ICC-01/04–01/07), Decision on a Number of Procedural Issues Raised by the Registry, 14 May 2009, para. 18; Sergey Vasiliev, 'Proofing the Ban on "Witness Proofing": Did the ICC Get It Right?', (2009) 20 *Criminal Law Forum* 193.

[78] Rules of Procedure and Evidence, Rules 65 and 171(1).

[79] Rome Statute, Art. 69(1); Rules of Procedure and Evidence, Rule 66(1).

[80] Rome Statute, Art. 68(2).

[81] International Covenant on Civil and Political Rights, (1966) 999 UNTS 171, Art. 14(3)(g).

in some national justice systems. Specifically, English common law has always prevented any adverse inference being drawn from an accused's failure to testify.[82]

While the accused cannot be compelled to 'testify', he or she may make an unsworn oral or written statement in his or her defence.[83] This is a practice admitted under many criminal codes throughout the world. In fact, continental European jurists are 'astonished' that it could be otherwise, as in their jurisdictions the accused is never sworn.[84] Under common law systems, an unsworn statement would in principle be inadmissible as evidence. The 'unsworn statement' seems to present itself as an exception to the general rule requiring that testimony be accompanied by an undertaking as to truthfulness.[85] It is also useful to a defendant as a technique of presenting his or her version of the facts without being subject to cross-examination.

Evidence obtained in violation of the Statute or in a manner contrary to internationally recognized human rights shall be inadmissible if it 'casts substantial doubt on the reliability of the evidence' or if its admission 'would be antithetical to and would seriously damage the integrity of the proceedings'.[86] A recent ruling of the European Court of Human Rights suggests that this may be implied in the right to a fair trial, even if such an exclusionary rule is not stated explicitly in the European Convention on Human Rights.[87] It hardly seems necessary to make a special rule dealing with unreliable evidence, as it should not be admitted in any case. In the ruling confirming the charges against Thomas Lubanga, Pre-Trial Chamber I dismissed a defence application to have evidence excluded. It agreed that the evidence in question had been obtained illegally, the result of a seizure that was illegal under Congolese criminal procedure. The Pre-Trial Chamber agreed this was a violation of the right to privacy, and therefore a breach of internationally recognized human rights.[88] But, after referring to precedents from the *ad hoc*

[82] But, in recent years, legislation adopted within the United Kingdom now allows prosecutors to propose such conclusions: Criminal Justice and Public Order Act 1994, s. 4(3). See *Murray* v. *United Kingdom* (1996) 22 EHRR 29, paras. 45–7; *Saunders* v. *United Kingdom* (1996) 23 EHRR 313, para. 68.
[83] Rome Statute, Art. 67(1)(h).
[84] Jean Pradel, *Droit pénal comparé*, Paris: Dalloz, 1995, p. 449, n. 1.
[85] Rome Statute, Art. 69(1).
[86] *Ibid.*, Art. 69(7).
[87] *Jalloh* v. *Germany* (App. No. 54810/00), Judgment, 11 July 2006.
[88] *Lubanga* (ICC-01/04–01/06), Decision on the Confirmation of the Charges, 29 January 2007, para. 82 (but see the puzzling, and ostensibly contradictory, para. 79).

tribunals, it said this was a minor issue that did not compromise the integrity of the proceedings.[89]

A distinct regime operates in the case of what is known as 'national security information'.[90] In domestic legal systems, special rules usually apply for the production of evidence deemed to raise major concerns of State security.[91] In some countries, the evidence is allowed but subject to a mechanism that protects its confidential nature. In others, its submission may be prohibited altogether. Although generalizations are always hazardous, it is probably fair to say that the heart of litigation on this subject under domestic legal systems concerns attempts by the defence to have access to information in the possession of State authorities. Prosecutors are less likely to find themselves in such an antagonistic relationship with State authorities.

The drafters of the Rome Statute began with much the same orientation. Thus, the initial concerns in this area, which first arose in the Ad Hoc Committee of the General Assembly in 1995 and continued during the work of the Preparatory Committee in 1996 and 1997, were directed to denying access by the defence to confidential information in the possession of the Prosecutor and, ordinarily, subject to disclosure as part of the preparation for a fair trial.[92] A decision by the Appeals Chamber of the International Criminal Tribunal for the former Yugoslavia in October 1997[93] seems to have redirected the attention of the drafters, who realized that, given the nature of the crimes to be tried by the Court, the heart of the problem was likely to lie with conflict between the Prosecutor and State authorities.

The provision that ultimately resulted, Article 72, is lengthy and confusing. Its complexity is exacerbated by the fact that much of its language was concocted during the Rome Conference itself, and did not benefit from the years of reflection provided by the Preparatory Committee process. The final version differs substantially from the various models considered during the Preparatory Committee phase. As a result, language is employed whose consequences are uncertain. Donald K. Piragoff, one of the experts involved in its drafting, speaking of 'the ambiguities of

[89] *Ibid.*, paras. 87–90.   [90] Rome Statute, Art. 72.

[91] *Blaškić* (IT-95-14-AR108*bis*), Objection to the Issue of Subpoenae Duces Tecum, 29 October 1997, (1998) 110 ILR 677, paras. 109, 124–6 and 141–6.

[92] Donald K. Piragoff, 'Protection of National Security Information', in Lee, *The International Criminal Court*, pp. 270–94 at p. 274.

[93] *Blaškić* (IT-95-14-AR108*bis*), Objection to the Issue of Subpoenae Duces Tecum, 29 October 1997, (1998) 110 ILR 677.

some of the provisions',[94] has certainly understated the matter. Basically, Article 72 leaves determination of whether or not matters affect national security to the State itself. The provision would seem to make things rather straightforward for a State that wishes to stonewall the Court. Where a State refuses a request for information in its possession, the Court may not order production.[95] It can only refer the non-compliance of the State concerned to the Assembly of States Parties or the Security Council although it can also draw 'evidentiary inferences'.

Decision

The English version of the Rome Statute refers to the final determination by the Trial Chamber as its 'decision' rather than 'judgment', the term that is commonly used at the *ad hoc* tribunals. 'Judgment' is a term that it reserves for the definitive ruling of the Appeals Chamber. But 'decision' also refers to rulings of the Trial Chamber on matters such as jurisdiction and admissibility. Article 81 refers to 'decision of acquittal or conviction' and 'decision under article 74'. The Rules of Procedure and Evidence speak of the Trial Chamber's 'decision' on the 'criminal responsibility of the accused'.[96] The draft statute submitted by the Preparatory Committee used the term 'judgment',[97] and the change was made in the course of the Rome Conference on the recommendation of the Working Group on Procedural Matters.[98] This choice of nomenclature may have been an attempt to avoid terminology that was too closely identified with one procedural regime or another.

In order to convict, the Court must be convinced of the guilt of the accused beyond reasonable doubt.[99] The words are more familiar to lawyers from common law systems than they are to those from Romano-Germanic systems, which generally require guilt to be proven to a degree

---

[94] Piragoff, 'Protection of National Security Information', p. 294. See also Rodney Dixon and Helen Duffy, revised by Christopher K. Hall, 'Article 72', in Otto Triffterer, ed., *Commentary on the Rome Statute of the International Criminal Court, Observers' Notes, Article by Article*, 2nd edn, Munich: C. H. Beck; Baden-Baden: Nomos; Oxford: Hart, 2008, pp. 1361–78.

[95] Rome Statute, Art. 72(7)(a).   [96] Rules of Procedure and Evidence, Rule 144(1).

[97] UN Doc. A/CONF.183/2, Arts. 72 and 80.

[98] UN Doc. A/CONF.183/C.1/SR.24, para. 1. In a footnote to one of its reports, the Working Group 'informed' the Drafting Committee that the phrase 'final decision of acquittal or conviction and sentence' should be used to refer to the final decision of the Trial Chamber throughout the Statute: UN Doc. A/CONF.183/C.1/WGPM/L.2.

[99] Rome Statute, Art. 66(3).

that satisfies the *intime conviction* of the trier of fact. The Strasbourg jurisprudence has no clear pronouncement on which standard is preferable in light of human rights norms.[100] An amendment specifying the 'reasonable doubt' standard of proof was defeated during the drafting of Article 14 of the International Covenant on Civil and Political Rights.[101] However, the Human Rights Committee has been less circumspect, clarifying that the prosecution must establish proof of guilt beyond reasonable doubt.[102] The International Military Tribunal at Nuremberg applied the standard of beyond reasonable doubt, stating explicitly in its judgment that Schacht and von Papen were to be acquitted because of failure to meet that burden of proof.[103] As for the *ad hoc* tribunals, they seem to have had no difficulty with the issue, and there are frequent statements in their judgments to the effect that the reasonable doubt standard applies.[104] The Rules of Procedure and Evidence of the *ad hoc* tribunals, adopted by the judges, specify: 'A finding of guilt may be reached only when a majority of the Trial Chamber is satisfied that guilt has been proved beyond reasonable doubt.'[105] One Trial Chamber of the International Criminal Tribunal for the former Yugoslavia observed that, although testimony 'raised grave suspicions' about the conduct of an accused, '[n]ot even the gravest of suspicions can establish proof beyond reasonable doubt'.[106]

Common law judges have devoted considerable effort to defining the notion of reasonable doubt, generally in an attempt to provide clear instructions for lay jurors. This is surely less important for experienced judges such as those likely to be elected to the Court. In *Delalić*, the Trial Chamber of the International Criminal Tribunal for the former Yugoslavia adopted a common law definition:

> A reasonable doubt is a doubt which the particular jury entertain in the circumstances. Jurymen themselves set the standard of what is reasonable

---

[100] *Austria* v. *Italy*, (1962) 9 *Yearbook* 740 at 784.

[101] UN Doc. E/CN.4/365; UN Doc. E/CN.4/SR.156.

[102] General Comment 13/21, UN Doc. A/39/40, pp. 143–7, para. 7.

[103] *France et al.* v. *Goering et al.*, (1946) 22 IMT 203.

[104] See the numerous references to the reasonable doubt standard in, for example, *Tadić* (IT-94-1-T), Opinion and Judgment, 7 May 1997; *Akayesu* (ICTR-96-4-T), Judgment, 2 September 1998; *Delalić et al.* (IT-96-21-T), Judgment, 16 November 1998. More recently, see *Brdjanin* (IT-99-36-T), Judgment, 1 September 2004, para. 23.

[105] Rules of Procedure and Evidence, UN Doc. IT/32, Rule 87(A); Rules of Procedure and Evidence of the International Criminal Tribunal for Rwanda, Rule 87(A); Rules of Procedure and Evidence of the Special Court for Sierra Leone, Rules 87(A) and 98.

[106] *Simić et al.* (IT-95-9-R77), Judgment in the Matter of Contempt Allegations Against an Accused and His Counsel, 30 June 2000.

in the circumstances. It is that ability which is attributed to them which is one of the virtues of our mode of trial: to their task of deciding facts they bring to bear their experience and judgment.[107]

Simply put, 'reasonable doubt' means a doubt that is founded in reason. It does not mean 'any doubt', 'beyond a shadow of a doubt', 'absolute certainty' or 'moral certainty'.[108] Nor, on the other end of the scale, does it imply 'an actual substantive doubt' or 'such doubt as would give rise to a grave uncertainty'.[109]

An important innovation reflecting the influence of continental legal systems is the right of the Court to alter the legal characterization of a charge. There has never been much problem with the idea that a judgment may convict an accused of a lesser but included offence. Thus, if a person is charged with murder, and the prosecution succeeds in demonstrating a violent attack but cannot confirm that the victim actually died, an accused might be found guilty of assault. Under the International Criminal Court regime, as developed in Regulation 55 of the Regulations of the Court, the Trial Chamber may modify the legal characterization of facts. This means that an accused person might be charged with war crimes yet convicted of crimes against humanity or even genocide. The idea is familiar enough to judges from the legal traditions of continental Europe, but quite shocking to many trained in the common law.[110] Regulation 55 provides:

1. In its decision under article 74, the Chamber may change the legal characterisation of facts to accord with the crimes under articles 6, 7 or 8, or to accord with the form of participation of the accused under articles 25 and 28, without exceeding the facts and circumstances described in the charges and any amendments to the charges.

2. If, at any time during the trial, it appears to the Chamber that the legal characterisation of facts may be subject to change, the Chamber shall give notice to the participants of such a possibility and having heard the evidence, shall, at an appropriate stage of the proceedings, give the participants the opportunity to make oral or written submissions. The Chamber may suspend the hearing to ensure that the participants have adequate time and facilities for effective preparation or, if necessary, it may order a hearing to consider all matters relevant to the proposed change.

---

[107] *Ibid.*, para. 600; citing *Green* v. *R.* (1972) 46 ALJR 545.
[108] *Victor* v. *Nebraska*, 127 L Ed 2d 583 (1994).
[109] *Cage* v. *Louisiana*, 498 US 39 (1990); *Sullivan* v. *Louisiana*, 113 S Ct 2078 (1993).
[110] Carsten Stahn, 'Modification of the Legal Characterization of Facts in the ICC System: A Portrayal of Regulation 55', (2005) 16 *Criminal Law Forum* 1.

3. For the purposes of sub-regulation 2, the Chamber shall, in particular, ensure that the accused shall:

    (a) Have adequate time and facilities for the effective preparation of his or her defence in accordance with article 67, paragraph 1(b); and

    (b) If necessary, be given the opportunity to examine again, or have examined again, a previous witness, to call a new witness or to present other evidence admissible under the Statute in accordance with article 67, paragraph 1(e).

The decision of the Trial Chamber must be reached by a majority of the three judges present, although the Statute encourages unanimity.[111] This is similar to the situation before the *ad hoc* tribunals. The *ad hoc* tribunals have established a tradition of dissent, with both majority and minority penning lengthy reasons. The Statute requires the Trial Chamber to deliver written reasons containing 'a full and reasoned statement' of its findings on the evidence and conclusions. Of course, the three judges of the Court's Trial Chambers who are assigned to a case must be present at all stages of the trial and during the deliberations. The Statute allows the Presidency to appoint an alternate judge who can be present in order to replace a member who is unable to continue attending. This wise practice was only adopted by the *ad hoc* tribunals in April 2006, after more than a decade of operation. In cases where a judge could not continue with a case, generally because of serious illness, the tribunals generally appointed a replacement.[112] That they recognized how unsatisfactory and potentially unfair such a situation created can be seen in their adoption of a new rule allowing for what are called 'reserve judges'.[113] Since then, a fourth judge sits on major cases, ready to step in if one of the three members of the panel can no longer participate.

Sentencing procedure

Upon determination of guilt, the Trial Chamber is to establish the 'appropriate sentence' in a distinct phase of the trial.[114] In so doing, the

---

[111] Rome Statute, Art. 74.

[112] *Karemera et al.* (ICTR-98-44-AR15*bis*.2), Reasons for Decision on Interlocutory Appeals Regarding Continuation of Proceedings with a Substitute Judge and on Nzirorera's Motion for Leave to Consider New Material, 22 October 2004, para. 52; *Krajisnik* (IT-00-39and40), Decision Pursuant to Rule 15*bis* (D), 16 December 2004.

[113] Rules of Procedure and Evidence of the International Criminal Tribunal for the former Yugoslavia, UN Doc. IT/32/Rev. 37, Rule 15*ter* (adopted 6 April 2006).

[114] *Ibid.*, Art. 76; Rules of Procedure and Evidence, Rule 143.

Statute instructs the Trial Chamber to consider the evidence presented and submissions made during the trial that are relevant to the sentence. Mitigating and aggravating factors relating to the commission of the crime itself, such as the individual role of the offender in the treatment of the victims, will form part of the evidence germane to guilt or innocence and thus will appear as part of the record of the trial. There is a strong presumption in favour of a distinct sentencing hearing following conviction. Though not mandatory, it must be held upon the request of either the Prosecutor or the accused, and, failing application from either party, the Court may decide to hold such a hearing.[115] The *ad hoc* tribunals held separate sentencing hearings and issued distinct sentencing decisions in their initial cases, although this was not mandated either by their statutes or by their rules.[116] Later, the rules of the two *ad hoc* tribunals were amended in order to eliminate any suggestion of a separate sentencing phase.

Failure to hold a separate sentencing hearing after conviction may put the accused at a real disadvantage during the trial. He or she may be in a position to submit relevant evidence in mitigation of sentence, for example concerning the individual's specific role in the crimes *vis-à-vis* accomplices, or efforts by the offender to reduce the suffering of the victim. The only way to introduce such evidence may be for the accused to renounce the right to silence and the protection against self-incrimination. Providing the accused with the right to a post-conviction sentencing hearing, where new evidence and submissions may be presented, thus enhances the right to silence of the accused at trial. From the Prosecutor's standpoint, there are also advantages to a sentencing hearing. Aggravating evidence, such as proof of bad character or prior convictions, might well be deemed inadmissible at trial, yet it would possibly pass the relevance test once guilt had been established and the only remaining issue is the determination of a fit penalty.

---

[115] Before the international and the United States military tribunals, there appears to have been no practice of holding distinct hearings to address matters concerning the sanction, once guilt had been established, although the British military tribunals seem to have followed this procedure in some cases: *United Kingdom v. Eck et al.* ('Peleus Trial'), (1947) 1 LRTWC 1, 13; *United Kingdom v. Grumfelt* ('Scuttled U-Boats Case'), (1947) 1 LRTWC 55, 65; *United Kingdom v. Kramer et al.* ('Belsen Trial'), (1947) 2 LRTWC 1, 122–5. See William A. Schabas, 'Sentencing and the International Tribunals: For a Human Rights Approach', (1997) 7 *Duke Journal of Comparative and International Law* 461.

[116] *Tadić* (IT-94-1-S), Sentencing Judgment, 14 July 1997; *Akayesu* (ICTR-96-4-T), Sentencing Judgment, 2 October 1998.

The purpose of the sentencing hearing is to provide for the submission of additional evidence or submissions relevant to the sentence. The *ad hoc* tribunals have considered such relevant information to include psychiatric and psychological reports, as well as testimony by the convicted person.

Appeal and revision

Decisions of acquittal or conviction by the Trial Chambers of the International Criminal Court are subject to appeal. Appeal against conviction is a fundamental right set out in the International Covenant on Civil and Political Rights. The Prosecutor may appeal an acquittal on grounds of procedural error, error of fact or error of law. The Appeals Chamber of the International Criminal Court has resisted any broadening of a right to appeal based upon customary law: 'Only final decisions of a criminal court determinative of its verdict or decisions pertaining to the punishment meted out to the convict are assured as an indispensable right of man.'[117] It held that 'the Statute defines exhaustively the right to appeal against decisions of first instance courts, namely decisions of the Pre-Trial or Trial Chambers'.[118]

There was difficulty with this provision at the Rome Conference, because some common law jurisdictions prohibit any prosecution appeal of an acquittal.[119] The defendant may appeal a conviction on grounds of procedural error, error of fact, error of law or '[a]ny other ground that affects the fairness or reliability of the proceedings or decision'. The Prosecutor is also entitled to appeal a conviction on behalf of the defendant.[120] Sentences may be appealed by both Prosecutor and convicted person 'on the ground of disproportion between the crime and the sentence'. If, during an appeal against sentence, the Court considers there are grounds to set aside a conviction, it may intervene to quash the judgment. Similarly, it may also intervene on sentence during an appeal taken against the conviction only.

---

[117] *Situation in the Democratic Republic of the Congo* (ICC-01/04–168), Judgment on the Prosecutor's Application for Extraordinary Review of Pre-Trial Chamber I's 31 March 2006 Decision Denying Leave to Appeal, 13 July 2006, para. 38.

[118] *Ibid.*, para. 20.

[119] Helen Brady and Mark Jennings, 'Appeal and Revision', in Lee, *The International Criminal Court*, pp. 294–304.

[120] Rome Statute, Art. 81.

In addition to decisions of the Trial Chamber on questions of guilt or innocence, and on the sentence, appeals regarding specific or interlocutory issues that are decided in the course of prosecution are allowed in certain cases.[121] Appeal is also permitted regarding decisions dealing with admissibility and jurisdiction, those granting or denying release of a person being investigated or prosecuted, certain decisions of the Pre-Trial Chamber, and any ruling 'that would significantly affect the fair and expeditious conduct of the proceedings or the outcome of the trial'. An example, drawn from the case law of the International Criminal Tribunal for the former Yugoslavia, is the jurisdictional appeal raised by Duško Tadić. It resulted in a seminal ruling of the Appeals Chamber issued prior to the beginning of the trial itself that pronounced on such matters as the legality of the creation of the Tribunal by the Security Council and the scope of its subject-matter jurisdiction, especially with respect to war crimes committed in non-international armed conflict.[122]

According to the Appeals Chamber of the International Criminal Court, 'not every issue may constitute the subject of an appeal' of an interlocutory decision. The issue must be one apt to 'significantly affect' the proceedings, that is, influence in a material way 'the fair and expeditious conduct of the proceedings' or 'the outcome of the trial'. But this alone is not enough, because an issue with such attributes must still be one 'for which in the opinion of the Pre-Trial or Trial Chamber, an immediate resolution by the Appeals Chamber may materially advance the proceedings'.[123] Moreover, according to the Appeals Chamber:

> Only an 'issue' may form the subject-matter of an appealable decision. An issue is an identifiable subject or topic requiring a decision for its resolution, not merely a question over which there is disagreement or conflicting opinion. There may be disagreement or conflict of views on the

---

[121] *Ibid.*, Art. 82. On the distinction between appeals on the merits and appeals, based on Art. 81, and on interlocutory issues, based on Art. 82, see *Lubanga* (ICC-01/04–01/06), Judgment on the Prosecutor's Appeal Against the Decision of Pre-Trial Chamber I entitled 'Decision Establishing General Principles Governing Applications to Restrict Disclosure Pursuant to Rule 81(2) and (4) of the Rules of Procedure and Evidence', 13 October 2006, paras. 12–19.

[122] *Tadić* (IT-94-1-AR72), Decision on the Defence Motion for Interlocutory Appeal on Jurisdiction, 2 October 1995.

[123] *Situation in the Democratic Republic of Congo* (ICC-01/04–168), Judgment on the Prosecutor's Application for Extraordinary Review of Pre-Trial Chamber I's 31 March 2006 Decision Denying Leave to Appeal, 13 July 2006. Followed in *Lubanga* (ICC-01/04–01/06), Decision on Third Defence Motion for Leave to Appeal, 4 October 2006.

law applicable for the resolution of a matter arising for determination in the judicial process. This conflict of opinion does not define an appealable subject. An issue is constituted by a subject the resolution of which is essential for the determination of matters arising in the judicial cause under examination. The issue may be legal or factual or a mixed one.[124]

According to Pre-Trial Chamber II, 'in striking the balance between the convenience of deciding certain issues at an early stage of the proceedings, and the need to avoid possible delays and disruptions caused by recourse to interlocutory appeals, the provisions enshrined in the relevant rules of the ad hoc Tribunals, and in the ICC Statute, favour as a principle the deferral of appellate proceedings until final judgment, and limit interlocutory appeals to a few, strictly defined, exceptions'.[125] Furthermore, Article 82 reflects 'a general trend to narrow the grounds for interlocutory appeals', rejecting a concept that interim appeal could be justified by its 'general importance to proceedings' or to 'international law generally'.[126]

Where leave to appeal is required, it must be granted by the Chamber whose decision is impugned. Under the circumstances, according to Judge Blattmann, the Chamber 'must tread carefully to apply the test provided in Article 82(1)(d), resisting any temptation to decide upon the substantive issues involved as that is reserved for the Appeals Chamber itself to determine'.[127] The Appeals Chamber has explained:

> Article 82(1)(d) of the Statute does not confer a right to appeal interlocutory or intermediate decisions of either the Pre-Trial or the Trial Chamber. A right to appeal arises only if the Pre-Trial or Trial Chamber is of the opinion that any such decision must receive the immediate attention of

---

[124] *Ibid.*, para. 9. Also *Lubanga* (ICC-01/04–01/06), Dissenting Opinion of Judge Pikis, 13 October 2006, para. 22.

[125] *Situation in Uganda* (ICC-02/04–01/05), Decision on Prosecutor's Application for Leave to Appeal in Part Pre-Trial Chamber II's Decision on the Prosecutor's Applications for Warrants of Arrest under Article 58, 19 August 2005, para. 19; *Lubanga* (ICC-01/04–01/06), Decision on the Defence and Prosecution Requests for Leave to Appeal the Decision on Victims' Participation of 18 January 2008, 26 February 2008, para. 13; *Situation in Uganda* (ICC-02/04–01/05), Decision on the Prosecutor's Applications for Leave to Appeal Dated the 15th Day of March 2006 and to Suspend or Stay Consideration of Leave to Appeal Dated the 11th Day of May 2006, 10 July 2006, para. 21.

[126] *Situation in Uganda* (ICC-02/04–01/05), Decision on Prosecutor's Application for Leave to Appeal in Part Pre-Trial Chamber II's Decision on the Prosecutor's Applications for Warrants of Arrest under Article 58, 19 August 2005, para. 16.

[127] *Lubanga* (ICC-01/04–01/06), Separate and Dissenting Opinion of Judge René Blattmann, 26 February 2008, para. 5. Also *Lubanga* (ICC-01/04–01/06), Dissenting Opinion of Judge René Blattmann, 8 May 2008, para. 6.

the Appeals Chamber. This opinion constitutes the definitive element for the genesis of a right to appeal. In essence, the Pre-Trial or Trial Chamber is vested with power to state, or more accurately still, to certify the existence of an appealable issue. By the plain terms of article 82(1)(d) of the Statute, a Pre-Trial or Trial Chamber may certify such a decision on its own accord. If it fails to address the appealability of an issue it may do so on the application of any party to the proceedings. It may be regarded as axiomatic that, if any power is conferred upon a court to make an order or issue a decision, the parties have an implicit right to move the Chamber to exercise it.[128]

Detailed review of the *travaux préparatoires* and the practice of international criminal tribunals with respect to interlocutory appeal supports the restrictive approach to Article 82(1)(d).

To date, with a few exceptions,[129] applications to the Pre-Trial Chambers for leave to appeal have been dismissed. In the first such ruling, Pre-Trial Chamber II said that determination of an application for leave to appeal should be guided by three principles: the restrictive character of the remedy provided for in Article 82(1)(d), the need for the applicant to satisfy the Chamber as to the existence of the specific requirements stipulated by this provision, and the irrelevance of or non-necessity at this stage for the Chamber to address arguments relating to the merit or substance of the appeal.[130] For the Pre-Trial Chamber, the restrictive terms for interlocutory appeal were deliberately incorporated by the drafters of the Statute, and seek to strike a balance between 'the convenience of deciding certain issues at an early stage of the proceedings, and the need to avoid possible delays and disruptions caused by recourse to interlocutory appeals'.[131]

It may seem odd to leave the keys to the appeals court in the hands of the judges whose decision is being attacked. But the Prosecutor's argument that, even in jurisdictions where such a procedure existed, there was always a way of getting the appeals jurisdiction to take on the case,

---

[128] *Situation in the Democratic Republic of the Congo* (ICC-01/04–168), Judgment on the Prosecutor's Application for Extraordinary Review of Pre-Trial Chamber I's 31 March 2006 Decision Denying Leave to Appeal 13 July 2006, para. 20.

[129] *Lubanga* (ICC-01/04–01/06–166), Decision on the Prosecution Motion for Reconsideration and, in the Alternative, Leave to Appeal, 23 June 2006; *Lubanga* (ICC-01/04–01/06), Decision on Third Defence Motion for Leave to Appeal, 4 October 2006.

[130] *Situation in Uganda* (ICC-02/04–01/05), Decision on Prosecutor's Application for Leave to Appeal in Part Pre-Trial Chamber II's Decision on the Prosecutor's Applications for Warrants of Arrest under Article 58, 19 August 2005, para. 15.

[131] *Ibid.*, para. 19.

failed to convince.[132] Nor is the claim that there is urgency in obtaining definitive determinations of law by the Appeals Chamber on controversial provisions of the Statute at such an early stage in the Court's existence at all compelling. Indeed, it may be quite productive and healthy to allow a variety of interpretative approaches within the Pre-Trial Chambers and Trial Chambers for some time. An impetuous approach risks stifling creativity and experimentation. The Appeals Chamber's ruling indicates that the Court will not easily depart from the procedural regime set out in the Statute or the Rules of Procedure and Evidence, allowing parties to devise their own remedies when the applicable law seems to offer none.[133]

During an appeal of a conviction or sentence, the execution of the decision or sentence is suspended, although the convicted person should remain in custody. Given the conviction, it can no longer be said that the person benefits from the presumption of innocence and as a result the same entitlement to provisional release does not exist. However, if an appellant is detained during the appeal and if the full sentence is served during that time, he or she must be released. In the event of acquittal, an accused is normally to be released immediately, although the Prosecution may apply to the Trial Chamber for an order imposing continued detention pending its appeal of the verdict. Interlocutory appeals are potentially disruptive of the normal course of trial, and afford the defence an opportunity to generate considerable delays in the proceedings. For that reason, such appeals do not normally suspend the ordinary trial proceedings.

Where the Appeals Chamber grants the appeal on a point of law or fact that materially influenced the decision, or because of unfairness at the trial proceedings affecting the reliability of the decision or sentence, it may reverse or amend the decision or sentence, or order a new trial before a different Trial Chamber. It may vary a sentence if it finds it is 'disproportionate to the crime'. In a defence appeal, the Appeals

---

[132] *Situation in the Democratic Republic of Congo* (ICC-01/04–168), Judgment on the Prosecutor's Application for Extraordinary Review of Pre-Trial Chamber I's 31 March 2006 Decision Denying Leave to Appeal, 13 July 2006.

[133] Along much the same lines, Pre-Trial Chamber II rejected the Prosecutor's application entitled 'Motion for Reconsideration', saying that '[r]eview of decisions by the Court is only allowed under specific circumstances, explicitly provided in the Statute and the Rules': *Situation in Uganda* (ICC-02/04–01/05), Decision on the Prosecutor's Position on the Decision of Pre-Trial Chamber II to Redact Factual Descriptions of Crimes from the Warrant of Arrest, Motion for Reconsideration, and Motion for Clarification, 28 October 2005, para. 18.

Chamber cannot modify a decision to the detriment of the convicted person, for example by increasing a sentence beyond that imposed at trial or by adding convictions under additional counts. It is possible for the Appeals Chamber to remand a factual issue back to the original Trial Chamber. The Appeals Chamber can also call evidence itself in order to determine an issue.[134]

Like the decision on guilt or innocence and the decision on sentence, an appeal is settled by a majority of the judges. Members of the Appeals Chamber may register their dissent and, if the experience of the *ad hoc* tribunals is any guide, dissenting judgments will be frequent and they will be long.[135] Some delegations at the Rome Conference believed that appeal decisions should be unanimous. But, here again, the practice of the *ad hoc* tribunals provided an influential model. Delegates pointed to the *Erdemović* decision of the Appeals Chamber of the International Criminal Tribunal for the former Yugoslavia, where the bench split three to two.[136] But it was the dissenting judgments penned by Judges Cassese and Stephen that ultimately prevailed, because their conclusions were incorporated into the Rome Statute.

It is also possible to seek revision of a conviction or sentence. Revision involves intervention at the appellate level that does not call into question findings of the Trial Chamber. It is based on new evidence, the discovery that decisive evidence at trial was false, forged or falsified, or a realization that a judge of the Trial Chamber participating in the trial was guilty of serious misconduct or breach of duty sufficient to justify removal from the bench.[137] When it grants review, the Trial Chamber may reconvene the original Trial Chamber, constitute a new Trial Chamber or dispose of the matter itself.

The Statute is silent on the subject of reconsideration of decisions of the Appeals Chamber. But there should be a remedy if it is established that the Appeals Chamber was in error on a point of law or fact, or if the proceedings were unfair. Nor is there any reason to deny review if

---

[134] Regulations of the Court, Regulation 62. On standards to be used in admitting new evidence upon appeal, see *Barayagwiza* (ICTR-97-19-AR72), Decision, 3 November 1999. The standard of the Appeals Chamber of the International Criminal Tribunal for Rwanda seems to be extraordinarily broad.

[135] See *Lubanga* (ICC-01/04–01/06), Dissenting Opinion of Judge Pikis, 13 October 2006; *Lubanga* (ICC-01/04–01/06), Dissenting Opinion of Judge Pikis to the Order of the Appeals Chamber issued on 4 December 2006, 11 December 2006; *Lubanga* (ICC-01/04–01/06), Separate Opinion by Judge Georghios M. Pikis, 14 December 2006.

[136] *Erdemović* (IT-96-22-A), Appeal Judgment, 7 October 1997.

[137] Rome Statute, Art. 84; Regulations of the Court, Regulation 66.

a judge who sits on the Appeals Chamber is subsequently found guilty of misconduct, in the same way as for the Trial Chamber. But, in the absence of a specific provision, the Appeals Chamber would have to craft its own remedy in the exercise of its inherent powers.

In the event of discovery of a miscarriage of justice as a result of new facts where a person has already suffered punishment, that individual is entitled to compensation, unless he or she was responsible for the non-disclosure of the fact or facts in question.[138] There is no comparable right in the applicable law of the *ad hoc* tribunals.[139] Invoking Article 85 of the Rome Statute, the presidents of the *ad hoc* tribunals tried, unsuccessfully, to obtain amendments to the statutes in this respect.[140] The applicable procedure for compensation in such circumstances is set out in the Rules of Procedure and Evidence.[141]

---

[138] *Ibid.*, Art. 85.
[139] *Rwamakuba* (ICTR-98-44C-A), Decision on Appeal Against Decision on Appropriate Remedy, 13 September 2007, para. 10.
[140] Letter Dated 19 September 2000 from the President of the International Criminal Tribunal for the Former Yugoslavia Addressed to the Secretary-General, annexed to Letter Dated 26 September 2000 from the Secretary-General Addressed to the President of the Security Council, UN Doc. S/2000/904; Letter Dated 26 September 2000 from the President of the International Criminal Tribunal for Rwanda Addressed to the Secretary-General, annexed to Letter Dated 28 September 2000 from the Secretary-General Addressed to the President of the Security Council, UN Doc. S/2000/925. See Stuart Beresford, 'Redressing the Wrongs of the International Justice System: Compensation for Persons Erroneously Detained, Prosecuted, or Convicted by the Ad Hoc Tribunals', (2002) 96 *American Journal of International Law* 628. See also Geert-Jan Alexander Knoops, *An Introduction to the Law of the International Criminal Tribunals*, Ardsley, NY: Transnational Publishers, 2003, pp. 191–9.
[141] Rules of Procedure and Evidence, Rules 173–175.

9

Punishment

Criminal law, in all domestic systems, culminates in a penalty phase. This is what principally distinguishes it from other forms of judicial and quasi-judicial accountability, be they traditional mechanisms like civil lawsuits or innovative contemporary experiments like truth commissions. And the International Criminal Court is no different. According to the Rome Statute, the basic penalty to be imposed by the Court is one of imprisonment, up to and including life imprisonment in extreme cases. Reflecting developments in international human rights law, the Court excludes any possibility of capital punishment, despite the seriousness of the offences that it will judge. Because there have as yet been no convictions by the Court, there is obviously no relevant case law on this subject. Clearly, the jurisprudence of the other international criminal tribunals provides very useful guidance as to the approach the Court is likely to take.

Most domestic criminal codes set out a precise and detailed range of sentencing options. Often, each specific offence is accompanied by the applicable penalty, including references to maximum and minimum terms. Whether international justice should follow this pattern has been debated for decades, dating back to the sessions of the International Law Commission in the 1950s. The final result in the Rome Statute, however, is a few laconic provisions establishing the maximum available sentence and, by and large, leaving determination in specific cases to the judges. This constitutes, incidentally, a rather dramatic exception to the general policy of the drafters of the Statute and the Rules, which was to define and delimit judicial discretion as much as possible. In determining the appropriate sentence, the judges have been given a very free hand.[1]

---

[1] See Claus Kreß, 'Investigation, Trial and Appeal in the International Criminal Court Statute (Parts V, VI, VIII)', (1998) 6 *European Journal of Crime, Criminal Law and Criminal Justice* 126; Rolf E. Fife, 'Penalties', in Roy Lee, ed., *The International Criminal Court: The Making of the Rome Statute*, The Hague: Kluwer Law International, 1999, pp. 319–44; Faiza P. King and Anne-Marie La Rosa, 'Penalties under the ICC Statute',

The reference point for the drafting of the Statute was usually 'customary international law', with particular attention to the case law of the *ad hoc* tribunals. To that extent, much of the exercise was one of codification. But, in the area of punishment, it seems appropriate to speak of progressive development rather than mere codification. After all, in the first great experiment in international justice, at Nuremberg and Tokyo, the maximum available penalty was death. In the late 1940s, capital punishment was imposed with unhesitating enthusiasm. There is in fact some old precedent for the notion that international law has recognized the death penalty as a maximum sentence in the case of war crimes.[2] As for the *ad hoc* tribunals for the former Yugoslavia and Rwanda, they are entitled to impose life imprisonment, but without any statutory qualification as to the appropriate circumstances. In several cases, the Rwanda Tribunal has sentenced offenders to life terms, noting that, had the offenders been judged in the corresponding domestic courts, the sentence would have been one of death.[3] The Rome Statute allows for a maximum sentence of life imprisonment, but subjects this to a limitation, namely, that it be 'justified by the extreme gravity of the crime and the individual circumstances of the convicted person'.[4] It constitutes, therefore, from the standpoint of public international law, the most advanced and progressive text on the subject of sentencing.

The great Italian penal reformer of the eighteenth century, Cesare Beccaria, said that 'punishment should not be harsh, but must be inevitable'.[5] According to the International Criminal Tribunal for the former Yugoslavia:

> It is the infallibility of punishment, rather than the severity of the sanction, which is the tool for retribution, stigmatization and deterrence. This is particularly the case for the International Tribunal; penalties are made

in Flavia Lattanzi and William A. Schabas, eds., *Essays on the Rome Statute of the International Criminal Court*, Rome: Editrice il Sirente, 2000, pp. 311–38.

[2] On sentencing for international crimes, see William A. Schabas, 'War Crimes, Crimes Against Humanity and the Death Penalty', (1997) 60 *Albany Law Journal* 736; William A. Schabas, 'International Sentencing: From Leipzig (1923) to Arusha (1996)', in M. Cherif Bassiouni, ed., *International Criminal Law*, 3rd edn, vol. III, Leiden: Martinus Nijhoff, 2008, pp. 613–34.

[3] *Serushago* (ICTR-98-39-S), Sentence, 2 February 1999, para. 17; *Kayishema and Ruzindana* (ICTR-95-1-T), Judgment, 21 May 1999, para. 6.

[4] Rome Statute of the International Criminal Court, (2002) 2187 UNTS 90, Art. 77(1).

[5] Cited in *Furundžija* (IT-95-17/1-T), Judgment, 10 December 1998, (1999) 38 ILM 317, para. 290.

more onerous by its international stature, moral authority and impact upon world public opinion, and this punitive effect must be borne in mind when assessing the suitable length of sentence.[6]

Yet the Rome Statute has virtually nothing to say about the purposes of sentencing, as if this question is so obvious as to require no comment or direction. The only real reference is in the preamble, which declares that putting an end to impunity for serious international crimes will 'contribute to the prevention of such crimes'.[7] But recognizing that the Court has a deterrent effect is not entirely the same as the suggestion that sentencing policy as such is a genuine deterrent.

There has been some comment from the *ad hoc* tribunals on the purposes of international sentencing. In the *Tadić* sentence, Judge McDonald said that 'retribution and deterrence serve as primary purposes of sentence'.[8] According to the International Criminal Tribunal for Rwanda:

> It is clear that the penalties imposed on accused persons found guilty by the Tribunal must be directed, on the one hand, at retribution of the said accused, who must see their crimes punished, and over and above that, on the other hand, at deterrence, namely to dissuade for good, others who may be tempted in the future to perpetrate such atrocities by showing them that the international community shall not tolerate the serious violations of international humanitarian law and human rights.[9]

Some pronouncements have taken a broader approach. In one sentencing decision, the International Criminal Tribunal for the former Yugoslavia said that the purposes of criminal law sanctions 'include such aims as just punishment, deterrence, incapacitation of the dangerous and rehabilitation'.[10] In another, it noted that retribution was 'an inheritance of the primitive theory of revenge', adding that it was

---

[6] *Ibid.*

[7] Tuiloma Neroni Slade and Roger S. Clark, 'Preamble and Final Clauses', in Lee, *The International Criminal Court*, pp. 421–50 at p. 427.

[8] *Tadić* (IT-94-1-S), Sentencing Judgment, 14 July 1997. See also *Delalić et al.* (IT-96-21-T), Judgment, 16 November 1998, (1999) 38 ILM 57, para. 1235; *Erdemović* (IT-96-22-T), Sentencing Judgment, 29 November 1996, para. 64; *Kupreškić et al.* (IT-96-16-T), Judgment, 14 January 2000, para. 838.

[9] *Rutaganda* (ICTR-96-3), Judgment and Sentence, 6 December 1999. See also *Serushago* (ICTR-98-39-S), Sentence, 2 February 1999, para. 20.

[10] *Tadić* (IT-94-1-T), Sentencing Judgment, 14 July 1997, para. 61. See also *Erdemović* (IT-96-22-T), Sentencing Judgment, 29 November 1996, paras. 58 and 60.

at cross-purposes with the stated goal of international justice which is reconciliation:

> A consideration of retribution as the only factor in sentencing is likely to be counter-productive and disruptive of the entire purpose of the Security Council, which is the restoration and maintenance of peace in the territory of the former Yugoslavia. Retributive punishment by itself does not bring justice.[11]

The Appeals Chamber of the International Criminal Tribunal for the former Yugoslavia has said that, while it accepted 'the general importance of deterrence as a consideration in sentencing for international crimes', it should 'not be accorded undue prominence in the overall assessment of the sentences to be imposed on persons convicted by the International Tribunal'.[12] According to the Appeals Chamber, '[a]n equally important factor is retribution. This is not to be understood as fulfilling a desire for revenge but as duly expressing the outrage of the international community at these crimes.'[13] Thus, said the Appeals Chamber, 'a sentence of the International Tribunal should make plain the condemnation of the international community' and show 'that the international community was not ready to tolerate serious violations of international humanitarian law and human rights'.[14]

The debate about capital punishment threatened to undo the Rome Conference. Unlike many other difficult issues, which had been widely debated and, in some cases, resolved during the Preparatory Committee sessions, the question of the death penalty had been studiously avoided throughout the pre-Rome process. At the December 1997 session of the Preparatory Committee, Norwegian diplomat Rolf Einar Fife, who directed the negotiations on sentencing, simply refused to entertain debate on the matter, saying this would be addressed at Rome. Capital punishment might not have been such an issue were it not for sharp debates that took place in another forum, the United Nations Commission on Human Rights. Beginning in 1997, progressive States

---

[11] *Delalić et al.* (IT-96-21-T), Judgment, 16 November 1998, para. 1231.

[12] *Tadić* (IT-94-1-A and IT-94-1-A*bis*), Judgment in Sentencing Appeals, 26 January 2000, para. 48. Also *Aleksovski* (IT-95-14/1-A), Judgment, 24 March 2000, para. 185; *Delalić et al.* (IT-96-21-A), Judgment, 20 February 2001, para. 801; *Todorović* (Case IT-95-9/1-S), Sentencing Judgment, 31 July 2001, paras. 29–30; *Krnojelac* (IT-97-25-T), Judgment, 15 March 2002, para. 508. See also *Kunarac et al.* (IT-96-23-T and IT-96-23/1-T), Judgment, 22 February 2001, paras. 840–1.

[13] *Aleksovski* (IT-95-14/1-A), Judgment, 24 March 2000, para. 185.

[14] *Ibid.*, references omitted.

had pushed through resolutions on abolition of the death penalty. A particularly difficult exchange took place in March and April 1998 and, although the abolitionists won the day, it appears that a handful of retentionist States decided that they would counterattack.[15]

The campaign was led by a persistent group of Arab and Islamic States, together with English-speaking Caribbean States, and a few others such as Singapore, Rwanda, Ethiopia and Nigeria. The Rome negotiations were a perfect occasion for them to attempt to promote their position, because adoption of the Statute would require consensus. A small but well-organized minority searching for a degree of recognition of the legitimacy of capital punishment was in a position to extort concessions, and to an extent they were successful. Desperate to resolve the issue and ensure support for the draft Statute as a whole, the majority of delegates agreed to include a new Article stating that the penalty provisions in the Statute are without prejudice to domestic criminal law sanctions,[16] as well as to authorize a declaration by the President at the conclusion of the Conference pandering to the sensitivity of the death penalty States on the issue.[17] Nevertheless, the exclusion of the death penalty from the Rome Statute can be nothing but an important benchmark in an unquestionable trend towards universal abolition of capital punishment.[18] It also provides a useful argument against Islamic fundamentalists who argue that the death penalty is an imperative in their own justice systems. Yet they ultimately agreed to a legal regime without the

---

[15] CHR Res. 1998/8. See Ilias Bantekas and Peter Hodgkinson, 'Capital Punishment at the United Nations: Recent Developments', (2000) 11 *Criminal Law Forum* 23.

[16] Rome Statute, Art. 80.

[17] UN Doc. A/CONF.183/SR.9, para. 53: 'The debate at this Conference on the issue of which penalties should be applied by the Court has shown that there is no international consensus on the inclusion or non-inclusion of the death penalty. However, in accordance with the principles of complementarity between the Court and national jurisdictions, national justice systems have the primary responsibility for investigating, prosecuting and punishing individuals, in accordance with their national laws, for crimes falling under the jurisdiction of the International Criminal Court. In this regard, the Court would clearly not be able to affect national policies in this field. It should be noted that not including the death penalty in the Statute would not in any way have a legal bearing on national legislations and practices with regard to the death penalty. Nor shall it be considered as influencing, in the development of customary international law or in any other way, the legality of penalties imposed by national systems for serious crimes.'

[18] 'The Question of the Death Penalty', UN Doc. E/CN.4/RES/2001/68; 'The Question of the Death Penalty', UN Doc. E/CN.4/RES/2005/59. See William A. Schabas, *The Abolition of the Death Penalty in International Law*, 3rd edn, Cambridge: Cambridge University Press, 2003.

death penalty. Several of them manifested this by voting in favour of the Statute, on 17 July 1998, and subsequently by signing it.

Available penalties

The basic sentencing provision in the Rome Statute declares that the Court may impose imprisonment 'for a specified number of years, which may not exceed a maximum of 30 years',[19] and that it may impose '[a] term of life imprisonment when justified by the extreme gravity of the crime and the individual circumstances of the convicted person'.[20] But there were widely varying views about life imprisonment at Rome. States favourable to the death penalty argued that life imprisonment was too timid a penalty, of course, and they used the lever of capital punishment in order to obtain as harsh a provision as possible for custodial sentences. Several European and Latin American States, on the other hand, were in principle opposed to life imprisonment, and at any event to its imposition without the possibility of parole or conditional release at some future date. In the debate, many States called life imprisonment a cruel, inhuman and degrading form of punishment, prohibited by international human rights norms.[21] The compromise was to allow life imprisonment, but with the proviso of mandatory parole review after a certain period of time, as well as the qualification that life imprisonment be imposed only 'when justified by the extreme gravity of the crime and the individual circumstances of the convicted person'. As a final gesture of respect for the feelings of the more liberal States, the report of the Working Group contained a footnote stating that '[s]ome delegations expressed concerns about an explicit reference to life imprisonment'.[22] The curious reference to 'extreme gravity of the crime' may seem out of place, since the Court is designed to try nothing but crimes of extreme gravity and, moreover, the most heinous offenders.[23] It must be viewed as a signal from the Rome Conference favourable to clemency in sentencing practice. The Rules of

---

[19] Rome Statute, Art. 77(1)(a).   [20] *Ibid.*, Art. 77(1)(b).

[21] Dirk Van Zyl Smit, 'Life Imprisonment as the Ultimate Penalty in International Law: A Human Rights Perspective', (1998) 9 *Criminal Law Forum* 1.

[22] *Ibid.*, p. 2, n. 2.

[23] During the drafting of the Rules of Procedure and Evidence, Spain proposed that life imprisonment be imposed only if one or more aggravating circumstance had been established and if there was a total absence of mitigating factors: Proposal Submitted by Spain on the Rules of Procedure and Evidence Relating to Part 7 of the Rome Statute of the International Criminal Court (Penalties), PCNICC/1999/WGRPE (7)/DP.2, p. 2, para. 7.

Procedure and Evidence declare that 'extreme gravity and the individual circumstances' are to be assessed with reference to 'the existence of one or more aggravating circumstances'.[24]

The Court is empowered to grant release after part of the sentence has been served. But this is not strictly speaking conditional release or parole, in the sense this has in most national legal systems, because the decision to free the prisoner is final and irreversible. Article 110 permits the Court to reduce the sentence if it finds that one or more of the following factors are present: the early and continuing willingness of the person to cooperate with the Court in its investigations and prosecutions; the voluntary assistance of the person in enabling the enforcement of the judgments and orders of the Court in other cases, and in particular providing assistance in locating assets subject to orders of fine, forfeiture or reparation which may be used for the benefit of victims; and other factors establishing a clear and significant change of circumstances sufficient to justify the reduction of sentence.

The Rome Statute also allows the Court to impose a fine, but only '[i]n addition to imprisonment',[25] and 'forfeiture of proceeds, property and assets derived directly or indirectly from that crime, without prejudice to the rights of bona fide third parties'.[26] There had been proposals to include forfeiture of 'instrumentalities' of crime as well as proceeds, but they were dropped. In the context of war crimes, 'instrumentalities' might include aircraft carriers and similar hardware, and this possibility seemed just a bit too awesome for any consensus to be reached!

In determining the sentence, the Court is to consider such mitigating and aggravating factors as the gravity of the crime and the individual circumstances of the offender.[27] The Statute also declares, in Article 27, that official capacity shall not, 'in and of itself, constitute a ground for reduction of sentence'. In reality, the fact that a convicted person held a senior government position will usually be an aggravating factor, as is confirmed by a number of sentencing rulings of the *ad hoc* tribunals.[28]

[24] Rules of Procedure and Evidence, ASP/1/3, pp. 10–107, Rule 145(3).
[25] Rome Statute, Art. 77(2)(a); Rules of Procedure and Evidence, Rule 146.
[26] Rome Statute, Art. 77(2)(b); Rules of Procedure and Evidence, Rules 147 and 218.
[27] Rome Statute, Art. 78(1).
[28] *Serushago* (ICTR-98-39-S), Sentencing, 2 February 1999, para. 28; *Kambanda* (ICTR-97-23-S), Judgment and Sentence, 4 September 1998, paras. 44 and 60; *Akayesu* (ICTR-96-4-T), Judgment, 2 September 1998, (1998) 37 ILM 1399, para. 36. ii; *Delalić et al.* (IT-96-21-T), Judgment, 16 November 1998, para. 1220; *Kayishema and Ruzindana* (ICTR-95-1-T), Judgment, 21 May 1999, para. 15; *Rutaganda* (ICTR-96-3), Judgment and Sentence, 6 December 1999; *Blaškić* (IT-95-14), Judgment, 3 March 2000, para. 788.

When a superior is being prosecuted on the basis of command responsibility, the level of culpability is closer to negligence than real intent and premeditation, and the Court will presumably temper justice with clemency. But 'calculated dereliction of an essential duty cannot operate as a factor in mitigation of criminal responsibility'.[29] In the past, international criminal law instruments dismissed the defence of superior orders, but said the fact that a person was acting under orders ought to be a mitigating factor in imposing sentence.[30] Although the Rome Statute, which authorizes a defence of superior orders in certain circumstances, is silent on its relevance to sentencing, the Rules suggest that most if not all unsuccessful defences, to the extent the grounds invoked have any resonance, will encourage a degree of mitigation.[31] The post-World War II tribunals accepted a wide range of mitigating factors, including superior orders, age, position in the military hierarchy, suffering of the victims, efforts by the defendant to reduce suffering, and duress.[32] The Rules of Procedure and Evidence list several mitigating and aggravating factors, including damage caused, harm to victims and their families, the nature of the unlawful behaviour and the means employed to execute the crime, the degree of participation, the degree of intent, the age, education and social and economic condition of the convicted person, conduct after the act, efforts to compensate victims, prior convictions for similar crimes, abuse of power and particular cruelty in the commission of the crime.[33]

The relevance of motive in terms of the actual elements of the crimes remains somewhat controversial. But, in the area of sentencing, there can be no doubt that it is germane. According to the International Criminal Tribunal for the former Yugoslavia:

> where the accused is found to have committed the offence charged with cold, calculated premeditation, suggestive of revenge against the individual victim or group to which the victim belongs, such circumstances

---

[29] *Delalić et al.* (IT-96-21-T), Judgment, 16 November 1998, para. 1250.

[30] Agreement for the Prosecution and Punishment of Major War Criminals of the European Axis, and Establishing the Charter of the International Military Tribunal (IMT), Annex, (1951) 82 UNTS 279, Art. 8; Statute of the International Criminal Tribunal for the former Yugoslavia, UN Doc. S/RES/827, Annex, Art. 7(4). See *Erdemović* (IT-96-22-T), Sentencing Judgment, 29 November 1996, paras. 21, 54 and 89–91; *Delalić et al.* (IT-96-21-T), Judgment, 16 November 1998, n. 1091.

[31] Rules of Procedure and Evidence, Rule 145(2)(a)(i).

[32] William A. Schabas, 'Sentencing and the International Tribunals: For a Human Rights Approach', (1997) 7 *Duke Journal of Comparative and International Law* 461.

[33] Rules of Procedure and Evidence, Rule 145(1)(c) and (2).

necessitate the imposition of aggravated punishment. On the other hand, if the accused is found to have committed the offence charged reluctantly and under the influence of group pressure and, in addition, demonstrated compassion towards the victim or the group to which the victim belongs, these are certainly mitigating factors which the Trial Chamber will take into consideration in the determination of the appropriate sentence.[34]

In imposing sentence of imprisonment, the International Criminal Court is to 'deduct the time, if any, previously spent in detention in accordance with an order of the Court. The Court may deduct any time otherwise spent in detention in connection with conduct underlying the crime.'[35] This seems only fair, although it was opposed by some delegations at the Rome Conference.

When sentence is pronounced for more than one offence, the Court must specify the sentence for each offence as well as a total period of imprisonment. The total period cannot be less than the highest individual sentence pronounced, nor may it exceed the total set out in Article 77(1)(b), that is, life imprisonment or a fixed term of thirty years. In effect, the Statute leaves to the judges of the Court the criteria to be applied in the imposition of multiple sentences. It imposes a ceiling, and from a practical standpoint in cases of the most serious crimes there will be little discretion to exercise, because individual offences will deserve the maximum available sentence.

Enforcement

The Court has no prison, and must rely upon States Parties for the enforcement of sentences of imprisonment.[36] States are to volunteer their services, indicating their own willingness to allow convicted prisoners to serve the sentence within their own prison institutions. The Statute explicitly refers to 'the principle that States Parties should share the responsibility for enforcing sentences of imprisonment, in accordance with principles of equitable distribution'.[37] Failing an offer from a State Party, the host State – the Netherlands – is saddled with this

---

[34] *Delalić et al.* (IT-96-21-T), Judgment, 16 November 1998, para. 1235.

[35] Rome Statute, Art. 78(2).

[36] Antonio Marchesi, 'The Enforcement of Sentences of the International Criminal Court', in Lattanzi and Schabas, *Essays on the Rome Statute*, pp. 427–46.

[37] Rome Statute, Art. 103(3)(a); Rules of Procedure and Evidence, Rule 201. See Trevor Pascal Chimimba, 'Establishing an Enforcement Regime', in Lee, *The International Criminal Court*, pp. 343–56 at pp. 348–50.

responsibility. A somewhat similar mechanism exists for the *ad hoc*
tribunals.[38] Within the Court, these issues are the responsibility of its
Enforcement Unit, which falls under the aegis of the Presidency.[39] The
2010 Review Conference adopted a Resolution entitled 'Strengthening the
Enforcement of Sentences' that confirmed 'that a sentence of imprisonment may be served in a prison facility made available in the designated
State through an international or regional organization, mechanism
or agency' and urged States 'to promote actively international cooperation at all levels, particularly at the regional and sub regional levels'.[40]
Originally, Norway had proposed a formal amendment to Article 103
recognizing the legitimacy of international or regional arrangements
enabling them to qualify for acceptance of sentenced persons, including
through receipt of voluntary financial contributions to upgrade prison
facilities and other assistance or supervision. One of the advantages that
it held out was facilitation of family visits.[41]

After sentencing an offender, the Court will designate the State where
the term is to be served,[42] and it may change this determination at
any time.[43] In choosing a State of detention, the Court must take into
account the views of the sentenced person, his or her nationality, and
'widely accepted international treaty standards governing the treatment of prisoners'. Furthermore, conditions of detention must be neither more nor less favourable than those available to prisoners convicted
of similar offences in the State where the sentence is being enforced.[44]
There can obviously be no question of sending a prisoner to a State with
prison conditions that do not meet international standards. However,
the reference to 'international treaty standards' is in fact rather vague,
and might be taken to exclude application of the rigorous and quite precise Standard Minimum Rules for the Treatment of Prisoners,[45] as these
are not a treaty but only a 'soft law' resolution of the United Nations
Economic and Social Council.

The Court's sentence is binding upon the State of enforcement, and
the latter is without any discretion whatsoever to modify it.[46] The Court

---

[38] David Tolbert, 'The International Tribunal for the Former Yugoslavia and the Enforcement of Sentences', (1998) 11 *Leiden Journal of International Law* 655.
[39] Regulations of the Court, Regulation 113.
[40] Strengthening the Enforcement of Sentences, RC/Res.3, paras. 2–3.
[41] 'Norway, Proposal of Amendment', UN Doc. C.N.713.2009.TREATIES-4.
[42] Rome Statute, Art. 103(1)(a).   [43] *Ibid.*, Art. 104.   [44] *Ibid.*, Art. 106(2).
[45] ECOSOC Res. 663C (XXIV); as amended, ECOSOC Res. 2076 (LXII). See Chimimba, 'Establishing an Enforcement Regime', p. 353.
[46] Rome Statute, Art. 105.

is required to review a sentence after two-thirds of the term have been served or, in the case of life imprisonment, after twenty-five years.[47] In deciding whether to shorten the term of imprisonment at this stage, the Court is to take into account the prisoner's willingness to cooperate with the Court, his or her assistance in enforcing an order of the Court such as in locating assets subject to fine, forfeiture or reparation, and any other factors 'establishing a clear and significant change of circumstances sufficient to justify the reduction of sentence'.[48]

When sentence is completed, if the prisoner is not a national of the State where the penalty is being enforced, he or she may be transferred to a State 'obliged to receive him or her', or to any other State that agrees.[49] It may well happen that such an individual is wanted elsewhere for criminal prosecution. The Statute bars prosecution for the same crimes, of course, according to the *ne bis in idem* principle.[50] But, where extradition is sought for other crimes, States may extradite a prisoner after release pursuant to their own laws and treaties. In this respect, however, the Statute imposes a rule of 'specialty' similar to that in effect in most bilateral extradition matters. The State where the sentence is served cannot prosecute or extradite for a crime committed prior to delivery of the prisoner for service of sentence, unless this has been authorized by the Court.[51] Thus, a prisoner could be prosecuted for a crime committed while serving the sentence, such as escaping lawful custody or assault on a prison guard.[52]

---

[47] *Ibid.*, Art. 110(3).
[48] *Ibid.*, Art. 110(4)(c); Rules of Procedure and Evidence, Rules 223–224.
[49] Rome Statute, Art. 107(1).
[50] *Ibid.*, Art. 20(2).
[51] *Ibid.*, Art. 108. The principle of complementarity would appear to impose, but indirectly, a rule of specialty on the Tribunal itself. It probably should not be able to prosecute for a crime for which surrender was not sought. But the International Criminal Tribunal for the former Yugoslavia has not considered itself bound by a rule of specialty: *Kovacevic* (IT-97-24-AR73), Decision Stating Reasons for Appeals Chamber's Order of 29 May 1998, 2 July 1998, para. 37.
[52] Escape is dealt with in Art. 111 of the Rome Statute.

10

Victims of crimes and their concerns

Victims have taken an increasingly prominent place in our contemporary system of international criminal law. There are several references to their role and their interests within the Rome Statute, including the right of victims to intervene in proceedings,[1] the establishment of a Victims and Witnesses Unit within the Registry,[2] and the recognition of the entitlement of victims to reparations.[3] The preamble to the Statute acknowledges that 'during this century millions of children, women and men have been victims of unimaginable atrocities that deeply shock the conscience of humanity'. In addition, the Rules of Procedure and Evidence express the following 'General principle': 'A Chamber in making any direction or order, and other organs of the Court in performing their functions under the Statute or the Rules, shall take into account the needs of all victims and witnesses in accordance with Article 68, in particular children, elderly persons, persons with disabilities and victims of sexual or gender violence.'[4]

If this seems self-evident to some, it is worth reflecting upon the varied and often quite insignificant roles given to victims in national systems of criminal justice. Some approaches, notably the 'civil law' or continental-type systems, enable victims to participate directly in proceedings (*partie civile*), and subsequently permit them to use issues adjudicated during the criminal trial so as to resolve matters that are fundamentally private in nature. To many French lawyers and legal academics, criminal or penal law falls within the rubric of *droit privé*, an assessment that common lawyers find utterly puzzling. Under the common law, criminal prosecution is seen as essentially a matter of public policy in which victims have a role that is marginal at the best

---

[1] Rome Statute of the International Criminal Court, (2002) 2187 UNTS 90, Arts. 15(3), 19(3) and 82(4).

[2] *Ibid.*, Arts. 43(6) and 68(4).   [3] *Ibid.*, Arts. 75, 79 and 110(4)(b).

[4] Rules of Procedure and Evidence, ASP/1/3, pp. 10–107, Rule 86.

of times.[5] Those on the 'defence side', in particular, are suspicious of efforts to promote victim participation, seeing this as a threat to distort further the purported 'equality of arms' balance said to exist between accused and accuser. Nevertheless, recent years have seen a softening of this resistance, perhaps a result of the growing popularity of restorative justice discourse.

It cannot be gainsaid that, until recently, international humanitarian law focused on the methods and materials of war, and had relatively little to say with respect to victims, at least to the extent that victims were considered to be 'innocent' civilian non-combatants (as contrasted with wounded soldiers or sailors, or prisoners of war). For example, the Regulations annexed to the fourth Hague Convention of 1907 do not use the term 'victims' at all. There are, perhaps, some indirect references, such as the preambular paragraph that declares the Convention's provisions to be 'inspired by the desire to diminish the evils of war, as far as military requirements permit', and that they are 'intended to serve as a general rule of conduct for the belligerents in their relations and in their relations with the inhabitants'.[6] It is really only with the 1949 Geneva Conventions that the victims of armed conflict start moving to the centre stage of international humanitarian law, adopted, as they were, by the Diplomatic Conference for the Establishment of International Conventions for the Protection of *Victims* of War. The 1977 Additional Protocols are even more explicit: the word 'victims' appears in the title.[7] And yet, even these instruments, although they address the situation of victims, fix the question within the general context of the interests of the State.

Victims did not fare particularly well in the initial efforts at prosecution before the international military tribunals at Nuremberg and Tokyo. Although today we may look upon the development of the concept of crimes against humanity as the supreme accomplishment of the Nuremberg Tribunal, at the time this category of crime, which focuses so appropriately on civilian victims, was relatively marginalized. The

---

[5] Christopher Muttukumaru, 'Reparation to Victims', in Roy S. Lee, ed., *The International Criminal Court, The Making of the Rome Statute, Issues, Negotiations, Results*, The Hague: Kluwer Law International, 1999, pp. 262–70 at pp. 263–4.

[6] Convention (IV) Respecting the Laws and Customs of War by Land, [1910] UKTS 9, Annex.

[7] Protocol Additional to the 1949 Geneva Conventions of 12 August 1949, and Relating to The Protection of Victims of International Armed Conflicts, (1979) 1125 UNTS 3; Protocol Additional to the 1949 Geneva Conventions and Relating to The Protection of Victims of Non-International Armed Conflicts, (1979) 1125 UNTS 609.

International Military Tribunal famously declared that aggression, not crimes against humanity, was the 'supreme international crime'.[8] Aggression was essentially a State-centred concept, holding one entity answerable for breaching its obligations to another. As for the victims of the Nazis prior to September 1939, before the Nazis were engaged in international armed conflict, their interests and sufferings were ultimately betrayed by the Nuremberg judgment.[9]

There is a reference to victims in the Security Council resolution establishing the International Criminal Tribunal for the former Yugoslavia, but it is hardly a mandate for them to play an active role in proceedings: 'the work of the International Tribunal shall be carried out without prejudice to the right of the victims to seek, through appropriate means, compensation for damages incurred as a result of violations of international humanitarian law'.[10] Nothing comparable can be found in the resolution establishing the International Criminal Tribunal for Rwanda.[11] And, in practice, their role in the work of the *ad hoc* tribunals has not been important.

Any real interest in the rights of victims that can be found in contemporary international criminal law comes from outside the international humanitarian law/international criminal law tradition. A victim-focused approach first developed within the distinct although related field of international human rights law. Victims have been entitled to participate in international human rights law mechanisms essentially since the system's early beginnings, in the late 1940s. After some initial hesitation about the authority of the United Nations to even consider individual petitions from victims of human rights,[12] the relevant bodies within the organization, more specifically the Commission on Human Rights (now the Human Rights Council) and the Sub-Commission on the Prevention of Discrimination and Protection of Minorities (now the Human Rights Council Advisory Committee), developed elaborate mechanisms in order

---

[8] *France et al.* v. *Goering et al.*, (1946) 22 IMT 203, p. 427.

[9] *Ibid.*: 'The Tribunal therefore cannot make a general declaration that the acts before 1939 were crimes against humanity within the meaning of the Charter, but from the beginning of the war in 1939 war crimes were committed on a vast scale, which were also crimes against humanity; and insofar as the inhumane acts charged in the Indictment, and committed after the beginning of the war, did not constitute war crimes, they were all committed in execution of, or in connection with, the aggressive war, and therefore constituted crimes against humanity.'

[10] UN Doc. S/RES/827 (1993), Annex. Security Council Resolution 808, which launched the process leading to establishment of the Tribunal, doesn't even use the word 'victim'.

[11] UN Doc. S/RES/955 (1994), Annex.   [12] UN Doc. E/259, Chapter V, §22.

to process the hundreds of thousands of communications received in Geneva and New York.[13] The right to a remedy for individual victims of human rights was recognized explicitly in both regional[14] and universal[15] human rights treaties.

By the 1980s, new instruments began to emerge that were aimed at enhancing the position of victims within the general protection of international human rights. In 1985, the Seventh United Nations Congress on the Prevention of Crime and the Treatment of Offenders adopted the 'Declaration of Basic Principles of Justice for Victims of Crime and Abuse of Power', a text that was subsequently endorsed by the United Nations General Assembly.[16] The Basic Principles recognize that victims should be treated with compassion and respect for their dignity, that they should have their right to access to justice and redress mechanisms fully respected, and that national funds for compensation to victims should be encouraged together with the expeditious development of appropriate rights and remedies. More or less in parallel, human rights treaty bodies and tribunals began establishing a body of jurisprudence approaching victim issues as 'horizontal' violations of human rights, and holding States responsible pursuant to their international treaty obligations even where there was no apparent link between the State and the perpetrator.[17]

This pioneering work was followed by efforts to develop more comprehensive guidelines on the right to remedy and reparation within the United Nations Sub-Commission and Commission, under the

---

[13] Nigel S. Rodley, 'United Nations Non-Treaty Procedures for Dealing with Human Rights Violations', in Hurst Hannum, ed., *Guide to International Human Rights Practice*, 2nd edn, Philadelphia: Pennsylvania University Press, 1992, p. 64; Marc J. Bossuyt, 'The Development of Special Procedures of the United Nations Commission on Human Rights', (1985) 6 *Human Rights Law Journal* 183.

[14] European Convention on Human Rights, (1955) 213 UNTS 221, Art. 13.

[15] International Covenant on Civil and Political Rights, (1976) 999 UNTS 171, Art. 2(3).

[16] GA Res. 40/34. Roger Clark, 'The 1985 United Nations Declaration of Basic Principles of Justice for Victims of Crime and Abuse of Power', in G. Alfredsson and A. Macalister-Smith, eds., *The Living Law of Nations*, Kehl, Strasbourg and Arlington: Engel, 1996, p. 355. See also the resolutions of the Economic and Social Council: 'Implementation of the Declaration of Basic Principles of Justice for Victims of Crime and Abuse of Power', ESC Res. 1989/57; 'Victims of Crime and Abuse of Power', ESC Res. 1990/22.

[17] Beginning with the Inter-American Court of Human Rights: *Velasquez Rodriguez* v. *Honduras*, 29 July 1988, Series C, No. 4. For the Human Rights Committee, see *Bautista de Arellana* v. *Colombia* (No. 563/1993), UN Doc. CCPR/C/55/D/563/1993, paras. 8.3 and 10; *Laureano* v. *Peru* (No. 540/1993), UN Doc. CCPR/C/56/D/540/1993, para. 10. For the European Court of Human Rights, see *Streletz, Kessler and Krenz* v. *Germany* (App. Nos. 34044/96, 35532/97 and 44801/98), 22 March 2001, para. 86.

leadership of two prominent human rights experts, Theo van Boven[18] and M. Cherif Bassiouni.[19] The basic principles that were proposed by Professors van Boven and Bassiouni include a duty on States to prosecute serious violations of human rights (flowing from the obligation to respect and ensure respect, which is codified in common Article 1 of the Geneva Conventions), the right of victims to a remedy and reparation, and the right to know the truth.

The attention given to the role and the rights of victims by the Rome Statute of the International Criminal Court, and by subsidiary instruments such as the Rules of Procedure and Evidence, is quite stunning when set aside the very secondary role they have been given historically by international criminal law and international humanitarian law. This is surely the result of the injection of human rights principles, derived from recent case law of the international treaty bodies and tribunals as well as the progressive development of law found in the van Boven and Bassiouni principles, and the work of bodies like the United Nations Congress on the Prevention of Crime and the Treatment of Offenders. The agenda was also promoted by certain specialized non-governmental organizations, like Redress, and by national delegations for whom a victim-based approach to criminal law could be derived from their own traditions, like France. But whether or not the International Criminal Court will actually serve the interests of victims in an effective and satisfactory way remains to be seen.

Other contemporary attempts at addressing impunity through criminal law measures must surely be a big disappointment if the standpoint of the victim becomes the benchmark of success. Few of the victims of serious violations of international humanitarian law in the former Yugoslavia or Rwanda can feel particularly satisfied with the

---

[18] Revised Set of Basic Principles and Guidelines on the Right to Reparation for Victims of Gross Violations of Human Rights and Humanitarian Law Prepared by Mr Theo van Boven Pursuant Sub-Commission Decision 1995/117, UN Doc. E/CN.4/Sub.2/1996/17; Note Prepared by the Former Special Rapporteur of the Sub-Commission, Mr Theo van Boven, in Accordance with Paragraph 2 of Sub-Commission Resolution 1996/28, UN Doc. E/CN.4/1997/104, Annex.

[19] The Right to Restitution, Compensation and Rehabilitation for Victims of Gross Violations of Human Rights and Fundamental Freedoms, Final Report of the Special Rapporteur, Mr M. Cherif Bassiouni, Submitted in Accordance with Commission Resolution 1999/33, UN Doc. E/CN.4/2000.62; Basic Principles and Guidelines on the Right to a Remedy and Reparation for Victims of Gross Violations of Human Rights and Serious Violations of International Humanitarian Law, UN Doc. A/RES/60/147.

modest output of two international tribunals established by the Security Council. To be fair, the *ad hoc* tribunals surely benefit the victims of crimes, particularly in their ability to clarify the historical truth,[20] one of the values that was stressed in the work of M. Cherif Bassiouni. They also stigmatize the perpetrators, fulfilling a denunciatory function. But there is no compensation or reparation, and rarely even an apology.[21] In a statement signed alongside her plea agreement, former Bosnian Serb leader Biljana Plavšić said that, by 'accepting responsibility and expressing her remorse fully and unconditionally, [she] hopes to offer some consolation to the innocent victims – Muslim, Croat and Serb – of the war in Bosnia and Herzegovina'.[22] The defence argued that her acknowledgment of the crimes and her personal accountability would contribute to 'rendering justice to victims'.[23] The Trial Chamber seemed to recognize that there was something to this, in sentencing her to eleven years' imprisonment, although it cautioned that 'undue leniency' could not 'fully reflect the horror of what occurred or the terrible impact on thousands of victims'.[24]

Victim participation in proceedings

One of the great innovations in the Rome Statute is the place it creates for victims to participate in the proceedings. The 'views and concerns' of witnesses may be presented at any stage of the proceedings. The Statute notes, as a limitation on this general principle, that it must be exercised in a manner which is not prejudicial to or inconsistent with the rights of the accused and a fair and impartial trial. Yet, at this early point in the judicial work of the Court, it is difficult to assess how much influence

---

[20] See, e.g., the discussion entitled 'Genocide in Rwanda in 1994?', in *Akayesu* (Case No. ICTR-96-4-T), Judgment, 2 September 1998, paras. 111–28.

[21] Former Rwandan Prime Minister Jean Kambanda, who pleaded guilty to genocide and crimes against humanity, 'offered no explanation for his voluntary participation in the genocide; nor has he expressed contrition, regret or sympathy for the victims in Rwanda, even when given the opportunity to do so by the Chamber': *Kambanda* (ICTR 97–23-S), Judgment and Sentence, para. 51.

[22] *Plavšić* (IT-00-39 and 40/1), Sentencing Judgment, 27 February 2003, para. 19; also *ibid.*, paras. 71–2.

[23] *Ibid.*, para. 68.

[24] *Ibid.*, para. 132. For examples of sentencing judgments that address the interests of victims, see also *Krstić* (Case No. IT-98-33-T), Judgment, 2 August 2001, para. 702; *Erdemović* (Case No. IT-96-22-A), Sentencing Appeal, 7 October 1997, para. 15; *Kayishema and Ruzindana* (Case No. ICTR-95-1-T), Sentence, 21 May 1999, para. 26; *Kordić et al.* (IT-95-14/2-T), Judgment, 26 February 2001, para. 852.

victims may really have. Nevertheless, the procedural issues relating to their participation have proven to be far more time-consuming and costly than most had anticipated.

The scale of participation has grown dramatically. In October 2008, the Registry reported that a total of 960 victims had applied to participate in judicial proceedings, in one or other of the situations or cases, and that this had been authorized by the Court for 126 of them.[25] In the *Lubanga* trial, ninety-three victims were given leave to participate.[26] In *Katanga et al.*, fifty-seven victims were participating through legal representatives, of whom nineteen were deemed indigent and received financial assistance from the Court.[27] This all began when Pre-Trial Chamber I, in the *Situation in the Democratic Republic of the Congo*, authorized representatives of victim representatives at the investigation stage, even before the Prosecutor had identified a suspect or accused person.[28] It was fairly evident that the Chamber, presided over by a French judge, Claude Jorda, was promoting a procedural model derived from the continental legal system whereby victims participate actively as parties in the criminal trial. Leave to appeal was denied,[29] and it has become clear that Judge Jorda's view, providing generous access of victims to the proceedings of the Court, is widely shared by other judges.

A definition of victims, which is of general application but which is especially relevant for the purposes of participation, is provided in Rule 85 of the Rules of Procedure and Evidence:

> For the purposes of the Statute and the Rules of Procedure and Evidence:
> (a) 'Victims' means natural persons who have suffered harm as a result of the commission of any crime within the jurisdiction of the Court;
> (b) Victims may include organizations or institutions that have sustained direct harm to any of their property, which is dedicated to religion,

[25] Report on the Activities of the Court, ASP/7/25, para. 8. Later in the same document, the Registry states that 168 victims participated in the *Situation in the Democratic Republic of the Congo* alone: *ibid.*, para. 26. Approximately twenty seem to be participating in the *Situation in Uganda*: *ibid.*, paras. 28–9. Eleven are participating in the *Situation in Darfur, Sudan*: *ibid.*, para. 37.

[26] *Lubanga* (ICC-01/04–01/06), Transcript of 8 April 2009, p. 14.

[27] Report on the Activities of the Court, ASP/7/25, para. 21.

[28] *Situation in the Democratic Republic of the Congo* (ICC-01/04), Decision on the Applications for Participation in the Proceedings of VPRS 1, VPRS 2, VPRS 3, VPRS 4, VPRS 5 and VPRS 6, 17 January 2006.

[29] *Situation in the Democratic Republic of the Congo* (ICC-01/04), Decision on the Prosecution's Application for Leave to Appeal the Chamber's Decision of 17 January 2006 on the Applications for Participation in the Proceedings of VPRS 1, VPRS 2, VPRS 3, VPRS 4, VPRS 5 and VPRS 6, 31 March 2006.

education, art or science or charitable purposes, and to their historic monuments, hospitals and other places and objects for humanitarian purposes.[30]

In the first ruling applying these provisions, a Pre-Trial Chamber held that 'the status of victim will be accorded to applicants who seem to meet the definition of victims set out in Rule 85 of the Rules of Procedure and Evidence'.[31]

Invoking Article 21(3) of the Statute, Trial Chamber I defined victims with reference to the Principles and Guidelines on the Right to a Remedy and Reparation for Victims of Gross Violations of International Human Rights Law and Serious Violations of International Humanitarian Law.[32] It establishes:

> 8. For purposes of the present document, victims are persons who individually or collectively suffered harm, including physical or mental injury, emotional suffering, economic loss or substantial impairment of their fundamental rights, through acts or omissions that constitute gross violations of international human rights law, or serious violations of international humanitarian law. Where appropriate, and in accordance with domestic law, the term 'victim' also includes the immediate family or dependants of the direct victim and persons who have suffered harm in intervening to assist victims in distress or to prevent victimization.
>
> 9. A person shall be considered a victim regardless of whether the perpetrator of the violation is identified, apprehended, prosecuted, or convicted and regardless of the familial relationship between the perpetrator and the victim.

The Trial Chamber also referred to relevant provisions of the Convention on the Rights of the Child establishing that 'the best interests of the child' are the 'primary consideration' in all matters concerning children. It referred to Article 12(2) of the Convention which declares that children are to be given the opportunity to be heard in judicial and administrative proceedings.[33] Judge Blattmann was more cautious, arguing that a cross-reference to the United Nations Declaration of 1985 had been specifically considered during the drafting of the Rome Statute and

---

[30] Rules of Evidence and Procedure, Rule 85.

[31] *Situation in the Democratic Republic of the Congo* (ICC-01/04), Decision on the Applications for Participation in the Proceedings of VPRS 1, VPRS 2, VPRS 3, VPRS 4, VPRS 5 and VPRS 6, 17 January 2006, para. 66.

[32] UN Doc. A/60/147, cited in *Lubanga* (ICC-01/04–01/06), Decision on Victims' Participation, 18 January 2008, para. 35.

[33] Convention on the Rights of the Child, (1990) 1577 UNTS 3, cited in *Lubanga* (ICC-01/04–01/06), Decision on Victims' Participation, 18 January 2008, paras. 36–7.

had been left out in the final version.[34] The Appeals Chamber held that the Trial Chamber had made no mistake in relying upon the Principles and Guidelines for the purpose of 'guidance'.[35]

According to Pre-Trial Chamber I, four criteria are to be applied in recognition of the status of victim: 'the victim must be a natural person; that he/she has suffered harm; that the crime from which the harm resulted must fall within the jurisdiction of the Court and that there must be a causal link between the crime and the harm'.[36] In *Situation in Uganda*, Pre-Trial Chamber II said harm would be considered to be the result of an incident when 'the spatial and temporal circumstances surrounding the appearance of the harm and the occurrence of the incident seem to overlap, or at least to be compatible and not clearly inconsistent'.[37]

Victim participation must be related to the charges in the case, according to the Appeals Chamber.[38] The Appeals Chamber reversed a holding by Trial Chamber I, Judge Blattmann dissenting, that interpreted Rule 85 as applying to the harm having resulted from the commission of a 'crime within the jurisdiction of the Court', even if this was not contemplated by the charges themselves.[39] Judge Blattmann noted that Article

---

[34] *Lubanga* (ICC-01/04–01/06), Separate and Dissenting Opinion of Judge René Blattmann, 18 January 2008, paras. 4–5. The Preparatory Committee Final Draft contained the following (at p. 109): '[7. The rules of procedure shall include provisions giving effect to the United Nations Declaration of Basic Principles of Justice for Victims of Crime and Abuse of Power.]'

[35] *Lubanga* (ICC-01/04–01/06 OA 9 OA 10), Judgment on the Appeals of the Prosecutor and the Defence Against Trial Chamber I's Decision on Victims' Participation of 18 January 2008, 11 July 2008, para. 33.

[36] *Lubanga* (ICC-01/04–01/06), Decision on the Applications for Participation in the Proceedings of a/0001/06, a/0002/06 and a/0003/06 in the Case of Thomas Lubanga Dyilo and of the Investigation in the Democratic Republic of the Congo, 18 July 2006, p. 7. Also *Lubanga* (ICC-01/04–01/06), Decision on the Applications for Participation in the Proceedings Submitted by VPRS 1 to VPRS 6 in the Case of Thomas Lubanga Dyilo, 29 June 2006, pp. 6–8; *Lubanga* (ICC-01/04–01/06), Decision on the Applications for Participation in the Proceedings of a/0001/06, a/0002/06 and a/0003/06 in the case of the Prosecutor v. Thomas Lubanga Dyilo and of the investigation in the Democratic Republic of the Congo, 28 July 2006, pp. 8–9.

[37] *Situation in Uganda* (ICC-02/04), Decision on Victims' Applications for Participation a/0010/06, a/0064/06 to a/0070/06, a/0081/06 to a/0104/06 and a/0111/06 to a/0127/06, ICC-02/04-101, 10 August 2007, paras. 12–14.

[38] *Lubanga* (ICC-01/04–01/06 OA 9 OA 10), Judgment on the Appeals of the Prosecutor and the Defence Against Trial Chamber I's Decision on Victims' Participation of 18 January 2008, 11 July 2008, para. 66.

[39] *Lubanga* (ICC-01/04–01/06), Decision on Victims' Participation, 18 January 2008, para. 93.

19(1) required the Court to establish it has jurisdiction over a *case*. He said he completely disagreed with the majority, which considered that the *Statute* did not limit the Chamber's jurisdiction to the crimes attributed to the accused where victim participation was concerned.[40]

The 'personal interests' of victims must be affected for them to be allowed to participate. For Judge Pikis of the Appeals Chamber, 'personal interests' means the personal interests of 'victims who suffered harm from the crime or crimes, the subject matter of investigation, confirmation, the trial, appeal, revision ... and reduction of sentence'.[41] Judge Song of the Appeals Chamber has written that the personal interests of victims include the right to receive reparations and 'to receive justice'.[42] This may extend to procedural matters as they are important to the outcome of substantive questions.

The two paragraphs of Rule 85 of the Rules of Procedure and Evidence distinguish between natural persons, for whom there must be 'harm', and organizations and institutions, which must have suffered 'direct harm'. Applying a purposive interpretation, Trial Chamber I held that people can be either direct or indirect victims of a crime within the jurisdiction of the Court.[43] Referring to Principle 8 of the Principles and Guidelines on the Right to a Remedy and Reparation for Victims of Gross Violations of International Human Rights Law and Serious Violations of International Humanitarian Law, the Trial Chamber said 'a victim may suffer, either individually or collectively, from harm in a variety of different ways such as physical or mental injury, emotional suffering, economic loss or substantial impairment of his or her fundamental rights'.[44] According to the Appeals Chamber:

> the harm suffered by a natural person is harm to that person, i.e. personal harm. Material, physical, and psychological harm are all forms of harm that fall within the rule if they are suffered personally by the victim. Harm suffered by one victim as a result of the commission of a crime within the jurisdiction of the Court can give rise to harm suffered by other victims. This is evident for instance, when there is a close personal relationship

---

[40] *Lubanga* (ICC-01/04–01/06), Separate and Dissenting Opinion of Judge René Blattmann, 18 January 2008, para. 7.

[41] *Lubanga* (ICC-01/04–01/06 OA 8), Separate Opinion of Judge Georghios M. Pikis, 13 June 2007, para. 13.

[42] *Lubanga* (ICC-01/04–01/06 OA 8), Separate Opinion of Judge Sang-Hyun Song, 13 June 2007, para. 10.

[43] *Lubanga* (ICC-01/04–01/06), Decision on Victims' Participation, 18 January 2008, para. 91.

[44] *Ibid.*, para. 92.

between the victims such as the relationship between a child soldier and the parents of that child. The recruitment of a child soldier may result in personal suffering of both the child concerned and the parents of that child. It is in this sense that the Appeals Chamber understands the Trial Chamber's statement that 'people can be the direct or indirect victims of a crime within the jurisdiction of the Court'. The issue for determination is whether the harm suffered is personal to the individual. If it is, it can attach to both direct and indirect victims. Whether or not a person has suffered harm as the result of a crime within the jurisdiction of the Court and is therefore a victim before the Court would have to be determined in light of the particular circumstances.[45]

Although the Appeals Chamber upheld the majority of the Trial Chamber in *Lubanga*, it said it ought to have spelled out the requirement that harm be personal, even if it need not be direct.[46]

The term 'indirect victims' has been used to designate persons who suffer harm as a result of harm perpetrated against direct victims.[47] Examples of indirect victimhood include parents of victims; persons who suffer harm while intervening to assist victims, and crimes generally directed at the civilian population.[48] However, the concept does not extend to persons who suffer harm as a result of the conduct of other victims, such as those who are victimized by child soldiers.[49]

Elaborate provision is made in the Rules of Procedure and Evidence to inform victims of various stages of the proceedings.[50] Victims must apply in writing for leave to present their 'views and concerns'.[51] The application may be contested by the Prosecutor and the defence, and may be rejected by the Chamber, even on its own initiative.[52] An application for participation may be made by a person acting with the consent of the victim. In the case of a child victim or one who is disabled, it may also be made by 'a person acting on behalf of a victim', apparently even without the victim's consent.[53] The Trial Chamber in *Lubanga* explained that 'the person acting on behalf of a victim does not have to be a relative or a legal guardian because, within the Rules, the "person acting" is

---

[45] *Lubanga* (ICC-01/04–01/06 OA 9 OA 10), Judgment on the Appeals of the Prosecutor and the Defence Against Trial Chamber I's Decision on Victims' Participation of 18 January 2008, 11 July 2008, para. 32. Judge Pikis dissenting: *Lubanga* (ICC-01/04–01/06), Partly Dissenting Opinion of Judge G. M. Pikis, 11 July 2008, para. 3.

[46] *Ibid.*, paras. 38–9.   [47] *Ibid.*, para. 32.

[48] *Lubanga* (ICC-01/04–01/06), Redacted Version of 'Decision on "indirect victims"', 8 April 2009, paras. 50–1.

[49] *Ibid.*, para. 52.   [50] Rules of Procedure and Evidence, Rule 92.

[51] *Ibid.*, Rule 89(1).   [52] *Ibid.*, Rule 89(2).   [53] *Ibid.*, Rule 89 (3).

undefined and unrestricted'.[54] Issues concerning representation in such matters have rather elaborate solutions within legal systems, but the Rules of Procedure and Evidence leave the determination of any difficulties, should they arise, to the judges. Where several applications have been filed, the Chamber may consider them 'so as to ensure the effectiveness of the proceedings and may issue one decision'.[55]

The right of victims to participate in proceedings will be based, initially, upon demonstration of a *prima facie* basis.[56] Victims may prove their status using a wide range of documents.[57] Because of the nature and circumstances of conflicts, victims may not always have access to adequate documentation in order to prove their identity. Where no documents are available, a statement signed by two credible witnesses has been held to be sufficient.[58]

Victims may apply to participate either directly or through a person acting with their consent, 'or a person acting on behalf of a victim, in the case of a victim who is a child or, when necessary, a victim who is disabled'.[59] Although victims are free to choose their legal representatives,[60] a Chamber may request victims or particular groups of victims to choose a common representative. The Registry is given a special role in facilitating this process.[61] Determination of when common legal representation is necessary in order to ensure the effectiveness of the proceedings is to be made by the Chamber.[62] Should the victims fail to choose a common representative within a time limit determined by the Chamber, it may request the Registrar to choose one or more common legal representatives.[63]

---

[54] *Lubanga* (ICC-01/04–01/06), Order Issuing Public Redacted Annexes to the Decisions on the Applications by Victims to Participate in the Proceedings of 15 and 18 December 2008, Annex A, 8 May 2009, p. 5.
[55] Rules of Procedure and Evidence, Rule 89(3).
[56] *Lubanga* (ICC-01/04–01/06), Decision on Victims' Participation, 18 January 2008, para. 99.
[57] *Situation in the Democratic Republic of the Congo* (ICC-01/04), Decision on the Requests of the Legal Representatives of Applicants on Application Process for Victims' Participation and Legal Representation, 17 August 2007, paras. 14–15.
[58] *Lubanga* (ICC-01/04–01/06), Decision on Victims' Participation, 18 January 2008, para. 86; leave to appeal denied: *Lubanga* (ICC-01/04–01/06), Decision on the Defence and Prosecution Requests for Leave to Appeal the Decision on Victims' Participation of 18 January 2008, 26 February 2008, para. 22.
[59] Rules of Procedure and Evidence, Rule 89(3).
[60] *Ibid.*, Rule 90(1).   [61] *Ibid.*, Rule 90(2).
[62] *Lubanga* (ICC-01/04–01/06), Decision on Victims' Participation, 18 January 2008, para. 123.
[63] *Ibid.*, Rule 90(3).

Victims who lack the means to pay for legal representatives may receive assistance from the Registry.[64] In practice, the legal representatives of victims are without exception paid for by the Court. Concern has been expressed by the Committee on Budget and Finance about 'the need to balance meaningful participation for victims and the cost implications of such participation'.[65]

In selecting common legal representatives, the Chamber and the Registry are to take 'all reasonable steps to ensure that ... the distinct interests of the victims ... are represented and that any conflict of interest is avoided'.[66] According to Trial Chamber I:

> it is necessary to apply a flexible approach to the question of the appropriateness of common legal representation, and the appointment of any particular common legal representative. As a result, detailed criteria cannot be laid down in advance. However, the Chamber envisages that considerations such as the language spoken by the victims (and any proposed representative), links between them provided by time, place and circumstance and the specific crimes of which they are alleged to be victims will all be potentially of relevance. In order to assist it in the consideration of this issue, the Trial Chamber directs the Victims Participation and Representation Section to make recommendations on common legal representation in its reports to the Chamber.[67]

The Regulations of the Court specify that, in choosing a common representative for victims, 'consideration should be given to the views of the victims, and the need to respect local traditions and to assist specific groups of victims'.[68]

Victims may participate in proceedings from the earliest stages, to the extent that their personal interests are affected. They may even intervene at the 'situation' stage, once the Prosecutor has decided to proceed with an investigation but before specific accused persons have been identified and arrest warrants or summonses to appear have been issued.[69]

---

[64] *Ibid.*, Rule 90(5).

[65] 'Report of the Committee on Budget and Finance on the Work of Its Twelfth Session, April 2009', ASP/8/5, para. 81.

[66] *Ibid.*, Rule 90(4).

[67] *Lubanga* (ICC-01/04–01/06), Decision on Victims' Participation, 18 January 2008, para. 124.

[68] Regulations of the Court, Regulation 79(2).

[69] *Situation in the Democratic Republic of the Congo* (ICC-01/04), Decision on the Applications for Participation in the Proceedings of VPRS 1, VPRS 2, VPRS 3, VPRS 4, VPRS 5 and VPRS 6, 17 January 2006, paras. 23–76; *Situation in Darfur, Sudan* (ICC-02/05), Decision on the Requests of the OPCD on the Production of Relevant

Pursuant to Article 68(3), victims are entitled to present their 'views and concerns' where their personal interests are affected. The Rules of Procedure and Evidence explain that participation 'may include opening and closing statements'. Legal representatives of victims are entitled to attend and participate in hearings, unless the Chamber considers that this should be confined to written observations or submissions.[70] The Prosecutor and the defence may respond to any submissions by victims, whether written or oral.[71] Rule 91 contemplates the questioning of witnesses by legal representatives of victims, although without the same extent and freedom to which the Prosecutor of defence counsel would be entitled.[72] More leeway is given to victim representatives where the hearing concerns only reparations.[73] According to the Appeals Chamber, the right to question witnesses necessarily implies matters which bear upon the guilt or innocence of the accused person.

> To exemplify this position one may envisage the adduction of evidence irrelevant to or inadmissible with regard to identification of the harm suffered by the victim. The evidence may have a source lacking credibility or may not bear relevance to the identification of such harm. In some such situations, participating victims may challenge the admissibility or relevance of evidence to be adduced where its admission would affect their personal interests.[74]

The Statute and the Rules of Procedure and Evidence say nothing about whether victims can actually lead evidence before the Court.

Supporting Documentation Pursuant to Regulation 86(2)(e) of the Regulations of the Court and on the Disclosure of Exculpatory Materials by the Prosecutor, 3 December 2007, paras. 2–3; *Situation in the Democratic Republic of the Congo* (ICC-01/04), Decision on the Requests of the OPCD on the Production of Relevant Supporting Documentation Pursuant to Regulation 86(2)(e) of the Regulations of the Court and on the Disclosure of Exculpatory Materials by the Prosecutor, 7 December 2007, paras. 2–3; *Situation in Darfur, Sudan* (ICC-02/05), Decision on Request for Leave to Appeal the 'Decision on the Requests of the OPCD on the Production of Relevant Supporting Documentation Pursuant to Regulation 86(2)(e) of the Regulations of the Court and on the Disclosure of Exculpatory Materials by the Prosecutor', 23 January 2008, p. 5.

[70] Rules of Procedure and Evidence, Rule 91(1), (2). See Regulations of the Court, Regulations 79–85.

[71] Rules of Procedure and Evidence, Rule 91(2).

[72] *Ibid.*, Rule 91(3).   [73] *Ibid.*, Rule 91(4).

[74] *Lubanga* (ICC-01/04–01/06 OA 9 OA 10), Judgment on the Appeals of the Prosecutor and the Defence Against Trial Chamber I's Decision on Victims' Participation of 18 January 2008, 11 July 2008, para. 102; *Lubanga* (ICC-01/04–01/06 OA 9 OA 10), Partly Dissenting Opinion of Judge G. M. Pikis, 11 July 2008; *Lubanga* (ICC-01/04–01/06 OA 9 OA 10), Partly Dissenting Opinion of Judge Philippe Kirsch, 23 July 2008.

During drafting of the Statute, a concrete proposal in this sense that had been included in the Preparatory Committee Final Draft, allowing victims to present evidence 'to establish the basis of criminal responsibility as a foundation for their right to pursue civil compensation',[75] was subsequently eliminated.[76] The Working Group at the Preparatory Commission was unable to agree on any more precise provision on this point.[77] The vague texts that were eventually adopted have effectively left the judges to decide upon the extent of victim participation in the hearing or trial itself.[78] Confirming a ruling of a Trial Chamber,[79] the Appeals Chamber decided, Judges Pikis and Kirsch dissenting, that victims may actually lead evidence pertaining to the guilt or innocence of the accused, and that they may challenge the admissibility or relevance of evidence presented by other parties.[80] Noting that Article 68(3) requires 'meaningful' participation by victims, the Appeals Chamber said:

> Evidence to be tendered at trial which does not pertain to the guilt or innocence of the accused would most likely be considered inadmissible and irrelevant. If victims were generally and under all circumstances precluded from tendering evidence relating to the guilt or innocence of the accused and from challenging the admissibility or relevance of evidence, their right to participate in the trial would potentially become ineffectual.[81]

Normally, the defence is entitled to disclosure of evidence well before trial, so as not to be taken by surprise. In specific cases, such as submission of an alibi or other special defence, the Prosecutor is also entitled to notice and a degree of disclosure from the defence. Given the silence of the Statute and the Rules on submission of evidence by the representatives of victims, regulation of disclosure in such cases is a matter to be determined by the judges on a case-by-case basis. The Appeals Chamber

---

[75] Preparatory Committee Final Draft, p. 109.

[76] Canada: Proposal Regarding Article 68, UN Doc. A/CONF.183/C.1/WGPM/L 58/ Rev.1; Report of the Working Group on Procedural Matters, UN Doc. A/CONF.183/C.1/ WGPM/L.2/Add.6.

[77] Gilbert Bitti and Håken Friman, 'Participation of Victims in the Proceedings', in Lee, *Elements and Rules*, pp. 456–74 at p. 461.

[78] Rules of Procedure and Evidence, Rule 89.

[79] *Lubanga* (ICC-01/04–01/06), Decision on Victims' Participation, 18 January 2008, para. 108.

[80] *Lubanga* (ICC-01/04–01/06 OA 9 OA 10), Judgment on the Appeals of the Prosecutor and the Defence Against Trial Chamber I's Decision on Victims' Participation of 18 January 2008, 11 July 2008, para. 94.

[81] *Ibid.*, para. 97.

said that, where a Trial Chamber decides that victims may present evidence, it can also rule on the modalities of disclosure.[82] Judge Kirsch, who dissented from the Appeals Chamber, said that the absence of disclosure obligations upon victims shows it was not envisaged that victims would either disclose or lead evidence germane to guilt or innocence.[83] As Judge Pikis pointed out in his dissenting opinion:

> The proof or disproof of the charges is a matter affecting the adversaries. The victims have no say in the matter. Their interest is that justice should be done, coinciding with the interest of the world at large that the criminal process should run its course according to law, according to the norms of a fair trial ... It is not the victims' concern, a matter directly related to the reception of evidence, to either prove or disprove the charges.[84]

The Appeals Chamber made clear that strict conditions would attach to the introduction of evidence, and that it was not introducing 'an unfettered right'.[85] A corollary of the right to produce evidence is the possibility of objecting to its production by parties to the proceedings (and perhaps by other victims).[86] The Appeals Chamber said that a Trial Chamber may take a decision on admissibility of evidence after hearing submissions from victims, thereby implicitly acknowledging the right of victims to object to the admissibility of evidence.[87]

Victim participation involves access to various aspects of the dossier, including confidential filings. Trial Chamber I held that Rule 131(2) provides participating victims with 'the right to consult the record of the proceedings, including the index, subject to any restrictions concerning confidentiality and the protection of national security information'.[88] The rationale for the Chamber's approach is that participating victims should be allowed access to material other than that which is publicly

---

[82] *Ibid.*, para. 100.

[83] *Lubanga* (ICC-01/04–01/06 OA 9 OA 10), Partly Dissenting Opinion of Judge Philippe Kirsch, 23 July 2008, para. 16.

[84] *Lubanga* (ICC-01/04–01/06 OA 9 OA 10), Partly Dissenting Opinion of Judge G. M. Pikis, 11 July 2008, para. 19.

[85] *Lubanga* (ICC-01/04–01/06 OA 9 OA 10), Judgment on the Appeals of the Prosecutor and the Defence Against Trial Chamber I's Decision on Victims' Participation of 18 January 2008, 11 July 2008, para. 96.

[86] In accordance with the criteria set out in the Rome Statute, Art. 69(4).

[87] *Lubanga* (ICC-01/04–01/06 OA 9 OA 10), Judgment on the Appeals of the Prosecutor and the Defence Against Trial Chamber I's Decision on Victims' Participation of 18 January 2008, 11 July 2008, para. 101.

[88] *Lubanga* (ICC-01/04–01/06), Decision on Victims' Participation, 18 January 2008, para. 105.

available only if they have demonstrated that their personal interests are materially affected.[89]

Protective measures

Even if victims do not participate actively in the trial process, as parties or interveners, their presence is virtually indispensable as witnesses. The protection of both victims and witnesses is a key responsibility of the Court.[90] From the earliest stages, the Court has manifested its understanding of its responsibilities to protect victims. In the *Situation in Darfur* referral, the Pre-Trial Chamber, on its own initiative, designated two *amici curiae* to advise it on appropriate measures for the protection of victims. The two were Professor Antonio Cassese, who had chaired the United Nations Commission of Inquiry that had recommended prosecution by the Court in its January 2005 report,[91] and Louise Arbour, the United Nations High Commissioner for Human Rights.[92] The Pre-Trial Chamber took note of the bi-annual report of the Prosecutor to the Security Council on the progress of prosecutions, in which he had explained that the continuing insecurity in Darfur was prohibitive of effective investigations inside Darfur, 'particularly in light of the absence of a functioning and sustainable system for the protection of victims and witnesses'.[93]

Professor Cassese's observations included a number of rather general comments about the role and rationale of the Court in the protection of victims. The Prosecutor took exception to some of this. In his response to Professor Cassese, he noted that 'at the heart of Professor Cassese's observations is the belief that the [Office of the Prosecutor] and the Chamber have a responsibility to enhance security for victims of crimes in Darfur'. That, said the Prosecutor, was going too far. He argued that, while the investigation 'should have the consequence of contributing to the protection of the civilian population in Darfur, by preventing further

---

[89] *Lubanga* (ICC-01/04–01/06), Transcript of 8 April 2009, p. 5.
[90] Rome Statute, Arts. 57(3)(c), 64(2), 64(6)(e) and 68; Rules of Procedure and Evidence, Rules 87–88.
[91] Report of the International Commission of Inquiry on Violations of International Humanitarian Law and Human Rights Law in Darfur, UN Doc. S/2005/60.
[92] *Situation in Darfur, Sudan* (ICC-02/05), Decision Inviting Observations in Application of Rule 103 of the Rules of Procedure and Evidence, 24 July 2006.
[93] Third Report of the Prosecutor of the International Criminal Court, Mr Luis Moreno-Ocampo, to the Security Council Pursuant to UNSC 1593 (2005) of 14 June 2006, p. 6.

crimes', this was not the mandate of the Court. Responsibility for the security of the civilian population in Darfur lay with the Government of Sudan, the Security Council, the African Union and other interested organizations.[94]

With respect to protection of victims and witnesses, there are a number of particular concerns, including the threat of reprisals, and ensuring that the investigation and trial themselves do not constitute further victimization of those who have already suffered terribly. At the investigation stage, the Prosecutor is required to 'respect the interests and personal circumstances of victims and witnesses, including age, gender as defined in Article 7, paragraph 3, and health, and take into account the nature of the crime, in particular where it involves sexual violence, gender violence or violence against children'.[95] The Prosecutor is entitled to withhold disclosure of evidence if this may lead to the 'grave endangerment' of a witness or his or her family.[96] Finally, the Pre-Trial Chamber is to ensure 'the protection and privacy of victims and witnesses'.[97]

Similar responsibilities are imposed upon the Trial Chamber.[98] Specifically, it is to take 'appropriate measures to protect the safety, physical and psychological well-being, dignity and privacy of victims and witnesses'. The Court is to have regard to all relevant factors, including age, gender, health, and the nature of the crime, 'in particular, but not limited to, where the crime involves sexual or gender violence or violence against children'.[99] With this in mind, the Trial Chamber may derogate from the principle of public hearings.[100] It may hold proceedings *in camera*, or permit evidence to be presented 'by electronic means'. Presumably, this refers to testimony where the witness testifies by video and cannot see the alleged perpetrator, a practice that is widely used in national justice systems involving children. The views

---

[94] *Situation in Darfur* (ICC-02/05), Prosecutor's Observations to Cassese's Observations on Issues Concerning the Protection of Victims and the Preservation of Evidence in the Proceedings on Darfur Pending Before the ICC, 11 September 2006, para. 8.

[95] Rome Statute, Art. 54(1)(b). On the particular difficulties involved in protecting child witnesses, see Stuart Beresford, 'Child Witnesses and the International Criminal Justice System: Does the International Criminal Court Protect the Most Vulnerable?', (2005) 3 *Journal of International Criminal Justice* 721.

[96] Rome Statute, Art. 68(5).

[97] *Ibid.*, Art. 57(3)(c); see also *ibid.*, Art. 57(3)(e).

[98] *Maryland* v. *Craig*, 497 US 836 (1990); Rome Statute, Art. 64(6)(e).

[99] Rome Statute, Art. 68(1).

[100] *Ibid.*, Art. 68(2). See also *ibid.*, Art. 69(1).

of the victim or witness are to be canvassed by the Court in making such a determination.[101] Neither the Statute nor the Rules of Procedure and Evidence explicitly authorize the possibility of anonymous witnesses, that is, a witness for one party whose identity is not disclosed to the other party. Article 68(1) of the Statute begins with the general rule that '[t]he Court shall take appropriate measures to protect the safety, physical and psychological well-being, dignity and privacy of victims and witnesses', and this might theoretically permit the practice. But the paragraph concludes with a restriction: 'These measures shall not be prejudicial to or inconsistent with the rights of the accused and a fair and impartial trial.' And therein lies the difficulty. At the International Criminal Tribunal for the former Yugoslavia, one of its very first rulings permitted non-disclosure of the names of witnesses. Judgments of the European Court of Human Rights suggested this was impermissible, but a majority of the Trial Chamber, with Judge Stephen dissenting, said the jurisprudence of the European Court of Human Rights only applied to 'ordinary criminal' jurisdictions.[102] The controversial decision was widely criticized,[103] and writers continued to discuss its merits long after the Prosecutor had abandoned the practice.

According to Rule 87(3) of the Rules of Procedure and Evidence:

> A Chamber may, on a motion or request under sub-rule 1, hold a hearing which shall be conducted in camera, to determine whether to order measures to prevent the release to the public or press and information agencies, of the identity or the location of a victim, a witness or other person at risk on account of testimony given by a witness by ordering, *inter alia*:
>
> (a) That the name of the victim, witness or other person at risk on account of testimony given by a witness or any information which could lead to his or her identification, be expunged from the public records of the Chamber;

---

[101] *Ibid.*, Art. 68(2).

[102] *Tadić* (IT-94-1-T), Decision on the Prosecutor's Motion Requesting Protective Measures for Victims and Witnesses, 10 August 1995, para. 28.

[103] Monroe Leigh, 'The Yugoslav Tribunal: Use of Unnamed Witnesses Against Accused', (1996) 90 *American Journal of International Law* 235; Natasha A. Affolder, '*Tadić*, the Anonymous Witness and the Sources of International Procedural Law', (1998) 19 *Michigan Journal of International Law* 445; Mercedeh Momeni, 'Balancing the Procedural Rights of the Accused Against a Mandate to Protect Victims and Witnesses: An Examination of the Anonymity Rules of the International Criminal Tribunal for the Former Yugoslavia', (1997) 41 *Howard Law Journal* 155.

(b) That the Prosecutor, the defence or any other participant in the proceedings be prohibited from disclosing such information to a third
party;

(c) That testimony be presented by electronic or other special means,
including the use of technical means enabling the alteration of pic-
tures or voice, the use of audio-visual technology, in particular video-
conferencing and closed-circuit television, and the exclusive use of
the sound media;

(d) That a pseudonym be used for a victim, a witness or other person at
risk on account of testimony given by a witness; or

(e) That a Chamber conduct part of its proceedings in camera.

The implication of this provision would seem to be that a truly anonymous witness does not fall within the 'special measures' permitted by
Article 68(1) of the Rome Statute. Rule 88 gives as an example of such
'special measures' those taken 'to facilitate the testimony of a trauma-
tized victim or witness, a child, an elderly person or a victim of sexual
violence'. This might involve taking testimony in a remote location, by
videolink or behind a screen, or permitting counsel, a legal representative, a psychologist or a family member to attend during the testimony
of the victim or the witness.[104] Judges are instructed to be 'vigilant in
controlling the manner of questioning a witness or victim so as to avoid
any harassment or intimidation, paying particular attention to attacks
on victims of crimes of sexual violence'.[105]

Reparations for victims

The Rome Statute allows the Court to address the issue of reparations
to victims, establishing general principles for 'restitution, compensation
and rehabilitation'.[106] The Court is empowered to 'determine the scope
and extent of any damage, loss and injury to, or in respect of, victims',
acting on its own initiative in cases where there is no specific request
from the victims themselves.[107] The purpose of this 'determination', it
appears, is to enable enforcement of the rights of victims before national

---

[104] Rules of Procedure and Evidence, Rule 88(2).   [105] *Ibid.*, Rule 88(5).

[106] Christopher Muttukumaru, 'Reparation to Victims', in Lattanzi and Schabas, *Essays on
the Rome Statute*, pp. 303–10.

[107] Rome Statute, Art. 75(1). See also Rules of Procedure and Evidence, Rules 94–99. The
idea that the Court could act on its own initiative was very controversial. Those favouring this argued that victims in underdeveloped parts of the world were unlikely to be in
a position to exercise the right on their own.

courts. Rule 97 of the Rules of Procedure and Evidence provides some indication of the guidelines that the Court will follow in assessing the amount of reparations to be ordered:

1. Taking into account the scope and extent of any damage, loss or injury, the Court may award reparations on an individualized basis or, where it deems it appropriate, on a collective basis or both.

2. At the request of victims or their legal representatives, or at the request of the convicted person, or on its own motion, the Court may appoint appropriate experts to assist it in determining the scope, extent of any damage, loss and injury to, or in respect of victims and to suggest various options concerning the appropriate types and modalities of reparations. The Court shall invite, as appropriate, victims or their legal representatives, the convicted person as well as interested persons and interested States to make observations on the reports of the experts.

According to Christopher Muttukumaru, Court rulings concerning reparations 'must be sufficiently practicable, clear and precise to be capable of enforcement in the courts of, or by the other relevant national authorities of, the States Parties'.[108] More specifically, the Court may 'make an order directly against a convicted person' specifying reparations, although it may not make an order against a State as such.[109] To some extent the Court can control enforcement of the order, but only if there are resources in the Trust Fund for victims.[110] It may also, in this context, request States to proceed with seizure of proceeds, property and assets, with a view to forfeiture and ultimate restitution.[111] States are required to give effect to such forfeiture orders.[112]

There were far more ambitious proposals for compensation of victims, but these fell by the wayside during the negotiations. The concept of international compensation is seductive, but it is not without many practical obstacles. Experience of the *ad hoc* tribunals suggests that by and large most defendants succeed in claiming indigence. For example, they are almost invariably represented by tribunal-funded counsel after making perfunctory demonstrations that they are without the means to pay for their own defence. The irony is that these are the very people who are widely believed to have looted the countries where they once ruled. It may simply be unrealistic to expect the new Court to be able to locate and seize substantial assets of its prisoners.

---

[108] Christopher Muttukumaru, 'Reparation to Victims', in Lee, *The International Criminal Court*, pp. 262–70 at p. 267.
[109] *Ibid.*, pp. 267–9.   [110] Rome Statute, Art. 75(2).
[111] *Ibid.*, Arts 75(4) and 93(1)(k).   [112] *Ibid.*, Art. 109.

Institutions for victims

Three institutions exist within the Court dedicated to the rights and interests of victims: the Trust Fund for Victims, the Victims and Witnesses Unit and the Office of Public Counsel for Victims.

The Rome Statute provides for the creation of a Trust Fund for Victims to hold fines and assets, and dispose of them. The Trust Fund is to be used 'for the benefit of victims of crimes within the jurisdiction of the Court, and of the families of such victims'.[113] The Trust Fund is one of the unique features of the International Criminal Court. Nothing similar has ever existed at an international criminal tribunal.

Because there have been no convictions, no proceeds resulting from the proceedings have been acquired by the Trust Fund for Victims. Nor does it seem likely, in the foreseeable future, that the Trust Fund will obtain any resources as a result of convictions, because all of the defendants to date have been declared indigent for the purposes of legal aid and other forms of assistance, including funded family visits. This has not prevented the establishment and operation of the Trust Fund, however.

The Trust Fund was established by decision of the Assembly of States Parties at its first session in September 2002. The Trust Fund is managed by a permanent secretariat and overseen by a five-person Board of Directors composed of prestigious international personalities. Its members serve in a voluntary capacity.[114] With its regulatory and administrative framework in place, the Fund actually began its operations early in 2007.

The Assembly of States Parties has interpreted the phrase 'benefit of victims' as consisting of two components, reparations and material support.[115] The Board of Directors of the Trust Fund has derived a focus on reparations from Article 75(1) of the Rome Statute, interpreting the concept with reference to the 'Basic Principles and Guidelines on the Right to a Remedy and Reparation for Victims of Gross Violations of International Human Rights Law and Serious Violations of International Humanitarian Law', which were adopted by the United Nations General

---

[113] *Ibid.*, Art. 79; Rules of Procedure and Evidence, Rule 98.

[114] Establishment of a Fund for the Benefit of Victims of Crimes Within the Jurisdiction of the Court, and of the Families of Such Victims, ASP/1/Res.6; Procedure for the Nomination and Election of Members of the Board of Directors of the Trust Fund for the Benefit of Victims, ASP/1/Res.7.

[115] Regulations of the Trust Fund for Victims, ASP/4/Res.3, Regulation 50(a)(i).

Assembly in 2005.[116] The Basic Principles identify five categories of reparations: restitution, compensation, rehabilitation, satisfaction and guarantees of non-repetition.

Even prior to the start of the Court's first trial, and thus any judicial determination that a crime within the jurisdiction of the Court had taken place, the Fund began allocating sums of money for projects that were said to benefit 'victims'. These were undertaken in Uganda and the Democratic Republic of the Congo, where active situations were being addressed by the Chambers. Defence counsel unsuccessfully challenged a decision to approve projects of the Trust Fund prior to any convictions being made by the Court. The defence argued that the Court would be pre-determining whether there were in fact victims of a crime within the jurisdiction of the Court, and that this was a violation of the presumption of innocence.[117]

Article 79(2) indicates that the Court may order money and other property collected through fines or forfeiture to be transferred to the Trust Fund. There is an awkward but presumably inadvertent redundancy in the double reference to an order by the Court. Coupled with the fact that Article 79 appears in Part 7, on penalties, it would be logical to conclude that proceeds of fines or forfeiture orders made in accordance with Article 77 are the only source of income for the Fund. Nevertheless, the Assembly of States Parties has determined that, in addition to the sources of income listed in Article 79(2), the Court may also be funded by voluntary contributions from governments, organizations, individuals, corporations and other entities, 'in accordance with relevant criteria adopted by the Assembly of States Parties', through '[r]esources collected through awards for reparations if ordered by the Court pursuant to rule 98 of the Rules of Procedure and Evidence' and '[s]uch resources, other than assessed contributions, as the Assembly of States Parties may decide to allocate to the Trust Fund'.[118] Income to the Trust Fund for Victims in 2008 stood at about €1 million, comprised essentially of voluntary contributions from States as well as a modest amount

---

[116] UN Doc. A/RES/60/147. See 'Report to the Assembly of States Parties on the Activities and Projects of the Board of Directors of the Trust Fund for Victims for the Period 1 July 2007 to 30 June 2008', ASP/7/13, para. 6.

[117] *Situation in the Democratic Republic of the Congo* (ICC-01/04), Decision on the Notification of the Board of Directors of the Trust Fund for Victims in Accordance with Regulation 50 of the Regulations of the Trust Fund, 11 April 2008, pp. 9, 11.

[118] Establishment of a Fund for the Benefit of Victims of Crimes within the Jurisdiction of the Court, and of the Families of Such Victims, ASP/1/Res.6, para. 2.

of interest on the existing balance. The annual cost of operating the Fund, budgeted for 2010 at about €1.4 million, has consistently exceeded the actual income of the Fund.[119]

Ruling on proposals from the Trust Fund, Pre-Trial Chamber I 'strongly recommended' that, before resorting to other activities or projects, the Trust Fund study and anticipate the resources that would be needed to execute an eventual reparation order.[120] Following the ruling, the Secretariat of the Fund 'expressed its fear that the approach urged by the Pre-Trial Chamber would create two categories of victims, those benefiting from reparations and those seeking assistance'.[121] The Secretariat of the Fund said it was 'financially unwise to set aside funds for a future order of reparations while there were victims in immediate need of physical or psychological rehabilitation or material support'.[122]

Specific details of the activities of the Fund are not provided to the public. According to the Board, due to 'the sensitive nature of its work and its association with the Court, the Trust Fund is limited in its ability to share details of the actual programmes and initiatives it supports, in order to protect its beneficiaries'.[123] The explanation seems a trifle contrived, given that the projects involve activities on the territory of sovereign States that can hardly be surreptitious or secret in nature. This looks more like a pretext to avoid public scrutiny. According to the Fund, projects have included: rehabilitating and reintegrating child soldiers, including girl combatants and abductees through family reunification, foster placement, and support for independent living; improving access to reproductive health services, counselling and psychosocial support for victims of rape, providing opportunities to improve household livelihoods through agricultural and microcredit initiatives; promoting Radio For Justice, a community-based radio approach that focuses on transitional and restorative justice to heal memories; and 'integrating

---

[119] ASP/8/10, pp. 135–9.

[120] *Situation in the Democratic Republic of the Congo* (ICC-01/04), Decision on the Notification of the Board of Directors of the Trust Fund for Victims in Accordance with Regulation 50 of the Regulations of the Trust Fund, 11 April 2008, pp. 7, 11.

[121] 'Report of the Bureau on the Assessment of the Regulations of the Trust Fund for Victims', ASP/7/32, para. 14.

[122] 'Report of the Bureau on the Assessment of the Regulations of the Trust Fund for Victims', ASP/7/32, para. 16.

[123] Report to the Assembly of States Parties on the Activities and Projects of the Board of Directors of the Trust Fund for Victims for the Period 1 July 2007 to 30 June 2008, ASP/7/13, para. 16.

a broad range of programme approaches to provide a comprehensive package of support services to target groups of affected individuals'.[124] In 2007, the Trust Fund approved eighteen projects for Uganda and sixteen for the Democratic Republic of the Congo.[125] These were subsequently endorsed by the Pre-Trial Chambers. According to the Board of Directors, the projects 'will likely benefit more than 380,000 victims'.[126] This sounds impressive, but, given the funds involved and the scale of the projects, the word 'benefit' is probably being used rather loosely. Possibly potential listeners of the community radio station are counted among the 'beneficiaries'.

Oversight of the Trust Fund is assigned to a five-person Board of Directors whose members serve in a voluntary capacity and are elected for a renewable term of three years.[127] The members are to be of different nationalities, elected on the basis of equitable geographical distribution and taking into account the need to ensure equitable gender distribution and equitable representation of the principal legal systems of the world.[128]

The Victims and Witnesses Unit is also a requirement of the Rome Statute.[129] The Registry is charged with the task of establishing the Unit. The Unit is to provide protective measures and security arrangements, counselling and other appropriate assistance for witnesses, victims who appear before the Court and others who are at risk on account of testimony given by them. Precise instructions concerning the responsibilities of the Victims and Witnesses Unit appear in the Rules of Procedure and Evidence. With respect to all witnesses, victims who appear before the Court, and others who are at risk on account of testimony given by witnesses, the Unit is charged with:

---

[124] *Ibid.*   [125] *Ibid.*, para. 22.   [126] *Ibid.*

[127] Establishment of a Fund for the Benefit of Victims of Crimes within the Jurisdiction of the Court, and of the Families of Such Victims, ASP/1/Res.6; Procedure for the Nomination and Election of Members of the Board of Directors of the Trust Fund for the Benefit of Victims, ASP/1/Res.7. Also Procedure for Filling Vacancies in the Board of Directors of the Trust Fund for Victims, ASP/4/Res.5; Amendment Regarding the Term of Office of Members of the Board of Directors of the Trust Fund for Victims, ASP/4/Res.7.

[128] Procedure for the Nomination and Election of Members of the Board of Directors of the Trust Fund for the Benefit of Victims, Resolution ASP/1/Res.7.

[129] Rome Statute, Art. 43(6). This summary provision is supplemented by very detailed provisions in other instruments: Rules of Procedure and Evidence, Rules 16–19; Regulations of the Court, ICC-BD/01–01–04, Regulation 41; Regulations of the Registry, Regulations 54–118.

(i) Providing them with adequate protective and security measures and formulating long- and short-term plans for their protection;

(ii) Recommending to the organs of the Court the adoption of protection measures and also advising relevant States of such measures;

(iii) Assisting them in obtaining medical, psychological and other appropriate assistance;

(iv) Making available to the Court and the parties training in issues of trauma, sexual violence, security and confidentiality;

(v) Recommending, in consultation with the Office of the Prosecutor, the elaboration of a code of conduct, emphasizing the vital nature of security and confidentiality for investigators of the Court and of the defence and all intergovernmental and non-governmental organizations acting at the request of the Court, as appropriate;

(vi) Cooperating with States, where necessary, in providing any of the measures described above.[130]

The Unit also has specific duties concerning witnesses:

(i) Advising them where to obtain legal advice for the purpose of protecting their rights, in particular in relation to their testimony;

(ii) Assisting them when they are called to testify before the Court;

(iii) Taking gender-sensitive measures to facilitate the testimony of victims of sexual violence at all stages of the proceedings.[131]

Due regard is to be given by the Unit to the particular needs of children, elderly persons and persons with disabilities. In order to facilitate the participation and protection of children as witnesses, the Unit may assign, with the agreement of the parents or the legal guardian, a child-support person to assist a child through all stages of the proceedings. The Unit is required to include staff with expertise in trauma, including trauma related to crimes of sexual violence.

The Unit must remain independent of the other organs of the Court.[132] According to Judge Steiner, sitting as a single judge in *Lubanga*, 'the Victims and Witnesses Unit can properly discharge its support functions vis-à-vis the Chamber only by distancing itself from the specific positions of the parties in any given matter and by providing the Chamber with objective information regarding the factual circumstances of the relevant witnesses and also specialized advice in respect of their needs

---

[130] Rules of Procedure and Evidence, Rule 17(2)(a).   [131] *Ibid.*, Rule 17(2)(b).

[132] *Situation in Uganda* (ICC 02/04–01/05), Decision on the Prosecutor's Application That the Pre-Trial Chamber Disregard as Irrelevant the Submission Filed by the Registry on 5 December 2005, 9 March 2006, para. 38.

in terms of protection; and that the Victims and Witnesses Unit must do so and, to date, has done so, irrespective of whether its conclusions are different from those advanced by the parties'.[133]

The Office of Public Counsel for Victims is the principal means by which the Registry fulfils its general mandate to assist victims in obtaining legal advice and organizing their legal representation, and providing their legal representatives with adequate support, assistance and information.[134] It is a requirement of the Regulations of the Court.[135] Its existence is without precedent, no similar body having been established by other international tribunals. The Office is designed to ensure the effective participation of victims in proceedings before the Court. Its role is to provide support and assistance to the legal representative for victims and to victims, including, where appropriate, legal research and advice and appearance before a Chamber in respect of specific issues. This may involve producing factual background documents on situations before the Court, and preparing research papers, legal opinions and bibliographies on aspects of international criminal law, especially those that are relevant to the rights of victims. The Office of Public Counsel for Victims has participated actively in litigation before the Pre-Trial Chamber.[136] The Office is fully independent of the other institutions of the Court.[137]

---

[133] *Lubanga* (01/04–01/06), Decision on Third Defence Motion for Leave to Appeal, 4 October 2006, p. 8.

[134] Rules of Procedure and Evidence, Rule 16(1)(b) and (c).

[135] Regulations of the Court, Regulation 81. Also Regulations of the Registry, Regulations 114–117.

[136] E.g., *Situation in the Democratic Republic of Congo* (ICC-01/04), Decision on the Prosecution's Application for Leave to Appeal the Chamber's Decision of 17 January 2006 on the Applications for Participation in the Proceedings of VPRS 1, VPRS 2, VPRS 3, VPRS 4, VPRS 5 and VPRS 6, 31 March 2006.

[137] Regulations of the Registry, Regulation 115; Report on the Activities of the Court, ASP/5/15, para. 77.

11

Structure and administration of the Court

The International Criminal Court is a distinct international organization headquartered in The Hague, in the Netherlands. It works in close
cooperation with the United Nations but is independent of it. The Court
is composed of four 'organs': the Presidency, the Chambers, the Office
of the Prosecutor and the Registry.[1] Other organizations also exist
within the Court, such as the Assembly of States Parties and the Review
Conference, as well as a considerable number of subsidiary bodies, such
as the Board of Trustees of the Trust Fund for Victims and the Victims
and Witnesses Unit.

Headquarters in The Hague

The seat of the Court is The Hague,[2] but it may sit elsewhere if it considers this desirable. The Netherlands was the only State to offer its services, despite rumours that circulated before and during the Diplomatic
Conference about Rome, Lyon and Nuremberg as possible candidates.[3]
The Hague is already the seat of the International Court of Justice as well
as of the International Criminal Tribunal for the former Yugoslavia, the
Special Tribunal for Lebanon and other international judicial organizations. Its candidacy must have seemed so unbeatable to possible com-
petitors that they declined even to throw their hats into the ring.

A 'headquarters agreement' between the International Criminal
Court and the Netherlands is required by Article 3(2) of the Rome
Statute. The final negotiated text of the Headquarters Agreement was
approved by the Assembly of States Parties in December 2006. Formal

---

[1] Rome Statute of the International Criminal Court, (2002) 2187 UNTS 90, Art. 34.
[2] *Ibid.*, Art. 3.
[3] Frank Jarasch, 'Establishment, Organization and Financing of the International
Criminal Court (Parts I, IV, XI–XIII)', (1998) 6 *European Journal of Crime, Criminal Law
and Criminal Justice* 9 at 18–19.

agreement was reached on 7 June 2007, with signature by the President of the Court and the Minister of Foreign Affairs of the Netherlands,[4] subject to ratification by the Dutch parliament.[5] The Headquarters Agreement entered into force on 3 March 2008.[6] The Agreement is completed by an exchange of letters confirming the joint interpretation of the Agreement by the parties and referencing the explanatory notes.

Until construction of the permanent premises is completed, the Netherlands provided the Court with a large office building in The Hague, known as 'the ARC', that was formerly used by the Dutch postal service, as a temporary home for the Court. The ARC is in a non-descript commercial neighbourhood, and offers nothing close to the gravitas required of a home for the Court. Even the International Criminal Tribunal for the former Yugoslavia is located in more elegant promises, the former headquarters of an insurance company situated not far from the International Court of Justice and other international institutions, as well as museums, embassies and major hotels. As a study by the Court explained, '[t]he Arc lacks the dignity of a court building. Its image as a modern office building does not correspond with the idea of a permanent universal court.'[7] The building also has serious shortcomings in terms of security, and is located at a considerable distance from the Detention Centre. It has proven to be inadequate for the needs of the Court, even on a temporary basis, and additional space has been obtained in neighbouring buildings. The Court has also established field offices in Kampala (Uganda), in N'Djamena and Abeche (Chad) and in Kinshasa and Bunia (the Democratic Republic of the Congo).

A design for the permanent premises of the Court was accepted in late 2009, following an international architectural competition. The buildings will be constructed at the Alexanderkazerne, a former military barracks in Scheveningen, which is a suburb of The Hague on the North Sea coast. Construction will probably begin in 2011, and it is hoped the Court will occupy its permanent home by 2014 or 2015.

---

[4] Report on the Activities of the Court, ASP/7/25, para. 84.
[5] Report on the Draft Headquarters Agreement Between the International Criminal Court and the Host State, ASP/5/25, para. 15.
[6] Headquarters Agreement between the International Criminal Court and the Host State, ASP/5/Res.3, Art. 30(1).
[7] Report on the Future Permanent Premises of the International Criminal Court, Comprehensive Progress Report, ASP/5/16, para. 91.

Relationship with the United Nations

The International Criminal Court is a new and independent international organization. The Court is formally distinct from the United Nations. Nevertheless, the United Nations has played a seminal role in its creation, and funded the process of establishment of the Court. The preamble to the Rome Statute refers to 'an independent permanent International Criminal Court in relationship with the United Nations system'. The Security Council has the right to refer cases to the Court, and also to block prosecution under certain circumstances.[8] Article 2 of the Rome Statute states: 'The Court shall be brought into relationship with the United Nations through an agreement to be approved by the Assembly of States Parties to this Statute and thereafter concluded by the President of the Court on its behalf.'

The Relationship Agreement between the Court and the United Nations was concluded on 4 October 2004. It was signed by Philippe Kirsch, President of the International Criminal Court, and Kofi Annan, Secretary-General of the United Nations, and entered into force immediately. The Agreement addresses issues such as the exchange of information, judicial assistance, cooperation on infrastructure and technical matters. Provision is made for the exchange of representatives, including: the participation of the Court as an observer at sessions of the General Assembly of the United Nations, to which the Court submits an annual report,[9] as well as administrative cooperation; the provision of conference services; and the use of the United Nations *laissez-passer* as a travel document by staff and officials of the Court. Under the Agreement, the United Nations will cooperate with the Court on judicial issues, for example if the Court requests the testimony of an official of the United Nations or one of its programmes, funds or offices. The Agreement also defines mechanisms of cooperation where the Security Council refers a situation to the Court in accordance with Article 13(b) of the Rome Statute.

The Presidency

The Presidency is responsible for the administration of the Court and a variety of specialized functions set out in the Statute.[10] The Presidency

---

[8] Rome Statute, Arts. 13 and 16.

[9] E.g. Report of the International Criminal Court, UN Doc. A/64/356.

[10] See also Regulations of the Court, ICC-BD/01–01–04, Regulation 11. Several of the Regulations delegate powers to the Presidency.

of the Court is elected by the judges. The President and the First and Second Vice-Presidents make up the Presidency. The Presidency is to decide upon the appropriate workload of the other fifteen judges.[11] The Presidency may also propose that the number of judges be increased, where this is considered necessary and appropriate, although any increase has to be authorized by the Assembly of States Parties.

Philippe Kirsch, who presided over the Rome Conference and the sessions of the Preparatory Commission, was elected first President of the Court in early 2003. More than any other individual, his adroit stewardship of the delicate negotiations at Rome was responsible for the successful adoption of the Statute and its entry into force. The two vice-presidents of the Court were Akua Kuenyehia and Elizabeth Odio Benito. Judge Kirsch was re-elected President for a second term in March 2006, with Akua Kuenyehia as First Vice-President and René Blattmann as Second Vice-President. In 2009, Judge Sang-Hyun Song was elected President, Judge Fatoumata Dembele Diarra was elected First Vice-President and Judge Hans-Peter Kaul was elected Second Vice-President.

The Chambers

There are three Divisions within the Chambers: the Appeals Division, the Trial Division and the Pre-Trial Division. The term 'Division' rather than 'Chamber' was used in order to resolve a dispute about whether there should be one or several pre-trial chambers.[12] The Appeals Division is composed of the President and four other judges. When the Statute was adopted, it was probably intended that members of the Appeals Division serve their entire nine-year term in the Division. This reflected widespread dissatisfaction with practice at the International Criminal Tribunal for the former Yugoslavia where judges have moved from one chamber to another during their terms. Once 'elevated' to the Appeals Chamber, judges do not then return to the other Divisions. Nevertheless, it is possible for a judge who has already served on the Pre-Trial or Trial Chambers to be named to the Appeals Chamber. These 'contaminated' judges cannot sit in proceedings in which they were previously involved at the pre-trial or trial stage.[13]

---

[11] Rome Statute, Art. 35.

[12] Jarasch, 'Establishment, Organization and Financing', p. 20.

[13] See Report of the Committee on Budget and Finance on the Work of Its Twelfth Session, ASP/8/5, paras. 107–8; Report of the Court on the New Composition of the Appeals Division and the Excusal of Judges, ASP/8/31.

The Trial Division and Pre-Trial Division are composed of not less than six judges. Judges in each of these divisions are to serve for at least three years within their division. Judges are assigned to the various divisions based on their qualifications and experience, and so as to ensure an appropriate combination of expertise in criminal and international law.[14] The Trial and Pre-Trial Divisions consist of judges with primarily criminal law experience and, though not stated as such in the Statute, there is the suggestion that those judges whose experience is predominantly in the field of international law will gravitate towards the Appeals Division. Reading between the lines, the Statute seems to be saying that the more practically oriented criminal law specialists should focus on trials, while their more cerebral brethren in the international law field should focus on appeals.

The Appeals Chamber sits as a full bench of the five judges belonging to the Appeals Division. The Trial Chamber sits in benches of three judges of the Trial Division. The Pre-Trial Chamber sits as either a three-judge panel or as a single judge. Various functions of the Pre-Trial Chamber may be delegated to a single judge.[15] Pre-Trial Chambers have designated single judges with specific responsibilities, such as matters relating to the unsealing of documents,[16] and victim issues.[17] Judges from the Trial and Pre-Trial Divisions may temporarily be assigned to the other division, although no judge who has participated in the pre-trial phase of a particular case may sit on the Trial Chamber of the same case.

The eighteen judges of the Court who now make up the Chambers are elected by the Assembly of States Parties. Any State Party may propose one candidate for the Court in any given election. That candidate need not be a national of the nominating State but must be a national of a State Party. There can be only one judge of any given nationality at any one time. Judges are to be of 'high moral character, impartiality and integrity', phraseology typical of international instruments.[18] They must also be qualified for appointment to the highest judicial offices in

---

[14] Rome Statute, Art. 39(1).

[15] *Ibid.*, Art. 57(2)(b); Rules of Procedure and Evidence, ASP/1/3, pp. 10–107, Rule 7; Regulations of the Court, Regulation 47.

[16] *Situation in Uganda* (ICC-02/04–01/05), Décision portant désignation d'un juge unique pour la levée des scellés, 31 May 2006.

[17] *Situation in Uganda* (ICC-02/04–01/05), Decision Designating a Single Judge on Victims Issues, 22 November 2006.

[18] Art. 2 of the Statute of the International Court of Justice speaks of 'a body of independent judges elected regardless of their nationality from among persons of high moral character'.

their respective States,[19] and are to have an excellent knowledge of and be fluent in at least one of the working languages of the Court, namely, English or French. The Statute allows for an 'advisory committee' on nominations.[20] But this is a timid affair indeed compared with the thoroughgoing screening procedure to ensure qualifications that was originally mooted by the United Kingdom, somewhat along the lines of the procedure in force for appointments to the European Court of Human Rights. However, many States resented any attempt to limit their right to designate their own candidates.[21]

The Statute requires that judges possess a degree of expertise in the subject matter of the Court. Here it creates two categories of candidates, those with criminal law experience and those with international law experience. Specific reference is made to international humanitarian law and the law of human rights. During an election there are two lists of candidates, one with the criminal law profile ('List A'), the other with the international law profile ('List B'). The drafters of the Rome Statute attached great importance to having judges with public international law expertise on the Court. In reality, however, there has been very little call for such specialized knowledge of public international law, either at the Court itself or at any of the other international criminal tribunals. To date, at any rate, most of the references consist of little more than occasional perfunctory citations to Article 31 of the Vienna Convention on the Law of Treaties. A nominee for the Court who meets both requirements may choose the list on which he or she will appear. A minimum of nine and a maximum of thirteen judges have to come from the criminal law profile, and a minimum of five and a maximum of nine from the international law profile.[22]

Although no specific percentages are set out, Article 36(8) commits the States Parties to 'take into account' the need to ensure representation of the principal legal systems of the world, equitable geographic representation, 'a fair representation of female and male judges', and legal expertise on specific issues such as violence against women or children. The wording is a watered-down version of draft provisions that spoke bluntly of 'gender balance'.[23] Those who felt that only 'balance'

---

[19]   Rome Statute, Art. 36(3).   [20]   *Ibid.*, Art. 36(4)(c).

[21]   Jarasch, 'Establishment, Organization and Financing', p. 21.

[22]   Procedure for the Election of the Judges for the International Criminal Court, ASP/1/ Res.3, para. 1.

[23]   Jarasch, 'Establishment, Organization and Financing', p. 21; Medard R. Rwelamira, 'Composition and Administration of the Court', in Roy Lee, ed., *The International*

would ensure adequate representation of women may soon see the day where male judges are in the minority! The requirement of fair gender representation reflects concerns that the new Court might resemble its close relation, the International Court of Justice, a fifteen-member body to which only one woman has ever been elected in its entire eighty-year history. The *ad hoc* tribunals, whose judges are designated by the Security Council or the Secretary-General, as the case may be, have shown some modest improvement in this respect. To the credit of these institutions, women judges have served as the presidents of the international tribunals for the former Yugoslavia, Rwanda and Sierra Leone. But the International Criminal Court shines in this respect when compared with the competition.

Judges who serve on a full-time basis at the seat of the Court are not allowed to engage in any other occupation of a professional nature. All judges, including the few who still do not work full-time, are forbidden from activities 'likely to interfere with their judicial functions or to affect confidence in their independence'.[24] Given these requirements, it would seem hazardous to allow senior civil servants or diplomats to stand for election to part-time positions, a practice that is tolerated in the case of some other international tribunals.

Salaries of the judges are set by the Assembly of States Parties and may not be reduced during their terms of office.[25] Annual salaries of the judges are set at €180,000. Part-time judges are entitled to a minimum annual allowance of €20,000, in addition to a *per diem* allowance when they are serving. A very generous pension scheme adopted when the Statute entered into force was subsequently reduced dramatically by the Assembly of States Parties. The new regime only applies to judges elected subsequent to the changes, however.

The Regulations declare that, in the exercise of their judicial functions, the judges are of 'equal status', irrespective of age, date of election or length of service. The Appeals Chamber has already warned against analogies with national justice systems, where judges are ranked hierarchically, generally reflecting experience and expertise. Thus, in the English common law system, for example, judges of the High Court would have an inherent authority to review the work of 'inferior' courts. The Appeals Chamber said: 'The Pre-Trial and Trial Chambers of the

Criminal Court: The Making of the Rome Statute: Issues, Negotiations, Results, The Hague: Kluwer Law International, 1999, pp. 153–73 at pp. 166–7; Cate Steains, 'Gender Issues', in Lee, *ibid.*, pp. 357–90 at pp. 376–7.
[24] *Ibid.*, Art. 40.   [25] *Ibid.*, Art. 49.

International Criminal Court are in no way inferior courts in the sense that inferior courts are perceived and classified in England and Wales. Hence, any comparison between them and inferior courts under English law is misleading.'[26]

The *ad hoc* tribunals began with only six trial judges, but the number was soon found to be insufficient. Initially, the Yugoslav Tribunal drew upon the five Appeals Chamber judges to assist with some trial work. Then, the Security Council agreed to add a three-judge chamber to each of the tribunals. There are at present more than thirty international judges working full-time on the Rwanda and Yugoslav Tribunals. It would seem likely, then, that the eighteen judges envisaged in the Rome Statute will eventually prove to be inadequate if the Court fulfils even the most modest of expectations. The Committee on Budget and Finance has suggested that consideration might be given to the appointment of *ad litem* judges who would sit in only one case. This system has been in force at the *ad hoc* tribunals for many years. Its introduction would require an amendment to the Statute.

The Regulations of the Court require the judges to prepare a Code of Judicial Ethics. Nothing comparable has existed at previous international criminal tribunals.[27] The Code was adopted by the judges at their March 2005 plenary session.[28] Judges are required to make a solemn undertaking in open court to exercise their functions impartially and conscientiously.[29] The Rome Statute's provisions concerning removal from office represent a very significant improvement over the *ad hoc* tribunals, which have left this important matter unaddressed. The problem has been not so much the need to provide a mechanism for dismissal of a judge in a rare but appropriate circumstance as confronting the uncertainty created for judges when such matters are not clarified. Independence and impartiality are inadequately protected when a judge does not know not only for what failing he or she may be removed, but by whom the process may be conducted.

Judges may be excused from their functions by the Presidency. They may also be disqualified from sitting in cases in which there can be reasonable doubts about their impartiality.[30] That they cannot sit in matters

---

[26] *Situation in the Democratic Republic of Congo* (ICC-01/04), Judgment on the Prosecutor's Application for Extraordinary Review of Pre-Trial Chamber I's 31 March 2006 Decision Denying Leave to Appeal, 13 July 2006, para. 30.

[27] Regulations of the Court, Regulation 126.

[28] ICC-BD/02–01–05.   [29] Rome Statute, Art. 45.

[30] *Ibid.*, Art. 41. See Rules of Procedure and Evidence, Rules 23–39. The Prosecutor was exonerated following a disciplinary hearing into charges of misconduct: see, *In Re*

in which they have previously been involved at the national level would seem obvious, but to avoid any doubt this rule is spelled out in the Statute. Two of the Appeals Chamber judges elected in 2009 have not been able to sit in matters where they had already been engaged at the pre-trial level. Judges from the other Divisions have replaced them on a case-by-case basis.

Judges of the International Criminal Court may be removed from office on grounds of serious misconduct, a serious breach of duties, or inability to exercise the functions required by the Statute. In the event of misconduct of a less serious nature, disciplinary measures may be imposed.[31] Removal is the result of a decision taken by the Assembly of States Parties.[32] Removal of a judge first requires a recommendation to this effect by a two-thirds majority of the other judges. Then, a two-thirds majority of the States Parties must agree.

Office of the Prosecutor

The prosecutorial arm of the Court is a separate and independent organ. Article 42(1) of the Statute identifies the basic function of the Office of the Prosecutor: 'It shall be responsible for receiving referrals and any substantiated information on crimes within the jurisdiction of the Court, for examining them and for conducting investigations and prosecutions before the Court.' The Office of the Prosecutor is headed by the Prosecutor, who is assisted by one or more Deputy Prosecutors. The Prosecutor and the Deputy Prosecutors are required to be of different nationalities.[33] Unlike the judges, however, neither Prosecutor nor Deputy Prosecutors are required to be nationals of a State Party. There is nothing in the official record to explain this, but when the Statute was being drafted it was widely believed that this might leave the door open to the participation of an American at a senior level of the Court despite the unlikelihood that the United States would join the institution. Ratification of treaties within the United States is an awkward and cumbersome process even if the administration is supportive, and allowing

Palme, Judgment No. 2757 of the Administrative Tribunal of the International Labour Organization, 9 July 2008.

[31] Rome Statute, Art. 47.   [32] *Ibid.*, Art. 46.

[33] *Ibid.*, Art. 42. On the Office of the Prosecutor, see John R. W. D. Jones, 'The Office of the Prosecutor', in Antonio Cassese, Paola Gaeta and John R. W. D. Jones, eds., *The Rome Statute of the International Criminal Court: A Commentary*, vol. I, Oxford: Oxford University Press, 2002, pp. 269–74.

for an American Prosecutor was one way of giving Washington a means to participate. In 1998, when the Statute was adopted, the Democratic administration was not unfriendly to the Court. The same could not be said of the Republican-controlled Congress, especially the important Senate Foreign Relations Committee, whose president at the time was Jesse Helms, a sworn enemy of the whole idea.

The Prosecutor is elected by secret ballot of an absolute majority of the Assembly of States Parties. The Deputy Prosecutors must also be elected by the Assembly of States Parties, but from a list of candidates proposed by the Prosecutor. The Prosecutor submits a list of three candidates for each position of Deputy Prosecutor to be filled. The term of both Prosecutor and Deputy Prosecutors is nine years.[34] Like the judges, they are not subject to re-election, a measure designed to ensure their independence at the personal level by removing any incentive to curry favour with States in order to promote a second mandate.

Both the Prosecutor and the Deputy Prosecutors are to be persons 'of high moral character' with 'extensive, practical experience' in criminal prosecutions. They must be fluent in at least one of the working languages of the Court. Selection of a Prosecutor proved to be more difficult than election of the judges. Early on, it was agreed that it was desirable for this highly sensitive position to be filled by consensus rather than by a volatile and unpredictable ballot.[35] When nominations formally came to an end in late 2002, not a single candidate had been proposed. The window that had been left open for an American candidate was abruptly closed when the United States administration shifted its position, in early 2002, and began openly attacking the Court. At the resumed first session of the Assembly of States Parties, in February 2003, it was agreed to reopen the nomination period, with a view to election of the Prosecutor at the second resumed session in April of the same year. An informal consensus was reached in late March, when Zeid Raad Al Hussein, President of the Assembly of States Parties, announced the designation of Luis Moreno-Ocampo of Argentina.

Moreno-Ocampo distinguished himself as deputy prosecutor during trials of Argentine military officials who had supported the dictatorship that held power between 1976 and 1983. Subsequently, he helped found one of the country's major human rights non-governmental organizations. It later emerged that Moreno-Ocampo had been highly

[34] Rome Statute, Art. 43(4).
[35] Procedure for the Nomination and Election of Judges, the Prosecutor and Deputy Prosecutors of the International Criminal Court, ASP/1/Res.2, Art. 29.

enough regarded by the United States Department of State that it had put his name forward, in 1993, to be first Prosecutor of the International Criminal Tribunal for the former Yugoslavia. The candidacy did not move forward because Argentina refused to endorse it.[36]

Two Deputy Prosecutors have been elected, one with responsibility for investigations and the other with responsibility for prosecutions. The scheme is equivalent to the structure within the United Nations international criminal tribunals, where the Prosecutor is assisted by a 'chief of investigations' and 'chief of prosecutions'. Belgian lawyer Serge Brammertz was elected Deputy Prosecutor (Investigations) in September 2003, at the second session of the Assembly of States Parties. During 2006, Deputy Prosecutor Brammertz took a leave of absence, so he could serve as Commissioner of the United Nations International Independent Investigation Commission into the assassination of former Lebanese Prime Minister Rafiq Hariri, responding to a request from the United Nations Secretary-General.[37] He subsequently resigned and took up the position of Prosecutor of the International Criminal Tribunal for the former Yugoslavia. The Prosecutor never put forward a replacement for him as Deputy Prosecutor (Investigations). In 2004, Fatou Bensouda, of The Gambia, was elected Deputy Prosecutor (Prosecutions). Fatou Bensouda served as Deputy Director of Public Prosecutions, Solicitor General, Attorney General and Minister of Justice in her home country. In May 2002, she joined the International Criminal Tribunal for Rwanda as a Trial Attorney. Both Bensouda and Brammertz are likely to be candidates for the job of Prosecutor of the Court when Moreno-Ocampo's nine-year term finishes in 2012.

The Prosecutor and the Deputy Prosecutors are all required to make a solemn undertaking in open court to exercise their functions impartially and conscientiously.[38] The Prosecutor may be removed by a majority of the Assembly of States Parties. The Deputy Prosecutor's removal must be recommended by the Prosecutor and then authorized by a majority of the Assembly.[39] Salaries of the Prosecutor and Deputy Prosecutor are set by the Assembly of States Parties and may not be reduced during their terms of office.[40]

---

[36] David J. Scheffer, 'Three Memories from the Year of Origin, 1993', (2004) 2 *Journal of International Criminal Justice* 353.

[37] Report on the Activities of the Court, ASP/5/15, paras. 63–4.

[38] Rome Statute, Art. 45.

[39] On removal and related matters, see Rules of Procedure and Evidence, Rules 23–39.

[40] Rome Statute, Art. 49.

Prosecutorial independence is assured by a number of measures and provisions. According to Article 42(1), '[t]he Office of the Prosecutor shall act independently as a separate organ of the Court'. Furthermore, '[a] member of the Office shall not seek or act on instructions from any external source'. The Prosecutor is also given administrative independence, having 'full authority over the management and administration of the Office, including the staff, facilities and other resources thereof'.[41] This administrative autonomy stands in contrast to the scheme at the *ad hoc* tribunals; nor was it contemplated by the International Law Commission in the draft Statute that it submitted to the General Assembly in 1994.

And yet the Prosecutor's so-called independence is everywhere constrained. Much of the initial litigation at the Court has involved attempts to trim the wings of the Prosecutor. He has vigorously defended his independence, but not always successfully. Many of the checks on prosecutorial independence are the result of negotiated compromises in the Statute. The concept of a genuinely independent prosecutor, with freedom to select cases and suspects for prosecution, was radical and unprecedented. Although strongly defended by non-governmental organizations and the 'like-minded' States, it was also bitterly contested by the United States and some others. In effect, the Rome Statute limits the actions of the Prosecutor in several important ways.

When the Prosecutor is acting on his own initiative, using the *proprio motu* powers defined by Article 15 of the Rome Statute, he is subject to the Pre-Trial Chamber from the earliest stage. Once he has determined that there is 'a reasonable basis to proceed with an investigation', the Prosecutor must apply to the Pre-Trial Chamber for authorization to proceed.[42] Cases may also come before the Court by referral from a State Party or from the Security Council, and even from a non-party State in the peculiar situation of Article 12(3). Then, it is the source of the referral that defines the scope of the prosecution, and not the Prosecutor. If the Prosecutor declines to proceed when a case has been referred, the State Party or the Security Council, as the case may be, is entitled to demand that his decision be reviewed by the Pre-Trial Chamber.[43] The United

---

[41] *Ibid.*, Art. 42(2).

[42] *Ibid.*, Art. 15(3). In the case of a prosecution for the crime of aggression, the Pre-Trial Division must approve of the investigation. This subject is discussed in more detail in the parts of this book dealing with procedure. See Chapters 4, 5, 7 and 8 above.

[43] *Ibid.*, Art. 53(3).

Nations Security Council can also block proceedings before the Court, in accordance with Article 16.

When the Government of Uganda referred the 'situation concerning the "Lord's Resistance Army" in northern and western Uganda', the Prosecutor responded to Uganda indicating his interpretation that 'the scope of the referral encompasses all crimes committed in Northern Uganda in the context of the ongoing conflict involving the [Lord's Resistance Army]'.[44] But, when the Security Council limited the ambit of a referral in a somewhat similar fashion, in referring 'the situation in Darfur since 1 July 2002', by excluding 'nationals, current or former officials or personnel from a contributing State outside Sudan which is not a party to the Rome Statute of the International Criminal Court',[45] the Prosecutor was silent (and deferential).

It has always been acknowledged that victims have an enhanced role under the Rome Statute by comparison with the other international tribunals. They, too, encroach upon the independence of the Prosecutor. One of the earliest debates about the Court concerned the role of victims at the investigation stage. Although the provisions of the Statute contain some ambiguities in this respect, to the Prosecutor it seemed reasonable that the recognition by Article 68(3) that the Court is to permit the views and concerns of victims 'to be presented and considered at stages of the proceedings determined to be appropriate by the Court and in a manner which is not prejudicial to or inconsistent with the rights of the accused and a fair and impartial trial' did not extend to the investigation stage when, in fact, no accused person has yet been identified. Indeed, until an accused has been identified, it appears difficult to determine the identity of the victim.

Since the beginning of its operations, the Office of the Prosecutor has been characterized by an impressive and unprecedented degree of transparency, at least by comparison with the equivalent bodies in the *ad hoc* tribunals. Rare indeed are examples of attempts by the prosecutors of the *ad hoc* tribunals for the former Yugoslavia, Rwanda, Sierra Leone and Lebanon to explain or justify their policies and their exercise of discretion.[46] By contrast, the Prosecutor of the International Criminal Court

---

[44] See *Situation in Uganda* (ICC-02/04–01/05), Decision to Convene a Status Conference on the Investigation in the Situation in Uganda in Relation to the Application of Article 53, 2 December 2005, paras. 3–4.

[45] UN Doc. S/RES/1593 (2005).

[46] The only real exception was the issuance, in 2000, of an explanation for the Prosecutor's decision not to proceed against NATO with respect to allegations of war crimes

has held public policy consultations and issued position papers and similar documents in order to explain his choices and determinations. It might be argued that the Statute has imposed such an obligation. Article 15(6) requires the Prosecutor to inform those who have provided information concerning a possible prosecution when he concludes that there is no reasonable basis to proceed further. Be that as it may, he has interpreted the provision liberally, issuing detailed public documents with respect to his decision not to initiate investigations concerning Iraq and Venezuela,[47] as well as general comments as to why certain situations fall outside the jurisdiction of the Court.[48] He is also under an obligation to account for his activities with respect to Security Council referrals, to the extent this is required by the Security Council itself.[49] The Prosecutor is required to put in place regulations to govern the operation, management and administration of the Office of the Prosecutor.[50] An elaborate draft was circulated in early 2003, but the Regulations, in a much thinner form, were only adopted in 2009.

The Prosecutor is to appoint legal experts as advisers on specific issues, such as sexual and gender violence and violence against children. Several have been made: Catharine A. MacKinnon of the University of Michigan Law School, on gender crimes; Juan Méndez, formerly United Nations Special Adviser on the Prevention of Genocide, on crime prevention; Tim McCormack, Melbourne Law School, on international humanitarian law; and Jose Alvarez, New York University, on international law.

The Prosecutor is also to hire investigators and other staff members. The same requirements as for judges, that is, experience with various judicial systems, geographic representivity and gender balance are to be sought. The Statute allows persons being investigated or prosecuted to request the disqualification of the Prosecutor or of a Deputy Prosecutor in a specific case.

committed during the 1999 Kosovo bombing campaign: 'Committee Established to Review the NATO Bombing Campaign Against the Federal Republic of Yugoslavia, Final Report to the Prosecutor', The Hague, 13 June 2000, PR/P.I.S./510-e. There are also some public indications of policy when the Prosecutors of the *ad hoc* tribunals make their bi-annual reports to the Security Council pursuant to Resolution 1534.

[47] Letter of Prosecutor dated 9 February 2006 (Venezuela); Letter of Prosecutor dated 9 February 2006 (Iraq).

[48] Communications Received by the Office of the Prosecutor of the ICC, 16 July 2003; Update on Communications Received by the Prosecutor, 10 February 2006.

[49] UN Doc. S/RES/1593 (2005), para. 8.

[50] Rules of Procedure and Evidence, Rule 9. Also Regulations of the Court, Regulation 7(1)(e).

The Registry

The Registry is responsible for the non-judicial aspects of the administration and servicing of the Court. These include a number of specific responsibilities concerning victims, witnesses, defence and outreach. The Registry also provides requisite support for ongoing judicial proceedings. The principal administrative officer of the Court is the Registrar, and he or she heads the Registry.[51] The Registrar is elected by the judges to a five-year term. A jurist from France, Bruno Cathala, was chosen in June 2003 as the Court's first Registrar. He was later replaced, in early 2008, by Silvana Arbia, of Italy. If required, the judges may also elect a Deputy Registrar to a five-year term or to such shorter term as they may decide. The Registrar and Deputy Registrar must make a solemn undertaking in open court to exercise their functions impartially and conscientiously.[52]

The activities of the Registry are subject to Regulations which address matters such as proceedings before the Court and the responsibilities of the Registry with respect to victims, witnesses, counsel, legal assistance and detention.

The Statute specifically provides for the use of 'gratis personnel' offered by States Parties, intergovernmental bodies and non-governmental organizations to assist with the work of any of the organs of the Court. Gratis personnel are to be employed only 'in exceptional circumstances'.[53] Many States have expressed their concern that frequent resort to such gratis personnel may distort the geographic balance of the Court's staff, favouring persons from wealthy countries.

Coordination Council

The Coordination Council is established pursuant to Regulation 2 of the Regulations of the Court.[54] It is comprised of the President (on behalf of the Presidency), the Prosecutor and the Registrar. The Council is to meet at least once a month, and on any other occasion, at the request of one of its members, in order to discuss and coordinate, where necessary, the administrative activities of the organs of the Court.

---

[51] Rome Statute, Art. 43. [52] *Ibid.*, Art. 45. [53] *Ibid.*, Art. 44(4).
[54] Regulations of the Court, Doc. ICC-BD/01–01–04, Regulation 3.

Advisory Committee on Legal Texts

The Advisory Committee on Legal Texts is established in accordance with Regulation 4 of the Regulations of the Court. The Committee is made up of three judges, one from each Division, elected from amongst the members of the Division. They serve for a term of three years. In addition, the Committee contains a representative of the Office of the Prosecutor, of the Registry, and of defence counsel. The Advisory Committee considers and reports on proposals for amendments to the Rules, the Elements of Crimes and the Regulations.[55]

Detention Unit

The Court operates its own detention unit, known as the Temporary Detention Centre, within a larger penitentiary facility of the Dutch Government. Detainees are held in the Dutch Government's Haaglanden Prison, in nearby Scheveningen, contiguous to the United Nations Detention Unit that is used by the International Criminal Tribunal for the former Yugoslavia. Twelve cells are available for the use of the Court. If the number of detainees exceeds twelve, the Court will negotiate with the Dutch authorities in order to obtain more detention space. Each cell has its own toilet and washing area; a communal shower unit is located within the wing. There are visiting rooms for family and counsel, and an outside yard for exercise. The Court is charged €289 per cell per day by the Dutch Government for this service.[56]

Several provisions of the Regulations of the Court address issues concerning detention.[57] Because overall responsibility for detention lies with the Registry, provisions of the Regulations of the Registry add more detailed norms concerning detention matters.[58] Together, these constitute an extremely comprehensive legal regime for detained persons, including the treatment of disciplinary problems, a complaints procedure, clothing, personal hygiene, treatment of disabled detainees, telephone calls and mail. The Court has an agreement with the International Committee of the Red Cross providing for visits to

---

[55] *Ibid.*, Regulation 4.
[56] Report of the Committee on Budget and Finance on the Work of its Sixth Session, ASP/5/1, para. 30.
[57] Regulations of the Court, Regulations 89–106.
[58] Regulations of the Registry, Doc. ICC-BD/03–01–06, Regulations 150–223.

detainees.[59] Regulation 94 of the Regulations of the Court calls for regular and unannounced inspections of the detention centre by an independent institution. Article 6 of the Agreement states that '[t]he visits of the ICRC delegates shall be unannounced and the time allocated for such visits shall not be restricted'.

The Detention Centre took custody of its first prisoner, Thomas Lubanga, in March 2006. On 20 June 2006, the former President of Liberia, Charles Taylor, was transferred to the Detention Centre in accordance with the Memorandum of Agreement between the Court and the Special Court for Sierra Leone.[60] On 28 and 29 June 2006, the International Committee of the Red Cross made its first visit to the Court's Detention Centre.[61] Apparently it intervened with the Court with respect to the hours in which the two detainees are confined to their cells, which it judged to be excessive. Charles Taylor has complained about the 'Eurocentric' food served in the Court's Detention Centre,[62] and a West African cook has had to be recruited in order to accommodate his dietary preferences.

Outreach

Outreach activities have become an important component of international criminal prosecution. In their early years, the International Criminal Tribunals for the former Yugoslavia and Rwanda did not attach much importance to explaining and promoting their activities among the populations of the territories over which they exercised jurisdiction, and only later came to appreciate the importance of such work.[63]

---

[59] Agreement between the International Criminal Court and the International Committee of the Red Cross on Visits to Persons Deprived of Liberty Pursuant to the Jurisdiction of the International Criminal Court, Doc. ICC-PRES/02–01–06.

[60] Report on the Activities of the Court, ASP/5/15, para. 80.

[61] Ibid., para. 103.

[62] Taylor (Case No. SCSL-2003-01-PT), Transcript of Status Conference, 21 July 2006.

[63] See, e.g., Eleventh Annual Report of the International Tribunal for the Prosecution of Persons Responsible for Serious Violations of International Humanitarian Law Committed in the Territory of the Former Yugoslavia since 1991, UN Doc. A/59/21-S/2004/627, paras. 314–16; Eleventh Annual Report of the International Criminal Tribunal for the Prosecution of Persons Responsible for Genocide and Other Serious Violations of International Humanitarian Law Committed in the Territory of Rwanda and Rwandan Citizens Responsible for Genocide and Other Such Violations Committed in the Territory of Neighbouring States between 1 January and 31 December 1994, UN Doc. A/61/265–S/2006/658, paras. 51 and 54–5. Also Victor Peskin, 'Courting Rwanda: The Promises and Pitfalls of the ICTR Outreach Programme', (2005) 3 Journal

A Security Council resolution called upon the two tribunals to improve their outreach programmes.[64] The Special Court for Sierra Leone showed itself to be more engaged with the local population from the outset of its work, largely due to the determination of its Prosecutor, David Crane. Nothing in the Rome Statute indicates any particular role for outreach in the work of the International Criminal Court. Nevertheless, building upon the experience of the *ad hoc* tribunals, the Court has developed some capacity in this area. It produces television and radio broadcasts, as well as taking advantage of modern information technologies using the internet.

Field activities are organized by Outreach Units in each situation country. For example, in the Democratic Republic of the Congo, the Court has held regular 'interactive sessions' in Ituri, Kisangani, North and South Kivu and Kinshasa. Outreach Units were closely with local NGOs, media, schools and academic institutions. The investment remains modest, and it is difficult to assess the effectiveness of the outreach activities, which look good on paper and in glossy annual reports but may have only very limited impacts. One account of outreach in the Democratic Republic of the Congo, by distinguished writer Adam Hochschild, did not give a particularly positive impression:

> The videos are in French, the language of Congo's government, although few of the teenagers in the room speak it well. Furthermore, Kuyaku, who comes from another part of the country, does not speak Swahili, eastern Congo's *lingua franca*. After showing the videos, he talks animatedly in a mixture of French and another Congolese language, Lingala, which a sprinkling of those in the audience know, while an assistant intermittently translates a few sentences into Swahili.

Hochschild reported a local official describing the trial as '*justice à l'occidentale*'.[65]

Defence bar

The Rome Statute explicitly affirms the right of an accused person 'to conduct the defence in person or through legal assistance of the accused's

---

of International Criminal Justice 950; Lal C. Vohrah and Jon Cina, 'The Outreach Programme', in Richard May *et al.*, eds., *Essays on International Criminal Tribunal for the Former Yugoslavia Procedure and Evidence in Honour of Gabrielle Kirk McDonald*, The Hague: Kluwer Law International, 2001, pp. 547–57.

[64] UN Doc. S/RES/1503 (2003), para. 1.

[65] Adam Hochschild, 'The Trial of Thomas Lubanga', *The Atlantic*, December 2009.

choosing'.[66] The participation of counsel is also provided for in various provisions of the Statute, such as questioning of a suspect,[67] proceedings concerning a unique investigative opportunity,[68] the confirmation of charges hearing,[69] exclusion of the accused from the courtroom[70] and consultation concerning a guilty plea.[71] The Statute and the Rules of Procedure and Evidence establish norms that apply to defence counsel, including a Code of Professional Conduct for Counsel to be adopted by the Assembly of States Parties pursuant to a proposal from the Registrar, following consultation with the Prosecutor.[72] An accused is free to choose his or her own counsel, but it is likely that most will be unable to finance their own defence. As a result, they will fall back on the Court to provide counsel. The Statute also contemplates the representation of the interests of the defence before an actual accused is identified. Obviously, in such circumstances, it is the Court, and not the unknown defendant, who must see that this duty is fulfilled. The Registrar is assigned responsibility for designation of defence counsel where required, as well as provision of various forms of material assistance to defence counsel. According to Regulation 76(1) of the Regulations of the Court, a Chamber may also appoint counsel, following consultation with the Registrar, 'in the circumstances specified in the Statute and the Rules or where the interests of justice so require'. When Pre-Trial Chamber I requested *amici curiae* to make submissions on the possibility of conducting investigations within Sudan, it also asked the Registrar to appoint an *ad hoc* counsel 'to represent and protect the general interests of the Defence in the Situation in Darfur, Sudan' during this particular phase of the proceedings.[73]

Proposals during the Preparatory Commission process to establish a defence counsel unit, similar to the Victims and Witnesses Unit, were criticized on the ground that there was no basis in the Statute for such an initiative. This shortcoming was subsequently rectified in the Regulations. Pursuant to Regulation 77, the Office of Public Counsel for the Defence has been established. This Office 'shall fall within the remit

---

[66] Rome Statute, Art. 67(1)(d). Although expressed without qualification, the right of an accused to defend himself or herself is subject to limitations: *Milošević* (IT-02-54-AR73.7), Decision on Interlocutory Appeal of the Trial Chamber's Decision on the Assignment of Defence Counsel, 1 November 2004; *Šešelj* (IT-03-67-AR73.4), Decision on Appeal Against the Trial Chamber's Decision (No. 2) on Assignment of Counsel, 8 December 2006.

[67] Rome Statute, Art. 55(2)(d).   [68] *Ibid.*, Art. 56(2)(d).

[69] *Ibid.*, Art. 61(1).   [70] *Ibid.*, Art. 63(2).   [71] *Ibid.*, Art. 64(1)(b).

[72] Rules of Procedure and Evidence, Rule 8.

[73] *Situation in Darfur, Sudan* (ICC-02/05–10), Decision Inviting Observations in Application of Rule 103 of the Rules of Procedure and Evidence, 24 July 2006, p. 6.

of the Registry solely for administrative purposes and otherwise shall function as a wholly independent office'.[74] The tasks of the Office of Public Counsel for the Defence include representing and protecting the rights of the defence during the initial stages of the investigation and providing support and assistance to defence counsel and to the person entitled to legal assistance, including, where appropriate, legal research and advice and appearing before a Chamber in respect of specific issues.[75]

Rule 20 of the Rules of Procedure and Evidence sets out the 'Responsibilities of the Registrar relating to the rights of the defence':

1. In accordance with article 43, paragraph 1, the Registrar shall organize the staff of the Registry in a manner that promotes the rights of the defence, consistent with the principle of fair trial as defined in the Statute. For that purpose, the Registrar shall, *inter alia*:

   (a) Facilitate the protection of confidentiality, as defined in article 67, paragraph 1(b);

   (b) Provide support, assistance, and information to all defence counsel appearing before the Court and, as appropriate, support for professional investigators necessary for the efficient and effective conduct of the defence;

   (c) Assist arrested persons, persons to whom article 55, paragraph 2, applies and the accused in obtaining legal advice and the assistance of legal counsel;

   (d) Advise the Prosecutor and the Chambers, as necessary, on relevant defence-related issues;

   (e) Provide the defence with such facilities as may be necessary for the direct performance of the duty of the defence;

   (f) Facilitate the dissemination of information and case law of the Court to defence counsel and, as appropriate, cooperate with national defence and bar associations or any independent representative body of counsel and legal associations referred to in sub-rule 3 to promote the specialization and training of lawyers in the law of the Statute and the Rules.

2. The Registrar shall carry out the functions stipulated in sub-rule 1, including the financial administration of the Registry, in such a manner as to ensure the professional independence of defence counsel.

3. For purposes such as the management of legal assistance in accordance with rule 21 and the development of a Code of Professional Conduct in accordance with rule 8, the Registrar shall consult, as appropriate, with any independent representative body of counsel or legal associations,

---

[74] Regulations of the Court, Regulation 77(2).   [75] *Ibid.*, Regulation 77(4) and (5).

including any such body the establishment of which may be facilitated by the Assembly of States Parties.

Counsel for the defence are required to have 'established competence in international or criminal law and procedure, as well as the necessary relevant experience, whether as judge, prosecutor, advocate or in other similar capacity, in criminal proceedings'. Defence counsel are also required to have 'an excellent knowledge of and be fluent in at least one of the working languages of the Court'.[76] When Pre-Trial Chamber I instructed the Registrar to designate *ad hoc* defence counsel in the *Situation in Darfur* investigation, the judges subsequently communicated by e-mail with the Registrar indicating the desirability of finding an appropriate candidate with fluency in both English and Arabic.[77] The Registrar noted that there were only three lawyers on his list who met these criteria, and he eventually settled on an individual who was fluent in Arabic and French and who professed a '"bonne" connaisance de l'anglais'. In making the determination, the Registrar relied upon a form completed by the lawyer two years earlier. The Registrar affirmed that the individual fulfilled the requirements of Rule 22. Weeks later, the designated counsel filed a motion challenging the jurisdiction of the Court that suggested a rather limited familiarity with the legal basis of the Court and the applicable principles of international law.[78]

Assembly of States Parties

The Assembly of States Parties is responsible for a wide range of administrative issues, including providing the officers of the Court with general guidelines, adoption of the budget, increases in the number of judges, and similar matters. The Assembly is also the forum for the adoption of amendments to the Statute. To some extent, it was also charged with completing the unfinished work of the Rome Conference, adopting the Elements of Crimes, the Rules of Procedure and Evidence, and other instruments necessary for the operation of the Court. These instruments were initially prepared by the Preparatory Commission, in accordance with instruction in the Final Act, but subject to formal adoption by the Assembly.

[76] Rules of Procedure and Evidence, Rule 22(1).
[77] *Situation in Darfur* (ICC-02/05), Décision du Greffier relative à la nomination de Me Hadi Shalluf en qualité de conseil ad hoc de la Défense, 25 August 2006, p. 2.
[78] *Situation in Darfur* (ICC-02/05), Conclusions aux fins d'exception d'incompétence et d'irrecevabilité, 9 October 2006.

Each State Party has one representative in the Assembly of States Parties.[79] Signatories of the Final Act can be observers in the Assembly. This 'generous' approach prevailed over those who wanted to confine attendance in the Assembly to signatories of the Statute itself.[80] The Assembly is authorized to establish a Bureau as well as subsidiary bodies.[81] Both the Bureau and the Assembly meet once a year, although they can be convened more frequently if necessary. The Bureau operates in the form of two Working Groups, one based in The Hague and the other in New York. The Working Group located in the Hague has responsibility for the interim and permanent premises; initiating the Court's strategic planning process; proposals to improve equitable geographic representation and gender balance in the recruitment of staff; the budget; and issues concerning the host State such as issuance of visas for participants in sessions of the Assembly and political dialogue at the ambassadorial level. The Working Group of the Bureau that is based in New York deals with participation in the Assembly of States Parties (including measures to increase both the number of ratifications and the participation of developing countries), arrears (including suggestions to promote timely payment and guidelines for submission of documentation regarding exemption requests), the independent oversight mechanism, and the New York Liaison Office.

Review Conference

The first Review Conference met in Kampala, Uganda, from 31 May to 11 June 2010, principally in order to consider amendments to the Statute. Other activities included a 'stocktaking' involving panel discussions on such issues as cooperation with the Court and the complementarity regime. Future Review Conferences may be convened by the Secretary-General of the United Nations at any time. They are to be called at the request of a State Party, but only after this has been approved by a majority of States Parties.[82] The Statute says that the Assembly of States Parties is also empowered to convene such a conference.[83] The Review Conference is open to those participating in the Assembly of States Parties and on the same conditions.

---

[79] Rome Statute, Art. 112(1).
[80] Jarasch, 'Establishment, Organization and Financing', p. 23.
[81] S. Rama Rao, 'Financing of the Court, Assembly of States Parties and the Preparatory Commission', in Lee, *The International Criminal Court*, pp. 399–420.
[82] Rome Statute, Art. 123.   [83] *Ibid.*, Art. 121(2).

Article 123 of the Rome Statute specifically refers to changes to the list of crimes contained in Article 5 of the Statute as the subject matter of the first Review Conference, but adds that this in no way limits its scope with respect to other amendments. Several amendments to the subject-matter jurisdiction were originally proposed by States Parties, with a view to expanding the provisions concerning prohibited weapons, including nuclear weapons, and the addition of terrorism and international drug trafficking to the categories of punishable crimes.[84] With one exception, concerning addition of provisions concerning prohibited weapons when used in non-international armed conflict, these proposals did not enjoy support that was broad enough for them to be included in the agenda of the Review Conference. The main accomplishment of the first Review Conference was the adoption of provisions on the prosecution of the crime of aggression.

The only requirement in the Statute concerning the first Review Conference is a decision on whether or not to retain Article 124, the provision allowing States Parties to deny the Court jurisdiction over war crimes for a seven-year period. Although there was very broad support for the elimination of the provision, a few States said that it should be retained, given that it had already contributed to the ratification of the Statute by two States, and that its retention would do no real harm. They pointed to the fact that several non-party States wished the provision to be retained. Eventually, the Review Conference decided not to delete Article 124, and to reconsider the issue in 2015.

Friends of the Court

The 'Friends of the Court' is an informal group of diplomats, originally active in New York but based in The Hague ever since the permanent premises of the Court were set up there, in late 2003. To some extent, it is a continuation of the 'Like-Minded Group' that played such an important role in the negotiations leading to adoption of the Rome Statute. The purpose of the 'Friends' is to operate at the political level and address problems confronting the Court, such as cooperation by States with investigations and increasing awareness about its activities. The 'Friends' may even include States that have not yet ratified or acceded to the Rome Statute. It has no official recognition within the legal documents of the Court and meets informally on an irregular basis, as issues arise.

---

[84] 'Report of the Bureau on the Review Conference', ASP/8/43.

Privileges and immunities

Like all other international organizations, the Court and its personnel require 'privileges and immunities' for their operations. These are broadly similar to the rights to which diplomats are entitled. Article 48 of the Rome Statute declares that '[t]he Court shall enjoy in the territory of each State Party such privileges and immunities as are necessary for the fulfilment of its purposes'. The text is modelled on a similar provision in the Charter of the United Nations. The international criminal tribunals established by the United Nations benefit from Article 105 of the Charter. But, because the Court is an independent international organization, distinct norms, including a separate treaty, are required. Article 48 continues:

> 2. The judges, the Prosecutor, the Deputy Prosecutors and the Registrar shall, when engaged on or with respect to the business of the Court, enjoy the same privileges and immunities as are accorded to heads of diplomatic missions and shall, after the expiry of their terms of office, continue to be accorded immunity from legal process of every kind in respect of words spoken or written and acts performed by them in their official capacity.
>
> 3. The Deputy Registrar, the staff of the Office of the Prosecutor and the staff of the Registry shall enjoy the privileges and immunities and facilities necessary for the performance of their functions, in accordance with the agreement on the privileges and immunities of the Court.
>
> 4. Counsel, experts, witnesses or any other person required to be present at the seat of the Court shall be accorded such treatment as is necessary for the proper functioning of the Court, in accordance with the agreement on the privileges and immunities of the Court.

More detailed provisions on the subject appear in the Agreement on Privileges and Immunities of the International Criminal Court, to which reference is made in paragraphs 3 and 4. Its text was adopted at the first meeting of the Assembly of States Parties, in September 2002, and it entered into force on 22 July 2004 after obtaining its tenth ratification.[85] The Agreement was opened for signature until 30 June 2004,

---

[85] P. Mochochoko, 'The Agreement on Privileges and Immunities in the International Criminal Court', (2002) 25 *Fordham International Law Journal* 638; Cecilia Nilsson, 'Contextualizing the Agreement on the Privileges and Immunities of the International Criminal Court', (2004) 3 *Leiden Journal of International Law* 559; S. Beresford, 'The Privileges and Immunities of the International Criminal Court: Are They Sufficient for the Proper Functioning of the Court or Is There Still Room for Improvement?', (2002) 3 *San Diego International Law Journal* 83; L. Zelniker, 'Towards a Functional

and some sixty-two States signed the instrument. States that did not sign the treaty by that date are required to accede to rather than ratify the instrument.

The Agreement provides for access to territory, inviolability of archives and documents; facilities in respect of communications and immunity of the Court's funds and property. The Agreement also protects persons involved with the Court's work, such as defence counsel and their assistants, witnesses, victims and experts.

The Court may also make *ad hoc* arrangements on privileges and immunities, where these are necessary, such as in the case of an investigation on the territory of a State that has not yet ratified or acceded to the Agreement.

Languages

The Court has two working languages, English and French, although it may designate other working languages on a case-by-case basis.[86] Judges, the Prosecutor, the Registrar and their deputies, as well as defence counsel, are all required to have fluency in at least one of these languages.[87] In practice, it seems that the Court works largely in English. In one hearing, a legal representative of victims, Hervé Diakiese, said: 'I know that the Court has two working languages, both English and French, but sometimes I feel that the first language is English and the second English too.'[88] Even where the Court operates in a francophone environment, like the Democratic Republic of the Congo, many administrative documents need to be translated into English so that staff members can work with them.[89]

The Court has six official languages: Arabic, Chinese, English, French, Russian and Spanish. Decisions of the Trial Chambers on guilt or innocence, sentence and reparations, all decision of the Appeals Division, and other decisions 'resolving fundamental issues before the Court', are to be published in all of the official languages.[90] The requirement is

---

International Criminal Court: An Argument in Favour of a Strong Privileges and Immunities Agreement', (2001) 24 *Fordham International Law Journal* 988.

[86] Rome Statute, Art. 50(2); Rules of Procedure and Evidence, Rule 41; Regulations of the Court, Regulations 39–40.

[87] Rome Statute, Art. 50.

[88] *Katanga et al.* (CC-01/04–01/07), Transcript of Confirmation Hearing, 15 July 2008, p. 40, lines 23–5.

[89] 'Report of the Court on Options for Outsourcing Translation Work', ASP/7/5, paras. 16–17.

[90] Rules of Procedure and Evidence, Rules 40 and 43.

consistent with United Nations practice, but may prove cumbersome in the case of judgments running into several hundreds of pages, something that has become somewhat of a custom of the prolific judges of the *ad hoc* tribunals. Although the *ad hoc* tribunals have only two official languages, as a general rule they have proven to be unable to issue judgments in both languages simultaneously.[91]

Funding

One of the unfortunate consequences of the fact that the Court is not a United Nations body is that it is responsible for its own funding. The Statute allows the Court to take money based on contributions assessed upon States Parties, following the basic scale already in use in the United Nations, a calculation that considers population and relative wealth.[92] In addition, the Court may take any funds provided by the United Nations. Specific mention is made of expenses that may be incurred in the case of Security Council referrals, for which it seems only natural that the United Nations must be responsible.[93] The wording suggests this form of mixed financing, but tilts towards the idea that United Nations contributions are to be based principally upon cases involving Security Council referral. But, in the first referral of a situation by the Security Council, the relevant resolution insisted that none of the costs associated with investigation and prosecution were to come from the budget of the United Nations.[94] At the Rome Conference, proposals that the Court should be funded strictly by the United Nations[95] were resisted, principally by the three biggest contributors to the United Nations budget, the United States, Germany and Japan.[96]

---

[91] The first major judgment of the International Criminal Tribunal for the former Yugoslavia, the *Tadić* jurisdictional decision, was initially issued in English only, prompting a harsh declaration by French-Canadian judge Jules Deschênes: *Tadić* (IT-94-1-AR72), Separate Declaration of Judge J. Deschênes on the Defence Motion for Interlocutory Appeal on Jurisdiction, 2 October 1995. Many months later, a French version of the judgment became available. Less frequently, judgments have been issued in French first with an English-language version following weeks or months later.

[92] Rome Statute, Art. 117.   [93] *Ibid.*, Art. 115.

[94] UN Doc. S/RES/1593 (2005), para. 7.

[95] UN Doc. A/CONF.183/SR.2, para. 64 (Canada); UN Doc. A/CONF.183/C.1/SR.18, para. 20 (Denmark), para. 32 (Sweden), para. 74 (Portugal), para. 109 (Norway) and para. 144 (Belgium).

[96] Jarasch, 'Establishment, Organization and Financing', p. 23. See also Rao, 'Financing of the Court'.

The actual budget of the Court is proposed by the Court but actually determined by the Assembly of States Parties. At its first session, in September 2002, the Assembly adopted a budget of approximately €30 million, to be met by assessments levied upon States Parties in accordance with the applicable scales of assessment within the United Nations.[97] By 2010, the budget had increased to about €100 million.[98] The highest assessment is Japan, at €19,884,061, followed by Germany at €11,540,739. The lowest assessment, €1,346, is imposed on several developing countries.[99] A twelve-member Committee on Budget and Finance reviews relevant technical issues.[100]

The Court is entitled to receive and use any voluntary contributions from governments, international organizations, individuals, corporations and other entities.[101] The practice of receiving voluntary contributions is already well entrenched within the United Nations and other international organizations, and many important programmes would be eliminated without this source of financing. Some important functions of the *ad hoc* tribunals have only been fulfilled as a result of voluntary contributions. At its first session, in September 2002, the Assembly of States Parties made a formal request to governments, international organizations, individuals, corporations and other entities making voluntary contributions to declare that these 'are not intended to affect the independence of the Court'. Furthermore, it assigned the Registrar the responsibility to assure himself or herself that this condition was respected.[102] The voluntary contributions are held in a number of specially designated trust funds.

Settlement of disputes

The Rome Statute is an international treaty subject to many general legal rules developed by custom over the centuries and partially codified in

---

[97] Detailed projections are set out in the report of the Assembly of States Parties. See ASP/1/3, pp. 253–317. See Rolf Einar Fife, 'The Draft Budget of the First Financial Period of the Court', (2002) 25 *Fordham International Law Journal* 606.

[98] Proposed Programme Budget for 2010 of the International Criminal Court, ASP/8/10, para. 2.

[99] Scales of assessments for the apportionment of the expenses of the International Criminal Court, Res. ASP/1/Res.14; Financial Statements for the Period 1 January to 31 December 2008, ICC-ASP/8/14, Annex 1.

[100] Establishment of the Committee on Budget and Finance, ASP/1/Res.4.

[101] Rome Statute, Art. 116.

[102] Relevant Criteria for Voluntary Contributions to the International Criminal Court, ASP/1/Res.11.

the 1969 Vienna Convention on the Law of Treaties.[103] A multilateral treaty is, in effect, a form of contract between the States that adhere to it. Disputes may arise between two or more States as to the interpretation or application of the Statute. Such cases are to be submitted to the Assembly of States Parties, which may attempt to settle the case or propose alternative means of settlement, including referring the case to the International Court of Justice.[104] However, this procedure can only work with States that have also accepted the jurisdiction of the International Court of Justice, or that agree to its jurisdiction in a specific case.

Reservations

It is not at all uncommon for States to formulate reservations or interpretative declarations at the time they sign or ratify international treaties. In the absence of any special rules in the treaty itself, such reservations are permissible provided they do not violate the 'object and purpose' of the treaty. Complex questions have arisen in recent years with respect to the legality of reservations to certain treaties, and the legal consequences of invalid reservations.[105] Theoretically, all of this is avoided by Article 120, which states simply: 'No reservations may be made to this Statute.'[106] But the provision has not prevented some States from making 'declarations' at the time of ratification. To the extent such declarations do not seek to limit the State's obligations under the Statute, they would seem to be permissible. In practice, it is not always easy to distinguish between a reservation and a declaration.[107] Several States have formulated declarations at the time of ratification of the Statute.

At least one declaration would seem to be analogous to a genuine reservation. Denmark, upon ratification of the Statute, declared that it did not extend to the Faroe Islands and Greenland. A reservation is defined by the Vienna Convention on the Law of Treaties as 'a unilateral statement, however phrased or named, made by a State, when signing, ratifying, accepting, approving or acceding to a treaty, whereby it purports to exclude or to modify the legal effect of certain provisions of the treaty

---

[103] Vienna Convention on the Law of Treaties, (1979) 1155 UNTS 331.
[104] Rome Statute, Art. 119.
[105] The matter is currently being studied by the International Law Commission, under the direction of rapporteur Alain Pellet. See UN Doc. A/CN.4/558 and Add.1.
[106] See Tuiloma Neroni Slade and Roger S. Clark, 'Preamble and Final Clauses', in Lee, *The International Criminal Court*, pp. 421–50 at pp. 431–2.
[107] *Belilos* v. *Switzerland*, Series A, No. 132, 29 April 1988.

in their application to that State'. The consequence is to limit Denmark's obligations under the Statute. The practice of the depositary of the Rome Statute, the Secretary-General of the United Nations, with respect to other treaties has not been to treat such territorial declarations as reservations in the classic sense.[108] Denmark withdrew its declaration in 2006.

Another suspect declaration was made by Uruguay at the time of ratification: 'As a State Party to the Rome Statute, the Eastern Republic of Uruguay shall ensure its application to the full extent of the powers of the State insofar as it is competent in that respect and in strict accordance with the Constitutional provisions of the Republic.' The declaration seems to subordinate Uruguay's obligations under the Rome Statute to its constitution, and to that extent it constitutes an impermissible reservation. There have been objections to the declaration by Uruguay. Finland formulated the following objection:

> [The] statement, without further specification, has to be considered in substance as a reservation which raises doubts as to the commitment of Uruguay to the object and purpose of the Statute. The Government of Finland would like to recall Article 120 of the Rome Statute and the general principle relating to internal law and observance of treaties, according to which a party may not invoke the provisions of its internal law as justification for its failure to perform a treaty. The Government of Finland therefore objects to the above-mentioned reservation made by the Eastern Republic of Uruguay to the Rome Statute of the International Criminal Court.

Other objections were submitted by Denmark, Ireland, Germany, Norway, the Netherlands and the United Kingdom. Uruguay has answered the objections as follows:

> It is noted for all necessary effects that the Rome Statute has unequivocally preserved the normal functioning of national jurisdictions and that the jurisdiction of the International Criminal Court is exercised only in the absence of the exercise of national jurisdiction. Accordingly, it is very

---

[108] Palitha T. B. Kohona, 'Some Notable Developments in the Practice of the UN Secretary-General as Depositary of Multilateral Treaties: Reservations and Declarations', (2005) 99 *American Journal of International Law* 433 at 446. Nevertheless, the rapporteur on reservations of the International Law Commission considers that such declarations meet the definition of reservations: Report of the International Law Commission on the Work of Its Fiftieth Session, 20 April–12 June 1998, 27 July–14 August 1998, UN Doc. A/53/10 and Corr.1, para. 498.

clear that the above-mentioned Act imposes no limits or conditions on the application of the Statute, fully authorizing the functioning of the national legal system without detriment to the Statute. The interpretative declaration made by Uruguay upon ratifying the Statute does not, therefore, constitute a reservation of any kind.

France formulated several declarations at the time of its deposit of the instrument of ratification. France argued strongly at the Rome Conference for the permissibility of reservations. The second French declaration says that 'the provisions of Article 8 of the Statute, in particular paragraph 2(b) thereof, relate solely to conventional weapons and can neither regulate nor prohibit the possible use of nuclear weapons'. No State objected to the French declaration, but New Zealand and Sweden submitted statements that suggest a very different understanding. New Zealand said:

> The Government of New Zealand notes that the majority of the war crimes specified in Article 8 of the Rome Statute, in particular those in Article 8(2)(b)(i)–(v) and 8(2)(e)(i)–(iv) (which relate to various kinds of attacks on civilian targets), make no reference to the type of the weapons employed to commit the particular crime. The Government of New Zealand recalls that the fundamental principle that underpins international humanitarian law is to mitigate and circumscribe the cruelty of war for humanitarian reasons and that, rather than being limited to weaponry of an earlier time, this branch of law has evolved, and continues to evolve, to meet contemporary circumstances. Accordingly, it is the view of the Government of New Zealand that it would be inconsistent with principles of international humanitarian law to purport to limit the scope of Article 8, in particular Article 8(2)(b), to events that involve conventional weapons only.

Sweden declared:

> In connection with the deposit of its instrument of ratification of the Rome Statute of the International Criminal Court and, with regard to the war crimes specified in Article 8 of the Statute which relate to the methods of warfare, the Government of the Kingdom of Sweden would like to recall the Advisory Opinion given by the International Court of Justice on 8 July 1996 on the Legality of the Threat or Use of Nuclear Weapons, and in particular paragraphs 85–87 thereof, in which the Court finds that there can be no doubt as to the applicability of humanitarian law to nuclear weapons.

The Rome Statute makes its own exception to the prohibition by allowing States to formulate a kind of reservation to Article 8. For a seven-year period, States may ratify the Statute but escape jurisdiction over war crimes.[109] The text is all that remains of an early scheme by which States Parties would be able to pick and choose the crimes over which the Statute would apply to them. The existing provision was inserted in the final draft of the Statute as a compromise aimed at garnering the support of France and perhaps a few other States.[110] It was resoundingly criticized by human rights non-governmental organizations at the close of the Rome Conference, although these concerns were probably exaggerated.[111] Since then, only two States, France and Colombia, have actually invoked Article 124. Serious war crimes likely to attract the attention of the Prosecutor and meet the Court's threshold for serious crimes will by and large also meet the definition of crimes against humanity, especially given the stiff gravity threshold imposed as part of the admissibility criteria. It would seem unlikely that the Court will be deprived of jurisdiction over very many specific offenders merely because of Article 124.[112]

It is not entirely clear what the effect of a declaration under Article 124 will be. If a State declares that it does not accept the Court's jurisdiction over war crimes, does this mean that its nationals cannot be prosecuted, even if the crime is committed on the territory of another State Party? Elizabeth Wilmshurst, who was a member of the United Kingdom delegation at the Rome Conference, has argued that the 'common sense view' resulting from the negotiations of the Statute is that a declaration under Article 124 in effect insulates nationals of the State from prosecution by the Court. Similarly, she has argued that, after expiry of the declaration, the Court will be blocked from prosecuting war crimes committed during the period of the declaration.[113]

Amendment

In domestic legal systems, criminal law requires a large degree of flexibility. Criminal behaviour evolves rapidly, and both procedural and

---

[109] Rome Statute, Art. 124.

[110] France was the twelfth State to ratify the Statute, in June 2000. See Slade and Clark, 'Preamble and Final Clauses', p. 443.

[111] See, e.g., the comments of the International Committee of the Red Cross: UN Doc. A/C.6/53/SR.12.

[112] See also Kelly Dawn Askin, 'Crimes Within the Jurisdiction of the International Criminal Court', (1999) 10 *Criminal Law Forum* 33 at 50, who notes that Art. 124 may in fact provide an incentive to States to ratify the Statute.

[113] Elizabeth Wilmshurst, 'Jurisdiction of the Court', in Lee, *The International Criminal Court*, pp. 127–41 at pp. 139–41.

substantive rules need to be adjusted regularly in order to cope with change. International justice is rather more cumbersome in this respect, and, to make matters worse, the drafters of the Statute attempted to reduce or eliminate judicial discretion in a variety of areas. Judges at the *ad hoc* tribunals were given a wide degree of latitude in their interpretation of the crimes themselves, the definition and application of defences, and the adjustment of rules of procedure and evidence. All of this was left to them by the relatively terse words of the statutes themselves. The Rome Statute, by contrast, sets out considerably more detailed rules with respect to defences and other general principles, and then further constrains any prospect of discretion by adding the detailed Elements of Crimes and Rules of Procedure and Evidence to the mix. Experienced judges will no doubt find imaginative ways of pushing these limits to the utmost, but the fact remains that their manoeuvrability has been considerably hampered. As a result, changes in the applicable law should require frequent adjustment by the States Parties. Minor alterations can be effected by the Assembly of States Parties at any time through modification of the Elements and the Rules.

Where amendment of the Statute is required, a complex and extremely cumbersome procedure is set out. Amendments during the first seven years from the entry into force of the Statute were excluded altogether. Although any State Party may propose an amendment at any time afterwards,[114] the Statute institutionalizes the initial amendment process by providing for a Review Conference.[115] The text of an amendment is to be submitted by the proposing State Party to the Secretary-General of the United Nations, who is to circulate it to all States Parties. The next Assembly of States Parties will consider the amendment or, alternatively, decide to convene a Review Conference. Amendments are to be adopted by the Assembly of States Parties or by a Review Conference by consensus, failing which a majority of two-thirds of all States Parties will be required.

But amendments adopted by the Assembly of States Parties or by a Review Conference do not automatically enter into force. The States Parties to the Statute must also deposit individual instruments of ratification or accession to such amendments. As a general rule, an amendment will not come into force until seven-eighths of the States Parties have filed instruments of acceptance. When an amendment has been

---

[114] Rome Statute, Art. 121.   [115] *Ibid.*, Art. 123.

accepted by seven-eighths of the States Parties, any State Party unhappy with the change may give notice that it withdraws from the Statute.

With respect to amendments to the subject-matter jurisdiction, there is a special regime. After the amendment is adopted, any State Party may ratify or accept the amendment, which appears to enter into force once the first State takes this initiative.[116] Article 121(5) has proven to be problematic, and various interpretations have been advanced that depart from the literal sense of the text. When it amended Article 8 by adding new crimes applicable in non-international armed conflict, the 2010 Review Conference declared that it was operating under a 'negative understanding' of the provision, by which the Court was without jurisdiction with respect to crimes committed by the nationals or on the territory of a non-party State.[117] Yet, at the same time, the Review Conference adopted a 'positive understanding' of Article 121(5) with respect to the crime of aggression, by which the amendment applies to all States Parties, unless they opt out with a special declaration.[118]

In the case of amendments to provisions of an institutional nature, these are in principle rather less controversial, and the Statute does not require that they be ratified by States Parties. Such amendments are to be adopted by consensus or by a two-thirds vote of the Assembly of States Parties or a review conference, and come into force six months later. The expression 'amendments of an institutional nature' is defined:[119] they include matters dealing with the number of judges, the composition of chambers, staff of the Court, and so on.

Signature, ratification, approval and accession

States were entitled to sign the Statute until 31 December 2000.[120] Although signature of a treaty may also, under certain circumstances, constitute a means of indicating its acceptance,[121] in the context of the Statute signature is only a preliminary act – 'a first step to participation'[122] – and must be followed by deposit of an instrument of ratification, approval or accession for the State to become a party to the Statute. Customary law, as codified in the 1969 Vienna Convention on the Law

---

[116] *Ibid.*, Art. 131(5).
[117] Resolution Amending Article 8 of the Rome Statute, RC/DC/1/Add.1, PP2.
[118] Rome Statute, Art. 15*bis*(3).   [119] *Ibid.*, Art. 122(1).   [120] *Ibid.*, Art. 125(1).
[121] Vienna Convention on the Law of Treaties, (1979) 1155 UNTS 331, Arts. 11–12.
[122] *Reservations to the Convention on the Prevention and Punishment of the Crime of Genocide (Advisory Opinion)*, [1951] ICJ Reports 16 at 28.

of Treaties, requires that between the time of signature and ratification a State is obliged to refrain from acts which would defeat the object and purpose of a treaty, until it shall have made its intention clear not to become a party to the treaty.[123]

The terms 'ratification', 'acceptance', 'approval' and 'accession' describe the international act by which a State establishes on the international plane its consent to be bound by a treaty.[124] Although all four terms are acceptable,[125] the acts they describe are colloquially referred to as 'ratification'. States which have already signed the Statute deposit instruments of ratification, acceptance or approval. Those that have not deposit instruments of 'accession'. Deposit of these instruments is done with the depositary, who is designated as the Secretary-General of the United Nations.

The Statute entered into force on the first day of the month after the sixtieth day following the date of the deposit of the sixtieth instrument of ratification, acceptance, approval or accession with the Secretary-General of the United Nations, that is, on 1 July 2002.[126] For States that ratify, accept, approve or accede after the entry into force of the Statute, it will enter into force for them on the first day of the month after the sixtieth day following the deposit of instruments of ratification, acceptance, approval or accession.[127] It is possible for States to withdraw from the Statute by sending a written notice to the Secretary-General of the United Nations. Withdrawal takes effect one year after the receipt of the notification, unless the State in question specifies a later date.[128] But a State that withdraws cannot escape obligations that arose while it was a party, including financial obligations.[129] A State that reacted to indictment of one of its senior officials by withdrawing from the Statute could not affect any pending investigation or trial. The Statute does not explain what would happen if there were enough withdrawals to bring the number of ratifications below sixty.

Authentic texts

The plenary sessions and working groups of the Rome Conference took place with simultaneous translation in all six official languages of the

---

[123] Vienna Convention on the Law of Treaties, Art. 18.
[124] *Ibid.*, Art. 2(1)(b).
[125] Some States prefer one or the other term for constitutional or historical reasons: Slade and Clark, 'Preamble and Final Clauses', p. 444.
[126] Rome Statute, Art. 126(1).   [127] *Ibid.*, Art. 126(2).
[128] *Ibid.*, Art. 127.   [129] *Ibid.*, Art. 127(2).

United Nations system, namely, English, French, Russian, Spanish, Arabic and Chinese. All documents were also available in these languages. The drafting committee, presided by M. Cherif Bassiouni, worked intensely on the various language versions in order to ensure the greatest degree of consistency and coherence. The six versions of the authentic text of the Statute, adopted the evening of 17 July 1998, are declared to be equally valid.[130] Because of the complexities of the Statute and the haste with which the Conference operated, there were inevitably some errors in the version that was actually voted upon on 17 July. Subsequently, corrections were circulated to the participants in the Conference for their concurrence, and the official text is now slightly different from the one voted upon at the conclusion of the Conference.[131]

---

[130] *Ibid.*, Art. 128.
[131] Roy Lee, 'The Rome Conference and Its Contributions to International Law', in Lee, *The International Criminal Court*, pp. 1–39 at pp. 11–12.

Appendices

Appendix 1

Rome Statute of the International Criminal Court

Adopted by the United Nations Diplomatic Conference of Plenipotentiaries on the Establishment of an International Criminal Court on 17 July 1998.[1]

Preamble

The States Parties to this Statute,

Conscious that all peoples are united by common bonds, their cultures pieced together in a shared heritage, and concerned that this delicate mosaic may be shattered at any time,

Mindful that during this century millions of children, women and men have been victims of unimaginable atrocities that deeply shock the conscience of humanity,

Recognizing that such grave crimes threaten the peace, security and well-being of the world,

Affirming that the most serious crimes of concern to the international community as a whole must not go unpunished and that their effective prosecution must be ensured by taking measures at the national level and by enhancing international cooperation,

Determined to put an end to impunity for the perpetrators of these crimes and thus to contribute to the prevention of such crimes,

Recalling that it is the duty of every State to exercise its criminal jurisdiction over those responsible for international crimes,

Reaffirming the Purposes and Principles of the Charter of the United Nations, and in particular that all States shall refrain from the threat or use of force against the territorial integrity or political independence of any State, or in any other manner inconsistent with the Purposes of the United Nations,

---

[1] As corrected by the *procès-verbaux* of 10 November 1998, 12 July 1999, 30 November 1999, 8 May 2000, 17 January 2001 and 16 January 2002.

Emphasizing in this connection that nothing in this Statute shall be taken as authorizing any State Party to intervene in an armed conflict or in the internal affairs of any State,

Determined to these ends and for the sake of present and future generations, to establish an independent permanent International Criminal Court in relationship with the United Nations system, with jurisdiction over the most serious crimes of concern to the international community as a whole,

Emphasizing that the International Criminal Court established under this Statute shall be complementary to national criminal jurisdictions,

Resolved to guarantee lasting respect for and the enforcement of international justice,

Have agreed as follows:

Part 1
Establishment of the Court

Article 1
The Court

An International Criminal Court ('the Court') is hereby established. It shall be a permanent institution and shall have the power to exercise its jurisdiction over persons for the most serious crimes of international concern, as referred to in this Statute, and shall be complementary to national criminal jurisdictions. The jurisdiction and functioning of the Court shall be governed by the provisions of this Statute.

Article 2
Relationship of the Court with the United Nations

The Court shall be brought into relationship with the United Nations through an agreement to be approved by the Assembly of States Parties to this Statute and thereafter concluded by the President of the Court on its behalf.

Article 3
Seat of the Court

1. The seat of the Court shall be established at The Hague in the Netherlands ('the host State').

2. The Court shall enter into a headquarters agreement with the host State, to be approved by the Assembly of States Parties and thereafter concluded by the President of the Court on its behalf.

3. The Court may sit elsewhere, whenever it considers it desirable, as provided in this Statute.

Article 4
Legal status and powers of the Court

1. The Court shall have international legal personality. It shall also have such legal capacity as may be necessary for the exercise of its functions and the fulfilment of its purposes.

2. The Court may exercise its functions and powers, as provided in this Statute, on the territory of any State Party and, by special agreement, on the territory of any other State.

Part 2
Jurisdiction, admissibility and applicable law

Article 5
Crimes within the jurisdiction of the Court

1. The jurisdiction of the Court shall be limited to the most serious crimes of concern to the international community as a whole. The Court has jurisdiction in accordance with this Statute with respect to the following crimes:

(a) The crime of genocide;
(b) Crimes against humanity;
(c) War crimes;
(d) The crime of aggression.

2. The Court shall exercise jurisdiction over the crime of aggression once a provision is adopted in accordance with articles 121 and 123 defining the crime and setting out the conditions under which the Court shall exercise jurisdiction with respect to this crime. Such a provision shall be consistent with the relevant provisions of the Charter of the United Nations.[*]

Article 6
Genocide

For the purpose of this Statute, 'genocide' means any of the following acts committed with intent to destroy, in whole or in part, a national, ethnical, racial or religious group, as such:

(a) Killing members of the group;
(b) Causing serious bodily or mental harm to members of the group;

---

[*] Article 5(2) was deleted by the 2010 Review Conference: Amendments to the Rome Statute of the International Criminal Court on the Crime of Aggression, RC/10, para. 1. The amendment is 'subject to ratification or acceptance and shall enter into force in accordance with article 121, paragraph 5': The Crime of Aggression, RC/10, para. 1.

(c) Deliberately inflicting on the group conditions of life calculated to bring about its physical destruction in whole or in part;
(d) Imposing measures intended to prevent births within the group;
(e) Forcibly transferring children of the group to another group.

Article 7
Crimes against humanity

1. For the purpose of this Statute, 'crime against humanity' means any of the following acts when committed as part of a widespread or systematic attack directed against any civilian population, with knowledge of the attack:

(a) Murder;
(b) Extermination;
(c) Enslavement;
(d) Deportation or forcible transfer of population;
(e) Imprisonment or other severe deprivation of physical liberty in violation of fundamental rules of international law;
(f) Torture;
(g) Rape, sexual slavery, enforced prostitution, forced pregnancy, enforced sterilization, or any other form of sexual violence of comparable gravity;
(h) Persecution against any identifiable group or collectivity on political, racial, national, ethnic, cultural, religious, gender as defined in paragraph 3, or other grounds that are universally recognized as impermissible under international law, in connection with any act referred to in this paragraph or any crime within the jurisdiction of the Court;
(i) Enforced disappearance of persons;
(j) The crime of apartheid;
(k) Other inhumane acts of a similar character intentionally causing great suffering, or serious injury to body or to mental or physical health.

2. For the purpose of paragraph 1:

(a) 'Attack directed against any civilian population' means a course of conduct involving the multiple commission of acts referred to in paragraph 1 against any civilian population, pursuant to or in furtherance of a State or organizational policy to commit such attack;
(b) 'Extermination' includes the intentional infliction of conditions of life, *inter alia* the deprivation of access to food and medicine, calculated to bring about the destruction of part of a population;
(c) 'Enslavement' means the exercise of any or all of the powers attaching to the right of ownership over a person and includes the exercise of such power in the course of trafficking in persons, in particular women and children;

(d) 'Deportation or forcible transfer of population' means forced displacement of the persons concerned by expulsion or other coercive acts from the area in which they are lawfully present, without grounds permitted under international law;

(e) 'Torture' means the intentional infliction of severe pain or suffering, whether physical or mental, upon a person in the custody or under the control of the accused; except that torture shall not include pain or suffering arising only from, inherent in or incidental to, lawful sanctions;

(f) 'Forced pregnancy' means the unlawful confinement of a woman forcibly made pregnant, with the intent of affecting the ethnic composition of any population or carrying out other grave violations of international law. This definition shall not in any way be interpreted as affecting national laws relating to pregnancy;

(g) 'Persecution' means the intentional and severe deprivation of fundamental rights contrary to international law by reason of the identity of the group or collectivity;

(h) 'The crime of apartheid' means inhumane acts of a character similar to those referred to in paragraph 1, committed in the context of an institutionalized regime of systematic oppression and domination by one racial group over any other racial group or groups and committed with the intention of maintaining that regime;

(i) 'Enforced disappearance of persons' means the arrest, detention or abduction of persons by, or with the authorization, support or acquiescence of, a State or a political organization, followed by a refusal to acknowledge that deprivation of freedom or to give information on the fate or whereabouts of those persons, with the intention of removing them from the protection of the law for a prolonged period of time.

3. For the purpose of this Statute, it is understood that the term 'gender' refers to the two sexes, male and female, within the context of society. The term 'gender' does not indicate any meaning different from the above.

Article 8
War crimes

1. The Court shall have jurisdiction in respect of war crimes in particular when committed as part of a plan or policy or as part of a large-scale commission of such crimes.

2. For the purpose of this Statute, 'war crimes' means:

(a) Grave breaches of the Geneva Conventions of 12 August 1949, namely, any of the following acts against persons or property protected under the provisions of the relevant Geneva Convention:
    (i) Wilful killing;
    (ii) Torture or inhuman treatment, including biological experiments;

(iii) Wilfully causing great suffering, or serious injury to body or health;

(iv) Extensive destruction and appropriation of property, not justified by military necessity and carried out unlawfully and wantonly;

(v) Compelling a prisoner of war or other protected person to serve in the forces of a hostile Power;

(vi) Wilfully depriving a prisoner of war or other protected person of the rights of fair and regular trial;

(vii) Unlawful deportation or transfer or unlawful confinement;

(viii) Taking of hostages.

(b) Other serious violations of the laws and customs applicable in international armed conflict, within the established framework of international law, namely, any of the following acts:

(i) Intentionally directing attacks against the civilian population as such or against individual civilians not taking direct part in hostilities;

(ii) Intentionally directing attacks against civilian objects, that is, objects which are not military objectives;

(iii) Intentionally directing attacks against personnel, installations, material, units or vehicles involved in a humanitarian assistance or peacekeeping mission in accordance with the Charter of the United Nations, as long as they are entitled to the protection given to civilians or civilian objects under the international law of armed conflict;

(iv) Intentionally launching an attack in the knowledge that such attack will cause incidental loss of life or injury to civilians or damage to civilian objects or widespread, long-term and severe damage to the natural environment which would be clearly excessive in relation to the concrete and direct overall military advantage anticipated;

(v) Attacking or bombarding, by whatever means, towns, villages, dwellings or buildings which are undefended and which are not military objectives;

(vi) Killing or wounding a combatant who, having laid down his arms or having no longer means of defence, has surrendered at discretion;

(vii) Making improper use of flag of truce, of the flag or of the military insignia and uniform of the enemy or of the United Nations, as well as of the distinctive emblems of the Geneva Conventions, resulting in death or serious personal injury;

(viii) The transfer, directly or indirectly, by the Occupying Power of parts of its own civilian population into the territory it occupies, or the deportation or transfer of all or parts of the population of the occupied territory within or outside this territory;

(ix) Intentionally directing attacks against buildings dedicated to religion, education, art, science or charitable purposes, historic monuments, hospitals and places where the sick and wounded are collected, provided they are not military objectives;

(x) Subjecting persons who are in the power of an adverse party to physical mutilation or to medical or scientific experiments of any kind which are neither justified by the medical, dental or hospital treatment of the person concerned nor carried out in his or her interest, and which cause death to or seriously endanger the health of such person or persons;

(xi) Killing or wounding treacherously individuals belonging to the hostile nation or army;

(xii) Declaring that no quarter will be given;

(xiii) Destroying or seizing the enemy's property unless such destruction or seizure be imperatively demanded by the necessities of war;

(xiv) Declaring abolished, suspended or inadmissible in a court of law the rights and actions of the nationals of the hostile party;

(xv) Compelling the nationals of the hostile party to take part in the operations of war directed against their own country, even if they were in the belligerent's service before the commencement of the war;

(xvi) Pillaging a town or place, even when taken by assault;

(xvii) Employing poison or poisoned weapons;

(xviii) Employing asphyxiating, poisonous or other gases, and all analogous liquids, materials or devices;

(xix) Employing bullets which expand or flatten easily in the human body, such as bullets with a hard envelope which does not entirely cover the core or is pierced with incisions;

(xx) Employing weapons, projectiles and material and methods of warfare which are of a nature to cause superfluous injury or unnecessary suffering or which are inherently indiscriminate in violation of the international law of armed conflict, provided that such weapons, projectiles and material and methods of warfare are the subject of a comprehensive prohibition and are included in an annex to this Statute, by an amendment in accordance with the relevant provisions set forth in articles 121 and 123;

(xxi) Committing outrages upon personal dignity, in particular humiliating and degrading treatment;

(xxii) Committing rape, sexual slavery, enforced prostitution, forced pregnancy, as defined in article 7, paragraph 2(f), enforced sterilization, or any other form of sexual violence also constituting a grave breach of the Geneva Conventions;

(xxiii) Utilizing the presence of a civilian or other protected person to render certain points, areas or military forces immune from military operations;

(xxiv) Intentionally directing attacks against buildings, material, medical units and transport, and personnel using the distinctive emblems of the Geneva Conventions in conformity with international law;

(xxv) Intentionally using starvation of civilians as a method of warfare by depriving them of objects indispensable to their survival, including wilfully impeding relief supplies as provided for under the Geneva Conventions;

(xxvi) Conscripting or enlisting children under the age of fifteen years into the national armed forces or using them to participate actively in hostilities.

(c) In the case of an armed conflict not of an international character, serious violations of article 3 common to the four Geneva Conventions of 12 August 1949, namely, any of the following acts committed against persons taking no active part in the hostilities, including members of armed forces who have laid down their arms and those placed *hors de combat* by sickness, wounds, detention or any other cause:

(i) Violence to life and person, in particular murder of all kinds, mutilation, cruel treatment and torture;

(ii) Committing outrages upon personal dignity, in particular humiliating and degrading treatment;

(iii) Taking of hostages;

(iv) The passing of sentences and the carrying out of executions without previous judgment pronounced by a regularly constituted court, affording all judicial guarantees which are generally recognized as indispensable.

(d) Paragraph 2 (c) applies to armed conflicts not of an international character and thus does not apply to situations of internal disturbances and tensions, such as riots, isolated and sporadic acts of violence or other acts of a similar nature.

(e) Other serious violations of the laws and customs applicable in armed conflicts not of an international character, within the established framework of international law, namely, any of the following acts:

(i) Intentionally directing attacks against the civilian population as such or against individual civilians not taking direct part in hostilities;

(ii) Intentionally directing attacks against buildings, material, medical units and transport, and personnel using the distinctive emblems of the Geneva Conventions in conformity with international law;

    (iii) Intentionally directing attacks against personnel, installations, material, units or vehicles involved in a humanitarian assistance or peacekeeping mission in accordance with the Charter of the United Nations, as long as they are entitled to the protection given to civilians or civilian objects under the international law of armed conflict;

    (iv) Intentionally directing attacks against buildings dedicated to religion, education, art, science or charitable purposes, historic monuments, hospitals and places where the sick and wounded are collected, provided they are not military objectives;

    (v) Pillaging a town or place, even when taken by assault;

    (vi) Committing rape, sexual slavery, enforced prostitution, forced pregnancy, as defined in article 7, paragraph 2 (f), enforced sterilization, and any other form of sexual violence also constituting a serious violation of article 3 common to the four Geneva Conventions;

    (vii) Conscripting or enlisting children under the age of fifteen years into armed forces or groups or using them to participate actively in hostilities;

    (viii) Ordering the displacement of the civilian population for reasons related to the conflict, unless the security of the civilians involved or imperative military reasons so demand;

    (ix) Killing or wounding treacherously a combatant adversary;

    (x) Declaring that no quarter will be given;

    (xi) Subjecting persons who are in the power of another party to the conflict to physical mutilation or to medical or scientific experiments of any kind which are neither justified by the medical, dental or hospital treatment of the person concerned nor carried out in his or her interest, and which cause death to or seriously endanger the health of such person or persons;

    (xii) Destroying or seizing the property of an adversary unless such destruction or seizure be imperatively demanded by the necessities of the conflict;

    (xiii) Employing poison or poisoned weapons; [not yet in force]

    (xiv) Employing asphyxiating, poisonous or other gases, and all analogous liquids, materials or devices; [not yet in force]

    (xv) Employing bullets which expand or flatten easily in the human body, such as bullets with a hard envelope which does not entirely cover the core or is pierced with incisions. [not yet in force]

(f) Paragraph 2 (e) applies to armed conflicts not of an international character and thus does not apply to situations of internal disturbances and tensions, such as riots, isolated and sporadic acts of violence or other acts of a similar nature. It applies to armed conflicts that take place in the territory of a State when there is protracted armed conflict between governmental authorities and organized armed groups or between such groups.

(3) Nothing in paragraph 2 (c) and (d) shall affect the responsibility of a Government to maintain or re-establish law and order in the State or to defend the unity and territorial integrity of the State, by all legitimate means.

Article 8*bis*[*]
Crime of aggression

1. For the purpose of this Statute, 'crime of aggression' means the planning, preparation, initiation or execution, by a person in a position effectively to exercise control over or to direct the political or military action of a State, of an act of aggression which, by its character, gravity and scale, constitutes a manifest violation of the Charter of the United Nations.

2. For the purpose of paragraph 1, 'act of aggression' means the use of armed force by a State against the sovereignty, territorial integrity or political independence of another State, or in any other manner inconsistent with the Charter of the United Nations. Any of the following acts, regardless of a declaration of war, shall, in accordance with United Nations General Assembly resolution 3314 (XXIX) of 14 December 1974, qualify as an act of aggression:

(a) The invasion or attack by the armed forces of a State of the territory of another State, or any military occupation, however temporary, resulting from such invasion or attack, or any annexation by the use of force of the territory of another State or part thereof;

(b) Bombardment by the armed forces of a State against the territory of another State or the use of any weapons by a State against the territory of another State;

(c) The blockade of the ports or coasts of a State by the armed forces of another State;

(d) An attack by the armed forces of a State on the land, sea or air forces, or marine and air fleets of another State;

(e) The use of armed forces of one State which are within the territory of another State with the agreement of the receiving State, in contravention of the conditions provided for in the agreement or any extension of their presence in such territory beyond the termination of the agreement;

---

[*] Article 8*bis* was added by the 2010 Review Conference: Amendments to the Rome Statute of the International Criminal Court on the Crime of Aggression, RC/10, para. 2. The amendment is 'subject to ratification or acceptance and shall enter into force in accordance with article 121, paragraph 5': The Crime of Aggression, RC/10, para. 1.

(f)   The action of a State in allowing its territory, which it has placed at the disposal of another State, to be used by that other State for perpetrating an act of aggression against a third State;

(g)   The sending by or on behalf of a State of armed bands, groups, irregulars or mercenaries, which carry out acts of armed force against another State of such gravity as to amount to the acts listed above, or its substantial involvement therein.

Article 9
Elements of Crimes

1. Elements of Crimes shall assist the Court in the interpretation and application of articles 6, 7, 8 and 8*bis*.* They shall be adopted by a two-thirds majority of the members of the Assembly of States Parties.

2. Amendments to the Elements of Crimes may be proposed by:

(a)   Any State Party;
(b)   The judges acting by an absolute majority;
(c)   The Prosecutor.

Such amendments shall be adopted by a two-thirds majority of the members of the Assembly of States Parties.

3. The Elements of Crimes and amendments thereto shall be consistent with this Statute.

Article 10

Nothing in this Part shall be interpreted as limiting or prejudicing in any way existing or developing rules of international law for purposes other than this Statute.

Article 11
Jurisdiction ratione temporis

1. The Court has jurisdiction only with respect to crimes committed after the entry into force of this Statute.

2. If a State becomes a Party to this Statute after its entry into force, the Court may exercise its jurisdiction only with respect to crimes committed after the entry into force of this Statute for that State, unless that State has made a declaration under article 12, paragraph 3.

---

* The reference to 'articles 6, 7 and 8' was changed to 'articles 6, 7, 8 and 8*bis*' by the 2010 Review Conference: Amendments to the Rome Statute of the International Criminal Court on the Crime of Aggression, RC/10, para. 6. The amendment is 'subject to ratification or acceptance and shall enter into force in accordance with article 121, paragraph 5': The Crime of Aggression, RC/10, para. 1.

Article 12
Preconditions to the exercise of jurisdiction

1. A State which becomes a Party to this Statute thereby accepts the jurisdiction of the Court with respect to the crimes referred to in article 5.

2. In the case of article 13, paragraph (a) or (c), the Court may exercise its jurisdiction if one or more of the following States are Parties to this Statute or have accepted the jurisdiction of the Court in accordance with paragraph 3:

(a) The State on the territory of which the conduct in question occurred or, if the crime was committed on board a vessel or aircraft, the State of registration of that vessel or aircraft;
(b) The State of which the person accused of the crime is a national.

3. If the acceptance of a State which is not a Party to this Statute is required under paragraph 2, that State may, by declaration lodged with the Registrar, accept the exercise of jurisdiction by the Court with respect to the crime in question. The accepting State shall cooperate with the Court without any delay or exception in accordance with Part 9.

Article 13
Exercise of jurisdiction

The Court may exercise its jurisdiction with respect to a crime referred to in article 5 in accordance with the provisions of this Statute if:

(a) A situation in which one or more of such crimes appears to have been committed is referred to the Prosecutor by a State Party in accordance with article 14;
(b) A situation in which one or more of such crimes appears to have been committed is referred to the Prosecutor by the Security Council acting under Chapter VII of the Charter of the United Nations; or
(c) The Prosecutor has initiated an investigation in respect of such a crime in accordance with article 15.

Article 14
Referral of a situation by a State Party

1. A State Party may refer to the Prosecutor a situation in which one or more crimes within the jurisdiction of the Court appear to have been committed requesting the Prosecutor to investigate the situation for the purpose of determining whether one or more specific persons should be charged with the commission of such crimes.

2. As far as possible, a referral shall specify the relevant circumstances and be accompanied by such supporting documentation as is available to the State referring the situation.

Article 15
Prosecutor

1. The Prosecutor may initiate investigations proprio motu on the basis of information on crimes within the jurisdiction of the Court.

2. The Prosecutor shall analyze the seriousness of the information received. For this purpose, he or she may seek additional information from States, organs of the United Nations, intergovernmental or non-governmental organizations, or other reliable sources that he or she deems appropriate, and may receive written or oral testimony at the seat of the Court.

3. If the Prosecutor concludes that there is a reasonable basis to proceed with an investigation, he or she shall submit to the Pre-Trial Chamber a request for authorization of an investigation, together with any supporting material collected. Victims may make representations to the Pre-Trial Chamber, in accordance with the Rules of Procedure and Evidence.

4. If the Pre-Trial Chamber, upon examination of the request and the supporting material, considers that there is a reasonable basis to proceed with an investigation, and that the case appears to fall within the jurisdiction of the Court, it shall authorize the commencement of the investigation, without prejudice to subsequent determinations by the Court with regard to the jurisdiction and admissibility of a case.

5. The refusal of the Pre-Trial Chamber to authorize the investigation shall not preclude the presentation of a subsequent request by the Prosecutor based on new facts or evidence regarding the same situation.

6. If, after the preliminary examination referred to in paragraphs 1 and 2, the Prosecutor concludes that the information provided does not constitute a reasonable basis for an investigation, he or she shall inform those who provided the information. This shall not preclude the Prosecutor from considering further information submitted to him or her regarding the same situation in the light of new facts or evidence.

Article 15*bis**
Exercise of jurisdiction over the crime of aggression
(State referral, *proprio motu*)

1. The Court may exercise jurisdiction over the crime of aggression in accordance with article 13 paragraphs (a) and (c), subject to the provisions of this article.

2. The Court may exercise jurisdiction only with respect to crimes of aggression committed one year after the ratification or acceptance of the amendments by thirty States Parties.

---

* Article 15*bis* was added by the 2010 Review Conference: Amendments to the Rome Statute of the International Criminal Court on the Crime of Aggression, RC/10, para. 3. The amendment is 'subject to ratification or acceptance and shall enter into force in accordance with article 121, paragraph 5': The Crime of Aggression, RC/10, para. 1.

3. The Court shall exercise jurisdiction over the crime of aggression in accordance with this article, subject to a decision to be taken after 1 January 2017 by the same majority of States Parties as is required for the adoption of an amendment to the Statute.

4. The Court may, in accordance with article 12, exercise jurisdiction over a crime of aggression, arising from an act of aggression committed by a State Party, unless that State Party has previously declared that it does not accept such jurisdiction by lodging a declaration with the Registrar. The withdrawal of such a declaration may be effected at any time and shall be considered by the State Party within three years.

5. In respect of a State that is not a party to this Statute, the Court shall not exercise its jurisdiction over the crime of aggression when committed by that State's nationals or on its territory.

6. Where the Prosecutor concludes that there is a reasonable basis to proceed with an investigation in respect of a crime of aggression, he or she shall first ascertain whether the Security Council has made a determination of an act of aggression committed by the State concerned. The Prosecutor shall notify the Secretary-General of the United Nations of the situation before the Court, including any relevant information and documents.

7. Where the Security Council has made such a determination, the Prosecutor may proceed with the investigation in respect of a crime of aggression.

8. Where no such determination is made within six months after the date of notification, the Prosecutor may proceed with the investigation in respect of a crime of aggression, provided that the Pre-Trial Division has authorized the commencement of the investigation in respect of a crime of aggression in accordance with the procedure contained in article 15, and the Security Council has not decided otherwise in accordance with article 16.

9. A determination of an act of aggression by an organ outside the Court shall be without prejudice to the Court's own findings under this Statute.

10. This article is without prejudice to the provisions relating to the exercise of jurisdiction with respect to other crimes referred to in article 5.

Article 15*ter*[*]
Exercise of jurisdiction over the crime of aggression
(Security Council referral)

1. The Court may exercise jurisdiction over the crime of aggression in accordance with article 13 paragraph (b).

---

[*] Article 15*ter* was added by the 2010 Review Conference: Amendments to the Rome Statute of the International Criminal Court on the Crime of Aggression, RC/10, para. 4. The amendment is 'subject to ratification or acceptance and shall enter into force in accordance with article 121, paragraph 5': The Crime of Aggression, RC/10, para. 1.

2. The Court may exercise jurisdiction only with respect to crimes of aggression committed one year after the ratification or acceptance of the amendments by thirty States Parties.

3. The Court shall exercise jurisdiction over the crime of aggression in accordance with this article, subject to a decision to be taken after 1 January 2017 by the same majority of States Parties as is required for the adoption of an amendment to the Statute.

4. A determination of an act of aggression by an organ outside the Court shall be without prejudice to the Court's own findings under this Statute.

5. This article is without prejudice to the provisions relating to the exercise of jurisdiction with respect to other crimes referred to in article 5.

Article 16
Deferral of investigation or prosecution

No investigation or prosecution may be commenced or proceeded with under this Statute for a period of 12 months after the Security Council, in a resolution adopted under Chapter VII of the Charter of the United Nations, has requested the Court to that effect; that request may be renewed by the Council under the same conditions.

Article 17
Issues of admissibility

1. Having regard to paragraph 10 of the Preamble and article 1, the Court shall determine that a case is inadmissible where:

(a) The case is being investigated or prosecuted by a State which has jurisdiction over it, unless the State is unwilling or unable genuinely to carry out the investigation or prosecution;

(b) The case has been investigated by a State which has jurisdiction over it and the State has decided not to prosecute the person concerned, unless the decision resulted from the unwillingness or inability of the State genuinely to prosecute;

(c) The person concerned has already been tried for conduct which is the subject of the complaint, and a trial by the Court is not permitted under article 20, paragraph 3;

(d) The case is not of sufficient gravity to justify further action by the Court.

2. In order to determine unwillingness in a particular case, the Court shall consider, having regard to the principles of due process recognized by international law, whether one or more of the following exist, as applicable:

(a) The proceedings were or are being undertaken or the national decision was made for the purpose of shielding the person concerned from criminal

responsibility for crimes within the jurisdiction of the Court referred to in article 5;
(b) There has been an unjustified delay in the proceedings which in the circumstances is inconsistent with an intent to bring the person concerned to justice;
(c) The proceedings were not or are not being conducted independently or impartially, and they were or are being conducted in a manner which, in the circumstances, is inconsistent with an intent to bring the person concerned to justice.

3. In order to determine inability in a particular case, the Court shall consider whether, due to a total or substantial collapse or unavailability of its national judicial system, the State is unable to obtain the accused or the necessary evidence and testimony or otherwise unable to carry out its proceedings.

Article 18
Preliminary rulings regarding admissibility

1. When a situation has been referred to the Court pursuant to article 13 (a) and the Prosecutor has determined that there would be a reasonable basis to commence an investigation, or the Prosecutor initiates an investigation pursuant to articles 13 (c) and 15, the Prosecutor shall notify all States Parties and those States which, taking into account the information available, would normally exercise jurisdiction over the crimes concerned. The Prosecutor may notify such States on a confidential basis and, where the Prosecutor believes it necessary to protect persons, prevent destruction of evidence or prevent the absconding of persons, may limit the scope of the information provided to States.

2. Within one month of receipt of that notice, a State may inform the Court that it is investigating or has investigated its nationals or others within its jurisdiction with respect to criminal acts which may constitute crimes referred to in article 5 and which relate to the information provided in the notification to States. At the request of that State, the Prosecutor shall defer to the State's investigation of those persons unless the Pre-Trial Chamber, on the application of the Prosecutor, decides to authorize the investigation.

3. The Prosecutor's deferral to a State's investigation shall be open to review by the Prosecutor six months after the date of deferral or at any time when there has been a significant change of circumstances based on the State's unwillingness or inability genuinely to carry out the investigation.

4. The State concerned or the Prosecutor may appeal to the Appeals Chamber against a ruling of the Pre-Trial Chamber, in accordance with article 82. The appeal may be heard on an expedited basis.

5. When the Prosecutor has deferred an investigation in accordance with paragraph 2, the Prosecutor may request that the State concerned periodically inform the Prosecutor of the progress of its investigations and any subsequent prosecutions. States Parties shall respond to such requests without undue delay.

6. Pending a ruling by the Pre-Trial Chamber, or at any time when the Prosecutor has deferred an investigation under this article, the Prosecutor may, on an exceptional basis, seek authority from the Pre-Trial Chamber to pursue necessary investigative steps for the purpose of preserving evidence where there is a unique opportunity to obtain important evidence or there is a significant risk that such evidence may not be subsequently available.

7. A State which has challenged a ruling of the Pre-Trial Chamber under this article may challenge the admissibility of a case under article 19 on the grounds of additional significant facts or significant change of circumstances.

Article 19
Challenges to the jurisdiction of the Court or the admissibility of a case

1. The Court shall satisfy itself that it has jurisdiction in any case brought before it. The Court may, on its own motion, determine the admissibility of a case in accordance with article 17.

2. Challenges to the admissibility of a case on the grounds referred to in article 17 or challenges to the jurisdiction of the Court may be made by:

(a) An accused or a person for whom a warrant of arrest or a summons to appear has been issued under article 58;

(b) A State which has jurisdiction over a case, on the ground that it is investigating or prosecuting the case or has investigated or prosecuted; or

(c) A State from which acceptance of jurisdiction is required under article 12.

3. The Prosecutor may seek a ruling from the Court regarding a question of jurisdiction or admissibility. In proceedings with respect to jurisdiction or admissibility, those who have referred the situation under article 13, as well as victims, may also submit observations to the Court.

4. The admissibility of a case or the jurisdiction of the Court may be challenged only once by any person or State referred to in paragraph 2. The challenge shall take place prior to or at the commencement of the trial. In exceptional circumstances, the Court may grant leave for a challenge to be brought more than once or at a time later than the commencement of the trial. Challenges to the admissibility of a case, at the commencement of a trial, or subsequently with the leave of the Court, may be based only on article 17, paragraph 1 (c).

5. A State referred to in paragraph 2 (b) and (c) shall make a challenge at the earliest opportunity.

6. Prior to the confirmation of the charges, challenges to the admissibility of a case or challenges to the jurisdiction of the Court shall be referred to the Pre-Trial Chamber. After confirmation of the charges, they shall be referred to the Trial Chamber. Decisions with respect to jurisdiction or admissibility may be appealed to the Appeals Chamber in accordance with article 82.

7. If a challenge is made by a State referred to in paragraph 2 (b) or (c), the Prosecutor shall suspend the investigation until such time as the Court makes a determination in accordance with article 17.

8. Pending a ruling by the Court, the Prosecutor may seek authority from the Court:

(a) To pursue necessary investigative steps of the kind referred to in article 18, paragraph 6;
(b) To take a statement or testimony from a witness or complete the collection and examination of evidence which had begun prior to the making of the challenge; and
(c) In cooperation with the relevant States, to prevent the absconding of persons in respect of whom the Prosecutor has already requested a warrant of arrest under article 58.

9. The making of a challenge shall not affect the validity of any act performed by the Prosecutor or any order or warrant issued by the Court prior to the making of the challenge.

10. If the Court has decided that a case is inadmissible under article 17, the Prosecutor may submit a request for a review of the decision when he or she is fully satisfied that new facts have arisen which negate the basis on which the case had previously been found inadmissible under article 17.

11. If the Prosecutor, having regard to the matters referred to in article 17, defers an investigation, the Prosecutor may request that the relevant State make available to the Prosecutor information on the proceedings. That information shall, at the request of the State concerned, be confidential. If the Prosecutor thereafter decides to proceed with an investigation, he or she shall notify the State in respect of the proceedings of which deferral has taken place.

Article 20
Ne bis in idem

1. Except as provided in this Statute, no person shall be tried before the Court with respect to conduct which formed the basis of crimes for which the person has been convicted or acquitted by the Court.

2. No person shall be tried by another court for a crime referred to in article 5 for which that person has already been convicted or acquitted by the Court.

3. No person who has been tried by another court for conduct also proscribed under article 6, 7, 8 or 8*bis** shall be tried by the Court with respect to the same conduct unless the proceedings in the other court:

4. Were for the purpose of shielding the person concerned from criminal responsibility for crimes within the jurisdiction of the Court; or

5. Otherwise were not conducted independently or impartially in accordance with the norms of due process recognized by international law and were conducted in a manner which, in the circumstances, was inconsistent with an intent to bring the person concerned to justice.

Article 21
Applicable law

1. The Court shall apply:

(a) In the first place, this Statute, Elements of Crimes and its Rules of Procedure and Evidence;
(b) In the second place, where appropriate, applicable treaties and the principles and rules of international law, including the established principles of the international law of armed conflict;
(c) Failing that, general principles of law derived by the Court from national laws of legal systems of the world including, as appropriate, the national laws of States that would normally exercise jurisdiction over the crime, provided that those principles are not inconsistent with this Statute and with international law and internationally recognized norms and standards.

2. The Court may apply principles and rules of law as interpreted in its previous decisions.

3. The application and interpretation of law pursuant to this article must be consistent with internationally recognized human rights, and be without any adverse distinction founded on grounds such as gender as defined in article 7, paragraph 3, age, race, colour, language, religion or belief, political or other opinion, national, ethnic or social origin, wealth, birth or other status.

---

* The reference to 'articles 6, 7 and 8' was changed to 'articles 6, 7, 8 and 8*bis*' by the 2010 Review Conference: Amendments to the Rome Statute of the International Criminal Court on the Crime of Aggression, RC/10, para. 7. The amendment is 'subject to ratification or acceptance and shall enter into force in accordance with article 121, paragraph 5': The Crime of Aggression, RC/10, para. 1.

Part 3
General principles of criminal law

Article 22
Nullum crimen sine lege

1. A person shall not be criminally responsible under this Statute unless the conduct in question constitutes, at the time it takes place, a crime within the jurisdiction of the Court.

2. The definition of a crime shall be strictly construed and shall not be extended by analogy. In case of ambiguity, the definition shall be interpreted in favour of the person being investigated, prosecuted or convicted.

3. This article shall not affect the characterization of any conduct as criminal under international law independently of this Statute.

Article 23
Nulla poena sine lege

A person convicted by the Court may be punished only in accordance with this Statute.

Article 24
Non-retroactivity ratione personae

1. No person shall be criminally responsible under this Statute for conduct prior to the entry into force of the Statute.

2. In the event of a change in the law applicable to a given case prior to a final judgment, the law more favourable to the person being investigated, prosecuted or convicted shall apply.

Article 25
Individual criminal responsibility

1. The Court shall have jurisdiction over natural persons pursuant to this Statute.

2. A person who commits a crime within the jurisdiction of the Court shall be individually responsible and liable for punishment in accordance with this Statute.

3. In accordance with this Statute, a person shall be criminally responsible and liable for punishment for a crime within the jurisdiction of the Court if that person:

(a) Commits such a crime, whether as an individual, jointly with another or through another person, regardless of whether that other person is criminally responsible;

(b) Orders, solicits or induces the commission of such a crime which in fact occurs or is attempted;

(c) For the purpose of facilitating the commission of such a crime, aids, abets or otherwise assists in its commission or its attempted commission, including providing the means for its commission;

(d) In any other way contributes to the commission or attempted commission of such a crime by a group of persons acting with a common purpose. Such contribution shall be intentional and shall either:

   (i) Be made with the aim of furthering the criminal activity or criminal purpose of the group, where such activity or purpose involves the commission of a crime within the jurisdiction of the Court; or

   (ii) Be made in the knowledge of the intention of the group to commit the crime;

(e) In respect of the crime of genocide, directly and publicly incites others to commit genocide;

(f) Attempts to commit such a crime by taking action that commences its execution by means of a substantial step, but the crime does not occur because of circumstances independent of the person's intentions. However, a person who abandons the effort to commit the crime or otherwise prevents the completion of the crime shall not be liable for punishment under this Statute for the attempt to commit that crime if that person completely and voluntarily gave up the criminal purpose.

3*bis*. In respect of the crime of aggression, the provisions of this article shall apply only to persons in a position effectively to exercise control over or to direct the political or military action of a State.*

4. No provision in this Statute relating to individual criminal responsibility shall affect the responsibility of States under international law.

Article 26
Exclusion of jurisdiction over persons under eighteen

The Court shall have no jurisdiction over any person who was under the age of 18 at the time of the alleged commission of a crime.

Article 27
Irrelevance of official capacity

1. This Statute shall apply equally to all persons without any distinction based on official capacity. In particular, official capacity as a Head of State or Government, a member of a Government or parliament, an elected representative or a government official shall in no case exempt a person from criminal

---

* Article 25(3)*bis* was added by the 2010 Review Conference: Amendments to the Rome Statute of the International Criminal Court on the Crime of Aggression, RC/10, para. 5. The amendment is 'subject to ratification or acceptance and shall enter into force in accordance with article 121, paragraph 5': The Crime of Aggression, RC/10, para. 1.

responsibility under this Statute, nor shall it, in and of itself, constitute a ground for reduction of sentence.

2. Immunities or special procedural rules which may attach to the official capacity of a person, whether under national or international law, shall not bar the Court from exercising its jurisdiction over such a person.

Article 28
Responsibility of commanders and other superiors

In addition to other grounds of criminal responsibility under this Statute for crimes within the jurisdiction of the Court:

1. A military commander or person effectively acting as a military commander shall be criminally responsible for crimes within the jurisdiction of the Court committed by forces under his or her effective command and control, or effective authority and control as the case may be, as a result of his or her failure to exercise control properly over such forces, where:
    (a) That military commander or person either knew or, owing to the circumstances at the time, should have known that the forces were committing or about to commit such crimes; and
    (b) That military commander or person failed to take all necessary and reasonable measures within his or her power to prevent or repress their commission or to submit the matter to the competent authorities for investigation and prosecution.

2. With respect to superior and subordinate relationships not described in paragraph (a), a superior shall be criminally responsible for crimes within the jurisdiction of the Court committed by subordinates under his or her effective authority and control, as a result of his or her failure to exercise control properly over such subordinates, where:
    (a) The superior either knew, or consciously disregarded information which clearly indicated, that the subordinates were committing or about to commit such crimes;
    (b) The crimes concerned activities that were within the effective responsibility and control of the superior; and
    (c) The superior failed to take all necessary and reasonable measures within his or her power to prevent or repress their commission or to submit the matter to the competent authorities for investigation and prosecution.

Article 29
Non-applicability of statute of limitations

The crimes within the jurisdiction of the Court shall not be subject to any statute of limitations.

Article 30
Mental element

1. Unless otherwise provided, a person shall be criminally responsible and liable for punishment for a crime within the jurisdiction of the Court only if the material elements are committed with intent and knowledge.

2. For the purposes of this article, a person has intent where:

(a) In relation to conduct, that person means to engage in the conduct;
(b) In relation to a consequence, that person means to cause that consequence or is aware that it will occur in the ordinary course of events.

3. For the purposes of this article, 'knowledge' means awareness that a circumstance exists or a consequence will occur in the ordinary course of events. 'Know' and 'knowingly' shall be construed accordingly.

Article 31
Grounds for excluding criminal responsibility

1. In addition to other grounds for excluding criminal responsibility provided for in this Statute, a person shall not be criminally responsible if, at the time of that person's conduct:

(a) The person suffers from a mental disease or defect that destroys that person's capacity to appreciate the unlawfulness or nature of his or her conduct, or capacity to control his or her conduct to conform to the requirements of law;
(b) The person is in a state of intoxication that destroys that person's capacity to appreciate the unlawfulness or nature of his or her conduct, or capacity to control his or her conduct to conform to the requirements of law, unless the person has become voluntarily intoxicated under such circumstances that the person knew, or disregarded the risk, that, as a result of the intoxication, he or she was likely to engage in conduct constituting a crime within the jurisdiction of the Court;
(c) The person acts reasonably to defend himself or herself or another person or, in the case of war crimes, property which is essential for the survival of the person or another person or property which is essential for accomplishing a military mission, against an imminent and unlawful use of force in a manner proportionate to the degree of danger to the person or the other person or property protected. The fact that the person was involved in a defensive operation conducted by forces shall not in itself constitute a ground for excluding criminal responsibility under this subparagraph;

(d) The conduct which is alleged to constitute a crime within the jurisdiction
     of the Court has been caused by duress resulting from a threat of immi-
     nent death or of continuing or imminent serious bodily harm against that
     person or another person, and the person acts necessarily and reasonably
     to avoid this threat, provided that the person does not intend to cause a
     greater harm than the one sought to be avoided. Such a threat may either
     be:
     (i)   Made by other persons; or
     (ii) Constituted by other circumstances beyond that person's control.

2. The Court shall determine the applicability of the grounds for excluding
criminal responsibility provided for in this Statute to the case before it.

3. At trial, the Court may consider a ground for excluding criminal responsibility other than those referred to in paragraph 1 where such a ground is
derived from applicable law as set forth in article 21. The procedures relating
to the consideration of such a ground shall be provided for in the Rules of
Procedure and Evidence.

Article 32
Mistake of fact or mistake of law

1. A mistake of fact shall be a ground for excluding criminal responsibility
only if it negates the mental element required by the crime.

2. A mistake of law as to whether a particular type of conduct is a crime
within the jurisdiction of the Court shall not be a ground for excluding criminal responsibility. A mistake of law may, however, be a ground for excluding criminal responsibility if it negates the mental element required by such a
crime, or as provided for in article 33.

Article 33
Superior orders and prescription of law

1. The fact that a crime within the jurisdiction of the Court has been committed by a person pursuant to an order of a Government or of a superior,
whether military or civilian, shall not relieve that person of criminal responsibility unless:

(a) The person was under a legal obligation to obey orders of the Government
     or the superior in question;
(b) The person did not know that the order was unlawful; and
(c) The order was not manifestly unlawful.

2. For the purposes of this article, orders to commit genocide or crimes
against humanity are manifestly unlawful.

Part 4
Composition and administration of the court

Article 34
Organs of the Court

The Court shall be composed of the following organs:

(a) The Presidency;
(b) An Appeals Division, a Trial Division and a Pre-Trial Division;
(c) The Office of the Prosecutor;
(d) The Registry.

Article 35
Service of judges

1. All judges shall be elected as full-time members of the Court and shall be available to serve on that basis from the commencement of their terms office.

2. The judges composing the Presidency shall serve on a full-time basis as soon as they are elected.

3. The Presidency may, on the basis of the workload of the Court and in consultation with its members, decide from time to time to what extent the remaining judges shall be required to serve on a full-time basis. Any such arrangement shall be without prejudice to the provisions of article 40.

4. The financial arrangements for judges not required to serve on a full-time basis shall be made in accordance with article 49.

Article 36
Qualifications, nomination and election of judges

1. Subject to the provisions of paragraph 2, there shall be 18 judges of the Court.

2.

(a) The Presidency, acting on behalf of the Court, may propose an increase in the number of judges specified in paragraph 1, indicating the reasons why this is considered necessary and appropriate. The Registrar shall promptly circulate any such proposal to all States Parties.

(b) Any such proposal shall then be considered at a meeting of the Assembly of States Parties to be convened in accordance with article 112. The proposal shall be considered adopted if approved at the meeting by a vote of two thirds of the members of the Assembly of States Parties and shall enter into force at such time as decided by the Assembly of States Parties.

(c)

    (i)   Once a proposal for an increase in the number of judges has been adopted under subparagraph (b), the election of the additional judges shall take place at the next session of the Assembly of States Parties in accordance with paragraphs 3 to 8, and article 37, paragraph 2;

   (ii)   Once a proposal for an increase in the number of judges has been adopted and brought into effect under subparagraphs (b) and (c) (i), it shall be open to the Presidency at any time thereafter, if the workload of the Court justifies it, to propose a reduction in the number of judges, provided that the number of judges shall not be reduced below that specified in paragraph 1. The proposal shall be dealt with in accordance with the procedure laid down in subparagraphs (a) and (b). In the event that the proposal is adopted, the number of judges shall be progressively decreased as the terms of office of serving judges expire, until the necessary number has been reached.

3.

(a) The judges shall be chosen from among persons of high moral character, impartiality and integrity who possess the qualifications required in their respective States for appointment to the highest judicial offices.

(b) Every candidate for election to the Court shall:

    (i)   Have established competence in criminal law and procedure, and the necessary relevant experience, whether as judge, prosecutor, advocate or in other similar capacity, in criminal proceedings; or

   (ii)   Have established competence in relevant areas of international law such as international humanitarian law and the law of human rights, and extensive experience in a professional legal capacity which is of relevance to the judicial work of the Court;

(c) Every candidate for election to the Court shall have an excellent knowledge of and be fluent in at least one of the working languages of the Court.

4.

(a) Nominations of candidates for election to the Court may be made by any State Party to this Statute, and shall be made either:

    (i)   By the procedure for the nomination of candidates for appointment to the highest judicial offices in the State in question; or

   (ii)   By the procedure provided for the nomination of candidates for the International Court of Justice in the Statute of that Court.

Nominations shall be accompanied by a statement in the necessary detail specifying how the candidate fulfils the requirements of paragraph 3.

(b) Each State Party may put forward one candidate for any given election who need not necessarily be a national of that State Party but shall in any case be a national of a State Party.

(c) The Assembly of States Parties may decide to establish, if appropriate, an Advisory Committee on nominations. In that event, the Committee's composition and mandate shall be established by the Assembly of States Parties.

5. For the purposes of the election, there shall be two lists of candidates:

List A containing the names of candidates with the qualifications specified in paragraph 3 (b)(i); and

List B containing the names of candidates with the qualifications specified in paragraph 3 (b)(ii).

A candidate with sufficient qualifications for both lists may choose on which list to appear. At the first election to the Court, at least nine judges shall be elected from list A and at least five judges from list B. Subsequent elections shall be so organized as to maintain the equivalent proportion on the Court of judges qualified on the two lists.

6.

(a) The judges shall be elected by secret ballot at a meeting of the Assembly of States Parties convened for that purpose under article 112. Subject to paragraph 7, the persons elected to the Court shall be the 18 candidates who obtain the highest number of votes and a two-thirds majority of the States Parties present and voting.

(b) In the event that a sufficient number of judges is not elected on the first ballot, successive ballots shall be held in accordance with the procedures laid down in subparagraph (a) until the remaining places have been filled.

7. No two judges may be nationals of the same State. A person who, for the purposes of membership of the Court, could be regarded as a national of more than one State shall be deemed to be a national of the State in which that person ordinarily exercises civil and political rights.

8.

(a) The States Parties shall, in the selection of judges, take into account the need, within the membership of the Court, for:
   (a) The representation of the principal legal systems of the world;
   (b) Equitable geographical representation; and
   (c) A fair representation of female and male judges.

(b) States Parties shall also take into account the need to include judges with legal expertise on specific issues, including, but not limited to, violence against women or children.

9.

(a) Subject to subparagraph (b), judges shall hold office for a term of nine years and, subject to subparagraph (c) and to article 37, paragraph 2, shall not be eligible for re-election.
(b) At the first election, one third of the judges elected shall be selected by lot to serve for a term of three years; one third of the judges elected shall be selected by lot to serve for a term of six years; and the remainder shall serve for a term of nine years.
(c) A judge who is selected to serve for a term of three years under subparagraph (b) shall be eligible for re-election for a full term.

10. Notwithstanding paragraph 9, a judge assigned to a Trial or Appeals Chamber in accordance with article 39 shall continue in office to complete any trial or appeal the hearing of which has already commenced before that Chamber.

Article 37
Judicial vacancies

1. In the event of a vacancy, an election shall be held in accordance with article 36 to fill the vacancy.
2. A judge elected to fill a vacancy shall serve for the remainder of the predecessor's term and, if that period is three years or less, shall be eligible for re-election for a full term under article 36.

Article 38
The Presidency

1. The President and the First and Second Vice-Presidents shall be elected by an absolute majority of the judges. They shall each serve for a term of three years or until the end of their respective terms of office as judges, whichever expires earlier. They shall be eligible for re-election once.
2. The First Vice-President shall act in place of the President in the event that the President is unavailable or disqualified. The Second Vice-President shall act in place of the President in the event that both the President and the First Vice-President are unavailable or disqualified.
3. The President, together with the First and Second Vice-Presidents, shall constitute the Presidency, which shall be responsible for:

(a) The proper administration of the Court, with the exception of the Office of the Prosecutor; and
(b) The other functions conferred upon it in accordance with this Statute.

4. In discharging its responsibility under paragraph 3 (a), the Presidency shall coordinate with and seek the concurrence of the Prosecutor on all matters of mutual concern.

Article 39
Chambers

1. As soon as possible after the election of the judges, the Court shall organize itself into the divisions specified in article 34, paragraph (b). The Appeals Division shall be composed of the President and four other judges, the Trial Division of not less than six judges and the Pre-Trial Division of not less than six judges. The assignment of judges to divisions shall be based on the nature of the functions to be performed by each division and the qualifications and experience of the judges elected to the Court, in such a way that each division shall contain an appropriate combination of expertise in criminal law and procedure and in international law. The Trial and Pre-Trial Divisions shall be composed predominantly of judges with criminal trial experience.   .

2.

(a) The judicial functions of the Court shall be carried out in each division by Chambers.

(b)

   (i) The Appeals Chamber shall be composed of all the judges of the Appeals Division;

   (ii) The functions of the Trial Chamber shall be carried out by three judges of the Trial Division;

   (iii) The functions of the Pre-Trial Chamber shall be carried out either by three judges of the Pre-Trial Division or by a single judge of that division in accordance with this Statute and the Rules of Procedure and Evidence;

(c) Nothing in this paragraph shall preclude the simultaneous constitution of more than one Trial Chamber or Pre-Trial Chamber when the efficient management of the Court's workload so requires.

3.

(a) Judges assigned to the Trial and Pre-Trial Divisions shall serve in those divisions for a period of three years, and thereafter until the completion of any case the hearing of which has already commenced in the division concerned.

(b) Judges assigned to the Appeals Division shall serve in that division for their entire term of office.

4. Judges assigned to the Appeals Division shall serve only in that division. Nothing in this article shall, however, preclude the temporary attachment of judges from the Trial Division to the Pre-Trial Division or vice versa, if the Presidency considers that the efficient management of the Court's workload so requires, provided that under no circumstances shall a judge who has participated in the pre-trial phase of a case be eligible to sit on the Trial Chamber hearing that case.

Article 40
Independence of the judges

1. The judges shall be independent in the performance of their functions.

2. Judges shall not engage in any activity which is likely to interfere with their judicial functions or to affect confidence in their independence.

3. Judges required to serve on a full-time basis at the seat of the Court shall not engage in any other occupation of a professional nature.

4. Any question regarding the application of paragraphs 2 and 3 shall be decided by an absolute majority of the judges. Where any such question concerns an individual judge, that judge shall not take part in the decision.

Article 41
Excusing and disqualification of judges

1. The Presidency may, at the request of a judge, excuse that judge from the exercise of a function under this Statute, in accordance with the Rules of Procedure and Evidence.

2.

(a) A judge shall not participate in any case in which his or her impartiality might reasonably be doubted on any ground. A judge shall be disqualified from a case in accordance with this paragraph if, *inter alia*, that judge has previously been involved in any capacity in that case before the Court or in a related criminal case at the national level involving the person being investigated or prosecuted. A judge shall also be disqualified on such other grounds as may be provided for in the Rules of Procedure and Evidence.

(b) The Prosecutor or the person being investigated or prosecuted may request the disqualification of a judge under this paragraph.

(c) Any question as to the disqualification of a judge shall be decided by an absolute majority of the judges. The challenged judge shall be entitled to present his or her comments on the matter, but shall not take part in the decision.

Article 42
The Office of the Prosecutor

1. The Office of the Prosecutor shall act independently as a separate organ of the Court. It shall be responsible for receiving referrals and any substantiated information on crimes within the jurisdiction of the Court, for examining them and for conducting investigations and prosecutions before the Court. A member of the Office shall not seek or act on instructions from any external source.

2. The Office shall be headed by the Prosecutor. The Prosecutor shall have full authority over the management and administration of the Office, including the staff, facilities and other resources thereof. The Prosecutor shall be assisted by one or more Deputy Prosecutors, who shall be entitled to carry out any of the acts required of the Prosecutor under this Statute. The Prosecutor and the Deputy Prosecutors shall be of different nationalities. They shall serve on a full-time basis.

3. The Prosecutor and the Deputy Prosecutors shall be persons of high moral character, be highly competent in and have extensive practical experience in the prosecution or trial of criminal cases. They shall have an excellent knowledge of and be fluent in at least one of the working languages of the Court.

4. The Prosecutor shall be elected by secret ballot by an absolute majority of the members of the Assembly of States Parties. The Deputy Prosecutors shall be elected in the same way from a list of candidates provided by the Prosecutor. The Prosecutor shall nominate three candidates for each position of Deputy Prosecutor to be filled. Unless a shorter term is decided upon at the time of their election, the Prosecutor and the Deputy Prosecutors shall hold office for a term of nine years and shall not be eligible for re-election.

5. Neither the Prosecutor nor a Deputy Prosecutor shall engage in any activity which is likely to interfere with his or her prosecutorial functions or to affect confidence in his or her independence. They shall not engage in any other occupation of a professional nature.

6. The Presidency may excuse the Prosecutor or a Deputy Prosecutor, at his or her request, from acting in a particular case.

7. Neither the Prosecutor nor a Deputy Prosecutor shall participate in any matter in which their impartiality might reasonably be doubted on any ground. They shall be disqualified from a case in accordance with this paragraph if, *inter alia*, they have previously been involved in any capacity in that case before the Court or in a related criminal case at the national level involving the person being investigated or prosecuted.

8. Any question as to the disqualification of the Prosecutor or a Deputy Prosecutor shall be decided by the Appeals Chamber.

(a) The person being investigated or prosecuted may at any time request the disqualification of the Prosecutor or a Deputy Prosecutor on the grounds set out in this article;
(b) The Prosecutor or the Deputy Prosecutor, as appropriate, shall be entitled to present his or her comments on the matter.

9. The Prosecutor shall appoint advisers with legal expertise on specific issues, including, but not limited to, sexual and gender violence and violence against children.

Article 43
The Registry

1. The Registry shall be responsible for the non-judicial aspects of the administration and servicing of the Court, without prejudice to the functions and powers of the Prosecutor in accordance with article 42.

2. The Registry shall be headed by the Registrar, who shall be the principal administrative officer of the Court. The Registrar shall exercise his or her functions under the authority of the President of the Court.

3. The Registrar and the Deputy Registrar shall be persons of high moral character, be highly competent and have an excellent knowledge of and be fluent in at least one of the working languages of the Court.

4. The judges shall elect the Registrar by an absolute majority by secret ballot, taking into account any recommendation by the Assembly of States Parties. If the need arises and upon the recommendation of the Registrar, the judges shall elect, in the same manner, a Deputy Registrar.

5. The Registrar shall hold office for a term of five years, shall be eligible for re-election once and shall serve on a full-time basis. The Deputy Registrar shall hold office for a term of five years or such shorter term as may be decided upon by an absolute majority of the judges, and may be elected on the basis that the Deputy Registrar shall be called upon to serve as required.

6. The Registrar shall set up a Victims and Witnesses Unit within the Registry. This Unit shall provide, in consultation with the Office of the Prosecutor, protective measures and security arrangements, counselling and other appropriate assistance for witnesses, victims who appear before the Court, and others who are at risk on account of testimony given by such witnesses. The Unit shall include staff with expertise in trauma, including trauma related to crimes of sexual violence.

Article 44
Staff

1. The Prosecutor and the Registrar shall appoint such qualified staff as may be required to their respective offices. In the case of the Prosecutor, this shall include the appointment of investigators.

2. In the employment of staff, the Prosecutor and the Registrar shall ensure the highest standards of efficiency, competency and integrity, and shall have regard, *mutatis mutandis*, to the criteria set forth in article 36, paragraph 8.

3. The Registrar, with the agreement of the Presidency and the Prosecutor, shall propose Staff Regulations which include the terms and conditions upon which the staff of the Court shall be appointed, remunerated and dismissed. The Staff Regulations shall be approved by the Assembly of States Parties.

4. The Court may, in exceptional circumstances, employ the expertise of gratis personnel offered by States Parties, intergovernmental organizations or non-governmental organizations to assist with the work of any of the organs of the Court. The Prosecutor may accept any such offer on behalf of the Office of the Prosecutor. Such gratis personnel shall be employed in accordance with guidelines to be established by the Assembly of States Parties.

Article 45
Solemn undertaking

Before taking up their respective duties under this Statute, the judges, the Prosecutor, the Deputy Prosecutors, the Registrar and the Deputy Registrar shall each make a solemn undertaking in open court to exercise his or her respective functions impartially and conscientiously.

Article 46
Removal from office

1. A judge, the Prosecutor, a Deputy Prosecutor, the Registrar or the Deputy Registrar shall be removed from office if a decision to this effect is made in accordance with paragraph 2, in cases where that person:

(a) Is found to have committed serious misconduct or a serious breach of his or her duties under this Statute, as provided for in the Rules of Procedure and Evidence; or
(b) Is unable to exercise the functions required by this Statute.

2. A decision as to the removal from office of a judge, the Prosecutor or a Deputy Prosecutor under paragraph 1 shall be made by the Assembly of States Parties, by secret ballot:

(a) In the case of a judge, by a two-thirds majority of the States Parties upon a recommendation adopted by a two-thirds majority of the other judges;
(b) In the case of the Prosecutor, by an absolute majority of the States Parties;
(c) In the case of a Deputy Prosecutor, by an absolute majority of the States Parties upon the recommendation of the Prosecutor.

3. A decision as to the removal from office of the Registrar or Deputy Registrar shall be made by an absolute majority of the judges.

4. A judge, Prosecutor, Deputy Prosecutor, Registrar or Deputy Registrar whose conduct or ability to exercise the functions of the office as required by this Statute is challenged under this article shall have full opportunity to present and receive evidence and to make submissions in accordance with the Rules of Procedure and Evidence. The person in question shall not otherwise participate in the consideration of the matter.

Article 47
Disciplinary measures

A judge, Prosecutor, Deputy Prosecutor, Registrar or Deputy Registrar who has committed misconduct of a less serious nature than that set out in article 46, paragraph 1, shall be subject to disciplinary measures, in accordance with the Rules of Procedure and Evidence.

Article 48
Privileges and immunities

1. The Court shall enjoy in the territory of each State Party such privileges and immunities as are necessary for the fulfilment of its purposes.

2. The judges, the Prosecutor, the Deputy Prosecutors and the Registrar shall, when engaged on or with respect to the business of the Court, enjoy the same privileges and immunities as are accorded to heads of diplomatic missions and shall, after the expiry of their terms of office, continue to be accorded immunity from legal process of every kind in respect of words spoken or written and acts performed by them in their official capacity.

3. The Deputy Registrar, the staff of the Office of the Prosecutor and the staff of the Registry shall enjoy the privileges and immunities and facilities necessary for the performance of their functions, in accordance with the agreement on the privileges and immunities of the Court.

4. Counsel, experts, witnesses or any other person required to be present at the seat of the Court shall be accorded such treatment as is necessary for the proper functioning of the Court, in accordance with the agreement on the privileges and immunities of the Court.

5. The privileges and immunities of:

(a) A judge or the Prosecutor may be waived by an absolute majority of the judges;
(b) The Registrar may be waived by the Presidency;
(c) The Deputy Prosecutors and staff of the Office of the Prosecutor may be waived by the Prosecutor;
(d) The Deputy Registrar and staff of the Registry may be waived by the Registrar.

Article 49
Salaries, allowances and expenses

The judges, the Prosecutor, the Deputy Prosecutors, the Registrar and the Deputy Registrar shall receive such salaries, allowances and expenses as may be decided upon by the Assembly of States Parties. These salaries and allowances shall not be reduced during their terms of office.

Article 50
Official and working languages

1. The official languages of the Court shall be Arabic, Chinese, English, French, Russian and Spanish. The judgments of the Court, as well as other decisions resolving fundamental issues before the Court, shall be published in the official languages. The Presidency shall, in accordance with the criteria established by the Rules of Procedure and Evidence, determine which decisions may be considered as resolving fundamental issues for the purposes of this paragraph.

2. The working languages of the Court shall be English and French. The Rules of Procedure and Evidence shall determine the cases in which other official languages may be used as working languages.

3. At the request of any party to a proceeding or a State allowed to intervene in a proceeding, the Court shall authorize a language other than English or French to be used by such a party or State, provided that the Court considers such authorization to be adequately justified.

Article 51
Rules of Procedure and Evidence

1. The Rules of Procedure and Evidence shall enter into force upon adoption by a two-thirds majority of the members of the Assembly of States Parties.

2. Amendments to the Rules of Procedure and Evidence may be proposed by:

(a) Any State Party;
(b) The judges acting by an absolute majority; or
(c) The Prosecutor.

Such amendments shall enter into force upon adoption by a two-thirds majority of the members of the Assembly of States Parties.

3. After the adoption of the Rules of Procedure and Evidence, in urgent cases where the Rules do not provide for a specific situation before the Court, the judges may, by a two-thirds majority, draw up provisional Rules to be applied until adopted, amended or rejected at the next ordinary or special session of the Assembly of States Parties.

4. The Rules of Procedure and Evidence, amendments thereto and any provisional Rule shall be consistent with this Statute. Amendments to the Rules of Procedure and Evidence as well as provisional Rules shall not be applied retroactively to the detriment of the person who is being investigated or prosecuted or who has been convicted.

5. In the event of conflict between the Statute and the Rules of Procedure and Evidence, the Statute shall prevail.

Article 52
Regulations of the Court

1. The judges shall, in accordance with this Statute and the Rules of Procedure and Evidence, adopt, by an absolute majority, the Regulations of the Court necessary for its routine functioning.

2. The Prosecutor and the Registrar shall be consulted in the elaboration of the Regulations and any amendments thereto.

3. The Regulations and any amendments thereto shall take effect upon adoption unless otherwise decided by the judges. Immediately upon adoption, they shall be circulated to States Parties for comments. If within six months there are no objections from a majority of States Parties, they shall remain in force.

Part 5
Investigation and prosecution

Article 53
Initiation of an investigation

1. The Prosecutor shall, having evaluated the information made available to him or her, initiate an investigation unless he or she determines that there is no reasonable basis to proceed under this Statute. In deciding whether to initiate an investigation, the Prosecutor shall consider whether:

(a) The information available to the Prosecutor provides a reasonable basis to believe that a crime within the jurisdiction of the Court has been or is being committed;
(b) The case is or would be admissible under article 17; and
(c) Taking into account the gravity of the crime and the interests of victims, there are nonetheless substantial reasons to believe that an investigation would not serve the interests of justice.

If the Prosecutor determines that there is no reasonable basis to proceed and his or her determination is based solely on subparagraph (c) above, he or she shall inform the Pre-Trial Chamber.

2. If, upon investigation, the Prosecutor concludes that there is not a sufficient basis for a prosecution because:

(a) There is not a sufficient legal or factual basis to seek a warrant or summons under article 58;
(b) The case is inadmissible under article 17; or
(c) A prosecution is not in the interests of justice, taking into account all the circumstances, including the gravity of the crime, the interests of victims and the age or infirmity of the alleged perpetrator, and his or her role in the alleged crime

The Prosecutor shall inform the Pre-Trial Chamber and the State making a referral under article 14 or the Security Council in a case under article 13, paragraph (b), of his or her conclusion and the reasons for the conclusion.

3.

(a) At the request of the State making a referral under article 14 or the Security Council under article 13, paragraph (b), the Pre-Trial Chamber may review a decision of the Prosecutor under paragraph 1 or 2 not to proceed and may request the Prosecutor to reconsider that decision.
(b) In addition, the Pre-Trial Chamber may, on its own initiative, review a decision of the Prosecutor not to proceed if it is based solely on paragraph 1 (c) or 2 (c). In such a case, the decision of the Prosecutor shall be effective only if confirmed by the Pre-Trial Chamber.

4. The Prosecutor may, at any time, reconsider a decision whether to initiate an investigation or prosecution based on new facts or information.

Article 54
Duties and powers of the Prosecutor with respect to investigations

1. The Prosecutor shall:

(a) In order to establish the truth, extend the investigation to cover all facts and evidence relevant to an assessment of whether there is criminal responsibility under this Statute, and, in doing so, investigate incriminating and exonerating circumstances equally;
(b) Take appropriate measures to ensure the effective investigation and prosecution of crimes within the jurisdiction of the Court, and in doing so, respect the interests and personal circumstances of victims and witnesses, including age, gender as defined in article 7, paragraph 3, and health, and take into account the nature of the crime, in particular where it involves sexual violence, gender violence or violence against children; and
(c) Fully respect the rights of persons arising under this Statute.

2. The Prosecutor may conduct investigations on the territory of a State:

(a) In accordance with the provisions of Part 9; or
(b) As authorized by the Pre-Trial Chamber under article 57, paragraph 3 (d).

3. The Prosecutor may:

(a) Collect and examine evidence;
(b) Request the presence of and question persons being investigated, victims and witnesses;

(c) Seek the cooperation of any State or intergovernmental organization or arrangement in accordance with its respective competence and/or mandate;

(d) Enter into such arrangements or agreements, not inconsistent with this Statute, as may be necessary to facilitate the cooperation of a State, intergovernmental organization or person;

(e) Agree not to disclose, at any stage of the proceedings, documents or information that the Prosecutor obtains on the condition of confidentiality and solely for the purpose of generating new evidence, unless the provider of the information consents; and

(f) Take necessary measures, or request that necessary measures be taken, to ensure the confidentiality of information, the protection of any person or the preservation of evidence.

Article 55
Rights of persons during an investigation

1. In respect of an investigation under this Statute, a person:

(a) Shall not be compelled to incriminate himself or herself or to confess guilt;

(b) Shall not be subjected to any form of coercion, duress or threat, to torture or to any other form of cruel, inhuman or degrading treatment or punishment;

(c) Shall, if questioned in a language other than a language the person fully understands and speaks, have, free of any cost, the assistance of a competent interpreter and such translations as are necessary to meet the requirements of fairness and

(d) Shall not be subjected to arbitrary arrest or detention; and shall not be deprived of his or her liberty except on such grounds and in accordance with such procedures as are established in this Statute.

2. Where there are grounds to believe that a person has committed a crime within the jurisdiction of the Court and that person is about to be questioned either by the Prosecutor, or by national authorities pursuant to a request made under Part 9 of this Statute, that person shall also have the following rights of which he or she shall be informed prior to being questioned:

(a) To be informed, prior to being questioned, that there are grounds to believe that he or she has committed a crime within the jurisdiction of the Court;

(b) To remain silent, without such silence being a consideration in the determination of guilt or innocence;

(c) To have legal assistance of the person's choosing, or, if the person does not have legal assistance, to have legal assistance assigned to him or her, in any case where the interests of justice so require, and without payment by the person in any such case if the person does not have sufficient means to pay for it; and

(d) To be questioned in the presence of counsel unless the person has voluntarily waived his or her right to counsel.

Article 56
Role of the Pre-Trial Chamber in relation to a unique investigative opportunity

1.

(a) Where the Prosecutor considers an investigation to present a unique opportunity to take testimony or a statement from a witness or to examine, collect or test evidence, which may not be available subsequently for the purposes of a trial, the Prosecutor shall so inform the Pre-Trial Chamber.

(b) In that case, the Pre-Trial Chamber may, upon request of the Prosecutor, take such measures as may be necessary to ensure the efficiency and integrity of the proceedings and, in particular, to protect the rights of the defence.

(c) Unless the Pre-Trial Chamber orders otherwise, the Prosecutor shall provide the relevant information to the person who has been arrested or appeared in response to a summons in connection with the investigation referred to in subparagraph (a), in order that he or she may be heard on the matter.

2. The measures referred to in paragraph 1 (b) may include:

(a) Making recommendations or orders regarding procedures to be followed;

(b) Directing that a record be made of the proceedings;

(c) Appointing an expert to assist;

(d) Authorizing counsel for a person who has been arrested, or appeared before the Court in response to a summons, to participate, or where there has not yet been such an arrest or appearance or counsel has not been designated, appointing another counsel to attend and represent the interests of the defence;

(e) Naming one of its members or, if necessary, another available judge of the Pre-Trial or Trial Division to observe and make recommendations or orders regarding the collection and preservation of evidence and the questioning of persons;

(f) Taking such other action as may be necessary to collect or preserve evidence.

3.

(a) Where the Prosecutor has not sought measures pursuant to this article but the Pre-Trial Chamber considers that such measures are required to preserve evidence that it deems would be essential for the defence at trial, it shall consult with the Prosecutor as to whether there is good reason for the Prosecutor's failure to request the measures. If upon consultation, the Pre-Trial Chamber concludes that the Prosecutor's failure to request such measures is unjustified, the Pre-Trial Chamber may take such measures on its own initiative.
(b) A decision of the Pre-Trial Chamber to act on its own initiative under this paragraph may be appealed by the Prosecutor. The appeal shall be heard on an expedited basis.

4. The admissibility of evidence preserved or collected for trial pursuant to this article, or the record thereof, shall be governed at trial by article 69, and given such weight as determined by the Trial Chamber.

Article 57
Functions and powers of the Pre-Trial Chamber

1. Unless otherwise provided in this Statute, the Pre-Trial Chamber shall exercise its functions in accordance with the provisions of this article.

2.

(a) Orders or rulings of the Pre-Trial Chamber issued under articles 15, 18, 19, 54, paragraph 2, 61, paragraph 7, and 72 must be concurred in by a majority of its judges.
(b) In all other cases, a single judge of the Pre-Trial Chamber may exercise the functions provided for in this Statute, unless otherwise provided for in the Rules of Procedure and Evidence or by a majority of the Pre-Trial Chamber.

3. In addition to its other functions under this Statute, the Pre-Trial Chamber may:

(a) At the request of the Prosecutor, issue such orders and warrants as may be required for the purposes of an investigation;
(b) Upon the request of a person who has been arrested or has appeared pursuant to a summons under article 58, issue such orders, including measures such as those described in article 56, or seek such cooperation pursuant to Part 9 as may be necessary to assist the person in the preparation of his or her defence;

(c) Where necessary, provide for the protection and privacy of victims and witnesses, the preservation of evidence, the protection of persons who have been arrested or appeared in response to a summons, and the protection of national security information;

(d) Authorize the Prosecutor to take specific investigative steps within the territory of a State Party without having secured the cooperation of that State under Part 9 if, whenever possible having regard to the views of the State concerned, the Pre-Trial Chamber has determined in that case that the State is clearly unable to execute a request for cooperation due to the unavailability of any authority or any component of its judicial system competent to execute the request for cooperation under Part 9.

(e) Where a warrant of arrest or a summons has been issued under article 58, and having due regard to the strength of the evidence and the rights of the parties concerned, as provided for in this Statute and the Rules of Procedure and Evidence, seek the cooperation of States pursuant to article 93, paragraph 1 (k), to take protective measures for the purpose of forfeiture, in particular for the ultimate benefit of victims.

Article 58
Issuance by the Pre-Trial Chamber of a warrant of arrest or a summons to appear

1. At any time after the initiation of an investigation, the Pre-Trial Chamber shall, on the application of the Prosecutor, issue a warrant of arrest of a person if, having examined the application and the evidence or other information submitted by the Prosecutor, it is satisfied that:

(a) There are reasonable grounds to believe that the person has committed a crime within the jurisdiction of the Court; and

(b) The arrest of the person appears necessary:

(c)

(i) To ensure the person's appearance at trial,

(ii) To ensure that the person does not obstruct or endanger the investigation or the court proceedings, or

(iii) Where applicable, to prevent the person from continuing with the commission of that crime or a related crime which is within the jurisdiction of the Court and which arises out of the same circumstances.

2. The application of the Prosecutor shall contain:

(a) The name of the person and any other relevant identifying information;

(b) A specific reference to the crimes within the jurisdiction of the Court which the person is alleged to have committed;

(c) A concise statement of the facts which are alleged to constitute those crimes;
(d) A summary of the evidence and any other information which establish reasonable grounds to believe that the person committed those crimes; and
(e) The reason why the Prosecutor believes that the arrest of the person is necessary.

3. The warrant of arrest shall contain:

(a) The name of the person and any other relevant identifying information;
(b) A specific reference to the crimes within the jurisdiction of the Court for which the person's arrest is sought; and
(c) A concise statement of the facts which are alleged to constitute those crimes.

4. The warrant of arrest shall remain in effect until otherwise ordered by the Court.

5. On the basis of the warrant of arrest, the Court may request the provisional arrest or the arrest and surrender of the person under Part 9.

6. The Prosecutor may request the Pre-Trial Chamber to amend the warrant of arrest by modifying or adding to the crimes specified therein. The Pre-Trial Chamber shall so amend the warrant if it is satisfied that there are reasonable grounds to believe that the person committed the modified or additional crimes.

7. As an alternative to seeking a warrant of arrest, the Prosecutor may submit an application requesting that the Pre-Trial Chamber issue a summons for the person to appear. If the Pre-Trial Chamber is satisfied that there are reasonable grounds to believe that the person committed the crime alleged and that a summons is sufficient to ensure the person's appearance, it shall issue the summons, with or without conditions restricting liberty (other than detention) if provided for by national law, for the person to appear. The summons shall contain:

(a) The name of the person and any other relevant identifying information;
(b) The specified date on which the person is to appear;
(c) A specific reference to the crimes within the jurisdiction of the Court which the person is alleged to have committed; and
(d) A concise statement of the facts which are alleged to constitute the crime.

The summons shall be served on the person.

Article 59
Arrest proceedings in the custodial State

1. A State Party which has received a request for provisional arrest or for arrest and surrender shall immediately take steps to arrest the person in question in accordance with its laws and the provisions of Part 9.

2. A person arrested shall be brought promptly before the competent judicial authority in the custodial State which shall determine, in accordance with the law of that State, that:

(a) The warrant applies to that person;
(b) The person has been arrested in accordance with the proper process; and
(c) The person's rights have been respected.

3. The person arrested shall have the right to apply to the competent authority in the custodial State for interim release pending surrender.

4. In reaching a decision on any such application, the competent authority in the custodial State shall consider whether, given the gravity of the alleged crimes, there are urgent and exceptional circumstances to justify interim release and whether necessary safeguards exist to ensure that the custodial State can fulfil its duty to surrender the person to the Court. It shall not be open to the competent authority of the custodial State to consider whether the warrant of arrest was properly issued in accordance with article 58, paragraph 1 (a) and (b).

5. The Pre-Trial Chamber shall be notified of any request for interim release and shall make recommendations to the competent authority in the custodial State. The competent authority in the custodial State shall give full consideration to such recommendations, including any recommendations on measures to prevent the escape of the person, before rendering its decision.

6. If the person is granted interim release, the Pre-Trial Chamber may request periodic reports on the status of the interim release.

7. Once ordered to be surrendered by the custodial State, the person shall be delivered to the Court as soon as possible.

Article 60
Initial proceedings before the Court

1. Upon the surrender of the person to the Court, or the person's appearance before the Court voluntarily or pursuant to a summons, the Pre-Trial Chamber shall satisfy itself that the person has been informed of the crimes which he or she is alleged to have committed, and of his or her rights under this Statute, including the right to apply for interim release pending trial.

2. A person subject to a warrant of arrest may apply for interim release pending trial. If the Pre-Trial Chamber is satisfied that the conditions set forth in article 58, paragraph 1, are met, the person shall continue to be detained. If it is not so satisfied, the Pre-Trial Chamber shall release the person, with or without conditions.

3. The Pre-Trial Chamber shall periodically review its ruling on the release or detention of the person, and may do so at any time on the request of the Prosecutor or the person. Upon such review, it may modify its ruling as to detention, release or conditions of release, if it is satisfied that changed circumstances so require.

4. The Pre-Trial Chamber shall ensure that a person is not detained for an unreasonable period prior to trial due to inexcusable delay by the Prosecutor. If such delay occurs, the Court shall consider releasing the person, with or without conditions.

5. If necessary, the Pre-Trial Chamber may issue a warrant of arrest to secure the presence of a person who has been released.

Article 61
Confirmation of the charges before trial

1. Subject to the provisions of paragraph 2, within a reasonable time after the person's surrender or voluntary appearance before the Court, the Pre-Trial Chamber shall hold a hearing to confirm the charges on which the Prosecutor intends to seek trial. The hearing shall be held in the presence of the Prosecutor and the person charged, as well as his or her counsel.

2. The Pre-Trial Chamber may, upon request of the Prosecutor or on its own motion, hold a hearing in the absence of the person charged to confirm the charges on which the Prosecutor intends to seek trial when the person has:

(a) Waived his or her right to be present; or
(b) Fled or cannot be found and all reasonable steps have been taken to secure his or her appearance before the Court and to inform the person of the charges and that a hearing to confirm those charges will be held.

In that case, the person shall be represented by counsel where the Pre-Trial Chamber determines that it is in the interests of justice.

3. Within a reasonable time before the hearing, the person shall:

(a) Be provided with a copy of the document containing the charges on which the Prosecutor intends to bring the person to trial; and
(b) Be informed of the evidence on which the Prosecutor intends to rely at the hearing.

The Pre-Trial Chamber may issue orders regarding the disclosure of information for the purposes of the hearing.

4. Before the hearing, the Prosecutor may continue the investigation and may amend or withdraw any charges. The person shall be given reasonable notice before the hearing of any amendment to or withdrawal of charges. In case of a withdrawal of charges, the Prosecutor shall notify the Pre-Trial Chamber of the reasons for the withdrawal.

5. At the hearing, the Prosecutor shall support each charge with sufficient evidence to establish substantial grounds to believe that the person committed

the crime charged. The Prosecutor may rely on documentary or summary evidence and need not call the witnesses expected to testify at the trial.

6. At the hearing, the person may:

(a) Object to the charges;
(b) Challenge the evidence presented by the Prosecutor; and
(c) Present evidence.

7. The Pre-Trial Chamber shall, on the basis of the hearing, determine whether there is sufficient evidence to establish substantial grounds to believe that the person committed each of the crimes charged. Based on its determination, the Pre-Trial Chamber shall:

(a) Confirm those charges in relation to which it has determined that there is sufficient evidence; and commit the person to a Trial Chamber for trial on the charges as confirmed;
(b) Decline to confirm those charges in relation to which it has determined that there is insufficient evidence;
(c) Adjourn the hearing and request the Prosecutor to consider:
  (i) Providing further evidence or conducting further investigation with respect to a particular charge; or
  (ii) Amending a charge because the evidence submitted appears to establish a different crime within the jurisdiction of the Court.

8. Where the Pre-Trial Chamber declines to confirm a charge, the Prosecutor shall not be precluded from subsequently requesting its confirmation if the request is supported by additional evidence.

9. After the charges are confirmed and before the trial has begun, the Prosecutor may, with the permission of the Pre-Trial Chamber and after notice to the accused, amend the charges. If the Prosecutor seeks to add additional charges or to substitute more serious charges, a hearing under this article to confirm those charges must be held. After commencement of the trial, the Prosecutor may, with the permission of the Trial Chamber, withdraw the charges.

10. Any warrant previously issued shall cease to have effect with respect to any charges which have not been confirmed by the Pre-Trial Chamber or which have been withdrawn by the Prosecutor.

11. Once the charges have been confirmed in accordance with this article, the Presidency shall constitute a Trial Chamber which, subject to paragraph 9 and to article 64, paragraph 4, shall be responsible for the conduct of subsequent proceedings and may exercise any function of the Pre-Trial Chamber that is relevant and capable of application in those proceedings.

Part 6
The trial

Article 62
Place of trial

Unless otherwise decided, the place of the trial shall be the seat of the Court.

Article 63
Trial in the presence of the accused

1. The accused shall be present during the trial.

2. If the accused, being present before the Court, continues to disrupt the trial, the Trial Chamber may remove the accused and shall make provision for him or her to observe the trial and instruct counsel from outside the court-room, through the use of communications technology, if required. Such meas-ures shall be taken only in exceptional circumstances after other reasonable alternatives have proved inadequate, and only for such duration as is strictly required.

Article 64
Functions and powers of the Trial Chamber

1. The functions and powers of the Trial Chamber set out in this article shall be exercised in accordance with this Statute and the Rules of Procedure and Evidence.

2. The Trial Chamber shall ensure that a trial is fair and expeditious and is conducted with full respect for the rights of the accused and due regard for the protection of victims and witnesses.

3. Upon assignment of a case for trial in accordance with this Statute, the Trial Chamber assigned to deal with the case shall:

(a) Confer with the parties and adopt such procedures as are necessary to facilitate the fair and expeditious conduct of the proceedings;
(b) Determine the language or languages to be used at trial; and
(c) Subject to any other relevant provisions of this Statute, provide for disclos-ure of documents or information not previously disclosed, sufficiently in advance of the commencement of the trial to enable adequate preparation for trial.

4. The Trial Chamber may, if necessary for its effective and fair functioning, refer preliminary issues to the Pre-Trial Chamber or, if necessary, to another available judge of the Pre-Trial Division.

5. Upon notice to the parties, the Trial Chamber may, as appropriate, direct that there be joinder or severance in respect of charges against more than one accused.

6. In performing its functions prior to trial or during the course of a trial, the Trial Chamber may, as necessary:

(a) Exercise any functions of the Pre-Trial Chamber referred to in article 61, paragraph 11;
(b) Require the attendance and testimony of witnesses and production of documents and other evidence by obtaining, if necessary, the assistance of States as provided in this Statute;
(c) Provide for the protection of confidential information;
(d) Order the production of evidence in addition to that already collected prior to the trial or presented during the trial by the parties;
(e) Provide for the protection of the accused, witnesses and victims; and
(f) Rule on any other relevant matters.

7. The trial shall be held in public. The Trial Chamber may, however, determine that special circumstances require that certain proceedings be in closed session for the purposes set forth in article 68, or to protect confidential or sensitive information to be given in evidence.

8.

(a) At the commencement of the trial, the Trial Chamber shall have read to the accused the charges previously confirmed by the Pre-Trial Chamber. The Trial Chamber shall satisfy itself that the accused understands the nature of the charges. It shall afford him or her the opportunity to make an admission of guilt in accordance with article 65 or to plead not guilty.
(b) At the trial, the presiding judge may give directions for the conduct of proceedings, including to ensure that they are conducted in a fair and impartial manner. Subject to any directions of the presiding judge, the parties may submit evidence in accordance with the provisions of this Statute.

9. The Trial Chamber shall have, *inter alia*, the power on application of a party or on its own motion to:

(a) Rule on the admissibility or relevance of evidence; and
(b) Take all necessary steps to maintain order in the course of a hearing.

10. The Trial Chamber shall ensure that a complete record of the trial, which accurately reflects the proceedings, is made and that it is maintained and preserved by the Registrar.

Article 65
Proceedings on an admission of guilt

1. Where the accused makes an admission of guilt pursuant to article 64, paragraph 8 (a), the Trial Chamber shall determine whether:

(a) The accused understands the nature and consequences of the admission of guilt;
(b) The admission is voluntarily made by the accused after sufficient consultation with defence counsel; and
(c) The admission of guilt is supported by the facts of the case that are contained in:
   (i) The charges brought by the Prosecutor and admitted by the accused;
   (ii) Any materials presented by the Prosecutor which supplement the charges and which the accused accepts; and
   (iii) Any other evidence, such as the testimony of witnesses, presented by the Prosecutor or the accused.

2. Where the Trial Chamber is satisfied that the matters referred to in paragraph 1 are established, it shall consider the admission of guilt, together with any additional evidence presented, as establishing all the essential facts that are required to prove the crime to which the admission of guilt relates, and may convict the accused of that crime.

3. Where the Trial Chamber is not satisfied that the matters referred to in paragraph 1 are established, it shall consider the admission of guilt as not having been made, in which case it shall order that the trial be continued under the ordinary trial procedures provided by this Statute and may remit the case to another Trial Chamber.

4. Where the Trial Chamber is of the opinion that a more complete presentation of the facts of the case is required in the interests of justice, in particular the interests of the victims, the Trial Chamber may:

(a) Request the Prosecutor to present additional evidence, including the testimony of witnesses; or
(b) Order that the trial be continued under the ordinary trial procedures provided by this Statute, in which case it shall consider the admission of guilt as not having been made and may remit the case to another Trial Chamber.

5. Any discussions between the Prosecutor and the defence regarding modification of the charges, the admission of guilt or the penalty to be imposed shall not be binding on the Court.

Article 66
Presumption of innocence

1. Everyone shall be presumed innocent until proved guilty before the Court in accordance with the applicable law.

2. The onus is on the Prosecutor to prove the guilt of the accused.

3. In order to convict the accused, the Court must be convinced of the guilt of the accused beyond reasonable doubt.

Article 67
Rights of the accused

1. In the determination of any charge, the accused shall be entitled to a public hearing, having regard to the provisions of this Statute, to a fair hearing conducted impartially, and to the following minimum guarantees, in full equality:

(a) To be informed promptly and in detail of the nature, cause and content of the charge, in a language which the accused fully understands and speaks;

(b) To have adequate time and facilities for the preparation of the defence and to communicate freely with counsel of the accused's choosing in confidence;

(c) To be tried without undue delay;

(d) Subject to article 63, paragraph 2, to be present at the trial, to conduct the defence in person or through legal assistance of the accused's choosing, to be informed, if the accused does not have legal assistance, of this right and to have legal assistance assigned by the Court in any case where the interests of justice so require, and without payment if the accused lacks sufficient means to pay for it;

(e) To examine, or have examined, the witnesses against him or her and to obtain the attendance and examination of witnesses on his or her behalf under the same conditions as witnesses against him or her. The accused shall also be entitled to raise defences and to present other evidence admissible under this Statute;

(f) To have, free of any cost, the assistance of a competent interpreter and such translations as are necessary to meet the requirements of fairness, if any of the proceedings of or documents presented to the Court are not in a language which the accused fully understands and speaks;

(g) Not to be compelled to testify or to confess guilt and to remain silent, without such silence being a consideration in the determination of guilt or innocence;

(h) To make an unsworn oral or written statement in his or her defence; and

(i) Not to have imposed on him or her any reversal of the burden of proof or any onus of rebuttal.

2. In addition to any other disclosure provided for in this Statute, the Prosecutor shall, as soon as practicable, disclose to the defence evidence in the Prosecutor's possession or control which he or she believes shows or tends to show the innocence of the accused, or to mitigate the guilt of the accused, or which may affect the credibility of prosecution evidence. In case of doubt as to the application of this paragraph, the Court shall decide.

Article 68
Protection of the victims and witnesses and their
participation in the proceedings

1. The Court shall take appropriate measures to protect the safety, physical and psychological well-being, dignity and privacy of victims and witnesses. In so doing, the Court shall have regard to all relevant factors, including age, gender as defined in article 7, paragraph 3, and health, and the nature of the crime, in particular, but not limited to, where the crime involves sexual or gender violence or violence against children. The Prosecutor shall take such measures particularly during the investigation and prosecution of such crimes. These measures shall not be prejudicial to or inconsistent with the rights of the accused and a fair and impartial trial.

2. As an exception to the principle of public hearings provided for in article 67, the Chambers of the Court may, to protect victims and witnesses or an accused, conduct any part of the proceedings *in camera* or allow the presentation of evidence by electronic or other special means. In particular, such measures shall be implemented in the case of a victim of sexual violence or a child who is a victim or a witness, unless otherwise ordered by the Court, having regard to all the circumstances, particularly the views of the victim or witness.

3. Where the personal interests of the victims are affected, the Court shall permit their views and concerns to be presented and considered at stages of the proceedings determined to be appropriate by the Court and in a manner which is not prejudicial to or inconsistent with the rights of the accused and a fair and impartial trial. Such views and concerns may be presented by the legal representatives of the victims where the Court considers it appropriate, in accordance with the Rules of Procedure and Evidence.

4. The Victims and Witnesses Unit may advise the Prosecutor and the Court on appropriate protective measures, security arrangements, counselling and assistance as referred to in article 43, paragraph 6.

5. Where the disclosure of evidence or information pursuant to this Statute may lead to the grave endangerment of the security of a witness or his or her family, the Prosecutor may, for the purposes of any proceedings conducted prior to the commencement of the trial, withhold such evidence or information and instead submit a summary thereof. Such measures shall be exercised in a manner which is not prejudicial to or inconsistent with the rights of the accused and a fair and impartial trial.

6. A State may make an application for necessary measures to be taken in respect of the protection of its servants or agents and the protection of confidential or sensitive information.

Article 69
Evidence

1. Before testifying, each witness shall, in accordance with the Rules of Procedure and Evidence, give an undertaking as to the truthfulness of the evidence to be given by that witness.

2. The testimony of a witness at trial shall be given in person, except to the extent provided by the measures set forth in article 68 or in the Rules of Procedure and Evidence. The Court may also permit the giving of viva voce (oral) or recorded testimony of a witness by means of video or audio technology, as well as the introduction of documents or written transcripts, subject to this Statute and in accordance with the Rules of Procedure and Evidence. These measures shall not be prejudicial to or inconsistent with the rights of the accused.

3. The parties may submit evidence relevant to the case, in accordance with article 64. The Court shall have the authority to request the submission of all evidence that it considers necessary for the determination of the truth.

4. The Court may rule on the relevance or admissibility of any evidence, taking into account, *inter alia*, the probative value of the evidence and any prejudice that such evidence may cause to a fair trial or to a fair evaluation of the testimony of a witness, in accordance with the Rules of Procedure and Evidence.

5. The Court shall respect and observe privileges on confidentiality as provided for in the Rules of Procedure and Evidence.

6. The Court shall not require proof of facts of common knowledge but may take judicial notice of them.

7. Evidence obtained by means of a violation of this Statute or internationally recognized human rights shall not be admissible if:

(a)   The violation casts substantial doubt on the reliability of the evidence; or
(b)   The admission of the evidence would be antithetical to and would seriously damage the integrity of the proceedings.

8. When deciding on the relevance or admissibility of evidence collected by a State, the Court shall not rule on the application of the State's national law.

Article 70
Offences against the administration of justice

1. The Court shall have jurisdiction over the following offences against its administration of justice when committed intentionally:

(a)   Giving false testimony when under an obligation pursuant to article 69, paragraph 1, to tell the truth;

(b) Presenting evidence that the party knows is false or forged;
(c) Corruptly influencing a witness, obstructing or interfering with the attendance or testimony of a witness, retaliating against a witness for giving testimony or destroying, tampering with or interfering with the collection of evidence;
(d) Impeding, intimidating or corruptly influencing an official of the Court for the purpose of forcing or persuading the official not to perform, or to perform improperly, his or her duties;
(e) Retaliating against an official of the Court on account of duties performed by that or another official;
(f) Soliciting or accepting a bribe as an official of the Court in connection with his or her official duties.

2. The principles and procedures governing the Court's exercise of jurisdiction over offences under this article shall be those provided for in the Rules of Procedure and Evidence. The conditions for providing international cooperation to the Court with respect to its proceedings under this article shall be governed by the domestic laws of the requested State.

3. In the event of conviction, the Court may impose a term of imprisonment not exceeding five years, or a fine in accordance with the Rules of Procedure and Evidence, or both.

4.

(a) Each State Party shall extend its criminal laws penalizing offences against the integrity of its own investigative or judicial process to offences against the administration of justice referred to in this article, committed on its territory, or by one of its nationals;
(b) Upon request by the Court, whenever it deems it proper, the State Party shall submit the case to its competent authorities for the purpose of prosecution. Those authorities shall treat such cases with diligence and devote sufficient resources to enable them to be conducted effectively.

Article 71
Sanctions for misconduct before the Court

1. The Court may sanction persons present before it who commit misconduct, including disruption of its proceedings or deliberate refusal to comply with its directions, by administrative measures other than imprisonment, such as temporary or permanent removal from the courtroom, a fine or other similar measures provided for in the Rules of Procedure and Evidence.

2. The procedures governing the imposition of the measures set forth in paragraph 1 shall be those provided for in the Rules of Procedure and Evidence.

Article 72
Protection of national security information

1. This article applies in any case where the disclosure of the information or documents of a State would, in the opinion of that State, prejudice its national security interests. Such cases include those falling within the scope of article 56, paragraphs 2 and 3, article 61, paragraph 3, article 64, paragraph 3, article 67, paragraph 2, article 68, paragraph 6, article 87, paragraph 6 and article 93, as well as cases arising at any other stage of the proceedings where such disclosure may be at issue.

2. This article shall also apply when a person who has been requested to give information or evidence has refused to do so or has referred the matter to the State on the ground that disclosure would prejudice the national security interests of a State and the State concerned confirms that it is of the opinion that disclosure would prejudice its national security interests.

3. Nothing in this article shall prejudice the requirements of confidentiality applicable under article 54, paragraph 3 (e) and (f), or the application of article 73.

4. If a State learns that information or documents of the State are being, or are likely to be, disclosed at any stage of the proceedings, and it is of the opinion that disclosure would prejudice its national security interests, that State shall have the right to intervene in order to obtain resolution of the issue in accordance with this article.

5. If, in the opinion of a State, disclosure of information would prejudice its national security interests, all reasonable steps will be taken by the State, acting in conjunction with the Prosecutor, the defence or the Pre-Trial Chamber or Trial Chamber, as the case may be, to seek to resolve the matter by cooperative means. Such steps may include:

(a) Modification or clarification of the request;
(b) A determination by the Court regarding the relevance of the information or evidence sought, or a determination as to whether the evidence, though relevant, could be or has been obtained from a source other than the requested State;
(c) Obtaining the information or evidence from a different source or in a different form; or
(d) Agreement on conditions under which the assistance could be provided including, among other things, providing summaries or redactions, limitations on disclosure, use of *in camera* or *ex parte* proceedings, or other protective measures permissible under the Statute and the Rules of Procedure and Evidence.

6. Once all reasonable steps have been taken to resolve the matter through cooperative means, and if the State considers that there are no means or

conditions under which the information or documents could be provided or disclosed without prejudice to its national security interests, it shall so notify the Prosecutor or the Court of the specific reasons for its decision, unless a specific description of the reasons would itself necessarily result in such prejudice to the State's national security interests.

7. Thereafter, if the Court determines that the evidence is relevant and necessary for the establishment of the guilt or innocence of the accused, the Court may undertake the following actions:

(a) Where disclosure of the information or document is sought pursuant to a request for cooperation under Part 9 or the circumstances described in paragraph 2, and the State has invoked the ground for refusal referred to in article 93, paragraph 4:

    (i) The Court may, before making any conclusion referred to in sub-paragraph 7 (a)(ii), request further consultations for the purpose of considering the State's representations, which may include, as appropriate, hearings *in camera* and *ex parte*;

    (ii) If the Court concludes that, by invoking the ground for refusal under article 93, paragraph 4, in the circumstances of the case, the requested State is not acting in accordance with its obligations under this Statute, the Court may refer the matter in accordance with article 87, paragraph 7, specifying the reasons for its conclusion and

    (iii) The Court may make such inference in the trial of the accused as to the existence or non-existence of a fact, as may be appropriate in the circumstances; or

(b) In all other circumstances:

    (i) Order disclosure; or

    (ii) To the extent it does not order disclosure, make such inference in the trial of the accused as to the existence or non-existence of a fact, as may be appropriate in the circumstances.

Article 73
Third-party information or documents

If a State Party is requested by the Court to provide a document or information in its custody, possession or control, which was disclosed to it in confidence by a State, intergovernmental organization or international organization, it shall seek the consent of the originator to disclose that document or information. If the originator is a State Party, it shall either consent to disclosure of the information or document or undertake to resolve the issue of disclosure with the Court, subject to the provisions of article 72. If the originator is not a State Party and refuses to consent to disclosure, the requested State shall inform the Court that it is unable to provide the document or information because of a pre-existing obligation of confidentiality to the originator.

Article 74
Requirements for the decision

1. All the judges of the Trial Chamber shall be present at each stage of the trial and throughout their deliberations. The Presidency may, on a case-by-case basis, designate, as available, one or more alternate judges to be present at each stage of the trial and to replace a member of the Trial Chamber if that member is unable to continue attending.

2. The Trial Chamber's decision shall be based on its evaluation of the evidence and the entire proceedings. The decision shall not exceed the facts and circumstances described in the charges and any amendments to the charges. The Court may base its decision only on evidence submitted and discussed before it at the trial.

3. The judges shall attempt to achieve unanimity in their decision, failing which the decision shall be taken by a majority of the judges.

4. The deliberations of the Trial Chamber shall remain secret.

5. The decision shall be in writing and shall contain a full and reasoned statement of the Trial Chamber's findings on the evidence and conclusions. The Trial Chamber shall issue one decision. When there is no unanimity, the Trial Chamber's decision shall contain the views of the majority and the minority. The decision or a summary there of shall be delivered in open court.

Article 75
Reparations to victims

1. The Court shall establish principles relating to reparations to, or in respect of, victims, including restitution, compensation and rehabilitation. On this basis, in its decision the Court may, either upon request or on its own motion in exceptional circumstances, determine the scope and extent of any damage, loss and injury to, or in respect of, victims and will state the principles on which it is acting.

2. The Court may make an order directly against a convicted person specifying appropriate reparations to, or in respect of, victims, including restitution, compensation and rehabilitation. Where appropriate, the Court may order that the award for reparations be made through the Trust Fund provided for in article 79.

3. Before making an order under this article, the Court may invite and shall take account of representations from or on behalf of the convicted person, victims, other interested persons or interested States.

4. In exercising its power under this article, the Court may, after a person is convicted of a crime within the jurisdiction of the Court, determine whether, in order to give effect to an order which it may make under this article, it is necessary to seek measures under article 93, paragraph 1.

5. A State Party shall give effect to a decision under this article as if the provisions of article 109 were applicable to this article.

6. Nothing in this article shall be interpreted as prejudicing the rights of victims under national or international law.

Article 76
Sentencing

1. In the event of a conviction, the Trial Chamber shall consider the appropriate sentence to be imposed and shall take into account the evidence presented and submissions made during the trial that are relevant to the sentence.

2. Except where article 65 applies and before the completion of the trial, the Trial Chamber may on its own motion and shall, at the request of the Prosecutor or the accused, hold a further hearing to hear any additional evidence or submissions relevant to the sentence, in accordance with the Rules of Procedure and Evidence.

3. Where paragraph 2 applies, any representations under article 75 shall be heard during the further hearing referred to in paragraph 2 and, if necessary, during any additional hearing.

4. The sentence shall be pronounced in public and, wherever possible, in the presence of the accused.

Part 7
Penalties

Article 77
Applicable penalties

1. Subject to article 110, the Court may impose one of the following penalties on a person convicted of a crime referred to in article 5 of this Statute:

(a) Imprisonment for a specified number of years, which may not exceed a maximum of 30 years; or
(b) A term of life imprisonment when justified by the extreme gravity of the crime and the individual circumstances of the convicted person.

2. In addition to imprisonment, the Court may order:

(a) A fine under the criteria provided for in the Rules of Procedure and Evidence;
(b) A forfeiture of proceeds, property and assets derived directly or indirectly from that crime, without prejudice to the rights of bona fide third parties.

Article 78
Determination of the sentence

1. In determining the sentence, the Court shall, in accordance with the Rules of Procedure and Evidence, take into account such factors as the gravity of the crime and the individual circumstances of the convicted person.

2. In imposing a sentence of imprisonment, the Court shall deduct the time, if any, previously spent in detention in accordance with an order of the Court. The Court may deduct any time otherwise spent in detention in connection with conduct underlying the crime.

3. When a person has been convicted of more than one crime, the Court shall pronounce a sentence for each crime and a joint sentence specifying the total period of imprisonment. This period shall be no less than the highest individual sentence pronounced and shall not exceed 30 years' imprisonment or a sentence of life imprisonment in conformity with article 77, paragraph 1 (b).

Article 79
Trust Fund

1. A Trust Fund shall be established by decision of the Assembly of States Parties for the benefit of victims of crimes within the jurisdiction of the Court, and of the families of such victims.

2. The Court may order money and other property collected through fines or forfeiture to be transferred, by order of the Court, to the Trust Fund.

3. The Trust Fund shall be managed according to criteria to be determined by the Assembly of States Parties.

Article 80
Non-prejudice to national application of penalties and national laws

Nothing in this Part affects the application by States of penalties prescribed by their national law, nor the law of States which do not provide for penalties prescribed in this Part.

Part 8
Appeal and revision

Article 81
Appeal against decision of acquittal or conviction or against sentence

1. A decision under article 74 may be appealed in accordance with the Rules of Procedure and Evidence as follows:

(a) The Prosecutor may make an appeal on any of the following grounds:

     (i) Procedural error,

     (ii) Error of fact, or

     (iii) Error of law;

(b) The convicted person, or the Prosecutor on that person's behalf, may make an appeal on any of the following grounds:

     (i) Procedural error,

     (ii) Error of fact,

     (iii) Error of law, or

     (iv) Any other ground that affects the fairness or reliability of the proceedings or decision.

2.

(a) A sentence may be appealed, in accordance with the Rules of Procedure and Evidence, by the Prosecutor or the convicted person on the ground of disproportion between the crime and the sentence;

(b) If on an appeal against sentence the Court considers that there are grounds on which the conviction might be set aside, wholly or in part, it may invite the Prosecutor and the convicted person to submit grounds under article 81, paragraph 1 (a) or (b), and may render a decision on conviction in accordance with article 83;

(c) The same procedure applies when the Court, on an appeal against conviction only, considers that there are grounds to reduce the sentence under paragraph 2 (a).

3.

(a) Unless the Trial Chamber orders otherwise, a convicted person shall remain in custody pending an appeal;

(b) When a convicted person's time in custody exceeds the sentence of imprisonment imposed, that person shall be released, except that if the Prosecutor is also appealing, the release may be subject to the conditions under subparagraph (c) below;

(c) In case of an acquittal, the accused shall be released immediately, subject to the following:

     (i) Under exceptional circumstances, and having regard, *inter alia*, to the concrete risk of flight, the seriousness of the offence charged and the probability of success on appeal, the Trial Chamber, at the request of the Prosecutor, may maintain the detention of the person pending appeal;

     (ii) A decision by the Trial Chamber under subparagraph (c)(i) may be appealed in accordance with the Rules of Procedure and Evidence.

    4. Subject to the provisions of paragraph 3 (a) and (b), execution of the decision or sentence shall be suspended during the period allowed for appeal and for the duration of the appeal proceedings.

Article 82
Appeal against other decisions

1. Either party may appeal any of the following decisions in accordance with the Rules of Procedure and Evidence:

(a) A decision with respect to jurisdiction or admissibility;
(b) A decision granting or denying release of the person being investigated or prosecuted;
(c) A decision of the Pre-Trial Chamber to act on its own initiative under article 56, paragraph 3;
(d) A decision that involves an issue that would significantly affect the fair and expeditious conduct of the proceedings or the outcome of the trial, and for which, in the opinion of the Pre-Trial or Trial Chamber, an immediate resolution by the Appeals Chamber may materially advance the proceedings.

2. A decision of the Pre-Trial Chamber under article 57, paragraph 3 (d), may be appealed against by the State concerned or by the Prosecutor, with the leave of the Pre-Trial Chamber. The appeal shall be heard on an expedited basis.

3. An appeal shall not of itself have suspensive effect unless the Appeals Chamber so orders, upon request, in accordance with the Rules of Procedure and Evidence.

4. A legal representative of the victims, the convicted person or a bona fide owner of property adversely affected by an order under article 75 may appeal against the order for reparations, as provided in the Rules of Procedure and Evidence.

Article 83
Proceedings on appeal

1. For the purposes of proceedings under article 81 and this article, the Appeals Chamber shall have all the powers of the Trial Chamber.

2. If the Appeals Chamber finds that the proceedings appealed from were unfair in a way that affected the reliability of the decision or sentence, or that the decision or sentence appealed from was materially affected by error of fact or law or procedural error, it may:

(a) Reverse or amend the decision or sentence; or
(b) Order a new trial before a different Trial Chamber.

For these purposes, the Appeals Chamber may remand a factual issue to the original Trial Chamber for it to determine the issue and to report back accordingly, or may itself call evidence to determine the issue. When the decision or sentence has been appealed only by the person convicted, or the Prosecutor on that person's behalf, it cannot be amended to his or her detriment.

3. If in an appeal against sentence the Appeals Chamber finds that the sentence is disproportionate to the crime, it may vary the sentence in accordance with Part 7.

4. The judgment of the Appeals Chamber shall be taken by a majority of the judges and shall be delivered in open court. The judgment shall state the reasons on which it is based. When there is no unanimity, the judgment of the Appeals Chamber shall contain the views of the majority and the minority, but a judge may deliver a separate or dissenting opinion on a question of law.

5. The Appeals Chamber may deliver its judgment in the absence of the person acquitted or convicted.

Article 84
Revision of conviction or sentence

1. The convicted person or, after death, spouses, children, parents or one person alive at the time of the accused's death who has been given express written instructions from the accused to bring such a claim, or the Prosecutor on the person's behalf, may apply to the Appeals Chamber to revise the final judgment of conviction or sentence on the grounds that:

(a) New evidence has been discovered that:
  (i) Was not available at the time of trial, and such unavailability was not wholly or partially attributable to the party making application; and
  (ii) Is sufficiently important that had it been proved at trial it would have been likely to have resulted in a different verdict;
(b) It has been newly discovered that decisive evidence, taken into account at trial and upon which the conviction depends, was false, forged or falsified;
(c) One or more of the judges who participated in conviction or confirmation of the charges has committed, in that case, an act of serious misconduct or serious breach of duty of sufficient gravity to justify the removal of that judge or those judges from office under article 46.

2. The Appeals Chamber shall reject the application if it considers it to be unfounded. If it determines that the application is meritorious, it may, as appropriate:

(a) Reconvene the original Trial Chamber;
(b) Constitute a new Trial Chamber; or
(c) Retain jurisdiction over the matter,

with a view to, after hearing the parties in the manner set forth in the Rules of Procedure and Evidence, arriving at a determination on whether the judgment should be revised.

Article 85
Compensation to an arrested or convicted person

1. Anyone who has been the victim of unlawful arrest or detention shall have an enforceable right to compensation.

2. When a person has by a final decision been convicted of a criminal offence, and when subsequently his or her conviction has been reversed on the ground that a new or newly discovered fact shows conclusively that there has been a miscarriage of justice, the person who has suffered punishment as a result of such conviction shall be compensated according to law, unless it is proved that the non disclosure of the unknown fact in time is wholly or partly attributable to him or her.

3. In exceptional circumstances, where the Court finds conclusive facts showing that there has been a grave and manifest miscarriage of justice, it may in its discretion award compensation, according to the criteria provided in the Rules of Procedure and Evidence, to a person who has been released from detention following a final decision of acquittal or a termination of the proceedings for that reason.

Part 9
International cooperation and judicial assistance

Article 86
General obligation to cooperate

States Parties shall, in accordance with the provisions of this Statute, cooperate fully with the Court in its investigation and prosecution of crimes within the jurisdiction of the Court.

Article 87
Requests for cooperation: general provisions

1.

(a) The Court shall have the authority to make requests to States Parties for cooperation. The requests shall be transmitted through the diplomatic channel or any other appropriate channel as may be designated by each State Party upon ratification, acceptance, approval or accession. Subsequent changes to the designation shall be made by each State Party in accordance with the Rules of Procedure and Evidence.

(b) When appropriate, without prejudice to the provisions of subparagraph (a), requests may also be transmitted through the International Criminal Police Organization or any appropriate regional organization.

2. Requests for cooperation and any documents supporting the request shall either be in or be accompanied by a translation into an official language of the requested State or one of the working languages of the Court, in accordance with the choice made by that State upon ratification, acceptance, approval or accession. Subsequent changes to this choice shall be made in accordance with the Rules of Procedure and Evidence.

3. The requested State shall keep confidential a request for cooperation and any documents supporting the request, except to the extent that the disclosure is necessary for execution of the request.

4. In relation to any request for assistance presented under this Part, the Court may take such measures, including measures related to the protection of information, as may be necessary to ensure the safety or physical or psychological well-being of any victims, potential witnesses and their families. The Court may request that any information that is made available under this Part shall be provided and handled in a manner that protects the safety and physical or psychological well-being of any victims, potential witnesses and their families.

5. The Court may invite any State not party to this Statute to provide assistance under this Part on the basis of an ad hoc arrangement, an agreement with such State or any other appropriate basis. Where a State not party to this Statute, which has entered into an ad hoc arrangement or an agreement with the Court, fails to cooperate with requests pursuant to any such arrangement or agreement, the Court may so inform the Assembly of States Parties or, where the Security Council referred the matter to the Court, the Security Council.

6. The Court may ask any intergovernmental organization to provide information or documents. The Court may also ask for other forms of cooperation and assistance which may be agreed upon with such an organization and which are in accordance with its competence or mandate.

7. Where a State Party fails to comply with a request to cooperate by the Court contrary to the provisions of this Statute, thereby preventing the Court from exercising its functions and powers under this Statute, the Court may make a finding to that effect and refer the matter to the Assembly of States Parties or, where the Security Council referred the matter to the Court, to the Security Council.

Article 88
Availability of procedures under national law

States Parties shall ensure that there are procedures available under their national law for all of the forms of cooperation which are specified under this Part.

Article 89
Surrender of persons to the Court

1. The Court may transmit a request for the arrest and surrender of a person, together with the material supporting the request outlined in article 91, to any State on the territory of which that person may be found and shall request the cooperation of that State in the arrest and surrender of such a person. States Parties shall, in accordance with the provisions of this Part and the procedure under their national law, comply with requests for arrest and surrender.

2. Where the person sought for surrender brings a challenge before a national court on the basis of the principle of ne bis in idem as provided in article 20, the requested State shall immediately consult with the Court to determine if there has been a relevant ruling on admissibility. If the case is admissible, the requested State shall proceed with the execution of the request. If an admissibility ruling is pending, the requested State may postpone the execution of the request for surrender of the person until the Court makes a determination on admissibility.

3.

(a) A State Party shall authorize, in accordance with its national procedural law, transportation through its territory of a person being surrendered to the Court by another State, except where transit through that State would impede or delay the surrender.

(b) A request by the Court for transit shall be transmitted in accordance with article 87. The request for transit shall contain:
  (i) A description of the person being transported;
  (ii) A brief statement of the facts of the case and their legal characterization; and
  (iii) The warrant for arrest and surrender;

(c) A person being transported shall be detained in custody during the period of transit;

(d) No authorization is required if the person is transported by air and no landing is scheduled on the territory of the transit State;

(e) If an unscheduled landing occurs on the territory of the transit State, that State may require a request for transit from the Court as provided for in subparagraph (b). The transit State shall detain the person being transported until the request for transit is received and the transit is effected; provided that detention for purposes of this subparagraph may not be extended beyond 96 hours from the unscheduled landing unless the request is received within that time.

4. If the person sought is being proceeded against or is serving a sentence in the requested State for a crime different from that for which surrender to

the Court is sought, the requested State, after making its decision to grant the request, shall consult with the Court.

Article 90
Competing requests

1. A State Party which receives a request from the Court for the surrender of a person under article 89 shall, if it also receives a request from any other State for the extradition of the same person for the same conduct which forms the basis of the crime for which the Court seeks the person's surrender, notify the Court and the requesting State of that fact.

2. Where the requesting State is a State Party, the requested State shall give priority to the request from the Court if:

(a) The Court has, pursuant to articles 18 or 19, made a determination that the case in respect of which surrender is sought is admissible and that determination takes into account the investigation or prosecution conducted by the requesting State in respect of its request for extradition; or

(b) The Court makes the determination described in subparagraph (a) pursuant to the requested State's notification under paragraph 1.

3. Where a determination under paragraph 2 (a) has not been made, the requested State may, at its discretion, pending the determination of the Court under paragraph 2 (b), proceed to deal with the request for extradition from the requesting State but shall not extradite the person until the Court has determined that the case is inadmissible. The Court's determination shall be made on an expedited basis.

4. If the requesting State is a State not Party to this Statute the requested State, if it is not under an international obligation to extradite the person to the requesting State, shall give priority to the request for surrender from the Court, if the Court has determined that the case is admissible.

5. Where a case under paragraph 4 has not been determined to be admissible by the Court, the requested State may, at its discretion, proceed to deal with the request for extradition from the requesting State.

6. In cases where paragraph 4 applies except that the requested State is under an existing international obligation to extradite the person to the requesting State not Party to this Statute, the requested State shall determine whether to surrender the person to the Court or extradite the person to the requesting State. In making its decision, the requested State shall consider all the relevant factors, including but not limited to:

(a) The respective dates of the requests;

(b) The interests of the requesting State including, where relevant, whether the crime was committed in its territory and the nationality of the victims and of the person sought; and

(c) The possibility of subsequent surrender between the Court and the requesting State.

7. Where a State Party which receives a request from the Court for the surrender of a person also receives a request from any State for the extradition of the same person for conduct other than that which constitutes the crime for which the Court seeks the person's surrender:

(a) The requested State shall, if it is not under an existing international obligation to extradite the person to the requesting State, give priority to the request from the Court;

(b) The requested State shall, if it is under an existing international obligation to extradite the person to the requesting State, determine whether to surrender the person to the Court or to extradite the person to the requesting State. In making its decision, the requested State shall consider all the relevant factors, including but not limited to those set out in paragraph 6, but shall give special consideration to the relative nature and gravity of the conduct in question.

8. Where pursuant to a notification under this article, the Court has determined a case to be inadmissible, and subsequently extradition to the requesting State is refused, the requested State shall notify the Court of this decision.

Article 91
Contents of request for arrest and surrender

1. A request for arrest and surrender shall be made in writing. In urgent cases, a request may be made by any medium capable of delivering a written record, provided that the request shall be confirmed through the channel provided for in article 87, paragraph 1 (a).

2. In the case of a request for the arrest and surrender of a person for whom a warrant of arrest has been issued by the Pre-Trial Chamber under article 58, the request shall contain or be supported by:

(a) Information describing the person sought, sufficient to identify the person, and information as to that person's probable location;

(b) A copy of the warrant of arrest; and

(c) Such documents, statements or information as may be necessary to meet the requirements for the surrender process in the requested State, except that those requirements should not be more burdensome than those applicable to requests for extradition pursuant to treaties or arrangements between the requested State and other States and should, if possible, be less burdensome, taking into account the distinct nature of the Court.

3. In the case of a request for the arrest and surrender of a person already convicted, the request shall contain or be supported by:

(a) A copy of any warrant of arrest for that person;
(b) A copy of the judgment of conviction;
(c) Information to demonstrate that the person sought is the one referred to in the judgment of conviction; and
(d) If the person sought has been sentenced, a copy of the sentence imposed and, in the case of a sentence for imprisonment, a statement of any time already served and the time remaining to be served.

3. Upon the request of the Court, a State Party shall consult with the Court, either generally or with respect to a specific matter, regarding any requirements under its national law that may apply under paragraph 2 (c). During the consultations, the State Party shall advise the Court of the specific requirements of its national law.

Article 92
Provisional arrest

1. In urgent cases, the Court may request the provisional arrest of the person sought, pending presentation of the request for surrender and the documents supporting the request as specified in article 91.

2. The request for provisional arrest shall be made by any medium capable of delivering a written record and shall contain:

(a) Information describing the person sought, sufficient to identify the person, and information as to that person's probable location;
(b) A concise statement of the crimes for which the person's arrest is sought and of the facts which are alleged to constitute those crimes, including, where possible, the date and location of the crime;
(c) A statement of the existence of a warrant of arrest or a judgment of conviction against the person sought; and
(d) A statement that a request for surrender of the person sought will follow.

3. A person who is provisionally arrested may be released from custody if the requested State has not received the request for surrender and the documents supporting the request as specified in article 91 within the time limits specified in the Rules of Procedure and Evidence. However, the person may consent to surrender before the expiration of this period if permitted by the law of the requested State. In such a case, the requested State shall proceed to surrender the person to the Court as soon as possible.

4. The fact that the person sought has been released from custody pursuant to paragraph 3 shall not prejudice the subsequent arrest and surrender of that person if the request for surrender and the documents supporting the request are delivered at a later date.

Article 93
Other forms of cooperation

1. States Parties shall, in accordance with the provisions of this Part and under procedures of national law, comply with requests by the Court to provide the following assistance in relation to investigations or prosecutions:

(a) The identification and whereabouts of persons or the location of items;

(b) The taking of evidence, including testimony under oath, and the production of evidence, including expert opinions and reports necessary to the Court;

(c) The questioning of any person being investigated or prosecuted;

(d) The service of documents, including judicial documents;

(e) Facilitating the voluntary appearance of persons as witnesses or experts before the Court;

(f) The temporary transfer of persons as provided in paragraph 7;

(g) The examination of places or sites, including the exhumation and examination of grave sites;

(h) The execution of searches and seizures;

(i) The provision of records and documents, including official records and documents;

(j) The protection of victims and witnesses and the preservation of evidence;

(k) The identification, tracing and freezing or seizure of proceeds, property and assets and instrumentalities of crimes for the purpose of eventual forfeiture, without prejudice to the rights of bona fide third parties; and

(l) Any other type of assistance which is not prohibited by the law of the requested State, with a view to facilitating the investigation and prosecution of crimes within the jurisdiction of the Court.

2. The Court shall have the authority to provide an assurance to a witness or an expert appearing before the Court that he or she will not be prosecuted, detained or subjected to any restriction of personal freedom by the Court in respect of any act or omission that preceded the departure of that person from the requested State.

3. Where execution of a particular measure of assistance detailed in a request presented under paragraph 1, is prohibited in the requested State on the basis of an existing fundamental legal principle of general application, the requested State shall promptly consult with the Court to try to resolve the matter. In the consultations, consideration should be given to whether the assistance can be rendered in another manner or subject to conditions. If after consultations the matter cannot be resolved, the Court shall modify the request as necessary.

4. In accordance with article 72, a State Party may deny a request for assistance, in whole or in part, only if the request concerns the production of any documents or disclosure of evidence which relates to its national security.

5. Before denying a request for assistance under paragraph 1 (l), the requested State shall consider whether the assistance can be provided subject to specified conditions, or whether the assistance can be provided at a later date or in an alternative manner, provided that if the Court or the Prosecutor accepts the assistance subject to conditions, the Court or the Prosecutor shall abide by them.

6. If a request for assistance is denied, the requested State Party shall promptly inform the Court or the Prosecutor of the reasons for such denial.

7.

(a) The Court may request the temporary transfer of a person in custody for purposes of identification or for obtaining testimony or other assistance. The person may be transferred if the following conditions are fulfilled:
   (i)   The person freely gives his or her informed consent to the transfer; and
   (ii) The requested State agrees to the transfer, subject to such conditions as that State and the Court may agree.
(b) The person being transferred shall remain in custody. When the purposes of the transfer have been fulfilled, the Court shall return the person without delay to the requested State.

8.

(a) The Court shall ensure the confidentiality of documents and information, except as required for the investigation and proceedings described in the request.
(b) The requested State may, when necessary, transmit documents or information to the Prosecutor on a confidential basis. The Prosecutor may then use them solely for the purpose of generating new evidence;
(c) The requested State may, on its own motion or at the request of the Prosecutor, subsequently consent to the disclosure of such documents or information. They may then be used as evidence pursuant to the provisions of Parts 5 and 6 and in accordance with the Rules of Procedure and Evidence.

9.

(a)
   (i)   In the event that a State Party receives competing requests, other than for surrender or extradition, from the Court and from another State pursuant to an international obligation, the State Party shall endeavour, in consultation with the Court and the other State, to meet both requests, if necessary by postponing or attaching conditions to one or the other request.

(ii) Failing that, competing requests shall be resolved in accordance with the principles established in article 90.

(b) Where, however, the request from the Court concerns information, property or persons which are subject to the control of a third State or an international organization by virtue of an international agreement, the requested States shall so inform the Court and the Court shall direct its request to the third State or international organization.

10.

(a) The Court may, upon request, cooperate with and provide assistance to a State Party conducting an investigation into or trial in respect of conduct which constitutes a crime within the jurisdiction of the Court or which constitutes a serious crime under the national law of the requesting State.

(b)

    (i) The assistance provided under subparagraph (a) shall include, *inter alia*:

        (1) The transmission of statements, documents or other types of evidence obtained in the course of an investigation or a trial conducted by the Court; and

        (2) The questioning of any person detained by order of the Court;

    (ii) In the case of assistance under subparagraph (b)(i)(a):

        (1) If the documents or other types of evidence have been obtained with the assistance of a State, such transmission shall require the consent of that State;

        (2) If the statements, documents or other types of evidence have been provided by a witness or expert, such transmission shall be subject to the provisions of article 68.

    (c) The Court may, under the conditions set out in this paragraph, grant a request for assistance under this paragraph from a State which is not a Party to this Statute.

Article 94
Postponement of execution of a request in respect of ongoing investigation or prosecution

1. If the immediate execution of a request would interfere with an ongoing investigation or prosecution of a case different from that to which the request relates, the requested State may postpone the execution of the request for a period of time agreed upon with the Court. However, the postponement shall be no longer than is necessary to complete the relevant investigation or prosecution in the requested State. Before making a decision to postpone, the

requested State should consider whether the assistance may be immediately provided subject to certain conditions.

2. If a decision to postpone is taken pursuant to paragraph 1, the Prosecutor may, however, seek measures to preserve evidence, pursuant to article 93, paragraph 1 (j).

Article 95
Postponement of execution of a request in respect of an admissibility challenge

Without prejudice to article 53, paragraph 2, where there is an admissibility challenge under consideration by the Court pursuant to article 18 or 19, the requested State may postpone the execution of a request under this Part pending a determination by the Court, unless the Court has specifically ordered that the Prosecutor may pursue the collection of such evidence pursuant to article 18 or 19.

Article 96
Contents of request for other forms of assistance under article 93

1. A request for other forms of assistance referred to in article 93 shall be made in writing. In urgent cases, a request may be made by any medium capable of delivering a written record, provided that the request shall be confirmed through the channel provided for in article 87, paragraph 1 (a).

2. The request shall, as applicable, contain or be supported by the following:

(a) A concise statement of the purpose of the request and the assistance sought, including the legal basis and the grounds for the request;

(b) As much detailed information as possible about the location or identification of any person or place that must be found or identified in order for the assistance sought to be provided;

(c) A concise statement of the essential facts underlying the request;

(d) The reasons for and details of any procedure or requirement to be followed;

(e) Such information as may be required under the law of the requested State in order to execute the request; and

(f) Any other information relevant in order for the assistance sought to be provided.

3. Upon the request of the Court, a State Party shall consult with the Court, either generally or with respect to a specific matter, regarding any requirements under its national law that may apply under paragraph 2 (e). During the consultations, the State Party shall advise the Court of the specific requirements of its national law.

4. The provisions of this article shall, where applicable, also apply in respect of a request for assistance made to the Court.

Article 97
Consultations

Where a State Party receives a request under this Part in relation to which it identifies problems which may impede or prevent the execution of the request, that State shall consult with the Court without delay in order to resolve the matter. Such problems may include, *inter alia*:

(a) Insufficient information to execute the request;
(b) In the case of a request for surrender, the fact that despite best efforts, the person sought cannot be located or that the investigation conducted has determined that the person in the requested State is clearly not the person named in the warrant; or
(c) The fact that execution of the request in its current form would require the requested State to breach a pre-existing treaty obligation undertaken with respect to another State.

Article 98
Cooperation with respect to waiver of immunity and consent to Surrender

1. The Court may not proceed with a request for surrender or assistance which would require the requested State to act inconsistently with its obligations under international law with respect to the State or diplomatic immunity of a person or property of a third State, unless the Court can first obtain the cooperation of that third State for the waiver of the immunity.

2. The Court may not proceed with a request for surrender which would require the requested State to act inconsistently with its obligations under international agreements pursuant to which the consent of a sending State is required to surrender a person of that State to the Court, unless the Court can first obtain the cooperation of the sending State for the giving of consent for the surrender.

Article 99
Execution of requests under articles 93 and 96

1. Requests for assistance shall be executed in accordance with the relevant procedure under the law of the requested State and, unless prohibited by such law, in the manner specified in the request, including following any procedure outlined therein or permitting persons specified in the request to be present at and assist in the execution process.

2. In the case of an urgent request, the documents or evidence produced in response shall, at the request of the Court, be sent urgently.

3. Replies from the requested State shall be transmitted in their original language and form.

4. Without prejudice to other articles in this Part, where it is necessary for the successful execution of a request which can be executed without any compulsory measures, including specifically the interview of or taking evidence from a person on a voluntary basis, including doing so without the presence of the authorities of the requested State Party if it is essential for the request to be executed, and the examination without modification of a public site or other public place, the Prosecutor may execute such request directly on the territory of a State as follows:

(a) When the State Party requested is a State on the territory of which the crime is alleged to have been committed, and there has been a determination of admissibility pursuant to article 18 or 19, the Prosecutor may directly execute such request following all possible consultations with the requested State Party;

(b) In other cases, the Prosecutor may execute such request following consultations with the requested State Party and subject to any reasonable conditions or concerns raised by that State Party. Where the requested State Party identifies problems with the execution of a request pursuant to this subparagraph it shall, without delay, consult with the Court to resolve the matter.

5. Provisions allowing a person heard or examined by the Court under article 72 to invoke restrictions designed to prevent disclosure of confidential information connected with national security shall also apply to the execution of requests for assistance under this article.

Article 100
Costs

1. The ordinary costs for execution of requests in the territory of the requested State shall be borne by that State, except for the following, which shall be borne by the Court:

(a) Costs associated with the travel and security of witnesses and experts or the transfer under article 93 of persons in custody;

(b) Costs of translation, interpretation and transcription;

(c) Travel and subsistence costs of the judges, the Prosecutor, the Deputy Prosecutors, the Registrar, the Deputy Registrar and staff of any organ of the Court;

(d) Costs of any expert opinion or report requested by the Court;

(e) Costs associated with the transport of a person being surrendered to the Court by a custodial State; and

(f) Following consultations, any extraordinary costs that may result from the execution of a request.

2. The provisions of paragraph 1 shall, as appropriate, apply to requests from States Parties to the Court. In that case, the Court shall bear the ordinary costs of execution.

Article 101
Rule of speciality

1. A person surrendered to the Court under this Statute shall not be proceeded against, punished or detained for any conduct committed prior to surrender, other than the conduct or course of conduct which forms the basis of the crimes for which that person has been surrendered.

2. The Court may request a waiver of the requirements of paragraph 1 from the State which surrendered the person to the Court and, if necessary, the Court shall provide additional information in accordance with article 91. States Parties shall have the authority to provide a waiver to the Court and should endeavour to do so.

Article 102
Use of terms

For the purposes of this Statute:

(a) 'surrender' means the delivering up of a person by a State to the Court, pursuant to this Statute.

(b) 'extradition' means the delivering up of a person by one State to another as provided by treaty, convention or national legislation.

Part 10
Enforcement

Article 103
Role of States in enforcement of sentences of imprisonment

1.

(a) A sentence of imprisonment shall be served in a State designated by the Court from a list of States which have indicated to the Court their willingness to accept sentenced persons.

(b) At the time of declaring its willingness to accept sentenced persons, a State may attach conditions to its acceptance as agreed by the Court and in accordance with this Part.

(c) A State designated in a particular case shall promptly inform the Court whether it accepts the Court's designation.

2.

(a) The State of enforcement shall notify the Court of any circumstances, including the exercise of any conditions agreed under paragraph 1, which could materially affect the terms or extent of the imprisonment. The Court shall be given at least 45 days' notice of any such known or foreseeable circumstances. During this period, the State of enforcement shall take no action that might prejudice its obligations under article 110.

(b) Where the Court cannot agree to the circumstances referred to in subparagraph (a), it shall notify the State of enforcement and proceed in accordance with article 104, paragraph 1.

3. In exercising its discretion to make a designation under paragraph 1, the Court shall take into account the following:

(a) The principle that States Parties should share the responsibility for enforcing sentences of imprisonment, in accordance with principles of equitable distribution, as provided in the Rules of Procedure and Evidence;

(b) The application of widely accepted international treaty standards governing the treatment of prisoners;

(c) The views of the sentenced person;

(d) The nationality of the sentenced person;

(e) Such other factors regarding the circumstances of the crime or the person sentenced, or the effective enforcement of the sentence, as may be appropriate in designating the State of enforcement.

4. If no State is designated under paragraph 1, the sentence of imprisonment shall be served in a prison facility made available by the host State, in accordance with the conditions set out in the headquarters agreement referred to in article 3, paragraph 2. In such a case, the costs arising out of the enforcement of a sentence of imprisonment shall be borne by the Court.

Article 104
Change in designation of State of enforcement

1. The Court may, at any time, decide to transfer a sentenced person to a prison of another State.

2. A sentenced person may, at any time, apply to the Court to be transferred from the State of enforcement.

Article 105
Enforcement of the sentence

1. Subject to conditions which a State may have specified in accordance with article 103, paragraph 1 (b), the sentence of imprisonment shall be binding on the States Parties, which shall in no case modify it.

2. The Court alone shall have the right to decide any application for appeal and revision. The State of enforcement shall not impede the making of any such application by a sentenced person.

Article 106
Supervision of enforcement of sentences and conditions of imprisonment

1. The enforcement of a sentence of imprisonment shall be subject to the supervision of the Court and shall be consistent with widely accepted international treaty standards governing treatment of prisoners.

2. The conditions of imprisonment shall be governed by the law of the State of enforcement and shall be consistent with widely accepted international treaty standards governing treatment of prisoners; in no case shall such conditions be more or less favourable than those available to prisoners convicted of similar offences in the State of enforcement.

3. Communications between a sentenced person and the Court shall be unimpeded and confidential.

Article 107
Transfer of the person upon completion of sentence

1. Following completion of the sentence, a person who is not a national of the State of enforcement may, in accordance with the law of the State of enforcement, be transferred to a State which is obliged to receive him or her, or to another State which agrees to receive him or her, taking into account any wishes of the person to be transferred to that State, unless the State of enforcement authorizes the person to remain in its territory.

2. If no State bears the costs arising out of transferring the person to another State pursuant to paragraph 1, such costs shall be borne by the Court.

3. Subject to the provisions of article 108, the State of enforcement may also, in accordance with its national law, extradite or otherwise surrender the person to a State which has requested the extradition or surrender of the person for purposes of trial or enforcement of a sentence.

Article 108
Limitation on the prosecution or punishment of other offences

1. A sentenced person in the custody of the State of enforcement shall not be subject to prosecution or punishment or to extradition to a third State for any

conduct engaged in prior to that person's delivery to the State of enforcement, unless such prosecution, punishment or extradition has been approved by the Court at the request of the State of enforcement.

2. The Court shall decide the matter after having heard the views of the sentenced person.

3. Paragraph 1 shall cease to apply if the sentenced person remains voluntarily for more than 30 days in the territory of the State of enforcement after having served the full sentence imposed by the Court, or returns to the territory of that State after having left it.

Article 109
Enforcement of fines and forfeiture measures

1. States Parties shall give effect to fines or forfeitures ordered by the Court under Part 7, without prejudice to the rights of bona fide third parties, and in accordance with the procedure of their national law.

2. If a State Party is unable to give effect to an order for forfeiture, it shall take measures to recover the value of the proceeds, property or assets ordered by the Court to be forfeited, without prejudice to the rights of bona fide third parties.

3. Property, or the proceeds of the sale of real property or, where appropriate, the sale of other property, which is obtained by a State Party as a result of its enforcement of a judgment of the Court shall be transferred to the Court.

Article 110
Review by the Court concerning reduction of sentence

1. The State of enforcement shall not release the person before expiry of the sentence pronounced by the Court.

2. The Court alone shall have the right to decide any reduction of sentence, and shall rule on the matter after having heard the person.

3. When the person has served two thirds of the sentence, or 25 years in the case of life imprisonment, the Court shall review the sentence to determine whether it should be reduced. Such a review shall not be conducted before that time.

4. In its review under paragraph 3, the Court may reduce the sentence if it finds that one or more of the following factors are present:

(a) The early and continuing willingness of the person to cooperate with the Court in its investigations and prosecutions;

(b) The voluntary assistance of the person in enabling the enforcement of the judgments and orders of the Court in other cases, and in particular providing assistance in locating assets subject to orders of fine, forfeiture or reparation which may be used for the benefit of victims; or

    (c) Other factors establishing a clear and significant change of circumstances sufficient to justify the reduction of sentence, as provided in the Rules of Procedure and Evidence.

    5. If the Court determines in its initial review under paragraph 3 that it is not appropriate to reduce the sentence, it shall thereafter review the question of reduction of sentence at such intervals and applying such criteria as provided for in the Rules of Procedure and Evidence.

Article 111
Escape

If a convicted person escapes from custody and flees the State of enforcement, that State may, after consultation with the Court, request the person's surrender from the State in which the person is located pursuant to existing bilateral or multilateral arrangements, or may request that the Court seek the person's surrender. It may direct that the person be delivered to the State in which he or she was serving the sentence or to another State designated by the Court.

Part 11
Assembly of States Parties

Article 112
Assembly of States Parties

    1. An Assembly of States Parties to this Statute is hereby established. Each State Party shall have one representative in the Assembly who may be accompanied by alternates and advisers. Other States which have signed this Statute or the Final Act may be observers in the Assembly.

    2. The Assembly shall:

(a) Consider and adopt, as appropriate, recommendations of the Preparatory Commission;

(b) Provide management oversight to the Presidency, the Prosecutor and the Registrar regarding the administration of the Court;

(c) Consider the reports and activities of the Bureau established under paragraph 3 and take appropriate action in regard thereto;

(d) Consider and decide the budget for the Court;

(e) Decide whether to alter, in accordance with article 36, the number of judges;

(f) Consider pursuant to article 87, paragraphs 5 and 7, any question relating to non-cooperation;

(g) Perform any other function consistent with this Statute or the Rules of Procedure and Evidence.

3.

(a) The Assembly shall have a Bureau consisting of a President, two Vice-Presidents and 18 members elected by the Assembly for three-year terms;

(b) The Bureau shall have a representative character, taking into account, in particular, equitable geographic distribution and the adequate representation of the principal legal systems of the world.

(c) The Bureau shall meet as often as necessary, but at least once a year. It shall assist the Assembly in the discharge of its responsibilities.

4. The Assembly may establish such subsidiary bodies as may be necessary, including an independent oversight mechanism for inspection, evaluation and investigation of the Court, in order to enhance its efficiency and economy.

5. The President of the Court, the Prosecutor and the Registrar or their representatives may participate, as appropriate, in meetings of the Assembly and of the Bureau.

6. The Assembly shall meet at the seat of the Court or at the Headquarters of the United Nations once a year and, when circumstances so require, hold special sessions. Except as otherwise specified in this Statute, special sessions shall be convened by the Bureau on its own initiative or at the request of one third of the States Parties.

7. Each State Party shall have one vote. Every effort shall be made to reach decisions by consensus in the Assembly and in the Bureau. If consensus cannot be reached, except as otherwise provided in the Statute:

(a) Decisions on matters of substance must be approved by a two-thirds majority of those present and voting provided that an absolute majority of States Parties constitutes the quorum for voting;

(b) Decisions on matters of procedure shall be taken by a simple majority of States Parties present and voting.

8. A State Party which is in arrears in the payment of its financial contributions towards the costs of the Court shall have no vote in the Assembly and in the Bureau if the amount of its arrears exceeds or equals the amount of the contributions due from it for the preceding two full years. The Assembly may, nevertheless, permit such a State Party to vote in the Assembly and in the Bureau if it is satisfied that the failure to pay is due to conditions beyond the control of the State Party.

9. The Assembly shall adopt its own rules of procedure.

10. The official and working languages of the Assembly shall be those of the General Assembly of the United Nations.

Article 113
Financial Regulations

Except as otherwise specifically provided, all financial matters related to the Court and the meetings of the Assembly of States Parties, including its Bureau and subsidiary bodies, shall be governed by this Statute and the Financial Regulations and Rules adopted by the Assembly of States Parties.

Article 114
Payment of expenses

Expenses of the Court and the Assembly of States Parties, including its Bureau and subsidiary bodies, shall be paid from the funds of the Court.

Article 115
Funds of the Court and of the Assembly of States Parties

The expenses of the Court and the Assembly of States Parties, including its Bureau and subsidiary bodies, as provided for in the budget decided by the Assembly of States Parties, shall be provided by the following sources:

(a) Assessed contributions made by States Parties;
(b) Funds provided by the United Nations, subject to the approval of the General Assembly, in particular in relation to the expenses incurred due to referrals by the Security Council.

Article 116
Voluntary contributions

Without prejudice to article 115, the Court may receive and utilize, as additional funds, voluntary contributions from Governments, international organizations, individuals, corporations and other entities, in accordance with relevant criteria adopted by the Assembly of States Parties.

Article 117
Assessment of contributions

The contributions of States Parties shall be assessed in accordance with an agreed scale of assessment, based on the scale adopted by the United Nations for its regular budget and adjusted in accordance with the principles on which that scale is based.

Article 118
Annual audit

The records, books and accounts of the Court, including its annual financial statements, shall be audited annually by an independent auditor.

Part 13
Final clauses

Article 119
Settlement of disputes

1. Any dispute concerning the judicial functions of the Court shall be settled by the decision of the Court.

2. Any other dispute between two or more States Parties relating to the interpretation or application of this Statute which is not settled through negotiations within three months of their commencement shall be referred to the Assembly of States Parties. The Assembly may itself seek to settle the dispute or may make recommendations on further means of settlement of the dispute, including referral to the International Court of Justice in conformity with the Statute of that Court.

Article 120
Reservations

No reservations may be made to this Statute.

Article 121
Amendments

1. After the expiry of seven years from the entry into force of this Statute, any State Party may propose amendments thereto. The text of any proposed amendment shall be submitted to the Secretary-General of the United Nations, who shall promptly circulate it to all States Parties.

2. No sooner than three months from the date of notification, the Assembly of States Parties, at its next meeting, shall, by a majority of those present and voting, decide whether to take up the proposal. The Assembly may deal with the proposal directly or convene a Review Conference if the issue involved so warrants.

3. The adoption of an amendment at a meeting of the Assembly of States Parties or at a Review Conference on which consensus cannot be reached shall require a two-thirds majority of States Parties.

4. Except as provided in paragraph 5, an amendment shall enter into force for all States Parties one year after instruments of ratification or acceptance

have been deposited with the Secretary-General of the United Nations by seven-eighths of them.

5. Any amendment to articles 5, 6, 7 and 8 of this Statute shall enter into force for those States Parties which have accepted the amendment one year after the deposit of their instruments of ratification or acceptance. In respect of a State Party which has not accepted the amendment, the Court shall not exercise its jurisdiction regarding a crime covered by the amendment when committed by that State Party's nationals or on its territory.

6. If an amendment has been accepted by seven-eighths of States Parties in accordance with paragraph 4, any State Party which has not accepted the amendment may withdraw from this Statute with immediate effect, notwithstanding article 127, paragraph 1, but subject to article 127, paragraph 2, by giving notice no later than one year after the entry into force of such amendment.

7. The Secretary-General of the United Nations shall circulate to all States Parties any amendment adopted at a meeting of the Assembly of States Parties or at a Review Conference.

Article 122
Amendments to provisions of an institutional nature

1. Amendments to provisions of this Statute which are of an exclusively institutional nature, namely, article 35, article 36, paragraphs 8 and 9, article 37, article 38, article 39, paragraphs 1 (first two sentences), 2 and 4, article 42, paragraphs 4 to 9, article 43, paragraphs 2 and 3, and articles 44, 46, 47 and 49, may be proposed at any time, notwithstanding article 121, paragraph 1, by any State Party. The text of any proposed amendment shall be submitted to the Secretary-General of the United Nations or such other person designated by the Assembly of States Parties who shall promptly circulate it to all States Parties and to others participating in the Assembly.

2. Amendments under this article on which consensus cannot be reached shall be adopted by the Assembly of States Parties or by a Review Conference, by a two-thirds majority of States Parties. Such amendments shall enter into force for all States Parties six months after their adoption by the Assembly or, as the case may be, by the Conference.

Article 123
Review of the Statute

1. Seven years after the entry into force of this Statute the Secretary-General of the United Nations shall convene a Review Conference to consider any amendments to this Statute. Such review may include, but is not limited to, the list of crimes contained in article 5. The Conference shall be open to those participating in the Assembly of States Parties and on the same conditions.

2. At any time thereafter, at the request of a State Party and for the purposes set out in paragraph 1, the Secretary-General of the United Nations shall, upon approval by a majority of States Parties, convene a Review Conference.

3. The provisions of article 121, paragraphs 3 to 7, shall apply to the adoption and entry into force of any amendment to the Statute considered at a Review Conference.

Article 124
Transitional provision

Notwithstanding article 12 paragraph 1, a State, on becoming a party to this Statute, may declare that, for a period of seven years after the entry into force of this Statute for the State concerned, it does not accept the jurisdiction of the Court with respect to the category of crimes referred to in article 8 when a crime is alleged to have been committed by its nationals or on its territory. A declaration under this article may be withdrawn at any time. The provisions of this article shall be reviewed at the Review Conference convened in accordance with article 123, paragraph 1.

Article 125
Signature, ratification, acceptance, approval or accession

1. This Statute shall be open for signature by all States in Rome, at the headquarters of the Food and Agriculture Organization of the United Nations, on 17 July 1998. Thereafter, it shall remain open for signature in Rome at the Ministry of Foreign Affairs of Italy until 17 October 1998. After that date, the Statute shall remain open for signature in New York, at United Nations Headquarters, until 31 December 2000.

2. This Statute is subject to ratification, acceptance or approval by signatory States. Instruments of ratification, acceptance or approval shall be deposited with the Secretary-General of the United Nations.

3. This Statute shall be open to accession by all States. Instruments of accession shall be deposited with the Secretary-General of the United Nations.

Article 126
Entry into force

1. This Statute shall enter into force on the first day of the month after the 60th day following the date of the deposit of the 60th instrument of ratification, acceptance, approval or accession with the Secretary-General of the United Nations.

2. For each State ratifying, accepting, approving or acceding to this Statute after the deposit of the 60th instrument of ratification, acceptance, approval or accession, the Statute shall enter into force on the first day of the month after

the 60th day following the deposit by such State of its instrument of ratification, acceptance, approval or accession.

Article 127
Withdrawal

1. A State Party may, by written notification addressed to the Secretary-General of the United Nations, withdraw from this Statute. The withdrawal shall take effect one year after the date of receipt of the notification, unless the notification specifies a later date.

2. A State shall not be discharged, by reason of its withdrawal, from the obligations arising from this Statute while it was a Party to the Statute, including any financial obligations which may have accrued. Its withdrawal shall not affect any cooperation with the Court in connection with criminal investigations and proceedings in relation to which the withdrawing State had a duty to cooperate and which were commenced prior to the date on which the withdrawal became effective, nor shall it prejudice in any way the continued consideration of any matter which was already under consideration by the Court prior to the date on which the withdrawal became effective.

Article 128
Authentic texts

The original of this Statute, of which the Arabic, Chinese, English, French, Russian and Spanish texts are equally authentic, shall be deposited with the Secretary-General of the United Nations, who shall send certified copies thereof to all States.

IN WITNESS, WHEREOF, the undersigned, being duly authorized thereto by their respective Governments, have signed this Statute.

DONE at Rome, this 17th day of July 1998.

Appendix 2

States Parties and signatories to the Rome Statute

Participant	Signature	Ratification, acceptance (A), accession (a)
Afghanistan		10 February 2003 (a)
Albania	18 July 1998	31 January 2003
Algeria	28 December 2000	
Andorra	18 July 1998	30 April 2001
Angola	7 October 1998	
Antigua and Barbuda	23 October 1998	18 June 2001
Argentina	8 January 1999	8 February 2001
Armenia	1 October 1999	
Australia	9 December 1998	1 July 2002
Austria	7 October 1998	28 December 2000
Bahamas	29 December 2000	
Bahrain	11 December 2000	
Bangladesh	16 September 1999	23 March 2010
Barbados	8 September 2000	10 December 2002
Belgium	10 September 1998	28 June 2000
Belize	5 April 2000	5 April 2000
Benin	24 September 1999	22 January 2002
Bolivia	17 July 1998	27 June 2002
Bosnia and Herzegovina	17 July 2000	11 April 2002
Botswana	8 September 2000	8 September 2000
Brazil	7 February 2000	20 June 2002
Bulgaria	11 February 1999	11 April 2002
Burkina Faso	30 November 1998	10 April 2004
Burundi	13 January 1999	21 September 2004
Cambodia	23 October 2000	11 April 2002
Cameroon	17 July 1998	
Canada	18 December 1998	7 July 2000
Cape Verde	28 December 2000	
Central African Republic	7 December 1999	3 October 2001

Participant	Signature	Ratification, acceptance (A), accession (a)
Chad	20 October 1999	1 November 2006
Chile	11 September 1998	
Colombia	10 December 1998	5 August 2002
Comoros	22 September 2000	18 August 2006
Congo	17 July 1998	2 May 2004
Congo, Democratic Republic of the	8 September 2000	11 April 2002
Cook Islands		18 July 2008 (a)
Costa Rica	7 October 1998	7 June 2001
Côte d'Ivoire	30 November 1998	
Croatia	12 October 1998	21 May 2001
Cyprus	15 October 1998	7 March 2002
Czech Republic	13 April 1999	
Denmark[1]	25 September 1998	21 June 2001
Djibouti	7 October 1998	5 November 2002
Dominica		12 February 2001 (a)
Dominican Republic	8 September 2000	12 May 2005
Ecuador	7 October 1998	5 February 2002
Egypt	26 December 2000	
Eritrea	7 October 1998	
Estonia	27 December 1999	30 January 2002
Fiji	29 November 1999	29 November 1999
Finland	7 October 1998	29 December 2000
France	18 July 1998	9 June 2000
Gabon	22 December 1998	20 September 2000
Gambia	4 December 1998	28 June 2002
Georgia	18 July 1998	5 September 2003
Germany	10 December 1998	11 December 2000
Ghana	18 July 1998	20 December 1999
Greece	18 July 1998	15 May 2002
Guinea	7 September 2000	14 July 2003
Guinea-Bissau	12 September 2000	
Guyana	28 December 2000	24 September 2004
Haiti	26 February 1999	
Honduras	7 October 1998	1 July 2002
Hungary	15 January 1999	30 November 2001
Iceland	26 August 1998	25 May 2000
Iran	31 December 2000	
Ireland	7 October 1998	11 April 2002
Israel[2]	31 December 2000	

Participant	Signature	Ratification, acceptance (A), accession (a)
Italy	18 July 1998	26 July 1999
Jamaica	8 September 2000	
Japan		17 July 2007 (a)
Jordan	7 October 1998	11 April 2002
Kenya	11 August 1999	15 March 2005
Korea, Republic of	8 March 2000	13 November 2002
Kuwait	8 September 2000	
Kyrgyzstan	8 December 1998	
Latvia	22 April 1999	28 June 2002
Lesotho	30 November 1998	6 September 2000
Liberia	17 July 1998	22 September 2004
Liechtenstein	18 July 1998	2 October 2001
Lithuania	10 December 1998	12 May 2003
Luxembourg	13 October 1998	8 September 2000
Macedonia	7 October 1998	6 March 2002
Madagascar	18 July 1998	
Malawi	2 March 1999	19 September 2002
Mali	17 July 1998	16 August 2000
Malta	17 July 1998	29 November 2002
Marshall Islands	6 September 2000	7 December 2000
Mauritius	11 November 1998	5 March 2002
Mexico	7 September 2000	28 October 2005
Moldova	8 September 2000	
Monaco	18 July 1998	
Mongolia	29 December 2000	11 April 2002
Montenegro		2 June 2006 (a)
Morocco	8 September 2000	
Mozambique	28 December 2000	
Namibia	27 October 1998	25 June 2002
Nauru	13 December 2000	12 November 2001
Netherlands[3]	18 July 1998	17 July 2001 (A)
New Zealand[4]	7 October 1998	7 September 2000
Niger	17 July 1998	11 April 2002
Nigeria	1 June 2000	27 September 2001
Norway	28 August 1998	16 February 2000
Oman	20 December 2000	
Panama	18 July 1998	21 March 2002
Paraguay	7 October 1998	14 May 2001
Peru	7 December 2000	10 November 2001

Participant	Signature	Ratification, acceptance (A), accession (a)
Philippines	28 December 2000	
Poland	9 April 1999	12 November 2001
Portugal	7 October 1998	5 February 2002
Romania	7 July 1999	11 April 2002
Russian Federation	13 September 2000	
Saint Kitts and Nevis		22 August 2006 (a)
Saint Lucia	27 August 1999	
Saint Vincent and the Grenadines	27 August 1999	3 December 2002
Samoa	17 July 1998	16 September 2002
San Marino	18 July 1998	13 May 1999
São Tomé and Príncipe	28 December 2000	
Senegal	18 July 1998	2 February 1999
Serbia		6 September 2001 (a)
Seychelles	28 December 2000	
Sierra Leone	17 October 1998	15 September 2000
Slovakia	23 December 1998	11 April 2002
Slovenia	7 October 1998	31 December 2001
Solomon Islands	3 December 1998	
South Africa	17 July 1998	27 November 2000
Spain	18 July 1998	24 October 2000
Sudan	8 September 2000	
Suriname		15 July 2008 (a)
Sweden	7 October 1998	28 June 2001
Switzerland	18 July 1998	12 October 2001
Syria	29 November 2000	
Tajikistan	30 November 1998	5 May 2000
Tanzania	29 December 2000	20 August 2002
Thailand	2 October 2000	
Timor-Leste		6 September 2002 (a)
Trinidad and Tobago	23 March 1999	6 April 1999
Uganda	17 March 1999	14 June 2002
Ukraine	20 January 2000	
United Arab Emirates	27 November 2000	
United Kingdom	30 November 1998	4 October 2001
United States of America[5]	31 December 2000	
Uruguay	19 December 2000	28 June 2002
Uzbekistan	29 December 2000	

Participant	Signature	Ratification, acceptance (A), accession (a)
Venezuela	14 October 1998	7 June 2000
Yemen	28 December 2000	
Zambia	17 July 1998	13 November 2002
Zimbabwe	17 July 1998	

[1] With a territorial exclusion: 'Until further notice, the Statute shall not apply to the Faroe Islands and Greenland.' Subsequently, on 17 November 2004 and 20 November 2006, respectively, the Secretary-General received from the Government of Denmark the following territorial applications: 'With reference to the Rome Statute of the International Criminal Court, done at Rome on 17 July 1998, [the Government of Denmark informs the Secretary-General] that by Royal [Decrees of 20 August 2004 entering into force on 1 October 2004, and 1 September 2006 entering into force on 1 October 2006, respectively] the above Convention will also be applicable in [Greenland and the Faroe Islands]. Denmark therefore withdraws its declaration made upon ratification of the said Convention to the effect that the Convention should not apply to the Faroe Islands and Greenland.'

[2] On 28 August 2002, the Secretary-General received from the Government of Israel the following communication: 'in connection with the Rome Statute of the International Criminal Court adopted on 17 July 1998 ... Israel does not intend to become a party to the treaty. Accordingly, Israel has no legal obligations arising from its signature on 31 December 2000. Israel requests that its intention not to become a party, as expressed in this letter, be reflected in the depositary's status lists relating to this treaty.'

[3] For the Kingdom in Europe, the Netherlands Antilles and Aruba.

[4] With a declaration to the effect that 'consistent with the constitutional status of Tokelau and taking into account its commitment to the development of self-government through an act of self-determination under the Charter of the United Nations, this ratification shall not extend to Tokelau unless and until a Declaration to this effect is lodged by the Government of New Zealand with the Depositary on the basis of appropriate consultation with that territory.'

[5] The US Government sent the following communication to the Secretary-General of the United Nations on 6 May 2002: 'This is to inform you, in connection with the Rome Statute of the International Criminal Court adopted on July 17, 1998, that the United States does not intend to become a party to the treaty. Accordingly, the United States has no legal obligations arising from its signature on December 31, 2000. The United States requests that its intention not to become a party, as expressed in this letter, be reflected in the depositary's status lists relating to this treaty.'

Appendix 3

Declarations and reservations

Unless otherwise indicated, the declarations and reservations were made upon ratification, acceptance, approval or accession.

Andorra

Declaration:

> With regard to Article 103, paragraph 1 (a) and (b) of the Rome Statute of the International Criminal Court, the Principality of Andorra declares that it would, if necessary, be willing to accept persons of Andorran nationality sentenced by the Court, provided that the sentence imposed by the Court was enforced in accordance with Andorran legislation on the maximum duration of sentences.

Australia

Declaration:

> The Government of Australia, having considered the Statute, now hereby ratifies the same, for and on behalf of Australia, with the following declaration, the terms of which have full effect in Australian law, and which is not a reservation:
>
> Australia notes that a case will be inadmissible before the International Criminal Court (the Court) where it is being investigated or prosecuted by a State. Australia reaffirms the primacy of its criminal jurisdiction in relation to crimes within the jurisdiction of the Court. To enable Australia to exercise its jurisdiction effectively, and fully adhering to its obligations under the Statute of the Court, no person will be surrendered to the Court by Australia until it has had the full opportunity to investigate or prosecute any alleged crimes. For this purpose, the procedure under Australian law implementing the Statute of the Court provides that no person can be surrendered to the Court unless the Australian Attorney-General issues a certificate allowing surrender. Australian law also provides that no person can be arrested pursuant to an arrest warrant issued by the Court without a certificate from the Attorney-General.

Australia further declares its understanding that the offences in Article 6, 7 and 8 will be interpreted and applied in a way that accords with the way they are implemented in Australian domestic law.

Belgium

Declaration concerning Article 31, paragraph 1 (c):

Pursuant to Article 21, paragraph 1 (b) of the Statute and having regard to the rules of international humanitarian law which may not be derogated from, the Belgian Government considers that Article 31, paragraph 1 (c), of the Statute can be applied and interpreted only in conformity with those rules.

Colombia

Declarations:

1. None of the provisions of the Rome Statute concerning the exercise of jurisdiction by the International Criminal Court prevent the Colombian State from granting amnesties, reprieves or judicial pardons for political crimes, provided that they are granted in conformity with the Constitution and with the principles and norms of international law accepted by Colombia.

   Colombia declares that the provisions of the Statute must be applied and interpreted in a manner consistent with the provisions of international humanitarian law and, consequently, that nothing in the Statute affects the rights and obligations embodied in the norms of international humanitarian law, especially those set forth in Article 3 common to the four Geneva Conventions and in Protocols I and II Additional thereto.

   Likewise, in the event that a Colombian national has to be investigated and prosecuted by the International Criminal Court, the Rome Statute must be interpreted and applied, where appropriate, in accordance with the principles and norms of international humanitarian law and international human rights law.

2. With respect to articles 61(2)(b) and 67(1)(d), Colombia declares that it will always be in the interests of justice that Colombian nationals be fully guaranteed the right of defence, especially the right to be assisted by counsel during the phases of investigation and prosecution by the International Criminal Court.

3. Concerning Article 17(3), Colombia declares that the use of the word 'otherwise' with respect to the determination of the State's ability to investigate or prosecute a case refers to the obvious absence of objective conditions necessary to conduct the trial.

4. Bearing in mind that the scope of the Rome Statute is limited exclusively to the exercise of complementary jurisdiction by the International Criminal Court and to the cooperation of national authorities with it, Colombia declares that none of the provisions of the Rome Statute alters the domestic law applied by the Colombian judicial authorities in exercise of their domestic jurisdiction within the territory of the Republic of Colombia.

5. Availing itself of the option provided in Article 124 of the Statute and subject to the conditions established therein, the Government of Colombia declares that it does not accept the jurisdiction of the Court with respect to the category of crimes referred to in Article 8 when a crime is alleged to have been committed by Colombian nationals or on Colombian territory.

6. In accordance with Article 87(1)(a) and the first paragraph of Article 87(2), the Government of Colombia declares that requests for cooperation or assistance shall be transmitted through the diplomatic channel and shall either be in or be accompanied by a translation into the Spanish language.

Egypt

Upon signature:
Declarations:

2. The Arab Republic of Egypt affirms the importance of the Statute being interpreted and applied in conformity with the general principles and fundamental rights which are universally recognized and accepted by the whole international community and with the principles, purposes and provisions of the Charter of the United Nations and the general principles and rules of international law and international humanitarian law. It further declares that it shall interpret and apply the references that appear in the Statute of the Court to the two terms fundamental rights and international standards on the understanding that such references are to the fundamental rights and internationally recognized norms and standards which are accepted by the international community as a whole.

3. The Arab Republic of Egypt declares that its understanding of the conditions, measures and rules which appear in the introductory paragraph of Article 7 of the Statute of the Court is that they shall apply to all the acts specified in that article.

4. Arab Republic of Egypt declares that its understanding of Article 8 of the Statute of the Court shall be as follows:
   (a) The provisions of the Statute with regard to the war crimes referred to in Article 8 in general and Article 8, paragraph 2 (b)

in particular shall apply irrespective of the means by which they were perpetrated or the type of weapon used, including nuclear weapons, which are indiscriminate in nature and cause unnecessary damage, in contravention of international humanitarian law.

(b) The military objectives referred to in Article 8, paragraph 2 (b) of the Statute must be defined in the light of the principles, rules and provisions of international humanitarian law. Civilian objects must be defined and dealt with in accordance with the provisions of the Protocol Additional to the Geneva Conventions of 12 August 1949 (Protocol I) and, in particular, Article 52 thereof. In case of doubt, the object shall be considered to be civilian.

(c) The Arab Republic of Egypt affirms that the term 'the concrete and direct overall military advantage anticipated' used in Article 8, paragraph 2 (b)(iv), must be interpreted in the light of the relevant provisions of the Protocol Additional to the Geneva Conventions of 12 August 1949 (Protocol I). The term must also be interpreted as referring to the advantage anticipated by the perpetrator at the time when the crime was committed. No justification may be adduced for the nature of any crime which may cause incidental damage in violation of the law applicable in armed conflicts. The overall military advantage must not be used as a basis on which to justify the ultimate goal of the war or any other strategic goals. The advantage anticipated must be proportionate to the damage inflicted.

(d) Article 8, paragraph 2 (b)(xvii) and (xviii) of the Statute shall be applicable to all types of emissions which are indiscriminate in their effects and the weapons used to deliver them, including emissions resulting from the use of nuclear weapons.

5. The Arab Republic of Egypt declares that the principle of the non-retroactivity of the jurisdiction of the Court, pursuant to articles 11 and 24 of the Statute, shall not invalidate the well established principle that no war crime shall be barred from prosecution due to the statute of limitations and no war criminal shall escape justice or escape prosecution in other legal jurisdictions.

France

I. Interpretative declarations:

1. The provisions of the Statute of the International Criminal Court do not preclude France from exercising its inherent right of self-defence in conformity with Article 51 of the Charter.

2. The provisions of Article 8 of the Statute, in particular paragraph 2 (b) thereof, relate solely to conventional weapons and can neither

regulate nor prohibit the possible use of nuclear weapons nor impair the other rules of international law applicable to other weapons necessary to the exercise by France of its inherent right of self-defence, unless nuclear weapons or the other weapons referred to herein become subject in the future to a comprehensive ban and are specified in an annex to the Statute by means of an amendment adopted in accordance with the provisions of articles 121 and 123.

3. The Government of the French Republic considers that the term 'armed conflict' in Article 8, paragraphs 2 (b) and (c), in and of itself and in its context, refers to a situation of a kind which does not include the commission of ordinary crimes, including acts of terrorism, whether collective or isolated.

4. The situation referred to in Article 8, paragraph 2 (b)(xxiii), of the Statute does not preclude France from directing attacks against objectives considered as military objectives under international humanitarian law.

5. The Government of the French Republic declares that the term 'military advantage' in Article 8, paragraph 2(b)(iv), refers to the advantage anticipated from the attack as a whole and not from isolated or specific elements thereof.

6. The Government of the French Republic declares that a specific area may be considered a 'military objective' as referred to in Article 8, paragraph 2 (b) as a whole if, by reason of its situation, nature, use, location, total or partial destruction, capture or neutralization, taking into account the circumstances of the moment, it offers a decisive military advantage.

   The Government of the French Republic considers that the provisions of Article 8, paragraph 2 (b)(ii) and (v), do not refer to possible collateral damage resulting from attacks directed against military objectives.

7. The Government of the French Republic declares that the risk of damage to the natural environment as a result of the use of methods and means of warfare, as envisaged in Article 8, paragraph 2 (b)(iv), must be weighed objectively on the basis of the information available at the time of its assessment.

III. Declaration under Article 124:

Pursuant to Article 124 of the Statute of the International Criminal Court, the French Republic declares that it does not accept the jurisdiction of the Court with respect to the category of crimes referred to in Article 8 when a crime is alleged to have been committed by its nationals or on its territory.

Israel

Upon signature:
Declaration:

Being an active consistent supporter of the concept of an International
Criminal Court, and its realization in the form of the Rome Statute, the
Government of the State of Israel is proud to thus express its acknowledgment of the importance, and indeed indispensability, of an effective court
for the enforcement of the rule of law and the prevention of impunity.

As one of the originators of the concept of an International Criminal
Court, Israel, through its prominent lawyers and statesmen, has, since the
early 1950s, actively participated in all stages of the formation of such a court.
Its representatives, carrying in both heart and mind collective, and sometimes personal, memories of the holocaust – the greatest and most heinous
crime to have been committed in the history of mankind – enthusiastically,
with a sense of acute sincerity and seriousness, contributed to all stages of the
preparation of the Statute. Responsibly, possessing the same sense of mission, they currently support the work of the ICC Preparatory Commission.

At the 1998 Rome Conference, Israel expressed its deep disappointment and regret at the insertion into the Statute of formulations tailored
to meet the political agenda of certain states. Israel warned that such an
unfortunate practice might reflect on the intent to abuse the Statute as a
political tool. Today, in the same spirit, the Government of the State of
Israel signs the Statute while rejecting any attempt to interpret provisions
thereof in a politically motivated manner against Israel and its citizens.
The Government of Israel hopes that Israel's expressions of concern of any
such attempt would be recorded in history as a warning against the risk of
politicization, that might undermine the objectives of what is intended to
become a central impartial body, benefiting mankind as a whole.

Nevertheless, as a democratic society, Israel has been conducting
ongoing political, public and academic debates concerning the ICC and
its significance in the context of international law and the international
community. The Court's essentiality – as a vital means of ensuring that
criminals who commit genuinely heinous crimes will be duly brought to
justice, while other potential offenders of the fundamental principles of
humanity and the dictates of public conscience will be properly deterred –
has never seized to guide us. Israel's signature of the Rome Statute will,
therefore, enable it to morally identify with this basic idea, underlying the
establishment of the Court.

Today, [the Government of Israel is] honoured to express [its] sincere hopes that the Court, guided by the cardinal judicial principles of
objectivity and universality, will indeed serve its noble and meritorious
objectives.

Jordan

Interpretative declaration:

The Government of the Hashemite Kingdom of Jordan hereby declares that nothing under its national law including the Constitution, is inconsistent with the Rome Statute of the International Criminal Court. As such, it interprets such national law as giving effect to the full application of the Rome Statute and the exercise of relevant jurisdiction thereunder.

Liechtenstein

Declaration pursuant to Article 103, paragraph 1 of the Statute:

Pursuant to Article 103, paragraph 1 of the Statute, the Principality of Liechtenstein declares its willingness to accept persons sentenced to imprisonment by the Court, for purposes of execution of the sentence, if the persons are Liechtenstein citizens or if the persons' usual residence is in the Principality of Liechtenstein.

Lithuania

Declaration:

'AND WHEREAS, it is provided in paragraph 1(b) of Article 103, the Seimas of the Republic of Lithuania declares that the Republic of Lithuania is willing to accept persons, sentenced by the International Criminal Court to serve the sentence of imprisonment, if such persons are nationals of the Republic of Lithuania.'

Malta

Declarations:

'Article 20, paragraphs 3(a) and (b).

With regard to article 20 paragraphs 3(a) and (b) of the Rome Statute of the International Criminal Court Malta declares that according to its constitution no person who shows that he has been tried by any competent court for a criminal offence and either convicted or acquitted shall again be tried for that offence or for any other criminal offence of which he could have been convicted at the trial for that offence save upon the order of a superior court made in the course of appeal or review proceedings relating to the conviction or acquittal; and no person shall be tried for a criminal offence if he shows that he has been pardoned for that offence.

It is presumed that under the general principles of law a trial as described in paragraphs 3(a) and (b) of Article 20 of the Statute would be considered a nullity and would not be taken into account in the application of the above constitutional rule. However, the matter has never been the subject of any judgment before the Maltese courts.

The prerogative of mercy will only be exercised in Malta in conformity with its obligations under International law including those arising from the Rome Statute of the International Criminal Court.'

New Zealand

Declaration:

1. The Government of New Zealand notes that the majority of the war crimes specified in Article 8 of the Rome Statute, in particular those in Article 8(2)(b)(i)–(v) and 8(2)(e)(i)–(iv) (which relate to various kinds of attacks on civilian targets), make no reference to the type of the weapons employed to commit the particular crime. The Government of New Zealand recalls that the fundamental principle that underpins international humanitarian law is to mitigate and circumscribe the cruelty of war for humanitarian reasons and that, rather than being limited to weaponry of an earlier time, this branch of law has evolved, and continues to evolve, to meet contemporary circumstances. Accordingly, it is the view of the Government of New Zealand that it would be inconsistent with principles of international humanitarian law to purport to limit the scope of Article 8, in particular Article 8 (2)(b), to events that involve conventional weapons only.

2. The Government of New Zealand finds support for its view in the Advisory Opinion of the International Court of Justice on the *Legality of the Threat or Use of Nuclear Weapons* (1996) and draws attention to paragraph 86, in particular, where the Court stated that the conclusion that humanitarian law did not apply to such weapons 'would be incompatible with the intrinsically humanitarian character of the legal principles in question which permeates the entire law of armed conflict and applies to all forms of warfare and to all kinds of weapons, those of the past, those of the present and those of the future.'

3. The Government of New Zealand further notes that international humanitarian law applies equally to aggressor and defender states and its application in a particular context is not dependent on a determination of whether or not a state is acting in self-defence. In this respect it refers to paragraphs 40–42 of the Advisory Opinion in the *Nuclear Weapons Case*.

Portugal

Declaration:

with the following declaration:

The Portuguese Republic declares the intention to exercise its jurisdictional powers over every person found in the Portuguese territory, that is being prosecuted for the crimes set forth in Article 5, paragraph 1 of the Rome Statute of the International Criminal Court, within the respect for the Portuguese criminal legislation ...

Slovakia

Declaration:

Pursuant to Article 103, paragraph 1 (b) of the Statute the Slovak Republic declares that it would accept, if necessary, persons sentenced by the Court, if the persons are citizens of the Slovak Republic or have a permanent residence in its territory, for purposes of execution of the sentence of imprisonment and at the same time it will apply the principle of conversion of sentence imposed by the Court.

Spain

Declaration under Article 103, paragraph 1(b):

Spain declares its willingness to accept at the appropriate time, persons sentenced by the International Criminal Court, provided that the duration of the sentence does not exceed the maximum stipulated for any crime under Spanish law.

Sweden

Statement:

In connection with the deposit of its instrument of ratification of the Rome Statute of the International Criminal Court and, with regard to the war crimes specified in Article 8 of the Statute which relate to the methods of warfare, the Government of the Kingdom of Sweden would like to recall the Advisory Opinion given by the International Court of Justice on 8 July 1996 on the Legality of the Threat or Use of Nuclear Weapons, and in particular paragraphs 85 to 87 thereof, in which the Court finds that there can be no doubt as to the applicability of humanitarian law to nuclear weapons.

Switzerland

Declaration:

In accordance with Article 103, paragraph 1, of the Statute, Switzerland declares that it is prepared to be responsible for enforcement of sentences of imprisonment handed down by the Court against Swiss nationals or persons habitually resident in Switzerland.

United Kingdom

Declaration:

The United Kingdom understands the term 'the established framework of international law', used in Article 8 (2)(b) and (e), to include customary international law as established by State practice and opinio iuris. In that context the United Kingdom confirms and draws to the attention of the Court its views as expressed, inter alia, in its statements made on ratification of relevant instruments of international law, including the Protocol Additional to the Geneva Conventions of 12th August 1949, and relating to the Protection of Victims of International Armed Conflicts (Protocol I) of 8th June 1977.

Uruguay

Interpretative declaration:

As a State Party to the Rome Statute, the Eastern Republic of Uruguay shall ensure its application to the full extent of the powers of the State insofar as it is competent in that respect and in strict accordance with the Constitutional provisions of the Republic. Pursuant to the provisions of part 9 of the Statute entitled 'International cooperation and judicial assistance', the Executive shall within six months refer to the Legislature a bill establishing the procedures for ensuring the application of the Statute.

21 July 2003

The Eastern Republic of Uruguay, by Act No. 17.510 of 27 June 2002 ratified by the legislative branch, gave its approval to the Rome Statute in terms fully compatible with Uruguay's constitutional order. While the Constitution is a law of higher rank to which all other laws are subject, this does not in any way constitute a reservation to any of the provisions of that international instrument.

It is noted for all necessary effects that the Rome Statute has unequivocally preserved the normal functioning of national jurisdictions and that the jurisdiction of the International Criminal Court is exercised only in the absence of the exercise of national jurisdiction.

Accordingly, it is very clear that the above-mentioned Act imposes no limits or conditions on the application of the Statute, fully authorizing the functioning of the national legal system without detriment to the Statute.

The interpretative declaration made by Uruguay upon ratifying the Statute does not, therefore, constitute a reservation of any kind.

Lastly, mention should be made of the significance that Uruguay attaches to the Rome Statute as a notable expression of the progressive development of international law on a highly sensitive issue.

Appendix 4

Objections

Finland

8 July 2003
With regard to the declaration made by Uruguay upon ratification:

> The Government of Finland has carefully examined the contents of these interpretative declarations, in particular the statement that 'as a State Party to the Rome Statute, the Eastern Republic of Uruguay shall ensure its application to the full extent of the powers of the State insofar as it is competent in that respect and in strict accordance with the Constitutional provisions of the Republic.' Such a statement, without further specification, has to be considered in substance as a reservation which raises doubts as to the commitment of Uruguay to the object and purpose of the Statute.
>
> The Government of Finland would like to recall Article 120 of the Rome Statute and the general principle relating to internal law and observance of treaties, according to which a party may not invoke the provisions of its internal law as justification for its failure to perform a treaty.
>
> The Government of Finland therefore objects to the above-mentioned reservation made by the Eastern Republic of Uruguay to the Rome Statute of the International Criminal Court. This objection shall not preclude the entry into force of the Statute between Finland and Uruguay. The Statute will thus become operative between the two states without Uruguay benefiting from its reservation.

Germany

7 July 2003
With regard to the declaration made by Uruguay upon ratification:

> The Government of the Federal Republic of Germany has examined the Interpretative Declaration to the Rome Statute of the International Criminal Court made by the Government of the Eastern Republic of Uruguay at the time of its ratification of the Statute.

The Government of the Federal Republic of Germany considers that the Interpretative Declaration with regard to the compatibility of the rules of the Statute with the provisions of the Constitution of Uruguay is in fact a reservation that seeks to limit the scope of the Statute on a unilateral basis. As it is provided in article 120 of the Statute that no reservation may be made to the Statute, this reservation should not be made.

The Government of the Federal Republic of Germany therefore objects to the aforementioned 'declaration' made by the Government of the Eastern Republic of Uruguay. This objection does not preclude the entry into force of the Statute between the Federal Republic of Germany and the Eastern Republic of Uruguay.

Ireland

28 July 2003

Ireland has examined the text of the interpretative declaration made by the Eastern Republic of Uruguay upon ratifying the Rome Statute of the International Criminal Court.

Ireland notes that the said interpretative declaration provides that the application of the Rome Statute by the Eastern Republic of Uruguay shall be subject to the provisions of the Constitution of Uruguay. Ireland considers this interpretative declaration to be in substance a reservation.

Article 120 of the Rome Statute expressly precludes the making of reservations. In addition, it is a rule of international law that a state may not invoke the provisions of its internal law as a justification for its failure to perform its treaty obligations.

Ireland therefore objects to the above-mentioned reservation made by the Eastern Republic of Uruguay to the Rome Statute of the International Criminal Court. This objection does not preclude the entry into force of the Statute between Ireland and the Eastern Republic of Uruguay. The Statute will therefore be effective between the two states, without Uruguay benefiting from its reservation.

Netherlands

8 July 2003
With regard to the declaration made by Uruguay upon ratification:

The Government of the Kingdom of the Netherlands has examined the interpretative declaration made by the Government of Uruguay and regards the declaration made by the Government of Uruguay to effectively be a reservation.

The Government of the Kingdom of the Netherlands notes that the application of the Statute by the Government of Uruguay will be limited by the bounds of national legislation. The reservation made by Uruguay therefore raises doubts as to the commitment of Uruguay to the object and purpose of the Statute.

Article 120 of the Statute precludes reservations.

On these two grounds the Kingdom of the Netherlands objects to the above-mentioned reservation made by Uruguay to the Rome Statute of the International Criminal Court.

This objection shall not preclude the entry into force of the Statute between the Kingdom of the Netherlands and Uruguay. The Statute will be effective between the two States, without Uruguay benefiting from its reservation.

Norway

29 August 2003

The Government of the Kingdom of Norway has examined the interpretative declaration made by the Government of Uruguay upon ratification of the Rome Statute of the International Criminal Court.

The Government of Norway notes that the interpretative declaration purports to limit the application of the Statute within national legislation, and therefore constitutes a reservation.

The Government of Norway recalls that according to Article 120 of the Statute, no reservations may be made to the Statute.

The Government of Norway therefore objects to the reservation made by the Government of Uruguay upon ratification of the Rome Statute of the International Criminal Court. This objection shall not preclude the entry into force of the Statute in its entirety between the Kingdom of Norway and Uruguay. The Statute thus becomes operative between the Kingdom of Norway and Uruguay without Uruguay benefiting from the reservation.

Sweden

7 July 2003
With regard to the declaration made by Uruguay upon ratification:

The Government of Sweden has examined the interpretative declaration made by the Eastern Republic of Uruguay upon ratifying the Rome Statute of the International Criminal Court (the Statute).

The Government of Sweden recalls that the designation assigned to a statement whereby the legal effect of certain provisions of a treaty is excluded or modified does not determine its status as a reservation to the treaty. The Government of Sweden considers that the declaration made by Uruguay to the Statute in substance constitutes a reservation.

The Government of Sweden notes that the application of the Statute is being made subject to a general reference to possible limits of the competence of the State and the constitutional provisions of Uruguay. Such a general reservation referring to national legislation without specifying its contents makes it unclear to what extent the reserving State considers itself bound by the obligations of the Statute. The reservation made by Uruguay therefore raises doubts as to the commitment of Uruguay to the object and purpose of the Statute.

According to article 120 of the Statute no reservations shall be permitted. The Government of Sweden therefore objects to the aforesaid reservation made by Uruguay to the Rome Statute of the International Criminal Court.

This objection shall not preclude the entry into force of the Statute between Sweden and Uruguay. The Statute enters into force in its entirety between the two States, without Uruguay benefiting from its reservation.

United Kingdom

31 July 2003

At the time of the deposit of its instrument of ratification, the Eastern Republic of Uruguay made two statements which are called 'interpretative declarations', the first of which states that 'as a State Party to the Rome Statute, the Eastern Republic of Uruguay shall ensure its application to the full extent of the powers of the State insofar as it is competent in that respect and in strict accordance with the Constitutional provisions of the Republic'.

The Government of the United Kingdom has given careful consideration to the so-called interpretative declaration quoted above. The Government of the United Kingdom is obliged to conclude that this so-called interpretative declaration purports to exclude or modify the legal effects of the Rome Statute in its application to the Eastern Republic of Uruguay and is accordingly a reservation. However, according to Article 120 of the Rome Statute, no reservations may be made thereto.

Accordingly, the Government objects to the above-quoted reservation by the Eastern Republic of Uruguay. However, this objection does not preclude the entry into force of the Rome Statute between the United Kingdom and Uruguay.

BIBLIOGRAPHY

Abass, A., 'The Competence of the Security Council to Terminate the Jurisdiction of the International Criminal Court', (2005) 40 *Texas International Law Journal* 263

Abtahi, Hirad, 'The Islamic Republic of Iran and the ICC', (2005) 3 *Journal of International Criminal Justice* 635

Ailslieger, Kristafer, 'Why the United States Should Be Wary of the International Criminal Court: Concerns over Sovereignty and Constitutional Guarantees', (1999) 39 *Washburn Law Journal* 80

Akande, Dapo, 'International Law Immunities and the International Criminal Court', (2004) 98 *American Journal of International Law* 419

'The Jurisdiction of the International Criminal Court over Nationals of Non-Parties: Legal Basis and Limits', (2003) 1 *Journal of International Criminal Justice* 618

Akhavan, Payam, 'The Lord's Resistance Army Case: Uganda's Submission of the First State Referral to the International Criminal Court', (2005) 99 *American Journal of International Law* 403

'The International Criminal Court in Context: Mediating the Global and Local in the Age of Accountability', (2003) 97 *American Journal of International Law* 712

Allen, Tim, *Trial Justice, the International Criminal Court and the Lord's Resistance Army*, London: Zed Books, 2006

Allmand, Warren, 'The International Criminal Court and the Human Rights Revolution', (2000) 46 *McGill Law Journal* 263

Alter, R. T., 'International Criminal Law: A Bittersweet Year for Supporters and Critics of the International Criminal Court', (2003) 37 *International Lawyer* 551

Amann, Diane Marie, 'Harmonic Convergence? Constitutional Criminal Procedure in an International Context', (2000) 75 *Indiana Law Journal* 809

Amann, Diane Marie, and Sellers, M. N. S., 'The United States of America and the International Criminal Court', (2002) 50 *American Journal of Comparative Law* 381

Ambos, Kai, 'Some Preliminary Reflections on the Mens Rea Requirements of the Crimes of the ICC Statute, and of the Elements of Crimes', in L. C.

Vohrah *et al.*, eds., *Man's Inhumanity to Man: Essays on International Law in Honour of Antonio Cassese*, The Hague: Kluwer Law International, 2003, pp. 11–40

'The Right of Non-Self-Incrimination of Witnesses before the ICC', (2002) 15 *Leiden Journal of International Law* 155

'General Principles of Criminal Law in the Rome Statute', (1999) 10 *Criminal Law Forum* 1

'The International Criminal Court and the Traditional Principles of International Cooperation in Criminal Matters', (1998) 9 *Finnish Yearbook of International Law* 413

'The Role of the Prosecutor of an International Criminal Court from a Comparative Perspective', [1997] *Review of the International Commission of Jurists* 45

'Establishing an International Criminal Court and International Criminal Code: Observations from an International Criminal Law Viewpoint', (1996) 7 *European Journal of International Law* 519

Andreasen, Scott W., 'The International Criminal Court: Does the Constitution Preclude Its Ratification by the United States?', (2000) 85 *Iowa Law Review* 697

Annan, Kofi, 'Advocating for an International Criminal Court', (1997) 21 *Fordham International Law Journal* 363

Apuuli, Kasaija Phillip, 'The ICC Arrest Warrants for the Lord's Resistance Army Leaders and Peace Prospects for Northern Uganda', (2006) 4 *Journal of International Criminal Justice* 179

'The International Criminal Court (ICC) and the Lord's Resistance Army (LRA) Insurgency in Northern Uganda', (2005) 15 *Criminal Law Forum* 408

Arbour, Louise, 'Will the ICC Have an Impact on Universal Jurisdiction?', (2003) 1 *Journal of International Criminal Justice* 585

'Friedmann Award Address: Litigation before the ICC: Not If and When, But How', (2001) 40 *Columbia Journal of Transnational Law* 1

'The Need for an Independent and Effective Prosecutor in the Permanent International Criminal Court', (1999) 17 *Windsor Yearbook of Access to Justice* 217

Arbour, Louise, and Bergsmo, Morten, 'Conspicuous Absence of Jurisdictional Overreach', in Herman von Hebel, Johan G. Lammers and Jolien Schukking, eds., *Reflections on the International Criminal Court: Essays in Honour of Adriaan Bos*, The Hague: T. M. C. Asser, 1999, pp. 129–40

Arbour, Louise, Eser, Albin, Ambos, Kai, and Sanders, Andrew, eds., *The Prosecutor of a Permanent International Criminal Court*, Freiburg im Breisgau: Edition Iuscrim, 2000

Armstead, J. Holmes, Jr, 'The International Criminal Court: History, Development and Status', (1998) 38 *Santa Clara Law Review* 745

Arnaut, Damir, 'When in Rome ... ? The International Criminal Court and Avenues for US Participation', (2003) 43 *Virginia Journal of International Law* 525

Arnold, Roberta, *The ICC as a New Instrument for Repressing Terrorism*, Ardsley, NY: Transnational Publishers, 2004

'The Mens Rea of Genocide under the Statute of the International Criminal Court', (2003) 14 *Criminal Law Forum* 127

Arsanjani, Mahnoush H., 'The Rome Statute of the International Criminal Court: Exceptions to the Jurisdiction', in Mauro Politi and Giuseppe Nesi, eds., *The Rome Statute of the International Criminal Court: A Challenge to Impunity*, Aldershot: Ashgate, 2001, pp. 49–54

'Reflections on the Jurisdiction and Trigger-Mechanism of the International Criminal Court', in Herman von Hebel, Johan G. Lammers and Jolien Schukking, eds., *Reflections on the International Criminal Court: Essays in Honour of Adriaan Bos*, The Hague: T. M. C. Asser, 1999, pp. 57–76

'The International Criminal Court and National Amnesty Laws', [1999] *ASIL Proceedings* 65

'The Rome Statute of the International Criminal Court', (1999) 93 *American Journal of International Law* 22

Arsanjani, Mahnoush H., and Reisman, W. M., 'The Law-in-Action of the International Criminal Court', (2005) 99 *American Journal of International Law* 385

Askin, Kelly Dawn, 'Women's Issues in International Criminal Law: Recent Developments and the Potential Contribution of the ICC', in Dinah Shelton, ed., *International Crimes, Peace, and Human Rights: The Role of the International Criminal Court*, Ardsley, NY: Transnational Publishers, 2000, pp. 47–64

'Crimes within the Jurisdiction of the International Criminal Court', (1999) 10 *Criminal Law Forum* 33

Austin, W. C., 'Who's Afraid of the Big Bad Wolf? The International Criminal Court as a Weapon of Asymmetric Warfare', (2006) 39 *Vanderbilt Journal of Transnational Law* 291

Bachrach, M., 'The Permanent International Criminal Court: An Examination of the Statutory Debate', (1998) 5 *ILSA Journal of International and Comparative Law* 139

Bacio Terracino, Julio, 'National Implementation of ICC Crimes: Impact on National Jurisdictions and the ICC', (2007) 5 *Journal of International Criminal Justice* 421

Baez, Jose A., 'An International Crimes Court: Further Tales of the King of Corinth', (1993) 23 *Georgia Journal of International and Comparative Law* 289

Bantekas, Ilias, 'Defences in International Criminal Law', in Dominic McGoldrick, Peter Rowe and Eric Donnelly, eds., *The Permanent International Criminal Court: Legal and Policy Issues*, Oxford and Portland, OR: Hart Publishing, 2004, pp. 263–85

Baronoff, David M., 'Unbalance of Powers: The International Criminal Court's Potential to Upset the Founders' Checks and Balances', (2002) 4 *University of Pennsylvania Journal of Constitutional Law* 800

Barrett, Matthew A., 'Ratify or Reject: Examining the United States' Opposition to the International Criminal Court', (1999) 28 *Georgia Journal of International and Comparative Law* 8

Bassiouni, M. Cherif, 'The ICC – Quo Vadis?', (2006) 4 *Journal of International Criminal Justice* 421

'The Permanent International Criminal Court', in Mark Lattimer and Philippe Sands, eds., *Justice for Crimes Against Humanity*, Oxford and Portland, OR: Hart Publishing, 2003

'Explanatory Note on the ICC Statute', (2000) 71 *Revue Internationale de Droit Penal* 1

'Negotiating the Treaty of Rome on the Establishment of an International Criminal Court', (1999) 32 *Cornell International Law Journal* 443

'Policy Perspectives Favouring the Establishment of the International Criminal Court', (1999) 52 *Journal of International Affairs* 795

'Observations on the Structure of the (Zutphen) Consolidated Text', (1998) 13*bis Nouvelles études pénales* 5

ed., *The Statute of the International Criminal Court: A Documentary History*, Ardsley, NY: Transnational Publishers, 1998

'From Versailles to Rwanda in Seventy-Five Years: The Need to Establish a Permanent International Criminal Court', (1997) 10 *Harvard Human Rights Journal* 11

'Observations Concerning the 1997–8 Preparatory Committee's Work', (1997) 29 *Denver Journal of International Law and Policy* 397; (1997) 13 *Nouvelles études pénales* 5

Baum, L. M., 'Pursuing Justice in a Climate of Moral Outrage: An Evaluation of the Rights of the Accused in the Rome Statute of the International Criminal Court', (2001) 19 *Wisconsin International Law Journal* 197

Bedont, Barbara, 'Gender-Specific Provisions in the Statute of the International Criminal Court', in Flavia Lattanzi and William A. Schabas, eds., *Essays on the Rome Statute of the International Criminal Court*, vol. I, Ripa Fagnano Alto: Editrice il Sirente, 2000, pp. 183–210

Bedont, Barbara, and Hall Martinez, Katherine, 'Ending Impunity for Gender Crimes under the International Criminal Court', (1999) 6 *Brown Journal of World Affairs* 65

Behrens, Hans-Jörg, 'Investigation, Trial and Appeal in the International Criminal Court Statute (Parts V, VI, VIII)', (1998) 6 *European Journal of Crime, Criminal Law and Criminal Justice* 113

Bekou, O., and Cryer, R., 'The International Criminal Court and Universal Jurisdiction – A Close Encounter?', (2007) 56 *International and Comparative Law Quarterly* 49

Benedetti, Fanny, and Washburn, John L., 'Drafting the International Criminal Court Treaty: Two Years to Rome and an Afterword on the Rome Diplomatic Conference', (1999) 5 *Global Governance* 1

Benison, Audrey I., 'International Criminal Tribunals: Is There a Substantive Limitation on the Treaty Power?', (2001) 37 *Stanford Journal of International Law* 75

'War Crimes: A Human Rights Approach to a Humanitarian Law Problem at the International Criminal Court', (1999) 88 *Georgetown Law Journal* 141

Benvenuti, Paolo, 'Complementarity of the International Criminal Court to National Jurisdictions', in Flavia Lattanzi and William A. Schabas, eds., *Essays on the Rome Statute of the International Criminal Court*, vol. I, Ripa Fagnano Alto: Editrice il Sirente, 2000, pp. 21–50

Benzing, M., 'The Complementarity Regime of the International Criminal Court: International Criminal Justice between State Sovereignty and the Fight Against Impunity', (2004) 7 *Max Planck Yearbook of UN Law* 591

Beresford, Stuart, 'Child Witnesses and the International Criminal Justice System: Does the International Criminal Court Protect the Most Vulnerable?', (2005) 3 *Journal of International Criminal Justice* 721

'The Privileges and Immunities of the International Criminal Court: Are They Sufficient for the Proper Functioning of the Court or Is There Still Room for Improvement?', (2002) 3 *San Diego International Law Journal* 83

Beresford, Stuart, and Lahiouel, Hafida, 'The Right to Be Defended in Person or Through Legal Assistance and the International Criminal Court', (2000) 13 *Leiden Journal of International Law* 949

Berg, Bradley E., 'The 1994 ILC Draft Statute for an International Criminal Court: A Principled Appraisal of Jurisdictional Structure', (1996) 28 *Case Western Reserve Journal of International Law* 221

Bergsmo, Morten, 'Occasional Remarks on Certain State Concerns about the Jurisdictional Reach of the International Criminal Court, and Their Possible Implications for the Relationship between the Court and the Security Council', (2000) 69 *Nordic Journal of International Law* 87

'The Jurisdictional Regime of the International Criminal Court (Part II, Articles 11–19)', (1998) 6 *European Journal of Crime, Criminal Law and Criminal Justice* 29

Berman, Franklin, 'The Relationship between the International Criminal Court and the Security Council', in Herman von Hebel, Johan G. Lammers and Jolien

Schukking, eds., *Reflections on the International Criminal Court: Essays in Honour of Adriaan Bos*, The Hague: T. M. C. Asser, 1999, pp. 173–80

Bevitz, J. B., 'Flawed Foreign Policy: Hypocritical US Attitudes Toward International Criminal Forums', (2002) 53 *Hastings Law Journal* 931

Bickley, L. S., 'US Resistance to the International Criminal Court: Is the Sword Mightier than the Law', (2000) 14 *Emory International Law Review* 159

Blakesley, Christopher L., 'Commentary on Parts 5 and 6 of the Zutphen Intersessional Draft: General Principles of Criminal Law', (1998) 13*bis Nouvelles études pénales* 69

'Model Draft Statute for the International Criminal Court Based on the Preparatory Committee's Text to the Diplomatic Conference, Rome, June 15–July 17, 1997, Parts 5 and 6', (1998) 13*ter Nouvelles études pénales* 83

'Jurisdiction, Definition of Crimes, and Triggering Mechanisms', (1997) 29 *Denver Journal of International Law and Policy* 233; (1997) 13 *Nouvelles études pénales* 177

'Obstacles to the Creation of a Permanent War Crimes Tribunal', (1994) 18 *Fletcher Forum of World Affairs* 77

Bleich, Jeffrey L., 'Complementarity', (1997) 13 *Nouvelles études pénales* 231; (1997) 29 *Denver Journal of International Law and Policy* 281

'Cooperation with National Systems', (1997) 13 *Nouvelles études pénales* 245; (1997) 29 *Denver Journal of International Law and Policy* 293

'The International Criminal Court: Report of the ILA Working Group on Complementarity', (1997) 25 *Denver Journal of International Law and Policy* 281

'Problems Facing the War Crimes Tribunal and the Need for a Permanent International Criminal Court', (1995) 16 *Whittier Law Review* 404

Blumenson, E., 'The Challenge of a Global Standard of Justice: Peace, Pluralism, and Punishment at the International Criminal Court', (2006) 44 *Columbia Journal of Transnational Law* 801

Blumenthal, D. A., 'The Politics of Justice: Why Israel Signed the International Criminal Court Statute and What the Signature Means', (2002) 30 *Georgia Journal of International and Comparative Law* 593

Boas, Gideon, 'Implementation by Australia of the Statute of the International Criminal Court', (2004) 2 *Journal of International Criminal Justice* 179

'Developments in the Law of Procedure and Evidence at the International Criminal Tribunal for the Former Yugoslavia and the International Criminal Court', (2001) 12 *Criminal Law Forum* 2

'Comparing the International Criminal Tribunal for the Former Yugoslavia and the ICC: Some Procedural and Substantive Issues', (2000) 4 *Netherlands International Law Review* 267

Boas, Gideon, Bischoff, James L., and Reid, Natalie L., *Elements of Crimes Under International Law*, Cambridge: Cambridge University Press, 2009

Boister, Neil, 'The Exclusion of Treaty Crimes from the Jurisdiction of the Proposed International Criminal Court: Law, Pragmatism, Politics', (1998) 3 *Journal of Armed Conflict Law* 27

Bolton, John R., 'The Risks and Weaknesses of the International Criminal Court from America's Perspective', (2001) 64 *Law and Contemporary Problems* 167

  'The Risks and the Weaknesses of the International Criminal Court from America's Perspective', (2000) 41 *Virginia Journal of International Law* 186

Bolton, John R., and Roth, K., 'Toward an International Criminal Court? A Debate', (2000) 14 *Emory International Law Review* 159

Boon, Kristen, 'Rape and Forced Pregnancy under the ICC Statute: Human Dignity, Autonomy and Consent', (2001) 32 *Columbia Human Rights Law Review* 625

Boot, Machteld, *Genocide, Crimes Against Humanity, War Crimes: Nullum Crimen Sine Lege and the Subject Matter Jurisdiction of the International Criminal Court*, Antwerp: Intersentia, 2002

Booth, Cherie, 'Prospects and Issues for the International Criminal Court: Lessons from Yugoslavia and Rwanda', in Philippe Sands, ed., *From Nuremberg to The Hague: The Future of International Criminal Justice*, Cambridge: Cambridge University Press, 2003

Bos, Adriaan, 'The Experience of the Preparatory Committee', in Mauro Politi and Giuseppe Nesi, eds., *The Rome Statute of the International Criminal Court: A Challenge to Impunity*, Aldershot: Ashgate, 2001, pp. 17–28

  'The International Criminal Court: Recent Developments', in Herman von Hebel, Johan G. Lammers and Jolien Schukking, eds., *Reflections on the International Criminal Court: Essays in Honour of Adriaan Bos*, The Hague: T. M. C. Asser, 1999, pp. 39–46

  'Dedicated to the Adoption of the Rome Statute of the International Criminal Court 1948–1998: The Universal Declaration of Human Rights and the Statute of the International Criminal Court', (1998) 22 *Fordham International Law Journal* 229

Bosly, H.-D., 'Admission of Guilt before the ICC and in Continental Legal Systems', (2004) 2 *Journal of International Criminal Justice* 1040

Bottini, G., 'Universal Jurisdiction after the Creation of the International Criminal Court', (2004) 36 *New York University Journal of International Law and Policy* 503

Brady, Helen, 'The System of Evidence in the Statute of the International Criminal Court', in Flavia Lattanzi and William A. Schabas, eds., *Essays on the Rome Statute of the International Criminal Court*, vol. I, Ripa Fagnano Alto: Editrice il Sirente, 2000, pp. 279–302

Branch, A., 'International Justice, Local Injustice: The International Criminal Court in Northern Uganda', (2004) 51:3 *Dissent* 22

Brandon, Ben, and Du Plessis, Max, eds., *The Prosecution of International Crimes, A Guide to Prosecuting ICC Crimes in Commonwealth States*, London: Commonwealth Secretariat, 2005

Brierly, J. L., 'Do We Need an International Criminal Court?', (1923) 8 *British Yearbook of International Law* 86

Broms, B., 'The Establishment of an International Criminal Court', in Yoram Dinstein and Mala Tabory, eds., *War Crimes in International Law*, The Hague, Boston and London: Martinus Nijhoff Publishers, 1996, pp. 183–96

Broomhall, Bruce, *International Justice and the International Criminal Court: Between Sovereignty and the Rule of Law*, Oxford: Oxford University Press, 2003

'NGOs, the ICC, and the Future of Global Justice', in *The Changing Face of International Criminal Law: Selected Papers*, Vancouver: International Centre for Criminal Law Reform and Criminal Justice Policy, 2002, pp. 217–20

'Toward US Acceptance of the International Criminal Court', (2001) 64 *Law and Contemporary Problems* 141

'The International Criminal Court: A Checklist for National Implementation', (1999) 13*quater Nouvelles etudes pénales* 113

'The International Criminal Court: Overview and Cooperation with States', (1999) 13*quater Nouvelles etudes pénales* 45

'Looking Forward to the Establishment of an International Criminal Court: Between State Consent and the Rule of Law', (1997) 8 *Criminal Law Forum* 317

Brown, Bartram S., 'US Objections to the Statute of the International Criminal Court: A Brief Response', (1999) 31 *New York University Journal of International Law and Politics* 855

'Primacy or Complementarity: Reconciling the Jurisdiction of National Courts and International Criminal Tribunals', (1998) 23 *Yale Journal of International Law* 383

Brown, Daniel J., 'The International Criminal Court and Trial in Absentia', (1999) 24 *Brooklyn Journal of International Law* 763

Brubacher, Matthew R., 'Prosecutorial Discretion within the International Criminal Court', (2004) 2 *Journal of International Criminal Justice* 81

Burke-White, William W., 'Implementing a Policy of Positive Complementarity in the Rome System of Justice', (2008) 19 *Criminal Law Forum* 59

'Proactive Complementarity: the International Criminal Court and National Courts in the Rome Statute', (2008) 49 *Harvard Journal of International Law* 53

'Complementarity in Practice: The International Criminal Court as Part of a System of Multilevel Global Governance in the Democratic Republic of Congo', (2004) 18 *Leiden Journal of International Law* 557

Butler, A. Hays, 'A Selective and Annotated Bibliography of the International Criminal Court', (1999) 10 *Criminal Law Forum* 121

Byron, Christine, 'Genocide', in Dominic McGoldrick, Peter Rowe and Eric Donnelly, eds., *The Permanent International Criminal Court: Legal and Policy Issues*, Oxford and Portland, OR: Hart Publishing, 2004, pp. 143–77

Byron, Christine, and Turns, David, 'The Preparatory Commission for the International Criminal Court', (2001) 50 *International and Comparative Law Quarterly* 420

Caflisch, Lucius, 'The Rome Statute and the European Convention on Human Rights', (2002) 23 *Human Rights Law Journal* 1

'Toward the Establishment of a Permanent International Criminal Jurisdiction', (1998) 4 *International Peacekeeping Newsletter* 110

Caianiello, M., and Illuminati, G., 'From the International Criminal Tribunal for the Former Yugoslavia to the International Criminal Court', (2001) 26 *North Carolina Journal of International Law and Commercial Regulation* 408

Calvo-Goller, Karin N., *The Trial Proceedings of the International Criminal Court*, Leiden and Boston: Martinus Nijhoff, 2006

Caracciolo, Ida, 'Applicable Law', in Flavia Lattanzi and William A. Schabas, eds., *Essays on the Rome Statute of the International Criminal Court*, vol. I, Ripa Fagnano Alto: Editrice il Sirente, 2000, pp. 211–29

Carnero Rojo, E., 'The Role of Fair Trial Considerations in the Rome Statute of the International Criminal Court: From "No Peace without Justice" to "No Peace with Victor's Justice"?', (2005) 18 *Leiden Journal of International Law* 829

Carpenter, A. C., 'The International Criminal Court and the Crime of Aggression', (1995) 64 *Nordic Journal of International Law* 223

Carter, Kim, 'Command Responsibility and Superior Orders in the Rome Statute', in *The Changing Face of International Criminal Law: Selected Papers*, Vancouver: International Centre for Criminal Law Reform and Criminal Justice Policy, 2002, pp. 169–81

Casey, Lee A., 'The Case Against the International Criminal Court', (2002) 25 *Fordham International Law Journal* 840

Casey, Lee A., and Rivkin, David B., Jr, 'The Limits of Legitimacy: The Rome Statute's Unlawful Application to Non-State Parties', (2003) 44 *Virginia Journal of International Law* 63

'The International Criminal Court vs. the American People', Heritage Foundation Paper No. 1249, 5 February 1999

Cassel, Dougal W., 'Empowering United States Courts to Hear Crimes within the Jurisdiction of the International Criminal Court', (2001) 35 *New England Law Review* 421

'The Rome Treaty for an International Criminal Court: A Flawed But Essential First Step', (1999) 6 *Brown Journal of World Affairs* 41

Cassese, Antonio, 'Is the ICC Still Having Teething Problems?', (2006) 4 *Journal of International Criminal Justice* 434

'The Statute of the International Criminal Court: Some Preliminary Reflections', (1999) 10 *European Journal of International Law* 158

Cassese, Antonio, Gaeta, Paola, and Jones, John R. W. D., eds., *The Rome Statute of the International Criminal Court: A Commentary*, Oxford: Oxford University Press, 2002

Cayley, Andrew T., 'The Prosecutor's Strategy in Seeking the Arrest of Sudanese President Al Bashir on Charges of Genocide', (2008) 6 *Journal of International Criminal Justice* 829

Chesterman, Simon, 'An Altogether Different Order: Defining the Elements of Crimes Against Humanity', (2000) 10 *Duke Journal of Comparative and International Law* 307

Chibueze, Remigius, 'United States Objection to the International Criminal Court: A Paradox of "Operation Enduring Freedom"', (2003) 9 *Annual Survey of International and Comparative Law* 19

Chin, Lionel Yee Woon, 'Not Just a War Crime Court: The Penal Regime Established by the Rome Statute of the International Criminal Court', (1998) 10 *Singapore Academy of Law Journal* 321

Clapham, Andrew, 'The Question of Jurisdiction under International Criminal Law over Legal Persons: Lessons from the Rome Conference on the International Criminal Court', in M. T. Kamminga and S. Zia-Zarifi, eds., *Liability of Multinational Corporations under International Law*, The Hague: Kluwer Law International, 2000, pp. 139–95

Clark, Roger S., 'Crimes Against Humanity and the Rome Statute of the International Criminal Court', in Mauro Politi and Giuseppe Nesi, eds., *The Rome Statute of the International Criminal Court: A Challenge to Impunity*, Aldershot: Ashgate, 2001, pp. 75–94

'The Mental Element in International Criminal Law: The Rome Statute of the International Criminal Court and the Elements of the Offences', (2001) 12 *Criminal Law Forum* 291

'The ICC Statute: Protecting the Sovereign Rights of Non-Parties', in Dinah Shelton, ed., *International Crimes, Peace, and Human Rights: The Role of the International Criminal Court*, Ardsley, NY: Transnational Publishers, 2000, pp. 207–18

'Commentary on Parts 1 and 4 of the Zutphen Intersessional Draft', (1998) 13*bis Nouvelles études pénales* 55

'The Proposed International Criminal Court: Its Establishment and Its Relationship with the United Nations', (1997) 8 *Criminal Law Forum* 411

Clark, Thomas Hethe, 'The Prosecutor of the ICC, Amnesties, and the "Interests of Justice": Striking a Delicate Balance', (2005) 4 *Washington University Global Studies Law Review* 389

Cogan, Jacob Katz, 'International Criminal Courts and Fair Trials: Difficulties and Prospects', (2002) 27 *Yale Journal of International Law* 111–41

'The Problem of Obtaining Evidence for International Criminal Courts', (2000) 22 *Human Rights Quarterly* 404

Concannon, B., Jr, 'Beyond Complementarity: The International Criminal Court and National Prosecutions: A View from Haiti', (2000) 32 *Columbia Human Rights Law Review* 201

Condorelli, Luigi, 'War Crimes and Internal Conflicts in the Statute of the International Criminal Court', in Mauro Politi and Giuseppe Nesi, eds., *The Rome Statute of the International Criminal Court: A Challenge to Impunity*, Aldershot: Ashgate, 2001, pp. 107–18

Condorelli, Luigi, and Ciampi, Annalisa, 'Comments on the Security Council Referral of the Situation in Darfur to the ICC', (2005) 3 *Journal of International Criminal Justice* 590

Cone, S. M., 'The Development of the World Trade Organization and the International Criminal Court', (2003/4) 48 *New York Law School Law Review* 743

Conso, Giovanni, 'The Basic Reasons for US Hostility to the ICC in Light of the Negotiating History of the Rome Statute', (2005) 3 *Journal of International Criminal Justice* 314

Converti, Antonio, 'The Rights of the Accused', in Flavia Lattanzi, ed., *The International Criminal Court: Comments on the Draft Statute*, Naples: Editoriale Scientifica, 1998, pp. 219–50

Corell, Hans, 'The Relationship between the International Criminal Court and the Host Country', in Herman von Hebel, Johan G. Lammers and Jolien Schukking, eds., *Reflections on the International Criminal Court: Essays in Honour of Adriaan Bos*, The Hague: T. M. C. Asser, 1999, pp. 181–8

Corrao, Maria Esilia, 'Jurisdiction of the International Criminal Court and State Consent', in Flavia Lattanzi, ed., *The International Criminal Court: Comments on the Draft Statute*, Naples: Editoriale Scientifica, 1998, pp. 79–94

Côté, Luc, 'International Justice: Tightening Up the Rules of the Game', (2006) 81 *International Review of the Red Cross* 133

Crawford, James, 'The ILC Adopts a Statute for an International Criminal Court', (1995) 89 *American Journal of International Law* 404

'The ILC's Draft Statute for an International Criminal Tribunal', (1994) 88 *American Journal of International Law* 140

Cryer, Robert, 'Sudan, Resolution 1593 and International Criminal Justice', (2006) 19 *Leiden Journal of International Law* 195

'General Principles of Liability in International Criminal Law', in Dominic McGoldrick, Peter Rowe and Eric Donnelly, eds., *The Permanent International Criminal Court: Legal and Policy Issues*, Oxford and Portland, OR: Hart Publishing, 2004, pp. 233–62

'Implementation of the International Criminal Court Statute in England and Wales', (2002) 51 *International and Comparative Law Quarterly* 733

'Commentary on the Rome Statute for an International Criminal Court: A Cadenza for the Song of Those Who Died in Vain?', (1998) 3 *Journal of Armed Conflict Law* 271

Cullen, Anthony, *The Concept of Non-International Armed Conflict in International Humanitarian Law*, Cambridge: Cambridge University Press, 2010

'The Definition of Non-International Armed Conflict in the Rome Statute of the International Criminal Court: An Analysis of the Threshold of Application Contained in Article 8(2)(f)', (2008) 12 *Journal of Conflict and Security Law* 419

Czarnetzky, J. M., 'An Empire of Law?: Legalism and the International Criminal Court', (2003) 79 *Notre Dame Law Review* 55

Danilenko, Gennady M., 'The Statute of the International Criminal Court and Third States', (2000) 21 *Michigan Journal of International Law* 445

Danner, Allison M., 'Enhancing the Legitimacy and Accountability of Prosecutorial Discretion at the International Criminal Court', (2003) 97 *American Journal of International Law* 510

'Navigating Law and Politics: The Prosecutor of the International Criminal Court and the Independent Counsel', (2002–3) 55 *Stanford Law Review* 1655

David, Marcella, 'Grotius Repudiated: The American Objections to the International Criminal Court and the Commitment to International Law', (1999) 20 *Michigan Journal of International Law* 337

Dawson, Grant M., 'Defining Substantive Crimes within the Subject Matter Jurisdiction of the International Criminal Court: What Is the Crime of Aggression', (2000) 19 *New York Law School Journal of International and Comparative Law* 413

De Bertodano, Sylvia, 'Judicial Independence in the International Criminal Court', (2002) 15 *Leiden Journal of International Law* 409

de Hemptinne, J., and Rindi, F., 'ICC Pre-Trial Chamber Allows Victims to Participate in the Investigation Phase of Proceedings', (2006) 4 *Journal of International Criminal Justice* 342

DeGuzman, Margaret McAuliffe, 'Gravity and the Legitimacy of the International Criminal Court', (2009) 32 *Fordham International Law Journal* 1400

'The Road from Rome: The Developing Law of Crimes Against Humanity', (2000) 22 *Human Rights Quarterly* 335

Del Buono, Vincent, 'International Advocacy Networks and the International Criminal Court', in *The Changing Face of International Criminal Law: Selected Papers*, Vancouver: International Centre for Criminal Law Reform and Criminal Justice Policy, 2002, pp. 201–16

Delmas-Marty, Mireille, 'Interactions between National and International Criminal Law in the Preliminary Phase of Trial at the ICC', (2006) 4 *Journal of International Criminal Justice* 2

Delmont, Adrian T., 'The International Criminal Court: The United States Should Ratify the Rome Statute Despite Its Objections', (2001) 27 *Journal of Legislation* 335

Derby, Daniel H., 'Model Draft Statute for the International Criminal Court Based on the Preparatory Committee's Text to the Diplomatic Conference, Rome, June 15–July 17, 1997, Part 4', (1998) 13*ter Nouvelles études pénales* 64

Dixon, Rodney, and Khan, Karim, *Archbold: Practice, Procedure and Evidence: International Criminal Courts*, 2nd edn, London: Sweet & Maxwell, 2005

Doherty, K., and McCormack, T. L. H., 'Complementarity as a Catalyst for Comprehensive Domestic Penal Legislation', (1999) 5 *University of California at Davis Journal of International Law and Policy* 147

Döhrmann, Knut, 'Preparatory Commission for the International Criminal Court: The Elements of War Crimes', (2000) 82 *International Review of the Red Cross* 771

   'The First and Second Sessions of the Preparatory Commission for the International Criminal Court', (1999) 2 *Yearbook of International Humanitarian Law* 283

Döhrmann, Knut, Doswald-Beck, Louise, and Kolb, Robert, *Elements of War Crimes under the Rome Statute of the International Criminal Court: Sources and Commentary*, Port Chester, NY: Cambridge University Press, 2002

Donat-Cattin, David, 'The Role of Victims in ICC Proceedings', in Flavia Lattanzi and William A. Schabas, eds., *Essays on the Rome Statute of the International Criminal Court*, vol. I, Ripa Fagnano Alto: Editrice il Sirente, 2000, pp. 251–78

   'Crimes Against Humanity', in Flavia Lattanzi, ed., *The International Criminal Court: Comments on the Draft Statute*, Naples: Editoriale Scientifica, 1998, pp. 49–78

   'The Role of Victims in the ICC Proceedings', in Flavia Lattanzi, ed., *The International Criminal Court: Comments on the Draft Statute*, Naples: Editoriale Scientifica, 1998, pp. 251–72

Doria, José, Gasser, Hans-Peter, and Bassiouni, M. Cherif, eds., *The Legal Regime of the International Criminal Court: Essays in Honour of Professor Igor Blishchenko*, Leiden and Boston: Martinus Nijhoff, 2009

Du Plessis, Max, and Gevers, Christopher, 'Into the Deep End – The International Criminal Court and Sudan', [2006] *African Yearbook on International Humanitarian law* 88

Duffy, Helen, 'National Constitutional Compatibility and the International Criminal Court', (2001) 11 *Duke Journal of Comparative and International Law* 5

Dugard, John, 'Obstacles in the Way of an International Criminal Court', (1997) 56 *Cambridge Law Journal* 337

Durham, Helen, 'The International Criminal Court and State Sovereignty', in Linda Hancock and Carolyn O'Brien, eds., *Rewriting Rights in Europe*, Aldershot: Ashgate, 2000, pp. 169–90

Economides, S., 'The International Criminal Court: Reforming the Politics of International Justice', (2003) 38 *Government and Opposition* 29

Edwards, George E., 'International Human Rights Law Challenges to the New International Criminal Court: The Search and Seizure Right to Privacy', (2001) 26 *Yale Journal of International Law* 343

El Zeidy, Mohamed, 'The Gravity Threshold Under the Statute of the International Criminal Court', (2008) 19 *Criminal Law Forum* 35

The Principle of Complementarity in International Criminal Law: Origin, Development and Practice, The Hague: Martinus Nijhoff, 2008

'Critical Thoughts on Article 59(2) of the ICC Statute', (2006) 4 *Journal of International Criminal Justice* 448

'Some Remarks on the Question of the Admissibility of a Case during Arrest Warrant Proceedings before the International Criminal Court', (2006) 19 *Leiden Journal of International Law* 1

'The Ugandan Government Triggers the First Test of the Complementarity Principle: An Assessment of the First State's Party Referral to the ICC', (2005) 5 *International Criminal Law Review* 83

'The Principle of Complementarity: A New Machinery to Implement International Criminal Law', (2002) 23 *Michigan Journal of International Law* 869

'The United States Dropped the Atomic Bomb of Article 16 of the ICC Statute: Security Council Power of Deferrals and Resolution 1422', (2002) 35 *Vanderbilt Journal of Transnational Law* 1503

Elaraby, Nabil, 'The Role of the Security Council and the Independence of the International Criminal Court: Some Reflections', in Mauro Politi and Giuseppe Nesi, eds., *The Rome Statute of the International Criminal Court: A Challenge to Impunity*, Aldershot: Ashgate, 2001, pp. 43–8

Elewa Badar, Mohamed, *Mens Rea in International Criminal Law*, Oxford: Hart Publishing (forthcoming)

'Drawing the Boundaries of Mens Rea in the Jurisprudence of the International Criminal Tribunal for the Former Yugoslavia', (2006) 6 *International Criminal Law Review* 313–48

'"Just Convict Everyone!" Joint Perpetration: From *Tadić* to *Stakić* and Back Again', (2006) 6 *International Criminal Law Review* 293

'Mens Rea – Mistake of Law and Mistake of Fact in German Criminal Law: A Survey for International Criminal Tribunals', (2005) 5 *International Criminal Law Review* 203

'From the Nuremberg Charter to the Rome Statute: Defining the Elements of Crimes Against humanity', (2004) 5 *San Diego International Law Journal* 73

Ellis, Mark S., 'The International Criminal Court and Its Implication for Domestic Law and National Capacity Building', (2002) 15 *Florida Journal of International Law* 215

England, Joel F., 'The Response of the United States to the International Criminal Court: Rejection, Ratification or Something Else?', (2001) 18 *Arizona Journal of International and Comparative Law* 941

Erb, Nicole Eva, 'Gender-Based Crimes under the Draft Statute for the Permanent International Criminal Court', (1998) 29 *Columbia Human Rights Law Review* 401

Fairlie, Megan A., 'Establishing Admissibility at the International Criminal Court: Does the Buck Stop with the Prosecutor, Full Stop?', (2005) 39 *International Lawyer* 817

'The Marriage of Common and Continental Law at the International Criminal Tribunal for the Former Yugoslavia and Its Progeny: Due Process Deficit', (2004) 4 *International Criminal Law Review* 243

Faulhaber, L. V., 'American Servicemembers' Protection Act of 2002', (2003) 40 *Harvard Journal on Legislation* 537

Ferencz, Benjamin B., *An International Criminal Court: A Step Toward World Peace: A Documentary History and Analysis*, Dobbs Ferry, NY: Oceana Publications, 1990

'Misguided Fears About the International Criminal Court', (2003) 15 *Pace International Law Review* 223

Fernandez De Gurmendi, Silvia A., 'The Working Group on Aggression at the Preparatory Commission for the International Criminal Court', (2002) 25 *Fordham International Law Journal* 589

'The Role of the Prosecutor', in Mauro Politi and Giuseppe Nesi, eds., *The Rome Statute of the International Criminal Court: A Challenge to Impunity*, Aldershot: Ashgate, 2001, pp. 55–8

Fernandez De Gurmendi, Silvia A., and Friman, Haken, 'The Rules of Procedure and Evidence of the International Criminal Court', (2000) 3 *Yearbook of International Humanitarian Law* 296

Fichtelberg, Aaron, 'Democratic Legitimacy and the International Criminal Court', (2006) 4 *Journal of International Criminal Justice* 765

Fife, Rolf Einar, 'The Draft Budget of the First Financial Period of the Court', (2002) 25 *Fordham International Law Journal* 606

'The International Criminal Court: Whence It Came, Where It Goes', (2000) 69 *Nordic Journal of International Law* 63

Figà-Talamanco, Niccolo A., 'Trials *in Absentia* and International Criminal Court', in Flavia Lattanzi, ed., *The International Criminal Court: Comments on the Draft Statute*, Naples: Editoriale Scientifica, 1998, pp. 209–18

Fischer, Horst, 'The Jurisdiction of the International Criminal Court for War
Crimes: Some Observations Concerning Differences between the Statute of
the Court and War Crimes Provisions of Other Treaties', in Volker Epping,
Horst Fischer and Heintschel Wolff von Heinegg, eds., *Brücken Bauen und
Begehen: Festschrift für Knut Ipsen zum 65. Geburtstag*, Munich: C. H. Beck,
2000, pp. 77–101

Fischer, Horst, Kreß, Claus, and Lüder, Sascha Rolf, eds., *International and
National Prosecution of Crimes under International Law: Current
Developments*, Berlin and Baden-Baden: Verlag Arno Spitz GmbH and
Nomos, 2001

Fletcher, George, and Ohlin, Jens David, 'The ICC – Two Courts in One?', (2006) 4
Journal of International Criminal Justice 428

Forsythe, David P., 'The United States and International Criminal Justice', (2002)
24 *Human Rights Quarterly* 974

'International Criminal Courts: A Political View', (1997) 15 *Netherlands
Quarterly of Human Rights* 5

Freeland, Steven, 'How Open Should the Door Be? – Declarations by Non-States
Parties under Article 12(3) of the Rome Statute of the International Criminal
Court', (2006) 75 *Nordic Journal of International Law* 211

Friman, H., 'Rights of Persons Suspected or Accused of a Crime', in Roy S. Lee, ed.,
*The International Criminal Court: The Making of the Rome Statute: Issues,
Negotiations, and Results*, The Hague: Kluwer Law International, 1999,
pp. 247–62

Fronza, Emanuela, 'Genocide in the Rome Statute', in Flavia Lattanzi and William
A. Schabas, eds., *Essays on the Rome Statute of the International Criminal
Court*, vol. I, Ripa Fagnano Alto: Editrice il Sirente, 2000, pp. 105–38

Gaeta, Paola, 'Is the Practice of "Self-Referrals" a Sound Start for the ICC?', (2004)
2 *Journal of International Criminal Justice* 949

'The Defence of Superior Orders: The Statute of the International Criminal
Court Versus Customary International Law', (1999) 10 *European Journal of
International Law* 172

Galasso, Mercurio, 'Appeal and Revision in Front of the International Criminal
Court', in Flavia Lattanzi, ed., *The International Criminal Court: Comments
on the Draft Statute*, Naples: Editoriale Scientifica, 1998, pp. 301–10

Gallant, Kenneth S., 'The Role and Powers of Defence Counsel in the ICC Statute',
(2000) 34 *International Lawyer* 21

'Individual Human Rights in a New International Organization: The Rome
Statute of the International Criminal Court', in M. Cherif Bassiouni, ed.,
International Criminal Law, vol. III, Dobbs Ferry, NY: Transnational
Publishers, 1999, pp. 693–722

'The International Criminal Court in the System of States and International
Organizations', (2003) 16 *Leiden Journal of International Law* 553

Gallarotti, Giulio M., and Preis, Arik Y., 'Politics, International Justice, and the United States: Toward a Permanent International Criminal Court', (1999) 4 *UCLA Journal of International Law and Foreign Affairs* 1

Gallavin, Chris, 'ICC Investigations and a Hierarchy of Referrals: Has Genocide in Darfur Been Predetermined?', in Ralph Henham and Paul Behrens, eds., *The Criminal Law of Genocide*, Aldershot: Ashgate, 2007, pp. 157–66

   'Prosecutorial Discretion within the ICC: Under the Pressure of Justice', (2006) 17 *Criminal Law Forum* 43

Gallon, Gustavo, 'The International Criminal Court and the Challenge of Deterrence', in Dinah Shelton, ed., *International Crimes, Peace, and Human Rights: The Role of the International Criminal Court*, Ardsley, NY: Transnational Publishers, 2000, pp. 93–104

Gargiulo, Pietro, 'The Controversial Relationship between the International Criminal Court and the Security Council', in Flavia Lattanzi and William A. Schabas, eds., *Essays on the Rome Statute of the International Criminal Court*, vol. I, Ripa Fagnano Alto: Editrice il Sirente, 2000, pp. 67–104

   'The Relationship between the ICC and the Security Council', in Flavia Lattanzi, ed., *The International Criminal Court: Comments on the Draft Statute*, Naples: Editoriale Scientifica, 1998, pp. 95–120

Garkawe, Sam, 'The Victim-Related Provisions of the Statute of the International Criminal Court: A Victimology Analysis', (2001) 8 *International Review of Victimology* 284

Garraway, Charles, 'Superior Orders and the International Criminal Court: Justice Delivered or Justice Denied', (1999) 836 *International Review of the Red Cross* 785

Gavron, Jessica, 'Amnesties in the Light of Developments in International Law and the Establishment of the International Criminal Court', (2002) 51 *International and Comparative Law Quarterly* 111

Gerber, Steven J., 'Commentary on Parts 10 and 11 of the Zutphen Intersessional Draft: General Principles of Criminal Law', (1998) 13*bis Nouvelles études pénales* 105

   'Model Draft Statute for the International Criminal Court Based on the Preparatory Committee's Text to the Diplomatic Conference, Rome, June 15–July 17, 1997, Parts 11, 12 and 13', (1998) 13*ter Nouvelles études pénales* 141

Gianaris, William N., 'The New World Order and the Need for an International Criminal Court', (1992) 16 *Fordham International Law Journal* 88

Gilmore, William C., 'The Proposed International Criminal Court: Recent Developments', (1995) 5 *Transnational Law and Contemporary Problems* 264

Gioia, Federica, 'State Sovereignty, Jurisdiction, and "Modern" International Law: The Principle of Complementarity in the International Criminal Court', (2006) 19 *Leiden Journal of International Law* 1095

Glasius, Marlies, *The International Criminal Court: A Global Civil Society Achievement*, London and New York: Routledge, 2006

Goldsmith, Jack, 'The Self-Defeating International Criminal Court', (2003) 70 *University of Chicago Law Review* 89

Goldstone, Richard J., and Fritz, Nicole, '"In the Interests of Justice" and the Independent Referral: The International Criminal Court Prosecutor's Unprecedented Power', (2000) 13 *Leiden Journal of International Law* 655

Gowlland-Debbas, Vera, 'The Relationship between the Security Council and the Projected International Criminal Court', (1998) 3 *Journal of Armed Conflict Law* 97

Graditzky, Thomas, 'War Crime Issues before the Rome Diplomatic Conference on the Establishment of an International Criminal Court', (1999) 5 *University of California at Davis Journal of International Law and Policy* 199

Graefrath, B., 'Universal Jurisdiction and an International Criminal Court', (1990) 1 *European Journal of International Law* 72

Grant, Sheryl, 'The International Criminal Court: The Nations of the World Must Not Give in to All of the United States Demands If the Court Is To Be a Strong, Independent, International Organ', (1999) 23 *Suffolk Transnational Law Review* 327

Gray, Kevin R., 'Evidence before the ICC', in Dominic McGoldrick, Peter Rowe and Eric Donnelly, eds., *The Permanent International Criminal Court: Legal and Policy Issues*, Oxford and Portland, OR: Hart Publishing, 2004, pp. 287–314

Greenawalt, Alexander K. A., 'Justice Without Politics? Prosecutorial Discretion and the International Criminal Court', (2007) 39 *New York University Journal of International Law and Politics* 583

Greenberg, Michael D., 'Creating an International Criminal Court', (1992) 10 *Boston University International Law Journal* 119

Groulx, Elise, 'Le troisième pilier: la profession juridique, véritable partenaire du système de justice pénale internationale', in Hélène Dumont and Anne-Marie Boisvert, eds., *La voie vers la Cour pénale internationale: Tous les chemins mènent à Rome*, Montreal: Themis, 2004, pp. 33–51

Gurulé, Jimmy, 'United States Opposition to the 1998 Rome Statute Establishing an International Criminal Court: Is the Court's Jurisdiction Truly Complementary to National Criminal Jurisdictions?', (2001–2) 35 *Cornell International Law Journal* 1

Hafner, Gerhard, 'An Attempt to Explain the Position of the USA towards the ICC', (2005) 3 *Journal of International Criminal Justice* 323

'The Status of Third States before the International Criminal Court', in Mauro Politi and Giuseppe Nesi, eds., *The Rome Statute of the International Criminal Court: A Challenge to Impunity*, Aldershot: Ashgate, 2001, pp. 239–54

Hafner, Gerhard, Boon, Kristen, Rübesame, Anne, and Huston, Jonathan, 'A Response to the American View as Presented by Ruth Wedgwood', (1999) 10 *European Journal of International Law* 108

Hall, Christopher Keith, 'The Powers and Role of the Prosecutor of the International Criminal Court in the Global Fight Against Impunity', (2004) 17 *Leiden Journal of International Law* 121

'The First Five Sessions of the UN Preparatory Commission for the International Criminal Court', (2000) 94 *American Journal of International Law* 773

'The Fifth Session of the UN Preparatory Committee on the Establishment of an International Criminal Court', (1998) 92 *American Journal of International Law* 331

'The First Proposal for a Permanent International Criminal Court', (1998) 322 *International Review of the Red Cross* 57

'The Jurisdiction of the Permanent International Criminal Court over Violations of Humanitarian Law', in Flavia Lattanzi, ed., *The International Criminal Court: Comments on the Draft Statute*, Naples: Editoriale Scientifica, 1998, pp. 19–48

'The Sixth Session of the UN Preparatory Committee on the Establishment of an International Criminal Court', (1998) 92 *American Journal of International Law* 548

'The Third and Fourth Sessions of the UN Preparatory Committee on the Establishment of an International Criminal Court', (1998) 92 *American Journal of International Law* 124

'The First Two Sessions of the UN Preparatory Committee on the Establishment of an International Criminal Court', (1997) 91 *American Journal of International Law* 177

Harris, David, 'Progress and Problems in Establishing an International Criminal Court', (1998) 3 *Journal of Armed Conflict Law* 1

Harris, Kenneth, 'Development of Rules of International Criminal Procedure Applicable to the International Adjudication Process: Arriving at a Body of Criminal Procedure Law for the ICC', (1998) 17 *Nouvelles études pénales* 389

Haslam, Emily, 'Victim Participation at the International Criminal Court: A Triumph of Hope over Experience?', in Dominic McGoldrick, Peter Rowe and Eric Donnelly, eds., *The Permanent International Criminal Court: Legal and Policy Issues*, Oxford and Portland, OR: Hart Publishing, 2004, pp. 315–35

Hatchell, M., 'Closing the Gaps in United State Law and Implementing the Rome Statute: A Comparative Approach', (2005) 12 *ILSA Journal of International and Comparative Law* 183

Hay, Juliet, 'Implementing the ICC Statute in New Zealand', (2004) 2 *Journal of International Criminal Justice* 191

Healy, Patrick, 'Canadian Cooperation with the International Criminal Court', in Hélène Dumont and Anne-Marie Boisvert, eds., *La voie vers la Cour pénale internationale: Tous les chemins mènent à Rome*, Montreal: Themis, 2004, pp. 483–8

Heller, Kevin Jon, 'The Shadow Side of Complementarity: The Effect of Article 17 of the Rome Statute on National Due Process', (2006) 17 *Criminal Law Forum* 255

Henham, Ralph, 'Some Issues for Sentencing in the International Criminal Court', (2003) 52 *International and Comparative Law Quarterly* 64

Henzelin, Marc, Heiskanen, Veijo, and Mettraux, Guénaël, 'Reparations to Victims before the International Criminal Court: Lessons from International Mass Claims Processes', (2006) 17 *Criminal Law Forum* 317

Hetesy, Z., 'The Making of the Basic Principles of the Headquarters Agreement', (2002) 25 *Fordham International Law Journal* 625

Higgins, Rosalyn, 'The Relationship between the International Criminal Court and the International Court of Justice', in Herman von Hebel, Johan G. Lammers and Jolien Schukking, eds., *Reflections on the International Criminal Court: Essays in Honour of Adriaan Bos*, The Hague: T. M. C. Asser, 1999, pp. 163–72

Hogan-Doran, J., and Van Ginkel, B. T., 'Aggression as a Crime under International Law and the Prosecution of Individuals by the Proposed International Criminal Court', (1996) 43 *Netherlands International Law Review* 321

Holcombe, A. Diane, 'The United States Becomes a Signatory to the Rome Treaty Establishing the International Criminal Court: Why Are So Many Concerned by This Action?', (2001) 62 *Montana Law Review* 301

Holmes, John, 'The International Criminal Court in Perspective: From the Rome Conference to the Years to Come', in Mauro Politi and Giuseppe Nesi, eds., *The Rome Statute of the International Criminal Court: A Challenge to Impunity*, Aldershot: Ashgate, 2001, pp. 29–38

'The Protection of Children's Rights in the Statute of the International Criminal Court', in Mauro Politi and Giuseppe Nesi, eds., *The Rome Statute of the International Criminal Court: A Challenge to Impunity*, Aldershot: Ashgate, 2001, pp. 119–22

Holthuis, H., 'Operational Aspects of Setting up the International Criminal Court: Building on the Experience of the International Criminal Tribunal for the Former Yugoslavia', (2002) 25 *Fordham International Law Journal* 708

'Operational Aspects of Setting Up the International Criminal Court: Building on the Experience of the International Criminal Tribunal for the Former Yugoslavia', (2002) 27 *International Legal Practitioner* 41

Horton, Regina, 'The Long Road to Hypocrisy: The United States and the International Criminal Court', (2003) 24 *Whittier Law Review* 1041

Howard, Robert J., 'An Economic Paradigm for the Debate Concerning the Jurisdictional Extent of the International Criminal Court', (1998) 8 *Touro International Law Review* 117

Hunt, David, 'The International Criminal Court, High Hopes, "Creative Ambiguity" and an Unfortunate Mistrust in International Judges', (2004) 2 *Journal of International Criminal Justice* 56

Hwang, Phyllis, 'Dedicated to the Adoption of the Rome Statute of the International Criminal Court: Defining Crimes Against Humanity: The Rome Statute of the International Criminal Court', (1998) 22 *Fordham International Law Journal* 457

Ingadottir, Thordis, 'The Trust Fund of the ICC', in Dinah Shelton, ed., *International Crimes, Peace, and Human Rights: The Role of the International Criminal Court*, Ardsley, NY: Transnational Publishers, 2000, pp. 149–62

Jamison, Sandra L., 'A Permanent International Court: A Proposal That Overcomes Past Objections', (1995) 23 *Denver Journal of International Law and Policy* 419

Jarasch, Frank, 'Establishment, Organization and Financing of the International Criminal Court (Parts I, IV, XI–XIII)', (1998) 6 *European Journal of Crime, Criminal Law and Criminal Justice* 9

Jescheck, H., 'The General Principles of International Criminal Law Set out in Nuremberg, as Mirrored in the ICC Statute', (2004) 2 *Journal of International Criminal Justice* 38

Jessberg, Florian, and Powell, Cathleen, 'Prosecuting Pinochets in South Africa – Implementing the Rome Statute of the International Criminal Court', (2001) 14 *South African Journal of Criminal Justice* 344

Johansen, R. C., 'The Impact of US Policy toward the International Criminal Court on the Prevention of Genocide, War Crimes, and Crimes Against Humanity', (2006) 28 *Human Rights Quarterly* 301

Jones, A. L., 'Continental Divide and the Politics of Complex Sovereignty: Canada, the United States and the International Criminal Court', (2006) 39 *Canadian Journal of Political Science* 227

Josipovic, Ivo, *The Hague: Implementing Criminal Law*, Zagreb: Hrvatski Pravni Centar, 2000

Joyner, Christopher C., and Posteraro, Christopher C., 'The United States and the International Criminal Court: Rethinking the Struggle between National Interests and International Justice', (1999) 10 *Criminal Law Forum* 359

Kaul, Hans-Peter, 'Construction Site for More Justice: The International Criminal Court After Two Years', (2005) 99 *American Journal of International Law* 370

'The International Criminal Court: Jurisdiction, Trigger Mechanism and Relationship to National Jurisdictions', in Mauro Politi and Giuseppe Nesi, eds., *The Rome Statute of the International Criminal Court: A Challenge to Impunity*, Aldershot: Ashgate, 2001, pp. 59–64

'Special Note: The Struggle for the International Criminal Court's Jurisdiction', (1998) 6 *European Journal of Crime, Criminal Law and Criminal Justice* 48

'Towards a Permanent International Criminal Court: Some Observations of a Negotiator', (1997) 8 *Human Rights Law Journal* 169

Kaul, Hans-Peter, and Kreß, Claus, 'Jurisdiction and Cooperation in the Statute of the International Criminal Court: Principles and Compromises', (1999) 2 *Yearbook of International Humanitarian Law* 143

Kelly, M. J., 'Case Studies "Ripe" for the International Criminal Court: Practical Applications for the Pinochet, Ocalan and Libyan Bomber Trials', (1999) 8 *Journal of International Law and Practice* 21

Kim, Y. S., 'The Preconditions to the Exercise of the Jurisdiction of the International Criminal Court: With Focus on Article 12 of the Rome Statute', (1999) 8 *Journal of International Law and Practice* 47

King, Faiza P., and La Rosa, Anne-Marie, 'Penalties under the ICC Statute', in Flavia Lattanzi and William A. Schabas, eds., *Essays on the Rome Statute of the International Criminal Court*, vol. I, Ripa Fagnano Alto: Editrice il Sirente, 2000, pp. 311–38

King, Henry T., Jr, and Theofrastous, T. C., 'From Nuremberg to Rome: A Step Backward for US Foreign Policy', (1999) 31 *Case Western Reserve Journal of International Law* 47

Kirsch, Philippe, and Holmes, John T., 'The Rome Conference on an International Criminal Court: The Negotiating Process', (1999) 93 *American Journal of International Law* 2

Kirsch, Philippe, and Oosterveld, V., 'The Preparatory Commission for the International Criminal Court', (2002) 25 *Fordham International Law Journal* 563

'Negotiating an Instrument of the Twenty-First Century: Multilateral Diplomacy and the International Criminal Court', (2001) 46 *McGill Law Journal* 1141

Kleffner, Jann K., 'The Impact of Complementarity on National Implementation of Substantive International Criminal Law', (2003) 1 *Journal of International Criminal Justice* 86

Kleffner, Jann, and Kor, G., eds., *Complementary Views on Complementarity*, The Hague: TMC Asser, 2006

Klip, André, 'Complementarity and Concurrent Jurisdiction', (2004) 19 *Nouvelles études pénales* 173

Koenig, Dorean M., 'Commentary on Parts 7 and 8 of the Zutphen Intersessional Draft: General Principles of Criminal Law', (1998) 13*bis Nouvelles études pénales* 95

Koenig, Dorean M., and Askin, Kelly D., 'International Criminal Law and the International Criminal Court Statute: Crimes Against Women', in Kelly D. Askin and Doreen M. Koenig, eds., *Women and International Human Rights Law*, Ardsley, NY: Transnational Publishers, 1999, pp. 3–29

Koenig, Dorean M., and Joyner, Christopher C., 'Model Draft Statute for the International Criminal Court Based on the Preparatory Committee's Text to the Diplomatic Conference, Rome, June 15–July 17, 1997, Parts 7 and 8', (1998) 13ter *Nouvelles études pénales* 111

Kramer, Ronald C., 'The Illegal War on Iraq: The "Role" of the International Criminal Court', in Dawn Rothe and Christopher W. Mullins, eds., *Symbolic Gestures and the Generation of Global Social Control: The International Criminal Court*, Lanham, MD: Lexington Books, 2006, pp. 87–103

Kreß, Claus, '"Self-Referrals" and "Waivers of Complementarity": Some Considerations in Law and Policy', (2004) 2 *Journal of International Criminal Justice* 944

'The Procedural Law of the International Criminal Court in Outline: Anatomy of a Unique Compromise', (2003) 1 *Journal of International Criminal Justice* 603

'Penalties, Enforcement and International Cooperation in the Statute of the International Criminal Court (Parts VII, IX, X)', (1998) 6 *European Journal of Crime, Criminal Law and Criminal Justice* 442

Kreß, Claus, Broomhall, Bruce, Lattanzi, Flavia, and Santori, Valeria, eds., *The Rome Statute and Domestic Legal Orders*, vol. II, *Constitutional Issues, Cooperation and Enforcement*, Baden-Baden: Nomos, 2005

Kreß, Claus, and Lattanzi, Flavia, eds., *The Rome Statute and Domestic Legal Orders*, vol. I, *General Aspects and Constitutional Issues*, Baden-Baden: Nomos, 2000

Krohne, S. W., 'The United States and the World Need an International Criminal Court as an Ally in the War Against Terrorism', (1997) 8 *Indiana International Comparative Law Review* 159

Kyriakakis, Joanna, 'Corporations and the International Criminal Court: The Complementarity Objections Stripped Bare', (2008) 19 *Criminal Law Forum* 115

La Haye, Eve, 'The Jurisdiction of the International Criminal Court: Controversies over the Preconditions for Exercising Its Jurisdiction', (1999) 46 *Netherlands International Law Review* 1

Latore, Roseann M., 'Escape Out the Back Door or Charge in the Front Door: US Reactions to the International Criminal Court', (2002) 25 *Boston College International and Comparative Law Review* 159

Lattanzi, Flavia, 'The International Criminal Court and National Jurisdictions', in Mauro Politi and Giuseppe Nesi, eds., *The Rome Statute of the International Criminal Court: A Challenge to Impunity*, Aldershot: Ashgate, 2001, pp. 177–96

'The Rome Statute and State Sovereignty: ICC Competence, Jurisdictional Links, Trigger Mechanism', in Flavia Lattanzi and William A. Schabas, eds., *Essays on the Rome Statute of the International Criminal Court*, vol. I, Ripa Fagnano Alto: Editrice il Sirente, 2000, pp. 51–66

'The Complementary Character of the Jurisdiction of the Court with Respect to National Jurisdictions', in Flavia Lattanzi, ed., *The International Criminal Court: Comments on the Draft Statute*, Naples: Editoriale Scientifica, 1998, pp. 1–18

ed., *The International Criminal Court: Comments on the Draft Statute*, Naples: Editoriale Scientifica, 1998

'The Recognition and Enforcement of Judgments and Sentences of the Court', in Flavia Lattanzi, ed., *The International Criminal Court: Comments on the Draft Statute*, Naples: Editoriale Scientifica, 1998, pp. 367–74

Laughland, John, *Le tribunal pénal international, gardien du nouvel ordre mondial*: Paris: Francois-Xavier de Guibert, 2003

Lavelle, Roberto, 'A Vicious Storm in a Teacup: The Action by the United Nations Security Council to Narrow the Jurisdiction of the International Criminal Court', (2003) 14 *Criminal Law Forum* 195

Leanza, Umberto, 'The Rome Conference on the Establishment of an International Criminal Court: A Fundamental Step in the Strengthening of International Criminal Law', in Flavia Lattanzi and William A. Schabas, eds., *Essays on the Rome Statute of the International Criminal Court*, vol. I, Ripa Fagnano Alto: Editrice il Sirente, 2000, pp. 7–20

Lee, Joanne, 'The International Criminal Court: An Historic Leap Forward for Humanity', in *The Changing Face of International Criminal Law: Selected Papers*, Vancouver: International Centre for Criminal Law Reform and Criminal Justice Policy, 2002, pp. 183–97

Lee, Roy S., ed., *States' Responses to Issues Arising from the ICC Statute: Constitutional, Sovereignty, Judicial Cooperation and Criminal Law*, Ardsley, NY: Transnational Publishers, 2005

'An Assessment of the ICC Statute', (2002) 25 *Fordham International Law Journal* 650

ed., *The International Criminal Court: Elements of Crimes and Rules of Procedure and Evidence*, Ardsley, NY: Transnational Publishers, 2001

'Creating an International Criminal Court – On Procedures and Compromises', in Herman von Hebel, Johan G. Lammers and Jolien Schukking, eds., *Reflections on the International Criminal Court: Essays in Honour of Adriaan Bos*, The Hague: T. M. C. Asser, 1999, pp. 141–54

ed., *The International Criminal Court: The Making of the Rome Statute: Issues, Negotiations, Results*, The Hague: Kluwer Law International, 1999

Lee, Roy S., Lietzau, W. K., Fletcher, G. P., Dicker, R., and Dubinsky, P. R., 'The International Criminal Court: Contemporary Perspectives and Prospects for Ratification', (2000) 19 *New York Law School Journal of International and Comparative Law* 505

Legomsky, Stephen H., 'Commentary on Part 9 of the Zutphen Intersessional Draft: General Principles of Criminal Law', (1998) 13bis *Nouvelles études pénales* 101

Leigh, Monroe, 'The United States and the Statute of Rome', (2001) 95 *American Journal of International Law* 124

Leir, Michael R., 'The Road from Rome to The Hague: The International Criminal Court Statute', in *The Changing Face of International Criminal Law: Selected Papers*, Vancouver: International Centre for Criminal Law Reform and Criminal Justice Policy, 2002, pp. 223–8

Levitine, Ilia B., 'Constitutional Aspects of an International Criminal Court', (1996) 9 *New York International Law Review* 27

Lietzau, William K., 'The United States and the International Criminal Court. International Criminal Law after Rome. Concerns from a US Military Perspective', (2001) 64 *Law and Contemporary Problems* 119

Llewellyn, Jennifer J., 'A Comment on the Complementary Jurisdiction of the International Criminal Court: Adding Insult to Injury in Transitional Contexts?', (2001) 24 *Dalhousie Law Journal* 192

Lohr, Michael F., and Lietzau, William K., 'One Road Away from Rome: Concerns Regarding the International Criminal Court', (1998/9) 9 *United States Air Force Journal of Legal Studies* 33

MacSweeney, Daniel, 'International Standards of Fairness, Criminal Procedure and the International Criminal Court', (1997) 68 *Revue internationale de droit pénal* 233

Mandel, Michael, 'The International Criminal Court: Rounding up the Usual Suspects While America Gets Away with Murder', in Hélène Dumont and Anne-Marie Boisvert, eds., *La voie vers la Cour pénale internationale: Tous les chemins mènent à Rome*, Montreal: Themis, 2004, pp. 193–206

Marchesi, Antonio, 'The Enforcement of Sentences of the International Criminal Court', in Flavia Lattanzi and William A. Schabas, eds., *Essays on the Rome Statute of the International Criminal Court*, vol. I, Ripa Fagnano Alto: Editrice il Sirente, 2000, pp. 427–46

'Initiation of Proceedings before the International Criminal Court', in Flavia Lattanzi, ed., *The International Criminal Court: Comments on the Draft Statute*, Naples: Editoriale Scientifica, 1998, pp. 121–38

Marler, M. K., 'The International Criminal Court: Assessing the Jurisdictional Loopholes in the Rome Statute', (1999) 49 *Duke Law Journal* 825

Marquardt, Paul D., 'Law without Borders: The Constitutionality of an International Criminal Court', (1995) 33 *Columbia Journal of Transnational Law* 73

Martinez, L., 'Prosecuting Terrorists at the International Criminal Court: Possibilities and Problems', (2002) 34 *Rutgers Law Journal* 1

May, Richard, 'The Relationship between the International Criminal Court and the International Criminal Tribunal for the Former Yugoslavia', in Herman von Hebel, Johan G. Lammers and Jolien Schukking, eds., *Reflections on the*

International Criminal Court: Essays in Honour of Adriaan Bos, The Hague: T. M. C. Asser, 1999, pp. 155–62

May, Richard, and Wierda, *Marieka, International Criminal Evidence*, Ardsley, NY: Transnational Publishers, 2002

Mayerfeld, J., 'Who Shall Be Judge?: The United States, the International Criminal Court, and the Global Enforcement of Human Rights', (2003) 25 *Human Rights Quarterly* 93

'The Mutual Dependence of External and Internal Justice: The Democratic Achievement of the International Criminal Court', (2001) 12 *Finnish Yearbook of International Law* 71

McCormack, Timothy L. H., 'Crimes Against Humanity', in Dominic McGoldrick, Peter Rowe and Eric Donnelly, eds., *The Permanent International Criminal Court: Legal and Policy Issues*, Oxford and Portland, OR: Hart Publishing, 2004, pp. 179–202

McCormack, Timothy L. H., and Robertson, Sue, 'Jurisdictional Aspects of the Rome Statute for the International Criminal Court', (1999) 23 *Melbourne University Law Review* 635

McCoubrey, Hilaire, 'War Crimes Jurisdiction and a Permanent International Criminal Court: Advantages and Difficulties', (1998) 3 *Journal of Armed Conflict Law* 9

'From Nuremberg to Rome: Restoring the Defence of Superior Orders', (2001) 50 *International and Comparative Law Quarterly* 386

McGoldrick, Dominic, 'Political and Legal Responses to the ICC', in Dominic McGoldrick, Peter Rowe and Eric Donnelly, eds., *The Permanent International Criminal Court: Legal and Policy Issues*, Oxford and Portland, OR: Hart Publishing, 2004, pp. 389–451

McGoldrick, Dominic, Rowe, Peter, and Donnelly, Eric, eds., *The Permanent International Criminal Court: Legal and Policy Issues*, Oxford and Portland, OR: Hart Publishing, 2004

McIntire, Alison M., 'Be Careful What You Wish for Because You Just Might Get It: The United States and the International Criminal Court', (2001) 25 *Suffolk Transnational Law Review* 249

McKay, Fiona, 'Are Reparations Appropriately Addressed in the ICC Statute?', in Dinah Shelton, ed., *International Crimes, Peace, and Human Rights: The Role of the International Criminal Court*, Ardsley, NY: Transnational Publishers, 2000, pp. 163–76

McKeon, Patricia A., 'An International Criminal Court: Balancing the Principle of Sovereignty Against the Demands for International Justice', (1997) 12 *St John's Journal of Legal Commentary* 535

McNerney, P., 'The International Criminal Court: Issues for Consideration by the United States Senate', (2001) 64 *Law and Contemporary Problems* 181

Megret, Frédéric, 'Epilogue to an Endless Debate: The International Criminal
    Court's Third Party Jurisdiction and the Looming Revolution of Inter-
    national Law', (2001) 12 *European Journal of International Law* 247
  'Three Dangers for the International Criminal Court. A Critical Look at a
    Consensual Project', (2001) 12 *Finnish Yearbook of International Law*
    244
Mekhemar, Lamia, 'The Status of the Individual in the Statute of the International
    Criminal Court', in Mauro Politi and Giuseppe Nesi, eds., *The Rome Statute
    of the International Criminal Court: A Challenge to Impunity*, Aldershot:
    Ashgate, 2001, pp. 123–30
Mekjian, G. J., and Varughese, M. C., 'Hearing the Victim's Voice: Analysis of
    Victims' Participation in the Trial Proceeding [*sic*] of the International
    Criminal Court', (2005) 17 *Pace International Law Review* 1
Meron, Theodor, 'Defining Aggression for the International Criminal Court',
    (2001) 15 *Suffolk Transnational Law Review* 1
  'Crimes under the Jurisdiction of the International Criminal Court', in Herman
    von Hebel, Johan G. Lammers and Jolien Schukking, eds., *Reflections on the
    International Criminal Court: Essays in Honour of Adriaan Bos*, The Hague:
    T. M. C. Asser, 1999, pp. 47–56
Meyer, Frank, 'Complementing Complementarity', (2006) 6 *International
    Criminal Law Review* 549
Mezzetti, Enrico, 'Grounds for Excluding Criminal Responsibility', in Flavia
    Lattanzi, ed., *The International Criminal Court: Comments on the Draft
    Statute*, Naples: Editoriale Scientifica, 1998, pp. 147–58
Milaninia, Nema, 'One Step Forward, Two Steps Backwards: Addressing
    Objections to the ICC's Prescriptive and Adjudicative Powers', (2006) 3:3
    International Studies Journal 31
Mochochoko, P., 'The Agreement on Privileges and Immunities in the International
    Criminal Court', (2002) 25 *Fordham International Law Journal* 638
Mokhtar, Aly, 'The Fine Art of Arm-Twisting: The US, Resolution 1422 and Security
    Council Deferral Power under the Rome Statute', (2004) 4 *International
    Criminal Law Review* 295
Momtaz, Djamchid, 'War Crimes in Non-International Armed Conflicts under
    the Statute of the International Criminal Court', (1999) 2 *Yearbook of
    International Humanitarian Law* 177
Morris, Madeline, 'High Crimes and Misconceptions: The ICC and Non-Party
    States', (2001) 64 *Law and Contemporary Problems* 13
  'Complementarity and Its Discontents: States, Victims, and the International
    Criminal Court', in Dinah Shelton, ed., *International Crimes, Peace, and
    Human Rights: The Role of the International Criminal Court*, Ardsley, NY:
    Transnational Publishers, 2000, pp. 177–202
Mosconi, Franco, and Parisi, Nicoletta, 'Co-operation between International
    Criminal Court and States Parties', in Flavia Lattanzi, ed., *The International*

Criminal Court: Comments on the Draft Statute, Naples: Editoriale Scientifica, 1998, pp. 311–38

Moshan, B. S., 'Women, War, and Words: The Gender Component in the Permanent International Criminal Court's Definition of Crimes Against Humanity', (1998) 22 *Fordham International Law Journal* 154

Moy, Abigail H., 'The International Criminal Court's Arrest Warrant and Uganda's Lord's Resistance Army: Renewing the Debate Over Amnesty and Complementarity', (2006) 19 *Harvard Human Rights Journal* 269

Mundis, D. A., 'The Assembly of States Parties and the Institutional Framework of the International Criminal Court', (2003) 97 *American Journal of International Law* 132

Murphy, John P., 'The Quivering Gulliver: US Views on a Permanent International Criminal Court', (2000) 34 *International Lawyer* 45

Murphy, Ray, 'Gravity Issues and the International Criminal Court', (2006) 17 *Criminal Law Forum* 281

Murungi, Betty Kaari, 'Implementing the International Criminal Court Statute in Africa', [2001] *International Legal Practitioner* 87

Muttukumaru, Christian P. J., 'Reparations for Victims', in Flavia Lattanzi and William A. Schabas, eds., *Essays on the Rome Statute of the International Criminal Court*, vol. I, Ripa Fagnano Alto: Editrice il Sirente, 2000, pp. 303–10

Mysak, M. D., 'Judging the Giant: An Examination of American Opposition to the Rome Statute of the International Criminal Court', (2000) 63 *Saskatchewan Law Review* 275

Neier, Aryeh, 'Waiting for Justice: The United States and the International Criminal Court', (1998) 15 *World Policy Journal* 33

Nesi, Giuseppe, 'The Organs of the International Criminal Court and Their Functions in the Rome Statute: The Assembly of States Parties', in Flavia Lattanzi and William A. Schabas, eds., *Essays on the Rome Statute of the International Criminal Court*, vol. I, Ripa Fagnano Alto: Editrice il Sirente, 2000, pp. 233–50

'The International Criminal Court: Its Establishment and Its Relationship with the United Nations System, Its Composition, Administration and Financing', in Flavia Lattanzi, ed., *The International Criminal Court: Comments on the Draft Statute*, Naples: Editoriale Scientifica, 1998, pp. 171–92

Neuner, Matthias, ed., *National Legislation Incorporating International Crimes*, Berlin: Berlinter Wissenschafts-Verlag/Wolf Legal Publishers, 2003

Newton, Michael A., 'Comparative Complementarity: Domestic Jurisdiction Consistent with the Rome Statute of the International Criminal Court', (2001) 167 *Military Law Review* 20

Nill, D. A., 'National Sovereignty: Must It Be Sacrificed to the International Criminal Court?', (1999) 14 *Brigham Young University Journal of Public Law* 119

Nilsson, Cecilia, 'Contextualizing the Agreement on the Privileges and Immunities of the International Criminal Court', (2004) 3 *Leiden Journal of International Law* 559

Noguchi, Motoo, 'Criminal Justice in Asia and Japan and the International Criminal Court', (2006) 6 *International Criminal Law Review* 585

Nowakowska-Malusecka, Joanna, 'Prosecuting War Crimes by the Ad Hoc Tribunals and by the Future Permanent International Criminal Court', in Paul L. C. Torremans, ed., *Legal Convergence in the Enlarged Europe of the New Millennium*, The Hague, Boston and London: Kluwer Law International, 2000, pp. 191–204

Nsereko, Daniel D. Ntanda, 'The International Criminal Court: Jurisdictional and Related Issues', (1999) 10 *Criminal Law Forum* 87

O'Connor, Gerard E., 'The Pursuit of Justice and Accountability: Why the United States Should Support the Establishment of an International Criminal Court', (1999) 27 *Hofstra Law Review* 927

O'Donohue, Jonathan, 'Towards a Fully Functional International Criminal Court: The Adoption of the 2004 Budget', (2004) 17 *Leiden Journal of International Law* 579

O'Shea, A., 'The Statute of the International Criminal Court', (1999) 116 *South Africa Law Journal* 243

Ohl, Shawn K., 'US Opposition to the International Criminal Court: Outside the Realm of Responsibility', (2000) 46 *Wayne Law Review* 2043

Olásolo, Héctor, 'Reflections on the International Criminal Court's Jurisdictional Reach', (2005) 16 *Criminal Law Forum* 279

The Triggering Procedure of the International Criminal Court, Leiden and Boston: Martinus Nijhoff, 2005

'The Triggering Procedure of the International Criminal Court, Procedural Treatment of the Principle of Complementarity, and the Role of Office of the Prosecutor', (2005) 5 *International Criminal Law Review* 121

'The Prosecutor of the ICC before the Initiation of Investigations: A Quasi-Judicial or a Political Body?', (2003) 3 *International Criminal Law Review* 87

Oosterveld, V., Perry, M., and McManus, J., 'The Cooperation of States with the International Criminal Court', (2002) 25 *Fordham International Law Journal* 767

Oosthuizen, Gabriel H., 'Some Preliminary Remarks on the Relationship between the Envisaged International Criminal Court and the UN Security Council', (1999) 46 *Netherlands International Law Review* 313

Orentlicher, Diane, 'Politics by Other Means: The Law of the International Criminal Court', (1999) 32 *Cornell International Law Journal* 489

'Judging Global Justice: Assessing the International Criminal Court', (2003) 21 *Wisconsin International Law Journal* 495

Pace, William R., 'The Relationship between the International Criminal Court and Non-Governmental Organizations', in Herman von Hebel, Johan G. Lammers and Jolien Schukking, eds., *Reflections on the International Criminal Court: Essays in Honour of Adriaan Bos*, The Hague: T. M. C. Asser, 1999, pp. 189–210

Palmisano, Giuseppe, 'The ICC and Third States', in Flavia Lattanzi and William A. Schabas, eds., *Essays on the Rome Statute of the International Criminal Court*, vol. I, Ripa Fagnano Alto: Editrice il Sirente, 2000, pp. 391–426

'Co-operation by Non-States Parties', in Flavia Lattanzi, ed., *The International Criminal Court: Comments on the Draft Statute*, Naples: Editoriale Scientifica, 1998, pp. 339–66

Paust, Jordan J., 'The Reach of ICC Jurisdiction over Non-Signatory Nationals', (2000) 33 *Vanderbilt Journal of Transnational Law* 1

'The Preparatory Committee's "Definition of Crimes" – War Crimes', (1997) 8 *Criminal Law Forum* 431

Paust, Jordan J., Sadat Wexler, Leila, and Wise, Edward M., 'Commentary on Part 2 of the Zutphen Intersessional Draft: General Principles of Criminal Law', (1998) 13*bis Nouvelles études pénales* 27

Pejic, Jelena, 'The United States and the International Criminal Court: One Loophole Too Many', (2001) 78 *University of Detroit Mercy Law Review* 267

'The International Criminal Court and the Human Rights Revolution', (2000) 34 *International Lawyer* 65

'Creating a Permanent International Criminal Court: The Obstacles to Independence and Effectiveness', (1998) 29 *Columbia Human Rights Law Review* 291

'The Tribunal and the ICC: Do Precedents Matter?', (1997) 60 *Albany Law Review* 841

Penrose, M. M., 'No Badges, No Bars: A Conspicuous Oversight in the Development of an International Criminal Court', (2003) 38 *Texas International Law Journal* 621

Peter, Matthew D., 'The Proposed International Criminal Court: A Commentary on the Legal and Political Debates Regarding Jurisdiction That Threaten the Establishment of an Effective Court', (1997) 24 *Syracuse Journal of International Law and Commerce* 177

Petera, A. Rohan, 'Towards the Establishment of an International Criminal Court', (1994) 20 *Commonwealth Law Bulletin* 298

Pfanner, Toni, 'The Establishment of a Permanent International Criminal Court: ICRC Expectations of the Rome Diplomatic Conference', (1998) 322 *International Review of the Red Cross* 21

Philips, Ruth B., 'The International Criminal Court Statute: Jurisdiction and Admissibility', (1999) 10 *Criminal Law Forum* 61

Pichon, J., 'The Principle of Complementarity in the Cases of the Sudanese Nationals Ahmad Harun and Ali Kushayb Before the International Criminal Court', (2008) 8 *International Criminal Law Review* 185

Pickard, Daniel B., 'Proposed Sentencing Guidelines for the International Criminal Court', (1997) 20 *Loyola of Los Angeles International and Comparative Law Journal* 123

Pocar, Fausto, 'The Rome Statute of the International Criminal Court and Human Rights', in Mauro Politi and Giuseppe Nesi, eds., *The Rome Statute of the International Criminal Court: A Challenge to Impunity*, Aldershot: Ashgate, 2001, pp. 67–74

Politi, Mauro, 'The Rome Statute of the ICC: Rays of Light and Some Shadows', in Mauro Politi and Giuseppe Nesi, eds., *The Rome Statute of the International Criminal Court: A Challenge to Impunity*, Aldershot: Ashgate, 2001, pp. 7–16
'The Establishment of an International Criminal Court at a Crossroads: Issues and Prospects after the First Session of the Preparatory Committee', (1997) 13 *Nouvelles études pénales* 115

Politi, Mauro, and Gioia, Federica, eds., *The International Criminal Court and National Jurisdictions*, Aldershot: Ashgate, 2008

Politi, Mauro, and Nesi, Giuseppe, eds., *The Rome Statute of the International Criminal Court: A Challenge to Impunity*, Aldershot: Ashgate, 2001

Popovski, Vesselin, 'The International Criminal Court: A Necessary Step Towards Global Justice', (2000) 31 *Security Dialogue* 405

Prescott, J. M., 'Litigating Genocide: A Consideration of the International Criminal Court in Light of the German Jews' Legal Response to Nazi Persecution, 1933–1941', (1999) 51 *Maine Law Review* 297

Proulx, V. J., 'Rethinking the Jurisdiction of the International Criminal Court in the Post-September 11th Era: Should Acts of Terrorism Qualify as Crimes against Humanity?', (2004) 19 *American University International Law Review* 1009

Rakate, P. K., 'An International Criminal Court for a New Millennium – The Rome Conference', (1998) 23 *South Africa Yearbook International Law* 217

Ralph, Jason, 'The International Criminal Court and the "Uneasy Revolution" in International Society', (2004) 8 *International Journal of Human Rights* 235

Ramanathan, Usha, 'India and the ICC', (2005) 3 *Journal of International Criminal Justice* 627

Rancilio, Peggy E., 'From Nuremberg to Rome: Establishing an International Criminal Court and the Need for US Participation', (1999) 77 *University of Detroit Mercy Law Review* 155

Rastan, Rod, 'What Is a "Case" for the Purpose of the Rome Statute?', (2008) 19 *Criminal Law Forum* 435

Ratner, S. R., 'The International Criminal Court and the Limits of Global Judicialization', (2003) 38 *Texas International Law Journal* 445

Reisman, W. Michael, 'On Paying the Piper: Financial Responsibility for Security Council Referrals to the International Criminal Court', (2005) 3 *American Journal of International Law* 615

'Learning to Deal with Rejection: The International Criminal Court and the United States', (2004) 2 *Journal of International Criminal Justice* 17

Relva, Hugo, 'The Implementation of the Rome Statute in Latin American States', (2003) 16 *Leiden Journal of International Law* 331

Retico, Vincenzo, 'The Trial of First Instance before the International Criminal Court', in Flavia Lattanzi, ed., *The International Criminal Court: Comments on the Draft Statute*, Naples: Editoriale Scientifica, 1998, pp. 193–208

Rinoldi, Dino, and Parisi, Nicoletta, 'International Co-operation and Judicial Assistance between States Parties and the International Criminal Court', in Flavia Lattanzi and William A. Schabas, eds., *Essays on the Rome Statute of the International Criminal Court*, vol. I, Ripa Fagnano Alto: Editrice il Sirente, 2000, pp. 339–90

Roach, S. C., 'Arab States and the Role of Islam in the International Criminal Court', (2005) 53 *Political Studies* 143

Roberge, Marie-Claude, 'The New International Criminal Court: A Preliminary Assessment', (1998) 325 *International Review of the Red Cross* 671

Roberts, G., 'Assault on Sovereignty: The Clear and Present Danger of the New International Criminal Court', (2001) 17 *American University International Law Review* 35

Roberts, Ken, 'Aspects of the International Criminal Tribunal for the Former Yugoslavia Contribution to the Criminal Procedure of the ICC', in Richard May *et al.*, eds., *Essays on International Criminal Tribunal for the Former Yugoslavia Procedure and Evidence: In Honour of Gabrielle Kirk McDonald*, The Hague and Boston: Kluwer Law International, 2001, pp. 559–73

Robinson, Darryl, 'Serving the Interests of Justice: Amnesties, Truth Commissions and the International Criminal Court', (2003) 14 *European Journal of International Law* 481

'Crimes Against Humanity: Reflections on State Sovereignty, Legal Precision and the Dictates of the Public Conscience', in Flavia Lattanzi and William A. Schabas, eds., *Essays on the Rome Statute of the International Criminal Court*, vol. I, Ripa Fagnano Alto: Editrice il Sirente, 2000, pp. 139–70

'Defining "Crimes Against Humanity" at the Rome Conference', (1999) 93 *American Journal of International Law* 43

Robinson, Darryl, and von Hebel, Herman, 'War Crimes in Internal Conflicts: Article 8 of the ICC Statute', (1999) 2 *Yearbook of International Humanitarian Law* 193

Roche, D., 'Truth Commission Amnesties and the International Criminal Court', (2005) 45 *British Journal of Criminology* 565

Rodman, K. A., 'Compromising Justice: Why the Bush Administration and the NGOs Are Both Wrong about the ICC', (2006) 20 *Ethics and International Affairs* 25

Rodriguez, Cara Levy, 'Slaying the Monster: Why the United States Should Not Support the Rome Treaty', (1999) 14 *American University International Law Review* 805

Roht-Arriaza, Naomi, 'Amnesty and the International Criminal Court', in Dinah Shelton, ed., *International Crimes, Peace, and Human Rights: The Role of the International Criminal Court*, Ardsley, NY: Transnational Publishers, 2000, pp. 77–82

Rosenne, Shabtai, 'Poor Drafting and Imperfect Organization: Flaws to Overcome in the Rome Statute', (2000) 41 *Virginia Journal of International Law* 164

'The Jurisdiction of the International Criminal Court', (1999) 2 *Yearbook of International Humanitarian Law* 119

Rothe, Dawn, and Mullins, Christopher W., *Symbolic Gestures and the Generation of Global Social Control: The International Criminal Court*, Lanham, MD: Lexington Books, 2006

Rowe, Peter, 'War Crimes', in Dominic McGoldrick, Peter Rowe and Eric Donnelly, eds., *The Permanent International Criminal Court: Legal and Policy Issues*, Oxford and Portland, OR: Hart Publishing, 2004, pp. 203–32

Rubin, Alfred P., 'The International Criminal Court: Possibilities for Prosecutorial Abuse', (2001) 64 *Law and Contemporary Problems* 153

'A Critical View of the Proposed International Criminal Court', (1999) 23 *Fletcher Forum of World Affairs* 139

'Challenging the Conventional Wisdom: Another View of the International Criminal Court', (1999) 52 *Journal of International Affairs* 783

Ruegenberg, Guido, 'The Independence and Accountability of Prosecutor of a Permanent International Criminal Court', [1999] *Zeitschrift für Rechtspolitik* 68

Rydberg, Å., 'The Protection of the Interests of Witnesses – The International Criminal Tribunal for the Former Yugoslavia in Comparison to the Future ICC', (1999) 12 *Leiden Journal of International Law* 455

Ryneveld, Dirk, and Mundis, Daryl A., 'The Contribution of the International Criminal Tribunal for the Former Yugoslavia to the Emergence of the ICC: Procedural and Evidentiary Aspects from a Practitioner's Perspective', in *The Changing Face of International Criminal Law: Selected Papers*, Vancouver: International Centre for Criminal Law Reform and Criminal Justice Policy, 2002, pp. 51–62

Ryngaert, Cedric, 'Applying the Rome Statute's Complementarity Principle: Drawing Lessons from the Prosecution of Core Crimes by States Acting Under the Universality Principle', (2008) 19 *Criminal Law Forum* 153

'Universal Jurisdiction in an ICC Era: A Role to Play for EU Member States with the Support of the European Union', (2006) 14 *European Journal of Crime, Criminal Law and Criminal Justice* 46

Sadat, Leila Nadya, 'Summer in Rome, Spring in The Hague, Winter in Washington? US Policy Towards the International Criminal Court', (2003) 21 *Wisconsin International Law Journal* 557

'The Least Dangerous Branch: Six Letters from Publius to Cato in Support of the International Criminal Court', (2003) 35 *Case Western Reserve Journal of International Law* 339

The International Criminal Court and the Transformation of International Law: Justice for the New Millennium, Ardsley, NY: Transnational Publishers, 2002

'Custom, Codification and Some Thoughts about the Relationship between the Two: Article 10 of the ICC Statute', (2000) 49 *DePaul Law Review* 909

Sadat, Leila Nadya, and Carden, S. Richard, 'The New International Criminal Court: An Uneasy Revolution', (2000) 88 *Georgetown Law Journal* 381

Sadat Wexler, Leila, 'A First Look at the 1998 Rome Statute for a Permanent International Criminal Court: Jurisdiction, Definition of Crimes, Structure, and Referrals to the Court', in M. Cherif Bassiouni, ed., *International Criminal Law*, vol. III, Dobbs Ferry, NY: Transnational Publishers, 1999, pp. 655–91

'Committee Report on Jurisdiction, Definition of Crimes, and Complementarity', (1997) 25 *Denver Journal of International Law and Policy* 221

'First Committee Report on Jurisdiction, Definition of Crimes and Complementarity', (1997) 13 *Nouvelles études pénales* 163; (1997) 29 *Denver Journal of International Law and Policy* 221

'The Proposed Permanent International Criminal Court: An Appraisal', (1996) 29 *Cornell International Law Journal* 665

Sadat Wexler, Leila, and Clark, Roger S., 'Commentary on Part 1 of the Zutphen Intersessional Draft: General Principles of Criminal Law', (1998) 13*bis Nouvelles études pénales* 17

Sadat Wexler, Leila, and Paust, Jordan J., 'Model Draft Statute for the International Criminal Court Based on the Preparatory Committee's Text to the Diplomatic Conference, Rome, June 15–July 17, 1997, Preamble, Parts 1 and 2', (1998) 13*ter Nouvelles études pénales* 1

Sailer, Todd M., 'The International Criminal Court: An Argument to Extend Its Jurisdiction to Terrorism and a Dismissal of US Objections', (1999) 13 *Temple International and Comparative Law Journal* 311

Sarooshi, Danesh, 'Prosecutorial Policy and the ICC, Prosecutor's Proprio Motu Action of Self-Denial?', (2004) 2 *Journal of International Criminal Justice* 940

'Aspects of the Relationship between the International Criminal Court and the United Nations', (2001) 32 *Netherlands Yearbook of International Law* 27

'The Statute of the International Criminal Court', (1999) 48 *International and Comparative Law Quarterly* 387

Satzger, Helmut, 'German Criminal Law and the Rome Statute – A Critical Analysis of the German Code of Crimes Against International Law', (2002) 2 *International Criminal Law Review* 261

Scaliotti, Massimo, 'Defences before the International Criminal Court: Substantive Grounds for Excluding Criminal Responsibility – Part 1', (2001) 1 *International Criminal Law Review* 111

'Defences before the International Criminal Court: Substantive Grounds for Excluding Criminal Responsibility – Part 2', (2002) 2 *International Criminal Law Review* 1

Schabas, William A., *The International Criminal Court: A Commentary on the Rome Statute*, Oxford: Oxford University Press, 2010

'Prosecutorial Discretion vs. Judicial Activism at the International Criminal Court', (2008) 6 *Journal of International Criminal Justice* 731

'First Prosecutions at the International Criminal Court', (2006) 25 *Human Rights Law Journal* 25

'The Unfinished Work of Defining Aggression: How Many Times Must the Cannonballs Fly, Before They Are Forever Banned?', in Dominic McGoldrick, Peter Rowe and Eric Donnelly, *The Permanent International Criminal Court: Legal and Policy Issues*, Oxford: Hart Publishing, 2004, pp. 123–41

'United States Hostility to the International Criminal Court: It's All About the Security Council', (2004) 15 *European Journal of International Law* 701

'Follow-up to Rome: Preparing for Entry Into Force of the Statute of the International Criminal Court', in Mauro Politi and Giuseppe Nesi, eds., *The Rome Statute of the International Criminal Court: A Challenge to Impunity*, Aldershot: Ashgate, 2001, pp. 197–216

'The International Criminal Court: The Secret of Its Success', (2001) 12 *Criminal Law Forum* 415

'Canadian Implementing Legislation for the Rome Statute', (2000) 3 *Yearbook of International Humanitarian Law* 337

'Life, Death and the Crime of Crimes: Supreme Penalties and the ICC Statute', (2000) 2 *Punishment and Society* 263

'The Penalty Provisions of the ICC Statute', in Dinah Shelton, ed., *International Crimes, Peace, and Human Rights: The Role of the International Criminal Court*, Ardsley, NY: Transnational Publishers, 2000, pp. 105–36

'The Follow up to Rome: Preparing for Entry Into Force of the International Criminal Court Statute', (1999) 20 *Human Rights Law Journal* 157

'General Principles of Criminal Law in the International Criminal Court Statute (Part III)', (1998) 6 *European Journal of Crime, Criminal Law and Criminal Justice* 84

'Penalties', in Flavia Lattanzi, ed., *The International Criminal Court: Comments on the Draft Statute*, Naples: Editoriale Scientifica, 1998, pp. 273–300

Scharf, Michael P., 'The ICC's Jurisdiction over the Nationals of Non-Party States: A Critique of the US Position', (2001) 64 *Law and Contemporary Problems* 67

'The United States and the International Criminal Court: A Recommendation for the Bush Administration', (2001) 7 *ILSA Journal of International and Comparative Law* 385

'The United States and the International Criminal Court: The ICC's Jurisdiction over the Nationals of Non-Party States: A Critique of the US Position', (2001) 64 *Law and Contemporary Problems* 67

'The ICC's Jurisdiction over the Nationals of Non-Party States', in S. B. Sewall and C. Kaysen, eds., *The United States and the International Criminal Court: National Security and International Law*, Lanham, MD, Boulder, CO, New York and Oxford: Rowman and Littlefield, 2000, pp. 213–36

'The Amnesty Exception to the Jurisdiction of the International Criminal Court', (1999) 32 *Cornell International Law Journal* 507

'The Draft Statute for an International Criminal Court', in M. Cherif Bassiouni, ed., *International Criminal Law*, vol. III, Dobbs Ferry, NY: Transnational Publishers, 1999, pp. 637–53

'Model Draft Statute for the International Criminal Court Based on the Preparatory Committee's Text to the Diplomatic Conference, Rome, June 15–July 17, 1997, Parts 9 and 10', (1998) 13*ter Nouvelles études pénales* 120

'The Politics of Establishing an International Criminal Court', (1995) 6 *Duke Journal of International and Comparative Law* 167

Scheffer, David J., 'Article 98(2) of the Rome Statute: America's Original Intent', (2005) 3 *Journal of International Criminal Justice* 333

'How to Turn the Tide Using the Rome Statute's Temporal Jurisdiction', (2004) 2 *Journal of International Criminal Justice* 26

'Restoring US Engagement with the International Criminal Court', (2003) 21 *Wisconsin International Law Journal* 599

'Staying the Course with the International Criminal Court', (2002) 35 *Cornell International Law Journal* 47

'A Negotiator's Perspective on the International Criminal Court', (2001) 167 *Military Law Review* 1

'The US Perspective on the International Criminal Court', (2000) 46 *McGill Law Journal* 269

'The International Criminal Tribunal, Foreword: Deterrence of War Crimes in the 21st Century', (1999) 23 *Maryland Journal of International and Trade Law* 1

'US Policy and the International Criminal Court', (1999) 32 *Cornell International Law Journal* 529

'The United States and the International Criminal Court', (1998) 93 *American Journal of International Law* 12

Schense, J., 'Necessary Steps for the Creation of the International Criminal Court', (2002) 25 *Fordham International Law Journal* 717

Schrag, Minna, 'Observations on the Rome Statute', (1999) 1 *International Law Forum* 34

Schuster, Matthias, 'The Rome Statute and the Crime of Aggression: A Gordian Knot in Search of a Sword', (2003) 14 *Criminal Law Forum* 1

Schwartz, Eric P., 'The United States and the International Criminal Court: The Case for "Dextrous Multilateralism"', (2003) 4 *Chicago Journal of International Law* 223

Seguin, John, 'Denouncing the International Criminal Court: An Examination of US Objections to the Rome Statute', (2000) 18 *Boston University International Law Journal* 85

Seibert-Fohr, A., 'The Relevance of the Rome Statute of the International Criminal Court for Amnesties and Truth Commissions', (2003) 7 *Max Planck Yearbook of United Nations Law* 553

Sellers Bickley, Lynn, 'US Resistance to the International Criminal Court: Is the Sword Mightier Than the Law?', (2000) 14 *Emory International Law Review* 213

Sereni, Andrea, 'Individual Criminal Responsibility', in Flavia Lattanzi, ed., *The International Criminal Court: Comments on the Draft Statute*, Naples: Editoriale Scientifica, 1998, pp. 139–46

Sewall, Sarah B., and Kaysen, Carl, eds., *The United States and the International Criminal Court: National Security and International Law*, Lanham, MD: Rowman and Littlefield, 2000

Shah, S. B., 'The Oversight of the Last Great International Institution of the Twentieth Century: The International Criminal Court's Definition of Genocide', (2002) 16 *Emory International Law Review* 351

Sharp, P., 'Prospects for Environmental Liability in the International Criminal Court', (1999) 18 *Virginia Environmental Law Journal* 217

Shaw, Malcolm N., 'The International Criminal Court – Some Procedural and Evidential Issues', (1998) 3 *Journal of Armed Conflict Law* 65

Shelton, Dinah, ed., *International Crimes, Peace, and Human Rights: The Role of the International Criminal Court*, Ardsley, NY: Transnational Publishers, 2000

Sluiter, Göran, 'Implementation of the ICC Statute in the Dutch Legal Order', (2004) 2 *Journal of International Criminal Justice* 158

'The Surrender of War Criminals to the International Criminal Court', (2003) 25 *Loyola of Los Angeles International and Comparative Law Review* 605

'An International Criminal Court Is Hereby Established', (1998) 3 *Netherlands Quarterly of Human Rights* 413

Smidt, M. L., 'The International Criminal Court: An Effective Means of Deterrence?', (2001) 167 *Military Law Review* 156

Spieker, Heike, 'The International Criminal Court and Non-International Armed Conflicts', (2000) 13 *Leiden Journal of International Law* 395

Ssenyonjo, Manisuli, 'Accountability of Non-State Actors in Uganda for War Crimes and Human Rights Violations: Between Amnesty and the International Criminal Court', (2005) 10 *Journal of Conflict and Security Law* 405

Stahn, Carsten, 'Why Some Doors May Be Closed Already: Second Thoughts on a "Case-by-Case" Treatment of Article 12(3) Declarations', (2006) 75 *Nordic Journal of International Law* 243

'Complementarity, Amnesties and Alternative Forms of Justice: Some Interpretative Guidelines for the International Criminal Court', (2005) 3 *Journal of International Criminal Court* 695

'Modification of the Legal Characterization of Facts in the ICC System: A Portrayal of Regulation 55', (2005) 16 *Criminal Law Forum* 1

'The Ambiguities of Security Council Resolution 1422 (2002)', (2003) 14 *European Journal of International Law* 85

Stahn, Carsten, El Zeidy, Mohamed, and Olásolo, Héctor, 'The International Criminal Court's Ad Hoc Jurisdiction Revisited', (2005) 99 *American Journal of International Law* 421

Stahn, Carsten, and Sluiter, Goran, *The Emerging Practice of the International Criminal Court*, Leiden: Brill, 2009

Stapleton, Sara, 'Ensuring a Fair Trial in the International Criminal Court: Statutory Interpretation and the Impermissibility of Derogation', (1999) 31 *New York University Journal of International Law and Policy* 535

Stephens, Beth, 'Accountability for International Crimes: The Synergy between the International Criminal Court and Alternative Remedies', (2003) 21 *Wisconsin International Law Journal* 527

Stevens, Lyn L., 'Towards a Permanent International Criminal Court', (1998) 6 *European Journal of Crime, Criminal Law and Criminal Justice* 236

Stoelting, David, 'Status Report on the International Criminal Court', (1999) 3 *Hofstra Law and Policy Symposium* 233

Strapatsas, N., 'Universal Jurisdiction and the International Criminal Court', (2002) 29 *Manitoba Law Journal* 1

Summers, M. A., 'A Fresh Look at the Jurisdictional Provisions of the Statute of the International Criminal Court: The Case for Scrapping the Treaty', (2001) 20 *Wisconsin International Law Journal* 57

Sunga, Lyal S., 'The Crimes within the Jurisdiction of the International Criminal Court (Part II, Articles 5–10)', (1998) 6 *European Journal of Crime, Criminal Law and Criminal Justice* 61

Supple, Shannon K., 'Global Responsibility and the United States: The Constitutionality of the International Criminal Court', (1999) 27 *Hastings Constitutional Law Quarterly* 181

Swart, Bert, and Sluiter, Göran, 'The International Criminal Court and International Criminal Co-operation', in Herman von Hebel, Johan

G. Lammers and Jolien Schukking, eds., *Reflections on the International Criminal Court: Essays in Honour of Adriaan Bos*, The Hague: T. M. C. Asser, 1999, pp. 91–128

Tallgren, Immi, 'Completing the "International Criminal Order": The Rhetoric of International Repression and the Notion of Complementarity in the Draft Statute for an International Criminal Court', (1998) 67 *Nordic Journal of International Law* 107

Tallman, D. A., 'Catch 98(2): Article 98 Agreements and the Dilemma of Treaty Conflict', (2005) 92 *Georgetown Law Journal* 1033

Tan, C. J., 'The Proliferation of Bilateral Non-Surrender Agreements among Non-Ratifiers of the Rome Statute of the International Criminal Court', (2004) 19 *American University International Law Review* 1115

Taulbee, J. L., 'A Call to Arms Declined: The United States and the International Criminal Court', (2000) 14 *Emory International Law Review* 105

Tepavac, Milan, 'Establishment of a Permanent International Criminal Court', (1998) 49 *Review of International Affairs* 25

Tiefenbrun, S. W., 'The Paradox of International Adjudication: Developments in the International Criminal Tribunals for the Former Yugoslavia and Rwanda, the World Court, and the International Criminal Court', (2000) 25 *North Carolina Journal of International Law and Commercial Regulation* 551

Tochilovsky, Vladimir, 'Rules of Procedure for the International Criminal Court: Problems to Address in Light of the Experience of the Ad Hoc Tribunals', (1999) 46 *Netherlands International Law Review* 343

Trahan, J., 'Defining "Aggression": Why the Preparatory Commission for the International Criminal Court Has Faced Such a Conundrum', (2002) 24 *Loyola of Los Angeles International and Comparative Law Review* 439

Triffterer, Otto, 'Causality, a Separate Element of the Doctrine of Superior Responsibility as Expressed in Article 28 Rome Statute?', (2002) 15 *Leiden Journal of International Law* 179

'The Preventive and the Repressive Function of the International Criminal Court', in Mauro Politi and Giuseppe Nesi, eds., *The Rome Statute of the International Criminal Court: A Challenge to Impunity*, Aldershot: Ashgate, 2001, pp. 137–76

ed., *Commentary on the Rome Statute of the International Criminal Court, Observers' Notes, Article by Article*, 2nd edn, Munich: C. H. Beck; Baden-Baden: Nomos; Oxford: Hart, 2008

Tucker, Robert W., 'The International Criminal Court Controversy', (2001) 18 *World Policy Journal* 71

Turns, David, 'Aspects of National Implementation of the Rome Statute', in Dominic McGoldrick, Peter Rowe and Eric Donnelly, eds., *The Permanent International Criminal Court: Legal and Policy Issues*, Oxford and Portland, OR: Hart Publishing, 2004, pp. 337–88

Tuzmukhamedov, Bakhtiyar, 'The ICC and Russian Constitutional Problems', (2005) 3 *Journal of International Criminal Justice* 621

Van Alebeek, Rosanne, 'From Rome to the Hague: Recent Developments on Immunity Issues in the ICC Statute', (2000) 13 *Leiden Journal of International Law* 485

Van Boven, Theo C., 'The Position of the Victim in the Statute of the International Criminal Court', in Herman von Hebel, Johan G. Lammers and Jolien Schukking, eds., *Reflections on the International Criminal Court: Essays in Honour of Adriaan Bos*, The Hague: T. M. C. Asser, 1999, pp. 77–90

'The European Union and the International Criminal Court', (1998) 5 *Maastricht Journal of European and Comparative Law* 325

Van de Kieft, Christopher M., 'Uncertain Risk: The United States Military and the International Criminal Court', (2002) 23 *Cardozo Law Review* 2325

Van der Voort, Karlijn, and Zwanenburg, Marten, 'From "Raison d'état" to "état de droit international": Amnesties and the French Implementation of the Rome Statute', (2001) 1 *International Criminal Law Review* 315

Van der Vyver, J. D., 'International Human Rights: American Exceptionalism: Human Rights, International Criminal Justice and National Self-Righteousness', (2001) 50 *Emory Law Journal* 775

'Personal and Territorial Jurisdiction of the International Criminal Court', (2000) 14 *Emory International Law Review* 1

Van der Wilt, Harmen, and Lyngdorf, Sandra, 'Procedural Obligations Under the European Convention on Human Rights: Useful Guidelines for the Assessment of "Unwillingness" and "Inability" in the Context of the Complementarity Principle', (2009) 9 *International Criminal Law Review* 39

Vandermeersch, Damien, 'The ICC Statute and Belgian Law', (2004) 2 *Journal of International Criminal Justice* 158

Venturini, Gabriella, 'War Crimes', in Flavia Lattanzi and William A. Schabas, eds., *Essays on the Rome Statute of the International Criminal Court*, vol. I, Ripa Fagnano Alto: Editrice il Sirente, 2000, pp. 171–82

Verweij, H., 'The International Criminal Court: Alive, Still Kicking', (2002) 25 *Fordham International Law Journal* 737

Vetter, Greg, 'Command Responsibility of Non-Military Superiors in the International Criminal Court (ICC)', (2000) 25 *Yale Journal of International Law* 89

Vierucci, L., 'The First Steps of the International Criminal Tribunal for the Former Yugoslavia', (1995) 6 *European Journal of International Law* 134

Villa-Vicencio, Charles, 'Why Perpetrators Should Not Always Be Prosecuted: Where the International Criminal Court and Truth Commissions Meet', (2000) 49 *Emory Law Journal* 205

Voigt, S. T., 'The United States Must Remain Steadfastly Opposed to the Rome Treaty International Criminal Court', (2003) 12 *Widener Law Journal* 619

Von Hebel, Herman, 'An International Criminal Court – A Historical Perspective', in Herman von Hebel, Johan G. Lammers and Jolien Schukking, eds., *Reflections on the International Criminal Court: Essays in Honour of Adriaan Bos*, The Hague: T. M. C. Asser, 1999, pp. 13–38

Von Hebel, Herman, Lammers, Johan G., and Schukking, Jolien, eds., *Reflections on the International Criminal Court: Essays in Honour of Adriaan Bos*, The Hague: T. M. C. Asser, 1999

Von Hebel, Hermann, and Robinson, Daryl, 'Crimes within the Jurisdiction of the Court', in Roy S. Lee, ed., *The International Criminal Court: The Making of the Rome Statute: Issues, Negotiations, and Results*, The Hague: Kluwer Law International, 1999

Wald, Patricia M., 'Is the United States' Opposition to the ICC Intractable?', (2004) 2 *Journal of International Criminal Justice* 19

  'Why I Support the International Criminal Court', (2003) 21 *Wisconsin International Law Journal* 513

Walsh, Martha, 'The International Bar Association Proposal for a Code of Professional Conduct for Counsel before the ICC', (2003) 1 *Journal of International Criminal Justice* 490

Ward, A., 'Breaking the Sovereignty Barrier: The United States and the International Criminal Court', (2001) 41 *Santa Clara Law Review* 1123

Warrick, Thomas S., 'Organization of the International Criminal Court: Administrative and Financial Issues', (1997) 25 *Denver Journal of International Law and Policy* 333; (1997) 13 *Nouvelles études pénales* 37

Washburn, John, 'The International Criminal Court Arrives – The US Position: Status and Prospects', (2002) 25 *Fordham International Law Journal* 873

Watters, L., 'Convergence and the Procedures of the International Criminal Court: An International and Comparative Perspective', (2002) 25 *Fordham International Law Journal* 419

Wedgwood, Ruth, 'The United States and the International Criminal Court: The Irresolution of Rome', (2001) 64 *Law and Contemporary Problems* 193

  'The International Criminal Court: An American View', (1999) 10 *European Journal of International Law* 93

  'Fiddling in Rome: America and the International Criminal Court', (1998) 77:6 *Foreign Affairs* 20

Weller, M., 'Undoing the Global Constitution: UN Security Council Action on the International Criminal Court', (2002) 78 *International Affairs* 693

Werle, Gerhard, and Jessberger, Florian, '"Unless Otherwise Provided": Article 30 of the ICC Statute and the Mental Element of Crimes under International Criminal Law', (2005) 3 *Journal of International Criminal Justice* 35

Wessel, J., 'Judicial Policy-Making at the International Criminal Court: An Institutional Guide to Analyzing International Adjudication', (2006) 44 *Columbia Journal of Transnational Law* 377

Wilkitzki, Peter, 'The German Law on Co-operation with the ICC', (2002) 2 *International Criminal Law Review* 195

Williams, Sharon A., 'The Rome Statute on the International Criminal Court: From 1947–2000 and Beyond', (2000) 38 *Osgoode Hall Law Journal* 297

Wilmshurst, Elizabeth, 'The International Criminal Court: The Role of the Security Council', in Mauro Politi and Giuseppe Nesi, eds., *The Rome Statute of the International Criminal Court: A Challenge to Impunity*, Aldershot: Ashgate, 2001, pp. 39–42

Wippman, David, 'Can an International Criminal Court Prevent and Punish Genocide?', in Neal Riemer, ed., *Protection Against Genocide: Mission Impossible?*, Westport, CT: Praeger Publishers, 2000, pp. 85–104

Wise, Edward M., 'Commentary on Parts 2 and 3 of the Zutphen Intersessional Draft: General Principles of Criminal Law', (1998) 13*bis Nouvelles études pénales* 43

'Model Draft Statute for the International Criminal Court Based on the Preparatory Committee's Text to the Diplomatic Conference, Rome, June 15–July 17, 1997, Part 3', (1998) 13*ter Nouvelles études pénales* 39

'General Rules of Criminal Law', (1997) 13 *Nouvelles études pénales* 267; (1997) 29 *Denver Journal of International Law and Policy* 313

Witschel, G., 'Financial Regulations and Rules of the Court', (2002) 25 *Fordham International Law Journal* 665

Wright, W. F., 'Limitations on the Prosecution of International Terrorists by the International Criminal Court', (1999) 8 *Journal of International Law and Practice* 139

Yang, L., 'On the Principle of Complementarity in the Rome Statute of the International Criminal Court', (2005) 4 *Chinese Journal of International Law* 121

Yee, Sien Ho, 'A Proposal to Reorganize Article 23 of the ILC Draft Statute for an International Criminal Court', (1996) 19 *Hastings International and Comparative Law Review* 529

Yengejeh, S. M., 'Rules of Procedure of the Assembly of States Parties to the Rome Statute of the International Criminal Court', (2002) 25 *Fordham International Law Journal* 674

Young, S. N. M., 'Surrendering the Accused to the International Criminal Court', (2000) 71 *British Yearbook of International Law* 317

Zahnd, Patrick, 'How the International Criminal Court Should Help Implement International Humanitarian Law', in Dinah Shelton, ed., *International Crimes, Peace, and Human Rights: The Role of the International Criminal Court*, Ardsley, NY: Transnational Publishers, 2000, pp. 35–42

Zappalà, Salvatore, 'Are Some Peacekeepers Better Than Others? UN Security Council Resolution 1497 (2003) and the ICC', (2003) 1 *Journal of International Criminal Justice* 671

'The Reaction of the US to the Entry into Force of the ICC Statute: Comments on UN SC Resolution 1422 (2002) and Article 98 Agreements', (2003) 1 *Journal of International Criminal Justice* 114

Zelniker, L., 'Towards a Functional International Criminal Court: An Argument in Favour of a Strong Privileges and Immunities Agreement', (2001) 24 *Fordham International Law Journal* 988

Zemach, A., 'Fairness and Moral Judgments in International Criminal Law: The Settlement Provision in the Rome Statute', (2003) 41 *Columbia Journal of Transnational Law* 895

Zimmermann, Andreas, 'The Creation of a Permanent International Criminal Court', (1998) 2 *Max Planck Yearbook of United Nations Law* 169

Zwanenburg, Marten, 'The Statute of an International Criminal Court and the United States: Peace without Justice?', (1999) 12 *Leiden Journal of International Law* 1

'The Statute for an International Criminal Court and the United States: Peacekeepers under Fire?', (1999) 10 *European Journal of International Law* 124

INDEX

abortion, 116–17
Abu Ghraib, 32
abuse of process, 239, 284–5
accused
    conducting own defence, 308
    confirmation hearings and, 291
    disrupting trial proceedings, 307
    presence at trial, 304–7, 452
    rights
        arrest, 274
        information, 211, 224, 455
        right to silence, 316–17, 323
        trials, 219–24, 455
    terminology, 289
    unsworn statements, 317
acquittals, appeals, 324, 464
actus reus, 237–8
ad hoc tribunals
    See also specific tribunals
    admissibility, 189
    aggression, 103
    co-perpetratorship, 226
    command responsibility, 233, 234,
        337
    confidentiality, 262
    crimes against humanity, 119–20,
        121
    criminal responsibility, 228
    delays, 223
    enforcement of penalties, 340
    establishment, 168
    ex parte hearings, 288–9
    funding, 395
    general principles of criminal law,
        206
    guilty plea procedure, 310
    history, 11–16

ICC jurisdiction and, 205
immunity defence, 244–5
joint criminal enterprise, 226
judgments, length, 394
judiciary, 376
jurisdiction, 191, 295
legal representation, 308, 309
majority decisions, 322
miscarriage of justice and, 330
model for ICC, 158
outreach and, 385–6
penalties, 332, 337, 340
precedents, 208–9, 223
procedures, 252
reference points for Rome Statute,
    332
reparation, 362
Rome Statute debates and, 249
sentencing, 323, 324
standard of proof, 320
superior orders defence and, 243
temporal jurisdiction, 74
transfer of cases to, 65
victims and, 346–7
witness proofing, 315
admissibility
    ad hoc tribunals, 189
    alternative models, 198–9
    appeals, 325
    challenges, 423–4
        postponement of cooperation,
            476
    complementarity and, 187–8,
        190–9, 295
    gravity, 200–3, 240
    issues, 421–2
    jurisdiction and, 188–9